**Hermeneia
—A Critical
and Historical
Commentary
on the Bible**

# Hosea

A Commentary on the
Book of the Prophet Hosea

by Hans Walter Wolff

Translated by
Gary Stansell

Edited by
Paul D. Hanson

**Fortress Press**      Philadelphia

Translated from the German *Dodekapropheton 1 Hosea* by Hans Walter Wolff; zweite, verbesserte und erweiterte Auflage. Biblischer Kommentar Altes Testament, Band XIV/1. © 1965 Neukirchner Verlag, Neukirchen–Vluyn.

Library of Congress Catalog Card Number 70–179634
ISBN 0–8006–6004–8

20–6004 Printed in the United States of America

Type set by Maurice Jacobs, Inc., Philadelphia

DER HOCHWÜRDIGEN
THEOLOGISCHEN FAKULTÄT
DER GEORG-AUGUST-UNIVERSITÄT
IN GÖTTINGEN
ALS ZEICHEN DES DANKES
FÜR DIE VERLEIHUNG
DES DOCTOR THEOLOGIAE
HONORIS CAUSA

---

Hosea 1:7–2:5
actual size fragment
4QXXII<sup>d</sup>
© Palestine
Archaeological
Museum

Hans Walter Wolff was born in 1911 at Barmen, Germany, and educated at Bethel, Göttingen, and Bonn. He served as a parish pastor from 1937–1949 and began teaching at the Kirchliche Hochschule in Wuppertal in 1947, where he was professor from 1951–1959. From 1959–1967 he taught at Mainz; in 1967 he became professor at the University of Heidelberg.

Wolff is the author of numerous books and articles, including his collected essays, commentaries on Hosea, Joel, and Amos, and his recent *Anthropologie des Alten Testaments* which is to appear in English in 1975. Other books in English include *Amos the Prophet* and *The Old Testament: A Guide to Its Writings*. He is editor of the German series Biblischer Kommentar Altes Testament.

**Contents**

The name *Hermeneia*, Greek ἑρμηνεία, has been chosen as the title of the commentary series to which this volume belongs. The word *Hermeneia* has a rich background in the history of biblical interpretation as a term used in the ancient Greek–speaking world for the detailed, systematic exposition of a scriptural work. It is hoped that the series, like its name, will carry forward this old and venerable tradition. A second, entirely practical reason for selecting the name lay in the desire to avoid a long descriptive title and its inevitable acronym, or worse, an unpronounceable abbreviation.

The series is designed to be a critical and historical commentary to the Bible without arbitrary limits in size or scope. It will utilize the full range of philological and historical tools including textual criticism (often ignored in modern commentaries), the methods of the history of tradition (including genre and prosodic analysis), and the history of religion.

*Hermeneia* is designed for the serious student of the Bible. It will make full use of ancient Semitic and classical languages; at the same time, English translations of all comparative materials—Greek, Latin, Canaanite, or Akkadian—will be supplied alongside the citation of the source in its original language. Insofar as possible, the aim is to provide the student or scholar with full critical discussion of each problem of interpretation and with the primary data upon which the discussion is based.

*Hermeneia* is designed to be international and interconfessional in the selection of its authors; its editorial boards were also formed with this end in view. Occasionally the series will offer translations of distinguished commentaries which originally appeared in languages other than English. Published volumes of the series will be revised continually, and, eventually, new commentaries will replace older works in order to preserve the currency of the series. Commentaries are also being assigned for important literary works in the categories of apocryphal and pseudepigraphical works of the Old and New Testaments, including some of Essene or Gnostic authorship.

The editors of *Hermeneia* impose no systematic–theological perspective upon the series (directly, or indirectly by its selection of authors). It is expected that authors will struggle to lay bare the ancient meaning of a biblical work or pericope. In this way the text's human relevance should become transparent, as is always the case in competent historical discourse. However, the series eschews for itself homiletical translation of the Bible.

The editors are heavily indebted to Fortress Press for its energy and courage in taking up an expensive, long–term project, the rewards of which will accrue chiefly to the field of biblical scholarship.

The translator of this volume is Professor Gary Stansell of St. Olaf College, Northfield, Minnesota. Translations of Latin quotations of the Reformers, identified by the abbreviation [Trans], were supplied by Professor Richard Dinda of Concordia College, Austin, Texas. The translator was assisted throughout his work by Professor Wolff, by the Reverend Erhard Gerstenberger, pastor in Essen, Germany, and by Professor Jörg Jeremias of the University of Munich.

The editor responsible for this volume is Paul D. Hanson of Harvard University.

May 1974

*Frank Moore Cross, Jr.*
For the Old Testament
Editorial Board

*Helmut Koester*
For the New Testament
Editorial Board

## 1. Abbreviations

Aside from numerous additions and occasional modifications, the abbreviations found in the *Theological Dictionary of the New Testament*, ed. Gerhard Kittel, tr. Geoffrey W. Bromiley, vol. 1 (Grand Rapids, Michigan, and London: Eerdmans, 1964), were followed. The following are important additional abbreviations used in this volume:

| | |
|---|---|
| AASOR | Annual of the American Schools of Oriental Research |
| *AfO* | *Archiv für Orientforschung* |
| AFLNW | Veroffentlichungen der Arbeitgemeinschaft für Forschung des Landes Nordrhein—Westfalen |
| *AJSL* | *American Journal of Semitic Languages and Literatures* Continued by *JNES* |
| Am | Amos |
| *AnBibl* | *Analecta Biblica* |
| *ANEP* | *The Ancient Near East in Pictures Relating to the Old Testament*, Pritchard, J. B., ed. (Princeton: Princeton Univ. Press, 1954). |
| *ANET²* | *Ancient Near Eastern Texts Relating to the Old Testament*, Pritchard, J. B. ed., (Princeton: Princeton Univ. Press, 1955²). Citations are made by translator: e.g., for "Keret Epic"—Ginsberg, *ANET²*, 142–49. |
| AO | Der Alte Orient |
| *AOBAT* | *Altorientalische Bilder zum Alten Testament*, ed., H. Gressmann (Tübingen, 1926²) |
| *AOT* | *Altorientalische Texte zum Alten Testament*, ed., H. Gressmann (Tübingen, 1926²) |
| *ArOr* | *Archiv Orientálni* |
| *ARW* | *Archiv für Religionswissenschaft* |
| ATANT | Abhandlungen zur Theologie des Alten und Neuen Testaments |
| ATD | Das Alte Testament Deutsch |
| *BASOR* | *Bulletin of the American Schools of Oriental Research* |
| BBB | Bonner Biblische Beiträge |
| BBLAK | Beiträge zur Biblischen Landes– und Altertumskunde |
| BC | Biblischer Commentar über das Alte Testament, eds., C. F. Keil and F. Delitzsch |
| *BDB* | F. Brown, S. R. Driver, C. A. Briggs, |

| | |
|---|---|
| | eds., *A Hebrew and English Lexicon of the Old Testament* (Oxford: Clarendon, 1953) |
| BEvTh | Beiträge zur Evangelischen Theologie |
| BFChrTh | Beiträge zur Förderung Christlichen Theologie |
| *BHH* | *Biblisch– historisches Handwörterbuch*, eds., Bo Reicke and Leonard Rost (Stuttgart: vol. 1, 1962; vol. 2, 1964; vol. 3, 1966) |
| BHTh | Beiträge zur historischen Theologie |
| *Bibl* | *Biblica* |
| *BJPES* | *Bulletin of the Jewish Palestine Exploration Society* |
| *BJRL* | *Bulletin of the John Rylands Library* |
| BK | Biblischer Kommentar. Altes Testament, eds., M. Noth, H. W. Wolff, and S. Herrmann |
| BOT | De Boeken van het Oude Testament, ed., A van den Born |
| BRL | *Biblisches Reallexikon*, ed., K. Galling (Tübingen, 1937) |
| BWANT | Beiträge zur Wissenschaft vom Alten und Neuen Testament |
| *BZ* | *Biblische Zeitschrift* |
| BZAW | Beihefte zur Zeitschrift für die alttestamentliche Wissenschaft |
| CAB | Cahiers d'Archeologie Biblique |
| *CBQ* | *The Catholic Biblical Quarterly* |
| CD | The Cairo Genizah Damascus Document |
| cf. | Confer, compare with |
| Chr | Chronicles |
| Cj. | Conjecture |
| Cor | Corinthians |
| COT | Commentaar op het Oude Testament, ed., G. C. Aalders |
| *CR* | *Corpus Reformatorum* |
| *CTCA* | *Corpus des tablettes en cuneiformes alphabetiques; decouvertes a Ras Shamra–Ugarit de 1929 a 1939*, ed., A. Herdner (Paris, 1963) |
| Dan | Daniel |
| *DTh* | *Deutsche Theologie:* Monatsschrift für die deutsche evangelische Kirche |
| Dtn | Deuteronomy |
| *DTT* | *Dansk Teologisk Tidsskrift* |
| EA | Martin Luther, *Sämmtliche Werke* (Erlangen Ausgabe, 1826ff) |
| Eccl | Ecclesiastes |
| Echter–B | Die Heilige Schrift in Deutscher |

|  |  |  |  |
|---|---|---|---|
|  | Übersetzung | KAT | Kommentar zum Alten Testament, ed., E. Sellin |
| ed. | Editor, edited by | | |
| [Ed.] | Editor of this volume of Hermeneia | *KB* | *Keilinschriftliche Bibliothek*, Berlin |
| *EKL* | *Evangelisches Kirchenlexikon*, eds., H. Brunotte and O. Weber (Göttingen, 1955ff) | KeH | Kurzgefasstes exegetisches Handbuch zum Alten Testament |
| | | Kgs | Kings |
| Est | Esther | KHC | Kurzer Hand-Commentar zum Alten Testament, ed., K. Marti |
| ÉtBi | Études Bibliques | | |
| *EvTh* | *Evangelische Theologie* | *KuD* | *Kerygma und Dogma* |
| Ex | Exodus | Lam | Lamentations |
| Ezek | Ezekiel | Lev | Leviticus |
| Ezr | Ezra | Lk | Luke |
| f | Designates one verse or page following the verse or page cited. | LUÅ | Lunds Universitets Årsskrift |
| | | Mal | Malachi |
| *FF* | *Forschungen und Fortschritte* | Mic | Micah |
| *FHG* | *Fragmenta historicorum Graecorum*, 5 vols., ed., C. Mueller, (Paris, 1841–70) | *MIOF* | *Mitteilungen des Instituts der Orientforschung* |
| FRLANT | Forschungen zur Religion und Literatur des Alten und Neuen Testaments | Mk | Mark |
| | | Mt | Matthew |
| | | Na | Nahum |
| | | *NAG* | *Nachrichten der Akademie der Wissenschaften in Göttingen* |
| Gen | Genesis | | |
| *GThT* | *Gereformeerd Theologisch Tijdschrift* | Neh | Nehemiah |
| Hab | Habakkuk | *NKZ* | *Neue Kirchliche Zeitschrift* |
| Hag | Haggai | NTD | Das Neue Testament Deutsch, eds., P. Althaus and J. Behm |
| HAT | Handbuch zum Alten Testament, ed., Otto Eissfeldt | | |
| | | *NThSt* | *Nieuwe Theologische Studiën* |
| HK | Handkommentar zum Alten Testament, ed., W. Nowack (Göttingen, 1292ff) | *NTT* | *Norsk Teologisk Tidsskrift* |
| | | Nu | Numbers |
| | | Ob | Obadiah |
| Hos | Hosea | *OLZ* | *Orientalistische Literaturzeitung* |
| HS | Die Heilige Schrift des Alten Testaments, eds., F. Feldmann and H. Herkenne (Bonn) | OTS | Oudtestamentische Studiën |
| | | p. (pp.) | Page(s) |
| | | *PEQ* | *Palestine Exploration Quarterly* |
| HSAT | Die Heilige Schrift der Alten Testaments, ed., E. Kautzsch (Tübingen, 1909) | *PJ* | *Palästinajahrbuch* |
| | | Prv | Proverbs |
| | | Ps | Psalms |
| *HUCA* | *Hebrew Union College Annual* | Q | Qumran documents |
| IB | The Interpreter's Bible, ed., G. Buttrick | 1 QH | Hodayot, the Psalms of Thanksgiving |
| | | 1 QIsaª | Isaiah scroll, exemplar a |
| *ibid.* | In the same place | 1 QM | Milhamah, the war of the Children of Light against the Children of Darkness |
| ICC | The International Critical Commentary of the Holy Scriptures of the Old and New Testament, eds., S. R. Driver, A. Plummer, and C. A. Briggs | | |
| | | *RB* | *Revue Biblique* |
| | | *RE³* | *Realencyklopädie für protestantische Theologie und Kirche*³ |
| *idem* | The same (person) | | |
| *Int* | *Interpretation* | *REJ* | *Revue des Etudes Juives* |
| Is | Isaiah | *RGG³* | *Die Religion der Geschichte und Gegenwart*³ |
| *JBL* | *Journal of Biblical Literature* | *RHPhR* | *Revue d'Histoire et de Philosophie Religieuses* |
| Jer | Jeremiah | | |
| *JJSt* | *The Journal of Jewish Studies* | *RHR* | *Revue de l'histoire des religions* |
| Jn | John | Rom | Romans |
| *JNES* | *Journal of Near Eastern Studies* | Sam | Samuel |
| Jon | Jonah | SAT | Die Schriften des Alten Testaments in Auswahl übersetzt und erklärt, ed., H. Gunkel |
| Josh | Joshua | | |
| *JPOS* | *Journal of the Palestine Oriental Society* | | |
| *JQR* | *Jewish Quarterly Review* | *SBU* | *Svensk Biblisk Uppslagsverk*, eds., I. Engnell & A. Fridrichsen, 2 vols. (Gävle, 1948–52) |
| *JTS* | *Journal of Theological Studies* | | |
| Ju | Judges | | |
| | | Song | Song of Songs |

| | |
|---|---|
| *SThZ* | *Schweizerische Theologische Zeitschrift* |
| StTh | Studia Theologica |
| *TDNT* | *Theological Dictionary of The New Testament*, ed., Gerhard Kittel and Gerhard Friedrich, tr. and ed., Geoffrey W. Bromiley |
| *TGI* | Galling, K. *Textbuch zur Geschichte Israels* (Tübingen, 1950) |
| ThB | Theologische Bücherei |
| *ThBl* | *Theologische Blätter* |
| *ThLZ* | *Theologische Literaturzeitung* |
| *ThQ* | *Theologische Quartalschrift* |
| *ThR* | *Theologische Rundschau* |
| ThSt(B) | Theologische Studien, ed. K. Barth |
| *ThStKr* | *Theologische Studien und Kritiken* |
| *ThT* | *Theologisch Tijdschrift* |
| *ThV* | *Theologia Viatorum* |
| *ThZ* | *Theologische Zeitschrift* |
| tr. | Translator, translated by |
| [Trans.] | Translator of this volume of Hermeneia |
| [Trans. by Ed.] | Translated by editor of this volume of Hermeneia |
| *TTK* | *Tidsskrift for Teologi og Kirke* |
| UUÅ | Uppsala Universitets Årsskrift, Uppsala |
| *VF* | *Verkündigung und Forschung* |
| Vol(s) | Volume(s) |
| *VT* | *Vetus Testamentum* |
| VTSuppl | Supplements to Vetus Testamentum |
| WA | Martin Luther, *Werke, Kritische Gesamtausgabe* (Weimar, 1883ff) |
| WC | The Westminster Commentaries |
| WMANT | Wissenschaftliche Monographien zum Alten und Neuen Testament |
| WO | Die Welt des Orients. Wissenschaftliche Beiträge zur Kunde des Morgenlandes |
| *WuD* | *Wort und Dienst* |
| *ZA* | *Zeitschrift für Assyriologie und verwandte Gebiete* |
| *ZAW* | *Zeitschrift für die altestamentliche Wissenschaft* |
| *ZDPV* | *Zeitschrift des deutschen Palästina–Vereins* |
| Zech | Zechariah |
| Zeph | Zephaniah |
| *ZKTh* | *Zeitschrift für Katholische Theologie* |
| *ZMR* | *Zeitschrift für Missionskunde und Religionswissenschaft* |
| *ZNW* | *Zeitschrift für die neutestamentliche Wissenschaft und die Kunde der älteren Kirche* |
| *ZRGG* | *Zeitschrift für Religions und Geistesgeschichte* |
| *ZS* | *Zeitschrift für Semistik und verwandte Gebiete* |
| *ZThK* | *Zeitschrift für Theologie und Kirche* |
| *ZWTh* | *Zeitschrift für wissenschaftliche Theologie* |

## 2. Short Title List

Ackroyd, "Hosea and Jacob"
P. R. Ackroyd, "Hosea and Jacob," *VT* 13
(1963): 245–59.

Albright, *Archaeology*
W. F. Albright, *Archaeology and the Religion of Israel*
(Baltimore: Johns Hopkins, 1956).

Albright, "High Place"
W. F. Albright, "The High Place in Ancient
Palestine," *Volume du Congres, Strasbourg 1956*,
VTSuppl 4 (Leiden, 1957), 242–58.

Allwohn, *Die Ehe*
A. Allwohn, *Die Ehe des Propheten Hosea in psychoanalytischer Beleuchtung*, BZAW 44 (Berlin; 1926).

Alt, "Hosea 5:8–6:6"
A. Alt, "Hosea 5:8–6:6, ein Krieg und seine
Folgen in prophetischer Beleuchtung," *Kleine
Schriften* 2, 163–87.

Alt, *Kleine Schriften*
A. Alt, *Kleine Schriften zur Geschichte des volkes Israel*,
3 Vols. (München, 1963[3], 1959[2], 1959[1]).

Alt, "Neue Erwägungen"
A. Alt, "Neue Erwägungen über die Lage von
Mizpa, Ataroth, Beeroth und Gibeon," *ZDPV* 69
(1953): 1–27.

Alt, "Stadtstaat"
A. Alt, "Der Stadtstaat Samaria," *Kleine Schriften*
3, 258–302.

Alt, "Feldzug"
A. Alt, "Tiglathpilesers III. erster Feldzug nach
Palästina," *Kleine Schriften* 2, 150–62.

Alt, "Ursprünge"
A. Alt, "Die Ursprünge des israelitischen Rechts,"
*Kleine Schriften* 1, 278–332.

Bach, *Aufforderungen*
R. Bach, *Die Aufforderungen zur Flucht und zum
Kampf im alt. Prophetenspruch*, WMANT 9
(Neukirchen, 1962).

Bach, "Erwählung"
R. Bach, "Die Erwählung Israels in der Wüste,"
unpublished dissertation, University of Bonn
(Bonn, 1952).

Barrois, *Manuel* I
A. G. Barrois, *Manuel d'Archeologie Biblique* 1
(Paris, 1939).

Barrois, *Manuel* II
A. G. Barrois, *Manuel d'Archeologie Biblique* 2
(Paris, 1953).

Barth, *Church Dogmatics*
K. Barth, *Church Dogmatics* IV, 2, tr. G. W.
Bromiley (Edinburgh: T & T Clark, 1958).

Baudissin, *Adonis*
W. W. Baudissin, *Adonis und Esmun* (Leipzig,
1911).

Bauer–Leander
H. Bauer and P. Leander, *Historische Grammatik
der Hebräischen Sprache des Alten Testaments* 1
(Halle, 1922).

Baumann, "Wissen um Gott"
E. Baumann, " 'Wissen um Gott' bei Hosea als
Urform von Theologie?" *EvTh* 15 (1955): 416–25.

Beer-Meyer
G. Beer and D. R. Meyer, *Hebräische Grammatik*
(Berlin, 1952–55).

Begrich, "Heilsorakel"
J. Begrich, "Das priesterliche Heilsorakel," *ZAW*
52 (1934): 81–92 [*Gesammelte Studien*, ThB 21
(München, 1964), 217–31].

Begrich, *Studien*
J. Begrich, *Studien zur Deuterojesaja*, BWANT 4
(Stuttgart, 1938) [Reprinted in ThB 20
(München, 1964)].

Benzinger, *Hebräische Archäologie*
I. Benzinger, *Hebräische Archäologie* (Leipzig,
1927[3]).

Bleeker
L. Bleeker, *De kleine Propheten* (Groningen, 1932).

Boecker, *Redeformen*
H. J. Boecker, *Redeformen des Rechtsleben. im A.T.*,
WMANT 14 (Neukirchen, 1964).

Bonnet, *Reallexikon*
H. Bonnet, *Reallexikon der ägyptischen Religionsgeschichte* (Berlin, 1952).

Boström, *Proverbiastudien*
G. Boström, *Proverbiastudien* (Lund, 1935).

Braun, "Der Fahrende"
H. Braun, " 'Der Fahrende'," *ZThK* 48 (1951):
32–38.

Brockelmann, *Syntax*
C. Brockelmann, *Hebräische Syntax* (Neukirchen,
1956).

Buber
M. Buber, *Bücher der Kündigung* (Köln, 1958).

Buber, *The Prophetic Faith*
M. Buber, *The Prophetic Faith*, tr. C. Witton–
Davies (New York: Macmillan, 1949).

Budde, "Der Abschnitt"
K. Budde, "Der Abschnitt Hosea 1–3 und seine
grundlegende religionsgeschichtliche Bedeutung,"
*ThStKr* 96/97 (1925): 1–89.

Budde, "Hosea 1 und 3"
K. Budde, "Hosea 1 und 3," *ThBl* 13 (1934):
337–42.

Budde, "Zu Text und Auslegung (4:1–19)"
K. Budde, "Zu Text und Auslegung des Buches
Hosea (4:1–19)," *JBL* 45 (1926): 280–97.

Budde, "Zu Text und Auslegung (5:1–6:6)"
K. Budde, "Zu Text und Auslegung des Buches
Hosea (5:1–6:6)," *JPOS* 14 (1934): 1–41.

Budde, "Zu Text und Auslegung (6:7–7:2)"
K. Budde, "Zu Text und Auslegung des Buches
Hosea (6:7–7:2)," *JBL* 53 (1934): 118–33.

Buss, "A Form–Critical Study"
M. J. Buss, "A Form–Critical Study in the Book
of Hosea with Special Attention to Method,"
Ph.D. dissertation, Yale University (New Haven,
1958).

Buss, *Prophetic Word*
   M. J. Buss, *The Prophetic Word of Hosea*, BZAW 3
   (Berlin, 1969).
Cazelles, "Os 8:4"
   H. Cazelles, "The Problem of the Kings in
   Os 8:4," *CBQ* 11 (1949): 14–25.
Coppens
   J. Coppens, *Les douze petits Prophetes* (Paris, 1950).
Coppens, "L'Histoire"
   J. Coppens, "L'Histoire matrimoniale d'Osee,"
   *Alttestamentliche Studien*, eds., H. Junker and
   J. Botterweck, BBB 1 (Bonn, 1950), 38–45.
Cowley, *Papyri*
   A. Cowley, *Aramaic Papyri of the Fifth Century B. C.*
   (Oxford, 1923).
Dalman, *Arbeit* I, II, III, IV, V, VI
   Gustaf Dalman, *Arbeit und Sitte in Palästina.*
   I    (Gütersloh, 1928)
   II   (Gütersloh, 1932)
   III  (Gütersloh, 1933)
   IV   (Gütersloh, 1935)
   V    (Gütersloh, 1937)
   VI   (Gütersloh, 1939)
Deden
   D. Deden, *De kleine Profeten*, Hosea–Micah, BOT
   (Roermond, 1953).
Dingermann, "Massora–Septuaginta"
   F. Dingermann, "Massora–Septuaginta der
   kleinen Propheten," (dissertation, University of
   Wurzberg, 1948).
Dobbie, "Hosea 9:8"
   R. Dobbie, "The Text of Hosea 9:8," *VT* 5
   (1955): 199–203.
Donner–Röllig, *KAI*
   H. Donner and W. Röllig, *Kanaanäische und
   aramäische Inschriften* 2 (Wiesbaden, 1964).
Duhm
   B. Duhm, *Die zwölf Propheten, in den Versmassen der
   Urschrift übersetzt* (Tübingen, 1910).
Eissfeldt, "Baʻalšamēm"
   O. Eissfeldt, "Baʻalšamēm und Jahwe," *ZAW* 57
   (1939): 1–31.
Eissfeldt, "Lade"
   O. Eissfeldt, "Lade und Stierbild," *ZAW* 58
   (1940/41): 190–215.
Eissfeldt, "Mein Gott"
   O. Eissfeldt, " 'Mein Gott' im Alten Testament,"
   *ZAW* 61 (1945–48): 3–16.
Fahlgren, *Sedākā*
   K. H. Fahlgren, *Sedākā* (Uppsala, 1932).
Fohrer, *Handlungen*
   G. Fohrer, *Die symbolischen Handlungen der Pro-
   pheten*, ATANT (Zürich, 1953).
Fohrer, "Vertrag"
   G. Fohrer, "Der Vertrag zwischen König und
   Volk in Israel," *ZAW* 71 (1959): 1–22.
de Fraine, "L'aspect"
   J. de Fraine, "L'aspect religieux de la royauté
   isráelite," *AnBibl* 3 (1954): 147–53.

Frey
   H. Frey, *Das Buch des Werbens Gottes um seine Kirche
   Der Prophet Hosea*, Die Botschaft des Alten
   Testaments, 23, 2 (Stuttgart, 1957).
Fück, "Hosea Kapitel 3"
   J. Fück, "Hosea Kapitel 3," *ZAW* 39 (1921):
   283–90.
Gaster, "Zu Hosea 7:3–6, 8–9"
   T. H. Gaster, "Zu Hosea 7:3–6, 8–9" *VT* 4
   (1954): 78f.
van Gelderen
   C. von Gelderen and W. H. Gispen, *Het Boek
   Hosea*, COT (Kampen, 1953).
Gemser, "rib"
   G. Gemser, "The *rib*—or Controversy—Pattern
   in Hebrew Mentality," *Wisdom in Israel and in the
   Ancient Near East*, ed., M. Noth, VTSuppl 3
   (Leiden, 1955), 120–37.
Gertner, "Masorah"
   M. Gertner, "The Masorah and the Levites.
   Appendix on Hosea 12," *VT* 10 (1960): 241–84.
Gesenius–Buhl
   W. Gesenius and F. Buhl, *Hebräisches und ara-
   mäisches Handwörterbuch zum AT* (Leipzig, 1915[16]).
Gesenius–Kautzsch
   *Gesenius' Hebrew Grammar*, E. Kautzsch (ed.) and
   A. E. Cowley (tr. and reviser) (Oxford, 1910[2]).
Gispen
   W. H. Gispen and C. van Gelderen, *Het Boek
   Hosea*, COT (Kampen, 1953).
Gordis, "Hosea 14:3"
   R. Gordis, "The Text and Meaning of Hosea
   14:3," *VT* 5 (1955): 88–90.
Gordis, "Studies"
   R. Gordis, "Studies in the Relationship of Biblical
   and Rabbinic Hebrew," *Louis Ginzberg Jubilee
   Volume* (New York: The American Academy for
   Jewish Research, 1945).
Gordon, "Hos 2:4–5"
   C. H. Gordon, "Hos 2:4–5 in the Light of New
   Semitic Inscriptions," *ZAW* 54 (1936): 277–80.
Gordon, *Literature*
   C. H. Gordon, *Ugaritic Literature* (Rome, 1949).
Goshen–Gottstein, "Ephraim"
   M. H. Goshen–Gottstein, " 'Ephraim is a well–
   trained heifer' and Ugaritic *mdl*," *Bibl* 41 (1960):
   64–66.
Gray, *KRT*
   J. Gray, *The KRT–Text in the Literature of Ras
   Shamra* (Leiden, 1964[2]).
Gressmann
   H. Gressmann, *Die älteste Geschichtsschreibung und
   Prophetie Israels* (von Samuel bis Amos und
   Hosea), SAT 2, 1 (Göttingen, 1921[2]).
Gressmann, *AOT*
   H. Gressmann, Altorientlische Texte zum AT
   (Tübingen, 1926[2]).
Gressmann, *Der Messias*
   H. Gressmann, *Der Messias* (Göttingen, 1929).

Grether
    Oskar Grether, *Hebräische Grammatik für den aka-
    demischen Unterricht* (München, 1955²).
Grether, *Name*
    O. Grether, *Name und Wort Gottes im A. T.*, BZAW
    64 (Giessen, 1934).
Gunkel–Begrich, *Einleitung*
    H. Gunkel and J. Begrich, *Einleitung in die Psalmen*
    (Göttingen, 1933).
Gunneweg, *Tradition*
    A. H. J. Gunneweg, *Mündliche und schriftliche
    Tradition der vorexilischen Prophetenbücher als Problem
    der neueren Prophetenforschung*, FRLANT 73
    (Göttingen, 1959).
Guthe
    .H. Guthe, *Hosea bis Chronik*, HSAT 2 (Tübingen,
    1923⁴).
Harper
    W. R. Harper, *Amos and Hosea*, ICC (Edinburgh:
    T & T Clark, 1905).
Heermann, "Ehe und Kinder"
    A. Heermann, "Ehe und Kinder des Propheten
    Hosea," *ZAW* 40 (1922): 287–312.
Hempel, *Althebräische Literatur*
    J. Hempel, *Die althebräische Literatur und ihr hel-
    lenistisch–jüdishces nachleben* (Potsdam, 1930).
Hempel, *Worte*
    J. Hempel, *Worte der Propheten* (Berlin, 1949).
Henke, "Beth Peor"
    O. Henke, "Zur Lage von Beth Peor," *ZDPV* 75
    (1959): 155–63.
Hentschke, *Stellung*
    R. Hentschke, *Die Stellung der vorexilischen Schrift-
    propheten zum Kultus*, BZAW 75 (Berlin, 1957).
Hitzig
    F. Hitzig, *Die zwölf kleinen Propheten*, KeH 1
    (Leipzig, 1838).
Horst, "Naturrecht"
    F. Horst, "Naturrecht und Altes Testament"
    *EvTh* 10 (1951–52): 253–73 [*Gottes Recht: Studien
    zum Recht im AT*, ThB 12 (München, 1961),
    235–59].
Horst, "Recht"
    F. Horst, "Recht und Religion im Bereich des
    Alten Testaments," *EvTh* 16 (1956): 49–75
    [*Gottes Recht: Studien zum Recht im AT*, ThB 12
    (München, 1961), 260–91].
Humbert, "Laetari et exultare"
    P. Humbert, "Laetari et exultare dans de vocabu-
    laire religieux de l'Ancien Testament," *RHPhR*
    22 (1942): 185–214 [*Opuscules d'un hebraisant*
    (Paris, 1958), 119–45].
Humbert, "En marge"
    P. Humbert, "En marge du dictionnaire hebrai-
    que," *ZAW* 62 (1950): 200–207.
Humbert, "So"
    P. Humbert, "Der Deltafürst So in Hosea 5:11,"
    *OLZ* 21 (1918): 223–26.
Humbert, "La logique"

P. Humbert, "La logique de la perspective no-
    made chez Osée et l'unite d'Osée 2:4–22,"
    BZAW 41 (Giessen, 1925), 158–66.
Humbert, "Les trois"
    P. Humbert, "Les trois premiens chapitres
    d'Osée," *RHR* 77 (1918): 157–71.
Jacob, "L'Heritage"
    E. Jacob, "L'Heritage cananeen dans le livre du
    prophéte Osée," *RHPhR* 43 (1963): 250–59.
Jacob, "La femme"
    E. Jacob, "La femme et le prophete. A propos
    d'Osée 12:13–14," *Hommage a W. Vischer* (Maqqel
    shaq ed, 1960), 83–87.
Janssen, *Exilzeit*
    E. Janssen, *Juda in der Exilzeit*, FRLANT 69
    (Göttingen, 1956).
Jepsen, *Quellen*
    A. Jepsen, *Die Quellen des Königsbuches* (Halle–
    Saale, 1956).
Johnson, *Vitality*
    A. R. Johnson, *The Vitality of the Individual in the
    Thought of Ancient Israel* (Cardiff, 1949).
Jolles, *Einfache Formen*
    André Jolles, *Einfache Formen* (Leipzig, 1930;
    Darmstadt, 1969⁵).
Joüon
    P. Joüon, *Grammaire de l'Hebrew Biblique* (Rome,
    1947).
Junker, "Os 4:1–10"
    H. Junker, "Textkritische, formkritische und
    traditions-geschichtliche Untersuchung zu Os
    4:1–10," *BZ* 4 (1960): 165–73.
Kapelrud, *Baal*
    A. S. Kapelrud, *Baal in the Ras Shamra Texts*
    (Copenhagen, 1955).
Keil
    C. F. Keil, *Biblischer Commentar über die zwölf
    kleinen Propheten* (Leipzig, 1888³).
Kittel, *Geschichte*
    R. Kittel, *Geschichte des Volkes Israel* 2 (Gotha,
    1925⁷).
Koch, "Vergeltungsdogma"
    K. Koch, "Gibt es ein Vergeltungsdogma im
    AT?" *ZThK* 52 (1955): 1–42.
Koehler, *Hebrew Man*
    L. Koehler, *Hebrew Man*, tr. P. R. Ackroyd
    (London: SCM, 1956) [*Der hebräische Mensch*
    (Tübingen, 1953)].
Koehler–Baumgartner
    L. Koehler and W. Baumgartner, *Hebräisches
    und aramäisches Lexicon zum AT* (Leiden, 1953;
    1967³).
Koehler, *Theology*
    L. Koehler, *Old Testament Theology*, tr. A. S. Todd
    (London: Lutterworth, 1957) [*Theologie des Alten
    Testaments* (Tübingen, 1953³)].
Kraeling, *Papyri*
    E. G. Kraeling, *The Brooklyn–Museum Aramaic
    Papyri* (New Haven: Yale, 1953).

Kraus, *Psalmen*
    H. J. Kraus, *Psalmen*, BK 15, 1, 2 (Neukirchen, 1960).
Kuhl, "Neue Dokumente"
    C. Kuhl, "Neue Dokumente zum Verständnis von Hosea 2:4–15," *ZAW* 52 (1934): 102–9.
Lindblom
    J. Lindblom, *Hosea, literarisch untersucht* (Åbo, 1927).
Lippl
    J. Lippl, *Die zwölf kleinen Propheten* (Hosea), HSAT 8, 3, 1 (Bonn, 1937).
Lohfink, "Os 4:4–6"
    N. Lohfink, "Zu Text und Form von Os 4:4–6," *Bibl* 42 (1961): 303–32.
Marti
    Karl Marti, *Das Dodekapropheton*, KHC (Tübingen, 1904).
May, "Fertility Cult"
    H. G. May, "The Fertility Cult in Hosea," *AJSL* 48 (1932): 73–98.
McCarthy, "Hosea 12:2"
    D. J. McCarthy, "Hosea 12:2—Covenant by Oil," *VT* 14 (1964): 215–21.
McKenzie, "Divine Passion"
    J. L. McKenzie, "Divine Passion in Osee," *CBQ* 17 (1955): 287–99.
Mowinckel, "Spirit"
    S. Mowinckel, " 'The Spirit' and the 'Word' in the Pre–exilic Reforming Prophets," *JBL* 53 (1934): 204–5.
Neher, *L'essence*
    Andre Neher, *L'essence du prophetisme* (Paris, 1955).
Nielsen, *Shechem*
    E. Nielsen, *Shechem* (Uppsala, 1955).
Nötscher
    F. Nötscher, *Zwölfprophetenbuch*, Echter B (Würzburg, 1948).
North, "Hosea's Introduction"
    F. S. North, "Hosea's Introduction to His Book," *VT* 8 (1958): 429–32.
North, "Essence"
    C. R. North, "The Essence of Idolatry," *Von Ugarit nach Qumran*, eds., J. Hempel and L. Rost, BZAW 77 (Berlin, 1958), 151–60.
Noth, *Aufsätze*, I and II
    M. Noth, *Aufsätze zur biblischen Landes– und Altertumskunde*, 2 vols., ed. H. W. Wolff (Neukirchen, 1971).
Noth, "Beiträge"
    M. Noth, "Beiträge zur Geschichte des Ostjordanlandes III: Die Nachbaren der israelitischen Stämme im Ostjordanlande," *ZDPV* 68 (1951): 1–50 [*Aufsätze zur biblischen Landes– und Altertumskunde* 1, ed. H. W. Wolff (Neukirchen, 1971), 434–75].
Noth, *History*
    M. Noth, *The History of Israel*, tr. P. Ackroyd (New York: Harper & Row, 1958²) [*Geschichte Israels* (Göttingen, 1959⁹)].
Noth, *Pentateuchal Traditions*
    M. Noth, *A History of Pentateuchal Traditions*, tr. B. W. Anderson (Englewood Cliffs: Prentice Hall, 1972) [*Überlieferungsgeschichte des Pentateuch* (Darmstadt, 1966³)].
Noth, *Personennamen*
    M. Noth, *Die israelitischen Personennamen im Rahmen der gemeinsemitischen Namengebung*, BWANT 3, 10 (Stuttgart, 1928).
Noth, "Stamme"
    M. Noth, "Israelitische Stämme zwischen Ammon und Moab," *ZAW* 60 (1944): 11–57 [*Aufsätze zur biblischen Landes– und Altertumskunde* 1, ed. H. W. Wolff (Neukirchen, 1971), 391–433].
Noth, *Laws*
    M. Noth, *The Laws in the Pentateuch and Other Studies*, tr. D. R. Ap–Thomas (Philadelphia: Fortress, 1966) [*Gesammelte Studien*, ThB 6 (München, 1957)].
Noth, "Covenant–making"
    M. Noth, "Old Testament Covenant–making in the Light of a Text from Mari," *Laws*, 108–17.
Noth, *World*
    M. Noth, *The Old Testament World*, tr. V. Gruhn (Philadelphia: 1966) [*Die Welt des Alten Testaments* (Berlin, 1957³)].
Nowack
    W. Nowack, *Die kleinen Propheten*, HK (Göttingen, 1897¹, 1922³).
Nyberg
    H. Nyberg, *Studien zum Hoseabuch* (Uppsala, 1935).
Nyberg, "Problem"
    H. Nyberg, "Das textkritische Problem des Alten Testaments am Hoseabuch demonstriert," *ZAW* 52 (1934): 241–54.
Östborn, *Yahweh and Baal*
    G. Östborn, *Yahweh and Baal: Studies in the Book of Hosea and Related Documents*, LUÅ 51, 6 (Lund, 1956).
Oettli
    A. Oettli, *Amos und Hosea: Zwei Zeugen gegen die Anwendung der Evolutionstheorie auf die Religion Israels*, BFChrTh 5, 4 (Gütersloh, 1901).
Oort, "Hosea"
    H. Oort, "Hosea," *ThT* 24 (1890): 345–64; 480–505.
Orelli
    C. von Orelli, *Die zwölf kleinen Propheten*, Strack–Zöcklers Kurzgefasster Kommentar zu den heiligen Schriften A. u. N.T. (München, 1908³).
Peter, "Echo"
    A. Peter, "Das Echo von Paradieserzählung und Paradiesmythus unter besonderer Berücksichtigung der prophetischen Endzeitschilderung," dissertation, Univ. of Würzburg (Würzburg, 1947).
Pfeiffer, *Introduction*
    R. H. Pfeiffer, *Introduction to the Old Testament*

(London: Adam and Charles Black, 1948).

Pope, *El*

M. H. Pope, *El in the Ugaritic Texts*, VTSuppl 2 (Leiden, 1955).

Procksch

O. Procksch, *Die kleinen prophetischen Schriften vor dem Exil*, Erläuterungen zum Alten Testament 3 (Stuttgart, 1910).

Quell, *Propheten*

G. Quell, *Wahre und falsche Propheten* (Gütersloh, 1952).

von Rad, *Theology*

G. von Rad, *Old Testament Theology*, tr. D. M. G. Stalker (New York: Harper, 1 1962, 2 1965).

Ratschow, *Werden*

C. H. Ratschow, *Werden und Wirken im A. T.*, BZAW 70 (Giessen, 1941).

Reider, "Studies"

J. Reider, "Etymological Studies in Biblical Hebrew," *VT* 2 (1952): 113–30.

Rendtorff, "Erwägungen"

R. Rendtorff, "Erwägungen zur Frühgeschichte des Prophetentums in Israel," *ZThK* 59 (1962): 145–67.

Rendtorff, "*ne'um Jahwe*"

R. Rendtorff, "Zum Gebrauch der Formel *ne'um Jahwe* im Jeremiabuch," *ZAW* 66 (1954): 27–37.

Richter, *Erläuterungen*

G. Richter, *Erläuterungen zu dunkeln Stellen in den kleinen Propheten*, BFChrTh 18 (Gütersloh, 1914).

Robertson, "Hos 10:11"

E. Robertson, "Textual Criticism of Hos 10:11," *Transact. Glasgow Univ. Or. Soc.* 8 (1938): 16–17.

Robinson, *Cross*

H. W. Robinson, *The Cross of Hosea* (Philadelphia: Westminster, 1949).

Robinson

Th. Robinson and F. Horst, *Die Zwölf Kleinen Propheten*, HAT 1, 14 (Tübingen, 1964).

Rohland, "Erwählungstraditionen"

E. Rohland, "Die Bedeutung der Erwählungstraditionen Israels für die Eschatologie der alttestamentlichen Propheten," dissertation, University of Heidelberg (Heidelberg, 1956).

Rost, "Erwägungen"

L. Rost, "Erwägungen zu Hos. 4:13f," in *Festschrift Alfred Bertholet*, eds., W. Baumgartner, O. Eissfeldt, K. Elliger, L. Rost (Tübingen, 1950), 451–60.

Rost, *Israel*

L. Rost, *Israel bei den Propheten*, BWANT 4, 19 (Giessen, 1937).

Rudolph, "Präparierte Jungfrauen?"

W. Rudolph, "Präparierte Jungfrauen?" *ZAW* 75 (1963): 65–73

Scharbert, *Schmerz*

J. Scharbert, *Der Schmerz im AT*, BBB 8 (Bonn, 1955).

Schmidt, "Die Ehe"

H. Schmidt, "Die Ehe des Hosea," *ZAW* 42 (1924): 245–72.

Schmidt, "Hosea 6:1–6"

H. Schmidt, "Hosea 6:1–6," *Sellin Festschrift*, ed., A. Jirku (Leipzig, 1927), 111–26.

Schmidt, "Anthropologische Begriffe"

W. Schmidt, "Anthropologische Begriffe im AT," *EvTh* 24 (1964): 374–88.

Schmidt, *Königtum*

W. Schmidt, *Königtum Gottes in Ugarit und Israel*, BZAW 80 (Berlin, 1961).

Schottroff, "*Gedenken*"

W. Schottroff, "*Gedenken*" im Alten Orient und im Alten Testament, WMANT 15 (Neukirchen, 1964).

Schunck, *Benjamin*

K. D. Schunck, *Benjamin*, BZAW 86 (Berlin, 1963).

Schwarzenbach, *Terminologie*

A. Schwarzenbach, *Die geographische Terminologie im Hebräischen des Alten Testaments* (Leiden, 1934).

Seierstad, *Die Offenbarungserlebnisse*

J. P. Seierstad, *Die Offenbarungserlebnisse der Propheten Amos, Jesaja und Jeremia* (Oslo, 1946, 1965²).

Sellin

E. Sellin, *Das Zwölfprophetenbuch*, KAT 12, 1 (Leipzig, 1929²).

Stamm, *Erlösen*

J. J. Stamm, *Erlösen und Vergeben im Alten Testament* (Bern, 1940).

Stamm, "Hosea 6:1–2"

J. J. Stamm, "Eine Erwägung zu Hosea 6:1–2," *ZAW* 57 (1939): 266–68

Testuz, "Deux fragments"

M. Testuz, "Deux fragments inedits des manuscrits de la Mer Morte," *Semitica* 5 (1955): 38–39.

Thomas, "Love"

W. Thomas, "The root אָהֵב 'love' in Hebrew," *ZAW* 57 (1939): 57–64.

Torczyner, "Bibelstellen"

H. Torczyner, "Dunkle Bibelstellen," BZAW 41, *Vom Alten Testament*, ed., K. Budde (Giessen, 1925), 274–80.

Tushingham, "A Reconsideration"

A. D. Tushingham, "A Reconsideration of Hosea Chapters 1–3," *JNES* 12 (1953): 150–59.

Vriezen, *Hosea*

Th. C. Vriezen, *Hosea: profeet en cultuur* (Groningen, 1941).

Vriezen, *Theologie*

Th. C. Vriezen, *Theologie des Alten Testament in Grundzügen* (Neukirchen, 1957).

Weiser

A. Weiser, *Das Buch der zwölf Kleinen Propheten*, ATD 24 (Göttingen, 1949).

Wellhausen

J. Wellhausen, *Die kleinen Propheten: Skizzen und Vorarbeiten Nr. 5* (Berlin, 1892; 1963⁴).

Westermann, "Begriffe"

C. Westermann, "Die Begriffe für Fragen und Suchen im Alten Testament," *KuD* (1960): 2–30.

Westermann, "Hoffen"
C. Westermann, "Das Hoffen im Alten Testament: Eine Begriffsuntersuchung," *ThV* 4 (1952): 19–70 [*Forsuchung am AT, Gesammelte Studien*, ThB 24 (Munich, 1964), 219–65].

Widengren, *Königtum*
G. Widengren, *Sakrales Königtum im AT und im Judentum* (Stuttgart, 1955).

Wildberger, *Eigentumsvolk*
H. Wildberger, *Yahwehs Eigentumsvolk*, ATANT 37 (Zürich/Stuttgart, 1960).

Wolff, "Begründung"
H. W. Wolff, "Die Begründung der prophetischen Heils– und Unheilssprüche," *ZAW* 52 (1934): 1–22 [*Gesammelte Studien* 9–35].

Wolff, "Ebene"
H. W. Wolff, "Die Ebene Achor," *ZDPV* 70 (1954): 76–81.

Wolff, *Gesammelte Studien*
H. W. Wolff, *Gesammelte Studien zum AT*, ThB 22 (München, 1964).

Wolff, "Der grosse Jesreeltag"
H. W. Wolff, "Der grosse Jesreeltag (Hosea 2, 1–3)," *EvTh* 12 (1952–53): 78–104 [*Gesammelte Studien* 151–81].

Wolff, "Heimat"
H. W. Wolff, "Hoseas geistige Heimat," *ThLZ* 81 (1956): 83–94 *Gesammelte Studien* 232–50.

Wolff, *Joel und Amos*
H. W. Wolff, *Joel und Amos*, BK 14, 2 (Neukirchen, 1969).

Wolff, "Wissen um Gott"
H. W. Wolff, " 'Wissen um Gott' bei Hosea als Urform der Theologie," *EvTh* 12 (1952–53): 533–54 [*Gesammelte Studien* 182–205].

Wolff, *Zitat*
H. W. Wolff, *Das Zitat im Prophetenspruch*, BEvTh 4 (München, 1937) [*Gesammelte Studien* 36–129].

Worden, "Influence"
T. Worden, "The Literary Influence of the Ugaritic Fertility Myth on the O.T.," *VT* 3 (1953): 273–97.

Wünche
A. Wünche, *Der Prophet Hosea übersetzt und erklärt mit Benutzung der Targumim, der jüdischen Ausleger Raschi, Aben Ezra und David Kimchi* (Leipzig, 1868).

Würthwein, "Ursprung"
E. Würthwein, "Der Ursprung der prophetischen Gerichtsrede," *ZThK* 49 (1952): 1–16 [*Wort und Existenz: Studien zum Alten Testaments* (Göttingen, 1970), 111–26].

Ziegler, *Duodecim prophetae*
J. Ziegler, ed., *Duodecim prophetae*, Septuaginta, Vetus Testamentum Graecum, 13, (Göttingen: 1963).

Zimmerli, "Jahwe"
W. Zimmerli, "Ich bin Jahwe," *Festschrift A. Alt*, ed., G. Eberling, BHTh 16 (Tübingen, 1953), 179–209 [*Gottes Offenbarung*, ThB 19 (München, 1963), 11–40].

Zimmerli, *Ezekiel*
W. Zimmerli, *Ezekiel*, BK 13 (Neukirchen, 1969).

Zolli, "Hosea 4:17–18"
J. Zolli, "Hosea 4:17–18," *ZAW* 56 (1938): 175.

Zolli, "Significato"
E. Zolli, "Il significato di *rd* e *rtt* in Osea 12:1 e 13:1," *Rivista degli Studi Orientali* 32 (1957): 371–74.

The English translation of the Book of Hosea printed
in this volume is new, based on the ancient texts
and following the exegetical decisions of the commentator. Within that translation words within
brackets [　] are regarded by the commentator as
interpolations, words within parentheses (　)
amplify the sense implied but not expressly stated by
the Hebrew text, words within angle brackets ⟨　⟩
represent a textual emendation which is discussed
in the textual notes.

Translations of ancient Greek and Latin texts are
taken from the *Loeb Classical Library* wherever possible. Translations made by the translator or editor
are so indicated. References to Ugaritic texts follow
the convention of A. Herdner (*CTCA*), with C.
Gordon's classification following in parentheses.

Wherever available, recent scholarly works are
cited in their published English versions. For the
convenience of those who continue to utilize original
foreign versions, page references to the latter are
given in brackets following the page references to the
English versions. In the case of journal articles
which have been reprinted in volumes of collected
essays, the bibliographical references to the latter
follow, again in brackets, the page references to the
original publications. Quotations from literature
not available in English translation have been
rendered by the translator.

The endpapers of this volume are reproduced
from Plates X and XI of *Discoveries in the Judean Desert of Jordan 5, Qumran Cave 4*, edited by John M.
Allegro with the collaboration of Arnold A. Anderson (Oxford: The Clarendon Press, 1968; © The
Paltestine Archaeological Museum). They are reproduced with the permission of the Palestine
Archaeological Museum and the Clarendon Press.
The front endpaper is a reproduction of 4Qp Hos[a]
(4Q166), of early Herodian date; it is Hosea 2:10–14
and commentary (left) and 2:8,9 and commentary
(right). The rear endpaper is a reproduction of
4Qp Hos[b] (4Q167), of early Herodian date; these
fragments contain citations from and commentary
on Hosea 1, 2 (?), 5, 6, and 8. The reproduction on
p. v, hitherto unpublished, is of Hosea 1:7 through
2:5 after 4QXII[d] (First Century B.C.); all rights
to this reproduction are reserved.

### 1. The Period

Prophetic proclamation is a special way of speaking to man in his time. Prophecy addressed Israel in the midst of her history. Any attempt to comprehend prophecy apart from the historical events surrounding it would only result in misunderstanding. This is just as true of Hosea as of any other prophet, although at first one might think that, since he is interested above all in the basic events of the history of God's people, he therefore is concerned with timeless truths. No other prophet says "now" as often as Hosea.[1] To be sure, we possess very little biographical information about him. Yet it is possible to date his sayings with a high degree of accuracy. At the most, the exact year may be disputed, but not the decade. This is extraordinary for such an early period. Though it is possible to date annals and similar historical works from the ancient Orient with this degree of accuracy, the same is not true of poetic, cultic, or Wisdom literature. We must take this into account in determining the special characteristics of prophetic speech.

Hosea's initial activity coincides with the last years of Jeroboam II, presumably at least five years before the king's death (747–46 B.C.)—752 at the latest. Not only is the threat in 1:4 directed at the Jehu Dynasty, but the entire chapter is also to be dated at the time of Jeroboam II. The only king named in 1:1b is Jeroboam II. This is understandable only if his name appeared in a superscription to a collection of Hosea traditions dating from Jeroboam's time which the redactor had at his disposal.[2] But chap. 1, which describes "how Yahweh began to speak through Hosea,"[3] already covers a period of at least five years.[4] Chap. 2:4–17 and chap. 3:1–5 also reflect a time of political security and economic plenty. There, as in 4:1–5:7, a major concern is the flourishing cult. The great political difficulties which began with the catastrophe of the Jehu Dynasty first appear in the prophet's threats (1:4; 3:4).

A second major period of Hosea's proclamation is linked with the crucial events of the Syro–Ephraimite War (5:8–11) and the subjugation by Tiglath–pileser III of extensive territory in Israel in the year 733 (5:14; 7:8f). At that time Hosea could look back upon a long series of palace revolts (7:7; 8:4); political vacillation between Egypt and Assyria (7:11); Hoshea ben Elah's submission to Assyria (5:13); and payment of heavy tribute (8:9f).[5]

The sayings contained in chaps. 9–12 are most intelligible if we relate them to the quiet period before and after the accession to the throne of Shalmaneser V in 727. To be sure, the mention of Shalman in 10:14 is not an allusion to Shalmaneser of Assyria, but more probably to the Moabite king Shalamanu, whom Tiglath–pileser III named among his tribute–paying vassals in the year 728.[6] Perhaps 9:3 and quite probably 11:5 and 12:2[7] presuppose Israel's mission to Egypt in 727, during the reign of Hoshea ben Elah (2 Kgs 17:4). The same may be said of 13:15,[8] although already here we find an obvious allusion to Assyria's punitive measure, which led to the death blow against the royal residence in Samaria.[9] "Where then is your king, that he may save you?" (13:10) likewise points to this final period, when King Hoshea already had been taken captive at the beginning of Assyria's attacks. Hence the latest group of texts which we can date with a fair amount of certainty has its origin around 725–24, immediately preceding or at the beginning of the siege of Samaria.

Thus Hosea with his prophecy accompanied his contemporaries in the Kingdom of Israel during a period of almost thirty years, the final and most agitated phase of Israel's history. He was the messenger of her end, nay more, the messenger of Israel's God, to whom he had to bear witness as Lord also of this end (11:8f; 14:5ff).

### 2. The Prophet Himself

Even the later editor of the Hosean traditions was more concerned with the dates relative to Israel's history than with those of Hosea's own life. In addition to the detailed information about the time of the prophet's activity,

---

| | |
|---|---|
| 1 | 4:16; 5:3, 7; 7:2; 8:8, 10, 13; 10:2, 3; cf. 13:13. |
| 2 | See pp. 3f. |
| 3 | 1:2a; see pp. 12f. |
| 4 | See pp. 11f. |
| 5 | See pp. 110–12, 136–37; cf. the relief of Tiglath–pileser III from the year 740 in *Die Religion in Geschichte und Gegenwort*, ed. K. Galling (Tübingen, 1958–65³), 1, Table 4, No. 3 opposite 817. |

| | |
|---|---|
| 6 | See p. 195. |
| 7 | See pp. 200, 211. |
| 8 | See pp. 228–29. |
| 9 | Cf. also 10:7 and the commentary. |

the editor names, besides Hosea himself, only his father, Beeri.[10] Neither his place of birth nor his office is mentioned, to say nothing of his age (cf. Jer 1:6), the year of his call (cf. Is 6:1), or similar details of his personal life. Our remaining knowledge of Hosea we owe exclusively to the fact that particulars of his life become the subject of his prophetic commission.

The most important of these is Hosea's *marriage*. We learn of his wife Gomer, the daughter of one Diblaim (1:3),[11] only because his execution of the divine command to marry "a whore" (1:2) is reported. The prophet's marriage is to expose the guilt of contemporary Israel, who has succumbed to the Canaanite fertility rites. Thus "the whore" Gomer was probably no exception in her own day; rather, she was simply one of many Israelite women who had submitted to the bridal rites customary among the Canaanites.[12]

We also learn of the two sons and daughter born of Hosea's marriage with Gomer. There was a slightly longer interval between the birth of the second child and the third—perhaps about three years (1:8)[13]—than between the first and second. Again, we are told about his children only because Hosea was commanded to give them unusual names: Jezreel, Without–Mercy, and Not–My–People (1:4f, 6, 9). They were signs pointing to Yahweh's decision to judge Israel because of her apostasy to the Baal cult.

We can only infer that one day Gomer, having committed adultery, left Hosea and became the legal wife of another man. It was most likely Gomer whom Hosea was later commanded to "love again", and whom he had to buy back for this purpose. Again, this was part of his proclamation of Yahweh's will in Israel (3:1f).[14]

Likewise, there is no direct evidence of the places in which Hosea lived and worked. We are completely certain that he was active in the Northern Kingdom. The cities he named are located chiefly in the regions of Ephraim and Benjamin. He most frequently mentions: the royal city of Samaria (7:1; 8:5f; 10:5, 7; 14:1);[15] the sanctuaries of Bethel (4:15; 5:8; 10:5; 12:5)[16] and Gilgal (4:15; 9:15; 12:12). He also mentions the Valley of Achor (2:17);[17] Adam on the Jordan (6:7);[18] Ramah and Gibeah (5:8);[19] and Gilead in Transjordan (6:8; 12:12).[20] The prophet never mentions Jerusalem or any other Judean city. Yet Judah falls within the immediate area of his interest, not only in the same sense as the foreign nations Assyria and Egypt (he also speaks of Judah as Ephraim's enemy [5:10]), but more importantly as a member of the ancient twelve tribes (10:11) standing together with Ephraim before Yahweh (5:12, 13, 14; 6:4).[21]

According to the content of his sayings, Hosea's public orations were most likely delivered in Samaria[22] or in the area of Bethel and Gilgal.[23] We can surmise where and when Hosea spoke in these cities only by examining the manner he chose to express himself. He primarily used the speech forms of the legal dispute (cf. רִיב in 2:4; 4:1, 4; 12:3)[24] or of the "watchman" of Ephraim (9:8; 5:8; 8:1).[25] It is therefore easily conceivable that he addressed public gatherings, for example, at the city gate (4:1–3; 5:1–7; 5:8–8:14; 12:1–14:1) or even at the cultic places (2:4–17; 4:4–19: 9:1–9). In either location, however, he spoke not as an official but as an independent prophet.[26]

We ought not think of Hosea, however, as a solitary figure in his opposition to Israel's conduct. He considered himself thoroughly allied with other prophets, a link in the chain of Yahweh's messengers that reached back to Moses (6:5; 9:7; 12:11, 14).[27] In addition, Hosea presents a clear picture of the true priest in Israel, which

---

10  On the meaning of "Beeri," see p. 5.
11  See p. 16.
12  See pp. 14f.
13  See p. 21.
14  See pp. 58, 61.
15  See p. 140.
16  On the epithet בֵּית אָוֶן ("Beth–aven"), see pp. 89f.
17  See p. 42.
18  See pp. 121f.
19  See pp. 112f.
20  See p. 122.
21  See p. 185; cf. also 8:14; 12:1b; 2:2, where, to be sure, Hosean authorship is uncertain; Judah is

assuredly secondary in 1:7; 5:5; 6:11; 12:3; see pp. xxxif.
22  On 5:1–7, see p. 96; on 5:8–7:16, p. 112; on 8:1–14, p. 140; on 10:9–15, p. 183.
23  On 4:4–19, see p. 76; on 12:1–15, p. 209; on 13:1–14:1, p. 224.
24  See pp. 66f.
25  See pp. 157f.
26  See p. 158.
27  See pp. 119f, 156f; also cf. the reminiscences of Amos in Hos 4:15; 8:14; 10:4 (11:10); 13:7f; see pp. 88f, 146f, 175ff, 194ff, 226ff.
28  See pp. 79ff, 121, 144ff.

was presumably kept alive in the Levitic circles of his own time (4:6; 6:6; 8:12).[28] These circles probably had a close connection with the prophetic groups. This relationship between prophets and Levites accounts for Hosea's familiarity with a large number of old Israelite traditions. It is possible that various series of Hosea's sayings bearing no stamp of a public oration[29] were delivered before this group of faithful followers among the opposition (9:10–10:8; 11:1–11; 14:2–9).[30]

Some of Hosea's words clearly indicate that it was difficult for him to speak publicly in Ephraim, at least temporarily; indeed, the outbreak of bitter hostility against him finally made public proclamation impossible, particularly after 733 (cf. especially 9:7–9, but also 12:1; 11:5b, 7a).[31] He had shared physically in his God's suffering over Israel's rebellion against him (8:1; 14:1). We do not know whether Hosea, with his small circle of followers, became oriented towards Judah or even took up residence there as a result of the attacks at the time the Kingdom of Israel collapsed. But his sayings did find their way to Judah, as their redaction makes clear.[32]

### 3. The Language of Hosea

In view of the book's transmission, we are unable to affirm that its every word belongs to the *verba ipsissima* of the prophet.[33] In a few instances it is certain that Hosea is not the author (e.g., 1:1, 7; 14:10); in several others, his own formulation has been fused with the language of the traditionists in such a way that it is no longer possible to separate them (e.g., 2:1–3; 7:10; 8:14; 11:10). For the most part, however, Hosea's own speech is unmistakable.

A large majority of his sayings have the basic form of the *divine speech*. In these sayings Yahweh speaks in the first person.[34] A smaller number of sayings are clearly formulated as *prophetic speech*. Here Yahweh is spoken of in the third person.[35] It should be noted that Yahweh's personal speech is found in extensive contexts, especially in sections which introduce a complex of sayings having a

unified theme. However, the "disputation style," with Yahweh in the third person, may appear in the midst of these complexes. This can result in a lively alternation from divine to prophetic speech (e.g., 4:10–15; 8:11–13; 12:1–15).

Conscious of the fact that he is Yahweh's messenger, the prophet most often utilizes the personal form of divine speech; he is the announcer of God's message. Other forms of divine speech are analogous to the language of the cult: (1) Yahweh's self–introduction ("I am Yahweh"), in connection with the proclamation of divine law (cf. 12:10 [9]; 13:4);[36] (2) the announcement of assurance that a prayer has been granted (oracle of salvation) within the framework of the lamentation liturgies (cf. 6:1–3; 8:1–3; 14:5–9).[37] Most of Hosea's prophetic sayings are reminiscent of those speech forms which have their *Sitz im Leben* in the legal dispute between two parties, especially when they bring their case before the elders at the city gate.

This explains the connection between the prophet's accusations and announcements of judgment (e.g., 4:1–3; 8:1–3; 13:1–3);[38] one hardly occurs without the other. Even the unity of longer passages is explicable in terms of the lawsuit, as for example, in the court proceedings against the unfaithful wife (2:4–17 [2–15])[39] or the rebellious son (11:1–9).[40] Such an interpretation also accounts for many of the abrupt changes from the first to the third persons of Yahweh and also from the second to the third persons of the accused party, especially in instances where the audience probably voiced an objection that is left unquoted.[41] Hosea's use of the key word ריב ("to contend, accuse," 2:4 [2]; 4:4; "lawsuit," 4:1; 12:3 [2]) clearly indicates that his proclamation of the divine word is modeled after the legal procedure in the city gate.

In our discussion of the form critical aspects of Hosea's sayings, three other features call for attention: (1) Words of genuine *lament* and *complaint* may be interspersed among the threats and accusations (4:6; 5:11; 7:8f;

---

29    See p. xxx.
30    See pp. 162ff, 172, 196, 234ff.
31    See pp. 156ff, 209ff.
32    See pp. xxxi, xxxii.
33    See pp. xxix–xxxii.
34    1:4f, 6, 9; 2:4–25; 4:4–9; 5:1–3; 5:8–7:16 (see
      p. 110); 8:1–12; 9:10–13, 15f; 10:9–15; 11:1–9, 11;
      12:10f; 13:4–14; 14:5–9.

35    3:5; 4:1–3; 5:4–7; 7:10; 8:13, 14; 9:1–9; 10:1–8;
      12:3–7, 13–15; 13:15–14:1, 2–4.
36    See pp. 214f, 223f.
37    See pp. 118f, 138, 233f.
38    See pp. 65f, 133f, 222.
39    See pp. 31ff.
40    See p. 193.
41    See pp. 74f, 133ff, 223.

8:8);[42] they attest to the compassion of Israel's God and his prophet for their people. (2) In the book of Hosea, the *exhortations* have their origin in the form of the "proposal to reach a settlement" (*Schlichtungsvorschlag*) in the lawsuit (2:4f [2f]; 4:15; 8:5 cj.; 14:2f [1f]; cf. 9:1; 10:12; 12:7 [6]).[43] (3) To a lesser extent we find forms peculiar to the law teacher: didactic exhortations (5:1)[44] and precepts (6:6; 8:6aβ).[45]

In this connection, the influence of Wisdom upon Hosea's language should be noted. We see it most visibly in the prophet's quotation of a proverb in 8:7[46] and in the close relationship of 2:23f to Wisdom's study of nature.[47] In addition, Hosea independently creates numerous metaphors. No other prophet—indeed, not one writer in the entire Old Testament—uses as many similes as Hosea does. He may take one metaphor and develop it in detail (11:1–4; 2:4–17 [2–15]); or, more frequently, he clothes the thought of each succeeding sentence in new imagery (e.g., 5:11–15; 7:4–12; 13:3, 15: 14:6–8 [5–7]). The most provocative are his similes for Yahweh and Israel. Not only does he picture Yahweh allegorically as a husband (2:4ff [2ff]),[48] a father (11:1ff), a physician (14:5 [4]; 7:1; 11:3; cf. 5:13; 6:1f), as shepherd (13:5f *G*) and fowler (7:12); but in even stranger similes as a lion (5:14; 13:7), a leopard (13:7) and a she–bear (13:8), as dew (14:6 [5]; cf. "dawn" and "downpour" in 6:3) and a luxuriant tree (14:9 [8]), as pus and rottenness (5:12). Corresponding to the first Yahweh similes named above, Israel appears as the wife (2:4ff [2ff]), then as the son (11:1ff), a sick person (5:13; 7:1, 9; 14:5 [4]; cf. 6:1f), a herd (13:5–8), a flighty dove and other birds of the air (7:11f; 9:11); further, Israel is said to be like a trained (10:11) as well as a stubborn heifer (4:16), a grapevine (10:1; 14:8 [7]), its grapes (9:10) and the wine of Lebanon (14:8 [7]), the early fig (9:10), and the lily (14:6 [5]), the forest of Lebanon and the olive tree (14:6f [5f]), a mother in labor as well as an unborn son (13:13). Israel is like a cake of bread (7:8), a slack bow (7:16), morning mist and dew (13:3a; cf. 6:4), chaff

blown from the threshing floor, and smoke that rises from the window (13:3b). Thus Hosea's audience must have been struck by the great number of metaphors he employed. In principle, he omits no sphere of life; but the imagery drawn from the vegetable and animal world and from family life clearly predominates.

As far as the transmitted text enables us to tell, the prophet's diction is not entirely poetic in character. On the whole his words are cast in an elevated prose that frequently changes into stricter poetic forms. Hosea's style is marked by the prominence of *parallelismus membrorum*; he shows a preference for synonymous parallelism, which he generally uses. By comparison, antithetic parallelism is a rarity. Synthetic parallelism, which fits quite well with his elevated prose, occurs more frequently. In accord with Hosea's enthusiastic manner of speech, a steplike parallelism (e.g., in 8:11; 13:6) seems to build to a climax.

Only with help from the thought-rhythm of *parallelismus membrorum* are we able, with some degree of certainty, to recognize a rhythmic structure in Hosea's sayings. Accordingly, we find the bicolon to be the most characteristic prosodic unit. But it is distinctive of Hosea to join these quite frequently with tricola, especially at the beginning and conclusion of a passage: 2:4a [2a], 5b [3b], 8 [7]; 5:1, 2; 8:11, 13b;[49] 9:3, 6;[50] 12:7 [6]; 14:1b [13:16b], etc. In this way the prophet brings his sayings to a climax. The lines usually receive three stresses. The change to short, two–stress lines must have had a startling affect that caught his audience's attention (e.g., 2:15b [13b]; 10:13a; 13:6b).[51] A more precise analysis is not possible, since the laws of meter for Hosea's time cannot be clarified, and since it is not certain that what has been recorded in the transmitted text corresponds to the words spoken.[52] The most important remarks on the poetic structure of the individual units of transmission are to be found in each case at the conclusion of the sections on "Form."[53] The arrangement of stress, line, and prosodic unit created by the *parallelismus*

---

42  See pp. 78ff, 114, 135f.
43  See pp. 32f, 89f, 134f, 194f.
44  See p. 97.
45  See pp. 120f, 141f.
46  See pp. 142; cf. 13:13 and pp. 227ff.
47  See pp. 53f.
48  On the motifs of the love songs in 2:9 [7], see p. 36; on 14:6–8 [5–7], see pp. 233f.

49  See p. 136.
50  See pp. 152.
51  See pp. 183, 224.
52  See p. xxx.
53  E.g., pp. 32f, 75, 152.

*membrorum* of 11:8–9 makes it the most highly poetic passage in the book.[54] In these verses the prophet also makes use of the stylistic device of *repetition* (11:8a), which he often employs elsewhere.[55] Finally, we have *alliteration* in 11:9b: a threefold א at the beginning of words in v 9bα; a twofold ק in v 9bβ. Clearer and more pleasing is the alliteration in 9:15, 16;[56] 12:2.[57] In two instances the *assonance*[58] becomes end rhyme, a rare phenomenon in Hebrew (2:7b [5b]; 8:7bα).[59]

### 4. The Theology of Hosea

Hosea names "Yahweh"[60] much more often than "God"[61] when he specifically mentions the one he serves as messenger. For Hosea knows only the God who, since the time of Moses (12:14 [13]), has revealed himself in the proclamation of his law and through his liberating acts: "I am Yahweh, your God from the land of Egypt" (12:10 [9]; 13:4). Nor does Israel know another as God and savior besides Yahweh (13:4b). Hosea is familiar with the interpretation of Yahweh's name in Ex 3:14, as he indicates in his negation of the old covenant formula.[62] Yahweh, the ancient God of Israel, is the God whom Hosea proclaims anew.

Except for the divine personal name, there is hardly any general mention of "God." Usually a suffix is attached to אֱלֹהִים, so that the word characterizes Yahweh as Israel's God: "Yahweh, your God" in 12:10 [9]; 13:4; 14:2 [1]; "Yahweh, their God" in 3:5; 7:10; "their God" in 4:12; 5:4; "your God" in 4:6; 9:1; 12:7a [6a], 7b [6b]; "my God" is said by the people in 2:25 [23]; 8:2; by Hosea in 9:17; "our God" in 14:4 [3]; "her God," i.e., Samaria's God, in 14:1 [13:16]. In those few instances in which "God" appears without a possessive pronoun (3:1; 8:6; 13:4b), the word also serves to elucidate Israel's right relationship to Yahweh alone;

otherwise, simply the word "God" appropriately stands only in the pre–Mosaic Jacob tradition (12:4 [3]; cf. v 7 [6]) and in formulaic expressions (4:1; 6:6).[63] The word אֵל emphasizes the incomparability of Israel's God.[64]

Hosea's language unequivocally shows that he is unable to speak of a divine being in a general religious sense; rather, he speaks precisely of Yahweh, who has attested and proved himself in history as the God of Israel.

Since this Yahweh is God not only of the past but of the present as well, the prophet can use new, extremely bold expressions in referring to him. He speaks of Yahweh, the judge of Israel, only once as "his Lord" (12:15 [14]). The above–named Yahweh similes should also be mentioned in this connection.[65] Because of Hosea's impudent, modernistic language, some of the similes must have sounded almost flippant to his audience. For example, Yahweh has Hosea describe him as "pus to Ephraim" and "rottenness to the house of Judah" (5:12), or as a "lion" that "rends and carries off his prey," from whom "none shall rescue" (5:14). There is also the imagery of the leopard and the enraged she–bear robbed of her cubs (13:7, 8).[66] The prophet's language itself strikes in the heart of his audience the terror of Yahweh's presently burning anger (5:10; 13:11). As far as we know, never before had anyone dared to speak of God in this fashion. Subordinating all consideration of pious tradition and aesthetic sensitivities, the prophet sought to bear witness to Yahweh's awesome, overpowering strength and present action.

Hosea also uses extreme imagery in his announcement of salvation. The power of God's saving deeds is elucidated by metaphors of the "dew" in 14:6 [5] and of the "luxuriant fruit tree" in v 9 [8]; yet the prophet is uncon-

---

54 See pp. 195f.
55 2:21f [19f] "to marry" (ארש); 3:1 "to love" (אהב) 4 times; 3:4 "without," "no," (אין) 5 times; 4:1 (אין) 3 times; 11:9 "not" (לא) 4 times; 14:2f "to return" (שוב).
56 See pp. 167f; cf. 14:9 [8] and p. 237.
57 See p. 211.
58 5:11; 7:8b: עָנָה—הֲפוּכָה; on 8:3b, see textual note "f"; on 8:7, see note "k"; on 12:9, see p. 214.
59 See p. 135.
60 יהוה occurs about 45 times in genuine sayings.
61 אֱלֹהִים occurs 26 times; אֵל 4 times; in addition to 2:1; 11:9; 12:1 [11:12], it probably occurs also

in 12:5aα [4aα]; see textual note "j" on 12:5.
62 See p. 21.
63 See p. 67; perhaps it also occurs in the textually uncertain verse 9:8a; see textual note "t" on 9:8.
64 11:9: "not man," "holy"; 2:1 [1:10]: "living God"; 12:1 [11:12], 5a [4a] (see textual note "j" on 12:5).
65 See p. xxiv.
66 See pp. 226f.

cerned that he thereby stands dangerously close to the imagery of the Canaanite vegetation cult.[67]

These expressions point to that which is most clearly recognizable in Hosea's best–known and fully allegorized metaphor of Yahweh as the loving yet rejected husband. Here Hosea's theology develops openly in dialogue with the *mythology* of his day in a remarkable process of adaptation of and polemic against this mythology.[68]

Hosea's use of the *mythologumenon* of Yahweh as Israel's husband has its roots in the prophet's recognition of Israel's specific guilt: the people have given themselves to "whoredom."[69] By her cultic practices and her dependence upon Canaanite mythology and thought, Israel has become unfaithful to Yahweh. The metaphor of the "first husband" (2:9 [7], 18 [16]) thus has the purpose of elucidating the accusation that Israel is guilty of whoredom and adultery.

Only in a derivative sense does this metaphor also emphasize that Yahweh is the exclusive Provider of all the gifts of the arable land (2:7 [5], 10 [8]). Hosea's adaptation of the divine husband concept to Yahwism presents Yahweh as the only God and thus states Yahwism's claim of exclusiveness. His modernistic language directly expresses the genuine profession of faith in Yahweh and clarifies its opposition to syncretism.

Two further observations plainly show how Hosea's use of mythical elements is dominated by his polemic against the Baal myth, and how the myth is broken precisely in the marriage parable. In the first place, it is Yahweh who provides the gifts of the arable land and who is free to take them back again (2:10 [8], 11 [9], 17 [15]). Here the concept of the conjugal union completely recedes, and Yahweh attests that he is—in contrast to Baal—Lord also over devastation and wilderness. In spite of Hosea's use of certain mythical fragments, his certitude that Yahweh alone is God disallows any suggestion of a plurality of divinities or even of a sexually differentiated Pantheon.

This brings us to the second point: Yahweh's partner in the marriage parable is not some goddess, but historical Israel. The legal categories of covenantal thought replace the mythico–cultic fertility concepts that are rooted in the ἱερὸς γάμος (sacral marriage) (cf. 1:9; 2:4 [2],

21f [19f]).

This unfolding of Hosea's theology in polemical dialogue with the cultus and mythology of Canaan provides us with a fundamental example of faith's dialogue with contemporary ideology.[70]

In spite of Hosea's daring, eristic usage of key words from the myth, the certitude remains dominant that the Yahweh who acts in the present and future is none other than the one who has begun his covenantal history with Israel at the time of her youth, with the exodus from Egypt (2:17 [15]; 11:1; 13:4); with the making of the covenant (1:9; 6:7; 8:1); and with the gift of divine law (2:21f [19f]; 8:12; 13:4f). Hosea views Israel's present and future together with her history.

It is quite remarkable how thoroughly Israel's history is embedded in Hosea's proclamation. He looks back over the last decade, when kings were murdered and the throne usurped (7:7; 8:4); over the last century, with the crimes of the Jehu Dynasty in 844 (1:4); on to the beginnings of kingship under Saul, where he locates the roots of the present kingship's transgression (13:10f; 9:15). Beyond this, he reaches back even more comprehensively to the period of the conquest (2:10 [8]; 9:10; 10:11f; 11:1ff; 13:5f). For Hosea the Conquest tradition is to be separated neither from the deliverance from Egypt (2:17 [15]; 11:1; 12:14 [13]; 13:4) nor from the Wilderness traditions (9:10; 13:5; 2:5 [3], 16f [14f]). The period of the conquest saw Israel's early encounter with the Baal cult (9:10) and with it the apostasy—determinative for Israel's present—from the God who had begun his saving history with her in Egypt and in the wilderness. Hosea's longest step back into history takes him to the Jacob traditions (12:4–5 [3–4], 7 [6], 13 [12]). They especially serve to lay bare Israel's present deceit against God and neighbor.

Hosea's use of historical traditions has considerably more significance than an arbitrary collection of examples from the past. If I am correct, there are three reasons for this. First, these historical retrospects disclose early, fundamental connections within Israel's history. Her apostasy to the Baal of Peor is an abominable transgression in view of the previous election of the fathers in the wilderness (9:10). Israel's wickedness and lies be-

67   See pp. 116f and 237.
68   See pp. 15f, 34, 44f.
69   1:2; 2:4–7 [2–5]; 3:3; 4:10–18; 5:3f; 6:10; 9:1.
70   Cf. E. Jacob, "L'Héritage cananéen dans le livre du prophète Osée," *RHPhR* 43 (1963): 250–59.

come transparent when set against the background of Yahweh's previous joy over the compliant heifer, Ephraim, and her election for service (10:11f; cf. also 9:15; 12:4f [3f], 13f [12f]).[71] Thus Hosea's interest in these connections of traditions proves to be a genuine interest in history. Of theological significance is the fact that in the light of Israel's beginnings, her present transgression is revealed as transgression against the God of love and election, against the Lord of saving history.

Second, the historical retrospects show how God's intensive struggle with Israel reaches from her past down to Hosea's present time. Yahweh's great lawsuit with his wife–turned–whore (2:4–17 [2–15]) and his accusing speech against the rebellious son (11:1–7) indicate how much the prophet is interested in the continuity of the defendant's previous life. Thus with the aid of history, Hosea presents Israel's transgression as "bound up," "stored up" transgression.[72] Here there is a genuine concern for more than isolated examples. Hosea pictures a loving God's continuous struggle with his stubborn people.

Third, it is not accidental that Hosea gives especially close attention to various beginnings: Jehu—the first king of the present dynasty (1:4); Gilgal and Saul—the beginning of the present kingship (9:15; 13:10f); Baal–Peor—the beginning of the cult of shame (9:10); the wandering in the wilderness and the deliverance from Egypt—the initial saving acts of Yahweh (2:17 [15]; 9:10; 11:1; 12:10 [9], 14 [13]; 13:4–6); the Jacob story—when Israel's deceitfulness began (12:4f [3f], 13f [12f]). Wherever Israel's beginnings are examined, her present immediately appears; indeed, the present is the end of the earlier beginnings of that history. In the light of the beginnings of Israel's history, a very essential aspect of Hosea's prophecy becomes understandable: the end of the ancient saving history now has actually begun. The most pregnant and also the most impressive statement illustrating this is found in the recasting of the old covenant formula as a formula of divorce (1:9; cf. 2:4 [2]);

but it is also expressed in the sayings which threaten Israel's return to Egypt, whereby the gift of the land is taken back (8:13; 9:3, 6).

Yet too little would be said if we contrasted the beginning of her saving history only with the end of Israel. There is also a future goal that corresponds to the beginning. But this we find only in Hosea's message of salvation.

First, however, let us consider the nature of the transgression Hosea uncovers in his indictment. He brings his accusation particularly against two groups within the nation: the priests and political leaders. He measures the priestly sacrifices and oracles and also the priests' activities in the fertility cult[73] against a remarkably positive ideal of a "knowledge of God." Hosea expects them to cultivate and use this "knowledge" in order to maintain the people's certitude in God's saving action and justice.[74] He charges the political leadership with zealous revolutionary intrigues and constant changes of direction in foreign policy which they carry out without ever seeking the will of Yahweh, the God of Israel.[75]

In his description of Israel's guilt, Hosea of course uses the familiar terms for sin and transgression as well.[76] Nor is it surprising that in his disputation with cultic circles he makes uncommonly frequent use of typically cultic concepts for guilt: defilement[77] and cultic transgression.[78] But that which is actually striking lies elsewhere. For Hosea, Israel's guilt is found above all in the dissolution of her personal relationship with her God, who has given himself to her in personal acts of love throughout the course of her history. This is most eloquently stated in the Yahweh similes of the loving husband (2:4–22 [2–20]), of the father (11:1f), and of the physician (14:5 [4]; 7:1; cf. 5:13; 6:1; 11:3). The prophet's metaphorical language provides us with an abundance of colorful, characteristically Hosean expressions for sin which can help every preacher avoid monotonous formulations. In addition to the particularly frequent imagery of "whoredom,"[79] we find the following

---

71 See pp. 185f, 217f.
72 Cf. 13:12 with v 10 and vv 1f; in addition, cf. the "twofold iniquity" of "then and now" in 10:10; see pp. 184f, 227f.
73 4:4–19; 6:1–6; 8:4–6, 11–13; 9:1; 10:1–8; 13:1–3.
74 4:1, 6; 6:6; 13:4–6; 2:10–15 [8–13], 21f [19f], and see pp. 79, 120f, 225f.
75 5:1f, 11ff; 7:3–16; 8:1–4, 7–10; 10:13–15; 13:10–

14:1 [13:16].
76 On חַטָּאת and עָוֹן, see p. 145.
77 טמא in 5:3; 6:10; 9:4.
78 אשם in 4:15; 10:2; 13:1; 14:1 [13:16]; see pp. 89f.
79 See p. xxvi.

expressions: Israel "no longer knows" (2:10 [8]; 5:4; 11:3) Yahweh; "forgets" (2:15 [13]; 4:6; 8:14; 13:6), "forsakes" (4:10) him; leaves him "to go after her lovers" (2:7 [5], 15 [13]; cf. 11:2); "flees from him" (7:13); "rebels against him" (7:13; 8:1); "disregards the instructions of his covenant" (6:7; 8:1); "turns to other gods" (3:1); "is unfaithful to him" (5:7; 6:7); "becomes stubborn" (4:16; 9:15). Moreover, numerous expressions denote her "false dealings" (7:1); "lies" (7:3; 10:13; 12:1 [11:12]); "deceit" (12:1 [11:12], 8 [7]); "falsehood" (10:2). As a result, Israel has lost her bearings,[80] is "unwise" (13:13); she "reels" (4:12) like a drunkard and "devotes herself to shame" (9:10).

The context in which these sayings in each case appear indicates how Hosea's God, in profound sorrow, laments the apostasy of his people; how he himself suffers under the distress their estrangement prepares for them. Our form critical analysis has already pointed out that Yahweh, having declared his judgment, laments over the impending disaster. After expressing his compassion, his words disclose the cause and then issue in a new threat.[81]

Corresponding to the divine suffering over Israel's sins is God's struggle to justly chastise her. Of course, numerous threats simply announce impending judgment; in his early period, Hosea first depicted it in terms of natural catastrophes (4:3; 5:7; 2:11ff [9ff]) and then later as military catastrophes (1:5; 7:16; 8:3; 10:14f; 14:1 [13:16]). It is more characteristic of Hosea when he announces that Yahweh personally will draw near to execute his punishment (5:12, 14; 7:12, 15; 12:10; 13:7ff), and that Yahweh will act not only as requiter (4:9; 12:3 [2]; 9:7),[82] but also as teacher (5:2, 9; cf. 10:10).[83] The most peculiar feature of Hosea's proclamation we find in the lawsuit speeches in which his God not only struggles with Israel but with himself as well; indeed, he calls his own decisions into question (2:4–17 [2–15]; 6:4; 11:8f following vv 1–7).

Thus according to Hosea, Yahweh's judgment in essence is his struggle for his people. The announcements of judgment take over the function of the exhortation to return, which had been unsuccessful in calling forth a response. In the beginning of his proclamation, Hosea's exhortations to repent become ultimatums (2:4f [2f]); later, they still appear occasionally (4:15; 8:5 G)[84] though they are met with stubborn resistance (4:16), refusal (11:5b), and the complete inability to return, since the actions of the people have rendered them incapable of conversion (5:4; 7:2). Or we find an all–too–fleeting, liturgically recited turn to Yahweh as a kind of self–appeasement expressed in affected phrases of confidence rather than an acknowledgment of guilt (6:1–3; 8:2). Thus Israel's God waits in vain for Israel's return to him (5:15; 6:4; 7:7, 10, 14, 16).[85] Instead, as in her cult, Israel merely executes strategic maneuvers in domestic (7:3ff) and foreign policy (5:13; 7:11). With his God, Hosea had hoped that the severe blows of judgment might accomplish what the exhortations were unable to do (2:8f [6f], 16f [14f]; 3:3–5). Nor could Tiglath–pileser's most severe attacks strike fear in their hearts. Even when the sword danced through Israel's cities, they held fast to their apostasy from Yahweh, as the final pronouncement of judgment in the lawsuit against the rebellious son states (11:6f).[86]

Under these circumstances, how could Hosea have proclaimed a message of salvation? In the prophet's early period, it had already become apparent that, after Israel had broken the covenant (1:9), a new beginning of the saving history was not to be expected from a reformation among the people in response to the prophet's warnings. Rather, it was to come only as a result of the preconditions which God himself created: in his judgment he would block Israel's path to her idols (2:8 [6]) and bring her anew to the wilderness, the place where his saving history had begun (2:16 [14]; cf. 3:4). There, according to the hope expressed by Hosea, Israel again would turn her thoughts to Yahweh (2:9 [7]), listen to his wooing words of love (2:16f [14f]), and return to him and his goodness (3:5). Already in this early phase of Hosea's

80  She is "without heart," i.e., "without understanding," 7:11; 4:11, 14; see pp. 38f.
81  See p. xxiii.
82  See pp. 82 and 156.
83  See pp. 99 and 113.
84  See p. 134; the sayings in 10:12; 12:7 [6], quotations of divine oracles from Hosea's early period, are only indirect exhortations to repent.

85  See pp. 127f.
86  See pp. 200f.

proclamation, when the political turmoil was yet to [illegible] come, this new beginning had its foundation in the efficacious intervention of Yahweh alone, who courted his beloved with his mighty though severe acts. The lawful opportunity for Israel's return was created only by the emphatic love of Yahweh (3:1).[87]

After 733, the later phase of Hosea's activity, when it also became clear that Yahweh's judgment could not bring Israel to obedience,[88] his unqualified love is expressly represented as the only precondition for healing Israel's apostasy and for giving her new life—a thought which breaks through in 11:8f. This saying must be seen strictly in relation to the powerful indictment leveled in 11:1–7 which, after a thorough discussion of the opponent's former life, pronounces the sentence: "My people are bent on apostasy from me" (11:7a).[89] This statement should be compared with 2:9f [7f], 16f [14f]; 3:4f. What is novel here is that the return, vainly awaited in Israel in spite of all the forces of judgment she experienced (11:7a), now takes place in Yahweh.[90] By saying no to his own burning anger, Yahweh does not become a different kind of God. It is precisely his love's victory which shows clearly that he has remained faithful to the beginning of the saving history (11:1) and that in his freedom and holiness, he acts independently of all human reaction. Yahweh's saving intention is at last conceptualized unambigiously in 14:5 [4]: "I will love them spontaneously"; the foregoing (14:2–4 [1–3]) invitation to return already presupposes this love.[91] Perhaps the remarkable combination of the Jacob and Moses tradition in 12:13 [14], 14 [15] means to say that a similar history of transgression preceded the deliverance from Egypt at the very outset of saving history.[92]

Yahweh brought lawsuits against his rebellious son (11:1–9) as well as against his wife (chaps. 2–3). When we compare the outcome of these trials with those laws formulated by early Deuteronomic circles which followed Hosea and were familiar with his words, we must consider the legally required punishment of the rebellious

son and the unfaithful wife in Dtn 21:18ff and 24:1ff. Then it becomes clear that in the end Hosea's prophecy points in the direction of Pauline theology.[93] God's struggle for his people and his suffering under their guilt is sealed by Jesus Christ (2 Cor 5:19–21), in whom this suffering bears fruit for all nations. In the light of this goal, the prophecy of Hosea in Israel becomes a model for the struggle carried on by Jesus' messengers on behalf of man in today's world.

### 5. The Transmission of Hosea's Prophecy

What path did Hosea's sayings take, from their proclamation to their final redaction in the present book of Hosea? The speaker as well as his audience can take the first step of putting the oral word into written form.

Judging from the first person style of the *memorabile*[94] in 3:1–5, it appears almost certain that the prophet himself is responsible for one part of the written tradition. The theme and the technique of composition of 2:4–17 [2–15] make it probable that together with 3:1–5 it formed an old literary unit.[95] In the immediate context, we find evidence of a different hand at work, as seen most clearly in the third person account in 1:2–6, 8f. Here one of Hosea's disciples[96] presents the beginning of his prophetic activity, likewise in the form of a *memorabile*.[97] The same disciple is probably responsible for the expansions of Hosea's own writings (2:4–17 [2–15]; 3:1–5) made by 2:18–25 [16–23], 1–3 [1:10–2:1], since these verses contain elements of composition similar to the *memorabile* in 1:2–6, 8f.[98] This disciple's primary concern is to interpret the old Hosean text by supplementing it with Hosea's later sayings.[99] However, since the sayings in 2:23–25, 1–3 presuppose a knowledge of the symbolic names of the prophet's children, he places 1:2–6, 8f first. In 2:18–25 he possibly takes up sayings which had already been fixed in writing, for the formula of divine utterance "saying of Yahweh" (נאם־יהוה) in vv 18, 23 also concludes a collection of the prophet's

---

87  See p. 63.
88  See pp. 129f, 147.
89  See pp. 193f.
90  See pp. 200–203.
91  See pp. 237f.
92  See pp. 217f.
93  Cf. Rom 8:3ff; see pp. 63f, 203.
94  See pp. 57f.

95  See pp. 33, 59.
96  See p. 11.
97  See p. 10.
98  See pp. 25f, 47f.
99  See p. 48.

sayings in 11:11bβ. Moreover, the concepts of the sayings in 2:18–25 are more closely related to 11:8f, 11 and 14:2–9 than to any other chapter.[100] Thus 1:2–6, 8f; 2:1–3:5 may be considered the first self–contained transmission complex in the book, a complex already having a literary prehistory of its own.

The second large transmission complex, introduced with the summons to "Hear the word of Yahweh" in 4:1a[101] and concluded by the formula of divine utterance (נאם־יהוה) in 11:11bβ,[102] presents quite a different picture. The framework provided by these formulas, which do not occur elsewhere within the transmission complex, belongs to its final stage of redaction. Its formation and growth are much more difficult to explain than that of the first complex. In contrast to chaps. 1–3, we find no formulas which introduce and conclude smaller units—aside from those mentioned above marking the outer limits of the transmission complex itself. Nevertheless, in certain instances it is possible to establish the beginning of the prophet's orations. The most important indications of this are the naming of the addressee, the distinct beginning of a new theme, and the absence of a copula that combines a saying with its forgoing context.[103] The sayings which commence in this fashion are usually connected with several other sayings. On the one hand, these sayings may be recognized as new rhetorical units by the change from a Yahweh speech to prophetic speech (i.e., from the style of the messenger speech to that of the disputation) or the change from the second person to the third of the audience (i.e., from the style of direct address to that of the account). On the other hand, an initial copula,[104] a pronoun[105] or pronominal suffix referring to the addressée, and the continuation of the former theme can make a connection with the preceding unit. From these two observations, we may conclude that the sayings within a series combined in this manner were proclaimed by the prophet on one and the same occasion. Thus they form a "kerygmatic unit." Between the rhetorical units, the audience may

have voiced its objections, or the speaker may have turned from one group to address another.[106] Both interruptions become understandable in the light of Hosea's preference for forms of speech taken from the legal dispute.[107]

The kerygmatic units build the first transmission units within the entire complex of chaps. 4–11. The peculiar way the sayings have been strung together, as described above, is explicable only if these kerygmatic units present sketches of scenes which were written down soon after the prophet had delivered his message. The frequently poor condition of the text may have resulted from the difficult circumstances under which it was first produced. Hosea's circle—those who were devoted to him from the outset and who supported him during perilous times[108]—were quite probably responsible for these sketches. Not all of them reflect the commotion of a public dispute (4:1–9:9; 10:9–15). Several passages seem more understandable if Hosea originally addressed them to the inner circle of the opposition (9:10–10:8; 11:1–11).[109] But in both cases, the traditions lists were presumably the same. Since these sketches probably date from various periods[110]—even though the main block (5:8–10:15) best fits the time around 733—their collection is to be considered a special undertaking which has left its stamp on the material in the introductory (4:1a) and concluding (11:11bβ) formulas. We find no evidence against the supposition that the sketches follow a chronological order. This is hardly surprising if the various elements of the transmission complex, as well as its final redaction, derive from Hosea's circle, who were experts in matters of tradition.[111]

A third transmission complex is found in chaps. 12–14. Apparently consisting of three[112] sketches, this composition is related to the second complex. We may also assume that in chaps. 12–14 the scenes took place both in public (12:8ff; 13:9ff)[113] and in private, among a closed circle of Hosea's followers (14:2–9).[114] In this respect, it seems unlikely that the present shape of the

---

100 See pp. 196f.
101 See p. 66.
102 See p. 196f.
103 4:1, 4; 5:1, 8; 8:1; 9:1, 10; 10:1, 9; 11:1.
104 ו or כ׳; see p. 138.
105 The pronoun is often placed first in the sentence; see p. 138.
106 E.g., see p. 75f, 110, 134f.

107 See pp. xxiii.
108 See pp. xxiif.
109 See pp. 163, 172, 196.
110 Merely cf. p. 76 with p. 197.
111 See p. xxiif.
112 See pp. 223f, 234.
113 See pp. 208, 223.
114 See p. 234f.

third complex goes back to the prophet himself, although it begins with Hosea's lament over his repudiation in the Northern Kingdom (12:1).[115] Without exception his sayings in chaps. 12–14 fit the last period of the Northern Kingdom, during the time of Shalmaneser V. One observes several small differences between this third complex and the sketches in chaps. 4–11: the deictic כִּי, which introduces Hosea's reply to his opponents, is completely absent in chaps. 12–14;[116] rhetorical units are repeatedly combined into one kerygmatic unit only by theme, but not by stylistic connectives (copula; pronoun).[117] Finally, the expression "[I am] Yahweh your God [from the land of Egypt],"[118] which belongs to liturgical traditions, occurs only in these chapters. The doxology inserted in 12:6 indicates that this transmission complex was soon proclaimed anew in a worship setting. This took place, in fact, in Judah, as we see from the Judaic redaction in 12:3a, which differs from all other Judaic glosses in the book.[119]

All three large complexes of transmission are parallel to each other in that they each move from accusation to threat, and then to the proclamation of salvation. Each may stem from different writers, but they all belong to the same circle of Hosea's contemporary followers,[120] who also were the forerunners of the Deuteronomic movement.

This is indicated by the numerous connections between the Hosean traditions and the language and theology of Deuteronomy, as the commentary on individual passages will show. Entire complexes of thought characteristic of Deuteronomic paraenesis occur first in Hosea. Thus, we find reminiscences of the exodus from Egypt, of divine guidance through the wilderness, and of the entry into the arable land, combined with the themes of Israel's satiation, presumption, and forgetting of Yahweh.[121]

In addition, there is the struggle against Israel's political alliances;[122] the manner in which תּוֹרָה (Torah) is spoken of;[123] Yahweh as Israel's "teacher";[124] Yahweh's "love";[125] "redemption";[126] the genuine prophet who is "with God";[127] "brotherhood";[128] the maṣṣēbôth of the Canaanites;[129] "grain, new wine, and olive oil."[130]

The transmission of the Hosean traditions, which were already fixed in writing during the prophet's lifetime, corresponds to these connections between Hosea and Deuteronomy. This process of transmission spans the time from the early Deuteronomic movement down to the Deuteronomistic circles of the exilic period. It is still possible to determine several of the steps in the redaction that covered a period of almost two hundred years. The earliest are the additions made by the initial traditionists—those who sketched the scenes in which Hosea proclaimed Yahweh's word. These we find in 8:14 and 11:10. Their style does not fit the context while their content is a combination of Hosean material and sayings from Amos.

Still another redactor took certain of Hosea's sayings—either literally or freely—and used them to gloss other sayings in order to elucidate or supplement them. Thus 2:10bβ picks up the thought of 8:4 and 13:2; 4:9 supplements chap. 4 with the very words of 12:3; 6:10b is taken from 5:3; 7:10a from 5:5a; 14:5b perhaps from 11:9a (likewise 14:4b?).[131]

A relatively early Judaic redaction supplemented Hosea's prophecy with a Judaic salvation eschatology. This is clearly recognizable in 1:7 and in the expansion of 3:5[132] in the first transmission complex; perhaps it also occurs in 9:4bβ.[133] This redaction may be connected with the late phase of Hosea's activity, when he looked with hope toward certain circles in Judah (12:1b).[134] It is easily distinguished from another, later Judaic redac-

---

115 See p. 209.
116 See p. 208.
117 See p. 224.
118 In 12:10; 13:4; 14:2.
119 See p. xxxii.
120 See pp. xxiif.
121 See pp. 40, 226.
122 See p. 211.
123 See pp. 137f.
124 See p. 99.
125 See p. 197.
126 See p. 127.
127 See p. 158.

128 See p. 28.
129 See pp. 173f.
130 See p. 37.
131 See textual note "h" on 14:5.
132 See textual note "g" on 3:5.
133 See p. 155.
134 See p. 210f.

tion which took Hosea's accusations and threats against the Northern Kingdom and applied them in like manner to Judah: 4:5aβ;[135] the word "Judah" in 4:15;[136] 5:5bβ; 6:11a; we have yet to consider whether 8:14 and 11:10 have a connection with the Judaic redaction of Amos.[137] In 12:3 *M*,[138] "Judah" has displaced an original "Israel." This differs from all of the aforementioned Judaic glosses in that they never replace one word with another but rather expand a verse, as can be seen most clearly in 4:15. This is further evidence for our supposition that chaps. 12–14 were once transmitted separately from the other complexes. Whether the brief glosses, such as "prophet" in 9:8a, "angel" in 12:5a, and "for all this" in 7:10b, were added before or after the final redaction of the book must remain an open question.

We are no longer able to determine when the three transmission complexes were combined into the present book of Hosea. This was probably accomplished with the final redaction, when the superscription in 1:1 was added. The superscription is written in the Deuteronomistic language of a circle of redactors who could have edited a series of preexilic prophetic books[139] as early as the 6th century. The closing words of 14:10 may also have their origin in this same circle; its language likewise belongs to the exilic or early postexilic period.[140]

135  See p. 77.
136  See textual note "w" on 4:15.
137  Cf. R. Tournay's review of H. W. Wolff's *Dodekapropheton 1. Hosea* (Neukirchen, 1961), *RB* 69 (1962): 271–74; see pp. 136, 147, 195, 203.
138  See textual note "h" on 12:3.
139  See p. xxi.
140  See p. 239.

# Hosea

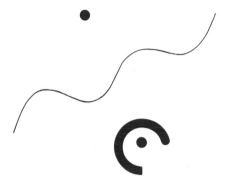

## The Title of the Book

**Bibliography**
K. Budde
"Der Abschnitt Hosea 1–3 und seine grund-
legende religionsgeschichtliche Bedeutung,"
*ThStKr* 96/97 (1925): 1–89.
A. D. Tushingham
"A Reconsideration of Hosea Chapters 1–3,"
*JNES* 12 (1953): 150–159; see the Bibliography
for 1:2–9.

# 1

1  **The word of Yahweh that came to Hosea
the son of Beeri, at the time of Uzziah,
Jotham, Ahaz, and Hezekiah, the kings of
Judah; and at the time of Jeroboam the
son of Joash, the king of Israel.**

## Form

Each expression contained in this introductory sentence
can also occur as a component of the superscriptions
found at the beginning of other prophetic writings. "The
word of Yahweh that came to . . ." (דבר־יהוה אשר היה
אל־) are the first words in Joel 1:1; Mic 1:1; Zeph 1:1
(Jer 1:1 *G*); the phrase also is found in Ezek 1:3; Jon 1:1;
Zech 1:1; Hag 1:1 and Mal 1:1 in a slightly varied
order. The name of the prophet's father is given with
"son of" (בן) in Joel 1:1; Jon 1:1; Zeph 1:1; Zech 1:1;
Is 1:1; Jer 1:1. "At the time of" (בימי) with the name of
the reigning kings of Judah indicates the time of a
prophet's activity in Mic 1:1; Zeph 1:1; Is 1:1 and
Jer 1:2; both the kings of Judah and Israel are named in
Am 1:1. These formal elements occur again in the superscription to Zephaniah. In the exilic and postexilic
prophets they are found only with modifications. The
prophet's name, the name of his father, and the time of
his activity are grammatically subordinate to "the word
of Yahweh" (דבר יהוה), the proper title of the book.

## Setting

The author of the superscription, a collector of prophetic
traditions, probably belonged to Judaic circles, since he
gives preeminence to the Davidic dynasty. He has used
ancient data that have not been preserved elsewhere.
Otherwise how might he have known the name of Beeri,
Hosea's father, which never again appears in the book
of Hosea? That Jeroboam II is the only Israelite king
mentioned here also suggests that he used a preexisting
source. Unlike the kings of Judah noted here, he provides
us with the name of Jeroboam's father. This is not of
great significance, since he must distinguish between
Jeroboam, the son of Joash, and Jeroboam I, the son of
Nebat.[1] Of decisive importance, however, is that the list
of the Judean kings extends far beyond the death of
Jeroboam II, which probably coincided with the death of
Uzziah of Judah.[2] The Judaic redactor apparently
intended to indicate a longer period of time than did the
source that provided him with both the names of the
Israelite king and Hosea's father, Beeri. Did his source
bear a superscription containing both these names?
If so, this source could not have included the complete
literary tradition of Hosea's sayings, since many of them
unquestionably originated during that period of disorder
when one king was followed quickly by another (e.g.,

---

1  Thus also Am 1:1; cf. 2 Kgs 14:23f.
2  See pp. xxiif.

8:4), that is, during the Syro–Ephraimite war (5:8ff), or the time of the Assyrian threat (9:3, etc.). One might assume that this was a superscription to the previously independent material in chaps. 1–3. These chapters, which in their framework reveal an intimate knowledge of Hosea's relationships, also name the members of his family (1:3, 4, 6, 9). Moreover, they undoubtedly contain sayings which belong to the politically quiet and prosperous time of Jeroboam II (1:4; 2:7, 10, 13). In addition, however, chaps. 1–3 also include sayings that are more understandable in the time after the events of 733, i.e., during the time of King Hoshea (2:1–3, 23–25),[3] although these sayings are still linked by catch-words with the theme of the prophet's family, which unites these chapters. Hence, it seems better to regard the names of Beeri and Jeroboam as having originally belonged in 1:2a. Then the time of Jeroboam II would characterize only the *beginning* of Hosea's work, but would not date all the sayings in chaps. 1–3. Therefore 1:1 appears to us to be the work of a Judaic redactor who took data from 1:2a and used it to create the present title of the book in 1:1. The redactor introduces Hosea to his readers as a contemporary of Isaiah (1:1) by listing the names of four Judean kings. With respect to the entire book, this historical information may be true at least to the extent that Hosea's activity in any case probably reached the first years of Hezekiah's reign.

The redactor was a member of a circle of Deuteronomistic theologians. The combination of "word of Yahweh" (דבר יהוה) with "came" (היה) and "to" (אל) is found in the Deuteronomistic History,[4] in Jeremiah,[5] and in Ezekiel.[6] Since Micah (without his father's name) and Zephaniah have essentially the same title,[7] we perhaps see in these books traces of a group which edited a series of preexilic prophetic writings. The validity of the ancient prophetic sayings of judgment—already made evident by the fall of the Northern Kingdom—became apparent to all after the kingdom of Judah was destroyed. The exilic period in the first half of the sixth century B.C. was an opportune time for completing a collection of preexilic prophetic sayings, especially since a theology of Yahweh's Word had intrinsically set the stage for such Deuteronomistic circles.[8] This appears to be the most probable time and setting of the writing of Hos 1:1.

## Interpretation

The very first words of the book provide the basis for its presentation of the accounts and sayings to its reader: they are "Yahweh's Word." Here דבר יהוה no longer means the individual prophetic utterances; rather, this refers to the prophet's total experience, which includes not only the words of revelation he is to proclaim (e.g., 2:18, 23f; 4:1), but also the divine commands that ordered and directed his own life (1:2; 3:1). The book contains prophetic narratives (1:2–9; 3:1–5), presented not because of a biographical interest, but because they preserve the Word of Yahweh. The singular "word" (דבר) signifies that with the variety of forms assumed by Yahweh's address there is a manifest uniformity of his will. The formulation of the book's title is in this respect an important step toward the formation of the canon.[9] But here the "Word of God" does not yet mean "Holy Scripture;"[10] instead it makes very clear that the Word of God is an event that confronts the prophet again and again: "that comes to" (אשר היה אל־).

In the relative clause begun by these words, all other data, including Hosea's name, are subordinated to the first two principal words: דבר יהוה. "Hosea" (הושע) is a name of thanksgiving ("He has helped"), formed simply by the perfect hipʻil of ישׁע,[11] attesting to the help experienced either in the birth of the child thus named, or in connection with some other event. The Israelite naturally thinks of Yahweh as his helper. The following observations speak against Koehler's derivation

---

3   See p. 12.
4   2 Sam 7:4, etc., a total of twelve times.
5   1:4, 11; 2:1, etc., a total of thirty times.
6   1:3; 3:16; 6:1, etc., a total of fifty times. For a complete survey, see O. Grether, *Name und Wort Gottes im AT*, BZAW 64 (Giessen, 1934), 67f; cf. W. Zimmerli, *Ezekiel*, BK XIII/1 (Neukirchen–Vluyn, 1969), 88f.

7   See above, p. 3.
8   Cf. E. Janssen, *Juda in der Exilzeit*, FRLANT 69 (Göttingen, 1956), 84ff.
9   Cf. O. Grether, *Name*, 145f.
10  Contra A. Weiser, *Das Buch der zwölf kleinen Propheten*, ATD 24 (Göttingen, 1949).
11  M. Noth, *Die israelitischen Personennamen im Rahmen der gemeinsemitischen Namengebung*, BWANT 46 (Stutt-

of the name from יוֹשִׁיעַ and יְהוֹ:[12] (1) the name occurs
in its complete form, הוֹשַׁעְיָה, in Neh 12:32; Jer 42:1;
43:2; (2) during the time of the monarchy, names were
formed predominantly by the perfect followed by a
noun, whereby the noun can be omitted, as e.g., in
"Nathan" (נָתָן) and "Ahaz" (אָחָז);[13] (3) noun–imperfect forms of names with יהו always appear differently, as
in יְ(ה)וֹיָקִ(י)ם, יְ, and יְ(ה)וֹיָרִיב. In extrabiblical
sources, the name is found in the Elephantine Papyri of
the fifth century B.C.[14] In the Old Testament four other
persons also bear this name: the earlier name of Joshua;[15]
the last king of Israel;[16] two different clan chieftains.[17]
In both the older examples,[18] the men are expressly
referred to as Ephraimites. Did the name originate in the
tribe of Ephraim, or—because of Joshua—was it a
particularly favorite name there? Should Hosea be considered a son of this leading tribe in the Northern Kingdom? This would certainly be the case if we were able
to connect the name of his father, Beeri, with the village
situated on the Ephraimite border, known today as
*el-bīre* (2 miles SW of Bethel), perhaps where the ancient
town of Beeroth was located.[19] But according to the
biblical tradition[20] this is undoubtedly a town in Benjamin. For the moment, we will have to leave the question
open whether Hosea actually comes from the "border-
land of Ephraim that was ravaged by war,"[21] or whether
he "perhaps comes from Beeroth in Benjamin."[22] Con-

sidered etymologically, it is unlikely that the father's
name was connected with a place–name. The proper
name "Beeri" (באְרי)[23] is a simple expression of the
parents' joy at the birth of a child and can be translated
"My Spring!" or perhaps better "O Spring!"[24] The
ancient name probably expressed delight at the birth of a
son, through whom the life of the clan would continue
as a "living spring" of water. It is simply important to the
author of the book's superscription that the prophet is
the son of a certain father; that is, he is a man among
men. A title of office, such as "prophet" (נָבִיא), is not
found here,[25] nor is the name of his place of origin.[26]

The redactor is more concerned with the data concerning Hosea's time than his person. The religious community in Jerusalem, of which he was a member, oriented
itself according to the Davidic dynasty, which for it was
the legitimate dynasty as well as the more familiar.
A. Jepsen[27] determined the time of each king's reign as
follows: Uzziah, 787–736; Jotham, 756–741; Ahaz,
741–725; Hezekiah, 725–697. In each case the years are
to be counted from the beginning of autumn. The date of
Ahaz' death and the beginning of Hezekiah's reign are
the least certain. According to 2 Kgs 18:13 it could be

gart, 1928), 175ff; also cf. 32 and 36.

12 L. Koehler and W. Baumgartner, *Hebräisches und
aramäisches Lexicon zum Alten Testament* (Leiden, 1953;
1967³), 228.

13 Noth, *Personennamen*, 21.

14 H. L. Ginsberg, "Letters of the Jews in Elephan-
tine," *Ancient Near Eastern Texts Relating to the
Old Testament*, ed. J. B. Pritchard (Princeton:
Princeton Univ., 1955²), 492; also found in
A. Cowley, *Aramaic Papyri of the Fifth Century B.C.*
(Oxford, 1923), No. 33, 4; 39, 1; also see the index;
further, E. G. Kraeling, *The Brooklyn–Museum
Aramaic Papyri* (New Haven: Yale Univ., 1953),
4,24; 6e; 9,23f.

15 Nu 13:8, etc.

16 2 Kgs 15:30, etc.

17 Neh 10:24; 1 Chr 27:20.

18 Nu 13:8; 1 Chr 27:20.

19 Cf. K. v. Rabenau, "Beeroth," *Biblisch–historisches
Handwörterbuch* 1, eds. B. Reiche and L. Rost
(Göttingen, 1964–66), 210f; also K. D. Schunck,
*Benjamin*, BZAW 86 (Berlin, 1963), 160, n. 50.

20 Josh 18:25; 2 Sam 4:2.

21 J. Hempel, *Die althebräische Literatur und ihr hel-
lenistisch–jüdisches Nachleben* (Potsdam, 1934), 130,
following G. Hölscher, *Die Profeten* (Leipzig, 1914),
205ff.

22 J. Hempel, *Worte der Profeten* (Berlin, 1949), 115.

23 Appearing elsewhere in the O.T. only in Gen. 26:34,
where it is the name of Esau's Hittite father-in-law;
cf. J. Lippl, *Die zwölf kleinen Propheten* (Hosea)
HSAT VIII, 3, 1 (Bonn, 1937) for the extrabiblical
occurrences in the Elephantine Papyri and the El
Amarna Tablets.

24 Noth, *Personennamen*, 224; the vocalic ending ' in a
name usually has a vocative meaning; *ibid.*, 38.

25 The word "prophet" does not occur in superscriptions until Hab 1:1; Hag 1:1; Zech 1:1; reference to
a prophet's occupation appears only in Am 1:1;
Jer. 1:1; Ezek 1:3a; cf. W. Zimmerli, *Ezekiel*, 28.

26 This is noted in the superscriptions in Am 1:1;
Mic 1:1; Na 1:1; Jer 1:1.

27 *Untersuchungen zur isr.-jüd. Chronologie*, BZAW 88
(Berlin, 1964), 42; cf. E. Kutsch, "Israel (II):
Chronologie der Könige von Israel und Juda,"
*RGG³*, 3:944.

715,[28] but according to 2 Kgs 18:1 the year is 729.[29] Since we have no knowledge of Hosea's sayings after the fall of the Northern Kingdom (Samaria fell in the spring of 721), Hos 1:1 does not support the year 715. The mention of Hezekiah would indicate that Hosea was active at least down to the time immediately preceding the assault on Samaria (724–23), since it is unlikely that the list of Judean kings was unintentionally taken over from Is 1:1. It is possible that the first important stage of the prophet's work was during the reign of Uzziah. In support of this is the fact that only Jeroboam II[30] is mentioned from the parallel list of Israelite kings. Our literary–critical observations[31] suggest that the name of Jeroboam, originally a part of 1:2, denotes the beginning of Hosea's prophetic work. The prominence given to Jeroboam's name may underline the intrinsic importance as well as the large extent of Hosea's preaching during his reign.

### Aim

The significance of the book's title lies in the fact that the editor has characterized Hosea's prophetic sayings and narratives with respect to their origin in three ways.

First, and of most importance, these collected words are God's Word, and as such they should be read. Second, they are words addressed to a man, meaning that God's word becomes audible through this man Hosea. Third, this Word of God is addressed to a particular time in history, namely, in the decades preceding the collapse of the state of Israel. In the Deuteronomistic redactor's opinion,[32] the authority of the words he preserves is not diminished by their belonging to a datable past. Rather, this is what provides the very basis for preserving them. In those days, the Word of Yahweh was issued in a decisive way to Israel, for which reason it was also to be heard and read later in Judah and in the period of the exile as Yahweh's valid Word. What is preserved is the Word of the Lord of history. This editor understood Israel's history as a history of the coming to fulfillment of Yahweh's Word.[33] He therefore consciously formulated the title otherwise than did the other—and to some extent older—redactors of the prophetic writings, who placed the prophet's name at the very beginning.[34]

28  Thus W. F. Albright, "The Chronology of the Divided Monarchy of Israel," *BASOR* 100 (1945): 22.

29  Cf. M. Noth, *The History of Israel*, tr. P. Ackroyd (New York: Harper and Row, 1958), 264 [*Geschichte Israels* (Göttingen, 1959) 239].

30  787–747, according to Jepsen.

31  See p. 4.

32  See p. 4.

33  Cf. G. von Rad, *Studies in Deuteronomy*, tr. D. Stalker (London: SCM, 1953), 66f [*Deuteronomium–Studien* (Göttingen, 1947), 46].

34  Am 1:1; Is 1:1; Jer 1:1 *M*; Ob 1; Na 1:1.

The Prophet's Family as a
Symbol of God's Judgment

## Bibliography

A. Allwohn
*Die Ehe des Propheten Hosea in psychoanalytischer
Beleuchtung*, BZAW 44 (Berlin, 1926).

J. A. Bewer
"The Story of Hosea's Marriage," *AJSL* 22
(1906): 120–130.

K. Budde
"Hos 1 und 3," *ThBl* 13 (1934): 337–342.

W. Caspari
"Die Nachrichten über Heimat und Hausstand
des Propheten Hosea und ihre Verfasser,"
*NKZ* 26 (1915): 143–168.

J. Coppens
"L'histoire matrimoniale d'Osée," BBB 1 (1950):
38–45.

√R. Gordis
"Hosea's Marriage and Message," *HUCA* 25
(1954): 9–35.

A. Heermann
"Ehe und Kinder des Propheten Hosea, eine
exegetische Studie zu Hos 1, 2–9," *ZAW* 40
(1922): 287–312.

P. Humbert
*Les trois premiers chapitres d'Osée, RHR* (Paris, 1918).

J. Lindblom
*Prophecy in Ancient Israel* (Philadelphia: Fortress,
1963²), 165–169.

√ H. G. May
"An Interpretation of the Names of Hosea's Children," *JBL* 55 (1936): 285–291.

✔ F. S. North
"Solution of Hosea's Marital Problems by Critical
Analysis," *JNES* 16 (1957): 128–130.

*Idem*,
"Hosea's Introduction to his Book," *VT* 8 (1958):
429–432.

Th. H. Robinson
"Die Ehe des Hosea," *ThStKr* 106 (1935):
301–313.

✔ H. H. Rowley
"The Marriage of Hosea," *BJRL* 39 (1956):
200–233; also found in his *Men of God. Studies in
OT History and Prophecy* (New York: Nelson, 1963),
66–97.

W. Rudolph
"Präparierte Jungfrauen?" *ZAW* 75 (1963):
65–73.

H. Schmidt
"Die Ehe des Hosea," *ZAW* 42 (1924): 245–272.

J. Steuber
*Dissertatio de conjugio Hoseae prophetae cum meretrice
ex jussu Dei, Ad Hoseam 1; Thesaurus theologico
philologicus sive Sylloge dissertationum elegantiorum ad
selectiora et illustriora Veteris et Novi Testamenti loca*
(Amsterdam, 1701).

P. Volz
"Die Ehegeschichte Hoseas," *ZWTh* (1898): 321–335.

✔ L. Watermann
"Hosea Chaps. 1–3 in Retrospect and Prospect," *JNES* 14 (1955): 100–109.

See the Bibliography for 1:1.

# 1

**2** How Yahweh began to speak[a] through Hosea.
　　Yahweh said to Hosea:
　　　"Go, take for yourself a wife of whoredom
　　　and children of whoredom!
　　　For the land goes[b] a–whoring away from Yahweh."

**3** Then he went and took Gomer, the daughter of Diblaim.
　　She conceived and bore him[c] a son.

**4** Then Yahweh said to him:[d]
　　　"Call his name Jezreel!
　　　For in a short time
　　　I will take vengence on the house of Jehu
　　　for the blood of Jezreel,
　　　and I will put an end to the kingdom of the house of Israel.

**5**　　On that day
　　　I will break the bow of Israel in the valley of Jezreel."

**6** And again she conceived and bore a daughter.
　　Then he[e] said to him:
　　　"Call her name 'Without–Mercy'!
　　　For I will no longer have mercy on the house of Israel; instead, I will withdraw it from them."[f]

a　*G*, Ἀρχὴ λόγου κυρίου ἐν (thus BQθ′; most of the other *G* manuscripts have πρός according to 1:1 = אֶל). Ωσηε does not justify changing the difficult Massoretic דִּבֶּר to the usual דְּבַר, especially since α′ reads: ἀρχὴ ἦν ἐλάλησεν.

b　Literally, "the land commits great fornication away from Yahweh"; Hosea likes to use *constructio praegnans*, whereby a verb of motion is to be added in accordance with the meaning of the sentence; cf. 2:17, 20; 3:5; 12:7; and *Gesenius' Hebrew Grammar*, ed. E. Kautzsch, tr. and rev. A. E. Cowley (Oxford, 1910) §119 ee-gg; O. Grether, *Hebräische Grammatik für den akademischen Unterricht* (München, 1955²) §87 h.

c　לו is not found in several manuscripts; αὐτῷ is likewise absent in several *G* manuscripts (cf. J. Ziegler [ed.], *Duodecim prophetae*, vol. 12, *Septuaginta vetus Testamentum Graecum* [Göttingen, 1967²] whereby the sentence is brought into agreement with the wording in vv 6 and 8.

d　One Hebrew manuscript reads אֵלִי (North, "Hosea's Introduction," 430), easily explained as a shortening of אֵלָיו.

e　*S* and *G*Luc have inserted their own words for יהוה to make the brief, ancient text easier to understand; further, *S* presupposes לֹא instead of לו.

f　*G*, ἀλλ' ἢ ἀντιτασσόμενος ἀντιτάξομαι αὐτοῖς does not support the conjecture שָׂנֹא אֶשְׂנָא (*BH³*); (שׂנא is always translated by μισεῖν; cf. 9:15; Am 5:21; Mic 3:2, where a person is the direct object). α′, ἐπιλήσομαι αὐτῶν (likewise *V*, *sed oblivione obliviscar eorum*) could presuppose נָשֹׁה אֶשֶּׁה = "I will completely forget them." However, this would require the accusative instead of ל (Lam 3:17). הַשֵּׂא אַשֶּׁה is also written very similarly (cf. Jer 4:10; 29:8 with ל, but the meaning is "to deceive"); נשׂא hipʻil in Ps 89:23 (with ב) and 55:16 (with עַל) means "to attack, assail" (W. Gesenius—F. Buhl, *Hebräisches und aramäisches Handwörterbuch zum AT* (Leipzig¹⁶, 1915). Then it would be translated: "I will utterly assail them." The suggestion remains uncertain with respect to meaning and syntax. We must attempt to understand *M* as an elliptical phrase: "No more will I have mercy on the house of Israel; instead, I will remove it from them completely" (*scil.* רְחָמְ׳; ארחם precedes thematically. For the meaning of נשׂא in the sense of "to carry off, take away" cf. 5:14; Jer 49:29; Mic 2:2; etc. Cf. Koehler-Baumgartner, 636b, No. 16 and 17). The older explanation of Heng-

**7** [But I will have mercy on the house[g] of
　　Judah; I will save them by Yahweh their
　　God; I will not save them by bow,
　　sword, and weapons of war, not by
　　horses and horsemen.][h]
**8** When she had weaned Without–Mercy,
　　she conceived and bore a son.
**9** Then he[i] said:
　　　"Call his name 'Not–My–People'!
　　　For you are Not–My–People,
　　　And I—I—Am–Not–There for you."[j]

stenberg reads: "I will remove from them [*scil.*
everything]"; but the object of the verb must be
completed from the context (cf. C. F. Keil, *Biblischer Commentar über die zwölf kleinen Propheten*
(Leipzig[3], 1888); נשא רחמים ל does not occur
elsewhere, but cf. נתן רחמים ל in Gen 43:14; Dtn
13:18; Jer 42:12 and שים רחמים ל in Is 47:6).
Following a negative phrase (cf. Gen 3:5; 17:5;
24:4; Is 7:8; 1 Sam 27:1), the meaning of כי as
"rather," "on the contrary" (supported by *G*) must
be absolutely retained. Only by doing so is the strong
emphasis on the sentence's climax (infinitive absolute) understandable. This makes unnecessary the
interpretation of נשא as "to forgive," which requires a difficult modal translation: "that I might
forgive them" (thus Budde, "Hos 1 und 3,"
Weiser, Th. H. Robinson, F. Horst, *Die zwölf
kleinen Propheten*, HAT I 14 [Tübingen, 1964[3]]), *et al.*

g　*G*, τοὺς δὲ υἱούς = בְּנֵי. This can be attributed to
　the influence of the plural suffix in the immediate
　context.
h　V 7 is an addition by Judaic redaction (see p. 21).
i　A few manuscripts of the translations presuppose לוֹ
　or אֵלָיו (North, "Hosea's Introduction," 431) as
　in vv 4 and 6, which *S* misread again as a first person
　suffix; cf. vv 4a and 6a.
j　*G*, καὶ ἐγὼ οὐκ Εἰμὶ (!) ὑμῶν; only a few of the
　later *G* manuscripts have inserted θεός before or
　after ὑμῶν (cf. Ziegler, *Duodecim prophetae*). Hence,
　the conjecture אֱלֹהֵיכֶם (*BH*[3] and Weiser) to alle-
　viate the textual difficulty is to be rejected; differ-
　ently, R. Smend, *Die Bundesformel*, ThSt [B] 68
　(Zürich, 1963), 38.

**Form**

This passage is an original narrative unit. It combines
four of Yahweh's commands to Hosea—of which the last
three apparently belong together—within the framework of an account of the births of Hosea's children.
Uniform in style, these commands place the naming of
the children in succession. In each instance, the brief
command "call the name" (קרא שם) is followed by a
"for" (כי) clause introducing a threat that at the same
time interprets the meaning of the name.

Vv 5 and 7 do not fit into this framework. V 5, in the
form of an independent threat, provides a second, different interpretation of the name Jezreel. It differs
stylistically from the interpretations of the children's
names: instead of the כי (vv 4, 6, 9), the connecting

formula והיה ביום ההוא introduces it.[1] In the style of a
gloss, v 7 takes up the most important catchword "I will
have mercy" (ארחם) from v 6. Its contents, however,
stand in antithesis to v 6; a promise to Judah contrasts
with the threat to Israel. In this chapter, both verses are
literarily secondary and therefore are omitted in the
following discussion.

The unit ends with 1:9. Although 2:1–3 presupposes
the naming of the children, it does not continue the
narrative of Yahweh's address to Hosea concerning his
family. But where does this unit begin? Does 1:2 belong
to the original narrative? The description of the wife
and children as "given to fornication" is of predominant
interest in v 2, as shown by the interpretation given in
the כי–clause. The fact that this goes unmentioned in the

1　As in 2:18, 23; concerning this formula, see *Joel*,
　BK XIV/2, 90, on Joel 2:18.

narrative's continuation[2] would argue against v 2 being a part of the original narrative. Yet the command for Hosea to marry is absolutely essential as an introduction, with its sentence structure indissolubly connected with that which follows: v 2, לֵךְ קַח; v 3, וַיֵּלֶךְ וַיִּקַּח. Moreover, Yahweh's command is followed by an interpretative כִּי–clause, which corresponds in style with the commands in subsequent verses. The difference is that in v 2 this כִּי–clause contains not a threat but an accusation. Hence, not Yahweh's coming act of judgment is announced (Yahweh is the subject in vv 5, 6, 9b$\beta$); rather, Israel's present guilt is characterized, which by anticipation provides the reason for the future judgment ("the land" is the subject in v 2b$\beta$). This demonstrates that v 2 is necessary as an introduction and belongs with vv 3–9. At the most, it could be asked whether an older, originally independent account might have been taken up and assimilated in v 2.

The accent of the composition falls on the divine sayings which, after the prelude in v 2, become threats. The narrative framework is somewhat monotonous[3] and contains little more than the formula introducing the words of Yahweh. These formulas become progressively shorter[4] and diminish as the threats become more comprehensive,[5] more severe,[6] and more direct.[7] But the variations within the schematic framework—the alternation of son and daughter; the weaning of the daughter

in v 8—together with the mention of the wife's name (v 3) suffice to eliminate any question of the narrative's historicity.

In view of this conclusion, the passage's literary genre is by no means an allegory,[8] but rather a *memorabile*.[9] Narratives which tell of prophetic symbolic actions belong to the literary genre of the *memorabile*. This particular example of the *memorabilia* exhibits two essential characteristics: God's command to perform a certain task, and its interpretation as a sign.[10] On the other hand a third element—the execution of the command[11]—may be omitted.[12] Here this third element occurs only after the command to marry (vv 2f)—thus confirming the nature of v 2 as an introduction (cf. Is 8:1f)—but not after the following commands to name the children.[13]

The account in 1:2–9 brings together four different symbolic actions that originally were separated from each other by various lengths of time. This is in contrast to all related *memorabilia* of symbolic action, which portray only isolated actions.[14] Here, then, we have the first example of the form's development into a collection of *memorabilia*. It is incorrect to regard this as "[the evolu-

---

2   See pp. 9f.

3   "She conceived and bore and he said, 'call [his] name' " (וַתַּהַר וַתֵּלֶד וַיֹּאמֶר קְרָא שֵׁם) remains the same, excepting small additions.

4   V 4: "And Yahweh said to him" (וַיֹּאמֶר יְהוָה אֵלָיו); v 6: "and he said to him" (וַיֹּאמֶר לוֹ); v. 9: "and he said" (וַיֹּאמֶר); for the same stylistic reason "to him" (לוֹ) (v 3) is omitted after "and she bore" (וַתֵּלֶד) in v 6 and v 8; cf. Gen 4:1f.

5   V 4: the King's dynasty is threatened; vv 6, 9: the nation.

6   V 6: "I will no longer have mercy" (לֹא אוֹסִיף אֲרַחֵם); v 9: "I am not there for you" (לֹא אֶהְיֶה לָכֶם).

7   Not until v 9 does Yahweh directly address the people.

8   *Contra* H. Gressmann, *Die älteste Geschichtsschreibung und Prophetie Israels (von Samuel bis Amos und Hosea)*, SAT 2, 1 (Göttingen, 1921²), 366; cf. H. Schmidt, "Die Ehe des Hosea," *ZAW* 42 (1924): 245ff. The Targum, some of the biblical interpreters in the ancient church after Jerome, and Calvin (*Corpus Reformatorum* LXX, 16) thought that the prophet's

morality had to be protected, and thus interpreted the passage, and especially v 2, as an allegory. Since the time of Origen, other interpreters, including the great Jewish expositors of the Middle Ages—Ibn Ezra, Kimchi, and Maimonides—on down to Hengstenberg, Keil, and König attempted to interpret 1:2–9 as a description of a visionary experience. On the other hand, there have been those who saw here the narrative of a historical event: Ireneus, Theodore of Mopsuestia, Theodoret, Cyril, and Augustine; in the Middle Ages, Albertus Magnus, *et al.*; since the time of Wellhausen, Duhm, Budde, and most exegetes, including Roman Catholics such as Lippl and Coppens.

9   See p. 57 for an explanation of the term.

10   Cf. 3:1; Is 8:1ff; 20:2ff; Jer 27:2ff.

11   3:2f; Is 20:2b.

12   Is 8:3f; Jer 27:2ff.

13   Cf. Zimmerli, *Ezekiel*, 103f.

14   These actions may last longer periods of time, such as Isaiah's "going about naked" (20:3) for three years, or they may lead to a permanent status, such as Jeremiah's celibacy (16:1ff).

tion of an independent] prophetic biography."[15] For the focus of attention is not upon the prophet's life;[16] rather, of central importance is the word of Yahweh that makes a claim on Hosea and his family. In Israel the concern for divine oracles dominated any interest in the "biographical." This resulted in the collection of these sayings, thus producing a new genre that stressed as its original setting the life of the prophet. To this extent the prophetic *memorabilia* are related to the *apophthegmata* of the Gospels.[17] The prophetic literature also contains such *apophthegmata*.[18] The *memorabilia* (ἀπομνημονεύματα) under discussion differ from *apophthegmata* in that for the former an event does not simply provide a framework for the sayings themselves as in the *apophthegmata*; instead, the sayings lead up to the event. In this way, the event character of what is reported in the *memorabilia* takes on central importance.[19] The prophetic call accounts belong to this genre, as do the accounts of symbolic action.

The basic significance of Yahweh's commands in these accounts of symbolic action is emphasized by the apparent rhythmic movement of the words. The meter in v 2 is the clearest: two Qinah clauses create synthetically parallel prosodic units, each consisting of 3+2.[20] The rhythm of the remaining words of Yahweh cannot be determined with equal certainty. Qinah clauses[21] as well as 3+3[22] can be recognized only if certain exceptions

to the rule are made. It makes little difference whether the system of accentuation or alternation is employed.[23]

**Setting**

The author of this passage is hardly the prophet himself. To be sure, F. S. North[24] thought it possible to reconstruct an original first–person account on the basis of several textual variants in vv 3, 4, 6, 9.[25] But the best attested text narrates the story in the third person. Of course it might be asked[26] whether "autobiography" in all ancient literature did not originally employ the third–person style, just as a small child at first is unable to speak of himself as "I"; and whether such impersonal speech might possibly have come from the prophet, since he supposedly wrote in a state of "ecstasy" in which his "self–consciousness disappeared." But for the first chapter of Hosea both questions must be answered negatively. A first–person account follows in chap. 3, and in any event, chap. 1 was not written out of recent experience, but in conscious retrospect of the past years. Hence it is more likely that a disciple of Hosea should be considered the author. The prophet had listeners who published *memorabilia* and prophetic sayings as accounts of the things they witnessed.[27]

Since the framework of the account reveals its author to have been well informed, we should consider him an "eyewitness" and thus a contemporary of Hosea. He

---

15  Cf. Hempel, *Althebräische Literatur*, 97.

16  If that were the case, the prophet's obedience to Yahweh's command would have to be described in each instance.

17  Concerning the usage of this term in form criticism of the New Testament, cf. H. Conzelmann, "Formen und Gattungen," *Evangelisches–Kirchenlexikon I*, eds. H. Brunotte and O. Weber (Göttingen, 1956), 1313.

18  E.g., Am 7:10–17; Is 7:1–19.

19  See below, pp. 57f; cf. Zimmerli, *Ezekiel*, 103; G. Fohrer, *Die symbolischen Handlungen der Propheten*, ATANT 25, (Zürich, 1953).

20  לך קח־לך is thereby read as one stress. The introductory formulas stand outside the meter, contrary to the arrangement of the sentences in *BH*³.

21  Three in v 4; one in v 5b; two in v 6; one in 9abα(?).

22  Two in v 6; one in v 9b (?).

23  For a discussion of this problem, cf. F. Horst, "Die Kennzeichen der hebräische Poesie," *ThR* 21 (1953): 97–121.

24  "Hosea's Introduction," 432.

25  See above, textual notes "c," "d," "e," and "i."

26  Cf. Allwohn, *Die Ehe*, 14f.

27  Cf. Luther's critical observations regarding authorship in his preface to Hosea (1532): "It appears that this prophecy of Hosea was not fully and completely written out, but that several parts and sayings from his sermons were selected and put together in a book" [Trans.] (Erlanger Ausgabe: 63, 74); from his "Table Talk": "None of the prophets' sermons were written down with completeness, but occasionally one saying, then another, was selected and then placed together. Thus the Bible was preserved with difficulty" [Trans.] (Tischreden 2, No. 1839); cf. H. Bornkamm, *Luther and the Old Testament*, tr. E. and R. Gritsch (Philadelphia: Fortress, 1969), 192 [*Luther und das Alte Testament* (Tübingen, 1948), 163].

knows the name of Hosea's wife (v 3) and when the third child was born (v 8). This last bit of information[28]—together with the previous births—makes it possible to infer when the account was written down. At the earliest, it was five years after Hosea's marriage and was therefore after the "beginning of Yahweh's speaking through Hosea" (v 2a). It was probably written during the reign of Jeroboam II, around 747–6 at the latest. But this conclusion cannot be drawn from v 4 without some qualification. This saying, of course, is directed against the Jehu dynasty, which implies Jeroboam II himself, or at least his son Zechariah, who reigned only half a year (2 Kgs 15:8), so that the time would be shifted only insignificantly. It should be noted, however, that this saying (v 4) concerning the naming of the first son preceded the entire written account by at least four years. Thus the account could have been written down several years after the collapse of the Jehu dynasty. Nevertheless, I consider the account to have been written during the reign of Jeroboam II, since his name in v 1b appears to have been taken[29] from v 2a, the superscription of 1:2–9.[30] Accordingly, this written account presupposes the same historical situation as the sayings of Hosea it preserves. The original purpose of the account was probably to support the prophet by the written dissemination of his words.

In the following context, chap. 2 contains such prophetic sayings almost exclusively; they are connected with chap. 1 by catchwords, threads of thought, and especially the widely varied motif of the prophet's family. The same holds true for the first–person account in chap. 3. In the remainder of the book, no other chapters reveal such a close connection with chap. 1. Although this arrangement could have come from the same contemporary responsible for chap. 1, its origin was somewhat later. As the expansion of the account in 1:5 already makes evident, the present shape of chaps. 1–3 probably presupposes the military activity of 733, as do 2:1–3, 18–25.[31] The history of transmission and growth of chap. 1 therefore should be considered together with the formation of chaps. 1–3.

## The Growth and Formation of Chapters 1–3

If we anticipate the results of our later discussion,[32] the following picture of the literary formation of chaps. 1–3 emerges. The account from Hosea's early period (1:2–4, 6, 8f) was combined with Hosea's own written words (2:4–17; 3:1–5), which represent a second period of his preaching and probably also come out of politically quiet times. The combination of both these literary components resulted at the same time in the addition of Hosea's sayings from 733 and later (1:5; 2:1–3, 18–25). The redactor's note in 1:2a may also belong to this process. 1:1, 7 and the additions in 3:5b originate from a Judaic redaction; 2:10bβ is a gloss.

The editor sets a gloomy stage with chap. 1, against which the miracle of Hosea's new message can appear even more joyous: with his judgment Yahweh prepares salvation (chaps. 2–3).

**Interpretation**

■ **2** The first four words exhibit a construct chain in which a verbal clause takes the place of the *nomen rectum*.[33] Syntactically, the "date" (v 2a) functions as a protasis, as the following "and he said" (ויאמר) shows,[34] and therefore means "in the beginning,"[35] despite the absence of a preposition. But regarding contents, v 2a should be related not only to the first of Yahweh's commands; rather, v 2a provides a superscription to vv 2b–9.[36] Otherwise, the repetition of "Yahweh" and "Hosea" would remain unclear, as well as the variation in expression.[37] V 2a places the following narrative chronologically before the passages in chaps. 2–3 that were added to it, and therefore may have been written by the editor of these first three chapters. The name of Hosea's father in v 1a and the date given in v 1b originally may have been part of v 2a.

---

28  See p. 21.
29  See p. 4.
30  See below, pp. 12f.
31  See pp. 25 and 48.
32  See pp. 25f, 33, 47f, 59.
33  Gesenius–Kautzsch §130d.
34  Cf. 11:1; Is 6:1; Gesenius–Kautzsch §111b.
35  As in 2 Sam 21:9 (ketib).

36  The Massoretic tradition understood it in the same way, as indicated by the *parasha*.
37  V 2a: ב דבר ("speak through Hosea"), v 2b: אל- ויאמר ("said to Hosea").

"The beginning" is therefore to be understood here in a relative rather than absolute sense of the prophet's call.[38] This is not an account of an initiation connected with the once–for–all event of the prophet's call, as in Is 6 and Jer 1; rather, four separate events are reported, the first of which (v 2b) is by no means the most important.[39] תחלה thus means the "first period" of Hosea's life as a prophet. It is defined by the phrase "Yahweh spoke through Hosea" (דבר יהוה בהושע). Whereas "and Yahweh said" (ויאמר יהוה) introduces a particular word from Yahweh, this solemn formula characterizes the total event of the prophet's revelation (cf. Am 3:8): Yahweh spoke "through Hosea." "Through" (ב) indicates that the prophet is Yahweh's instrument.[40] Although the translation "with" or "to"[41] can be supported by remote parallels,[42] they are to be rejected, since in chap. 1 the preposition אל is used for "to speak to" or "with."[43] "In" meaning "in his heart"[44] would most likely be בלבו[45] or something similar. The superscription in v 2a does not offer an account of Hosea's spiritual experiences or his personal life, but rather marks the first part of his service as Yahweh's messenger.[46]

Hosea's activity as messenger begins, to be sure, with the reception of Yahweh's commands concerning himself. According to Gen 4:19 and Ex 34:16 "take for yourself [a wife]" (לקח לו [אשה]) is the usual expression for marriage.[47] This first command to Hosea cannot have been given later than 751, providing that 1:2–9 was written at the latest in 747–6 and at the earliest five years after his marriage.[48] What kind of woman is meant by "wife of whoredom" (אשת זנונים)? It cannot simply mean a soliciting prostitute[49]—which would have to read אשה זונה;[50] nor is it an intensive form of זונה.[51] As a plural abstract[52] זנונים refers to a personal quality, not an activity.[53] Recent commentators usually think of "a young woman given to prostitution,"[54] or a "woman inclined to adultery."[55] But this interpretation meets with two difficulties: (1) the children of both sexes possess the same character as their mother: they are called "children of whoredom" (ילדי זנונים); (2) this supposed inclination of the wife plays no part in the following narrative. In view of these difficulties, the suggestion that this term was chosen in retrospect[56] would have to be related either to chap. 3 or to an act of adultery read into chap. 1.[57] It must be maintained, however, that in the narrator's opinion Yahweh's command described to the prophet the kind of person he was to marry. The problems are resolved if we observe the other usage of זנונים in Hosea; 4:12 and 5:4 denounce the "spirit of whoredom" (רוח זנונים) as the spirit of a people fallen away from Yahweh. Should not זנונים be strictly considered an abstract plural, insofar as it describes a personal trait recognizable already before the marriage? Accordingly, does Yahweh direct Hosea to a woman em-

---

38 Thus Budde, "Hos 1 und 3," and Lippl.
39 See pp. 9f.
40 As in 12:11b; cf. 1 Kgs 22:28; Koehler-Baumgartner, 104a, No. 13.
41 Budde, "Hos 1 und 3," Sellin, *et al.*
42 2 Sam 23:2; Hab 2:1; Zech 1:9.
43 Vv 2b, 4: cf. v 1; v 6: ל.
44 Schmidt, "Die Ehe," 255; also K. Marti, *Das Dodekapropheton*, KHC XIII (Tübingen, 1904), H. Guthe, HSAT II (Bonn, 1923–4). Calvin: "God therefore has spoken in Hosea. Here I have no doubt that the prophet represents himself as the instrument of the Holy Spirit" (trans. by Ed.). (*Deus ergo locutus est in Hosea. Hoc loco mihi dubium non est, qui propheta se constituat tamquam organum spiritus sancti. CR* LXX, 203).
45 Eccl 2:15; compare, on the other hand especially 12:11b.
46 Luther: "the point at which the Lord begins to speak through Hosea" (trans. by Ed.) (*initium quo coepit dominus loqui per Ozeam* [V: "in"!] *Weimarer Ausgabe* 13, 3).
47 See below, p. 52.
48 See pp. 11f.
49 Gressmann, E. Sellin, *Das Zwölfprophetenbuch*, KAT XII, 1 (Leipzig, 1922¹).
50 Josh 2:1; Ju 11:1.
51 Keil, Allwohn, "Die Ehe."
52 Gesenius–Kautzsch, § 124f; cf. D. Leibel, "Über die Etymologie von זנונים," (in Hebrew) *Lesonénu* 20 (1956): 153.
53 Cf. first of all J. Fück, "Hosea Kapitel 3," *ZAW* 39 (1921): 286; Budde, "Hos 1 und 3," E. Sellin, *Das Zwölf prophetenbuch*, KAT XII, 1 (Leipzig, 1929–30²⁻³).
54 Lippl.
55 Kohler–Baumgartner, 92a; 261b: "given to prostitution."
56 Schmidt, "Die Ehe;" it would be better to speak of God's foreknowledge.
57 See p. 21.

bued with the spirit of a faithless people, who is a "worshiper of Baal,"[58] and thus require Hosea to marry simply any woman from among rebellious Israel?[59] This interpretation would also explain the term "children of whoredom;" this first important catchword provides the accent that dominates the entire chapter. Here it is not the wife's morality, but Israel's apostasy from Yahweh that is called into question.[60] Yet to what extent was the word זנונים chosen to signify Israel's apostasy, since it clearly suggests sexual activity? To what degree does it characterize a previously recognizable personal quality of the woman Hosea is to marry? Here we should take note of the inroads of a Canaanite sexual rite into Israel in which young virgins offered themselves to the divinity and expected fertility in return. They surrendered themselves to strangers inside the holy precincts.

### The Sex Cult

Cf. C. Clemen, "Miszellen zu Lukians Schrift über die syrische Göttin," BZAW 33 (Berlin, 1918): 89ff and W. Baumgartner, "Herodots babylonische und assyrische Nachrichten," *ArOr* 18 (1950): 69–109, also in his *Zum Alten Testament und seiner Umwelt* (Leiden, 1959), 282–331. G. Boström demonstrated the existence of such a sex cult in Canaan. This was a fertility rite in which the women had sexual relations with strangers to bring new vitality to the clan.[61] Although occurring only once in a person's lifetime, the rite was occasionally repeated because of a vow that had been made. But this must be carefully distinguished from the institution of permanent prostitutes hired for the cult.[62]

The evidence for such a rite in Babylon is found in Herodotus I, 199.[63] For Byblos, see Lukian, *De Syria dea* § 6. Concerning the goddess Venus, Augustine gives this account: ". . . to whom the Phoenicians offered the gift of prostituting their daughters, before they married them to husbands" [trans. by Ed.] (*cui etiam Phoenices donum dabant de prostitutione filiarum, antequam eas iungeret viris. De Civitate Dei IV, 10*). Also, cf. *Testament of the Twelve Patriarchs, Judah* 12:2: "It is the custom of the Amorites that those who want to be married must sit in the gate for seven days and engage in prostitution." Within the Old Testament this sex cult perhaps is presupposed in Lev 19:29 and Prv 7:13ff (in view of the repetition of vows in marriage); in Dtn 23:18, 19 (here professional prostitution and the one–time occurrence of a sex rite stand side by side); and in the mythological background of Ju 11:33, 37ff (originally Jephtha's vow probably referred to the sacrifice of the virgins. The most important evidence for this is the emphasis placed on "mourning of their virginity"; Cf. Boström, *Proverbiastudien*, 117ff). Frequent references to this cult stand in the background of Hosea's sayings.[64] Although Rudolph[65] thinks it possible "that occasionally there were such practices in the Baal–infested Yahweh religion of Hosea's time as well," he nevertheless cautions against the view that the rites of initiation for the bride were "generally practiced" at that time.

If we compare these rites with the usage of "whoredom" (זנונים) in 2:4, where the word refers to certain visible marks which can be removed from the woman's person, then in 1:2 we have a reference to an official sacral act in which the evidence of its execution was dis-

58 Thus already W. Riedel, *Alttestamentliche Untersuchungen* (Leipzig, 1902); more recently, Coppens, "L'histoire," 44.

59 Thus Coppens, "L'histoire," 44; "From the point of view of the cult current in the Northern Kingdom, every Israelite woman could be called a whore." Of the older interpreters, Osiander stands closest to Coppens.

60 Luther, *WA* 13, 3: "I believe that we must say the same thing about a whore, because she has been called 'the mother of whoredom' to signify that the people are now fornicating and are going to fornicate away from God" [Trans.] (*Ego existimo idem dicendum de fornicaria, quod vocata fuerit uxor fornicationum, ut significaret fornicantem iam et fornicaturum a Deo populum*).

61 G. Boström, *Proverbiastudien* (Lund, 1935), 150.

62 *Ibid.,* 108.

63 "Every native–born woman must once in her life sit in the temple of Aphrodite and have intercourse with some stranger." [Loeb modified].

64 Cf. above all 4:13f and L. Rost, "Erwägungen zu Hos 4:13f," *Festschrift Bertholet*, eds. W. Baumgartner, O. Eissfeldt, K. Elliger, and L. Rost (Tübingen, 1950), 451–460. Rost interprets this cultic practice primarily as a "rite of initiation," whereby in Canaan the power of procreation is expected from Baal, since the womb is opened in his sanctuary.

65 Rudolph, "Präparierte Jungfrauen?" 72; further, see pp. 86f.

played on the woman's body.[66] Apparently Hosea had this cultic act chiefly in mind when he spoke of "a–whoring away from Yahweh." Then "wife of whoredom" (אשת זנונים) refers to any young woman ready for marriage (as in 4:13f) who had submitted to the bridal rites of initiation then current in Israel. The cultic symbols made her easily recognizable as an average, "modern" Israelite woman. She whom Hosea is to marry is therefore not an especially wicked exception; she is simply representative of her contemporaries in Israel. With his command, had Yahweh intended to change Hosea's intention not to marry a woman from a people who worshiped Baal (cf. Jer 16:1ff)? In any case, the command to perform an action that was in itself atrocious (cf. Am 7:17a) draws a picture of Israel's readiness for Yahweh's judgment. Since the prophet is expected to take a "wife of whoredom," it becomes startlingly clear to him and his people how complete Israel's corruption and guilt have become.[67] The way in which v 2 is formulated does not derive from Hosea's later experiences; rather, his later understanding and perception were rooted in this first command from Yahweh.

Instead of a realistic interpretation[68]—which has become traditional—or a metaphorical one,[69] we suggest a metaphorical–ritual explanation: she was a young Israelite woman, ready for marriage, who had demonstrably taken part in the Canaanite bridal rite of initiation that had become customary.[70] How this topic was later treated can be seen in Jer 3:6ff and Ezek 16:23.[71]

"Children of whoredom" (ילדי זנונים) is dependent upon "take for yourself" (קח־לך) and is its second object. To elucidate this abbreviated manner of speaking a second verb is required, such as ". . . and she will give birth to . . . ." The "children of whoredom" born to the "wife of whoredom," according to our interpretation,

were not necessarily born before the marriage and by no means were they born outside of marriage. They are so named because the mother had acquired her ability to bear children in marriage by her participation in a pagan rite which in Yahweh's judgment was "whoredom."[72] Thus they are "children of whoredom" not because they have an unknown father, but because they owe their existence to a pagan god.

The כי–clause explains both this peculiar characterization of the wife and children, and also why Hosea was hardly free to choose a different kind of wife: "The *land* unfaithfully turns away from Yahweh as a whore." With this generalization, the final sentence of judgment upon Israel is passed. "The land" (הארץ) represents the nation, not simply because a feminine noun alone fits the metaphor, but above all because that which is condemned suggests it.[73] The phrase "a–whoring away from Yahweh" calls to mind, in addition to the bridal rites of initiation discussed above, a profusion of Canaanite fertility cults in whose theology "the land" appears in the form of a Mother Goddess. In her encounter with a youthful god (the Baal of heaven or a local Baal) she conceives by means of the σπέρμα of the rain.[74] In its ritual form the ἱερὸς γάμος was celebrated orgiastically by cultic representatives of the divinities.[75] As a result of these sex rites, certain practices became customary in Israel which, in terms of the ancient ordinances of Yahweh, could only be judged as barbaric licentiousness. Since the time of David, when the old Canaanite cities were united with the tribal districts of Israel to form a state, this mythological theology, with its cults and accompanying phenomena, had had a powerful influence on Israel.[76] Occasionally, severe measures were taken against it, for example by Elijah (1 Kgs 18). But in the century preceding Hosea, it was increasingly able to

---

66 See p. 33f.
67 Differently, Rudolph, "Präparierte Jungfrauen?"
68 His wife was a whore, temple prostitute, or a person inclined to prostitution.
69 She was a worshiper of Baal.
70 In view of Hos 1:2, Coppens' arguments ("L'histoire," 38) scarcely obviate Robert Bellarmin's warning not to allow Holy Scripture in the layman's hands: ". . . for the sake of avoiding offense, the laity must be called away from reading the Holy Scripture. . ." [Trans.] (*ob scandali evitationem laici a Sacri Codicis lectione arcendi sunt*).
71 Cf. Zimmerli, *Ezekiel*, 344, 538f.

72 Cf. 5:7; L. Rost, "Erwägungen," 458, explains the sacrifice of the firstborn also in terms of this rite: a child conceived in the sanctuary must be given back to the divinity; thereafter, the legitimate marriage can begin.
73 הארץ occurs again as a personification in 2:23; for its meaning in Hosea, see p. 51.
74 See pp. 38ff.
75 Concerning so–called sacral prostitution, cf. pp. 87ff and Noth, *History*, 143 [133].
76 Noth, *History*, 216f [200].

gain a foothold in Israel, despite Jehu's revolution (for which Hosea had no praise: 1:4). This led to a "Baalization" of Yahweh himself.[77] Yahweh's first words to Hosea summon him to oppose this post–Elijah syncretism and provide him with a catch–phrase denoting its practice in Israel: "a–whoring away from Yahweh."

This formula provides us with the astonishing idea of a legal marriage between Yahweh—who in Israelite thought was considered transsexual[78]—and Israel, as it occupied the land. Before Hosea's time this concept is absent in the Old Testament. Likewise, the characterization of a cult as "whoredom" is not to be found in the ancient Near East. We should note that Hosea adopted the idea of a marriage between a god and his people from Canaanite tradition and used it in his polemic. In this eristic appropriation, the sexual aspect, so important in Canaanite thinking, was excluded with respect to Yahweh, but appears in the description of Israel's relation to the "whores," who are the Canaanite cults. The adoption of this motif is conceived of only in terms of Israel, not Yahweh. "The land" is the subject in v 2b$\beta$. The marriage imagery in Hosea, and later in Jeremiah and Ezekiel, describes Yahweh's relation to Israel only insofar as it is an expression of the historically and legally oriented covenant relationship.

The occurrence of the words "away from Yahweh" (מאחרי יהוה) within the divine address has suggested the hypothesis that only מאחרי is original.[79] But this stylistic unevenness, in which the third person appears within Yahweh's first–person speech, occurs frequently in Hosea, and often (though not only) in expressions of a formulary nature.[80] The words Hosea received from Yahweh already take on a style of proclamation in which Yahweh appears in the third person.

This first command from Yahweh immediately casts light upon the problem in Israel: "commit fornication," a form of the root זנה, occurs four times. In this introduction, Israel's guilt is exposed as unfaithful apostasy from Yahweh by participation in the Canaanite cult and

way of life. The command that Hosea marry a woman who had taken part in this cult possesses no independent symbolic meaning whatsoever; certainly it does not mean that Yahweh seeks communion with his unfaithful people. Rather, it shows that within Hosea's purview such women were representative of contemporary Israel. As a "whore" the wife's character is typical of Israel's; however, the action which the prophet is commended to perform is not typical of Yahweh's action (yet cf. 3:1), but only prepares for it. It is Yahweh's plan that Hosea begin a family whose children are to become the bearers of his word of judgment on this nation.

■ 3 "Then he went and took [Gomer]" (וילך ויקח) picks up the exact words of the command in v 2: "go, take" (לך קח); but only these words. In this way, without further ado, the narrator relates how as a simple matter of course Hosea's conduct corresponded precisely with Yahweh's will. Whether or not Hosea's inner resistance had to be overcome[81] is of no importance to the narrator; he intends that something else affect the reader.

Hosea married "Gomer, the daughter of Diblaim" (גמר בת־דבלים). The preference for concrete detail in the *memorabile*[82] is indicated by the fact that the wife's name is mentioned. The name is given for no other reason than to designate the woman chosen by Hosea—at Yahweh's command—from among a large number of people. According to our interpretation of "wife of whoredom" (v 2)[83] Hosea's own choice was not denied him. This rules out the supposition that "Gomer" is the nickname of a notorious prostitute; etymologically, this would also be improbable. "Gomer" is not related to the Arabic *gamratun*,[84] but is a shortened form of גְּמַרְיָהוּ[85] derived from גמר, meaning "to accomplish." Nor is the name to be explained as the expression of a

77   Cf. 2:18 and pp. 49f; cf. Buber, *The Prophetic Faith*, 118.

78   Cf. J. Hempel, "Die Grenzen des Anthropomorphismus Jahwehs im Alten Testament," *ZAW* 57 (1939): 82ff.

79   Budde, "Hosea 1 und 3."

80   (1:7); 2:22; 3:1; 4:1, 10, 15, (16); 5:4, 6, 7; 6:6; (7:10; 8:13); 8:1; 9:3, 4, 5; 10:12; 12:6; 13:5;

cf. Allwohn, *Die Ehe*, 7, and I. P. Seierstad, *Die Offenbarungserlebnisse der Propheten Amos, Jesaja und Jeremia* (Oslo, 1946), 202f.

81   Hempel, *Worte*, 94; cf. Jer 1:6.

82   See pp. 57f.

83   Cf. pp. 13f.

84   "Burning coal," Koehler–Baumgartner, 189a.

85   Jer 29:3; 36:10–12, 25.

wish,[86] in which case an imperfect verb would be expected. Rather, the name expresses thanks that by Yahweh's (or Baal's?) guidance the birth was successfully accomplished.[87] בת־דבלים stands in apposition to this popular female name. The translation "two–figged kitchen maid" takes דבלים as a dual form of דְּבֵלָה, meaning a prostitute who is "cheap to have."[88] But this is linguistically improbable, since the usage of בת presupposed by this interpretation has no evidence to support it. For the same reason, this appositional phrase cannot specify Gomer's place of birth;[89] it simply states the father's name.[90] The casual way in which the narrator mentions a name which would have been impossible to invent indicates that he must have been a contemporary of Hosea.

"She conceived and bore him a son" (ותהר ותלד־לו בן): In a concise style the narrator avoids everything that would be superfluous or distracting and especially whatever might place himself in the foreground. The *memorabile* neither embellishes nor deliberates, but simply provides factual data.[91] Thus the author strives to achieve quickly his goal of presenting the commands of Yahweh which name Hosea's children. Here we have an example of a modest "service with words." "To him" (לוֹ) indicates that the child was born within wedlock, thus confirming our interpretation of "children of whoredom."

■ **4** In this verse the narrative makes its first main point. In the preceding verses, only passing reference is made to biographical details. But now, as though it were the intention from the outset, the narrative enlarges upon the naming of the first child. This took place immediately after his birth.[92] "Call his name" (קרא שמו): Although the mother usually gives the child its name,[93] here the father[94] does this at God's command. The unusual name "Jezreel," otherwise used for a place or region, must have caused lively public discussion. With such a provocative riddle Hosea's prophetic ministry began,[95] which was in the year 750 at the latest.[96] It is not surprising that the misgivings elicited by the growing boy named Jezreel later on evoked new responses from Hosea regarding the meaning of the name.[97] According to the narrator, Yahweh's commission to name the child included at the same time the name's first interpretation (v 4b). Since the name Jezreel, which is used as a catch-word in Hosea's preaching, is inseparably linked with a person, the shadow of the *incarnatio verbi*[98] is projected into the future: *umbra futurorum*.[99]

"In a short time" (עוד מעט),[100] emphasized by its position in the sentence, sets a time limit for the fulfillment of judgment. The prophetic word assaults the "now" of its hearers. There are at least four years left before Jehu's dynasty comes to an end. "To punish"[101] is the meaning of פקד in this context, as the parallel" pun-

---

86  L. Koehler, "Zur Weiterführung des alttestamentlichen Wörterbuch," *ZAW* 32 (1912): 8: "May this birth of a female child be the last one."

87  Yahweh-Baal "has accomplished it"; cf. Noth, *Personennamen*, 195, 175, who, moreover, suspects that here the name is incorrectly pointed after the name of the nation גֹּמֶר (Gen 10:2f; 1 Chr 1:5f; Ezek 38:6) instead of גָּמַר or גָּמֵר; but *G* already has Γομερ.

88  E. Nestle, "Miszellen," *ZAW* 29 (1909): 233f, supported by W. Baumgartner, "Miszellen," *ZAW* 33 (1913): 78, who cites parallels taken from Latin literature. Cf. also Noth, *Personennamen*, 240.

89  In any case, it would not be identifiable. Nu 33:46 and Jer 48:22 mention דְּבְלָתָיִם. Otherwise, only the plurals בָּנֵי and בָּנוֹת are combined with place–names, thus making a misunderstanding impossible; cf. Guthe.

90  To be sure, the name is otherwise unknown and its form is unusual. The ending ־ִים is of course found in names of places and regions, as in אֶפְרַיִם. But otherwise this ending never occurs in personal names. Cf. M. Noth, *The Old Testament World*, tr.

V. I. Gruhn (Philadelphia: Fortress, 1966), 57f [*Die Welt des Alten Testaments* (Berlin, 1957³), 49f]; idem, *Personennamen*, 38f.

91  See pp. 57f.

92  Cf. J. Benzinger, *Hebräische Archäologie*, (Leipzig, 1927³), 124.

93  Gen 4:1; Ju 13:24; 1 Sam 1:20; Is 7:14, etc.

94  This is related elsewhere only about Abraham (Gen 16:15; 17:19), Jacob (Gen 35:18), Moses (Ex 2:22), David (2 Sam 12:24), and Isaiah (Is 8:3).

95  Cf. H. Gunkel's introduction to H. Schmidt, *Die Grossen Propheten*, SAT II 2 (Göttingen, 1923²), xxiv.

96  See p. 13.

97  Cf. 1:5; 2:2, 24, 25; see p. 28.

98  Jn 1:14.

99  Col 2:17; Heb 10:1.

100  Cf. Jer 51:33; Hag 2:6; Ex 17:4; Ps 37:10.

101  Cf. 2:15; 12:3; Am 3:2, 14.

ish" ‖ "put an end to" (והשבתי ‖ ופקדתי) indicates and *G* confirms (ἐκδικήσω "avenge"). It is close in meaning to the word "to revenge" (נקם), which *G* translates by the same word.[102]

What act of punishment is meant by the words "blood of Jezreel" (דמי יזרעאל)? The name Jezreel, "God sows,"[103] denotes primarily the fruitful plain between the highlands of Samaria and Galilee. The ancient city of the same name, known today as *Zerʿin*, is situated on the highland's eastern border at the entrance of the broad valley of the *Nahr Jâlûd* leading to the Jordan. There the dynasty of Omri established a second capital, probably intended especially for the governing of the tribes of Israel, in the same way Samaria primarily governed the Canaanite populace.[104] Here "Jezreel" refers to this capital. דָּמִים is the bloodguilt (Ex 22:1 [2]) of a murderer, an אִישׁ דָּמִים (2 Sam 16:7f).[105] "Blood-guilt of Jezreel" does not imply the execution of Naboth (1 Kgs 21), since for that the Omrides were responsible (2 Kgs 9:7). It refers to the bloodthirsty extermination of the House of Omri in 845–4 by Jehu, one of the military officers.[106] Many of the members of the royal families met their death[107] including Joram, the dynasty's last representative (2 Kgs 9:24), old, guiltladen Queen Jezebel (v 33), and King Ahaziah of Judah (v 27). Is Jehu merely accused here of doing more than he had been commanded?[108] Or is his dynasty's reign principally accused of illegitimacy, as that of his successors was?[109] Did Hosea know of the prophetic designation of Jehu (2 Kgs 9:1ff) and his "zeal" for Yahweh (2 Kgs 10:16)? With respect to these questions, only two things seem

at once to be clear: (1) The bloodguilt resulting from this political struggle for power provokes Yahweh's judgment; (2) according to v 4, Hosea assesses Jehu's revolution otherwise than did the prophetic circles gathered around Elijah and Elisha (2 Kgs 10:30). We probably should not conclude, however, that this represents a conscious opposition to them. In Hosea's earliest period, there was yet no connection with the prophetic traditions of the ninth century,[110] nor with ideas associated with the Rechabites (2 Kgs 10:15ff). Rather, in comparison with them, Hosea had a new, independent word to say. If we take into account the general reason in v 2 substantiating the judgment announced in v 4, Hosea could have held Jehu additionally responsible for not preventing the internal "Canaanization" of Yahweh in his struggle against the Omrides, who had made room next to Yahweh for the Tyrian Baal and the Canaanite cult in general.[111] In any case, the murder committed by Jehu is included in the words "a–whoring away from Yahweh" (v 2bβ) and constitutes its very first example. The judgment announced in v 4 applies in the first instance not to cultic but to political abuses.[112] Hosea's first child, named Jezreel, is to be a constant reminder that the reigning dynasty—from the hour of its founding onward—is not in accordance with God's will. A monarchy in Israel that bases its power upon bloodletting can expect only a "No" from Yahweh. This message was yet to be of the utmost importance more than once in the next twenty years.

עַל־בֵּית יֵהוּא: The word בֵּית denotes the (royal) family, the reigning house, or dynasty. The whole dynasty is

---

102 Cf. G. Schrenk, *Theological Dictionary of the New Testament* II, ed. G. Kittel, tr. G. Bromiley (Grand Rapids: Eerdmans, 1964), 442ff; J. Scharbert, 'Das Verbum פקד in der Theologie des AT," *BZ* NF 4 (1960): 209–26: the word's basic meaning is "to examine, supervise" something or someone. Cf. 2 Kgs 9:7: וְנִקַמְתִּי דְּמֵי עֲבָדַי; *G* translates ἐκδικήσεις and interprets this as a prophetic word addressed to Jehu!

103 Cf. *Biblisches Reallexikon*, K. Galling (Tübingen, 1937), 308, and Noth, *World*, 23f, 60f [19, 53].

104 Cf. A. Alt, "Der Stadtstaat Samaria," *Kleine Schriften zur Geschichte des Volkes Israel* III (München, 1959), 264ff; 268f.

105 Cf. "City of blood" (עִיר דָּמִים) in Ezek 22:2; Na 3:1.

106 Noth, *History*, 228f [210].

107 Murdered were seventy persons of the King's house

in Israel (2 Kgs 10:7) and forty-two of the King's house in Judah (v 14).

108 2 Kgs 9:7. Is this comparable to the accusation against Assyria, according to Is 10:5ff, as M. Buber interprets it: *The Prophetic Faith*, tr. C. Witton-Davies (New York: Macmillan, 1949), 122.

109 Hos 3:4; 7:3; 8:4.

110 Cf. A. Jepsen, *Nabi; Sociologische Studien zur alttestamentlichen Literatur und Religionsgeschichte* (München, 1934), and G. von Rad, *Der heilige Krieg im alten Israel*, ATANT 20 (Zürich, 1951), 56; but on the other hand, cf. H. W. Wolff, "Hoseas geistige Heimat," *ThLZ* 81 (1956): 83ff [also in his *Gesammelte Studien zum Alten Testament*, ThB 22 (München, 1964), 232–50].

111 Cf. with this the Deuteronomistic criticism of Jehu in 2 Kgs 10:28ff.

112 The king is named first also in 3:4.

held responsible for the guilt of its founder, whose sins Yahweh is completely free to requite, even after a hundred years. והשבתי is parallel to ופקדתי and interprets it: the "punishment" consists in "putting to rest," "dismissal,"[113] i.e., the termination or destruction of the royal family.

ממלכות denotes "royal dominion," "kingship," the power and majesty of the king[114] (as in 1 Sam 15:28; 2 Sam 16:3; Jer 26:1), not his kingdom,[115] for שבת in the hip'il prefers persons[116] or functions[117] as its objects. "House of Israel" (בית ישראל) in Hosea always means the nation of Israel as a people (cf. 1:6; 12:1) as represented by the clan chieftains;[118] therefore it is not to be interpreted parallel to "house of Jehu" (בית יהוא)— as the "reigning dynasty in the Northern Kingdom;" the connection of "house of Israel" with ממלכות also rules out this interpretation.[119] This threat then means that with the destruction of Jehu's dynasty comes the end of the entire monarchy in Israel (cf. 10:15 cj.). Yet the monarchy, after the murder of the Jehu dynasty's last representative, endured more than twenty frail years. Of the six successors to Jeroboam II, Menahem was the only one to die a natural death. In this respect, the "king's glory" came to an end with the king living at this time, Jeroboam II. Concerning the Yahweh traditions in which Hosea stood, the question arises as to where the emphasis lies: Does Hosea threaten the end of the *kingship* in Israel or the kingship in *Israel*? That is, does Hosea take up premonarchic or Judean traditions?[120] When the entire verse is taken into account, the first possibility is more likely. And here we ought not overlook the relationship to Amos (7:9).

■ **5** Here an independent saying of Hosea is secondarily inserted into the older narrative. It cannot have originally belonged in its present context, as is indicated by its different structure[121] and vocabulary: it has "Israel" instead of the phrase which occurs in the surrounding context, "House of Israel" (vv 4 and 6). There is no reason, however, to reject v 5 as inauthentic. "Israel" in fact occurs more frequently than "House of Israel" in Hosea. According to L. Rost[122] the word occurs thirty-one times (of which twenty-seven are genuine),[123] in contrast to five instances of "House of Israel." שבר קשת occurs again in 2:20 together with additions. The brevity of the diction in v 5, combined with the easily remembered wordplay "Israel–Jezreel," is typical of genuine prophecy. Such a saying bores its way into one's memory. This verse cannot be a *vaticinium ex eventu* which was later inserted here, being related either to the judgment upon the house of Jehu or to the final catastrophe of the Southern Kingdom. For these events actually happened differently[124] than described here. The saying is best understood in terms of the turbulent events of 733, when the Valley of Jezreel was in fact lost to Tiglath–pileser III.[125] It continues the thought of v 4, and betrays the same intention as vv 6 and 9 with the entire nation being included in the judgment on the royal house. As its main weapon, "bow" (קשת) represents the whole of military strength and fighting potential. "To break" the bow means the destruction of this power. This is said to Israel very probably because its weaponry also constituted its guilt in the sight of Yahweh in the very same way as acts of violence constituted the transgressions of the royal house. In the prophet's mind, the kind of punishment threatened corresponded to the very reason for the punishment. The same idea provides the basis for the insertion of this saying into its present context (cf. 1 Kgs 21:19): since unjust acts were committed in Jezreel (v 4), Yahweh's punishment will be suffered in the Valley of Jezreel (v 5). God's exacting righteousness expiates sin at the place where it is committed; there his righteousness is present for those whom he punishes. "Valley of Jezreel" (עמק יזרעאל) is the historical battle-

---

113 Buber, *The Prophetic Faith.*
114 With Gesenius–Buhl.
115 Thus Koehler–Baumgartner, 534a, No. 2.
116 Am 8:4; Jer 36:29; Ps 8:3.
117 Hos 2:13, etc.
118 5:1; see pp. 97f.
119 Cf. the commentary on 5:1 and 10:15 (cj.).
120 Thus I. Engnell, "Hosea," *SBU* 1 (1948): 873ff.

121 See p. 9.
122 *Israel bei den Propheten*, BWANT IV, 19 (Stuttgart, 1937), 19f.
123 *Ibid.*, 24, n. 1.
124 Against Marti, *et al.*; cf. 2 Kgs 15:10 in *G*[L] and 17:5f. Ibleam is situated in the mountains several miles south of the Jezreel Valley.
125 Cf. Noth, *History*, 260f [236]; see below, p. 48.

field of Palestine.[126] Therefore, it is quite possible that "battle of Jezreel" is a "byword for a large destructive battle."[127] In v 5, however, the words should be taken literally, as the preposition ב suggests and the reminiscence of the campaign of 733 of Tiglath–pileser III makes probable.

■ 6 That "to him" (לו) does not occur after "and she bore" (ותלד) (cf. v 3) can be explained by the "increasing economy of expression,"[128] and therefore by no means supports the idea that the second child was illegitimate and Gomer an adulteress.[129] Yahweh's command is both the origin and the aim of this biographical sketch of the prophet's family. That a daughter is now born simply indicates that these events have not been reordered by imposing on them an invented, lifeless framework. The *memorabile* preserves real events with their unexpected changes, but for the sake of stressing one main fact.

The form of the name לא רחמה is a negated perfect: "She finds no mercy."[130] But who is the subject of this sentence, i.e., who is not to receive Yahweh's mercy? In analogy to other related symbolical names,[131] the answer is not to be found in the child herself, even though this confusingly suggests itself in this very case. The question would then arise how a father could so name his child, as though he intended to withhold his care and affection from her during her entire life. With regard simply to its form, a negated sentence usually does not function as a name. The context gives the subject as "the land receives no mercy" (הארץ לא רחמה) which in v 2bβ is the main premise for this threat, too. The feminine passive verb form, however, is probably to be understood simply as impersonal[132] and translated "There is no mercy!" so that for the name, we translate "Without–Mercy."

In the interpretative כי–clause (v 6b) Yahweh renounces his mercy for the future. "I will no longer" (לא אוסיף עוד) implies that the House of Israel experienced God's love down to and including the time of Jereboam II,[133] even when Yahweh had threatened to remove its royal house, thereby returning Israel to the time of the charismatic leaders, when he himself was Israel's king and military strength. Now—at least one year later—Yahweh declares that his love had ended. רחם means the natural love parents have for their children (רֶחֶם = womb), a close tie that joyfully and unconditionally embraces the child as the weaker person, especially in time of need. Therefore רחם often is best translated as "mercy"[134] and is appropriate as a description of Yahweh's covenant relationship with Israel.[135] The threat's negative formulation, "I will no longer have mercy"[136] indicates that it is derived entirely from Yahweh's intimate relationship with Israel. This second announcement of judgment in the original narrative is more intense than the first. Now the entire "House of Israel" is included. Furthermore, the tone is more severe, as is evident from the antithetically formulated closing ("instead I will completely withdraw [my mercy] from them")[137] and from the intensified verb form (infinitive absolute); but the lashing severity of its sound is fully perceptible only when the words are spoken.

■ 7 Verse 7 is easily recognizable as a gloss on v 6. It takes up the key words "I will no longer have mercy on the house . . ." (לא ארחם את־בית v 6) and, applying them positively, connects them with a promise to Judah, which is written in an artificial style. V 7b also is reminiscent of Hosea's vocabulary (cf. 2:20). The "by Yahweh" (ביהוה) after the immediately preceding first–person speech of Yahweh, "and I will save them" (והושעתים) seems particularly awkward. This is concealed by trans-

126  Ju 4:13; 6:33ff; 7:1ff; 1 Sam 29:1ff; 31; 2 Kgs 23:29.

127  Thus F. Nötscher, *Zwölfprophetenbuch*, Echter-Bibel (Würzburg, 1948), with reference to the "day of Midian" in Is 9:3 [4].

128  Budde, "Der Abschnitt," 18; see p. 10.

129  See pp. 13f.

130  The accent provided by the Massoretes excludes the possibility of an abbreviated participial form without a מ.

131  Cf. 1:4, 9 and Is 7:3; 8:3.

132  Cf. Heermann, "Ehe und Kinder," 310, who refers to "never happened" (לֹא נִהְיָתָה) in Ju 19:30; Jer 48:19; Ezek 21:12 [7].

133  2 Kgs 13:23; 14:26f.

134  Cf. Bultmann, *TDNT* 2, 477 and L. Koehler, *Old Testament Theology*, tr. A. S. Todd (London: Lutherworth, 1957), 240, n. 24 [*Theologie des Alten Testaments* (Tübingen, 1953³), 233, n. 22].

135  Cf. 2:21; Ex 33:19; 1 Kgs 8:50; Ps 103:13 and see the commentary on 2:21.

136  Its antithesis, positively formulated, would be "to be angry," as in Dtn 13:18; Am 1:11; Zech 1:12.

137  Cf. textual note "f."

lations such as "[I will help them] as Yahweh their God";[138] or "since I am Yahweh, their God."[139] ב functions in v 7a in the same way as in v 7b. Moreover, v 7 interrupts the continuity of the otherwise clearly structured passage. The absence of any corresponding promise in vv 4 and 9 indicates that v 7 is a parenthetic note. Nevertheless, it admonishes the reader to view the threatening verses of this chapter in terms of the entire saving history. It cannot be proved with certainty that the glossator was looking back to Jerusalem's deliverance from Sennacherib in 701, when no Judean troops were deployed;[140] yet he had probably written these words before the fall of Judah in 587.

■ 8 The account's stereotyped style becomes even more abbreviated in v 8. This was hardly acceptable to the ancient translators. Just as *S* inserted its own word for יהוה in v 6, now *G* and *S* presuppose עוד after ותהר, as in v 6; several late *G* manuscripts presuppose לו after ותלד as in v 3.[141] Because of the abbreviated diction, we must especially evaluate the additional note that the third child was conceived after the second had been weaned.

A child was nursed for three years[142] and then the weaning was festively celebrated.[143] The Egyptian "Instructions of Ani," admonishing that one's elderly mother be cared for, gives as the reason: "Her breasts were in thy mouth for three years."[144] For ancient times we will probably have to assume that the length of time a child nursed was longer rather than shorter than this, since according to 1 Sam 1:23ff a child that had just been weaned was independent enough to be taken from his mother's care and presented to the sanctuary. Although the narrator obviously limits himself to the necessary details, why did he think it important to relate that more than three years had passed before Hosea's third

child was born? Although the prophet's sayings are otherwise the only reason for his narrative, it apparently seemed important to him to note that God waited a considerable amount of time before he issued the third threat.[145] Why did God wait? As Hosea's disciple, the author must have been thinking only of "return" (2:9; 3:5).

■ 9 The name of the third child likewise simply conveys a message. The translation of the name as "Not–My–Clan" in the sense of "not my flesh and blood," suggesting that Gomer's adultery is exposed here,[146] is not supported by the text; this is evident from (1) the literal agreement of the interpretative כי–clause after the name; (2) the nature of the other symbolical names;[147] (3) our previous interpretation of אשת זנונים.[148]

The כי–clause (v 9b) can be understood as an answer to the question asked later, when there had been no return: "How can the threat of Yahweh's judgment be reconciled with his covenant promises and his election?"[149] This answer picks up the vocabulary of the narrative in Ex 3f,[150] but, in antithesis to the covenant formula there (cf. Ex 6:7), it here is a formula of divorce (cf. 2:4aβ). Verse 9b is composed of two strictly parallel nominal clauses. The last four words are comprehensible only when thus interpreted:"I am not" (לא־אהיה; note the maqqeph) functions as a predicate noun, thus standing parallel to "not by people" (לא עמי). This makes sense, however, only if אהיה is used as in Ex 3:14 and replaces the name of Yahweh. Thus "for you" (לכם) replaces the corresponding nominal suffix in לא עמי.[151] Thus the meaning of the sentence is: "You are not my people and I am not your אהיה." The import of such a statement, saturated as it is by tradition, can be made clear in the English language only by way of suggestion. Although אהיה is a kind of proper name, its sound also

138 Lippl.

139 M. Schumpp, *Das Buch der zwölf Propheten*, Herders Bibelkommentar 10, 2 (Freiburg, 1950).

140 2 Kgs 19:32–34; cf. Is 29:5ff; 30:27ff.

141 Ziegler, *Duodecim prophetae*.

142 2 Macc 7:27; according to Rabbinic sayings, children were nursed for two years; in Palestine in modern times, from two to three years; cf. J. Benzinger, *Hebräische Archäologie* (Leipzig, 1927³), 123.

143 Gen 21:8; 1 Sam 1:24.

144 Wilson, *ANET*, 420.

145 In the *memorabile*, one main fact is elucidated by

genuine accompanying details; cf. pp. 57f.

146 O. Procksch, *Die kleinen prophetischen Schriften vor dem Exil: Erläuterungen zum Alten Testament* 3 (Stuttgart, 1910), 23.

147 See pp. 20.

148 See pp. 13ff.

149 Cf. Am 3:2; Jer 7:4; and Heermann, "Ehe und Kinder," 311.

150 "My people" (עמי) in 3:7, 10; "I am" (אהיה) in 3:12, 14; 4:12, 15.

151 *G* also understood אהיה as a divine name (cf. textual note "i") as is indicated by the possessive ὑμῶν and the capital letter in "Εἰμί" as is used in all the

makes the meaning of the Tetragrammaton more easily heard than "Yahweh." The promise that Yahweh would be efficaciously present for Israel is here negated.

This final sentence of the chapter is like the last remark of a discussion about the ancient exodus and election traditions of Israel. It possesses the cutting abruptness of a "final word" spoken face to face with one's partner in the discussion. It should be noted that no direct address is found in our passage until the third and final threat.[152] The nominal clauses emphasize the finality of the threats. The threat uttered in v 6 reaches its completion in v 9. Yahweh states that Israel has broken the covenant; she has now returned to her position among the "nations" (גוים). The question whether Yahweh might also be אהיה for other nations, perhaps for Judah, is not considered. A prophetic saying always had only one addressee. According to the context, Hosea himself likewise belongs among those addressed by Yahweh, and thus among those rejected by him. He who presents God's word thus stands among those whom Yahweh divorces.

In this verse we see more clearly than in vv 2 and 4 that Hosea is concerned with the oldest premonarchic traditions of Yahwism. The new revelation he had received from God allowed him to pass sentence on Israel in the light of her earliest experiences, when she wandered towards freedom as Yahweh's people, far removed from the ways and customs of the Canaanites, without monarchy or militia. But at the same time this new word from Yahweh required Hosea to confront with a severe "No!" the popular notion that Israel's origins were a means of self–assurance. Yahweh's rejection—the reverse side of his free election—must be proclaimed to those who forsook him like an unfaithful wife. He divorces himself from those (v 9) who forsake him (v 2bβ), who permanently fall away without regard for his threatening words.[153]

**Aim**

For what purpose has one of Hosea's disciples written the account now found in vv 2–9? Here he presents the words of Yahweh addressed to Hosea before he offers his readers a collection of the prophet's own sayings. He describes the first part of Hosea's ministry as a series of symbolic actions, thus indicating that Hosea was constrained by Yahweh both in his preaching and in his personal life. Hosea's office as Yahweh's messenger begins when he receives a personal command. When he marries a woman who had participated in Canaanite customs and rituals, the children become symbols of an Israel rejected by Yahweh. And thus, as a partner in Israel's guilt, the prophet with his family stands under the word of Yahweh. It is not surprising then, that the final, most severe word from Yahweh includes the prophet and his family with Israel: "You are not my people and I am not there for you" (v 9).

Compelled by the command of Yahweh, the prophet's symbolic actions were of such a nature that they bound him once and for all to the word of Yahweh. In the marriage from which the children came, the guilt of faithless Israel lived before his very eyes. The children with these peculiar names forced the people to hear the word of Yahweh, since they raised questions that elicited from the prophet again and again (vv 4 and 5) those words which had been divinely entrusted to him. After these symbolic actions have taken place, the prophet cannot evade his task. This account intends to offer as an abiding presence the prophet's family as a provocative, threatening sign of God. With a prostitute for a wife and mother, the family is the reflection of Israel gone astray from Yahweh; because of the childrens' names, the family is the archtype of Israel rejected by Yahweh.

At the same time, this account anticipates from afar the events of the New Testament. The word of God made visible in these symbolic actions of the prophet and his family announces the message of the incarnation of the Word. Moreover, as the prophet is included in God's judgment on Israel, so too the son of God would be numbered with the transgressors.[154] Yet we note these analogies, as it were, only in passing.[155] We should not consider them apart from the intrinsic scopus of the pericope, just as the prophet's disciple does not introduce us to his master without immediately attesting to the content of Hosea's message. And in this lies his very purpose.

What is the intention of Hosea's message, according to this account? He shows Israel how she stands before

---

minuscules for personal nouns; cf. in v 6; Οὐκ ἠλεημένη; and in v 9: Οὐ λαός μου.
152 Cf. H. Nyberg, *Studien zum Hoseabuche*
(Uppsala, 1935).
153 V 8; see p. 21.
154 Cf. Is 53:12 and Mk 15:27.

God's law. By taking an overview of the pericope, we note three important characteristics:

(1) Israel's guilt is stated at the beginning of the passage. The motive clause (v 2), with its dire reference to Israel's unfaithful apostasy from Yahweh, precedes the three threats (vv 4, 6, 9).[156] The reason Yahweh addresses his people through Hosea is that Israel no longer looks to him, to his mercy and covenant fidelity for her life, children, kingship, and freedom. Instead, following Canaanite practice, she looks to Baal and his rituals, and to her own strength. Israel has offended Yahweh, and therefore a blunt catchword about her whoredom begins Hosea's message.

(2) God's judgment is simply the consequence of Israel's attitude and conduct, and therefore this judgment consists of a remarkably negative reaction from Yahweh. Since Israel seeks love and help elsewhere, Yahweh discontinues any demonstration of his fatherly love, which is his essential activity (v 6). The covenant, the essential element of Yahweh's and Israel's life, proves to have been broken (v 9). Yahweh did not dissolve the covenant; he states that Israel has become the people of another god, thereby drawing her own consequences. As the judgment threatened in these verses becomes more comprehensive, Yahweh becomes less active: after the devastating blow against the dynasty (v 4), the withdrawal of his mercy is threatened (v 6), and finally only the dissolution of the covenant remains to be confirmed as an accomplished fact (v 9). Therefore, the prophetic judgment speech essentially makes evident to Israel what the people themselves have done.

(3) The judgment announced here is accomplished only step by step. We have already noted how each threat is more intensive than the last. The threats become more and more inclusive (at first they apply only to the reigning dynasty, but finally to the whole nation); extreme (first Yahweh removes the king, then his love, and at last himself); and intensified (first the future is summed up, then the new legal situation is presented directly to the listener). In the same breath, Yahweh's active punishment (v 4) is replaced by passivity (v 6), and even a complete withdrawal (v 9). After the initial declaration of punishment, with each passing year hope disappears that Israel, because of Yahweh's threat, will return to her own Lord. Israel's failure to return[157] heightens the judgment until finally Yahweh divorces himself from Israel. In this way, the pericope's message of judgment discloses what Israel is justifiably to encounter in Hosea's time.

But thus far, according to the narrator's stated intention, only the first part of Yahweh's "speaking through Hosea" has been presented (v 2a). In spite of its unequivocal, severe sentence of judgment, with the sound of ultimacy in these "final words," chap. 1 is nevertheless correctly understood only when it is read as a Preface. Although the glossator who wrote v 7 was, for our literary sensitivities, somewhat hasty and awkward, he understood that in this chapter everything had not yet been said. He of course had Judah in mind. But the original narrator knew that Israel—who had turned from Yahweh and was in turn rejected by him, in keeping with the law—was yet to hear from Hosea something of saving importance in completely different words. He intended that first these bitter sayings about Yahweh's divorce of Israel be carefully heard; then the new message following in chaps. 2 and 3 could be correctly understood.

Without a recognition of Israel's "legal" situation before Yahweh, as it is attested here, we will only misunderstand the origin and the secret of the cross of Jesus Christ.[158]

---

155  See above, pp. 17 and 21.
156  See p. 42.
157  V 8; see p. 21.
158  Cf. 1 Pt 2:10.

## The Great Day of Jezreel

### Bibliography

L. B. Gorgulho
"A Perspectiva Ecumenica de Oséias 2, 1–3,"
Revista Ecclesiastica Brasileira 22 (1962): 607–15.

E. Rohland
"Die Bedeutung der Erwählungstraditionen
Israels für die Eschatologie der alt. Propheten."
Unpublished Diss. University of Heidelberg
(1956), 117f.

H. W. Wolff
"Der grosse Jesreeltag (Hosea 2, 1–3)," *EvTh* 12
(1952–53): 78–104, also in his *Gesammelte Studien
zum Alten Testament*, ThB 22 (München, 1964),
151–81.

See the Bibliography for 1:1 and 1:2–9.

# 2

**1 [1:10]** **(Yet) the number of the people of Israel
shall be**[a] **like the sand of the sea,
which cannot be measured**[b] **or
counted.
Instead of saying to them: "You are not
my people,"
then**[c] **they shall be called:
"Sons of the living God."**
**2 [1:11]** **The people of Judah shall then be united**[d]
**with the people of Israel;
they shall choose one head
and take possession of the land.**[e]
**For great is the day of Jezreel.**
**3 [2:1]** **Call your brothers**[f] **"My–People"
and your sisters**[f] **"Mercy."**

a   *G* has Καὶ ἦν (= וַיְהִי), which makes an intentional
connection with 1:9; for *G* correctly translated
והיה in 2:1b and 1:5 with the usual καὶ ἔσται
(e.g., Gen 9:14; Is 14:3; Am 6:9). In presupposing
וְלֹא יְהְיֶה (Nyberg), *S* apparently had reflected
further upon the contrast to 1:9. *M* is supported by
α′ and σ′ and the sense of the context in vv 1f.

b   *Nipha tolerativum* (Gesenius–Kautzsch § 51c, "it
cannot be measured or numbered"; "is immeasurable, innumerable") as a passive expresses at the
same time a general subject (Gesenius–Kautzsch
§144k, Grether §87 b4).

c   See textual note "a" to 2:18, p. 46.

d   Literally: "Those of Judah and of Israel shall
gather themselves together."

e   Literally: "They shall go up from the land," which
can mean "spring up" (Dtn 29:22) as well as "revolt"
(Ex 1:10); see p. 28.

f   *G* reads the singular forms (τῷ ἀδελφῷ . . . τῇ
ἀδελφῇ), interpreting the verse in terms of 1:6, 9
and 2:25, perhaps because it considered v 4 a part
of 2:3 (in spite of v 6!). But the plural forms found
in *M* are necessary because of v 1f and are supported by α′ and *V*.

## Form

A series of perfect consecutives in 2:1f sets off this new
unit from its previous context; as a prophetic saying about
the future it stands in contrast to the rigidly styled report
concerning the prophet's family in 1:2–9 with its imperfect consecutives. *G*, however, connected the two
units.[1] The exhortation in v 3 presupposes the promise of
salvation in vv 1f, which clearly sets off v 3 from the
lawsuit in 2:4ff, even though both vv 3 and 4 begin with
an imperative.

But do the announcement of salvation and the exhortation originally belong together? Although the name
"My–People" (v 3) recalls its negative counterpart in
v 1b, neither is the changing of the name to "Sons of

the living God" picked up by v 3, nor does the name "Mercy" occur previously in v 1f. The imperative verb in v 3 seems abrupt after the announcement of salvation that is rounded off by the כי–clause in v 2b. Hence, the connection of vv 1–2 with v 3 is quite free and is similar to the loosely knit structure of the prophetic sayings in 2:18–25.[2] This literary composition corresponds to that form of prophetic saying in which a prediction is accompanied by imperatives. The essential basis for this is that the prophet defines the present time of his listeners in terms of the future.[3]

This picture of the future begins with two free–ranging sentences (v 1), followed by three simple sentences that become increasingly shorter, with at first six, then four, and finally only three words (v 2a). In this way a person would speak who carefully and deliberately views a portrait that suddenly lights up before him. As the enjoyment of his discovery deepens, he speaks increasingly faster, but with brevity, in order to describe his experience. The closing sentence (v 2b), clearly marked by the כי, interprets the entire enigma, providing it with an easily remembered motto: "For great is the day of Jezreel."

### Setting

The peculiar linguistic style of this passage raises the question of its origin. The very first sentences appear to be non–Hosean not only because of their detailed prolixity but especially because of their passive construction (v 1b). What seems most unusual is that, in comparison with other salvation speeches in Hosea (2:16–25), the "I" of Yahweh in the active voice completely recedes, while the subject in each verse is "the people." Moreover, the idea of a reunion of Israel and Judah under one head (v 2) recalls Ezek 37:15ff (especially vv 21f). Thus it has been supposed that the author belonged in the exilic period; in particular, the last sentence in v 2a has been interpreted as a reference to the return from the exile.[4] Finally, it has been considered unlikely that Hosea would reinterpret the names of his children as given in

chap. 1; had he done this at all, then it would be recorded in several instances, in which case the reinterpretation in 2:1f would differ from 2:23f, 25.

On the other hand, are not the spontaneous changing of the name "My–People" to "Sons of the living God," the completely new application of the name Jezreel, and the concept of the children as "brothers" and "sisters" more understandable from Hosea himself than from a later hand that would have added material reminiscent of Ezekiel? The name Jezreel has already undergone two different interpretations (1:4, 5) in the proclamation of judgment. To speak of a "great day of Jezreel" then becomes clearly intelligible only when the same person had already given other interpretations of the name that would prepare for a new application of it, including that of a proclamation of salvation. The straightforward usage of the word Jezreel in 2:23f and the beginning of v 25—to be understood as an interpretation of the name[5]—both suggest that after the events of 733, Hosea repeatedly proclaimed salvation, having in mind the area of the Jezreel Valley that had experienced an especially severe judgment. Like Isaiah, who during the same period expected a day of liberation for the "people who walked in darkness" (8:23–9:6), Hosea similarly proclaims the great day of Jezreel as the important turning point for all of Israel.[6]

Just as the expression "the day of Jezreel" is best clarified in relation to Hosea's own historical situation, so the language itself strongly reflects its Hosean origin. He prefers to introduce a comparison with כ.[7] Although he says "sons of Israel" less often than "Israel,"[8] yet the expression is found also in 3:1, 4, 5 (4:1). Nor is the root "to gather" (קבץ) unknown to him (8:10; 9:6). Israel's disunity is mentioned again in 5:8ff. The word "head" (ראש), used to avoid the words "king" (מֶלֶךְ) and "prince" (נָשִׂיא Ezek 37:22), is more understandable from Hosea than from the disciples of Ezekiel; the same holds true for "Sons of the living God."[9]

Nevertheless, is not the structure of the speech non–

---

1  Cf. textual note "a."
2  See p. 47.
3  Cf. Jer 4:5–8; 6:22–25; Is 40:1f; Zech 9:9f; and Wolff, "Der grosse Jezreeltag," 84f.
4  Procksch, Budde, "Der Abschnitt;" Robinson, *et al.*
5  See the commentary on 2:25.
6  For the reasons, see p. 48.
7  Cf. 2:1a; cf. 2:5, 17; 3:1; 4:9, 16; 5:10, 12, 14; 6:4;

8:8; 11:11; 13:7; etc.
8  See the commentary on 1:5.
9  See p. 27.

Hosean? First, we should take note of Hosea's divine utterances in the first–person style of the messenger speech. Also at the end of this type of saying, after the announcement of God's action, there is frequently a transition to a description of Israel's attitude changed by God's action.[10] Even the interpretation of the symbolic action in 3:4f—to be understood as the conclusion of Hosea's own written account[11]—has as its subject only the "people of Israel." Hence, 2:1–3 probably belongs to those sayings of Hosea that describe the effects of Yahweh's action. That means, however, with respect to the sequence of Hosea's proclamation, that 2:1–3 belongs not at the beginning but at the end of the series of sayings in 2:4–25. Likewise, the expression the "great day of Jezreel" indicates that this passage belongs with the sayings about Jezreel in 2:23f, 25.

Chap. 2:1–3 was presumably moved to its present position at the head of this chapter by the same editor of Hosea's sayings responsible for the compilation of chap. 1. The purpose of the rearrangement, whereby a clarifying antitheses ("yet") was placed after the initial words of doom, was to exhibit immediately the entire range of tension in the prophet's message. The diffuse style in the first sentences could in part originate from the editor, since the connection formed by והיה (literally, "and it shall be") indicates his own peculiar style found also in other passages.[12] Here he placed together vv 1f and v 3 so that the three symbolic names in chap. 1 now have a complete antithesis in 2:1ff, just as he also loosely connected other fragments of sayings.[13] As to the details, it must remain an open question to what degree the editor, who must have been among Hosea's audience,[14] left his own stamp upon these words. It is just as probable that he had some effect on the present form of the passage as it is that the passage's basic content comes from Hosea.

### Interpretation

■ **1** The very beginning of the saying announces an immeasurable increase of the people of Israel. This was spoken in a time in Israel when there were, relatively speaking, a small number of people. According to 2 Kgs 15:19f, in the kingdom of Israel in 738 there lived 60,000 free, landed proprietors who were required to pay King Menahem's tribute to Tiglath–pileser III. According to the Display Inscriptions of Sargon II,[15] after the conquest of Samaria in 721, the Assyrians deported 27,290 inhabitants from the capital city of the Northern Kingdom. One hundred years earlier, in the battle of Qarqar (854), 20,000 soldiers of the Syrian Kingdom of Damascus were mustered against the victorious Shalmaneser III, while Ahab commanded only 10,000 troops from Israel. The victor reported: "I fought with them with (the support of) the mighty forces of Ashur, which Ashur, my lord, has given to me, . . . I slew 14,000 of their soldiers with the sword . . . with their corpses I spanned the Orontes before there was a bridge."[16] In contrast to the overwhelming power of Assyria, the population of Israel at that time must have appeared unimpressive. Hence, those contemporaries of Hosea who heard these words could have understood them only as the announcement of an absolute miracle.

The future miracle will fulfill this promise. The metaphor of the sand of the sea recalls the promise to the patriarchs,[17] although there is no recognizable literary dependency. The new message Hosea proclaims is always related to the ancient traditions. This message is new in that it proclaims a complete transformation of Yahweh's judgment, which Hosea himself had announced in 4:3, 10; 9:12a, 16b; 14:1 as a catastrophic decimation of the population. Whereas the dwindling number of people was a sign of Yahweh's judgment, the eschatological increase in their number can be understood only as the abrogation of this judgment. The miracle consists primarily in the fact that Yahweh's love overcomes his anger (11:9). Hence, with these words of the prophet, the promise to the patriarchs has become a new eschatological promise of salvation.

This interpretation is not forced on the material;

10   Cf. 2:8–9, 16, 17a–17b, 21, 22a–22b, 25abα–bβ.
11   See p. 59.
12   2:1ab; 1:5; 2:18, 23: see p. 47.
13   Cf. pp. 74f on 2:23f, 25.
14   See pp. 11f.
15   Oppenheim, *ANET²*, 285.
16   *Ibid.*, 279.
17   Gen 32:13 (J); cf. 15:5; 22:17.

18   Koehler–Baumgartner, 560a, No. 6.

rather, it is provided by the continuation of the verse itself, which speaks of a renaming (v 1b). במקום אשר (literally, "in the place where") need not denote a location, which would be meaningless in this context. Here, where the passive construction places all the emphasis on the changing of the name, the expression means "instead of,"[18] especially since the relative clause is also in the imperfect. The passive construction, which exegetes have been inclined to regard as nonprophetic, suggestively presents the essentials with an antithetic expression.

The name "Not–My–People" meant the dissolution of the covenant as the ultimate radicalization of Yahweh's judgment.[19] The use of this name reaches back to the earlier preaching of Hosea, making vv 1–3 appropriate for summarizing at the beginning of the book the surprising change which would be developed later by the prophet. The new name "Sons of the living God" is Hosea's own creative formulation. It is uncertain whether the expression "living God" (אל־חי) was current before Hosea.[20] Hos 6:2 and 13:14 teach us to understand the "living God" as he who gives life, who possesses lordly might over the powers of destruction, and who thereby distinguishes himself from the Baals (2:10–12). The expression "Sons of the living God" is hardly otherwise comprehensible than as Hosea's own creation. Here we should recall not only that Hosea elsewhere names Israel God's "son" (11:1), but above all that here Hosea presents a contrasting metaphor to the "children of whoredom," who owe their existence to a foreign god. Because of this, they shall come to a terrible death in Yahweh's judgment.[21] Should Israel again become united with Yahweh, an unsuspected fertility will be given them. From such thoughts of Hosea the formulation of this new name could have arisen.

Such a supposition aids us in understanding the context.[22] Since the people of the future promise will exist only because of the life–giving power of Yahweh, they will become immeasurably great in number; thus v 1b gives the reason for v 1a. Therefore they are not renamed "My–People" as in 2:3, 25, which would attest only to the renewal of the covenant, but would not explain Israel's future abundance of population. Accordingly, v 1

is clearly a unit.

■ 2 Following this portrayal of Israel's new existence, v 2a describes three important events: (1) "Judeans and Israelites will be united." The accent is upon union: ונקבצו . . . יחדו (literally, "gather themselves together"). It is remarkable how differently the joint return from exile is formulated in Ezek 37:21. Nothing in v 2 refers to a stay "among the nations" far from their own land as is found in Ezekiel. As to the background of the verse, the time before the collapse of the Northern Kingdom appears better suited. During that period, Jerusalem and Samaria had for a time not only been separated, but were even engaged in battle against each other (734; cf. 5:8ff). As Hosea considered both Jerusalem and Samaria under the wrath of Yahweh (5:14) he also saw the end of their enmity and even of their political separation in the future time of salvation.

(2) "They shall appoint themselves a common head." Here again there is no reference to the exile, since "head" (ראש) hardly means an "army" as a designation for returning pilgrims.[23] According to 1 Sam 8:5, the object of "appoint for themselves" (ושמו להם) is a sovereign who is to be appointed. The emphasis on "one head" means that those who up to this time had been separated would place "him" as their head in order to seal their union. Who is meant? Is he a king? The selection of the word ראש by Hosea is conceivable, inasmuch as for him the word king belongs only in the context of a judgment speech.[24] The word "head" refers back to the time of the premonarchic leaders (Nu 14:4; Ju 11:8), who were later replaced by a monarchy (1 Sam 15:17). Once again the early period of Israel's history provides the colors for the picture of the eschatological time of salvation (cf. 2:17). However, this is no evidence for a messianism in Hosea; nor is Yahweh thought of as "head," since Israel and Judah themselves appoint their common head. The elections of the kings of that time—certainly criticized by Hosea (8:4)—increased the inner strife between the two kingdoms, and provided the background for Hosea's choice of words. The eschatological election of one head lends stability to the eschatological unification; more than this is not said here, which in true prophetic manner hints at more than it describes in detail.

---

19   See the commentary on 1:9.
20   Cf. Ps 42:3; 84:3; Josh 3:10.
21   5:7; 9:10ff, 15ff; 11:7; 13:1; cf. 1:2 and p. 15.
22   Differently Budde, "Der Abschnitt," 23f.
23   Budde, "Der Abschnitt."
24   1:4; 3:4; 5:1; 7:3; 8:4, 10; 10:15; 13:10f; see p. 62.

(3) "And take possession of the land." This third event is even more brief and therefore more obscure for us.[25] Again, it is improbable that this is to be explained in terms of the exile. This is demonstrated by a comparison with the corresponding terminology in Ezek 37:21f,[26] as well as by a specific examination of its linguistic usage: neither in Hosea nor in other prophetic books is ארץ found in a similar context where "earth" = "the nations."[27] Wellhausen suggested "land of their exile" (אֶרֶץ גְּלוּתָם); Duhm, "the lands" (הָאֲרָצוֹת); but in view of the context, both suggestions are arbitrary.

If the interpretation of a return from exile is also untenable in this sentence, and thus for the entire verse, then according to OT linguistic usage we would next think of this as an eschatological pilgrimage.[28] This idea fits well with Hosea's general cultic interest, but not with the context of the saying. If these two entities that are to be politically united should also be viewed as being cultically united, then certainly it would have to be expressed more clearly, especially since the main point, namely, the destination of the pilgrimage, is left unmentioned.

Finally, it must be taken into consideration that עלה מן הארץ in Ex 1:10 means "take possession of the land."[29] This meaning fits v 2 best of all when we understand the passage in terms of the state of affairs after 733. Under one head, the united nation shall again possess the land that had, to a considerable degree, become part of the Assyrian province.[30] Moreover, the expression becomes understandable in Hosea in this context of thought and is seen in a new light. With reference to the phrase עלה מן, Th. C. Vriezen[31] has called attention to 2:25a ("I will sow her for myself") and suggested accordingly that "to go up" (עלה, 2:3) means "to sprout up" (i.e., of seed).[32]

Thus the concluding sentence, "For great is the day of Jezreel," also takes on a clear meaning. The name "Jezreel" first reminds us of its etymology: "God sows." In this sense it somewhat obscurely contains the reason for the promised event. On that day when God sows, a rich "sprouting up" in the land will be experienced. Hence this final sentence would again provide inconspicuously the substantiation for the promise of an innumerable people in v 1a. Yet this concept, which rounds off the entire unit, is barely perceptible. Now the promise of an increase in population is no longer in the foreground, but rather a united Israel's "springing up" from the land, freely taking possession of it, after God has brought the deportees back[33] into the land. Then the day of Yahweh's great deed will have been completed and a richly populated Israel will live again in freedom in her land. However, this does not exclude the possibility that the word "Jezreel" also has a historical and geographical connotation, that is to say, that Hosea thought of the "day of Jezreel"—similar to Isaiah's use of the "day of Midian" in 9:3—as a battle of liberation in the valley of Jezreel; the verse would thus serve as an antithesis to 1:5.[34] The various allusions in the context suggest many possibilities of interpreting these prophetic expressions.

■ 3 The exhortation adjoined to vv 1–2 draws from the promised events conclusions which apply to the present. Hosea addresses his contemporaries in the Northern Kingdom, to whom alone the salvation speech first applied (v 1). According to v 2 the meaning of their "brothers and sisters" probably would be first of all the neighboring Judeans. Just as the name Jezreel allows for various emphases in meaning, now the new aspect of brotherhood is derived from the symbol of the prophet's family.[35] The hostile brother and sister, Judah and

---

25 For a survey of the many attempts to explain this *crux interpretum*, cf. Wolff, "Der grosse Jezreeltag," 94f.
26 "... from the nations ... to their land ... I will make ... one nation in the land" (... מִבֵּין הַגּוֹיִם ... אֶל־אַדְמָתָם וְעָשִׂיתִי אֹתָם לְגוֹי אֶחָד בָּאָרֶץ).
27 On 2:20 see p. 51.
28 1 Sam 1:3; 10:3; Is 2:3; Jer 31:6; Ex 34:24, etc., thus H. Schmidt, "Die Ehe"; also Wolff, "Der grosse Jezreeltag," 95.
29 M. Lambert, "Notes exégétiques," *REJ* 39 (1899): 300; G. Beer, *Exodus*, HAT 1, 3 (Tübingen, 1939), 14; also H. Gressmann, *Der Messias* (Göttingen,

1929), 235.
30 See p. 48.
31 *Hosea, profeet en cultuur* (Groningen, 1941), 13; 22.
32 Cf. Dtn 29:22.
33 = "has sown" v 25a; see p. 54.
34 Cf. Keil; Nötscher.
35 Cf. Dtn 3:18, 20; 10:9; 17:15; 18:2, 7, 15, 18.

Israel, are to address each other with the signs of the new covenant, "my people" (עמי), and of grace, "she has found pity" (רחמה).[36] Following the catastrophe of 733, Hosea, in the expectation of a joint day of salvation, thereby calls upon the enemies of the year 734 (5:8ff) to be reconciled to one another.

### Aim

The dominant theme of the entire passage is the coming day of salvation (v 2b). Its main characteristics are a vast increase in population (v 1a), a reunification of the two separated kingdoms (v 2a) under joint leadership (v 2aβ¹), and the regaining of freedom in the land (v 2aβ²). The act of God that laid the foundation for this is recalled in vv 1b and 2b; but in the passage as a whole it recedes behind the future life and work of the community of God which it has established. This is described as the fulfillment of ancient Israel's hope (v 1a) and life (v 2a). This prophetic saying was addressed to the community of God which was threatened and even conquered by a world power. Torn by inner strife, they experienced God's judgment; but now this proclamation of salvation summons them not only to hope, but also expressly to union and harmony.

With the appearance of Jesus Christ, the great day of liberation dawned (Mt 4:15f), but more comprehensively than Hosea's "day of Jezreel" could have led one to expect. Through Jesus Christ "Not–My–People" are renamed "Sons of the living God," thus accomplishing an unawaited increase of God's community. Since the people outside Israel—who are Not–My–People and Without–Pity—are to become a part of the blessed people of God (Rom 9:24f; 1 Pt 2:10), these words take on a meaning unforseen by the prophet. In this way the prophet's words are becoming fulfilled. But this is not yet completed with respect to Israel (Rom 10:1; 11:26) or the nations (Rev 7:9ff). God's community of the new covenant, as the "little flock" (Lk 12:32), continues to be in need of the prophetic word. In the joint "election" of its revealed master and sovereign Jesus Christ, it awaits both the healing of its brokenness and a life of freedom on a new earth. But especially does it await the addition to its own number of those to whom the promise first applied. Thus together with Israel, it faces the great day of Jezreel when the harvest of what God has sown in Jesus Christ (Jn 12:24) ripens in its field, the world.

But in the meantime, in the light of the prophetic proclamation confirmed by Jesus Christ, God's community stands under the prophet's admonition: "Call your brother 'My–People' and your sister 'There–Is–Mercy'!" God's people of today have a new word for their contemporaries in Israel and among the nations. They can see them only as men who, by God's mercy and covenant, have been made their brothers. The ecumenical as well as the missionary task is to bring about reconciliation on the basis of God's redemption (v 3), in the expectation of the new life he promises his people (v 1f).

---

36    See the commentary on 1:6.

Legal Proceedings Against
Unfaithful Israel

**Bibliography**

J. M. Allegro
"A recently discovered Fragment of a Com-
mentary on Hosea from Qumran's Fourth Cave,"
*JBL* 78 (1959): 142–48.
U. Devescovi
"La nuova alleanza in Osea," *Biblia e Oriente*, 1
(1959): 172–80.
C. H. Gordon
"Hos 2:4–5 in the Light of New Semitic Inscrip-
tions," *ZAW* 54 (1936): 277–80.
P. Humbert
"La logique de la perspective nomade chez Osée
et l'unité d'Osée 2:4–22," *BZAW* 41 (Berlin,
1925): 158–66.
C. Kuhl
"Neue Dokumente zum Verstandis von Hosea
2:4–15," *ZAW* 52 (1934): 102–9.

See the Bibliography for 1:1 and 1:2–9.

# 2

**4 [2]**  Accuse your mother! Accuse!
  For she is not my wife,
    and I am not her husband.
  Let her[a] remove the marks of her
    prostitution from her[a] face,
  and the signs of her adultery
    from between her breasts!

**5 [3]**  Lest I strip her naked
    and expose her as on the day of
    her birth.
  I will make her like a wilderness,
    change her into a barren land
    and let her die of thirst.

**6 [4]**  Also upon her children I will have
    no mercy,
  for they are children of whoredom.

**7 [5]**  Indeed! Their mother has played the whore;
  she that conceived them acted
    shamefully.
  For she said:
  "I will go after my lovers.
    They give me my bread and my water,
      my wool[b] and my flax,[b]
      my oil and my drink.[c]"

**8 [6]**  Therefore I will now hedge up her[d] way
    with thorns;
  I will build a rampart of stone
    against her,
  so that she cannot find her paths.

a   *G* (ἐξαρῶ . . . ἐκ προσώπου μου) presupposes
    אָסִיר . . . מִפָּנַי, and thus has the threat begin
    already in v 4. But the "lest" in v 5a makes it certain
    that *M* is correct, where v 4b is an exhortation.

b   Instead of these gifts of creation, which α' renders
    correctly as ἔριον and λίνον, *G* names the man–
    made articles τὰ ἱμάτια καὶ τὰ ὀθόνια ("clothes and
    linen") and thereby transfers the text's setting
    from a peasant to a city culture; likewise in v 11.
    Perhaps פִּשְׁתִּי is to be read, which would result in a
    fourfold end–rhyme in v 7b (cf. Albright, "The
    Gezer Calendar," *BASOR* 92 [1943]: 22, n. 34, and
    D. N. Freedman, "פשׁת in Hos 2:7," *JBL* 74
    [1955]: 275). With the exception of Hos 2:7, 11 (*M*)
    פִּשְׁתִּים occurs only in the plural in the Old Tes-
    tament (thirteen times), five of which are in
    conjunction with the singular צֶמֶר (Lev 13:48,
    52, 59; Dtn 22:11; Prv 31:13).

c   *G* (πάντα ὅσα μοι καθήκει), likewise *S*, does not
    necessarily presuppose a different Hebrew text, as
    Nyberg assumes ("which are my needs" וְשִׁדְּיָ);
    for though שִׁקּוּיַ is understood as τὸ πόμα in Ps
    102:10, there is already in Prv 3:8 with ἐπιμέλεια
    ("refreshment," "care") the beginning of a free
    translation: "all that I have a right to." *G* interprets
    the text for its readers in such a way that all human
    needs are meant.

d   With the form of address in the second person,
    "your way," *M* contradicts the context and the
    reading in *G S*, which require a third feminine
    suffix. With *M* and *G* we read the singular noun,
    contrary to *S* (דְּרָכֶיהָ, which Nowack adopts).

**9 [7]** Then she shall pursue her lovers,
    but not overtake them.
And she shall seek them,
    but not find (them).[e]
Then she shall say:
"I will set out and return
    to my first husband.
For then it was better for me than now."

**10 [8]** She did not know
    that I gave her
    the grain, the new wine,
    and the olive oil;
    that I lavished upon her
    silver and gold
    [which they made into Baal].

**11 [9]** Therefore I will take back[g] my grain
    in its time,
    the new wine in its season;
I will remove my wool and my flax[h]
    which[i] were to cover her nakedness.

**12 [10]** Now I will uncover her genitals
    in the sight of her lovers.
And no one shall snatch her from my hand.

**13 [11]** I will bring an end to all her pleasures,[j]
    her feasts, her new moon
    and sabbath celebrations,
    and all her appointed festivals.

**14 [12]** I will lay waste her vines and fig trees,
    of which she said:
"These are my wages as a whore,
    which my lovers have given me."
I will make them a wilderness[k]
    so that the beasts of the field[l]
    shall devour them.

**15 [13]** I will call her to account
    for the feast days of the Baals,
when she burns incense[m] to them,
    decks herself with ring and jewelry
    and goes after her lovers;
but she forgot me, says Yahweh.

**16 [14]** Therefore I myself will now allure her.
    I will bring[n] her into the wilderness
    and woo her heart.

**17 [15]** Then I will give her from there
    her vineyards[o]
and the Valley of Achor
    as a gateway of hope.
There she shall willingly follow[p]
    as in the days of her youth,
    as at the time when she came out
    of the land of Egypt.

The change from singular to plural presupposed by *M* (and *S*) in v 8ab (*S* and *G* נִתְבָתָה) is probably older than their harmonization (*G* has both in the singular; Nowack reads both in the plural).

e  Dependent on the preceding text, *G* usually inserts αὐτούς (*S* also presupposes תִּמְצָאֵם); on the other hand, Theodoret of Cyrus and Jerome do not.

f  *G* expands (αὐτὴ δὲ ἀργυρᾶ καὶ χρυσᾶ ἐποίησε τῇ Βααλ) and harmonizes the plural subject of the asyndetic relative clause with the singular in v 10a, and makes v 10b coordinate with v 10a. The feminine article before Βααλ at a later period indicates that it was pictured as a cow (Tob 1:5: τῇ Βααλ τῇ δαμάλει), but originally it intended that this word be read as "disgrace" (ἡ αἰσχύνη); cf. O. Eissfeldt, "Lade und Stierbild," *ZAW* 58 (1940–41): 201f. The last two words in the verse (in Hebrew) are a gloss; (see p. 37).

g  Neither *G T* nor the Massoretic accentuation support translating the verb as a *verbum relativum* (as in Gen 30:31; Ju 19:7, etc. = *G* πάλιν). But שׁוב as a *verbum relativum* denotes not only the repetition of an action, but also the return to a previous condition (Dtn 23:14; 2 Kgs 24:1. Gen 26:18 mediates between both meanings). Cf. Hos 11:9

h  Read פִּשְׁתִּי; cf. textual note "b."

i  *G* did not recognize the infinitive with ל as a relative clause; as a purpose clause, it had to be negated.

j  *G* also understood the nouns in the entire line as collectives and translated them as plurals as in v 14: תאנה, אתנה and חית השדה; in v 15: נזם and חליה.

k  *G* misreads יער as עֵיד (μαρτύριον).

l  *G* adds "birds of heaven and reptiles of the earth"; since these do not belong in the thicket (יער) as do "wild animals," *G* probably has harmonized it secondarily with 2:20; similarly, *G* expands 4:3.

m  תָּקְטֵר is probably to be read in accordance with the customary prophetic linguistic usage (cf. 4:13; 11:2; Am 4:5; Jer 1:16; 11:17; 18:15, etc.).

n  *G* resulted from textual corruption internal to the Greek text: καὶ τάξω instead of καὶ κατάξω; cf. Ziegler, *Duodecim prophetae*, 121.

o  *G* generalizes with τὰ κτήματα αὐτῆς = "her possessions" and thereby actualizes the text for the city congregations of the Jewish diaspora; σ' correctly reads τοὺς ἀμπελῶνας αὐτῆς.

p  Literally, "and there she will answer, respond, be compliant." For the meaning of ענה cf. 2:23f and L. Delekat, "Zum hebräischen Wörterbuch," *VT* 14 (1964): 41f. For *constructio praegnans*, whereby a verb of motion is to be added according to the meaning of the sentence, cf. 1:2; 3:5; Ps 28:1; Is 41:1; Gesenius–Kautzsch § 119ee–gg; Grether § 87h.

## Form

The sayings in vv 4–17 are set off from their context as a kerygmatic unit. In each saying Yahweh is the "first husband" (vv 9b, 4, 15, 17) of Israel, his unfaithful wife (vv 4, 7, 9, 14f, 16), who wrongly expects the gifts of the land to come from her "lovers" (vv 7, 9, 12, 14f) instead of from him (vv 10, 11, 17). Besides the content, the style also indicates that the passage is a unit. It is a divine speech in which the wife herself is not addressed, as later in vv 18, 21f, but is always spoken of in the third person. The allegory is consistent to the end, except for v 10b, where the third person plural occurs.[1]

Such unusual consistency of theme and form in so comprehensive a complex of tradition is understandable in view of the uniform, common origin of the genres of speech employed in these sayings. They all have their setting in a legal process against an unfaithful wife. This explains why the accused wife is spoken of in the third person. The deceived husband brings his children forward to confirm his accusation (v 4a). The ultimatum–like admonition of the defendant (v 4b) is accompanied by a threat of punishment, if she becomes obdurate (vv 5f). In the following sayings, as indicated by the introductory "therefore," the form of an announcement of judgment occurs three times (vv 8f, 11–15, 16f), in each instance preceded by the proof substantiating the judgment (vv 7, 10, 15b). Likewise in v 16, "therefore" (לכן) should not be interpreted as a "connecting particle" which, like the formula והיה ביום ההוא in vv 18 and 23,[2] connects a new speech unit secondarily.[3] Rather, לכן in v 16, as in vv 8 and 11, belongs to the internal structure of the kerygmatic unit. Similar to the admonition, the judicial decrees seek to heal the broken marriage (vv 4b, 9, 17). They are, therefore, to be interpreted chiefly as attempts to achieve conciliation.[4]

Speaking in behalf of Yahweh, the prophet freely employs various forms of speech used before an assembled court. For Yahweh is plaintiff, judge, executor of punishment, and arbitrator all in one person. In other examples of a court procedure dealing with marriage, the plaintiff is of course distinguished from the elders of the city as the judges (Dtn 22:15), and from the "men of the city" as the executors of punishment (Dtn 22:21). Yahweh changes roles in the individual sayings, and thus a certain tension is understandable. In v 4 the plaintiff addresses his children; yet the judge speaks about them in the third person (vv 6f). The entire procedure that emerges here is not a reconstruction of a legal process. Rather, it is a loosely knit collection of sayings which, according to their genre, have the same setting, and which, according to their content, concentrate throughout on the subject of the court proceedings. In the kerygmatic unit thus defined, a variation in style and theme sets off the following rhetorical units: vv 4a, 4b–5, 6–7, 8f,[5] 10, 11–15, 16f. The suggestion to place vv 8f after v 15 because of the sequence of thought[6] fails to recognize the nature of this collection of sayings. Although their setting is the same, the structure is loosely knit,[7] in which the threefold "therefore" (vv 8, 11, 16) nevertheless regularly picks up the proof of guilt in each of the preceding verses (vv 7, 10, 15b).[8]

The kerygmatic unit thus cannot immediately be regarded as a rhetorical unity, as is likewise demonstrated by the varying degrees of poetic diction in the individual sayings. A regular *parallelismus membrorum* is found only in vv 4–10 and vv 16f. Here the most frequently occurring is the synonymous type, corresponding with a sort of drumming style, whereas synthetic parallelism seldom

---

1    Cf. p. 37.
2    See p. 9.
3    Thus J. Lindblom's review of *Hosea*, BK XIV 1, fascicle 2–4 in *ThLZ* 87 (1962): 835.
4    Cf. L. Koehler, "Justice in the Gate," in *Hebrew Man* (London: SCM, 1956), 150ff; G. Gemser, "The *rîb*-Pattern in Hebrew Mentality," VT Suppl. 3 (Leiden, 1955): 120–37, esp. 129; H. J. Boecker, *Redeformen des Rechtsleben im AT*, WMANT 14 (Neukirchen, 1964), 117–21.
5    Only with reservation is it possible to divide the unit of transmission in vv 4–9 into originally independent and self–contained sayings. Nor is the deletion of glosses of any benefit. On the one hand, v 7 presupposes v 6 (הורתם . . . אמם = "their mother" . . . "who conceived them"); on the other hand, it is essential as a preparation for v 8 (לכן) and v 9 (a quotation). Again, v 6 presupposes the distinction between mother and children in vv 4f, but it changes in style (from second to third persons) and in content (the children are now threatened).

Here we have a structure comprising verses which are inextricably woven together, which nevertheless, according to style and subject matter, are discontinuous. To say that this structure is the result of a literary combination of fragments of prophetic sayings is only a partial explanation. Also reflected here is the genuine, persistent conflict— with the thoughts somewhat disconnected—within the prophet himself, who again and again attempts to declare the will of a God who cannot abandon his faithless people.
6    J. Halévy, *Le Livre d'Osée*, Revue Sémitique 10 (Paris, 1902); Procksch; Humbert, "La logique."
7    See pp. 35f.
8    See p. 41.

occurs (vv 6, 9). There is a kind of graduated parallelism in vv 16f in which only the beginning of the new line corresponds with the ending of the previous line, while the rest of the line goes on (the pattern is a–b//b–c). Within vv 11–15 parts of sentences are only occasionally parallel (v 11a). On the whole, merely the forms of the verbs, introducing prosodic units of unequal length, exhibit an external synthetic parallelism. Like the waves of a flood, the sentences roll forward in a persistent style.

In those sayings which are more intensively poetic in character, Hosea usually uses the bicolon. He also favors the tricolon, particularly at the beginning and ending of a unit (vv 5b, 7bβ, 8, 16). But the irregularities in these sayings are also to be noted. They occur especially at the beginning and with the introduction of the quotation, while cola with anacrusis are not always ascertainable. A regular alternating rhythm is an exception (v 5b). Usually the accents in each colon are followed by varying numbers of unaccented syllables. Generally there are three stresses per colon; but cola having two (v 7b) or four (v 17) stresses also occur.

### Setting

These prophetic sayings presuppose a thriving economic situation in Israel (vv 7, 10, 11) and the undisturbed organization of religious festivals in Palestine (vv 13, 15). Since disturbances in foreign relations and domestic affairs are not yet reflected here, the best date is probably in the early period of Hosea's ministry, during the last years of Jeroboam II, i.e., around 750. Also in support of this date is the relationship of the imagery with the content of chap. 1—especially the divorce formula in 2:4 compared with the negated covenant formula in 1:9.

The transmission of these verses probably goes back to Hosea himself. Later editors (cf. 1:2–9; 2:18–25) could not have taken older rhetorical units and created a literary structure that is such a completely indivisible kerygmatic unit. According to 3:1 Hosea was responsible for some of the written tradition. And chap. 3 represents a continuation of a preceding section, the beginning of which is most likely to be found in 2:4–17.

### Interpretation

■ **4** The God of Israel appears first as plaintiff against his unfaithful wife. He summons the accusing party for the beginning of the legal dispute. The word "accuse" (ריב) denotes the succession of speeches before the court[9] and thus the judicial procedure as a whole. In a narrower sense, combined with בְּ, it means a speech that calls one to account, that assails with rebuke,[10] or makes an accusation. E. Würthwein,[11] contra J. Begrich[12] and Koehler–Baumgartner, 888f, maintains that the primary and most frequent meaning of ריב is "accusation," but without giving attention to the accompanying preposition. Here this meaning applies.

It is surprising that in this allegorical speech the children are drawn to the father's side against the mother. But do not both mother and children represent Israel? Do Israelites take sides against Israel? Here the collective idea, in its various forms, noticeably breaks down— whether Hosea summons the people of Israel against the land of Israel; the youth against the leaders; the morally superior against those chiefly responsible for Israel's guilt; or a genuine new repentance against complacent transgression. The allegory contains many possibilities of interpretation. This bold distinction between mother and children opens up new paths enabling Hosea's audience within guilty Israel to take the side of Yahweh.

The mother's guilt is juridically established by the accusation made with a reciprocal divorce formula. In substance this formula corresponds to the negation of the covenant formula in 1:9. The wife has culpably separated herself from her husband by committing adultery and now intends to be legally divorced. There follows, however, not a corresponding order for her punishment, but an admonition which is to spare her the punishment (v 5). The children are to assist in this, not in the execution of punishment.[13] The unfaithful wife is to put aside everything that reminds her of her adultery. It is noticeable that Yahweh's purpose is not rejection but reconciliation. זנונים and נאפופים are objects which can be placed on or removed from the face or breast. These were probably certain marks or emblems, e.g., headbands,

---

9   ריב with "with" (עָם) occurs in 4:1 and 12:3.
10  Gen 31:36; Ju 6:32.
11  "Der Ursprung der prophetischen Gerichtsrede," *ZThK* 49 (1952): 4.
12  *Studien zur Deuterojesaja*, BWANT IV, 25 (Stuttgart, 1938), 31 [also in ThB 20 (München, 1963²), 37].
13  Cf. Gordon, "Hos 2:4–5," 279f.

belts,[14] rings, necklaces, or similar jewelry,[15] placed on a woman who had participated in the Canaanite sex cult. They could also be scratches on the breast resulting from ecstatic frenzy.[16] For Hosea such cultic marks are signs of willful prostitution and adultery. Therefore he employs abstract plurals to name these objects.[17]

■ **5** The admonition in v 4b becomes an ultimatum in v 5 by virtue of the threat contained in the פן–clause. If the children's entreaty of their mother is futile, then Yahweh himself must take severe measures against her; he would rather not. By stripping her "naked" he indicates his own freedom from the obligation to clothe her, a legal obligation the man assumes with marriage (Ex 21:10). The husband's right to do this is stipulated by ancient oriental law, if the wife initiates divorce pre-ceedings.[18] Israel's divorce because of her whoredom brings with it even more vexing consequences. The naked wife becomes helpless, unable to live any longer, as at "the time of her birth" (Ezek 16:4–8) when Yahweh found her (9:10; 11:1ff). If, after her adultery, the divorce from Yahweh becomes legally binding, she would be given up not only to the shame of being stripped naked (Ezek 16:36ff; Na 3:5ff) but to death as well. Yet it is significant that Hosea does not speak of death by fire or stoning, the usual punishment for adultery (Gen 38:24; Lev 21:9; Dtn 22:23). The theme of Israel's divorce from Yahweh, with its consequences, remains dominant, as v 5b indicates, where the discourse moves from image to the literal sense: the accused wife shall become an arid plain that Yahweh allows to die of thirst (cf. Ex 17:3). At this point we recognize the connection between Hosea's allegory and Canaanite mythology. The wife represents the land; her children represent its inhabitants, the offspring of the marriage between the land and the god of heaven. Hosea employs this imagery to demonstrate that the arable land inhabited by Israel owes its fertility only to its initmate relationship with Yahweh. Should it marry another god, the land will become a desert. Therefore the children are to take care that the signs of whoredom, i.e., the sanctuaries of Baal, are removed from the face of the land. Thus Hosea uses the Canaanite myth to attack the Canaanite faith in Baal. In so doing, he stands far removed from a nomadic or

Rechabite ideal.[19] The wilderness is a land of death; the arable land is "Yahweh's land" (9:3).

■ **6** Unexpectedly, the "children" are no longer addressed from v 6 onward. A completely different sentence of punishment with a twofold motivation (vv 6f) that applies first of all to the children themselves is added to the summons for them to admonish their mother (vv 4f). Vv 6–7 comprise a new rhetorical unit which recalls above all the content of 1:6; it has been joined to the foregoing as a gloss (like 1:7a) in the process of the tradition's taking written form. Now the children are more severely attacked than the mother was previously. The preceding saying, employing Canaanite imagery in its polemic, is thereby guarded against the misunderstanding that the people (represented by the children) are guiltless and thus free from punishment in contrast to the land (represented by the mother). They are "children of whoredom." As the reason for Yahweh's withdrawal of his mercy, this can only mean that they, too, are guilty of whoredom.

■ **7** With v 7 the mother likewise becomes increasingly the representative of the nation, as the content of her own words indicate (on v 7b see below). Only in this sense is the new כי–clause, together with v 6b, meaningful as a substantiation for v 6a. If v 7 should be connected with v 5, excluding v 6 as a secondary addition,[20] then it must not only be explained why the children are no longer addressed here, as likewise in v 6, but why, after the reason given in v 4aβ, a second reason should have been added, especially since the פן–clause (v 5) is entirely oriented toward v 4. In relation to v 6, however, v 7 indicates that the land and its inhabitants—the people as a whole and as individuals—are equally unfaithful. The accent lies on the proof of guilt as such. Thus the original causal כי (v 6b), repeated twice in v 7ab, has more of a deictic function. With these demonstrative particles, the fragment of a prophetic saying in vv 6f—first preventing a misunderstanding of vv 4f (see above)—prepares for an understanding within the framework of the literary composition of Yahweh's punitive measures in vv 8f.

The mother is denounced as a "prostitute who chases

14   Cf. Letter of Jeremiah 42 [43].
15   Hos 2:15; Gen 35:4; Ex 32:2.
16   Zech 13:6.
17   See the commentary on 1:2.

18   Kuhl, "Neue Dokumente," 105f.
19   Th. C. Vriezen, *Hosea, profeet en cultuur* (Groningen, 1941), 8, *contra* Humbert, "La logique," 159.
20   Budde, "Der Abschnitt."

men."[21] The disgrace of her prostitution is proved by her own words (v 7b). The quotation formulated by Hosea is consistent with the continuous allegory ("my lovers"). But it may employ expressions that occurred in connection with the departure to the sex rites and with the hymns of the fertility cult.[22] Hence, the form of the quotation emphasizes that Israel wantonly, consciously, and deliberately divorced herself from Yahweh. This prostitute, who runs after her lovers, is unusually persistent. Most prostitutes wait for their lovers to come to them.[23] In cultic mythology, the "lovers" are the Baals (v 15) of the various cultic places; each Baal is responsible for its own district. In the cultic ritual, it is the "partners" —representing Baal—who are sought out by those participating in the fertility cult.

מאהבים, pi'el participle of אהב, is used in the Old Testament—following Hosea—only in the sense of adulterous lovers, and is found especially in Jeremiah and Ezekiel.[24] According to W. Thomas,[25] אהב is formed on the biliteral root הב (Arabic *habba*), an onomatopoetic form meaning to "breath heavily, to gasp for breath, to pant." Accordingly, "אהב belongs to that category of words in which the ideas of breathing and emotion, in this case desire, are combined."[26] The root אהב is based on the idea of a yearning desire that visibly and perceptibly hungers for its opposite.[27] The intensive stem in the Hebrew again brings out this original meaning. This explains the exclusive use of the pi'el stem for passionate, extramarital love in the book of Hosea.

The gifts of Baal are praised in the hymnic participial style. However, according to the quotation (v 7b), what Israel expects from the Canaanite cult is the wages given a prostitute.[28] This list indicates that the whorelike

mother no longer represents the land (as in vv 5 and 14), but clearly the people. As the gifts from her lovers she names the staples of Palestine that are most important for its inhabitants: bread and water provide the basic nutriments; wool and flax furnish raw material for clothing. Sheep's wool (Prv 27:26) from herdsmen (2 Kgs 3:4) is made into warm clothing (Job 31:20) while flax—cultivated in the coastal plain region and in the Jordan Valley[29]—affords clothing that is cool (Ezek 44:17f). The industrious wife weaves them both (Prv 31:13), but they are not to be interwoven with each other (Dtn 22:11). In addition to food and clothing, oil (שמן) for anointing provides the necessary care for the skin.[30] שקוים is an infrequent word and probably means beverages, such as wine and beer,[31] which were special luxuries beyond the necessities of life. Thus everything that nourishes, protects, and gives pleasure was expected in return for worshiping the Baals.

■ **8** Since the time of Oort, Condamin, and Procksch, v 8f is often placed after v 15. To be sure, the content of v 10 fits easier with v 7 than with v 9, but the transition from v 9 to v 16 is even more difficult.[32] Stylistically, v 8f is undoubtedly more closely connected with v 7 than with v 15. The quotation in v 9b is formulated in antithesis to v 7b: "then she shall say: 'I will set out and return' " (אמרה אלכה ואשובה); "For she said: 'I will go after . . .' " (אמרה אלכה אחרי). This connection should not be sacrificed in favor of a vague idea about the correct order of the thoughts contained in vv 4–15.[33]

In a prophetic saying "therefore" (לכן) generally introduces the announcement of some action Yahweh is about to take in response to man's deeds or his sufferings. It occurs more frequently in Amos (seven times), Micah (six times), Isaiah (fourteen times), Jeremiah and Ezekiel (about fifty times each) than in Hosea (only in 2:8, 11,

21  Gressmann, *Geschichtsschreibung*.
22  With "to go after" (הלך אחרי) cf. Dtn. 4:3; with "who gives me" (נתני) cf. Ps 136:25; 145:15.
23  Gen 38:14ff; Jer 3:2.
24  Cf. Koehler–Baumgartner, 16.
25  "The root אָהֵב 'love' in Hebrew," *ZAW* 57 (1939): 57–64, esp. 62.
26  Such as אף, נחם, etc.; cf. Koehler–Baumgartner.
27  For the corresponding usage in Ugaritic texts cf. *CTCA* 3.III.4, 67; V.18 (Gordon *'nt* III.4, 67; V.18); cf. A. D. Tushingham, "A Reconsideration," 151ff.
28  Cf. 2:14; 9:1; Mic 1:7 with Gen 38:16.
29  Gezer Calendar in Albright, *ANET²*, 320; H. Donner–W. Röllig, *Kanaanäische und Aramäische Inschriften* 2 (Wiesbaden, 1964), 182; Josh 2:6; cf. G. Dalman, *Arbeit und Sitte in Palästina V* (Gütersloh, 1937), 23f.
30  Lipit–Ishtar Lawcode § 27, Kramer, *ANET²*, 160; Code of Hammurabi § 178, Meek, *ANET²*, 174; Middle Assyrian Law § 36, Meek, *ANET²*, 183; cf. L. Dürr, "Altorientalisches Recht bei den Propheten Amos und Hosea," *BZ* 23 (1935–36): 154–57.
31  *BRL*, 110f.
32  See p. 41.
33  See pp. 32 and 36f.

16; 13:3) or Deutero–Isaiah (three times). In the older prophets, לכן almost always marks the transition from the proof of guilt to the threat of punishment. But here and in v 16f there is an exception, since the threat has been replaced by Yahweh's corrective measures.

The formula הנני with a participle[34] introduces a threat or a promise from God in 118 instances. It introduces the words of a human speaker only seven times.[35] It signals Yahweh's immediate intervention and compellingly invites the listeners' attention.[36] Yahweh blocks (שׂך) the path of his unfaithful wife with a wall of thorns or a stone embankment. The maquis of Palestine has thorn bushes of every size.[37] Perhaps the allegory already implies that the land becomes a total wilderness (vv 11ff), which would make the route to the Baal sanctuaries impossible. גדר is a heaped-up rampart of stone about one meter high used mostly as a fence to mark the boundaries for vineyards.[38] The statement in v 8bβ with a negated jussive after the preceding participial construction is to be interpreted as a purpose clause.[39] נתיבותיה are the byways leading to the lovers (v 7b) which in the allegory represent the pilgrims' roads to the sanctuaries. To prevent his people from continuing their breach of faith, Yahweh places obstacles in their path.

■ 9  The lovers are no longer to be found. They will be passionately pursued (רדף) and sought for[40] according to the Canaanite ritual. But the objects of Israel's wicked yearning will be forsaken and turned into a wilderness. And thus through great disappointment the wife, Israel, regains her senses. The theme "seeking but not finding" belongs to the rituals of love and marriage, as is clearly indicated by Song 3:1–4.[41] Hosea puts the wife's new attitude in the form of a quotation (cf. 6:1–3; 8:2; 14:3f) just as he previously had done with her wicked intentions

(v 7b). The desire to return to her "first husband" presupposes a divorce that was initiated by the woman herself.[42] The announced conversion is clearly recognizable here as a return to the original relationship Yahweh himself had created.[43] According to the marriage laws in Dtn 24:1ff, this would be legally impossible between two people. "Then"—when things went better for Israel than at the present—refers to the early period of her history, including the wandering in the wilderness (11:1–3). Yahweh, her God from the beginning, can now be found and is able to help Israel, if the gods of Palestine are dethroned and have disappeared. Hosea presupposes that, alongside the Canaanized forms of worship in Israel, there still exists a knowledge of Yahweh's distinctiveness. However, the people's new turning to the ancient confession of faith in Yahweh is brought about only by Yahweh's corrective measures. God's actions proceeding from his love now achieve what the admonition (vv 4f) was unable to accomplish, since all the members of the nation are equally guilty (vv 6f). Yet the measures spoken of in v 5 are now suspended. This group of sayings began with an accusation against Israel because of her wanton divorce for purposes of prostitution. Now, in the announcement of Israel's desire to return to her husband, the sayings attain their goal for the first time.

■ 10  If v 10 is interpreted as the continuation of v 9, the wife's desire to return must be condemned as a "semblance of repentance."[44] Yet neither the choice of words nor the emphasis of the verse refers back to vv 8f, but rather to v 7, "my lovers who give me" ∥ "I gave her" (אנכי נתתי ∥ מאהבי נתני). Within its present literary structure, v 10 is directly related to v 11: לכן presupposes v 10, where the reason for the punishment is given. The words "she does not know . . ." can be the evidence for

34  It occurs 125 times in the Old Testament.

35  P. Humbert, "La formule hébraique en hineni suivi d'un participe," REJ 97 (1934): 58–64.

36  Cf. K. Oberhuber, "Zur Syntax das Richterbuches," VT 3 (1953): 10.

37  G. Dalman, Arbeit und Sitte in Palästina II (Gütersloh, 1932), 319f.

38  G. Dalman, Arbeit II, 59f. Concerning the internal object of figura etymologia, cf. Gesenius–Kautzsch § 117f.

39  Gesenius–Kautzsch § 165a; Grether § 83b.

40  On בקשׁ as a cultic term, cf. 5:6, 15.

41  Cf. E. Jacob, "L'Héritage cananéen dans le livre

du prophète Osée," RHPhR 43 (1963): 256.

42  See the commentary on v 4.

43  H. W. Wolff, "Das Thema Umkehr in der alttestamentlichen Prophetie," ZThK 48 (1951): 135f, [also in Wolff, Gesammelte Studien, 130–50].

44  Vriezen, Hosea, 9. Cf. 5:6; 6:1–4.

guilt only if this is an invective against a punishable carelessness, a thoughtless "forgetting" (cf. v 15b) of the knowledge of God's saving works handed down in Israel. Since the time of David and Solomon, the more highly cultivated half of the empire had been influenced by Canaanite culture.[45] This of course produced harmful results. Hosea sees the traditional Israelite beliefs pushed aside, as is also indicated by the three–word formula "grain, new wine, olive oil." It belongs to the vocabulary of Deuteronomy[46] and is therefore new evidence for Hosea's close connection with those groups of Levites who formed an opposition party in the Northern Kingdom, groups to which Deuteronomy ultimately may be traced.[47] It is significant that the controversy over apostasy to the Canaanite religion does not proceed from the doctrine of creation, but from a confession of the historical works and gifts of Yahweh: "I have given."[48] Since these commodities come directly from Yahweh, they are not called bread, wine, and oil—the humanly processed goods—but "grain, new wine, and olive oil." Since there was no shortage of silver and gold in the flourishing economy of Jereboam II's reign, these characteristics of economic wealth for Hosea are gifts from Yahweh as well. "Gold" (זהב) is placed at the end to emphasize it as the most precious of all.

"They made into Baal" (עשׂו לבעל) appears to be foreign to the context because of the plural verb form[49] and the singular בעל (cf. 2:7ff, 15). The phrase is probably a gloss whose purpose is to elucidate Israel's transgression with words taken from 8:4 and 13:2. Yahweh's gifts are given to idols (cf. v 15aβ) or are even used to make pagan cultic images. Is 44:17, as 8:4 and 13:2, makes this second meaning the more likely. The gloss is now connected with the rest of the sentence as an asyndetic relative clause, which should be regarded as the mechanical appropriation of a marginal notation rather than as an example of Hosea's literary style, for in the sayings which follow in vv 14–15 he does not leave out the אשר for the sake of the meter.[50]

■ 11 The threat in v 11 is introduced by "therefore" (לכן), which connects it with the motivation in v 10. The punishment corresponds to the guilt. If God the Provider has been forgotten, he will demonstrate his lordship over his gifts by withdrawing them. "Grain" and "new wine" emphasize the fact that v 11 belongs with v 10; "wool" and "flax" recall v 7. The first person singular suffix throughout the verse indicates that the natural resources of Palestine belong to him who creates and provides them; and that if Israel forsakes Yahweh, it cannot expect to receive them. "The time" and "the season" of the grain and the new wine is harvest time (Ps 1:3). Even then, when the maturing of the harvest is awaited, Yahweh will remain in charge. These punitive measures remain within the context of universal, oriental marriage laws. The woman who "humiliates her husband" is cast out with no means of support.[51] The additional phrase "to cover her nakedness" singles out the particular functions of wool and flax in a woman's life, so that the words have a directly personal effect.

■ 12 With "and now" (ועתה) Hosea frequently introduces the amplification of something previously alluded to (5:3; 10:3; 13:2). Here it introduces the consequences of the harvest failure described in detail in vv 12–15, but in such a way that Yahweh, with his own hand (v 12b), is presented again and again as the immediate cause of the punishment; note the verbs in the first person at the beginning of every sentence in vv 11–15a! Verse 12 first of all picks up v 11bβ. If Yahweh removes her means of clothing herself, the unfaithful wife must stand naked and publicly exposed.[52] With her genitals exposed,

45  Cf. A. Alt, "Der Stadtstaat Samaria," *Kleine Schriften zur Geschichte des Volkes Israel* 3 (München, 1953–9), 265f; "Das Reich Davids und Salomos," *Kleine Schriften* 2, 49ff.

46  7:13; 11:14; 12:17; 14:23; 18:4; 28:51; cf. L. Koehler, "Archeologisches Nr. 22, 23," *ZAW* 46 (1928): 218–20.

47  Cf. H. W. Wolff, "Hoseas geistige Heimat," *ThLZ* 81 (1956): 83–94, [also in Wolff, *Gesammelte Studien*, 232–50]. For the occurrence of this formula in Ugarit, see the excursus to v 15.

48  Cf. נתן in 2:17; Dtn 26:1, 2, 3, 9, 11; 11:14; 7:13 and G. von Rad, "The Theological Problem of the Old Testament Doctrine of Creation," in *The Problem of the Hexateuch and other essays*, tr. E. W. Trueman Dicken (New York: McGraw–Hill, 1966), 131–43.

49  Only the plural form of this verb does not fit the allegory. See pp. 34ff.

50  Cf. F. Horst, "Die Kennzeichen der hebräischen Poesie," *ThR* 21 (1953): 114.

51  Cod. Hammurabi, § 141: Meek, *ANET²*, 172.

52  With נבלות cf. Akk. *baltu = genitalia*, according to P. Humbert, "La Logique," 163; differently, Koehler–Baumgartner.

she is given up to complete contempt, disgrace, and shame.[53] Yahweh finds it necessary to carry out the threat of his ultimatum–like admonition in v 5a. Then her lovers will stand by like helpless spectators. None is equal to the severe grasp (5:14) of Yahweh's "hand" (Ps 32:4). He demonstrates that he is the first and the last stage of appeal.

■ **13** Although the allegory of the marriage continues uninterrupted, the metaphor of the wife's exposure before her lovers (v 12) finds its interpretation in v 13. If Yahweh removes the natural resources of the arable land, the feasts must come to an end. For Hosea it is primarily during these festivals that Israel's adulterous activity takes place. He describes this series of feasts as "her pleasures," and expressly repeats the third feminine suffix with each one. Yahweh has nothing to do with any of them. חג may point to the week–long main festival of the year in celebration of the vintage,[54] which is placed first as the most important of the festivals. The festival of the new moon may have included special sexual rituals; this may have been the time of the ἱερὸς γάμος.[55] "Sabbath" stands next to "new moon," as in Am 8:5; Is 1:13; 2 Kgs 4:23, but it can hardly be understood as the day of the full moon. Instead, in descending order, it is listed as the most frequent, weekly celebrated (Ex 20:8ff) festival, and is mentioned last before various other, not especially important festivals. In Jereboam II's kingdom, the sabbath was observed as a kind of "tabu–day" when one rested from his daily work. This is evident from Am 8:5 as well as from Hos 2:13, inasmuch as the introductory השבתי ironically alludes to the Sabbath. Perhaps the verb שבת is a denominative of שָׁבָת.[56] Yahweh will bring an end to these holy days, because they are dedicated to Baalism and thus represent Israel's adulterous relationship with her lovers.

■ **14** This verse does not refer back to v 11 in such a way that vv 12 and 13 must be understood as an interruption of the continuity.[57] Rather, v 14 further describes how

Yahweh will dispose of these cultic festivals. It shows more clearly than v 11 that the threat to the harvest includes the condemned cult of Baal as well. "Vines and fig trees" belong together: fig trees were planted in the vineyards (Lk 13:6); and grapes could be grafted onto the fig trees.[58] More importantly, the fruit of each matured about the same time (Mic 7:1) in August and September. The great autumn festival (חג; cf. v 13) came after the grape and fig harvest. If Yahweh destroys grapevine and fig trees, all the joyous feasts must come to an end; the archetypal image of peace and prosperity is in this way destroyed.[59]

The whore Israel calls the vine and fig tree her "wages, hire" (אתנה) from her lovers, the Baals. This form of the word is found only here in the Old Testament; it appears that Hosea chose it as a wordplay on "fig tree" (תאנה) instead of the usual אֶתְנָן.[60] It probably derives from "to pay a prostitute's hire," "to prostitute oneself" (תנה, cf. 8:9f), and thus recalls with Ju 11:40 the four–day festival in which young maidens lost their virginity.[61] Yahweh will turn the vineyards and fig trees into a wilderness. Should any fruit continue to grow among the thorns and weeds (Is 32:12f), the wild animals that live in thickly forested areas (יער) will devour them (Is 5:5).

■ **15** In v 15 Hosea for the first time refers to Israel's "lovers" (vv 7, 9, 12, 14) by the name of "Baals." Is the plural indicative of numerous Baal divinities, or does it merely derive from the imagery of adulterous relations with other men?[61a]

### The Baal Divinities

The assumption that the Canaanite religion knew an immense number of various localized Baals is incorrect. In Ugarit in Northern Syria, during the middle of the second millenium B.C., we find Baal represented as the king of the gods. He is the son of Dagon, the god of grain,[62] and appears as the immanent divinity while El, the father of the

53   Cf. Lam 1:8; Ezek 16:37; 23:39.
54   Ex 23:16; Ju 21:19ff; 1 Kgs 12:32.
55   Thus Boström, *Proverbiastudien*, 135f; Prv 7:19f; see the commentary on 5:7.
56   Cf. R. North, "The Derivation of Sabbath," *Biblica* 36 (1955): 182–201.
57   Budde, "Hos 1 und 3."
58   G. Dalman, *Arbeit und Sitte in Palästina* 4 (Gütersloh, 1935), 328f.
59   1 Kgs 5:5; Mic 4:4; Zech 3:10.
60   9:1; Dtn 23:19; Mic 1:7; etc.
61   Boström, *Proverbiastudien*, 119.
61a  Thus O. Eissfeldt "Baʿalšamēm und Jahwe," *ZAW* 57 (1939): 17.

gods, was considered a high god. Concerning the relationship of El's kingship to Baal's, cf. W. Schmidt, *Königtum Gottes in Ugarit und Israel*, BZAW 80 (Berlin, 1961) 52–4. As a stormgod Baal is the provider of all fertility. When he falls into the hands of Mot, the god of death, everything withers and decays (cf. v 12). Yet when Anath, Baal's wife and sister, destroys Mot, Baal comes to life again. Overcome by his embrace, Anath conceives and bears a calf. Thus we have here the mythical archetype of sacral prostitution (cf. v 14).

The priests of Baal wore the mask of a bull in their cultic worship, as Baal himself is similarly portrayed on a stela in the temple;[63] although in human form, he has the horns of a bull on his forehead.[64] His right hand wields a club, while the left hurls a thunderbolt. As the god of vegetation, he was the lord who provided fertility for all of life.[65]

Of particular interest to our discussion is *CTCA* 16.III–V (Gordon 126.III)[66] in which the awaited "rain of Baal" is described as being "sweet for the earth." There we find the same series of three words which occurs in v 10a: "spent is the bread (grain) from their jar, spent is the wine from their bottles, spent is the oil from their cruses."

O. Eissfeldt[67] supposed that, in the area inhabited by the Israelites, Baʿalšamēm was the real opponent of Yahweh throughout the Old Testament when the cult of Baal is mentioned. According to the evidence, Baʿalšamēm enjoyed special regard as the lord of heaven in Byblos, Tyre, and in Aramaic Syria. In any case the individual Baal divinities often gained dominion over large areas and became identified secondarily with other Baals.

In addition to v 15, Hosea speaks of "Baals" (בעלים) also in 2:19 and 11:2. In these two passages, the context itself does not suggest the plural (cf. especially 2:18), just as the imagery of marital unfaithfulness does not require a plurality of lovers in 2:7, 9, 12, 15. 3:1 (cf. v 3), where the parable has "friend," but the interpretation in v 1b has "other gods," shows that Eissfeldt's hypothesis is not valid for Hosea. Hence, the conclusion that Hosea did have a number of Baals in mind is unavoidable. If we take only the Old Testament into consideration, in addition to the ancient Baal–Berith (בַּעַל בְּרִית) of Shechem (Ju 8:33; 9:4), there is the Baal of Samaria;[68] the Baal of Carmel;[69] Baalzebub (בַּעַל זְבוּב) of Ekron;[70] and Baal of Hermon.[71] Concerning Baal of Tabor see below, p. 98; on Baal of Peor, p. 165. That all these easily could become identified as one does not alter the fact that they originally—and this applies to the religious practices in Hosea's time—must be distinguished from Baʿalšamēm. Hence, there is good reason for the plural בעלים in Hosea, not only because of the numerous Baal sanctuaries (Jer 2:28), but more importantly, because of the numerous, distinguishable Baals. In Hosea "Baal" has become a collective term for Canaanite deities ( = foreign gods in 3:1; cf. 13:4), since with Baal not even Asherah is mentioned.[72]

As a generic term for foreign deities, "Baalim" was taken over from Hosea—in addition to Jeremiah (2:23; 9:13)—only by the Deuteronomistic and Chronistic Histories.[73] In Ugarit Baal also seems to

---

62  Ju 16:23; 1 Sam 5:2ff.

63  *The Ancient Near East in Pictures Relating to the Old Testament,* ed. James B. Pritchard (Princeton: Princeton Univ., 1954), 490.

64  The bull is a symbol of fertility; cf. the commentary on 8:5ff.

65  Cf. A. S. Kapelrud, *Baal in the Ras Shamra Texts* (Copenhagen, 1952); M. H. Pope, *El in the Ugaritic Texts*, VT Suppl. 2 (Leiden, 1955); G. Ostborn, *Yahweh and Baal; Studies in the Book of Hosea and Related Documents*, LUÅ 51, 6 (Lund, 1956); W. F. Albright, *Archaeology and the Religion of Israel* (Baltimore: Johns Hopkins, 1956), 73ff; W. Schmidt, "Baals Tod und Auferstehung," *ZRGG* 15 (1963): 1–13. See the commentary on 8:5.

66  For an English translation, see C. H. Gordon, *Ugaritic Literature* (Rome, 1949), 80.

67  Eissfeldt, "Baʿalšamēm, 1–31.

68  1 Kgs 16:32; this Baal is probably identical with Melkart, the chief god of the Phoenecian kingdom of Tyre; cf. Alt, "Stadtstaat," 274f.

69  1 Kgs 18:19ff.

70  2 Kgs 1:2ff, "the lord of the flies" is probably a corruption of "the exalted lord" (בַּעַל זְבוּל); concerning *zbl* as a divine title, cf. Schmidt, *Königtum*, 7f.

71  Ju 3:3; cf. A. Alt, "Das Gottesurteil auf dem Karmel," *Kleine Schriften* 2, 138ff.

72  1 Kgs 18:19; 2 Kgs 23:4, 7.

73  The word is used as a collective name for masculine divinities in Ju 2:11; 8:33; 10:10; 1 Kgs 18:18; 2 Chr 17:3; 24:7; 28:2; it appears with אֲשֵׁרוֹת (Asheroth) in Ju 3:7; 2 Chr 33:3; 34:4; with עַשְׁתָּרוֹת (Ashtaroth) in Ju 10:6; 1 Sam 7:4 (where, significantly, הַבְּעָלִים takes the place of אֱלֹהֵי הַנֵּכָר ["foreign gods"] in 7:3), and 12:10.

be used occasionally as a generic term for local deities, while its usage as a proper noun predominates.[74] Its meaning as "lord, owner, proprietor," makes it especially appropriate as a generic term.[75]

"The days of the Baals" are the Canaanite cultic feasts,[76] with their outdoor festivities upon the sacred high places and underneath the holy trees (4:13). Three particulars are mentioned in the text: (1) The burnt offering. The word קטר pi'el is ordinarily used in reference to the pagan cult.[77] Thus, Old Testament prophecy considered the practice of making the sacrifice go up in smoke apostasy to pagan gods, aside from the fact that it was offered to those gods. The burnt offering was as characteristic of the ancient vegetarian culture in Canaan as the meal offering was of the culture of the shepherds living on the steppes, the latter being the culture in which Israel had its origins.[78] (2) The wearing of jewelry. According to Ex 32:2f (cf. Gen 35:4) נזם are the earrings belonging to the cult of the bull. It is uncertain whether חליה also means jewelry worn on the ears.[79] (3) The ceremonial procession. Since the statement "Israel goes after her lovers" is stated third, it is more likely that it indicates a procession within the sanctuary rather than a pilgrimage to it.[80] Leading such cultic processions which "went after her lovers" were standards bearing an image of a bull (in Mari) or a similar religious symbol.[81] Yahweh will "call Israel to account" for this entire ceremony. In Hosea פקד stands parallel to זכר (= to remember [guilt], 8:13; 9:9); to שוב hip'il (= to turn back, i.e., to pay back the deeds of, 4:9; 12:3); and to שלם (= to requite, 9:7). פקד describes a specific way in which God reacts to transgression; it presupposes a relationship of responsibility. According to Hosea, when God practices פקד, the punishment itself stands in the

foreground; nevertheless, the basic accent of sorrowful regret and concerned grief does not entirely escape notice.[82] This note of sorrow becomes apparent in the final sentence of the verse: "but she forgot me." This recalls the theme found in the motivation for Yahweh's punishment in v 10: "she no longer knows. . . ." That שכח is the opposite of ידע in Hosea is made evident by 4:6 and 13:4–6.[83] The connection of v 15 with v 10 makes it clear that "forgetting" Yahweh in effect means not only forgetting the תורה (4:6; cf. 13:4ff), but also the gifts Yahweh provides (cf. 8:14).

In Dtn the object of "forgetting" can be "the covenant" (4:23, 31), the "commandments" (25:19; 26:13), and also "Yahweh" himself as Israel's savior (6:12–14; 8:11, 14, 18f). Especially these last passages indicate once again the close connection of Hosea with the thought of the Deuteronomic circles. For there, too, the ones who "forget Yahweh" are described as those who "follow after other gods" (6:14; 8:19). Because of the related terminology, v 15b has been considered a secondary addition stemming from a Deuteronomistic redaction.[84] Stylistically, however, it is so smoothly connected with its context and, in view of 4:6, its content is so clearly Hosean, that this literary–critical hypothesis would deprive not only this genuine saying of its climax, but also the Deuteronomic circles of their early theological antecedents.

Hosea's God is personally affected by Israel's apostasy. Therefore, he who is forgotten will visit judgment on those who forgot. In the end, it is for "pastoral" reasons that the threat not only is introduced but also concluded by the description of Israel's guilt.[85] In Hosea, "says Yahweh" (נאם יהוה) concludes a rhetorical unit only in one other instance (11:11); in 2:18 it introduces the saying; in v 23 it occurs in the middle of the saying. In

---

74 *CTCA* 9 (Gordon 14); translated in Gordon, *Literature*, 109; see also Kapelrud, *Baal*, 44.

75 Cf. also W. Baudissin, "Baal und Bel," *RE*³, 323–40.

76 Cf. 9:5 and the Akk. *um ili* = "festival"; cf. Pfeiffer, *ANET*², 434, 16; Gressmann, *AOT*, 275, 16; B. Landsberger, *Der kultische Kalender der Babylonier und Assyrer*, Leipziger semitische Studien VI 1/2 (Leipzig, 1915), 12.

77 By contrast, the hip'il form, found primarily in Leviticus, is used for the worship of Yahweh.

78 Cf. pp. 85ff. and V. Maag, "Erwägungen zur deuteronomistischen Kultzentralization," *VT* 6 (1956): 14ff.

79 Dalman, *Arbeit* 5, 349. Cf. H. Schmökel, *Ur, Assur, und Babylon* (Stuttgart, 1955), Table 79 (jewelry of Ishtar priestesses).

80 "To go" (בוא) and "to go up" (עלה) in 4:15; עלה in 2:2.

81 O. Eissfeldt, "Lade und Stierbild," *ZAW* 58 (1940–1): 200ff; esp. 209.

82 Cf. v 15b and Koehler–Baumgartner.

83 Cf. H. W. Wolff, "'Wissen um Gott' bei Hosea als Urform der Theologie," *EvTh* 12 (1952–3): 539–43, [also in Wolff, *Gesammelte Studien*, 188–92].

84 Marti.

85 Cf. Wolff, "Die Begründung der prophetischen

each of these instances, this formula of divine utterance verifies the fact that Yahweh is speaking in the first person in the immediate context. Its function, therefore, is not necessarily that of dividing a unit from one that follows.

Cf. F. S. North, "The Expression 'the Oracle of Yahweh' as an Aid to Critical Analysis," *JBL* 71 (1952): x; and R. Rendtorff, "Zum Gebrauch der Formel *neʾum Jahwe* im Jeremiabuch," *ZAW* 66 (1954): 27–37. Did Hosea use this formula, or does it stem from the book's redaction? It is surprising that its occurrence is so infrequent, since Hosea often uses the form of divine speech; moreover, other formulas indicative of divine address are almost totally lacking; 3:1 and 4:1 are exceptions.[86]

■ **16** For a third time, a divine speech begun by לכן introduces the consequences resulting from Israel's transgression. לכן in vv 8 and 11 refers back to the guilt described in vv 7 and 10; the same is true of v 16 in relation to v 15b. This structural connection makes it necessary to take vv 16f with the preceding verses.[87] To be sure, v 15aβb and v 10, forming a kind of circle, give the motivation for the threat in vv 11–15a, which declares a crop failure and the lands's desolation. It appears as though this new "threat" (v 16) is motivated by the thought that the preceding punishment would not fully accomplish all that Israel's guilt required. Even more intensively than vv 10 and 7, v 15b had expressed that God himself suffers under Israel's unfaithfulness. Already in vv 4f and above all in vv 8f, Yahweh had intended, both as plaintiff and judge, to take only such measures that would heal this broken relationship. It is in this sense that vv 11–15a need some kind of completion. In v 16 Israel is to be brought again to the wilderness; this theme replaces that of the land's desolation, which was also mentioned in vv 5 and 8f. Now the expected judgment appears differently than before. Israel does not have to leave her own land because life there has somehow become unbearable.[88] For here the land is not described as desolate; rather, the land, with its vineyards, is to be repossessed by Israel as she comes out of the wilderness. Thus, although vv 16f probably do not form an original rhetorical unit with the previous verses,

here we certainly have a kerygmatic unit according to the sense of the present literary composition. Essentially, Israel's return to the wilderness first accomplishes the same purpose as that mentioned in the foregoing verses: Israel is to have nothing more to do with her would–be "suitors" but is to be Yahweh's alone (cf. vv 9, 12). Now, however, this new saying (vv 16f) kerygmatically goes beyond the intention of all that has been said up to this point: not only is Yahweh's severe action announced— against which the Baals are powerless (v 12)—but Yahweh will speak a new, indeed, a tender and loving word to Israel in the wilderness. The saying not only tells of the wife's new confession to her husband (v 9b), but more importantly, it declares that Yahweh will give her once again the gift of the vineyards.

At the beginning, the prophetic speech compellingly[89] directs the listeners' attention again to a quite unusual act of Yahweh: "I will allure her." In 7:11 Hosea calls the dove "easily seduced" (פּוֹתָה); it is "inexperienced" and "unintelligent" (אֵין לֵב). The dove represents Israel, who is easily mislead politically by the powerful nations. פתה piʿel means, accordingly, "to treat one as easily seduced." Thus Yahweh is represented here in a crudely anthropomorphic picture as a "seducer" who allures a young woman with many other suitors (cf. Ex 22:15). Like Jeremiah, who as an individual later stood before Yahweh on his people's behalf,[90] Israel as a nation will experience Yahweh's overpowering persuasion. Yahweh will lead her away to a solitary place in the wilderness— where there are no Baals—and there he will be alone with her. As in vv 4–15, now the accent lies not upon the description of certain future historical events, but upon Yahweh's personal action. In vain one would ask whether Hosea referred to the desert or the land's desolation by warfare in vv 11–15. Similarly, it would be fruitless to ask whether he means a return to a nomadic existence or to exile. The former is more probable in view of Yahweh's aloneness with Israel mentioned in v 16 and because of the promise to give her the vineyards "from there" in v 17. Chapters 12:10b and 13:4–6 also make this the more likely interpretation. The second possibility accords with Ezekiel's (20:33–44) new adaptation of this theme. He speaks of a "wilderness of the nations."

---

Heils– und Unheilssprüche," *ZAW* 52 (1934): 5f [also in Wolff, *Gesammelte Studien*, 13f].

86  See pp. 66f.
87  See p. 32.

88  Thus Humbert, "La logique," 164.
89  On לכן הנני, see pp. 35f.
90  Jer 20:7— פתה ‖ חזק: "seduce" ‖ "prevail over."

Hosea's comparison with the "day when she came out of Egypt" (v 17bβ) apparently influenced Ezekiel's terminology as well as his own comparison of the coming judgment with those events "in the wilderness of the land of Egypt" (v 36).[91] For Hosea, nature and history used by Yahweh as a means are of little importance and are replaceable. What is decisive and constant, however, is that Yahweh himself tells of his own coming, above all to make his people listen to him again: "I will speak to her heart." This expression (דבר על לבה) belongs to the language of courtship. Shechem "spoke to the heart" of Dinah, since "his soul was drawn to her and he loved her" (Gen 34:3). Ruth (2:13) was amazed that Boaz "spoke to her heart," as though she enjoyed his special confidence. Such a manner of speaking brings comfort (cf. also Is 40:2). The Levite in Ju 19:3 most accurately reflects Yahweh's attitude. He speaks "to the heart" of his wife who had gone astray, with the intention of bringing her back. The reason for "speaking to the heart" is therefore love and the awareness of belonging together; its object is to overcome sorrow and resentment (cf. also 2 Chr 32:6), obstinacy and estrangement.[92]

■ **17** It is surprising that there is no immediate response from the wife following the report of Yahweh's comforting words. Instead, we are told of Yahweh's action: "I will give to her her vineyards." Yahweh's words to her were apparently a sole declaration of his love which must now be sealed by his acts, not unlike "the gifts given to a young woman by her suitor."[93] Since this intimate conversation between Yahweh and Israel took place in the desert, and "from there" she will be led to the new gift of the vineyards, it is now beyond all doubt that Yahweh—and not Baal—is the provider of Israel's needs. They do not move to the wilderness as the ideal place of God's presence; rather, it is only a stopping place that

seems well suited for proving anew Yahweh's absolute sovereignty and miraculous power. His aim is to give her "her vineyards," namely, those "she had possessed earlier, which legally belong to the spouse who is faithful; they were taken away only because of her unfaithfulness (v 14)."[94] As Yahweh's new gift, the "vineyards" represent the arable land in its totality. They are a pledge of the comforting new beginning following Yahweh's judgment;[95] a source of deepest, heart–gladdening joy (Ps 104:15); and a sign of well–being in a secure peace provided by a power greater than herself.[96] "I will give from there" (נתתי משם) means as much as to lead back from the eastern wilderness to the arable land west of the Jordan. The mention of the "Valley of Achor" refers to this route. The valley is located, in any case, to the west of the Jordan Valley at the ascent to the fertile plain of the West Jordan highlands.

### The Valley of Achor

The precise location of the Valley of Achor is disputed.[97] On the basis of a survey of the locations in question, I have suggested the water-supplying *Wadi en-Nuwēʿime*, northwest of *Tell es-Sultan*, as its location. A broadly sweeping valley bottom approximately one half mile wide and one mile long, it is bordered on its western side by a semicircle of ascending mountains[98] and on its eastern side[99] by slightly hilly country opposite the Jordan Valley at *Khirbet el-Mefjer*.[100] A broad strip of vegetation accompanies the *wadi* at its southern end at the foot of the mountain (picture A). But also the dry, somewhat hilly northern part is traversed

---

91 Cf. 1QM 1:2f: "When the Sons of Light who are now in exile return from the 'desert of the nations' [ממדבר העמים] to pitch camp in the desert of Jerusalem, the children of Levi, Judah, and Benjamin, who are now among those exiles [of the wilderness, גולת המדבר], shall wage war against these peoples—that is against each and every one of their troops." The text is in E. L. Sukenik, *'Ôṣar hammegillôth haggenûzôth* (Jerusalem, 1955), Table 16. Eng. trans., Theodor H. Gaster, *The Dead Sea Scriptures* (New York: Anchor Book, 1964²), 301.

92 M. Luther, *WA* XIII, 9 (*ad loc.*): "Through my apostles I shall teach you a sweet doctrine different

from the law." [Trans.] (*Docebo te per meos apostolos dulcem doctrinam, aliam quam lex est*).

93 Budde, "Hos 1 und 3."

94 Keil.

95 Cf. Gen 9:20 with 5:29.

96 2 Kgs 18:31; see p. 38.

97 Cf. H. W. Wolff, "Die Ebene Achor," *ZDPV* 70 (1954): 76–81, and M. Noth, *ZDPV* 71 (1955): 42–55.

98 Wolff, "Ebene," 76, table 1, picture B.

99 *Ibid.*, picture A left.

100 Is this Gilgal? Cf. J. Muilenburg, "The Site of Ancient Gilgal," *BASOR* 140 (1955): 11–27.

by herds of sheep and goats.[101] Noth[102] agreed with my rejection of the older suggestions concerning the Valley's location;[103] however, against my new suggestion he made, among others, two objections: (1) The *Wadi en-Nuwēʿime* would not be an עמק in the sense the word is used in the Old Testament; (2) It would be located in the area of the Benjamin-Ephraimite border, whereas in Josh 15:7 the "Valley of Achor" helps describe the Judean-Benjamite border. As to (1), the counter-question remains unanswered: What, then, might be the Old Testament name of *Wadi en-Nuwēʿime*? Such a broadly stretching fertile valley would hardly be called a נַחַל,[104] but possibly a גְ. However, this "plain," like a genuine עמק, provides enough space for dwellings, cultivated land, and pasture. That this plain is not surrounded by mountains is in accordance with the use of עמק for the western coastal plain.[105] With respect to (2), a certain difficulty unquestionably remains. Noth's argument, however, is not so convincing when we consider that the area of Benjamin facing the Jordan gradually becomes smaller and includes little more than the immediate surrounding area of the valley bottom of the *Wadi en-Nuwēʿime*. Since there are hardly any prominent, fixed landmarks in the larger surrounding area, one surely could have determined the boundary of Judah from a well-known place on the other side, especially since the expression "hinterland of the Achor Valley" in Josh 15:7 is conspicuous.

Noth regards this as improbable and now, therefore, suggests the *buqēʿa* below *Khirbet Mird*, a 4 × 2 mile valley surrounded by mountains that is situated in the Judean desert, near the Greek Orthodox monastery *Mar Saba* by the *Wadi en-Nar*. In the meantime, J. T. Milik and F. M. Cross have stated that in this *buqēʿa* three small villages were settled in the 8th and 7th centuries. Accordingly, they have agreed with Noth.[106] But this interpretation involves three difficulties: (1) This valley is situated 9–12 miles from Jericho. Does Josh 7:24ff imply such a distance? (2) How could Hosea have ever named this valley—situated in the midst of a desert—a "gateway of hope?" It neither has the nature of a gateway, nor can it have had any connection with the Benjamite idea of

Israel's entry into the land. (3) The Judean-Benjamite border—if we follow Noth—would have bowed out curiously far toward the south.[107]

Since there is for the present little certainty about the location of the Valley of Achor, I still consider Hosea's description of it as a "gateway of hope" as a reference to the bay-type of valley floor northwest of Jericho. Like a verdant gateway, it invitingly ascends to the fertile hill country and its vineyards.

For Hosea and his contemporaries, the sound of the word "Achor" (עכור) was probably more important than its geographical location. "Achor" is reminiscent of "Achan" (עָכָן) upon whom Yahweh's wrath "brought misfortune" after he had "brought misfortune" (עכר, Josh 7:24–26) upon Israel. That God radically changes this valley of misfortune and wrath into a "Gateway of Hope" is an illuminating sign of the breakthrough of his love for Israel. This gateway already conveys a foretaste of the vineyards in Palestine. In v 17b the wife who was courted and presented with gifts finally becomes the subject: literally, "she shall answer" (וענתה). This is more than an answer in the sense of an exchange of words. Comprehensively, it says: she does what the call expected (cf. 2:23f; Is 65:12); in accordance with the words addressed to her, she accepts the hand of her Benefactor. She is now prepared to begin her marriage relationship anew.[108] That וענתה implies both an answer and a "following after" is indicated by the next word "there" (שמה) which syntactically presupposes a *constructio praegnans*,[109] (as in 1:2b; 2:20b, and 3:5b), i.e., a verb of motion is implied: "she answers and follows after" = "she follows willingly."

This willingness to follow in the approaching days is like the attitude of the wife Israel during "her youth." For Hosea, Israel's life had begun with the "ascent from Egypt" (cf. 11:1 and Ju 19:30). In her youth she acted willingly (10:11). Jeremiah (2:2) interprets Hosea for us when he lists her characteristics from the time of her "engagement" (cf. Ezek 16:43) as loyal devotion (חֶסֶד), love (אַהֲבָה), and discipleship (לֶכֶת אַחֲרֵי). In the Penta-

101 Cf. the group of tents in picture B.

102 *Josua*, HAT 7 (Tübingen, 1953²), 88.

103 Cf. Dalman, *PJB* 8 (Berlin, 1912), 62; Koehler-Baumgartner, 702a.

104 A. Schwartzenbach, *Die geographische Terminologie im Hebräischen des AT* (Leiden, 1934), 30.

105 Cf. *ibid.*, 34.

106 Cf. *RB* 63 (1956): 74–6.

107 Cf. also K. D. Schunck, *Benjamin*, BZAW 86 (Berlin, 1963), 39ff, 144ff, 161.

108 Cf. Ex 21:10; עָנָה = *debitum conjugale*, Humbert, "La logique," 165.

109 Grether, §87h.

teuchal sources there is no such positive evaluation of Israel's attitude in the days of her youth.[110] Hosea knows nothing of the people's murmuring "repeated continuously and almost monotonously" in the units forming the "Wandering in the Wilderness" theme.[111] For Hosea, the exodus from Egypt and the wandering through the wilderness happened during a time when Yahweh called Israel, presented her with his gifts, and she responded with grateful discipleship. Yahweh promises an eschatological return of this earlier time.

## Aim

The series of sayings in 2:4–17 is concerned with the question of how Yahweh deals with unfaithful Israel. Although dissimilar according to form and content, these sayings are nevertheless connected by one basic fact: God suffers under Israel's deceitful love affair. He refuses to accept as final the divorce his wife both desired and initiated (v 4a). He cannot bear her illusion that she could actually exist from what her false lovers provide (v 7). His love unrequited, he laments that he is forgotten (vv 10, 15). Because God suffers in his love for Israel, he therefore woos her once again (v 16f).[112] This basic motif makes understandable that, stylistically, the parable of the unfaithful wife continues through to the very end of the passage. In terms of ancient Israel's faith in Yahweh, it is an unprecedented modernism that Hosea so consistently utilizes the Canaanite mythologoumenon of divine marriage. But he transfers to Yahweh and Israel, i.e., to God and his historical people, what the myth says of the god and the goddess, what the cult celebrated as a holy marriage, and what in the study of nature was observed as the "mating" of heaven and earth. But above all, Hosea introduces the concept of adultery and divorce, thereby destroying the myth from the inside in a way that is without analogy.[113] Hence, in the end a mythical element is changed into a parable that severely polemicizes against the introduction of Canaanite mythology into Israel.

Impelled by his suffering and love for his people, God seeks a variety of paths by which to lead her back. The diversity of the sayings combined here is a moving witness to how Hosea's God competes to win Israel back. Here we have what might be called a small compendium of answers to the question: "What shall I do to you, O Ephraim?" (6:4). At first, people are summoned against people; reason is called out against folly, integrity against unfaithfulness (v 4a). In a word of warning, God seeks out listeners and advocates, as though improvement were possible (vv 4b, 5) through utmost rigor. But Israel's infatuation with the false gods is so total (vv 6f) that Yahweh can no longer address his beloved people with words, but only with acts which are proclaimed as his. He creates conditions in which the heathen gods can no longer be reached (v 8) and demonstrates that they are impotent (v 12). He accomplishes both by the desolation of the land and its sanctuaries (vv 8f, 11–15). This very last way brings Israel back into the wilderness. There God's address again comprises word and action. Yet this word does not make demands; rather, it seals Yahweh's courtship with gifts (vv 16f).[114] Thus we have the announcement of at least three different ways in which Yahweh proceeds: (1) he admonishes Israel to turn voluntarily from her pagan gods; (2) he threatens destruction of all possibilities for pagan worship in Palestine; and, (3) after leading Israel away from the land, he courts Israel with loving words and acts that represent the eschatological, new beginning of Israel's history.

The interrelation of these thoughts shows that Yahweh passionately strives, in various ways, to achieve *one* aim: that Israel turn to him anew. Although the catchword "return" occurs only in v 9, the warning (vv 4f) and the words of courtship (vv 16f), according to their intention, also seek Israel's return. Even the obscure saying of judgment (vv 11–15a) appears to be related indirectly to this future expectation (vv 10, 15b). Yet, not the admonition, but only Yahweh's acts are able to attain

110 Cf. J. Rieger, *Die Bedeutung der Geschichte für die Verkündigung des Amos u. Hosea* (Giessen, 1929), 113.

111 M. Noth, *A History of Pentateuchal Traditions*, tr. B. W. Anderson (Englewood Cliffs: Prentice Hall, 1972), 122 [*Überlieferungsgeschichte des Pentateuch* (Darmstadt, 1966³), 134].

112 Cf. J. Scharbert, "Der Schmerz im AT," *BBB* 8 (1955): 162, 219.

113 Cf. H. Schrade, *Der verborgene Gott* (Stuttgart, 1947), 168.

114 J. Calvin, *CR* LXX, 243 (on 2:15): "The prophet had said in the previous verse: 'I shall address her heart.' Now he adds: 'Now I shall make known the sure and clear testimony of my goodwill that they may know that I have been reconciled to them' " [Trans.] (*Dixerat propheta proximo versu,*

the goal, as is noted twice in vv 9b and 17b. In both instances the presupposition is a harsh judgment: in v 8 it occurs alone, while in vv 16f it appears together with words of promise and acts of salvation. Yahweh's judgment takes Israel back to the time of her wandering in the wilderness as the prerequisite for her return and for the eschatological new beginning of the history of God's people. Thus the church experiences its total renewal only as *église du désert*.[115]

John the Baptist appeared in the wilderness (Mk 1:2ff) with his baptism of repentance as a gift of God.[116] This may be better understood as the beginning of the eschatological time of salvation if we see the evangelist's quotation of Is 40:2f in connection with Hos 2:16f.[117] The path Jesus chose began in the wilderness. It was the place not only of John's work and Jesus' own temptation (Mk 1:9–13), but where he quietly and undisturbedly conversed with his Father (Mk 1:35, 45; Lk 5:16, etc.). The Judaism of New Testament times expected that the age of salvation would have its beginning in the wilderness. Therefore revolutionary, messianic movements frequently moved to the desert.[118] The New Testament Church thought of the wilderness as its eschatological place of shelter from its persecutor and tempter (Rev 12:6, 14).

Yahweh's judgment effects Israel's return, rekindling her "first love" for him (vv 9b, 17b; cf. Rev 2:4f). This is finally accomplished by God's new, intimate word (cf. Is 40:2f) spoken to her in the wilderness, and by his gift of the vineyards given anew when he leads her back again from the wilderness (vv 16f). Only with this saying (vv 16f) is it entirely clear that the judgment's purpose is new life for God's people. The wilderness is not idealized. The God of the wilderness demonstrates to his own that he is the Provider of civilization. Everything depends upon Israel's return to Yahweh. How important for Hosea is Yahweh's future action in bringing about the return of all of Israel? This answer is clear if we compare Hos 2:4ff with Ezek 20:33–44. There, in a similar tradition complex[119] much greater importance is laid upon man's action. The culmination of Hosea's message points us toward Rom 5:8 and Eph 2:4ff.[120]

*Loquar ad cor eius: nunc addit, Ego proferam certum et illustre testimonium favoris mei, ut sentiant me sibi reconciliatum esse*).

115 M. Luther, *WA* XIII, 8 (on v 11): "If today the belly of the pope were hungry, there would not be so many papists" [Trans.] (*Si egeret hodie venter papae, non tam multi essent papistae*).

116 Cf. E. Lohmeyer, *Das Evangelium des Markus* (Göttin-gen, 1951), 14f.

117 Cf. L. Koehler, *Kleine Lichter* (Zürich, 1945), 86.

118 Acts 21:38; Mt 24:26; Jos. *Ant.* XX: 8:6, 10; *Bell* II: 13:4; on this, see G. Kittel, *TDNT* 2, 658f.

119 See pp. 41–42.

120 Cf. H. Wh. Robinson, *The Cross of Hosea* (Philadelphia, Westminster, 1949), 48.

## The Day of the New Covenant

### Bibliography

W. Baumgartner
"Kennen Amos und Hosea eine Heilseschatologie?" *SThZ* 30 (1913): 30–42, 95–124, 152–70.

See the Bibliography for 1:1 and 2:4–17.

# 2

18 [16]  **On that day, says Yahweh,**
**then**[a] **you**[b] **will call out: "My husband,"**
**and you**[b] **will no longer call me**
**"My Baal."**[c]

19 [17]  **I will remove the names of the Baals**
**from her mouth,**
**that they no longer be mentioned**
**by their name.**[d]

20 [18]  **I will make for them a covenant on that day**
**with the beasts of the field, the birds of the**
**air, and the creeping things of the ground;**
**I will abolish**[e] **bow, sword,**
**and weapons from the land;**
**I will provide rest and security**[f]
**for them.**[g]

21 [19]  **I will make you my own**[h] **forever.**
**I will make you my own in salvation**
**and justice,**
**in unfailing loyalty and in mercy.**

22 [20]  **I will make you my own in faithfulness.**
**Then you shall know**[i] **Yahweh.**

23 [21]  **On that day, then**[j] **I will answer,**[k]
**says Yahweh.**

a  והיה is used as a temporal adverb, as indicated by the absence of the copula preceding the next verb (cf. Koehler–Baumgartner, 229b).

b  *G* reads καλέσει twice, while α′σ′θ′ read καλέσεις at least for the second occurrence. In view of the context (vv 4–17, 19a) and the tendency of *G* to harmonize, the third person is much more likely to be secondary than the second person. *G* inserts με in v 18a, thus harmonizing it with v 18b.

c  *G* (βααλιμ) is also inexact, harmonizing v 18b with vv 15 and 19.

d  With the plural τὰ ὀνόματα αὐτῶν, *G* harmonizes the close of the verse with v 19a.

e  With its three objects (קשת וחרב ומלחמה) אשבור stylistically represents a zeugma, even if מלחמה is taken as a collective concept for weapons or perhaps a definite weapon, like a club, which according to Is 30:32, is swung (cf. H. Gunkel, *Die Psalmen*, HK II, 2 [Göttingen, 1926⁴] on Ps 76:4). For only a bow can be "broken" (1:5; Ps 46:10). Yet the hand of Yahweh is capable of more. אשבור מן is *constructio praegnans* (see textual note "p" on p. 31), which suggests a second verb "and I will remove" or something similar.

f  Literally: "I let them rest in safety" ("I will make them lie down in safety" RSV). *G* freely renders לבטח with ἐπ' ἐλπίδι; σ′ (ἐν εἰρήνῃ) and θ′ (ἐν πεποιθήσει) are more exact.

g  With σε *G* harmonizes v 20 with v 21f, in spite of the correct αὐτοῖς in v 20a; α′σ′θ′ correctly translate with αὐτούς.

h  Literally: "to marry." ארש pi'el denotes the legal act constituting marriage. The customary translation "to betroth" as we use the term incorrectly separates the act described here from the time of the public act of marriage (see p. 52).

i  An unimportant strand of Masoretic (45MSS)—and of Greek (Cyril of Alexandria)—tradition, which has been taken up by *V*, reads כִּי אֲנִי יהוה instead of אֶת־יהוה, thus interpreting Hosea in terms of Ezek (cf. Wolff, "Erkenntnis Gottes im AT," *EvTh* 15 [1955]: 428ff.).

j  See textual note "a" above.

k  אענה is not found in *G*. Has this thematic catchword in *M* been placed in its present position secondarily? It could also reflect oral discourse, which is fre-

I will answer the heavens,
    and they[l] shall answer the earth;
24 [22]   the earth shall answer the grain,
    the new wine, and the olive oil,
    and they shall answer Jezreel.
25 [23]   ...[m] and I will sow her[m] for myself
    in the land.
    I will have mercy on Without–Mercy,
    I will say to Not–My–People:
    "You are my people!"
      and he will say: "My God!"[n]

quently intensified by repetition. Cf. Gen 25:30. *G* often varies freely within its context (see textual notes "b," "d," "g," "i," "l," "n").

l    *G* (ὁ οὐρανός) probably is an inner-Greek corruption of an original αὐτός (cf. Ziegler, *Duodecim prophetae*, 132).

m    A protasis containing an antecedent for the suffix appears to have been lost (see the commentary on 2:25).

n    *G* expands this to a complete formula of confession: κύριος ὁ θεός μου εἶ σύ.

## Form

In 2:4–17 we found a collection of prophetic sayings that have been carefully connected with each other, according to both form and content. In clear contrast to these verses, 2:18–25 consists of a loosely knit series of sayings and fragments of sayings. The redactional formula[1] "on that day" (והיה ביום ההוא) divides our passage into three units: vv 18–19, 20–22, 23–25. Each of these units probably combines two (originally) distinct parts, as is evident from the different personal objects: second feminine singular in vv 18, 21f; third feminine singular in v 19 (v 25aα); third plural in v 20; Jezreel in vv (23–) 24; and Without–Mercy and Not–My–People, in addition to the third feminine suffix, in v 25. Thus there are six units, more or less joined together, whose fragmentary nature is particularly noticeable at the beginning of vv 20 and 25. Whereas the unfaithful wife (third feminine singular) is the subject throughout vv 4–17, here, the theme changes, as does the person: Baal, vv 18f; covenant of peace, v 20; covenant of marriage, vv 21f; answer, vv 23f; divine covenant, v 25.

Nevertheless, this miniature collection[2] is a genuine unit. Two things unify it: (1) Each of the sayings is in the form of a divine speech. Moreover, the divine "I" is usually the subject; man's response to the divine initiative in vv 22b and 25bβ is in the terse style typical of Hosea (cf. vv 9b, 17b). Accordingly, one might think that v 19 originally preceded v 18,[3] if the change from second to third person did not indicate the verses to be fragments of different sayings. (2) Each of the sayings serves to characterize "that day" (vv 18, 20, 23) as a day of salvation. Within this unified genre of promises, proclamations of salvation (third person in vv 19, 20, 23f, 25) alternate with assurances of salvation (second person in vv 18, 21f).

## Setting

The formula "that day," occurring three times, is suggestive of the function this collection of sayings performs in its present context: it is to elucidate the era of salvation (vv 9, 17) that is expected as a result of the judgment in vv 4–17. Verse 18 interprets as "and she will answer" the word וענתה in v 17b; v 19 is to safeguard that Israel's new attitude is the result of what Yahweh has done (vv 8f, 11–15, 16f); vv 21f interpret Yahweh's courtship (v 16) as an act of binding engagement; vv 20 and 23–25 explain the withdrawal of judgment, similar to v 17a.

Are these sayings, which provide such elucidation, genuine words of Hosea? Since the threats in vv 4–17 clearly intend to bring about salvation, it is hardly possible to deny vv 18–25 to Hosea merely because they are oracles of salvation.[4] P. Humbert[5] was convinced of a meaningful connection of the sayings in vv 4–22. In addition, the thematic connection of 2:4–25 with 11:8ff and 14:2ff should not be overlooked.[6] Nevertheless, there are certain difficulties regarding the details. Whereas vv 18f and 21f exhibit the same theme and language as vv 4–17, this does not hold true to the same degree for vv 20, 23f and 25. Verse 20 seems alien to its context because its characterization of Israel in the third plural ("for them," להם; "I will provide rest for them," והשכבתים) interrupts the connection of vv 18f

---

1    See pp. 47f.

2    Gressmann, *Der Messias*, 87.

3    Gressmann, *Der Messias*, 182, n. 1, regards v 18 as a gloss on v 19.

4    Budde, "Der Abschnitt," R. H. Pfeiffer, *Introduction to the O T* (London: Adam and Charles Black, 1948), *et al.*

5    "La Logique," 166.

6    Th. C. Vriezen, "Prophecy and Exhatology," VT Suppl. 1 (1953): 206f; cf. especially 2:23f with 14:9b!

with 21f, where Israel still appears in the metaphor of the wife (as in vv 4–17). Moreover, in v 20 the formula ביום ההוא has a different position than in vv 18 and 23. Finally, the concept of the covenant and the covenant partners in v 20 is different from that found in 6:7 and 8:1. Verses 23–25 have been considered inauthentic because Jezreel, Without–Mercy, and Not–My–People are no longer spoken of as Hosea's children, as in chap. 1; the theme of the unfaithful wife in vv 4–17, which still echoes in vv 18f and 21f, is finally left behind.

These observations concerning vv 20 and 23–25, however, prove nothing more than that vv 18–25 present a secondary collection of sayings which vary in language and theme. Hosea also uses the word "covenant" (ברית) in different ways (cf. 12:2 and 10:4 with 6:7 and 8:1). And why should the symbolic names of Hosea's children —similar to the marriage–metaphor—not continue to be used in his proclamation? The image of peace as continuous fertility accords with its antithesis in the judgment speech in vv 4–17, even in the formulation of the details.[7]

Since this literary composition is far less logically connected than vv 4–17 we should probably not ascribe it to Hosea, but to the redactor responsible for 1:2–6, 8f. This is suggested by the expression "on that day" (והיה ביום ההוא)[8] which does not appear again in the book. This formula is evidence of his concern to elucidate the final event in 2:4–17 with the help of Hosea's later sayings. Moreover, 3:1–5 precisely continues the tone of 2:4–17, but shows no signs of the definite accent on salvation found in vv 18–25. Verses 18–25 presuppose that the judgment threatened in 1:2–6, 8f; 2:4–17; and 3:1–5 has already taken place. Verse 20 looks back to a desolation and ruin of the land (cf. v 14); vv 23f look back to a drought (cf. vv 5, 11) or a capture of the fertile

land of Palestine (cf. v 16). Also, vv 21f and 25 mention only salvation, without even suggesting that Yahweh's judgment is the way leading to salvation.[9]

This passage could probably be dated in the year 733, when the Northern Kingdom was overthrown by Tiglath–pileser III.[10] At that time, only the Samaritan highlands remained under the rule of Pekah, King of Israel. The rest of his territory was divided into three Assyrian provinces: the coastal plain south of Carmel became the province of Dor; the region east of the Jordan became the province of Gilead; and Galilee, together with the Jezreel Valley, became the province of Megiddo.[11] The struggle for the fertile Jezreel Valley and its subsequent loss could very well have been of utmost importance, as the appointment of Megiddo as administrative capital indicates.[12] These events seem to form the historical background of Hosea's new interpretations of his oldest child's symbolic name. At that time he must have been at least seventeen years old.[13] When these events began Hosea could more accurately describe his earlier judgment upon the Israelite dynasty (1:4) as a battle in the Jezreel Valley (1:5). Similarly, in 2:23f he can now allude to the economic straits of the rump state after the fertile Jezreel Valley—the supplier of grain for the whole land—had been desolated and cut off; with v 25a he hints at the farmers' loss of land or the deportation of the upper class of that region. Accordingly, the collection of sayings in vv 18–25 would not have existed until after the fall of Pekah; at the earliest, during the beginning of King Hoshea's reign (732–23). But in view of its relationship to chaps. 11 and 14:2–9, a more probable time would be the reign of Shalmaneser V, beginning in 727.[14] While Hosea's earlier sayings (1:2–4, 6, 8f; 2:4–17; 3:4f) were first being fulfilled, a redactor completed an earlier document written by the prophet

---

7   Cf. "beasts of the field" (חית השדה) in v 20a with v 14b; "grain, new wine, olive oil" (הדגן והתירוש והיצהר) in v 24 with v 10; "I will sow her for myself in the land" in v 25a with "I will bring her into the wilderness" in v 16a.

8   Cf. vv. 18, [20], 23 with 1:5 and also 2:1f; see p. 9.

9   How different, by comparison, are those sayings stemming from economically prosperous times in vv 8f, 16f and 3:4f!

10  Noth, *History*, 260f [236].

11  Cf. 2 Kgs 15:29; Is 8:23; see Tiglath–pileser's annals from 734–3, lines 227–34 in Oppenheim, *ANET*[2], 283; also A. Alt, "Das System der as-

syrischen Provinzen," *Kleine Schriften zur Geschichte das Volkes Israel* 2 (München, 1953–9), 188–205.

12  Alt, *ibid.*, 197–9; 210f; see the commentary on 1:5.

13  See the commentary on 1:4, p. 138f.

14  See pp. 197 and 217.

15  A. Alt, "Jesaja 8:23–9:6: Befreiungsnacht und Krönungstag," *Kleine Schriften* 2, 208.

(2:4–17; 3:1–5) by adding to it both the old collection of *memorabilia* (1:2–4, 6, 8f) and Hosea's more recent sayings (1:5; 2:18–25). The addition of vv 18–25 to vv 4–17 probably offers a historical as well as literary–historical parallel to the addition of Is 8:23–9:6 to 8:21f.[15]

## Interpretation

■ **18** "And on that day" (והיה ביום ההוא) is usually followed by an imperfect verb as it is here;[16] in the older prophetic literature it can also be followed by a perfect consecutive.[17] Thus the tense of the verb is not compelling evidence for the redactional character of the formula.[18] In more than two thirds of its occurrences, the formula introduces a promise.[19] In Hosea it introduces one threat (1:5) as compared to three promises (2:18, 20, 23). Perhaps this expression echoes the old, popular expectation of the day of Yahweh as a day of salvation (Am 5:18). The description of this day of salvation does not point first of all to the new conditions of life, but rather to the proclaimed new confession of Israel. The result of Yahweh's judgment (v 9b) and salvation (v 17b) is thus stated more precisely than before. Israel is addressed as an unfaithful wife; it is as though words taken directly from Yahweh's courtship (v 16) were cited here. She is provided with the new words she will address to Yahweh. The change of address from one to the other should be understood in terms of the metaphor of marriage Hosea uses. "My husband" (אישׁי) is apparently an endearing expression; it addresses the husband as one who belongs to and who even enjoys a deep personal relationship with the "wife" (אשׁה).[20] On the other hand, the address "my lord," "my Baal" (בעלי) emphasizes the legal position of the husband as lord and "owner" of the wife. There is not necessarily a correspondingly genuine and personal devotion to her as his wife.[21] Hence, this saying announces that Israel will not just respect Yahweh somewhat reluctantly, since he is its legal lord, but it knows itself to be placed in a completely new, loving relationship with him. In addition to

the primary sense of the saying, there is a punlike polemic against the cult. The word for "lord" in this parable is the same Hebrew word that denotes the Canaanite god, Baal. This undertone is intentional. It presupposes the existence of a syncretism in which Yahweh was worshiped as Baal.

## Yahweh as Baal

The Israelite names prevalent at that time can serve as an illustration of this. The words יהוה and בעל occurred together, functioning as elements that signified the respective divine names. Already in the earliest period of the monarchy, two of Saul's sons were named "Jonathan" (יונתן 1 Sam 13:16) "Eshbaal" (אשׁבעל 2 Sam 2:8, α′ σ′ θ′); among David's sons there were "Adonijah" (אדניה) and "Shephatiah" (שׁפטיה 2 Sam 3:4) together with "Beeliada" (בעלידע 2 Sam 5:16, *G*ᴮᴸ; cf. 1 Chr 14:7). On the Samarian ostraca, probably dating from the third decade of the 8th century,[22] there are ten names formed on the word Baal, with eleven names formed on Yahweh. The former occur more frequently among lower classes (eight, compared with six Yahweh names) than among the upper class (two, compared with five Yahweh names).[23] In addition to this evidence, the occurrence of the name בעליה[24] most clearly indicates how Israel's life among the ancient, settled, Canaanite population led to the identification of one god with the other.[25] It is difficult to determine in detail whether Yahweh was worshiped as Baal, or whether they were worshiped together.

The papyri from the Judean military colony Elephantine on the Nile peninsula (fifth century) provide an unequivocal example of the "Baalization" of Yahweh. Here, with the name of Yahweh, we find the name of the goddess Anathbethel, or

---

16   2:23; Is 7:18, 21, 23; Jer 4:9; Ezek 38:10; 39:11; Joel 3:18, etc.; cf. textual note "a" and H. W. Wolff, *Joel und Amos*, BK XIV/2 (Neukirchen, 1969), 90, on Joel 4:12 [3:18].

17   1:5; Am 8:9; Mic 5:9; Is 22:20.

18   *Contra* Robinson, 15; see p. 48.

19   Gressmann, *Der Messias*, 83.

20   2:9, Gen 2:23f; cf. Gen 29:32, 34; 30:15, 20; 2 Sam

14:5; 2 Kgs 4:1.

21   Ex 21:22; Dtn 22:22; 24:2; cf. Gen 20:3.

22   Noth, *World*, 98 [76]; W. F. Albright, *Archeology and the Religion of Israel* (Baltimore: Johns Hopkins, 1941), 41, 160; differently, Alt, "Stadtstaat," 296.

23   Noth, *Personennamen*, 120.

24   "Bealiah," 1 Chr 12:6 [5].

25   Noth, *Personennamen*, 120f, 141.

Anathyahu, and a third divinity, Ishumbethel.[26] It appears that this group of Jews in Egypt practiced the kind of syncretism against which Hosea speaks. "Yahweh" is combined with a goddess, as Baal is with Anath in Ugarit.[27] In view of this, the form of address "my Baal" might be understood as an element of the cultic representation of the sacral marriage.

The cult–polemical aspect of the verse is only a secondary emphasis. If it were of main importance, then "Yahweh" (יהוה) or "my God" (אלהי v 25b) instead of "my husband" (אישי) would be expected in the first part of the passage. Nevertheless, this secondary emphasis is intended to be heard along with the allegory's primary emphasis on the marriage imagery. Since Israel recognizes Yahweh alone as her legally constituted lord, in forsaking him she exchanges her God for Baal. The juxtaposition of vv 18 and 19 strongly underscores this secondary aspect. However, the change of address from second to third person (no longer present in *G*), as well as the different meaning of each verse, indicates that they are fragments of different rhetorical origins.

■ **19** This verse is clearly directed against the Canaanized cult. If it is Yahweh who removes the names of the Baal from the wife's mouth, then her new confession—as found in 2:8f, 16f—is represented exclusively as a work of Yahweh, and not as her own accomplishment. The plural "Baals" (בעלים), as in v 15 and 11:2, means "pagan gods."[28] Their various names may have been Ba'alšamēm, Melcart, Baal of Carmel, Asherah, Astarte, Anath, Milcom, Chemosh.[29] The second half of the verse has no indication of a heightening, as though "the names of Baal [were] first removed from their mouth and second, from their thoughts."[30] Rather, it states the effect of Yahweh's work, for זכר nip'al is the passive

of זכר hip'il, which combined here with "name" (בְּשֵׁם) denotes the solemn occasion in the cult when the god is represented by the mention of his name.[31] This recalls the prayerful invocation of the name (= קרא in 1 Kgs 18:26) as well as the proclamation commissioned by the gods (= דבר in Dtn 18:2; cf. Jer 2:8; 23:13).[32] Chapter 2:8–17 described how Yahweh reforms Israel's worship by removing the name of Baal. Its result was announced already in v 18.

■ **20** The following sayings complete the picture of "that day," which is announced by the prophet as a day of salvation. After the restoration of Israel's worship, the restoration of the world becomes the theme. It, too, is entirely the result of Yahweh's action. In this saying there is no transition from the first person announcement of Yahweh's deed (וכרתי–אשבור–והשכבתים) to a description of the new conditions of life in which other entities become subjects of the narrative. Cf. on the other hand, Ezek 34:25a, 26, 29, with vv 25b, 27, 28; and Lev 26:6aα, bα with aβ, bβ. This supports the Hosean authorship of v 20. The promise consists of three parts:

1) The restoration of man's relationship to the animal kingdom is described as the enactment of a covenant. The formula כרת ברית recalls the ancient rite of cutting animals in two. The person who enacted the covenant passed through the middle of the two halves of the animal. This act set a curse in motion which would result in his being cut in two should he not keep his obligations. It would be more precise to describe this "covenant making" as the assuming of self–imposed obligations in a ceremonial act.[33] Verse 20, however, does not present the act of granting a covenant in the form in which it usually occurs in the Old Testament; rather, Yahweh appears as the covenant mediator between Israel and a third party, with whom enmity has existed up to this

26 Ginsberg, *ANET*[2], 491; Noth, *History*, 294f [266f]; Cowley, *Papyri*, No. 22:123 = יהו; 22:124 = אשמביתאל; 22:125 = ענתביתאל; 44:3 = ענתיהו; further, see Kraeling, *Papyri*, 87ff.

27 See pp. 38ff on 2:15, and G. Widengren, *Sakrales Königtum im AT und im Judentum* (Stuttgart, 1955), 12, 77ff.

28 See p. 39.

29 Cf. 1 Kgs 11:33; 18:19 and p. 39 on 2:15 and pp. 49f on 2:18. According to the Eshmun'azar Inscription from Sidon, Astarte probably was also called שֵׁם-בָּעַל; Rosenthal, *ANET*[3], 662; Hans Bietenhard, *TDNT* 5, 258, n. 117.

30 Thus Allwohn, *Die Ehe*, 26.

31 Josh 23:7; Am 6:10; Ps 20:8; Zech 13:2; cf. Is 48:1; Ps 38:1; 70:1.

32 Cf. H. Bietenhard, *TDNT* 5, 258, lines 17ff and W. Schottroff, *"Gedenken" im Alten Orient und im Alten Testament*, WMANT 15 (Neukirchen, 1964), 249–51, 275f.

33 Cf. Gen 15:9f, 17f; Jer 34:18; J. Begrich, "Berit," *ZAW* 60 (1944): 1–11.

time. Mari Text II, 37[34] sheds some light on this unusual act of Yahweh. According to the Mari Text, Zimrilim of Mari commissions someone who, by slaying donkeys, makes a covenant between two groups of people that are under the king's jurisdiction.[35] Like the royally commissioned executor of the covenant from Mari, here Yahweh is not a covenant partner. To be sure, "for them" (להם) indicates that he knows himself to be obligated to the partner, Israel, and acts especially on her behalf. But the relationship effected by the enactment of the covenant does not have to do with Yahweh; rather, it involves a mediation of peace between Israel and the estranged animal kingdom (cf. Gen 3:15). Yahweh proves his covenant loyalty toward Israel by mediating a covenant between opposing forces within creation (cf. Ezek 34:25–30; Gen 9:8–17). Such an act would correspond to the original meaning of the word ברית, which possibly is connected with the Akk. *birit*, a preposition (= "between") used as a noun in the sense of "mediation."[36] כרת ברית (עם) is genuinely Hosean: 12:1; cf. 10:4.

Yahweh establishes a covenant of peace for Israel with the "beasts of the field, the birds of the air, and the creeping things of the ground." These are animals that can harm the population, their vineyards, and their crops. Thus the sentence of judgment in 2:14 is removed; a paradisiacal harmony between man and the animals is established. The three phrases naming the animals recall Gen 1:30, where they and mankind are placed under the same divine regulation concerning food (cf. Is 11:6–8; 65:25).[37] Just as Hosea traces the founding of Israel as the community of God back to a ברית (6:7; 8:1), he also attributes the eschatological restoration of creation to a ברית which is a divine act of pacification especially for the benefit of Israel. Regarding the content,

here we have the first reference to a "new covenant" of the endtime (cf. Jer 31:31).

2) Israel will also be at peace with the hostile nations. That *Israel* is meant is evident not only from the context "for them" (להם), continued by "I will provide rest for them" (השכבתים), but also from the meaning of ארץ.

In addition to 2:20, ארץ occurs in Hosea nineteen times. In ten of these instances it means "land" in the sense of a dwelling place for a single people.[38] In six instances "land" means ground, cultivated land,[39] or waste land (2:5; 13:5). But Hosea never uses the word in the sense of "earth" or "world" for the entire area populated by the nations, as distinguished from the heavens and ocean (Gen 1:1, 10; 2:4). Hence, we may suppose that also in 2:20 the meaning of "land" is that area in which Israel lived; cf. also Lev 26:6b. Thus Hosea does not announce a cosmic kingdom of peace that includes the entire heathen world, as in Is 2:4 and Zech 9:10. Yahweh promises a tangible act of redemption, which is closely related to Is 9:3f both historically and according to its content.[40]

3) Yahweh removes the injury wrought by animals and war to create rest and security for Israel. Instead of לבטח ("trustful," "without care," "peaceful"),[41] Lev 26:6 reads אין מחריד ("without anyone disturbing"). Yahweh creates living conditions in which one can sleep in peace, unafraid of the enemy.[42] This is the result of Yahweh's two-pronged action for bringing peace. The idea of peace with the animals and with the nations is combined elsewhere only in Ezek 34:25–28 and Lev 26:6. The injury caused by animals and war occurs in a threatening context in Jer 15:2f, but there this double motif has already become part of a series of four. In Job 5:19–23 this connection of animals and war is included in a sapiential series of six "troubles" from which one is to be

---

34   *Archives Royales de Mari II*. Musée du Louvre. Département des Antiquités Orientales. Textes cunéiformes Tome XXIII, publ. par Ch.–F. Jean (Paris, 1941).

35   For details, cf. M. Noth, "Old Testament Covenant–Making in the Light of a Text from Mari," in *The Laws in the Pentateuch and other Studies*, trans. D. R. Ap–Thomas (Philadelphia: Fortress Press, 1967), 108–17. On Hos 2:20, see especially H. W. Wolff, "Jahwe als Bundesvermittler," *VT* 6 (1956): 316–20.

36   Thus Noth, "Covenant–Making," 112.

37   Hosea frequently uses such a series: cf. 2:20b, 7b,

10, 13, 21f; see the commentary on 2:23f.

38   Land of Egypt (2:17; 7:16; 11:5; 12:10; 13:4); of Assyria (11:11); of Israel (1:2; see p. 15); 4:1 (twice), 3; 10:1; 9:3 ("land of Yahweh").

39   Cf. 2:2 (but see the commentary on 2:2), 23, 24, 25; 6:3.

40   See p. 48.

41   Cf. textual note "f."

42   Cf. Is 32:18; Mic 5:3; Jer 23:6; 33:16.

saved. Because of the austerity of the divine speech and the terseness of its three parts, Hos 2:20 belongs, form critically speaking, at the very beginning of this series of motifs. It may be interpreted in terms of the political situation in 733,[43] when Tiglath–pileser III made deep advances into Israelite territory, immediately after the Syro–Ephraimite war. In addition to the general distress of war, there was probably widespread desolation and destruction of the cultivated land. As in all times of economic scarcity, crop damage by animals was especially feared. In this situation, which appeared as a fulfillment of the threat in 2:14, the announcement of salvation in v 20 promises an undisturbed and secure life.

■ **21, 22** In spite of the change of address to the second person feminine singular in vv 21f, the editor has joined these verses immediately to the previous ones (as v 19 is connected with v 18 and v 25 to vv 23f). In so doing he indicates that Yahweh's new, intimate relationship with Israel is the foundation for the future conditions of economic and political peace, thus providing a further interpretation of 2:16–17. This purpose is served by making use of Hosea's metaphor of Israel as a wife. Yahweh does not address her as the old unfaithful whore (vv 4–17), but simply as a young woman who looks forward to a new life (v 17b). Only now does the change announced in vv 16f become entirely clear: the old marriage is not to be reconstituted, but a completely new one is to be created. The threefold occurrence of the words: "I will make you my own" (וארשתיך לי) solemnly attests to the binding, legal act of marriage. ארש pi'el should be distinguished from לקח ("to lead home," 1:2; cf. Dtn 20:7) and שגל ("to lie with," Dtn 28:30). ארש pi'el marks the end of the premarital status, however, in that it denotes the act of paying the bridal price (מֹהַר), thus removing the last possible objection the

bride's father might raise.[44] The customary translation "to become engaged," as the word is used today, is not the sense intended here.[45] As in v 18, the chosen bride is addressed as though a new sentence were being related from the suitor's speech in v 16b. Freely translated into everyday language, the verse would read: "I will eliminate your father's last objections to our marriage by paying the amount he demands; I will do everything to win your complete and lasting companionship." "Forever" (לעולם) is legal terminology for a lifelong, final, unalterable commitment.[46] עולם occurs nowhere else in Hosea; it is completely absent in Amos, and is found in Micah only once in this sense (2:9). It occurs in Isaiah three times, two of which (30:8; 9:6 [cf. 32:14]) also recall the word's legal sense.[47]

The five nouns prefixed with ב denote the "bridal price" Yahweh "pays" for Israel. In the language of marital law, ב (*pretii*) introduces the מֹהַר (2 Sam 3:14), which generally amounted to 50 silver shekels (Dtn 22:29). With the introduction of Yahweh's bridal gifts, Hosea ends the parable and speaks of that reality which is constitutive for the life of the nation, even as the father, who receives the marriage gifts, is replaced by Israel. Taken together, the five concepts serve to guarantee the indissolubility of the community. Fahlgren[48] and Koch[49] have shown that צדק means the faithful performance of duties in the community that helps those in need.[50] משפט denotes a corresponding way of life that maintains and restores the community's existence through just legal decisions.[51] After the word–pair משפט / צדק— which also occurs three times in Amos—Hosea goes on to three other words. חסד denotes kindhearted actions that, by spontaneous love and the faithful meeting of responsibilities, create or establish a sense of community.[52] Beyond this, רחמים emphasizes a loving sensitivity

43   Cf. Robinson, 14.
44   Ex 22:15f [16f]; Dtn 22:23–29; Gen 34:12; 1 Sam 18:25; 2 Sam 3:14; cf. F. Horst, "Ehe im AT," *RGG*³ 2, 316f; Boecker, *Redeformen*, 170–75.
45   Cf. Sehling, "Eherecht," *RE* 5, 219 (l. 52)–220 (l. 24).
46   Cf. Ex 21:6 and E. Jenni, "Das Wort ʿōlām im AT," *ZAW* 64 (1952): 235–39.
47   Cf. E. Jenni, "Das Wort ʿōlām im AT," *ZAW* 65 (1953): 13.
48   K. H. Fahlgren, ṣ*edaqa* (Uppsala, 1932), 78.
49   K. Koch, "Gibt es ein Vergeltungsdogma im Alten Testament?" *ZThK* 52 (1955): 2; cf. review of K.

Koch's "Ṣdq im AT," Diss. Univ. Heidelberg (1953) *ThLZ* 79 (1954): 54f.
50   Cf. 10:12; Am 5:7, 24; 6:12; Ju 5:11; Ps 98:2.
51   5:11; 6:5; 10:4; Am 5:7, 24; 6:12; Ezek 20:11; cf. L. Koehler, *Hebrew Man*, tr. P. R. Ackroyd (London: SCM, 1956), 149ff; [*Der Hebräische Mensch* (Tübingen, 1953), 150ff].
52   4:1; 6:4, 6; 10:12; 12:7; Gen 20:13; Jer 2:2; Josh 2:12; 1 Sam 15:6; cf. N. Glueck, *Hesed in the Bible*, tr. A. Gottschalk, ed. E. Epstein (Cincinnati: The Hebrew Union College, 1967) with H. J. Stoebe, "Die Bedeutung des Wortes *häsäd* im AT," *VT* 2 (1952): 244–54; idem, "Gnade I," *EKL* 1, 1604f.

founded on an indissoluble togetherness, which is sympathetically moved to pity, especially for those in need of help.[53] אֱמוּנָה is given particular emphasis as the last word in the series. It summarily underlines the truly divine constancy and dependability of that intimate, living community that has been established.[54]

■ **22b** The outcome expected from Yahweh's payment of the bridal price is described: Israel will acknowledge him as the generous Lord of her life. As in the case of the naming of the "bridal price," here too the marriage imagery has receded into the background. יָדַע should be interpreted in view of its other uses in Hosea: what Yahweh has painfully felt to be absent in Israel (2:10, 15; 4:1, 6; 6:6) shall be no longer. Now there will be acknowledgment of and thankful response to Yahweh's gifts.[55] His covenant relationship with Israel, which was to have been legally abrogated as a result of Israel's separation from God (2:4), would be restored by Yahweh's eschatological action and again become legally binding in all respects. It is not without reason that the words about the enactment of the covenant (v 20) stand in the background of this composition of prophetic sayings. Regarding the contents, the new covenant announced in Jer 31:33f is prefigured in Hos 2:21f by Yahweh's new gifts and by Israel's response as well.

■ **23, 24** An oracle expressing assurance of Yahweh's favorable response (*Erhörungswort*), introduced by the formula "on that day" as in v 18,[56] further describes the "day of salvation." The word identifying this type of saying is "I will answer" (אֶעֱנֶה).[57] It is emphasized both by its repetition and by the addition of the formula of divine utterance (*Gottesspruchformel*).[58] נְאֻם־יהוה frequently occurs at the beginning of salvation oracles.[59] The supplication of Jezreel presupposed here is, remarkably, not heard directly by Yahweh. Instead, a series of "mediators" convey Yahweh's help. As we have already observed,[60] Hosea often lists objects in a series. Here we see the influence of didactic motifs that derive from the sapiental study of nature.[61] The series Yahweh–heaven–earth–grain–new wine–olive oil–Jezreel follows the route of human nutrition from Yahweh to the heavens that provide rain, to the ground made fertile by the rains, to the threshing floors, the wine press and the olive press, and finally to man. Vv 23f are quite unlike the sapiental studies of nature found in the miracle stories of the ancient Orient and encyclopedic lists of natural phenomena of the Egyptians. There we find merely enumerations of items. But the background of these verses indicates a genuine scientific representation of relationships within nature. In this regard, Israel had apparently accomplished something new in the ancient Orient since the time of Solomon.[62] Only the listing of objects in a series derives immediately from wisdom, since Israel elsewhere expresses that bread comes from the earth

53 Cf. the commentary on 1:6 and Stoebe, *ibid*.

54 G. Quell, *TDNT* 1, 233; A. Weiser, *TDNT* 6, 185.

55 Cf. vv 9b, 17b, 25bβ; on these verses see Wolff, " 'Wissen um Gott,' " 548f and Wolff, "Erkenntnis," 429; differently, E. Baumann, " 'Wissen um Gott' als Urform der Theologie von Hosea?" *EvTh* 15, (1955): 420.

56 See the commentary on 2:18.

57 Cf. 14:9; Ps 34:5; 118:5, 21; Is 65:24; Zech 13:9.

58 Cf. textual note "k" on pp. 46f.

59 Is 41:14; Jer 30:10; etc.; cf. J. Begrich, "Das priesterliche Heilsorakel," *ZAW* 52 (1934): 87; [also in his *Gesammelte Studien*, ThB 21 (München, 1964), 224f], and Rendtorff, "*neʾum Jahwe*," 31.

60 See p. 51, n. 37.

61 Cf. Am 3:3–6; Jer 15:2f; 51:20–23; Is 65:13f; and J. Lindblom, "Wisdom in the OT Prophets," VT Suppl 3 (1955): 192–204; or does the formation of such a series have its roots in formulas of incantation? G. Eisler ("Der älteste deutsche Sauberspruch," *FF* 30 [1956]: 104–11) has called attention to "the oldest German incantation" as an example of very ancient Indogermanic poetry. The incanta-

tion pertains to a disease in a horse's hoof caused by worms. Translated from old Saxon, it reads: "Go away, Nesso, with your nine little Nessies, away from the marrow to the bone, away from the bone to the flesh, away from the flesh to the skin, away from the skin to its sole." Since in this incantation, as in vv 23f, there is a precise description of the route a matter must proceed, so that it is impossible for this route to be missed, there must certainly be an original relationship between magic and wisdom. Cf. the Neo–Babylonian "Incantation against Toothache" in Speiser, *ANET²*, 100. But Hosea's critical intellect raises objections against deriving the series of objects in vv 23f directly from magic.

62 A. Alt, "Die Weisheit Salomos," *Kleine Schriften* 2, 90–99; G. von Rad, "Job 38 and Ancient Egyptian Wisdom," in *The Problem of the Hexateuch*, 281–91.

(Ps 104:14) and that rain makes the land fertile (Ps 65:10f). In the book of Hosea, it is instructive to note how Israel's liberation from the nature myths of the cult of Baal permitted the free study of nature to flourish (cf. Gen 1). As in 6:3, here ארץ means the ground which receives rain from the heavens.

"Grain, new wine, and olive oil"[63] make supplication and seek an assuring answer. Thus דגן must refer to the (scanty) yield of grain on the threshing floor, while תירוש and יצהר indicate the meager produce in the pressing vats.[64] Accordingly we could freely translate: "the land shall answer the threshing floor and the press, and they shall answer Jezreel."

Why does Jezreel stand at the end of the sequence and what is its significance? This cannot mean the Jezreel Valley as such (cf. הארץ in vv 23b, 24a), but only the starving people of Israel. Nevertheless, it is possible that the Jezreel Valley is conceived of as a fertile plain, especially in this verse, making it likely that reference is intended to those people who receive their food from the Valley of Jezreel. The people are called "Jezreel," which recalls the symbolic name of Hosea's first son (1:4). In connection with Tiglath–pileser III's conquest in 733, the name apparently pointed to the place of judgment (1:5); but it also stood parallel to the names of the second child and the third (1:6, 9) and thus became a symbolic name for the judged nation. Here a drought is probably the reason Yahweh's "answer" is promised to the condemned nation. The day of salvation will be a day of new dialogue with Yahweh (cf. vv 16f, 18, 21f); then he will also respond to their supplication for food and nourishment (cf. v 20).

■ **25** The salvation oracle (vv 23f) has a clearly marked ending that does not necessarily require a continuation. On the other hand, v 25a requires some preceding sentence, since the suffix of זרעתיה ("I will sow *her*") now has no antecedent and therefore is unclear. Even if we vocalize the suffix as masculine—with critics from Wellhausen to Robinson and Weiser—and relate it to Jezreel in v 24b, there is nevertheless a change in the theme. Vv 23f speak of an answer to Jezreel in time of famine, but in v 25a Jezreel would in that case become the object of Yahweh's sowing. Hence this conjecture

hardly eliminates the difficulty of the third feminine singular suffix found in the transmitted texts of both *M* and *G*. It is therefore more likely that the protasis has been lost, perhaps as a result of homoeoteleuton, providing the sentence ended with "Jezreel." It is very probable that the name of Hosea's first son was mentioned in connection with v 25, since the names of his other two children are repeated from 1:6, 9. According to the parables in 2:4–19, 21f, the third feminine suffix is reminiscent of the mother. Did the lost protasis mention Jezreel's mother? In any case, in accordance with what follows, v 25a should be understood as a reinterpretation of Jezreel. First symbolizing judgment, the name now signifies grace and renewal of the covenant. The other two names are changed by the removal of their negative particles (v 25aβb); the historical and geographical meaning of Jezreel (cf. 1:4f) is removed by the interpretation: "God sows." But what would be the meaning of sowing the "mother of Jezreel" in the land? The promise of a great increase in population[65] would very likely be differently and more clearly expressed.[66] Since the accent lies on "in the land" (בארץ), v 25a more probably refers to the return of the population of the Jezreel Valley who were deported by Tiglath–pileser III in 733, or possibly to the reestablishment of the expropriated peasants' rights to their land. Thus as an important region, Jezreel represents all three of the new Assyrian provinces that had been located in the old Kingdom of Israel.[67] The verse's continuation explains this event as an act of God's grace by using two more metaphors: the daughter "Without–Mercy"[68] is given his mercy; to the son "Not–My–People" it is said: "You are my people." Both sentences state that Israel, having suffered judgment, will by Yahweh's mercy again become his covenant people. The new "planting" in the land serves this end (cf. vv 16f, 20). The concluding sentence, which still belongs to the third part of the verse, designates the new confession to Yahweh by his people as: "My God!" It is one of the characteristically brief, closing sentences in Hosea, as in v 22b (cf. also vv 9b, 17b, 18), which states that Israel's response to its God is the result of Yahweh's eschatological salvation. God's mercy upon his covenant people calls forth their new confession.

63 See the commentary on 2:10.
64 Cf. 9:1f; Nu 18:27; and Dalman, *Arbeit* 3, 161.
65 Nowack.
66 Cf. Jer 31:27f and see the commentary on 2:2.
67 See pp. 48f.
68 See the commentary on 1:6.

The prayerful call "My God" expresses in its terseness complete trust in God's faithful relationship with his people.[69] In Rom 9:25 and 1 Pt 2:10, the nations which are not a part of Israel are placed under this promise.

**Aim**

This collection of various prophetic sayings from Hosea serves one purpose: to elucidate "that day" (vv 18, 20, 23). On "that day" Yahweh's punishment of the people who had turned away from him (vv 4–17) is to have accomplished its intended salvatory aim. The collection is an exposition of vv (9 and) 16f in particular. The editor presents the individual sayings as though he intends to make known the details of God's courtship "in the wilderness" (v 16). Two things distinguish this new day of salvation:

1) Yahweh will make a new covenant.

a) Irrespective of what Yahweh's deeds are, their aim is to bring about new communion with Israel. This is most clearly presented in the sayings about the new marriage (vv 21f), and the restoration of God's covenant (v 25); but it is also evident in the "answer" to Jezreel's lament in time of famine (vv 23f). The announcements stating that the names of the Baals will be removed (v 19) and that the ravages of war and animals will be eliminated (v 20) do not of course directly mention God's new relationship to Israel; yet they obviously serve this purpose. For the worship of Baal had indeed destroyed the old covenant; total peace in the land is expressly introduced as a "covenant for the benefit of" Israel.

b) Yahweh's new covenantal deeds establish a genuine relation insofar as they evoke Israel's response. The new covenant is in no way preconditioned by Israel's own works. She will live in the peace and security Yahweh prepares for her (v 20b). Her task is to respond faithfully with thanksgiving: the wife Israel will "recognize" (v 22b) the gifts of the new marriage covenant; she will acknowledge that she is Yahweh's: "My husband" (v 18) and "My God" (v 25). No longer will she call to him without receiving an answer (vv 23f). For Hosea, genuine dialogue between Israel and her God belongs to the consummation of the day of salvation.

c) The covenant is indeed a *new* covenant. To this new covenant belongs a new entrance (v 25a) into a new land (v 20). A new marriage will begin in nuptial love (v 21f; cf. Is 62:5). But what is essentially new in comparison with the old covenant is that Yahweh provides everything for its establishment and its endurance, including mercy for the guilty (v 25; cf. v 21) and healing for their guilt (v 19). This is, therefore, not the restoration of the old covenant; new wine is not being poured into old wineskins. Here is the announcement of a marriage that establishes a new, final communion between God and his people (cf. Mk 2:18–22). Jer 31:31–34 adds little more to this than the appropriate catchword "new covenant." The basic outline of this theme is Hosean. We find in Hosea the origins of that proclamation which reached its culmination in the New Testament's metaphor of Christ as the bridegroom of his bride, the church.[70]

2) The new covenant brings with it new conditions in all areas of life. A characteristic of this brief collection of prophetic sayings is that the sphere of God's most intimate relationship with people (vv 18f, 21f) and the public spheres of economic and political life (vv 20, 23f) are inseparably juxtaposed; indeed, they even seem to be interwoven (v 25). The intimacy of Israel's new relationship with her God brings about a new world order, because the God of Israel is the lord of heaven, of earth and its produce (vv 23f), of the animal kingdom, and of the weapons of the nations (v 20). Just as apostasy from Yahweh inevitably resulted in national disaster (vv 4–17), so the new covenant must inevitably make all things new (cf. 2 Cor 5:17; Rev 21:5). For the people of the new covenant, however, this means they must first seek the kingdom of God and its righteousness; everything else will be added thereafter (Mt 6:33). Just as the people of the promise, who confess their belief in God (vv 18, 22b, 25b), are cared for (vv 23f), protected (v 20), and liberated (v 25a) by him, so Jesus also will care for the people that follow him into the wilderness to hear his word (Mk 6:32–44). Hos 2:18–25 can help the people of the New Covenant to grasp more fully in faith and hope the gift of life as they stand in God's presence and in the world.

---

69 Cf. O. Eissfeldt, "'Mein Gott' im AT," *ZAW* 61 (1945–8): 3–16; esp. 8; [also in his *Kleine Schriften,* Vol. 3, ed. R. Sellheim and F. Maass (Tübingen,

1966), 35–47, esp. 39].
70 Cf. J. Jeremias, *TDNT* 4, 1097ff

## How Yahweh's Love Works

**Bibliography**

J. Fück

"Hosea Kapitel 3," *ZAW* 39 (1921): 283–90.

See the Bibliography for 1:2–9.

# 3

**1**    And Yahweh said to me:
    "Go once again, love a woman
      who ⟨loves⟩ᵃ a friend and practices
       adultery,
     as Yahweh loves the children of Israel,
      although they turn to other gods
      and love cakes of raisins."

**2**    So I bought herᵇ for myself
     for fifteen shekels of silver,
     for a homer of barley and a lethech
      of barley,ᶜ

**3**    and I said to her:
    "For many days you shall remain at home
      as mine,
     you shall not play the harlot,
      or belong to another man,
     and neither will I ⟨have intercourse⟩ᵈ
      with you."

**4**    For the children of Israel shall remain
      for many days
     without king or leader,
      without sacrificeᵉ or pillar,
       without ephod or teraphim.ᶠ

---

**a**   *G* and *S* have vocalized אֲהֻבַת. α′ and σ′ presuppose *M*: "beloved of a friend," thus reading רֵעַ next to the passive participle; *G* and *S* misread רֵעַ as רָע. The context speaks in favor of the active participle: the example of God's love in 1b stands precisely parallel to the prophet's symbolic act commanded in 1a. In 1bβγ the active participles (particularly וְאֹהֲבֵי א") presuppose that אֹהֶבֶת was read as an active participle. The passive participle may have originated from 2:7, 12 (מְאַהֲבֶיהָ – מְאַהֲבַי).

**b**   כרה is an imperfect qal with suffix; cf. Gesenius–Kautzsch § 20h, Beer–Meyer § 142b, Grether § 9k for *dagesh forte dirimens*. A corresponding verb is hardly present in Ugaritic (*CTCA* 14.102 [Gordon Krt 102]: nkr), as J. Gray supposes (*The KRT–Text in the Literature of Ras Shamra* [Leiden, 1955], 37), but rather an adjective used as a noun: "a foreigner" (J. Aistleitner, *Wörterbuch der ugarit. Sprache* [Berlin, 1963], 206).

**c**   *G* offers a "genuine variant" (H. Nyberg, "Das textkritische Problem des AT am Hoseabuch demonstriert," *ZAW* 52 [1934]) with νέβελ οἴνου, which scarcely can be traced back to a misreading of *M*, even if one assumes instead of יַיִן either שֵׁכָר as in Ps 69:13 or תִּירוֹשׁ as in Hos 2:10, 24.

**d**   לֹא אַלַךְ (J. Meinhold, *Studien zur israelitischen Religionsgeschichte* I, 1 [Bonn, 1903], 71, n. 1; Sellin; cf. Am 2:7) may have been lost as homoeoteleuton. Ibn Ezra and David Kimchi already inserted לֹא אָבוֹא. The parallelism to the previous sentence, underscored by וְגַם, requires such a supposition. Otherwise the interpretation of אֵלַיִךְ in the sense of עָלַיִךְ would be sufficient: "and I also will be against you" (A. Wünsche, *Der Prophet Hosea übersetzt und erklärt mit Benutzung der Targumim, der jüdischen Ausleger Raschi, Aben Ezra und David Kimchi* (Leipzig, 1868). Or has *M* understood וְגַם as adversative (cf. Neh 5:8): "but I (will hold) to you"? This nominal sentence, however, not only would be unusual in its form (cf. Hag 2:17 *M*), but it also is not presupposed by the words of interpretation in v 4f.

**e**   *G* and *S* presuppose מִזְבֵּחַ instead of מצבה so that cultic place stands next to cultic place as in 10:1f.

**f**   *T* translates מְחַוֵּי ("proclaimer, interpreter") as a clarification.

**5**     **Then the children of Israel shall return,**
      **seek Yahweh their God,**
        **[and David their king ]**[g]
      **and with trembling**[h] **approach Yahweh**
        **and his goodness**
        **[in the latter days ].**[g]

g    Additions of Judaic redaction (Wellhausen, Budde, "Hosea 1 und 3"). The presence of "David their king" between the clauses containing the name of Yahweh appears to be an addition. Nor does this fit as a second object of בקשׁ. The solemn closing formula clashes with the simple word אחר at the beginning of the verse.

h    *Constructis praegnans*; see the textual note to 1:2b.

## Form

Can this chapter be considered an original unit? Does v 5 not treat a theme which is foreign to the previous verses and therefore appear to be connected loosely and perhaps secondarily by "thereafter"?[1] Are not vv 4–5 sharply set off from vv 1–3?[2] The first verses present a first person account by the prophet, while the final two verses are a prophetic saying about Israel. Verses 1–3 are concerned exclusively with Yahweh's action as reflected in the actions of the prophet; but vv 4–5 pertain just as exclusively to Israel's future destiny which could be announced without the foregoing verses.

Verse 4, however, is not merely connected with v 3 in a superficial manner. The three accented words at the beginning of v 4 refer back to the vocabulary of v 3. This is an external indication that the negations of v 4 can be understood only as an interpretation of the negations in v 3. This combination of an account with an interpretation belongs to the special genre of accounts of the prophets' symbolic actions. These accounts, together with the call accounts, can be considered to belong to the basic literary genre called the *memorabile*.

## Memorabile

According to André Jolles,[3] the *memorabile* (ἀπομνημόνευμα) originates in the "intellectual preoccupation with the factual," just as the legend is concerned with the imitable, and the saying with practical knowledge. As a basic literary genre "it stresses one fact, which it sets above a series of subordinate data and to which all details are uniquely and cleverly related"; thus in this genre "independent facts" become a "connected reality."[4] With its concrete assertions it becomes credible. As a "segment of history" the *memorabile* "endeavors to set apart something unique from a common occurrence, which as a whole signifies the meaning of this occurrence." In this whole the details are arranged in such a way that, in their relationships and in their entirety, by clarifying, discussing, comparing, and contrasting, they together bring the significance of the event into prominence.[5]

The first–person account by the prophet, with its concrete statements, is intended to be read as a reference to a real event. To be sure, there have been doubts as to the reality of the prophet's experience. It has been supposed that this is a vision[6] or an allegory.[7] But certain details speak against this, such as the impossibility of interpreting v 2 as an allegory. Decisive, however, is the recognition that the passage belongs to the particular genre of the *memorabile* of symbolic action.

1) The *memorabile* is to be distinguished from a section of a novella, a parable, or an allegory. Each of these are composed of imaginary elements, whereas in the *memorabile* a historical event is condensed to one central

1    Fück, "Hosea Kapitel 3," 290; similarly B. Duhm, "Anmerkungen zu den zwölf kleinen Propheten," *ZAW* 31 (1911), W. R. Harper, *Amos and Hosea*, ICC (Edinburgh: T. and T. Clark, 1905), and W. Nowack, *Die kleinen Propheten*, HK (Göttingen, 1897[1], 1922[3]), *et al.*

2    Robinson, 16.

3    *Einfache Formen* (Leipzig, 1930; Darmstadt, 1969[5], reprint of the unrevised fourth ed.).

4    *Ibid.*, 211.

5    *Ibid.*, 203.

6    Calvin, *CR* LXX, 256: "There is no doubt but that God here has depicted the kind of grace He promises the Israelites. This He has done under a metaphor or vision. You see, those who imagine that the prophet married a woman who had been a whore are too dense." [Trans.] (*Non dubium est, quin Deus depinxerit hic gratiam qualem promittit Israelitis, idque sub figura aut visione. Nam nimis crassi sunt qui imaginantur prophetam duxisse uxorem quae scortata fuerat.*)

7    P. Humbert, *Les trois premiers chapitres d'Osée*. RHR (Paris, 1918); H. Gressmann, *Die älteste Geschichtsschreibung und Prophetie Israels* (von Samuel bis Amos und Hosea), SAT 2/1 (Göttingen, 1921[2]); H. G. May, "An Interpretation of the Names of Hosea's Children," *JBL* 55 (1936).

point. In the *memorabile*, when regarded as a "segment of history," a concern for the factual suppresses any underlying intention to narrate a story.[8] Thus no autobiographical interest directs Hosea's account; rather, the passage is presented simply in order to set forth the primary fact of God's command to perform the symbolic action. To this all the details (vv 2–3) are related. The precision of these details serves not the reconstruction of Hosea's life, but the understanding of a remarkable occurrence, into which the individual events coalesce. This coalescence takes place in the *memorabile*, the genre "in which the concrete is effected throughout."[9] As a *memorabile* the account is composed of facts combined into a rounded whole. When viewed in terms of the biographical question, however, this passage remains an annoying fragment; as an allegory, it would be overloaded with unintelligible facts.

2) Second to be considered is that the subject of this particular *memorabile* is the prophet's symbolic action. An essential part of this act is its completion; for it represents the prophesied, future event, which is divinely commanded, as a *present* event.[10] This content changes the basic form to the extent that the reported event characterizes at the same time a coming event. The symbolic action is meaningful only as it occurs between God's command and the event as it actually takes place. Hence the three main elements belonging to the account of a symbolic action are: God's command (v 1); report of its execution (vv 2f); and the interpretation (vv 4f).[11] The third element in an account of a prophet's symbolic act is always present because of its particular relatedness.[12]

Why then has there been some question as to the unity of the chapter? Simply because its peculiar style went unnoticed. The three elements are not always congruent with respect to their content, as, e.g., in 1:2f; Jer 13:1–11; Ezek 12:1–11; 2 Kgs 13:15–19. More is accomplished than the command indicated, and the interpretation (vv 4f) goes beyond the previous symbolic action. Certainly

the command sets the action in motion, and that which is presented as accomplished gives rise to the interpretation; but the customary repetition of the wording is intimated only in v 4 (cf. v 3). Instead of the customary repetitive style one finds the stylistic device of continuation, in the sense of a step–by–step interpretation. If at first only "love" is commanded (v 1), then the description of the prophet's obedience, without repeating this key word, shows its surprising consequences (vv 2f). If the symbolic action ultimately presents love as severity (v 3), the interpretative proclamation goes beyond this in describing love's healing consequences (v 5). Thus only in the end does God's act as portrayed become completely understandable as "love." If v 5 is separated from the foregoing verses, not only does the peculiar style of the whole passage go unrecognized, but there unavoidably follows a misunderstanding of the chapter's key word אהב (repeated fourfold in v 1) as "wrathful scorn,"[13] in which case v 2 also remains inexplicable.

The prophetic account, because of its halting progression, appears incoherent at certain points. The indefinite command "love *a* woman" (v 1) does not sufficiently prepare for the suffix "I bought *her* for myself" (v 2). This lively style is driven by a clear intention to witness which presses toward the fulfillment of v 1 in v 5. Contrary to the general rules of interpreting an account of symbolic action, this intention appears already in v 1b, since an anticipatory interpretation of the symbolic action is brought into the command (cf. 1:2, 4, 6, 9). To delete v 1b[14] would distort the original into a predetermined pattern. Hosea shows that from the very beginning his action stands in the light of the message which he goes on to proclaim by interpreting the action.

The direct discourses indicate a disposition for synonymous rhyme of thought: 1a ∥ b; 1bβ ∥ γ; 3 ∥ 4; 4aβ ∥ γ ∥ b; uncertain are 3aβ ∥ b; 5aα ∥ β ∥ b. I am unable to find a regular rhythm, not to mention a prosodic arrangement which is carried through.[15] The prophet writes elevated prose.

---

8  Cf. v 1 with vv 2f and vv 2f with vv 4f.
9  Jolles, *Einfache Formen*, 211.
10  Cf. Zimmerli, *Ezekiel*, 103f.
11  Cf. Fohrer, *Handlungen*, 5.
12  See above, commentary on 1:2.
13  Fück, "Hosea Kapitel 3," 288.
14  Thus Fohrer, *Handlungen*, 23.
15  G. Fohrer, "Die Gattung der Berichte über sym-

bolische Handlungen der Propheten," *ZAW* 64 (1952): 106; cf. S. Mowinckel, "Der Metrische Aufbau von Jesaja 62,1–12," *ZAW* 65 (1953): 167–187.
16  Thus J. Lindblom, *Hosea literarisch untersucht* (Åbo, 1927); Robinson.

**Setting**

The text itself indicates neither the period of Hosea's ministry in which it was written, nor the concrete circumstances within which it is to be interpreted. Therefore the relationship of chap. 3 to its context must be examined.

Chap. 3 has often been compared with chap. 1. Is this account in the first person parallel to the third person account?[16] The birth of the three children in chap. 1 already excludes this in view of 3:3. Do the events of chap. 3 precede those of chap. 1?[17] To affirm this is to approach the view that chap. 3 is parallel at least to 1:2f. The absence of the article in 3:1a, "love *a* woman," and the characterization of the wife as an adulteress make both these related views understandable. The "again" in 3:1 must then of course be interpreted as a later addition. However, it is an essential presupposition for the comparison that the wife in 3:1 committed adultery against Hosea. Thus "again" becomes not only understandable, but necessary. Then the action of chap. 3 must follow after the events of chap. 1.[18] This interpretation has been applied only in view of a second marriage.[18a] According to this view, the indefinite "a woman" (אשה) in 3:1 points to another wife, as does the silence in chap. 1 concerning Gomer's desertion. Because of the literary character and the original function of both chapters, neither argument is compelling. It lies beyond the scope of chap. 1 to provide a glimpse of the marriage's continuation.[19] As the writer of chap. 3, Hosea does not presuppose any knowledge of chap. 1. With regard to the time it was written, chap. 3 is probably older than the third person account of chap. 1, which summarizes Hosea's previous experiences. We are inclined to view the origin of chap. 1 together with the redaction and editing of chaps. 2 and 3.

Chap. 3 should be understood in terms of chap. 2, not chap. 1. Certainly it is not coincidental that chap. 3 is the immediate continuation of chap. 2, since it corresponds completely with its theme. Chap. 3:3f can be compared with the measures of isolation announced in 2:8, chap. 3:5 with the expected return in 2:9, and 3:1 with Yahweh's love promised to his unfaithful wife in 2:16f. Chap. 3 functions as the prophet's personal seal upon the foregoing series of threats and promises. It is probable that chap. 3 originally formed the conclusion to 2:4–17, which was also written by Hosea.[20] The analysis of the genre of 3:1–5 thus indicates that the text is intended to be a kerygmatic unit and does not aim at biographical completeness.[21] Moreover, to connect chap. 3 with chap. 1 rather than with chap. 2 is to draw upon arguments that are foreign to the text.

**Interpretation**

■ **1** According to our understanding of the relationship of chaps. 2 and 3, a portrayal of the circumstances in which Yahweh appeared to the prophet is not to be expected previous to "and" in v 1.[22] Any preceding biographical reference or a description of a theophany would merely delay the all–important confirmation of the message in chap. 2. By means of the account of a specific command from Yahweh, together with its consequences, chap. 3 summarizes all of the foregoing, bringing it to an impressive conclusion. "And Yahweh said to me"—this is the older style utilized by the prophets to depict their own particular experience of divine revelation.[23] All other considerations recede behind the question of "whence" their experience. "When a person received divine revelation he perceived it in the same manner in which one hears the speech of another."[24] The later expression "The word of Yahweh came to me"[25] no longer attests so simply to the immediacy of this great experience. "Again" (עוד) belongs already to the context of the divine address, as *G* correctly understood, and as a comparison of Zech 1:17; 11:15 with Ex 3:15 demonstrates. "Once again," if it is not considered a gloss, need not presuppose the account of Hosea's first love, so that it would be necessary to assume that in chap. 1:2, "beginning" (תחלת), there is a fragment of a

17 Robinson, *Cross*, 14ff.
18 Budde, "Hosea 1 und 3," Sellin, Weiser, J. Coppens, *Les douze petits Prophètes* (Paris, 1950).
18a Heermann, "Ehe und Kinder," 287–312; Th. C. Vriezen, *Oud-israelitische geschriften* (Den Haag, 1948); Fohrer, *Handlungen*, 52.
19 See pp. 9f and 13.
20 See p. 48f on 2:18–25.

21 See pp. 57f.
22 Robinson.
23 Cf. Am 7:15, 8; 8:2; Is 7:3; 8:1, 3; Jer 3:6, 11; 11:6, etc.
24 I. P. Seierstad, *Die Offenbarungserlebnisse der Propheten Amos, Jesaja, und Jeremia* (Oslo, 1946), 196.
25 Jer 1:4, 11, 13, etc.

misplaced first–person account. The word is meaningful and necessary here because it makes certain that the woman to be won over "once again" is not just any adulteress, but that she committed adultery against Hosea. "Go" (לך) as a general formula of summons underscores that now a new act from the prophet is expected. Thus עוד does not mean "furthermore" or "continually," as though the command from God would allow Hosea only one love, whom he unceasingly cherished. On the other hand, M. Buber asks, "Is it possible to order love?"[26] God's command does. For "love" (אהב) neither connotes "to fall in love,"[27] nor is it a euphemism for sexual intercourse,[28] nor is it the legal act of marriage.[29] Rather, as elsewhere in Hosea, אהב means a spontaneous helping (11:1) and healing (14:5) that is the opposite of anger and hatred (9:15). Whereas אהב describes the fatherly raising of the child in 11:1 and the physician's healing of illness in 14:5, here in v 1 it portrays the husband's act of winning back the unfaithful wife. Whereas God's call (11:1; 9:15) or conversion (14:5) of Israel is depicted in those passages, in v 1 the act commanded by God is no less than a portrayal of God's action. Consequently the command "Love!" must be interpreted solely in light of these statements about God.

The prophet is to love "a woman" who "loves a friend." "Friend" (רע) is the desired lover also in Jer 3:1, 20; Song 5:16.[30] The second usage of אהב means love as lustful desire, since it occurs "in adultery." A genuine act of adultery by the woman is presupposed here, of which there is no mention in chap. 1. Above all 3:3 speaks against the assumption that the description of the wife conveys merely religious faithlessness.[31]

Hosea's act of love toward his unfaithful wife mirrors Yahweh's own love: "as Yahweh loves the people of Israel." It is, therefore, not that "something of the incomprehensible and indestructible love of God becomes apparent to Hosea in his own love for his adulterous wife,"[32] but precisely the opposite: at the discovery of

God's love he perceives how he must act toward his wife. One would expect "as I love" (כאהבתי) in the Yahweh speech (v 1) rather than the third person ("Yahweh loves"). Has the pronominal suffix erroneously been added?[33] Or does the "stylistic carelessness"[34] emphasize that Yahweh places himself before his messenger "as a model to be copied?"[35] With the use of the third person ("Yahweh"), the intention to proclaim suddenly interrupts what is stylistically a report. It is important that "Yahweh" be mentioned before the "other gods" are named.

The love of God is undeserved love, for those loved by him are characterized immediately in a concessive nominal clause[36] as in love with someone else. "Turning to other gods" is a genuine Hosean reproach (cf. 13:4). "Other gods" (אלהים אחרים) corresponds to "Baals" (בעלים) in 2:15, 19 and 11:2. Hosea apparently knows the Decalogue (12:10; 13:4; 4:2) and therefore knows the term "other gods" (Ex 20:3), which does not appear in Amos, Isaiah, and Micah. Again, Hosea's relationship to Deuteronomy becomes all the more evident: אלהים אחרים occurs in Dtn 5:7; 6:14; 7:4; 8:19; 11:16, 28; 13:3, 7, 14; 17:3; 18:20; 28:14, 36, 64; 29:25; פנה אל־א״א in Dtn 31:18, 20.[37] Amos, Isaiah, and Micah, moreover, know nothing of the "love of Yahweh," although it is found in Deuteronomy.[38] After this it appears again only in Mal 1:2! On the basis of Ju 5:31 and the occurrence of the word "love" in ancient Near Eastern treaties, W. L. Moran[39] has argued that with the introduction of the concept of covenant, "love" immediately was used to describe the relationship between Yahweh and Israel, even before the time of Hosea.

Yahweh's love finds no response: "and love" (ואהבי) should not be interpreted as a second attribute of "gods' "

---

26  Buber, *The Prophetic Faith*, 112.
27  Budde, "Hosea 1 und 3" contra Sellin.
28  G. Quell, *TDNT* I, 23.
29  לקח ("take") in 1:2; Dtn 24:1ff; ארש ("to marry") in 2:21f; Dtn 22:23ff.
30  Cf. J. Fichtner, "Der Begriff des 'Nächsten' im AT," *WuD* 4 (1955): 25ff; *idem, TDNT* 6, 313.
31  Coppens, 44.

32  Weiser.
33  Budde, "Hosea 1 und 3," Sellin.
34  Allwohn, *Die Ehe*; see p. 16.
35  Buber, *The Prophetic Faith*.
36  Gesenius–Kautzsch § 141e.
37  Cf. Dtn 29:17; 30:17.
38  4:37; 7:8, 13; 10:15, 18; 23:6.
39  "The Ancient Near Eastern Background of the Love

(אלהים),[40] but rather as a second predicate to "they" (והם).[41] Therefore it is not "the other gods" who "love the cakes of raisins,"[42] but the Israelites themselves, since the woman who "loves a friend" (v 1aβ) is meant to correspond to Israel. Moreover, the "cakes of raisins" were eaten by the participants in the cult[43] and apparently also enjoyed by Hosea's contemporaries as gifts from Baal.[44] "Sacrificial cakes (כַּוָּנִים) for the queen of heaven" are mentioned in Jer 7:18; 44:19; they belong therefore to the cult of the Mother Goddess.[45] These words are a harsh rebuff to Israel: only out of sensual love for pleasure does Israel forsake her God. But Yahweh does not expel her; his love for pitiable Israel nevertheless remains true. This is the model for Hosea's attitude.

■ **2** The prophet gives an account of his obedience to God's command, expressing the concrete realization of his love for the unfaithful woman with the words "I bought her for myself." The infrequent "bought" (כרה) signifies not only that he pays a price (Dtn 2:6), but further that he must also bargain for her.[46] Accordingly, the woman became his legal possession. Her equivalent value consists of money and barley. "Silver" (כסף) means "shekel of silver" (שֶׁקֶל־כֶּסֶף, e.g., Gen 23:15), the customary silver pieces used in trade, which may have weighed approximately 11.5 grams.[47] To the fifteen pieces of silver a supply of barley is added; barley was worth only half the value of wheat, and was used more for fodder than for bread in times of plenty.[48] It therefore was hardly used in the sanctuary.[49] A "homer" (חמר). as a dry measure consists of about eleven bushels,

and a "lethech" (לתך) is half of that:[50] thus Hosea delivers almost seventeen bushels of grain. Since a "seah" (סְאָה) of barley[51] cost a shekel in time of famine[52] one figured about fifteen shekels for one–and–a–half homers during normal times.[53] The entire price for the woman thus amounted to about thirty shekels. That would equal the price of a slave according to Ex 21:32 (cf. Lev 27:4). Hosea does not say to whom he paid the price, nor where the woman lived. She could have been either someone's personal slave[54] or a temple prostitute.[55] "Who loves a friend" (אהבת רע) in v 1a perhaps makes the first interpretation more probable. Nothing in the context indicates a return to the parents' house, as Cornill,[56] Nötscher, et al., suppose, in view of Lev 22:13 and Ju 19:2. Hosea's report is limited to that which is decisive for the symbolic act: he who receives God's undeserved love must be prepared for obedience and personal sacrifice. The amount comprising the purchase price indicates not only the event's historicity,[57] but also suggests that Hosea was not particularly wealthy.

■ **3** All in all the account of the purchase has no importance by itself, although it raises many questions for us today. While v 2 demonstrates the initial realization of Yahweh's command to love in v 1, it also forms a transition to the words addressed to the woman who has been won back. These words alone form a transition to the interpretation (v 4a) of the prophetic act. Yahweh issues a charge which is to be "for many days"; here this does not mean "forever,"[58] but "temporarily." While it is true that "many" (רבים) can represent inclusively the whole that comprehends many particulars,[59]

of God in Deuteronomy," *CBQ* 25 (1963): 77–87.

40 Thus according to Wellhausen, Duhm, Gressmann, Sellin, Lippl, Nötscher.
41 Thus *G*, Wünsche, Nowack, Weiser, Robinson.
42 Budde, "Hosea 1 und 3."
43 2 Sam 6:19; 1 Chr 16:3; cf. Is 16:7; Song 2:5.
44 Cf. 2:7, 14 and Dalman, *Arbeit* 4, 353f.
45 Cf. Rudolph, *Jeremia*, HAT 12 (Tübingen, 1947), 47f.
46 Job 6:27; 40:30.
47 *BRL*, 187.
48 1 Kgs 5:8; 2 Sam 17:28; Ezek 4:9 (used for bread during time of war).
49 *BRL* 177, 183; Dalman, *Arbeit* 2, 254.
50 *BRL*, 367.
51 Twelve quarts, the thirtieth part of a homer.
52 2 Kgs 7:1, 16, 18.
53 *BRL*, 177f.

54 Budde, "Hosea 1 und 3."
55 Schmidt, "Die Ehe"; cf. 4:14; 2 Kgs 23:7; Am 2:7; Dtn 23:17f; Mic 1:7.
56 C. H. Cornill, *Der israelitische Prophetismus* (Strassburg, 1909), 49.
57 See p. 57.
58 P. Humbert, *Les trois*, 162: "ironic and tantamount to 'forever.' "
59 Cf. Is 2:3a//2b; 52:14f; 53:11ff; see H. W. Wolff, *Jes 53 im Urchristentum* (Berlin, 1952³), 29; above all, see J. Jeremias, *Die Abendmahlsworte Jesu* (Göttingen, 1960³), 171–74.

yet "forever" in Hosea is expressed by לְעוֹלָם (2:21). Moreover, the words of interpretation in vv 4f indicate that the command is temporary and looks forward to the "thereafter" (אחר) in v 5. This interpretation of the entire chapter is consistent with the Hosean concept of a temporary judgment that serves the purpose of renewal (cf. 2:8f, 16f). The woman, who could no longer resist temptation, was saved from it. Thus love dominates these severe measures. Here ישב means "to remain at home" as in Lev 12:4f—instead of being permitted to go out—and to be completely resigned to household duties.[60] She is there solely for Hosea (לי = "as mine"); consequently her prostitution, her relations with any other man, is made *de facto* impossible. Even Hosea himself will refrain temporarily from any intimate relations with her.[61] Hosea's wife experiences nothing more than his words and his presence, just as in the desert the wife Israel, having been denied the pleasures of fertile Palestine, only later received the vineyards from Yahweh (2:16f).

■ **4** In this verse "for" (כי) introduces the interpretation of the symbolic action for Israel (cf. 1:2b, 4b, 6b, 9b) and thereby provides the intrinsic reason for the prophetic action. The *tertium comparationis* is the temporary separation. In place of the threefold (*M* twofold) negation in v 3, a fivefold (sixfold in substance) "without" (אין) appears in v 4. In view of v 3 we must note that with the three pairs of negations,[62] legitimate as well as illegitimate contact is prevented, just as in 2:11f Yahweh's good gifts (cf. 2:10, 17) also were taken from rebellious Israel. The kingdom falls under judgment as in 1:4; 5:1; 8:4; 10:15; 13:10f, because it exists in defiance of Yahweh's will. The "leaders" (שרים) also come under this judgment. This word includes the military leaders (5:10; 7:16) as well as the administrative officials (13:10), who are not to be separated from the king (7:3; 8:4; 13:10). Thus Israel will first lose its political existence, in which she believed herself capable of securing her life independent of Yahweh. Further, the offering of sacrifices

becomes impossible. Yahweh had not commanded them, and therefore they could not cover Israel's guilt.[63] Sacrificial worship will cease, together with the sanctuaries situated at the holy pillars around which Israel assembled for its festivals. The most famous ones stood in Shechem[64] and Bethel.[65] Following Hosea, Deuteronomy (16:22) condemns them as hated by God. As a second step, therefore, the people's cultic activity is denied them (cf. 2:13, 15). Finally, the customary ways of inquiring into the will of God are removed. The ephod, although difficult to define in detail,[66] served this purpose as well as the teraphim,[67] which may be envisioned as a divine image or a face mask.[67a] These are mentioned quite frequently in the land of Benjamin, as K. D. Schunck has shown.[68] Ephod and teraphim also appear together elsewhere in Ju 17:5; 18:14, 17f, 20. Thus Yahweh will withdraw himself from Israel, together with every means of approaching him that had become an idol. Politically and cultically Israel will be virtually driven back into the desert (cf. 2:8f, 11–15).

■ **5** The significance and objective of such harsh words is new life. "Then" (אחר) very clearly denotes Hosea's two–phased eschatology that appeared already in 2:9, 17. Although here one root of apocalyptic with its division of history into periods becomes visible, yet it is genuine prophetic eschatology, since the undetermined time of the first phase, which begins already with its proclamation, completely serves the second phase. The eschaton will begin "thereafter" and "on that day" (2:18, 20, 23) as the final age (cf. לעולם in 2:21), which is not a qualitative opposite to history, but rather brings the beginnings of saving history to its consummation.[69] Both phases intersect from the standpoint of time: the second phase begins in and with the first; for it not only is implied in and with the first phase, but is predicated upon and effected by it. It is Yahweh's action that creates new life (2:8f, 16f, 21f, 25). Hence, in v 5 the return to Yahweh begins with the political and cultic nadir. Since Yahweh removes from Israel the possibility of self–

60 1 Sam 1:23.

61 For "to go in to" (הלך אל) cf. Am 2:7 and textual note "d" on p. 56.

62 The clear arrangement of the material in pairs is unmistakable in v. 4b.

63 6:6; 8:11, 13; cf. Am 5:25 and Koehler, *Theology*, 181 [171].

64 Gen 33:20; Josh 24:26.

65 Gen 28:18, 22; 35:14; cf. *BRL*, 368ff.

66 Cf. 1 Sam 23:9ff; 30:7ff; perhaps it was a priest's garment with an oracle–pocket; cf. Ex 28:4, 12, 15, 25–28.

67 Ezek 21:26; Zech 10:2; cf. textual note "f"; also 4:12 and Hab 2:18f.

67a Gen 31:19, 34; 1 Sam 19:13ff; 15:23.

68 *Benjamin*, 11.

reliance, they again recognize who had led them out of bondage (cf. 2:9). Such a conversion, brought about by God's efficacious action, is just as unknown among the gods of the ancient Orient as is apostasy from those gods (cf. Jer 2:10f).

Two further statements elucidate <u>Israel's return.</u> (1) <u>"They shall seek" Yahweh;</u> "seek" (בקשׁ) also stands parallel to "return" (שׁוב) in 7:10 and parallel to "turn toward, aim at, look for" (שׁחר) in 5:15. Hosea still knows this word as cultic terminology for the futile visitation of the sanctuaries (2:9) with sacrificial animals (5:6). The pilgrimages to the sanctuaries, where it was believed God's presence could be found, but which no longer accomplished this purpose, are abandoned in favor of a humble (7:10) visit to the "lost" God, who had deprived Israel of her sanctuaries and withdrawn himself from them (cf. 5:15 with 3:4). (2) "They shall approach Yahweh with trembling." These words describe the utter excitement in the return to Yahweh that had been missing in the old cultic exercises. In view of their goal (טובו = "his goodness"), fear[70] ultimately is overcome by joy.[71] This turning about is described as the elemental movement of a return to Yahweh which is initiated by his judgment. This return will strive for and attain that which Israel's political and cultic activity until then had failed to accomplish.

Just as this return is defined by two verbs ("return" and "seek"), so in the second and third clauses the object, Yahweh, is defined by two appositional phrases. (1) Yahweh "their God" is the God of the old covenant[72] who is not bound to the Palestinian sanctuaries.[73] The conversion promised by Hosea and effected by Yahweh himself has as its object the Initiator of Israel's history. (2) This same object (Yahweh) is elucidated as the source of the prosperous life for Israel by the addition of *"and his goodness"* (וטובו) in the last part of the sentence. The vineyards, the cultivated land, and the olive groves that are temporarily removed may belong to the gifts of "his goodness" (2:10f, 17, 23f), but not the

political and cultic institutions that have been removed according to v 4. Hosea never names these as the gifts provided by Yahweh's goodness. On the other hand, to see only Yahweh's "word" as his "goodness" is a non–Hosean spiritualization.[74] טובו <u>probably includes the natural resources of Palestine, as</u> it is also used in Jer 2:7; however, the word is primarily a designation of Yahweh's attitude toward Israel and is an all–inclusive summary of the concepts that in 2:21f express his indissoluble faithfulness.

The additions to the text[75] have their origin in Judaic messianic eschatology (cf. 1:7). "David their King" (דוד מלכם) appears only in Jer 30:9 where it also stands in an otherwise unknown connection with "Yahweh their God" (יהוה אלהיהם). "In the latter days" (באחרית הימים) likewise belongs to Judaic eschatology: Is 2:2; Mic 4:1; Jer 23:20; 30:24; Ezek 38:16; as in v 5 the phrase appears last in a sentence in Gen 49:1; Nu 24:14; Jer 48:47; in Dtn 4:30 it appears with the concept of return to Yahweh.

**Aim**

The chapter's theme is stated unequivocally by the fourfold "to love" (אהב) in v 1. This underscores Yahweh's love as a model for Hosea's love; it stands in contrast to the fickle lovers for whom His love remains true. Its overpowering strength first becomes recognizable as it is reflected in the prophet's symbolic action. The command to Hosea is certainly annoying as a personal request. How much more so, if <u>the law codified in Dtn 24:1ff</u> already obtained in Hosea's geographical area?[76] <u>Even a lawfully divorced and remarried wife must not return to her first husband.</u> Now, however, <u>the love which represents Yahweh's love is to bring home an adulteress who had legally come into another's possession!</u> God does what is impossible according to the law. A Pauline concept becomes visible here.[77] Jeremiah was the first after Hosea to thoroughly reflect upon this problem,[78] and then Ezekiel.[79]

69 Cf. E. Jacob, "Der Prophet Hosea und die Geschichte," *EvTh* 24 (1964): 289.
70 11:11; Mic 7:17; Is 19:16.
71 Jer 33:9.
72 2:25; 12:10; 13:4; cf. 1:7.
73 13:4–6; 11:1; 9:10; 2:16.
74 Thus R. Gordis (*VT* 5 [1955]: 90) "The Text and Meaning of Hosea XIV 3," has considered whether

the root of טוב in v. 5 is related to דבה ("evil report") as in 14:3; Neh 6:19; Ps 39:3b; cf. the same problem in Am 8:12.
75 Cf. textual note "g."
76 Cf. Lev 21:7.
77 Rom 8:3.
78 Cf. Jer 3:1 with 3:22–4:2.
79 16:32ff; 23:37ff.

In the development of the theme, the strongest accents lie in vv 3 and 4. With a series of negations, these verses describe the punitive measures of God's love by means of the enacted parable and its interpretation. The negations apply for "many days." The efficacious power of God's love is manifested in the fact that it does not choose the cheap and easy way for itself (v 2) or its beloved (v 3). The lasting and difficult measures of deprivation are to be recognized as the necessary acts of love.[80] These measures are surrounded by the accented "love" motif in v 1 and by the goal described in v 5. They seek to attain nothing other than Israel's return to communion with her God. This goal and the reason for God's action in v 1 are emphasized by the three synonymous closing phrases. What is decisive is the message that God's people cannot find the good apart from him. Therefore love impels them toward him alone.

In this chapter the formation of the kerygma is no less important than the kerygma itself. Yahweh commands that his love be represented through the prophet. Now Hosea is a witness, not only as a messenger of the Word, but also in that he draws the consequences for himself from the message he received. By his obedience he confirms that the proclaimed love of Yahweh becomes an event which leads Israel through judgment to salvation.

---

80    Calvin, *CR* LXX, 256: "A summation of this chapter is that God wishes to keep in good faith the hearts of the faithful in exile, lest they become overwhelmed by lack of hope and fall completely away. We see, therefore, that this prophecy lies midway between the denunciation which the prophet used earlier and the promise of pardon. Here God lifts up the hearts of the faithful, that they may realize for certain that they are loved even while they are being castigated." [Trans.] (*Summa huius capitis est, quod Deus vult retinere bona spe animos fidelium in exsilio, ne desperatione obruti, prorsus deficiant. Videmus itaque hoc vaticinium medium esse inter denuntiationem qua prius usus est propheta, et promissionem veniae. Hic Deus erigit animos fidelium, ut certo statuant se amari, etiam dum castigantur.*)

## Yahweh's Lawsuit Against Israel

### Bibliography

H. J. Boecker
*Redeformen des Rechtslebens im AT*, WMANT 14
(Neukirchen, 1964), 149–59.

K. Budde
"Zu Text und Auslegung des Buches Hosea [on
4:1–19]," *JBL* 45 (1926): 280–97.

H. Junker
"Textkritische, formkritische, und traditions-
geschichtliche Untersuchung zu Os 4:1–10," *BZ*
NF 4 (1960): 165–73.

# 4

1     **Hear the word of Yahweh, O sons of Israel,**
      **for Yahweh has a lawsuit with**
        **the inhabitants of the land.**
      **For there is no trustworthiness or loyalty,**
      **no knowledge of God in the land.**

2     **Cursing, cheating, murdering, stealing,**
      **and adultery break out ⟨in the land⟩ᵃ,**
      **and there is one deed of blood**
      **after another.**

3     **Therefore the land shall witherᵇ**
      **and whoever livesᶜ there shall fade away,**
    **withᵈ the beasts of the fieldᵉ and**
      **the birds of the air;**
        **even the fish of the sea shall be**
        **swept away.ᶠ**

a    *G* Κέχυται ἐπὶ τῆς γῆς is reading פָּרַץ בָּאָרֶץ; v 3 makes it probable that "land" was also once present in v 2. The text of *M* could be the result of homoeo-teleuton, having originally read ‏ופרצו בארץ‏". וּפָרַץ, meaning "and plunder" (Nötscher), is (a) un-likely in Hosea, since also in 4:10 פרץ means "to expand in number"; furthermore, (b) a finitive verb is to be expected in correlation to נגעו, since the series of infinitive absolutes as subject requires a predicate.

b    The parallel word אמלל (see p. 68) demonstrates that here, as in Jer 12:4; 23:10; Am 1:2 (cf. Joel 1:10), the meaning of II אבל applies (= Akk. *abālu*; cf. Koehler–Baumgartner, following Driver, *Gaster Anniversary Volume* [1936], 73ff) rather than I אבל = "to mourn."

c    *G* σὺν πᾶσιν τοῖς κατοικοῦσιν αὐτήν has changed the singular to plural, harmonizing it with v 1 (יושבי).

d    Here ב denotes "sharing with" (Koehler–Baum-gartner, 103f No. 11; Brockelmann, *Syntax* § 106b); ב–*essentiae* (Robinson, following Gesenius–Kautzsch § 119i) is ruled out by the meaning of the verse, since the "inhabitants of the land" first of all means man-kind, as in v 1.

e    Following 2:20, *G* completes the line with καὶ σὺν τοῖς ἑρπετοῖς τῆς γῆς = וּבְרֶמֶשׂ הָאֲדָמָר.

f    Does *G* ἐκλείψουσιν presuppose יָסְפוּ (Nyberg)?

### Form

The saying in vv 1–3 is set off from vv 4ff, as the change in addressee makes clear. In vv 1–3 the prophet ad-dresses the land and all its inhabitants, while vv 4–6 are directed to the priest. This saying, an example of the prophetic judgment speech, is a self–contained unit that requires no continuation after v 3. Vv 1bβ–2 furnish proof for the case by stating the offense negatively (v 1bβ) and positively (v 2). The evidence is introduced by כי and formulated in a nominative clause (v 1bβ) and a ver-bal clause in the perfect (v 2). Verse 3 announces the legal consequences; על-כן introduces the judicial sentence, which is stated in the imperfect tense.[1] The change in the tense of the verbs, with the transition from כי to על-כן, eliminates the generally accepted view[2] that v 3 continues the description of the "case." The misinterpretation of אבל[3] is probably the chief reason for this misunderstanding. As early as the Middle Ages the Jewish exegetes Rashi and Kimchi interpreted v 3 as an announcement of judgment,[4] which is made all the more certain by v 3b. There are no compelling grounds on which to delete v 3aβb as a gloss[5] (especially in view of the difference between v 3 and 2:20, which G followed in making its addition; cf. textual note "e").

The judgment speech is introduced by the prophet as such in v 1b, for its sense and purpose is to present "Yahweh's lawsuit (ריב) with the inhabitants of the land." The same formula occurs in 12:3, where it announces God's action as judge (cf. 12:3b). In 4:1 Hosea uses ריב more comprehensively than in 2:4,[6] even though the accusation comes first. But now the accusation serves as the motivation (v 1bβ–2) for the punishment and is thus inseparably connected with it (v 3). Yahweh stands as judge before Israel.[7]

This probably also accounts for the "proclamation formula" that now begins the passage in v 1a: "Hear the word of Yahweh, O sons of Israel!" Among Hosea's sayings, this formula has a weak precursor in 5:1.[8] In a variety of forms, it occurs in Amos (3:1; 4:1; 7:16; 8:4), Micah (3:1, 9; 6:1), and Isaiah (1:10). As a fixed formula "hear the word of Yahweh" (שמעו דבר-יהוה), with the addressee in the vocative, first occurs in Jeremiah (2:4; 7:2; 19:3; 22:11, altogether fifteen times) and Ezekiel (6:3; 13:2; 21:3, altogether ten times).[9] Generally, the messenger formula follows the proclamation formula in Jeremiah and Ezekiel. Here, instead of the messenger formula, the introduction of the judgment speech follows the proclamation formula. It should be noted how the announcement of the judicial sentence (and its motivation) is connected secondarily with the proclamation formula and is thus distinguished from the genuine combination of the accusation with the summons to hear that is addressed to the court (Mic 6:2; cf. Jer 2:12f). It should also be distinguished from the paraenetic proclamation of divine law in the cult, which begins with a similar summons to hear.[10] It is true that the identity of plaintiff and judge is reminiscent of cultic legal paraenesis. But the sentence of judgment with its motivation, although introduced as a ריב and structured in analogy to casuistic legal instruction (cf. Ex 21:1ff), more probably has its setting in the announcements of judgment given by the court assembled at the city gate.[11]

### Setting

If we are correct in identifying v 1a as secondary to the following verses, the beginning of 4:1 probably was written by the same redactor responsible for the superscription in 1:1.[12] "Word of Yahweh" (דבר-יהוה) is found in Hosea only in 1:1 and 4:1. "Sons of Israel" (בני ישראל, v 1) does not occur again in chaps. 4–14, but in the preceding chapter in 3:1, 4, 5 (and 2:1, 2). This observation supports our assumption that a redactor formulated this verse in dependency upon the preceding context.[13] Finally, to assume that v 1a was added by a redactor better accounts for the grammatical complexity created by the two subordinate כי–clauses than to suppose that the passage is a rhetorical unit.

To the older booklet containing 1:2–3:5, the redactor has added sayings of Hosea that had a separate transmission. He placed this judgment speech (4:1–3), comprehensive in every respect, at the very beginning, lending it emphasis by adding the proclamation formula. Since this saying announces nothing but disaster, which is described as a catastrophic drought, it could have originated in the first period of Hosea's activity, even as 1:2–4, 6, 8f; and 2:11–15. Thus the second collection of Hosean traditions, like the first, probably begins with sayings from Hosea's early period.

---

1  Cf. Boecker, *Redeformen*, 152f.
2  Sellin, Lippl, Weiser, Robinson, *et al.*
3  Cf. textual note "b."
4  Wünsche, 136.
5  Sellin, Lippl.
6  See p. 95.
7  Cf. Gemser, "*rîb*," 120–37, esp. 129.
8  See pp. 72ff.

9  For a complete survey, see Grether, *Name*, 69.
10  Dtn 6:4; Ps 50:7; 81:9.
11  With Begrich, *Studien*, 19–42, [27–49], against Würthwein, "Ursprung," 1ff [111ff]; cf. H. E. von Waldow, "Anlaß und Hintergrund der Verkündigung Deuterojesajas," unpub. diss. University of Bonn (Bonn, 1953), 37ff; Boecker, *Redeformen*, 149–59.

**Interpretation**

■ **1** With the introductory proclamation formula "Hear the word of Yahweh, O sons of Israel!" the redactor again expressly admonishes his readers to regard also this second section of Hosea's sayings as God's word. He had already indicated at the very beginning of the first section (1:1) that the whole book is the word of God. After 3:5 a new beginning seems necessary, since Hosea has now completed the first cycle, having gone from threats of judgment to promises of salvation; now the cycle begins a second time. He must first make Israel aware that "Yahweh has a lawsuit with the land's inhabitants." The connection of the preposition "with" (עם) with "lawsuit" (ריב) indicates that the legal proceedings before the assembled court are still vividly remembered; this word, however, no longer signifies just the speech of the accusing party, as originally (2:4; Mic 6:2; Is 3:13; Job 9:3; 33:13), but the speech of a unique plaintiff who immediately appears as judge.[14] The accused and sentenced are called "the inhabitants of the land," i.e., they have received the land as Yahweh's salutary gift (9:3; 2:10; 13:6; cf. בארץ in v 1bβ [2b cj.], 3a).

Israel's offense consists in this, that she has removed herself from Yahweh's lordship while dwelling in his land. There is (a) no "trustworthiness" (אמת) "in the land." This word does not occur again in Hosea, but it is related to "faithfulness" (אֱמוּנָה 2:22); it denotes an unconditional reliability in which one has confidence in the other (cf. Ex 18:21; Josh 2:12), especially in his word (1 Kgs 10:6; 22:16) and service (Josh 24:14; 1 Sam 12:24). Moreover, there is (b) no "loyalty."[15] Whereas אמת emphasizes the enduring quality of responsible relationships, חסד underlines its intensity. Both words are often combined in a formula representing an indissoluble bond of loyalty (Gen 47:29; Josh 2:14; Ps 85:11), especially God's faithful relationship with his people (Ex 34:6; 2 Sam 15:20; Ps 89:15). Verse 2 shows that the meaning here is a lack of community responsibility among those who live together in the land. It has its roots in (c) a lack of "knowledge of God." As the parallel theme in v 2 again makes clear, "knowledge of God" is not a second, different kind of "religious" sphere in addition to the "ethical," as though one's relationship to God can be separated from his relationship with the neighbor. Rather, the phrase means knowledge of his teachings as the source of a harmonious community life within Israel (cf. 4:6; 6:6). "Knowledge of God" (דעת אלהים) is not Hosea's original formulation, which must necessarily be interpreted in analogy to his marriage; rather, the prophet makes use of an ancient formula of priestly–cultic origin. This is evident from the selection of the words דעת אלהים (4:1; 6:6; cf. 4:6; הדעת ‖ תורת אלהיך ["knowledge" ‖ "law of your God"] and 8:2; 13:4) in addition to the other formula ידע את־יהוה ("to know Yahweh" 2:2; 5:4; 6:3).[16] Verse 2 proves conclusively that דעת אלהים signifies the intimate knowledge of the revealed law of God (see below). This lack of "knowledge" is a transgression because it has its origin in the rejection of (4:6) and contempt for (8:12) the gift of divine revelation. Thus v 1bβ characterizes Israel's guilt as an absence of faithful relationships among the members of God's people, which has its roots in contempt for God's will.

■ **2** Disobedience of God's commands spreads throughout the land as the result of this lack of "knowledge of God." Five absolute infinitives name five acts forbidden by divine authority in apodictic law, which is genuine Israelite law.[17] The vocabulary and word order do not precisely correspond with the Decalogue, the best known example of a series of apodictic laws. A similar free grouping of offenses occurs in Jer 7:9. But in Hosea—unlike Jer 7:9—all the offenses have to do with one's neighbor, since: (1) אלה means cursing and damning of another person[18] by the ceremonial—but misused—invocation of God's name.[19] The Decalogue calls this "using God's name for evil" (Ex 20:7). (2) כחש denotes lying deception and cheating of the neighbor[20] as es-

---

12   See p. 4.

13   Cf. Rost, *Israel*, 24.

14   As in 12:3; see p. 66; cf. Jer 2:9.

15   On חסד, see the commentary on 2:21.

16   Against Baumann, " 'Wissen um Gott,' " 416–25; cf. Wolff, " 'Wissen um Gott,' " 537f, 547 [186f, 197]; *idem*, "Erkenntnis," 429f.

17   Cf. A. Alt, "Die Ursprünge des israelitischen

Rechts," *Kleine Schriften* 1, 302–32.

18   E.g., the deaf, parents, the prince or king, God.

19   10:4; Ju 17:2; cf. Ex 21:17; 22:27; Lev 19:14; 20:9; Ex 20:12; Dtn 27:16.

20   7:3; 10:13; 12:1; cf. 9:2; 12:8.

pecially practiced in the law courts[21] and in trade.[22] Cheating of a blind person is also placed under the curse in apodictic law.[23] The word כחשׁ appears in a series of apodictic laws only in Lev 19:11.[24] (3) רצח denotes premeditated murder.[25] (4) In ancient apodictic law, גנב first of all signifies kidnapping, as A. Alt has demonstrated from the commandment's position within the total structure of the Decalogue.[26] Likewise in the series in v 2, the position of גנב is between such transgressions that have to do with the neighbor's person, his life and his marriage (cf. also Jer 7:9). In Ex 21:16 the word occurs in an apodictic series of crimes worthy of death, where it certainly also means kidnapping; cf. Lev 9:11 and Ex 20:15 with v 17. (5) נאף denotes adultery, as in 4:13f; 7:4; 2:4; 3:1; cf. Jer 7:9 and the apodictic series in Ex 20:14; Lev 20:10.

Thus Hosea juxtaposes those transgressions that (a) concern one's neighbor and (b) by divine law require the death penalty, because they (c) are totally irreconcilable with the life of God's people. These crimes "break out 'in the land';" they fill the vacuum created by the absence of a sense of trustworthiness in the community and the lack of knowledge of God's will. The brief closing sentence—"and there is one deed of blood after another"—emphasizes that the foregoing series of offenses above all presents crimes against the neighbor's person that require the death penalty; the series forms an uninterrupted sequence.[27] In view of the address in v 1, it is hardly possible to suppose (with van Gelderen) that Hosea's reference to "acts of blood" was related to the quick succession of revolts against the throne in 746 (2 Kgs 15:10, 14).

The malicious deeds mentioned by the prophet show the opposite side of the flourishing economy at the time of Jeroboam II that led to an early form of capitalism and at the same time produced a social crisis of the first order, without which the subsequent political crisis cannot be comprehended.[28] Hosea sees that those who then lived in the land were no longer Yahweh's people.

**■ 3** Therefore Hosea announces Yahweh's approaching judgment in the form of a great drought. The land itself will so completely wither[29] that it can no longer support any form of life. Its population will "fade away." אמל pu'al denotes first the withering of vegetation (Is 16:8; Joel 1:12), but can also mean, in antithesis to "to bear children" (ילד 1 Sam 2:5), to become childless (Jer 15:9). In this sense Hosea sees the whole population fading, shriveling (4:10; 9:12, 14). The universal drought also snatches away the wild animals and birds, even the fish of the sea. Thus the judgment by fire causes even more death than the flood (Gen 7:21–23). נֶאֱסָף is an elliptic expression[30] which, in light of the phrases "to be gathered to his people" (נֶאֱסַף אֶל־עַמָּיו Gen 25:8, 17; 35:29, etc.) and "to his fathers" (אֶל־אֲבוֹתָיו Ju 2:10), "to his grave" (אֶל־קְבֹרֹתָיו 2 Kgs 22:20) should be understood as a term for "to die." Those who are intent on living their life in violence against their neighbors must learn that in bringing death to others they bring terrible consequences upon themselves (4:9; 5:5). It is noticeable that the judgment results not from the direct actions of Yahweh himself, but from an "organic structure of order," "a sphere in which one's actions have fateful consequences," which Yahweh puts into effect. This conception results from a "synthetic view of life."[31]

**Aim**

As a genuine "heading," with conciseness of style and structure, this brief saying is expressive of the unity of prophetic theology, anthropology, and cosmology, which is rooted in its ecclesiology. (1) God's people as a community which Yahweh has created exists by its knowledge of God (v 1b), which is a concrete knowledge of God's commandments (v 2). If knowledge of the covenant God—who provides a salutary order for the life of Israel—disintegrates, the community of God's people also disintegrates. (2) Yahweh's will protects the life of the neighbor. God's people live only as a community

21 Apodictic series in Ex 23:1–3, 6–9.
22 12:8; cf. the apodictic series in Dtn 25:13–16.
23 Dtn 27:18; Lev 19:14.
24 But cf. also v 12; Jer 7:9; Ex 20:16.
25 6:9; cf. the apodictic series in Ex 20:13; cf. 21:12, 14; Dtn 27:24.
26 "Das Verbot des Diebstahls im Dekalog," *Kleine Schriften* 1, 333–40.
27 On דמים, see p. 18.
28 Cf. J. Hempel, *Das Ethos des AT*, BZAW 67 (Giessen, 1938), 115; also H. J. Kraus, "Die prophetische Botschaft gegen das soziale Unrecht Israels" *EvTh* 15 (1955): 298.
29 On אבל, see textual note "b."
30 As in Nu 20:26; Is 57:1; CD 19:35.
31 K. Koch, "Vergeltungsdogma" 1–42; F. Horst,

of brothers. If one's fellowman is under attack in Israel (v 2), then Israel ceases to exist as God's people; that means it ceases to live at all (v 3). (3) Just as God's people live for the sake of the life of the community, so also the land, with its plants and animals, exists only for the sake of God's people. Therefore they bring the created world with them in their own death (v 3; cf. 2:10ff). Hence, all life in the cosmos depends ultimately upon knowledge of God, that is, upon living under the manifest will of him who has ordered the life of his people into a helpful community. If it rejects this salutary order, it brings the world with it to its destruction.

In 4:1–3 is a comprehensive, severely formulated saying that, as its head, sets the tone of the second collection of Hosean traditions. One might compare it first with the Yahwist's flood narrative (Gen 6:5ff) on the one hand, and the apocalyptic view of world–judgment (Is 24:1ff) on the other.[32] What is characteristic of Yahweh's lawsuit in this prophetic saying is its concentration upon the people of God's transgression against the life of the community established by the salutary words of Yahweh. Upon this community all existence completely depends. In this respect, 4:1–3 as a word of judgment is an Old Testament prelude to the New Testament witness that God's word establishes brotherly love, upon which all existence is completely dependent. For he who does not have the Son of God does not have life.[33]

---

"Recht und Religion im Bereich des AT," *EvTh* 16 (1956): 71f [also in his *Gottes Recht: Studien zum Recht im AT*, ThB 12 (München, 1961), 287f].

32　Concerning the influence of Hos 4:2f upon Is 24:1ff,

cf. O. Ploeger, *Theocracy and Eschatology*, tr. S. Rudman (Richmond: John Knox, 1968), 55 [*Theokratie und Eschatologie*, WMANT 2 (1959), 71].

33　1 Jn 2:5; 3:14ff; 5:12; cf. Eph 1:9f.

## A Spirit of Whoredom in Israel's Worship

**Bibliography**

W. L. Holladay
"On every high hill and under every green tree,"
*VT* 11 (1961): 170–76.

N. Lohfink
"Zu Text und Form von Os 4:4–6," *Biblica* 42
(1961): 303–32.

L. Rost
"Erwägungen zu Hos 4:13f," "in *Festschrift Alfred
Bertholet*, eds. W. Baumgartner, O. Eissfeldt, K.
Elliger, L. Rost (Tübingen, 1950), 451–60.

J. Zolli
"Hosea 4:17–18," *ZAW* 56 (1938): 175.

See the Bibliography for 4:1–3.

# 4

**4**  No, not just anyone ⟨should be accused⟩[a],
　　　nor should just anyone ⟨be reproved⟩[a]!
　　But ⟨my lawsuit is with you⟩[b], O Priest,
**5**  so that you shall stumble in the day(light)
　　　and [also the prophet shall stumble
　　　with you at night][c]
　　　your mother[d] shall ⟨perish⟩[e] as well.

a　With Budde, "Zu Text und Auslegung (4:1–19)," I
read יָרֵב and יוּכָח; otherwise the antithesis between
the negation in v 4a and the positive statement in
v 4 b would hardly be recognizable. *M*'s vocalization
produces forms that are more common: "None
should accuse, none should reprove."

b　With H. Oort, "Hozea," *ThT* 24 (1890), Guthe,
Budde, "Zu Text und Auslegung (4:1–19)," Junker,
"Os 4:1–10" *et al.*, I read וְעִמְּךָ רִיבִי כֹהֵן, since the
continuation in v 5 suggests that the priest is addressed here. Indeed, the words are an announcement of Yahweh's intervention which brings the
priest's downfall (see the commentary on 5a). There
need be no article before the vocative (cf. Josh 10:12;
Mic. 1:2 and Brockelmann, *Syntax* § 10). It is not
clear how כמ was added to the text. Was it originally
כֹּמֶר (cf. 10:5; Koehler–Baumgartner, 442a), which
became later abbreviated as a result of haplography,
on which כֹהֵן would simply be an explanatory gloss?
Or was כֹּמֶר a gloss on כֹהֵן? Junker's explanation
for the corrupt text is more plausible: the reading
וְעִמְּכֶם (cf. C. van Gelderen, *Het Boek Hosea*, COT
(Kampen, 1953), as noted in A. van Hoonacker,
*Les douze petits Prophètes*, EtBi [Paris, 1908], which
understood כֹהֵן as a collective noun, "was later corrected by changing the suffix to ךָ. This was first
written above the line and brought into the text
later." However, כמ was incorrectly retained in the
process "and was combined with the following word
רִיבִי" (Junker, Os 4:1–10," 166). With König and
Robinson, Lohfink ("Os 4:4–6") reconstructs the
transmitted text by taking כ as the result of dittography; this leaves the word מָרִיב, which is not
otherwise attested.

c　The change to the third person and the interpolation
(נם) which mentions the prophet—who is not mentioned with the priest again in this context—indi-

6    My people perish[f] for lack of knowledge.
        Because you have rejected knowledge,
        I also reject you[g] as my priest[h].
        You have forgotten the teaching of
           your God;
           therefore I will also forget your sons.

7    The more they increased, the more they
        sinned against me.
        ⟨They⟩[i] exchanged their glory for
           dishonor.

8    They exist[j] on the sin of my people;
        ⟨they⟩[k] are greedy[j] for their iniquity.

9    [Then it shall be the same for the priest
        as for the people:
        I will punish him[l] for his[l] ways[m],
        repay him[l] for his[l] deeds.][n]

cates this clause to be a gloss (cf. Budde, "Zu Text und Auslegung [4:1–19]"). Because its style is similar to 5:5bβ (cf. 6:11a נם), the clause probably originated from the Judaic redaction of the book. לילה is likely part of the gloss; an original parallelism would probably require הלילה in correlation with היום (Neh 4:16; cf. Zech 1:8 and Koehler–Baumgartner, 373, no. 9, 374); see p. 77 and Wolff, "Heimat," 89ff [241ff]. For a discussion of the counter arguments, cf. Lohfink, "Os 4:4–6," 328ff.

d    Budde reads אָרֶיךָ (cf. Nu 27:21; 1 Sam 28:6), Robinson and Weiser אוֹתְךָ; Lohfink ("Os 4:4–6," n. 1) lists other conjectures. *M* is supported by *G S V* (*T*: כְּנִישָׁה = "congregation," "synagogue," which is an interpretation of "mother").

e    *M* ("and I am at rest") provides no antecedent for אמך. *V* gives it a pregnant interpretation with the words *tacere feci*; but this meaning of II דמה is not attested elsewhere; the pi'el form (Koehler–Baumgartner suggests וְדִמֵּיתִי) is not found in the Old Testament; only I דמה occurs in Hosea (12:11). Perhaps וְנִדְמְתָה (Jer 47:5) should be read, since II דמה nip'al is used by Hosea, above all in the following verse (v 6; 10:7). It can also have an individual as its subject (10:15); similarly Nowack.

f    *G* (ὡμοιώθη) may entirely presuppose *M* (plural), since it (like α′ σ′ θ′) often has a singular when a Hebrew collective noun is constructed with a plural verb (F. Dingermann, "Massora–Septuaginta der kleinen Propheten," diss. Univ. Würzburg (Würzburg, 1948), 8; cf. Gesenius–Kautzsch § 145b. The plural more clearly distinguishes this verse from the singular וְנִדְמְתָה conjectured in v 5b.

g    The marginal Masora already considered the final א in ואמאסאך superfluous. Is it merely a copyist's error, as all recent critics think? Or is it reminiscent of a nonextant voluntative form with suffix, as it was regarded in the nineteenth century (e.g., van Gelderen).

h    Literally: "to act as priest for me."

i    In reference back to v 6, *M* ("I will exchange") introduces a threat. The Masora transmitted הֵמִירוּ as *tiqqun sopherim*, which *S T* also read. It fits the context of vv 7a–8, 10 better than *M*.

j    "The imperfects represent the habitual nature of their acts" (Budde, "Zu Text und Auslegung [4:1–19]"). Literally: "they eat" = "they nourish themselves" and "lift up their throats."

k    נַפְשָׁם is to be preferred, following twenty MSS *G S T* σ′ θ′, for when נפש is the object of נשא, its suffix always agrees with the subject (Dtn 24:15; Prv 19:18; Ps 25:1; 86:4; 143:8).

l    *S* noted the disagreement between the singular forms in the Hebrew and the plural forms in the surrounding context (vv 8, 10) and therefore offers plural suffixs.

m    The Achmimic and Sahidic translations read τὰς ἀνομίας; Cyril of Alexandria: τὰς ἀδικίας; cf. 12:3.

n    See pp. 82f.

**10** They shall eat, but not be satisfied;
they shall fornicate, but not increase.

Indeed! They have forsaken Yahweh to
devote themselves to ⟨fornication⟩.[o]

**11** ⟨ ⟩[p] New wine takes from my people
understanding[q].

**12** ⟨ ⟩[q] They seek advice from their wood;
and expect answers from their staff.

Indeed! A spirit of whoredom leads[r]
astray,
so that they turn away unfaithfully
from their God.

**13** On the mountain tops they hold
sacrificial meals,
on the hills they burn offerings,
under oak, poplar, and terebinth,
because their shade is so pleasant.
Therefore your daughters play the whore,
your sons' brides commit adultery.

**14** I will not punish your[s] daughters
because they play the whore
nor your[s] sons' brides because they
commit adultery.
For these men go aside with whores
and share sacrificial meals with
temple prostitutes.
Thus an unknowing[t] people comes to
ruin 15 / ⟨with whores⟩[u].
You, O Israel, do not make ⟨yourself⟩[v]
guilty!
[and Judah][w]
Do not come to Gilgal!

Nor go up to Beth-aven!
Swear not[x]: "As Yahweh lives!"

**16** Indeed! Like a stubborn heifer, Israel is
stubborn. Should Yahweh now feed
them like lambs in a broad meadow?
17 / Ephraim is united with idols. Let him
do as he likes![y] 18 / When their carousing

o/p Contrary to *M* and *T*, we take the first two words
of v 11 as part of v 10 with *G*, and read זְנוּנִים with
Koehler–Baumgartner instead of זְנוּת וְיַיִן or זְנוּת יַיִן
in the best MSS, for in Hosea זְנוּת occurs elsewhere
only in 6:10 (probably secondary). In the light of
Jeremiah (3:2, 9; 13:27, זְנוּת may have been the
later customary spelling. Hosea's chief word for
whoredom is זְנוּנִים: 1:2(2x); 2:4, 6; 4:12; 5:4; here
and throughout, *G* reads πορνεία; *V*, singular *fornicatio* only here, otherwise plural; זְ never occurs
elsewhere with תִּירוֹשׁ (Koehler–Baumgartner, 1027f,
but here already in *G*); the singular יִקַּח also suggests
that only תִּירוֹשׁ is the subject, without יַיִן. Since it
is highly probable that זְנוּנִים is the original reading,
we do not accept Budde's suggestion, in itself possible, to read זֹנוֹת instead of זְנוּת, whereby a personal
object ("they retain whores") would stand in antithesis to v 10bα ("they forsake Yahweh").

q Literally: "takes away my people's understanding."
We follow *G* instead of *M T S V* and take עַמִּי with
v 11, which is supported by the usual arrangement
of the sentence.

r To explain the text, *T S V* insert an accusative object
("them"), which presupposes הִתְעָם. Like *M*, *G*
has no suffix.

s Because of the הֵם in v 14aβ, Sellin, Budde ("Zu
Text und Auslegung [4:1–19]"), *et al.*, suggest reading third person suffixes; however, this overlooks the
fact that the addressees are to be distinguished from
the accused; see pp. 74f; 87f.

t לֹא־יָבִין is an asyndetic relative clause.

u The first two words in v 15 (μετὰ πόρνης) are taken
as part of v 14 by *G*, which reads עִם זֹנָה instead of
אִם זֹנָה. Since the singular זֹנָה is unexpected after the
plural forms in v 14a, is it possible that זֹנֶה was the
original vocalization, even though prepositions with
the absolute infinitive seldom occur, with evidence
for such being uncertain (Brockelmann, *Syntax* § 46)?
See textual note "w" below on אִם in *M*.

v *G* (μὴ ἀγνόει) presupposes the second person אַל־
תֶּאְשַׁם, which is probably the original, since the
context is formulated in direct address to Israel; see
p. 89.

w In *M* "Judah" is now the subject of this sentence,
but it probably is a gloss that was later inserted into
the text. Perhaps this interpolation (which is still
recognizable as such in *G*) in the transmitted text
followed by *M* was the reason for the change to יֶאְשַׁם
and for the misreading of עִם as אִם. *G* does not presuppose וְ before אַל־תָּבֹאוּ, which belongs instead
to the insertion (καὶ Ιουδα).

x *T* adds לַשֶּׁקֶר, probably with Jer 5:2 in mind.

y *G* (ἔθηκεν ἑαυτῷ σκάνδαλα) and α′ θ′ (ἀνέπαυσεν
ἑαυτῷ) do not presuppose the imperfect hip'il as in
*M*, but the perfect, which harmonizes the verb with
the adjoining descriptive sentences. *G*'s text is expanded: הִנִּיחַ לוֹ מוֹקְשִׁים = "he shall come to ruin
by himself." α′ confirms the consonants in *M*:
ἀνέπαυσεν ἑαυτῷ ἄρχων συμποσιασμοῦ αὐτῶν,

is past (?)[z], they surely fornicate. They ⟨even love⟩[aa] the dishonor ⟨of the⟩ shameless[bb]. 19 / A wind shall wrap ⟨them⟩[cc] with its wings. Thus they shall come to shame on their [altars][dd].

but connects it with v 18a and translates סר as שַׂר (likewise *T*): "The lord of their orgy is at rest."

z　In *G* does ἡρέτισε Χαναναίους reflect בָּחַר סֹבְאִים? Hoonacker reads בַּר from ברר. According to Zolli ("Hosea 4:17–18"), *G* and the ancient encyclopedists understood the Canaanites as נוע or כנע, the intoxicated ones. *G* speaks of election of the Canaanites; α′ σ′ θ′ ε′ of drinking parties (σ′: ἐπέκλινε τὸ συμπόσιον αὐτῶν; θ′: ἐπέκλινε τὸν οἶνον αὐτῶν) which presupposes הִטָּה (Gen 24:14; 1 Kgs 8:58) or סָבָא instead of סָר in *M*: "he drinks their beer." Since the time of Houtsma (*Bijdrage tot de kritiek en verklaring van Hosea*, ThT 9 (1875), 55–75) בְּסֹד סֹבְאִים is often conjectured, which with the tense noted in v 17a (perfect), would give the required location of the activity: "in the company of the carousers." The suggested reading הִנִּיחַ לוֹ סָבָא סָבְאָם = "they sit down and drink their beer" is closer to the Greek versions, but the singular subject does not fit with v 18b. Should it be supposed that the text was even more seriously damaged and thus read, in parallel to what follows, סָבָא סָבְאוּ (cf. H. Torczyner, "Dunkle Bibelstellen," BZAW 41 [Giessen, 1925], 277)?

aa　The obscure אהבו הבו in *M* is most simply explained with σ′ and the foregoing parallel *figura etymologica* as a misreading of אָהֹב אָהֲבוּ (Koehler–Baumgartner).

bb　The third femine suffix with no antecedent could be a misreading of the plural ending ־ים (or has the imagery in v16a influenced the gender of the suffix?). Wellhausen, Budde, ("Zu Text und Auslegung [4:1–19]"), Zolli ("Hosea 4:17–18"), *et al.*, following *G* (ἐκ φρυάγματος αὐτῆς; *G*^AQ etc.: αὐτῶν) suggest מִגְּאֹנָה or מִגְּאֹנָם "they love dishonor more than their pride," in which Israel's pride is "of course Yahweh" (Budde). After G. R. Driver's discovery of II מָגֵן ("Studies in the Vocabulary of the Old Testament VI," *JTS* 34, 383f; cf. Koehler–Baumgartner) this questionable emendation has become superfluous.

cc　Here the third femine suffix is likewise unclear (see textual note "bb"). I read אוֹתָם with Weiser, Nötscher, *et al.*

dd　The femine plural of זֶבַח does not occur elsewhere. The form is probably the result of haplography of an original מִמִּזְבְּחוֹתָם (Wellhausen) which *G S* presuppose.

## Form

The new addressee in v 4 marks the beginning of a new kerygmatic unit. The priest who is now addressed was not yet mentioned in vv 1–3. אַךְ can function as a restrictive particle ("however") which continues something previously said, as the present literary connection with vv 1–3 intends it to be understood. But the particle can also emphasize the beginning of an oration especially in Hosea.[1] Verses 4ff do not form a rhetorical unit with vv 1–3. This is made evident both by the address to the

---

1　12:9; see the commentary on 4:4.

priest and by the new theme "cult" which brings into focus yet another aspect of the offense which provoked Yahweh's punishment. And yet the "lack of knowledge" theme is also taken up,[2] which would indicate that vv 1–3 and vv 4ff perhaps belong to the same scene in which one speech undoubtedly followed shortly after the other. But the people who were condemned in vv 1–3 for their crimes against the community are now pardoned and the priest in charge of the cult is held responsible.

This new theme continues to the end of the chapter. Also in vv 11ff, the "common people" (v 14b) are defended against the responsible cultic representatives (v 14) as "Yahweh's people" (עמי v 12, as in vv 6, 8). Moreover, vv 16ff are connected to the foregoing by כי; the announcement of punishment expected after v 14 does not occur until v 19. Catchwords provide a connection between the closing verses and the beginning of the unit in several places: The accused have given themselves to *fornication* (זנה v 18; cf. vv 10–15aα¹) and *dishonor* (קלון v 18; cf. v 7) and like the priests in vv 7f, 10, shall also come to shame at their altars (v 19). The spirit (רוח) of guilt (v 12) proves to be the spirit of judgment in v 19. The entire passage contains neither introductory nor concluding formulas, and thus there is no distinctly recognizable transition from one addressee to another. We do not find the clear beginning of a new speech until 5:1.

But this long transmission unit (4:4–19) is by no means an original rhetorical unit. There are too many breaks in its structure, especially in the transitions from the second person of those who are accused (singular vv 4–6), lamented (plural vv 13b, 14aα), or admonished (v 15) to the third person (singular vv 12a, 14b, 16f; plural vv 7f, 10, 12b, 13a, 14aβ, 18f). In addition, Yahweh not only speaks in the first person (vv 4–9, 12a, 14) but is also spoken of in the third person (vv 10b, 12b, 15b, 16). Likewise, following the threats (second person) and their motive clauses in vv 5f, the indictments (vv 7f, 10b, 15aα¹, 16–18) repeatedly change to announcements of disaster (third person vv 9, 10a, 18a?, 19) and in one instance to an admonition (v 15). The largest break seems to lie at the end of v 10; the priest or priests are threatened in vv 1–10, while in the following verses it is clearly "Israel" (vv 15aα, 16) or "Ephraim" (v 17).

This jagged style is due to later *literary* activity only in three instances. The most obvious secondary addition is the word "Judah" in v 15aβ, a Judaic gloss which also resulted in a change of the second to the third person form of the verb in $M$.[3] The brief expansion[4] in v 5aβ, combined with a change from the second to the third person, is of the same origin. Both additions were intended to actualize the Hosean traditions for a later day in Judah.[5] On the other hand, v 9 perhaps contains an earlier saying of Hosea (cf. 12:3), which, to be sure, was inserted later between vv 8 and 10. Verse 9 speaks of those who are accused in the third person singular, and thus interrupts the original connection of vv 8 and 10,[6] where the plural is used. This is substantiated by the catchword "to devour" (אכל vv 8, 10a), which is indicative of the connection of thought between the two verses. Junker[7] did not give sufficient attention to these details when he interpreted v 9 as a threat which originally belonged with v 8 as its motivation. As an addendum, v 9 originally could have been a marginal note on v 6, rather than on vv 7f, and could have been inserted into its present position when the text was later copied. All the other literary problems referred to above must be clarified in terms of their genre and the nature of the primary Hosean tradition.[8]

We can attempt to define the smaller units of speech by noting the various genre elements. Our passage contains the following units: vv 4–6: a threat to the priests in talion style, with its motivation; vv 7f, 10: announcement of the judicial sentence to a number of priests in v 10, preceded by the accusation in vv 7f; vv 11–15aα¹: a weighing of the nation's transgressions against the guilt of their false leaders in the form of an accusing speech. After the warning directed to the people (v 15)[9], an accusation in vv 16–18 presents the evidence of guilt and leads to a final proclamation of the judicial sentence. It should be noted that the lament clauses are inserted into the accusations, as is most evident in vv 6a, 13b–14aα,b; they lament the consequences brought upon the people by the transgressions of the accused priests. In part, this is done in such a manner that those concerned

---

2 Junker, "Os 4:1–10," 168f.
3 See textual note "w."
4 See textual note "c."

5 See the commentary on 4:5, 15.
6 See textual note "l."
7 "Os 4:1–10," 169.

are themselves addressed (vv 13b, 14aα). Perhaps vv 11–12a should also be understood as a lament (because of v 4a) which is inserted into the accusation. This change from accusation to lament probably derives from speech forms used in legal proceedings: at the gate the plaintiff now speaks to the defendant, now to the injured party. This explains much that now appears as literary unevenness. Compare, for example, the alternation of accusation and complaint in the dialogues of Job.[10] But the way the theme is woven through the passage and the style of the connections noted above, as well as the absence of clear introductory and concluding formulas, make it impossible to establish unequivocally the limits of the small rhetorical units.

Nor does an analysis of the style take us essentially further. The first part of the passage is in elevated language, as is evidenced by the balanced construction of the prosodic units. Usually, two lines of three stresses are synonymously parallel; this may be seen most clearly in vv 6–10a and 12b–13a. At the beginning of v 4 there is a tricolon. In correspondence to this, does the tricolon in vv 11–12a also begin a new speech? But it could also form a conclusion like that found in vv 14aβ, b, 15aα[1]. In each of the tricola, two lines are synonymously parallel (vv 4a, 12a, 14aβ); the third line is antithetically (4b) or synthetically (vv 11, 14b–15aα[1]) parallel to the others and in each case is one stress longer. From v 13 on the balanced construction of the prosodic units begins to diminish. Parallelism and meter are no longer recognizable from vv 16ff. Is this because of a faulty transmission of the text? Or is it to be explained by the fact that the text's poetic structure gradually changed to prose as the prophetic dispute runs its course? The messenger speech at the beginning evidently is more clearly stylized than is the later disputation. The stricter style facilitates a correct literary transmission. The discussion itself (cf. 7:3–6) might have required a change in the prophet's diction. But here we return again to the question of how and in what sense our passage should be regarded as a unit.

## Setting

The nature of the passage's unity should not be considered apart from the question of its setting within the history of its transmission. What setting would enable us to understand how such a patchwork structure became a transmission unit? On the one hand, the setting should account for the juxtaposition of divine speech with prophetic speech; of direct address with the style of the report. On the other hand, it should clarify the present connection of themes, the dovetailing of catchwords, as well as the absence of formulas indicative of the beginning and ending of smaller units. The assumption that this passage presents a private revelation given to the prophet which he wrote down himself before proclaiming it publicly[11] does not sufficiently explain the text's form. This assumption clarifies neither the change from the messenger speech to the disputation style nor the transition from second to third person. The other hypothesis, namely, that the passage is a later, literary combination of individual sayings which had been proclaimed previously and first handed down independently, is improbable, for there is a continuous connection of one saying with the other. The present shape of the tradition strongly suggests that vv 4–19 represent a quick sketch or outline of the prophet's words, which was written down soon after he had spoken them. Hosea could have written it himself, should we not wish to suppose that, in view of 2:4–17; 3:1–5,[12] he would have made a more thorough connection of the individual sayings with regard to style and content. It is more likely that the traditionists of Hosea's sayings were members of his prophetic circle (cf. Is 8:16). This prophetic–Levitic group, which formed an opposition party to the official priests, were experts in the transmission of Hosea's words.[13] If these are various sayings, all belonging to a definite, still vividly remembered occasion, which were soon afterward given written form, then it becomes understandable why one theme dominates this transmission unit, and why it is set off from related sayings by

8  See pp. 75f.
9  See pp. 89f.
10  7:12ff; 9:13ff; 22:5ff. See C. Westermann, "Der Aufbau des Buches Hiob," BHT 23 (1956): 46ff, and H. Richter, "Studien zu Hiob: Der Aufbau des Hiobbuches, dargestellt an den Gattungen des Rechtslebens," diss. Univ. of Leipzig (Leipzig, 1954), 76ff (cf. the review of this work in ThLZ 81 (1956): 629ff).
11  Lindblom, 71.
12  See p. 33.
13  Cf. H. W. Wolff, "Heimat," 94 [249f].

the introductory formulas in 4:4 and 5:1. In addition, this would explain why, in the course of the controversy, the form of Hosea's words changes from the divine speech in the messenger style (vv 4–9, 12a, 14) to the disputation style in which the prophet speaks on Yahweh's behalf (vv 10b, 12b, 16b) and why viewpoints and addresses change so rapidly—the accused are spoken to in the second and then in the third person. The genre elements suggest that this scene is most comparable to the legal procedure in the city gate. The objections which the opponents surely must have raised[14] were apparently unworthy of quotation. In 6:1–3 we find an exception.[15] Hosea quotes the words of his opponents (9:7) less frequently than the other prophets.[16] If the most important sayings from this scene were written down shortly afterward, it would explain both the irregularities in the transmitted text and also the occurrence of the same theme in later transmission units. Quite naturally then, the transmission unit and the kerygmatic unit are coincident with each other. This scene's stirring, inner development from beginning to bitter end could have lead to the event's prompt recording (cf. Is 8:16).

This scene probably took place at one of the important high places on the mountains of Ephraim (vv 13, 17). It seems more likely that the priests in Bethel, rather than in Samaria, would be accused of forgetting the "teaching of your God" (v 6), since the history of Bethel was connected with the older Israelite Yahwistic tradition.[17]

The passage presents us with little helpful criteria for establishing its date. There are no references to political upheavals. Instead, the catchword "whoredom" (vv 10–15, 18) predominates; it is found in those sayings from Hosea's early period (1:2; 2:6f; 3:3), but occurs less frequently later on.[18] It would therefore seem pos-

sible to date our passage in the final years of Jeroboam II, at approximately the same time as 4:1–3. The important catchword "knowledge" (דעת vv 1, 6) connects the two passages. Moreover, there is at least a literary connection of v 4a with vv 1–3. It is possible that Hosea himself, pointing up the words he had proclaimed shortly beforehand, placed v 4a into this context as an antithetical explanation to vv 1–3.

**Interpretation**

■ **4** After the completed judgment speech in 4:1–3, אך begins a new saying. This particle often occurs at the beginning of a speech.[19] It gives emphasis to the immediately following words, especially those spoken in the heat of controversy.[20] Thus אך frequently introduces a sentence which is quickly followed by an antithesis.[21] This should be presupposed here, if a meaningful connection is to be recognized in this poorly transmitted text. ריב in v 4b picks up the negated ריב in v 4a. In v 4a the primary meaning of "to accuse," "to hold court against"[22] (ריב), is complemented by יכח hip'il. Whereas the subject of the verb ריב was originally a participant in the court proceedings, the subject of "to judge" (יכח) is a neutral person (Gen 31:37; Job 9:33; 16:21), who first of all dispassionately (Lev 19:17) states what is right. Thus he gives a legal opinion or admonition (Am 5:10; Is 29:21; Ezek 3:26), and at times passes final judgment on a case.[23] These two concepts, occurring as a word–pair in v 4, approach the same meaning (cf. Mic 6:2), since in the antithetic parallel in v 4b, ריב comprises the aspects of legal suit and of judicial decision.[24] The word thus represents both concepts and probably leans strongly in the direction of the meaning "sentence," as 12:3 and the following verses[25] make evident.

14 Wolff, *Das Zitat im Prophetenspurch*, BEvTh 4 (München, 1937), 20ff; 76ff [also in his *Gesammelte Studien*, 47ff, 85ff].

15 See the commentary.

16 Cf. Am 2:12 (7:10–13); 9:10; Is 5:19; 28:9, 15; 29:15; 30:10–11, 16; Mic 3:11; Jer 5:12ff; Ezek 21:5.

17 Cf. Ju 20:18; 1 Sam 7:16 with 1 Kgs 16:32; 2 Kgs 10:27.

18 Only in 5:3f [6:10], 9:1.

19 12:9; Gen 26:9; 29:14; 1 Sam 25:21; Ps 73:1; Is 19:11; 36:5; 45:24; Jer 10:19; 16:19; Lev 23:27.

20 12:9 [8]; Is 45:14; cf. Gen 34:15; Is 14:15.

21 12:9 [8]; Jer 5:4ff; Is 45:14ff.

22 Cf. 2:4; see p. 33.

23 Gen 31:42; Prv 9:8; Mic 4:3; cf. Boecker, *Redeformen*, 45–47.

24 As in 4:1; cf. 1 Sam 25:39; see the commentary on 4:1.

25 See commentary on v 5aα.

But the lawsuit is first negated and then affirmed. Where does the prophet himself stand in relation to this antithesis? If v 4a be interpreted as it stands in *M*, it might be understood as a quotation of a priest's admonition that the prophet keep silent,[26] his response to Hosea's words in 4:1–3; cf. ריב in 4:1. Hosea could have had experiences similar to those of Amos in Bethel (cf. Am 7:12f). In this case, v 4a would be Hosea's reply after the priest had forbidden him to make an accusation: "Of course no one should contend, no one should reprove." Then Hosea could have continued—like Amos (7:16f)—with an even more caustic attack: "But ⟨my lawsuit is with you⟩, O Priest!" This interpretation, however, is implausible: according to the continuation in vv 5f, we must assume that the "I" in v 4 is also Yahweh, not the prophet. Hence, v 4 is a messenger speech, not a disputation. The twofold occurrence of "man" (איש) in v 4a is hardly an indirect reference to the priest who supposedly had neglected to bring forth the accusation mentioned in vv 1b–2, as Junker[27] suggests on the basis of 2 Kgs 6:27. Then אך would have to be interpreted as a conditional particle ("But if no one makes the accusation—not even you, Priest!—then my lawsuit is with you yourself!"). In this interpretation the "I" of the prophet or Yahweh in v 4b would have to be emphasized in contrast to the two occurrences of איש in v 4a. The probable solution will have to begin with the fact that אך at the beginning of a speech first of all emphasizes the following ambiguous words.[28] Accordingly, one would expect that the twofold איש in v 4a should be interpreted as the object of the verb, in antithetic parallelism to the partner of the lawsuit named in v 4b: "Certainly, not just anyone ⟨should be accused⟩; not just someone ⟨should be reproved⟩.[29] But ⟨my lawsuit is with you⟩, O Priest!" In view of the condition of the text

this interpretation of course remains uncertain. In its favor, however, is that it is consonant with the Yahweh speech required by the context. This new saying by the prophet lends precision to the previous verses (1–3), in that now the priest is the first among the people to be accused, rather than an unspecified member of the nation. The כהן addressed here is probably a high official of an important sanctuary, like Amaziah of Bethel (Am 7:10). The mention of the priest's "mother" (v 5) and his "sons" (v 6) speaks against a collective interpretation of "priest";[30] furthermore, כֹּהֵן in the vocative never has a collective meaning.[31]

■ 5 The announcement of Yahweh's lawsuit against the priest is immediately followed by the results. The perfect consecutive, "You shall stumble" (וכשלת) has a future, resultative meaning and therefore describes not the priest's offense,[32] but its consequences. Also in its other occurrences in Hosea, כשל denotes the results of an offense (5:5; 14:2). Generally in prophetic sayings this word in the perfect consecutive describes "stumbling" as the punishment brought on by the immediately preceding announcement of Yahweh's action.[33] Hence, v 5aα makes it necessary to emend v 4b as is suggested above.[34] Because Yahweh punishes the priest, he shall stumble "in the daylight"[35] when one does not normally stumble—as in the dark (Jn 11:9f). In v 5aβ, whose style already indicates that it is a gloss (see textual note "c"), this meaning is misunderstood; in reference to the nocturnal revelations of the prophets,[36] it states that the prophet stumbles "by night." Like Amaziah, the high priest of Bethel (Am 7:12f), Hosea knows no prophets who carried out official duties in the sanctuaries of the Northern Kingdom.[37] In the Jerusalem temple, however, prophets stood side by side with the priests as the cultic personnel.[38] Hence, it was apparently impor-

26    *T* and Rashi interpret v 4a in a similar way, according to Wünsche, 139f; cf. also Sellin.
27    "Os 4:1–16," 166.
28    See p. 76.
29    See textual note "a."
30    Recently Junker, "Os 4:1–3," 168ff.
31    Concerning this, cf. Lohfink, "Os 4:4–6," 305ff.
32    Thus Sellin, Harper, Deden, *De kleine Profeten, Hosea–Micah*, BOT (Roermond, 1953).
33    Is 8:15; 28:13; 31:3; Jer 6:21; cf. Is 3:8.
34    See textual note "b."
35    Cf. Neh 4:16; also *G S T; V* mistranslates with *hodie;* also see textual note "c."

36    Mic 3:6; Jer 23:25f; Zech 1:8; 4:1.
37    H. W. Wolff, "Heimat," 83–90 [232–43]; and R. Hentschke, *Die Stellung der vorexilischen Schriftpropheten zum Kultus*, BZAW 75 (Berlin, 1957), 153.
38    Is 28:7; Mic 3:11; Jer 2:8; 4:9; 5:31; 6:13; 8:10; 14:18; 18:18; 23:11.

tant to the Judaic traditionist to attest that Hosea's words also applied to Jeremiah's opponents and their successors.

The unexpected change to the first person (וְדָמִיתִי) in v 5b in the transmitted text appears strange; thus אִמֶּךָ has no antecedent, which has prompted various conjectures.[39] Should not v 5b, in parallel to v 5aα, announce a further consequence of Yahweh's act of judgment? In this case, an original וְנִדְמְתָה would better correspond with Hosea's diction.[40] Like Amos, who threatened both the children and wife of Amaziah (Am 7:17), Hosea, in announcing judgment upon the priest's sons (v 6b), could have also included his mother. Jeremiah's threat to King Jehoiachin also included his mother.[41] II דמה nipʿal means first of all "to be silenced," "to have to keep silent" (Is 6:5; Jer 47:5; Ezek 32:2; Ps 49:13, 21); but it may also have the more general sense of "to die," "to be destroyed" (in Zeph 1:11 it stands parallel to כרת nipʿal; in Is 15:1 to שדד puʿal; cf. Ob 5).[42] Perhaps

Hosea had some reason—unknown to us—for declaring that the guilty priest's mother would be silenced or killed; if not, by referring to her, too, he may have underlined the totality of the judgment on the priest's dynasty,[43] just as in v 6bβ. This is hardly a reference to a cultic place, as in 2 Sam 20:19, where a city is called "a mother in Israel."[44] Since the text's transmission is uncertain, the conjectures offered[45] in place of the concrete statement about the "mother" of the prophet are to be rejected, especially since the parallelism "you ∥ your sons" in v 6bα –β[46] corresponds to the parallelism "you ∥ your mother" in v 5aα –b.

■ 6 The priest's offense is not mentioned until v 6. The condition of the people mirrors the priest's guilt. In a tone of lament Yahweh speaks first of the downfall of his people. This is indicated by the word "destroyed" (נדמו), which picks up the וְנִדְמְתָה (cj.) from 5b.[47] That which now threatens the priest's dynasty has already happened to the people in the sight of Yahweh, as

39 See textual note "d."

40 Cf. textual note "e."

41 Jer 22:26; cf. 13:18; Ps 109:12ff; 1 Sam 15:33. On the "scheme encompassing three generations," which is found in the ancient Orient and the Old Testament, cf. Lohfink, "Os 4:4–6," 308–11. In this "scheme" the curse of a person includes both his ancestors who are still living and his descendants.

42 M. Luther, *WA* 13, 17: " 'I shall make him to be silent.' 'To be silent' is in the Hebrew and properly means 'still sein.' Consequently, Virgil, too, calls the shadows 'silent' because they are nothing. That there be silence properly means here 'to be nothing.' Today I shall hold your mother, the synagogue, in check and thus I shall reduce her to nothing that nothing may be heard about her, not even about her worship" [Trans.]. (*Tacere faciam. Silere est in hebraeo et significat proprie styll syn. Unde et Virgilius silentes umbras nominat, quod nihil sint. Significat autem hic proprie nihil esse, ut sit silentia: compescam hodie matrem tuam, synagogam, atque adeo eam in nihilum redigam, ut de ea nihil audiatur, cultum quidem suum.*)

43 J. Calvin, (*CR* XLII, 273), similar to *T* (see textual note "d") and Luther (see n 42), interpreted the "mother" as the "community": "Here the name 'mother' is taken for the actual name of the church in which we know the Israelites were accustomed to take pride against God, just as the papists do today. They boast of their mother, the Church. This is for them, as they say, the shield of Ajax. Should anyone reveal their corruptions, they immediately flee to that protection. Why go on? Are we or are we

not the Church of God? Because then the prophet saw that the Israelites were abusing this false title, he said, 'I shall at the same time destroy your mother.' That is, that boasting of yours in the nobility of Abram's tribe and that holy title 'The Church' will not prevent the Lord from taking horrible vengeance on all, because he will tear out by the roots and destroy that very name of your mother. That is, he will dissipate the very (sacrificial) smoke which you raise when you cover your disgraceful activities under the name 'The Church' " [Trans.]. (*Matris nomen hic accipitur pro ipso ecclesiae nomine, quo scimus Israelitas solitos fuisse superbire adversus deum, quemadmodum hodie faciunt papistae: jactant matrem suam ecclesiam: et hic est ipsis clypeus Aiacis, ut loquuntur. Si quis corruptelas eorum ostendat, statim confugiunt ad illam umbram, Quid? annon sumus ecclesia Dei? Quum ergo Israelitas videret propheta abuti fallaci hoc titulo, dicit, Ego simul perdam matrem vestram: hoc est, Non impediet vestra ista gloriatio, et nobilitas generis Abrahae, et ecclesiae sacer titulus, quominus sumat Dominus de omnibus horrendam vindictam, quia ab ipsa radice avellet et abolebit ipsum quoque nomen matris vestrae, hoc est, discutiet fumum illum quem jactatis, quum tegitis vestra flagitia sub ecclesiae titulo.*)

44 Cf. "Sons of Zion" (בְּנֵי צִיּוֹן) Ps 149:2.

45 E.g., the rather pale "to you" (אֹתְךָ) or the much too uncertain "your Urim" (אֻרֶיךָ; see textual note "d"), or an allegory on the nation (in view of 2:4).

46 Cf. also p. 80.

47 A verb seldom begins a sentence without a ו, but its quite frequent occurrence in the songs of lamentation should be noted; cf. Lam 1:2, 3, 7, etc.; also Hos

Hosea has previously proclaimed (4:1–3). Now, however, Yahweh suffers with his people. In Hosea "my people" (עמי) is always an expression of God's mercy or compassion (2:3, 25; 4:8, 12; 6:11b; 11:7; cf. 4:14b). The reason for the catastrophe, as in 4:1–3, is the lack of knowledge of God's will which has been passed on to them.[48] Yahweh's lament over the distress of his people is an accusation against the priests. Such a "reporting" lament over personal loss (a lamenting for oneself) as an element of the accusation is a speech form used before the court (Ju 20:5b). As the punishment of the priest's dynasty corresponds with the people's distress in vv 5b–6a, so the punishment in 6baβ corresponds with the priest's sin. Much like the *lex talionis*, the decisive verbs are repeated in both places.[49] The punishment from Yahweh, who speaks in the emphatic form (גם־אני v 6bβ²), corresponds to the priest's transgression, who is addressed in the emphatic form (אתה v 6bα¹). The *talion* formulas in the legal statutes are presented in nominal form; in each instance the same noun is repeated (cf. Gen 9:6a). But in Hosea, the punishment is expressed merely by the repetition of the same verb; the punishment is publicly proclaimed as the act of God. "The genuine talion formulas," however, "including Gen 9:6a, are concerned with a nemesis which belongs entirely to the essence of the deed and therefore also can be linguistically derived from it."[50] Hosea's style is more reminiscent of the curses, as in Ps 137:5; Josh 7:25; 1 Sam 15:33, which are similar to the international treaties in the ancient Orient and are perhaps part of ancient Israel's covenant tradition to which Hosea surely alludes in this context.[51]

What is the priest's transgression? He has destroyed the people of God by "rejecting knowledge" and "forgetting the directions of his God." The connection with vv 1–3, recognizable in v 4a and especially v 6a, suggests that "knowledge" (הדעת v 6) corresponds to the דעת אלהים in v 1, i.e., to the knowledge of God's revealed will; it is the content of this divine will to which 4:2

refers. The content of the "knowledge of God" in Hosea, in addition to divine law, is the basic deeds of salvation performed by Yahweh in Israel's earliest period: the exodus from Egypt (11:1); the election and wandering in the wilderness (9:10; 13:5f); the gift of the land and its natural resources (2:10). In each of these, Yahweh's covenant with Israel (8:1; 6:7) is to be the object of this "knowledge." To be sure, there have been frequent attempts to interpret דעת subjectively, as, for example, the attitudes of "heartfelt devotion" and of an "inward relationship to God,"[52] attitudes which the priest should have as an example to his people. On the other hand, it should be remembered that—in addition to the whole context of Hosea's theology[53]—מאס means "to reject" or "to scorn" a concrete object;[54] and that as a material parallel to דעת, תורה ("instruction") does not signify the priestly function of giving "instruction," but denotes the "instruction of your God" entrusted to him, which he has "forgotten" (!). Since in addition Hosea speaks of the written תורה (8:12), it seems the most probable that he saw the priest's guilt in his conscious negligence of his duties of transmitting and teaching the law, duties which were given him when Yahweh first revealed himself as the covenant God of Israel.[55] Since to Israel the Torah was God's instruction for life (Dtn 32:47), by neglecting his primary duty the priest bears responsibility for the destruction of the people of God.

Accordingly, Hosea gives a surprisingly positive picture of the priest's work. In any case what André Neher[56] expressed in a general way proves correct with regard to Hosea: "The priests are not attacked by the prophets because they are priests, but because they are priests no longer." Hosea's portrayal of the priest is similar to the Chronicler's description of the teaching Levites.[57] Dtn 33:10 and 31:9ff give further support to the assumption that this description has its precursor, at least as far as the priests' activities are concerned, in those groups of priests which formed an opposition party in the Northern Kingdom; with these groups Hosea was closely

10:7; Jer 47:5; on this see K. Schlesinger, "Zur Wortfolge im hebräischen Verbalsatz," *VT* 3 (1953): 386.

48 See p. 67; on this expression, cf. Is 5:13.

49 Cf. the *talion* formulas in Ex 21:23–25, 36; Lev 24:18–20; Dtn 19:21.

50 Lohfink, "Os 4:4–6," 313.

51 Lohfink ("Os 4:4–6," 314–25) attempts to prove this.

52 Weiser, 41, 45.

53 Cf. Wolff, " 'Wissen um Gott' " 533ff [182ff].

54 In Hosea מאס occurs again only in 9:17; cf. Am 5:21 and especially Is 5:24; 30:12; Jer 6:19.

55 Cf. Dtn 33:10; Ezek 44:23; Mal 2:7.

56 *L'essence du prophétisme* (Paris, 1955), 295.

57 2 Chr 15:3; 17:7–9; 19:8ff; 35:3; Neh 8:5–8.

associated.[58] The threat to the priest's mother in v 5b remains obscure. However, it is a matter of speculation whether this bears some relationship to the righteous priest who, according to the example of the Levite, regards neither father nor mother (Dtn 33:9) and who takes his place with the orphans and the sojourner (Dtn 14:29). W. F. Albright[59] thinks "the classical illustration of a 'Levite' . . . in the Bible is Samuel, who was vowed to Yahweh at Shiloh by his mother before he was born." Since the sons of the priests are also threatened, it appears that the priesthood was hereditary. Again perhaps this is not in accordance with the ideal Levite, who "ignored his children" (Dtn 33:9). Nothing indicates that there was some reason for this threat against the sons, as in 1 Sam 2:29–34. But according to 4:8, this would not be impossible.

The lament in v 6a, which accuses the priests indirectly, forms a transition to the twofold threat of punishment and its motivation in v 6b. With v 6b, the judgment addressed to the priest in v 5aαb, which also began with a twofold threat, is evenly rounded off. The middle section, an unusual divine lament, gives the motivation for the punishment. It corresponds to the introductory warning (v 4) which precedes the announcements of judgment upon the priest and shows Yahweh's compassion for his people. Yahweh condemns the priest because he is guilty of destroying the people of God. By withholding the proclamation of God's saving law, he is unfaithful to his calling.[60]

■ **7** The new prophetic saying beginning in v 7 also concerns priests. But it no longer addresses a single priest, as in vv 4–6; instead, v 7 speaks about them in the third person plural, as in the continuation in vv 8 and 10. According to form and content, the proof of guilt and the threat of disaster are new. Hence, vv 7f and 10 should not be interpreted as immediately continuing the statement concerning the sons (v 6b) of the priest threatened in vv 4–6. Yet this saying continues the general theme of "the transgressions of the priesthood." At first it is also in the form of the messenger speech. Yahweh speaks in the first person in vv 7 and 8, but he is spoken about in the third person in v 10b. The passage's abrupt beginning is probably due to the way it was transmitted.

Here the traditionist adds yet another saying from the same scene. The prophet may have spoken these words after the priest—following the prophet's first reproof in vv 4–6—had attempted to defend himself by referring to the customary practice of numerous priests throughout the land. Or, it might have followed an apology subsequent to the last threat to the "sons" in v 6b. This could explain (1) why there is an abrupt transition to the plural ("priests"); (2) why the threat in the second person (vv 4–6) changes to an accusation, giving proof of guilt (vv 7, 8, 10b), with a public announcement of the judicial sentence (v 10a). This happens in the presence of those who, in the meantime, have gathered around the priests and the prophet at the sanctuary. It is significant that in this second saying, the accusation predominates, while in the first the threat stands in the foreground. Whereas vv 4–6 only mentioned the priest's guilt in passing, v 7 merely touches upon the consequences of the guilt.

The saying begins with a comparison in which כְּ with an infinitive construction and suffix is found instead of כַּאֲשֶׁר with a finite verb (cf. Ex 1:12). רֻבָּם is a verbal form of the root רבב, which means "to be or to become numerous." "Corresponding to their increase in number is the fact that they sin against me," that is, "the more numerous they became, the more they sinned against me." It could also be translated, "As many as they are, so many were their sins against me," which means "they all sin against me."[61] Even the Targum related this sentence to the priests. The justification is found in the verse's connection with v 8, where the accused are distinguished from the people themselves. If the verse is not form critically analyzed, v 7 is interpreted in isolation from its context as referring to the people; here 9:10–15 might be useful for a comparison. We assume that Hosea has taken up a catchword spoken by the priest, who, in defense against the prophet's attack in vv 4–6, has made an appeal to the large number of his colleagues. With a genuine prophetic antithesis, Hosea answers that the great number of priests does not justify the sins, but only multiplies them. If we compare this saying about the increase in the number of priests with 10:1 and 8:11, which speak of the multiplica-

---

58 Further evidence in Wolff, "Heimat," 90–94 [243–50]; cf. also A. Neher, *L'essence*, 166–75; differently R. Rendtorff, "Erwägungen zur Frühgeschichte

des Prophetismus in Israel," *ZThK* 59 (1962): 151f.
59 *Archeology*, 109.
60 M. Luther, *WA* 13, 17: "Where there is a true

tion of sanctuaries, we can see—especially in view of 10:1b—that the healthy economy of the peaceful decades under Jeroboam II was accompanied by the flowering of multifaceted religious activity. There was time for the celebration of feasts which were arranged according to ancient Canaanite models and foreign patterns, the latter having been made accessible by foreign trade. The expansion of religious activity, with its increase in cultic personnel, meant for Hosea only an increase of sin. Transgression against Yahweh occurred all the more frequently. חטא means primarily "to miss (the mark)."[62] The idea that the large number increases the danger of apostasy from Yahweh is typically Hosean (cf. 8:11; 10:1, also 13:6); it occurs again in Deuteronomy (8:13; cf. 32:15). This is quite understandable in view of Hosea's connection with the small opposition party.

"Their glory" should have consisted in their cultivation of the "knowledge of God" (דעת אלהים). In this they should have lived for Yahweh.[63] The priests' real honor at the same time should have achieved the rich blessings of an increase in Israel's population (cf. 9:11). But they have "exchanged it for dishonor." The continuation explains how Hosea understood this dishonor: they lived from the sins of the people (v 8); they expect life and prosperity from the rites of prostitution in Canaan, but they will be deceived (v 10). In Jeremiah's interpretation of his spiritual father, Hosea, Yahweh himself is Israel's glory; the worthless Baal is her dishonor (2:11).

■ 8 The priests' sin and shame consist plainly in their eagerness for the people's transgressions. Here חטאת probably does not refer directly to the sin–offering, although this would be linguistically possible and, in the prophet's metaphorical speech, could even be the object of the priests' "eating." But עון in the parallel clause indicates that here, as in 8:13; 9:9; 13:12, and also 10:8, it means offense against God's will (Harper). In terms of its root meaning, חטאת emphasizes more the objective side of a transgression, whereas עון expresses

the subjective side of an offense.[64] The priests' own guilt becomes apparent in their reaction to the sins of the people: "They feed on them," "they yearn for them with greedy throats." Here נֶפֶשׁ has its original, concrete meaning of "throat, gullet," as in Prv 27:7; Mic 7:1; Is 5:14; 29:8. נשא נפש therefore graphically describes yearning greediness.[65] Whereas the words חטאת and עון describe the sins of the people only in general terms, the verbs indicate what the real sins of the people are, namely, sacrificial worship which is contrary to Yahweh's will, and that which, according to priestly doctrine, makes such worship necessary. The priests receive their own portion from the meat and cereal offerings.[66] It remains unclear whether in Hosea חטאת already implies the secondary meaning of "sin–offering."[67]

Like 4:8, 8:11 considers Israel's sacrifices as transgression (cf. 4:13 and 5:6). In this regard Hosea is of the same mind as Amos (4:4f). Exactly as in 6:6 the sacrifices, which are against God's will, are set in antithesis to the priests' real duty—characterized in a positive sense in 4:6 as "knowledge of God" (דעת אלהים) and "teaching of your God" (תורת אלהיך). The criticism of the cultic sacrifices is aimed at the selfish interests of the priests who in the sacrifices seek their own private gain. As in v 6a, Yahweh, in the form of the messenger speech, again sympathetically takes the side of Israel, calling them anew "my people." With their sacrificial cult, the priests do not serve the people of God with the divine gifts entrusted to them; instead, at the people's expense they store up their own profit and advantage. As in v 6 the priests' sins against God (v 7a) and against the people (v 8) are one and the same.

■ 10 The legal consequences of such conduct, established by God and proclaimed by the prophet, are stated in v 10a.[68] Like the priests in v 8, whoever tries to satisfy himself will remain hungry. And, like the priests in v 7, whoever dedicates himself to the cult of Baal, expecting fertility and population increase from the "sacral marriage" (ἱερὸς γάμος) will become a dying generation

---

knowledge of God, there is the priesthood of God," [Trans.]. (*Sacerdotium dei est, ubi est vera cognitio dei*).

61  Similarly Robinson.

62  Cf. Prv. 8:36; 19:2; Job 5:24; Is 65:20; Ju 20:16; and Koehler, *Theology*, 168f [158f].

63  "Priest to me" (כהן לי v 6) is antithetic to "sin against me" (חטא לי v 7a).

64  Cf. Koheler, *Theology*, 168f [158f].

65  Cf. Dtn 24:15; Jer 22:27; Ps 86:4.

66  Cf. v 13a; see pp. 85f.

67  Keil; cf. Lev 6:26.

68  On the connection of this verse with vv 7f, but excluding v 9, see p. 74.

(cf. 9:11; 13:1). Here זנה hip'il probably does not mean "to lead astray into fornication" (as in 5:3; Ex 34:16; Lev 19:29; 2 Chr 21:11, 13), but "to commit fornication," "to have relations with a זוֹנָה" (as in v 18). In distinction to the passages listed above, here the verb has no object, and the same subject serves the following verb יפרצו. Since the verse speaks of the priests, this is to be thought of chiefly as a reference to their official sexual relations with the sacral prostitutes[69] in the performance of the "sacral marriage."[70] As in 4:2 and Ex 1:12, פרץ means "to increase." The increase in population expected from the fertility cult will not materialize.

Verse 10b states the intrinsic necessity of the punishment. Of necessity the priests' life deteriorates "because they have forsaken Yahweh to worship whoredom." Since vv 7f are in the form of a messenger speech, the word "Yahweh" is surprising. This uneven style might have originated in the traditionist's sketch of this scene. Perhaps he took a new saying of Hosea's, originally in the disputation style, and joined it to the foregoing messenger speech with כי (in such a way vv 12bf have apparently been combined with the preceding saying). Or the traditionist might have changed the first person to the third to create a clear, didactic antithesis. Finally, however, it also should be considered that Hosea himself can make a transition from the messenger to the disputation style within the same saying (cf. 1:2; 3:1), particularly in the motive clause. It can be demonstrated from other prophetic books that the prophet himself adds the motivation to Yahweh's words of judgment revealed to him.[71] In each case the express mention of "Yahweh" emphasizes the abrupt antithesis: "Yahweh they have forsaken to cherish harlotry." Thus they have exchanged their "honor" for "shame" (v 7b).

For the first time in the prophetic writings—and in the general history of religion, for that matter—the concept "apostasy" appears, denoted by the word "to forsake" (עזב). The idea was already familiar to ancient Israel, whose faith in Yahweh precluded forsaking him for other gods. Significantly, all the law codes in the Old Testament contain a commandment forbidding worship of other gods; usually the commandment is prominently placed among the other commandments. However, the commandment against worshiping other gods is foreign to all known ancient oriental legal codes and lawbooks.[72] Hosea uses the word עזב only in v 10, but characteristically he connects it with זנה, a combination which again appears in Dtn 31:16 (cf. 28:20). Jeremiah uses the word more than twelve times, usually in relation to the idea of turning to other gods.[73]

Israel's apostasy is like whoredom. "To devote themselves to fornication" (לשמר זנונים) apparently is not without an ironic undertone. שמר can especially denote worship of a god (Ps 31:7; Prv 27:18); thus זנונים[74] would appear to have replaced Yahweh in Israel's worship. But it is more likely that לשמר followed by a nonpersonal object belonged originally in Hosea's circle of disciples and, as in Deuteronomy (sixteen times), had the content of the דעת אלהים as its object.[75] The priests have replaced this, the true object of their careful observance and cultic practice, with זנונים, i.e., with Canaanite sex rites. This could be undertaken only in unfaithfulness to Yahweh.[76]

With its antithesis in 7b and 10b this saying is a very precise answer to the priest's objections to the threat in vv 4–6. Hosea severely censures the priests for surrendering themselves to an egotistic, sacrificial cult and its shameful sex rites as the fruitless result of their apostasy from Yahweh, by whose saving instruction they should actually live (4:6).

■ 9 An announcement of punishment has been secondarily inserted into the transmitted text. The connecting formula והיה, used to expand upon a transmitted text, occurred beforehand in 1:5; 2:1, 18, 23.[77] Does v 9 refer to the priest or the people? It is difficult to tell because the answer depends upon the tone of the sentence as well as its context. With the double כי the subject of comparison may precede that to which it is compared

---

69 See the commentary on 4:14.
70 See pp. 15f.
71 E.g., Am 4:1–2; 7:14f–16f; Is 5:8–9f; cf. H. W. Wolff, "Begründung," 6f [14ff], and E. Würthwein, "Amos–Studien," *ZAW* 62 (1950): 22f [also in his *Wort und Existenz. Studien zum Alten Testament* (Göttingen, 1970), 80f].
72 M. Noth, *The Laws in the Pentateuch and Other Studies*, tr. D. R. Ap–Thomas (Philadelphia: Fortress Press, 1966), 51f [*Gesammelte Studien*, ThB 6 (München, 1957) 70ff].
73 1:16; 2:13, 17, 19; 5:7, 19, etc.
74 Or זנות, see textual note "o/p."
75 "Keep all the words of the law" (לשמר את־כל־דברי התורה) as in Dtn 17:19; cf. 32:46; 13:19; 15:5.
76 See pp. 13f and the commentary on 12:13f on שמר.

82

("it will be for the people as for the priest," as in Gen 18:25; 44:18; Dtn 1:17; 1 Kgs 22:4; Hag 2:3) or vice versa ("it will be for the priest as for the people," as in Lev 7:7; Ju 8:18). The former occurs more frequently, since often the subject has already been mentioned; in this case it would appear as a "psychological subject"[78] which precedes the comparison, the actual goal of the statement. Accordingly, in Hosea there are numerous similies in which the thing being compared more often precedes the image of comparison[79] than follows it.[80] According to the rule of frequency, the people would be the subject[81] rather than the priest. But in view of the enumerated exceptions, certainty can be reached only from a consideration of the preceding context, or rather that text on which v 9 is a gloss, since we can no longer determine the accentuation of v 9. V 9a most likely relates to vv 4–6, where, as in v 9a, (1) "priest" (כהן) is in the singular; (2) the priest's fate is compared with the people's; and (3) the punishment is described as return of the sin to the sinner. In v 6b, the guilt and punishment of the priest are twice elucidated by the repetition of the same verbs ("reject," "forget"). This is clearly expressed and summarized in v 9b by the idea that Yahweh "causes his deeds to return to him." He who forsakes Yahweh and rejects his salvation creates his own punishment: he will be helplessly forsaken and rejected. Yahweh is the executor of punishment only in the sense that he actually provides for the inner causal connection between deed ("his ways" דרכיו) and fate ("to avenge" פקד);[82] indeed, he creates this connection[83] and allows the wicked deed to return[84] like a boomerang to its agent.[85] If v 9 was originally a gloss on vv 4–6 as we have suggested, and was later inserted incorrectly after v 8, then "priest" (ככהן) must be considered the subject. The priest's fate is identified with that of

the people in accord with Yahweh's judgment in v 6 and in accord with the juxtaposition of vv 1–3 with vv 4–6. Finally, when it is noted that v 9b corresponds literally with 12:3b [2b] (cf. also 12:15b [14b]) it becomes entirely clear that this gloss is an old saying of Hosea's about the people which has been secondarily applied to the priest. The glossator noted that vv 4–6 threatened the priest in the same way as 12:3 [2] threatened the people. Whereas Hosea, in the already existing context in chap. 4, emphasized that the priests are responsible for the people's situation (vv 6, 14), the glossator stated only the similarity of their liability to divine judgment. The priest has no special hope because of his advantageous position before God.

■ 11  After the change to the objective style of the report ("Yahweh" את־יהוה) in v 10b, the saying returns to the form of the messenger speech ("my people" עמי; cf. vv 4–8 [9]) in vv 11f. This indicates the beginning of a new saying. If "new wine" (תירוש) alone was the original subject of the sentence[86] then what is meant? L. Koehler's[87] explanation that תירוש is an archaic word for "wine" (יין) can hardly be demonstrated from the book of Hosea. Hosea not only knows the word (7:5; 9:4; 14:8), but as a drink clearly distinguishes it (7:5; 9:4) from תירוש, which often occurs with "grain" and "olive oil" (2:10, 24; 7:14) as a natural product of the harvest (2:11; see p. 37) and winepress (9:2); this usage is by no means restricted to formulaic phrases. Thus, in contrast to wine, Hosea understands תירוש either as juice of the grape,[88] or as fresh must[89] stored in the wine vat.[90] The derivation of the word from the root "to tread, to press" (ירש) confirms its meaning as (unfermented) freshly pressed grape juice, in distinction to יין, which is fermented and ready for consumption. This grape juice "takes away the heart." In Hosea "heart" (לב) is

---

77  See p. 26.
78  Brockelmann, *Syntax* § 27ab.
79  2:1, 5, 17; 3:1; 5:10, 12, 14; 6:4; 7:4, 7, 16; 8:8, 12; 9:1, 4, 9; 10:7; 11:8, 11; 12:10, 12; 13:3, 7, 8; 14:6, 7b, 8, 9.
80  4:7, 16; 6:3; 7:6, 12; 9:10, 11; 10:4; 14:7a.
81  Brockelmann, *Syntax* § 109d.
82  See pp. 18 and 40.
83  Cf. 1 Kgs 8:32: "bringing his conduct upon his head" (לָתֵת דַּרְכּוֹ בְּרֹאשׁוֹ).
84  אשׁיב; cf. Joel 4:4b, 7b; Ob 15b.
85  On this subject, see K. Koch, "Vergeltungsdogma," 10ff, and F. Horst, "Recht," 71ff [287ff].
86  See textual note "o/p."
87  "Archäologisches Nr. 22, 23," *ZAW* 46 (1928): 218–20.
88  As in Is 24:7; 65:8; Ju 9:13.
89  Mic 6:15; Prv 3:10.
90  *BRL*, 538.

the seat of life (13:8) and of one's self–awareness (13:6); above all it is the organ of reflective thinking (7:2); it provides a sense of direction (7:11), and correctly perceives what is heard (2:16). The heart draws rational conclusions (11:8, in antithesis to enflamed wrath; cf. 7:6); in the heart well–considered decisions are made (7:14; 10:2). "To take away[91] the heart" from the people therefore means to rob them of their rational ability to orient themselves; to hand them over to deception. In the same sense Gen 31:20 speaks of "to steal the heart."[92] This happens to "my people" (עמי) says Yahweh's messenger, in a tone of sympathetic complaint (as in v 6a).

But how can "grape juice" destroy the ability to think clearly? Would this not be the expected result of drinking wine (Prv 23:29–35)? It was first mentioned in the secondary addition to this verse and probably did not originally stem from Hosea. Light on the question is shed by 7:14, where—as in 4:11—Hosea uses תירוש to speak of the vintage and its produce in the wine vats as the object of senseless, passionate pleasure. The longing for a good wine harvest drives the people to wailing in the Canaanite fertility cults rather than to praying to Yahweh. It should be noted that in 7:14 crying to Yahweh "with their hearts," i.e., with deliberate consideration, stands in contrast to the ecstatic rites of the Canaanites. Also in 7:14 new wine (and grain) is the object of their yearning, even as irrationality is a part of their disloyalty to Yahweh.

■ 12 In 7:14 it is said that the people, according to the customs of Baal–worship, wail and gash themselves instead of calling upon Yahweh from the heart (בִּלְבָם); similarly, in v 12 the outcome of their greed for the harvest is the Canaanite practice of visiting oracles. Hosea's choice of words ironically expresses the irrationality of the confused people which was characterized beforehand in v 11. Yahweh's people seeks answers from "its wood" and "its staff." שאל ב means to seek counsel from oracles in Ju 1:1; 2 Sam 2:1; Ezek 21:26. Speechless wood is expected to give information and a lifeless staff is "to proclaim" (cf. Hab 2:18f; Is 44:9–20), for instance, concerning the land's cultivation and the prospects of the harvest. Because of Hosea's demythologizing of the Canaanite cultic objects, it is impossible to say whether "wood" means the Asherah, the cultic pole that was set up next to the altar;[93] or the divine image similar to the Teraphim;[94] or a tree which gives oracles.[95] It is equally difficult to decide whether the "staff" means the small Ashera;[96] the Urim and Thummim that are part of the Ephod;[97] or whether it means the staves of rhabdomancy.[98] In any case, with the suffixes "its" wood and "its" staff, Hosea sharply attacks the use of these oracles as signs of Israel's willful apostasy from Yahweh.[99]

The saying (v 12b) now connected to v 12a as its motivation goes to the very root of such false practices. The כי connects a new speech fragment which, unlike vv 11–12a, is in the disputation style ("their God" [אלהיהם]). It is in the third person plural and, like vv 7f, 10 and vv 13a, 14aβ, probably no longer speaks of the people, as do the interpolated verses 11–12a in the third person singular. The new word התעה expresses the same deceiving and misleading activities as in v 11.[100] The people now live as an animal gone astray (Ex 23:4) or as a drunken person whose loss of sobriety means that he also looses his self–control and his way (Is 28:7). The saying in v 12b discloses the cause of this in a more profound sense than does v 11. Almost axiomatic, it says: "A spirit of whoredom leads astray"; "makes [them] reel." Yahweh's people have been relinquished to a mis-

91 לקח 2:11; 13:11.

92 Cf. "to lead astray" (התעה) in the continuation in v 12b and A. R. Johnson, *The Vitality of the Individual in the Thought of Ancient Israel* (Cardiff, 1949), 79ff; W. Schmidt, "Anthropologische Begriffe im AT," *EvTh* 24 (1964): 384f.

93 Dtn 16:21; Ju 6:25ff; cf. *BRL*, 35 and O. Eissfeldt, "Ashera," *RGG*[3] 1, 637f.

94 See the commentary on 3:4; further, Ezek 21:26; Hab 2:18f.

95 As in Gen 12:6; Dtn 11:30; Ju 4:5; 9:37; (cf. 2 Sam 5:23f).

96 Harper; cf. E. Meyer, *Geschichte des Altertums* 2[2]

(Stuttgart, 1931[2]), 149; Philo names the Asherim ῥάβδοι as does *G* (מקל).

97 Nu 27:21; Dtn 33:8; see the commentary on 3:4.

98 Thus as early as Cyril of Alexandria; cf. Keil and van Gelderen.

99 Luther, *WA* 13, 19: "So it also happens today that we bring answers from our own pursuits: 'You have worn this vestment for so long, you have prayed for so long; therefore you will be holy' " [Trans.]. (*Ita fit et hodie, ut responsa feramus ex nostris studiis: tam diu portasti hanc vestem, tam diu orasti, ergo sanctus eris.*)

100 See above on יקח לב.

leading, higher power. Much like Micah (3:5) and Jeremiah (23:13, 32) Hosea sees this power in the spiritual leaders who have fallen away from Yahweh. It is these very priests who exchange their honor for shame (v 7) and who make prostitution the object of the cultic exercises (vv 10f). Their spirit leads the people astray. רוּחַ זְנוּנִים means, therefore, not the indwelling spirit in those led astray, like the feeling of jealousy a husband has for his wife (Nu 5:14, 30); rather, it characterizes the power of apostasy as an overwhelming force which comes upon the people from the outside. This is similar to the "spirit of confusion" which proceeds from Yahweh in Is 19:14, whose activity as a רוּחַ עִוְעִים is also described by תעה hip'il; or it is like the spirit of deep sleep in Is 29:10.[101] The difference is that Hosea does not conceive of the spirit of whoredom as proceeding from Yahweh, nor, on the other hand, does he assume that it is an independent spiritual being.[102] Instead, this spirit is embodied in the priesthood, making them guilty.[103] In this connection it is important to note that Hosea, in speaking of a "spirit of harlotry," views the guilty persons directly in the light of their own actions.[104] As an infecting, seductive power, this spirit makes all of Israel incapable of finding its way, so that "they go a–whoring away from their God." In its present literary context v 12bβ relates to the "people" in v 12a. However, in its original rhetorical context with vv 13f (note the third person plural), v 12bβ would have to be related to the priests, thus giving an interpretation of רוּח זנונים, since in vv 13b, 14aα the people are addressed. The dual preposition מתחת expresses the move toward emancipation from Yahweh[105] even more strongly than מאחרי in 1:2. מאחרי means: formal break of personal relationships (cf. 2:15); but מתחת signifies the rebellious betrayal of an obligatory relationship of obedience

and submission,[106] and thus more clearly than v 11, it calls the rebelliousness of the false cults an irrational activity of a wicked intoxication. Rebellion against the God of revelation means for Hosea the departure from a reasoned life which is free of deception and sure of its goal.

■ **13** The new accusation beginning with v 12b continues immediately in vv 13f. The same third person plural is the subject of v 13a. The larger context strongly suggests that the third plural refers to the priests. The content and style of v 12b already indicated its connection with vv 7, 8, 10. The people are spoken of merely incidentally in vv 11–12a, where the tone is that of a lament rather than an accusation (similarly v 6a). Likewise in the continuation (v 14aβ) the priests, the primary object of the accusation, are clearly distinguished from the fathers—who from now on are directly addressed in vv 13b, 14aα—and from the rest of the people (v 14b). Here in the direct address the forum becomes visible before which the accusation against the priests (in the third person) has been made since vv 7ff. H. Schmidt[107] has pointed out "that we must take note of the unusually exited tone of the lament and accusation" in order to define correctly also in this instance who the defendants actually are.[108] When we conceive of the actual court scene, with its various types of discourse addressed to one group and then to another by the prophet, then the sudden transitions to direct address can be correctly evaluated. This makes it unnecessary to change the suffixes to the third person or to delete v 13b.[109]

If the priests are actually the accused, then it is not surprising that the theme from vv 7f, 10, 12b continues here, namely, the adulterous breech of faith through participation in the sacrificial cult and the sex rites. For the first time there is a description of the cultic places, especially the high sanctuaries, which is basically iden-

101 Cf. Johnson, *Vitality*, 34ff; D. Lys, "*rûach*" *le Souffle dans l'AT*, Etudes d' Histoire et de Philosophie Religieuses *56* (Paris, 1962), 75; Schmidt, "Anthropologische Begriffe," 383.

102 A. Jepsen, *Nabi* (München, 1934), 21, n. 1.

103 Cf. 1 Kgs 22:22ff; Zech 13:2; also see the commentary on 5:4.

104 Cf. G. Pidoux, "L'homme dans l'Ancien Testament," *Cahiers théologiques* 32 (1953): 21: The spirit is an aspect of the soul or its power: it signifies the soul in its activity. On זנונים, see pp. 13ff.

105 Cf. Brockelmann, *Syntax* § 119a.

106 "Revolted from" (פָּשַׁע מִתַּחַת) 2 Kgs 8:20, 22; cf.

107 Ex 6:7; 18:10; cf. "away from" (מֵעַל) in 9:1, 12b.

107 Schmidt, "Die Ehe," 266.

108 Cf. G. Richter, *Erläuterungen zu dunklen Stellen in den kleinen Propheten* (Gütersloh, 1914); see also van Gelderen, 118.

109 Thus Budde, "Zu Text und Auslegung [4:1–19]," 291; Robinson, *et al.*

tical with their description in Dtn 12:2. They are situated on the tops of high mountains (הרים) or lower hills (גבעות).[110] The high places have "a minimum of furnishings."[111] In addition to the altar—on which the sacrifice was placed or burned—and the Asheroth and *maṣṣēbôth* (where oracles were given),[112] there was especially one or more sacred trees. Hosea names the most important kinds of trees, instead of using the general expression "under every green tree."[113] אלון is the oak tree, abundant of shade, whose best known varieties grow in Haurân and therefore are called the "oaks of Bashan" in Is 2:13; Ezek 27:6; Zech 11:2. לבנה occurs elsewhere only in Gen 30:37; this is probably the poplar,[114] though not the white poplar, which grows only in very moist ground; the poplar Hosea mentions grows everywhere in the highlands of Palestine and especially on the mountains. "The pleasant smell of its white blossoms could in fact attract one to its rather insignificant shade."[115] אלה is the terebinth,[116] which, like the oak, grows a majestic crown affording deep shade.

What takes place in the sanctuaries located high on the mountains? The iterative imperfects[117] are indiative of a constant activity there. זבח pi'el and קטר pi'el together denote the regular occurrence of the sacrifices offered to Baal on the cultic high places.[118] These two words occur chiefly in the Deuteronomistic History.[119] זבח pi'el means not only the slaughter of the sacrificial animal (זבח qal in 8:13), but especially the eating of its meat (8:13) at the meal of *communio*.[120] Moreover, קטר pi'el can indicate the burning of certain nonedible parts of the sacrificial animal before the idols (11:2). Amos, Hosea's contemporary, mentions the sacrificial burning (קטר Am 4:5) of "that which is leavened";[121] Lev 2:11 forbids the offering of honey by fire in the cult of Yahweh; Song 4:6 speaks of a moun-

tain of myrrh (cf. Prv 7:17) and a hill on which incense was burned.[122] The "shade" of the trees is praised because it increases the pleasure of the sacrificial meals. As in v 8, Hosea censures the priests' lustful desires with irony.

In addition, the trees' shadows serve the other activites of the cultic high places, namely, the sex rites. These rites are alluded to by Hosea's catchword (זנה) already in vv 10f and v 12; they are expressly mentioned again in vv 13b, 14. Sacrificial meals and sexual rites are also mentioned together in 5:6f; Ezek 18:6, 11, 15; 22:9; Is 57:5, 7; and Prv 7:14ff. Ex 32:6 and Nu 25:1f paint an appropriate, comprehensive picture of the cultic activity of Baalism.

Among the sex rites themselves, Hosea distinguishes between the cultic acts of the priests (v 14aβ) and the customs of the other participants in the cult (vv 13b, 14aα). Verse 13b refers to the latter, which are most probably the bridal rites. This is evident from the fact that Hosea reminds the fathers who are present of what their daughters and daughters–in–law are doing. Rost[123] has shown that within the context of laws relating to the family, כלה means both daughter and daughter–in–law. In the first place (and this is important for our discussion), the word denotes "the bride till now a virgin, who takes on the status of a wife through marriage," who is placed under the *paterna potestas* of the father–in–law. The "whoring" and "adultery" of the daughters and daughters–in–law above all refer to that initial act of intercourse in the sacred forest.[124] Hosea abhors this bridal rite, which is fully understandable when we read Herodotus' (I, 199) detailed portrayal of it:

---

The foulest Babylonian custom is that which compels every woman of the land once in her life to sit in

---

110 Cf. Schwarzenbach, *Terminologie*, 9f: הר is parallel to גבעה thirty–one times in the Old Testament. גבעה occurs sixty times, thirty–nine of which are in the prophetic literature.

111 Noth, *World*, 177 [141]; for a detailed presentation see A. G. Barrois, *Manuel d'Archéologie Biblique* 2 (Paris, 1953), 345–55.

112 See the commentary on v 12a.

113 Dtn 12:2; 1 Kgs 14:23; Jer 2:20, etc.; the phrase occurs ten times in the Old Testament in connection with foreign cults.

114 Gen 30:37 G: στύραξ, *styrax officinalis*; Arab. *libne*; also ᶜabhar.

115 Dalman, *Arbeit* 1, 67; van Gelderen, on the other hand, thinks it is white poplar, with *G α'*: λεύκη.

116 *Pistacia palaestina*; Arab. *buṭm*, Dalman, *Arbeit* 1, 66.

117 Brockelmann, *Syntax* § 42d.

118 11:2; cf. Am 4:4f; on קטר, see p. 15.

119 1 Kgs 3:3; 11:8, etc.; cf. Koehler–Baumgartner, 249a.

120 "Sacrifice with" (זבח עם) 4:14; cf. Ex 34:15; Gen 31:54.

121 Cf. Ex 23:18.

122 Cf. Lev 2:1f, 15f.

123 "Erwägungen," 453.

124 See the discussion, following Boström and Rost, on

the temple of Aphrodite and have intercourse with some stranger. Many women who are rich and proud and disdain to consort with the rest, drive to the temple in covered carriages drawn by teams, and there stand with a great retinue of attendants. But most sit down in the sacred plot of Aphrodite, with crowns of cord on their heads; there is a great multitude of women coming and going; passages marked by line run every way through the crowd, by which the stranger men pass and make their choice. When a woman has once taken her place there she goes not away to her home before some stranger has cast money into her lap and had intercourse with her outside the temple; but while he casts the money, he must say, "I demand thee in the name of Mylitta" (that is the Assyrian name for Aphrodite). It matters not what be the sum of the money; the woman will never refuse, for that were a sin, the money being by this act made sacred. So she follows the first man who casts it and rejects none. After their intercourse she has made herself holy in the goddess's sight and goes away to her home; and thereafter there is no bribe however great that will get her. So then the women that are fair and tall are soon free to depart, but the uncomely have long to wait because they cannot fulfil the law; for some of them remain for three years, or four. There is a custom like to this in some parts of Cyprus.

---

The Canaanite bridal rites were quite similar, as Dtn 23:19 and Ezek 16:31, 34 make evident, which refer to a gift (of money?) called "harlot's hire" in the Old Testament. The similarity is also apparent from the book of Jeremiah, where it is said that the virgins lustfully wait for the "strangers" (2:25) upon the high places in the sacred forest (2:20; 3:2); according to Ezek 16:15 their beauty was not of little importance in this connection. Like Herodotus' report, sexual intercourse also in Canaan probably took place in the outlying thickets, outside the sanctuary, as v 14aβ ("to go aside" [יפרדו]) indicates. The introduction of such bridal rites[125] into the region of the tribes of Israel must have caused general degradation of Israelite customs (cf. Ezek 18:5ff), for the worshipers of Yahweh were incomparably strict with the purity and chastity of marriage.[126] In addition to these bridal rites, which were more or less prac-

ticed only once, it should be noted in this context that, as "temple prostitutes" (זונות or קדשות), the daughters of Israelite fathers assumed public, permanent functions.[127] Especially in terms of Yahweh's law, Hosea, as far as we know, was the first who was compelled to call the whole procedure "whoring and adultery." Following Hosea's lead, Deuteronomy (22:14ff), in order to ward off this practice, introduced a law concerning the contesting of a virgin's purity.[128]

Now, however, Hosea excuses the daughters and daughters-in-law who indulge in these strictly forbidden practices as well as the heads of families whom he addresses here and holds responsible. For in their sin the prophet sees only the wicked consequences of the priests' bad example in carrying out their cultic duties. V 13b is connected with vv 12–13a by "therefore" (על־כן). Hosea thus characterizes this apostasy from the marriage law by the community of Yahweh as the inevitable consequence of the priests' "spirit of whoredom." Previously Hosea also had characterized the people's lack of knowledge (v 6a) and their use of oracles (v 12) as the priests' fault. The following verse fully confirms that here an indirect pardon is indicated by על־כן in the same sense as v 4a and that v 13 is more of a lament than an accusation.

■ 14 Again in the style of a solemn Yahweh speech which continues to address the fathers as in v 13b, the messenger proclaims that the daughters and daughters-in-law will not be punished.[129] To interpret v 14a as a question (Nyberg) destroys the clear sense of the context; above all, it obscures the fact that in v 14aβ the prophet returns to the cause of the priests' guilt—distinctly referred to by "for these men" (כי־הם). After v 13b has already anticipated the dire consequence for the people, the plaintiff now points an accusing finger at the priests, thereby elucidating the accusation in vv 12b–13a. The first usage of the term "temple prostitutes" (קדשות) clearly refers to the actions of the cultic officials. The same word is used for the professional prostitutes in Dtn 23:18, with whom the "sacral marriage" is

---

p. 14.
125  Sometimes the rites were repeated to honor a vow that had been made: Lev 19:29; Dtn 23:19; Prv 7:14.

126  Noth, *Laws*, 54ff [74ff].
127  See the commentary on v 14.
128  Rost, "Erwägungen," 458.
129  On פקד, see pp. 18 and 40.

officially celebrated by the priests in the cult.[130]

There is extrabiblical evidence for sacral prostitutes in Syria and Phoenicia. Egyptian art dating from the time of the New Kingdom shows the Syrian goddess *qadeš*, together with the god Min, standing upon a lion ready for sexual intercourse. This is probably an archetypal image of the temple prostitutes and the sacral marriage.[131] In Ugarit the *qdšm*, who received a regular income, are attested repeatedly in parallel to the priests.[132] "Nothing can better denote the degeneration of the worship services in Israel than the word קדשות,"[133] which harshly illustrates the inroads of Canaanite customs into Israel. Hosea accuses the priests that, aside from their official cultic activities with the temple prostitutes,[134] they "turn aside with whores." According to our observations about Hosea's diction in v 13b, this could mean that the priests sought out the more beautiful among the brides who came to the rites of initiation at the high places and went aside with them into the forest. This the priests (who according to v 7 have increased in number) may have done as a part of their official duties, although this function, according to Herodotus, was performed by "the strangers" (but cf. Jer 2:25). Furthermore, the זנות, as distinguished from the קדשות, should probably be thought of as groups of public prostitutes.[135]

After the blunt accusation that the priests have initiated such pagan practices in Israel, for the last time there follows a brief lament over the people (cf. vv 4a, 6a [11–12a]; 13b–14aα): "a people without understanding comes to ruin" (v 14b). "To be thrust down" (לבט nip'al) occurs elsewhere only in Prv 10:8, 10. The word ילבט, together with the asyndetic relative clause לא־יבין, appears to have been selected for the sake of the threefold alliteration. The sentence is proverbial in style.[136] According to Hosea's intention, those over whom Yahweh laments are not only the inexperienced people, the youth—as most commentators have interpreted it—but all of Israel, insofar as they have not been instructed because the priests have withheld from them their own understanding of God's will. Thus in the phrase "an unknowing people" (עם לא־יבין) in v 14b, we recognize the "people who lack knowledge" (עם מבלי הדעת) in v 6a. Similarly in Dtn 4:6, Israel's "understanding" (בינה) is traced to the teaching of Yahweh's laws and statutes; in Jer 9:11 [12] the man of understanding (יבן) is taught by the "mouth of Yahweh." Note the parallel of "understand ∥ know" (בין∥ידע) in 14:10; Is 1:3; 11:2.

Perhaps the beginning of v 15 belongs to v 14b:[137] the evil destruction of Israel is the result of the whore or of their whoring(?). This state of affairs is part of the priests' guilt; it is the consequence of their negligence (v 6) and wicked example (vv 12b–14a). Having said this, Hosea, in the climax of this scene, has provided the

130 See pp. 9f and 15f.
131 Cf. *ANEP*, No. 473; 474; 470; a reproduction of lesser quality is in Gressmann, *Altorientalische Bilder zum Alten Testament* (Berlin, 1927²), 270, 272; cf. H. Bonnet, *Reallexikon der ägyptischen Religionsgeschichte* (Berlin, 1952), 362, 462; Albright, *Archeology*, 75f.
132 *CTCA* 77 and 75 (Gordon 63 and 81); cf. Barrois, *Manuel* 2, 341. For Mesopotamia, mention is made of the hierodule in the Code of Hammurabi, §§ 110, 127, 182, and in The Middle Assyrian Laws, § 40, Meek, *ANET²*, 170, 171, 174, 183.
133 L. Bleeker, *De kleine Propheten* (Groningen, 1932).
134 On "sacrifice" (זבח pi'el) see the commentary on v 13a.
135 Cf. the harlot Rahab in Josh 2:1ff; Code of Hammurabi § 178 (Meek, *ANET²*, 174; cf. The Middle Assyrian Laws, Tablet A, § 40: Meek, *ANET²*, 183) refers to various groups of harlots: the bride (or sister) of the deity as the high priestess (*entum*), the priestess (*nadîtum*), the hierodule (*qadištum*), the disciples (*kulmašitum*), the deaconesses (*šugê/itum*), and the (*SAL*)–*ZIKRUM* (which is more likely "a particular spelling" for the *sekertum*, the "separated" [von Soden], than a masculinely dressed woman as described in Dtn 22:5 [Driver–Miles]). § 181 attests that fathers dedicated their daughters to such service in the temple. Cf. G. R. Driver–J. C. Miles, *The Babylonian Laws* 1 (Oxford: Clarendon Press, 1956²), 358–83 ("Women of Religion"). § 27 of the Lipit-Ishtar Law Code (Kramer, *ANET²*, 160) of the early post–Sumerian era (nineteenth century B.C.) speaks of a man who had offspring from "a prostitute from the public quarters" (*kar-kid*), because his wife had remained barren.
136 Pfeiffer, *Introduction*, 572; van Gelderen.
137 Thus *G*; see textual note "u."
138 Differently, Engnell, "Hosea," *SBU*, who takes 1:7; 2:2; 3:5; 6:11, as well as 4:15, as evidence for Hosea's pro–Judah position.

conclusive basis both for the antithesis at the beginning (v 4) and for the legitimacy of the judgment speech (vv 5f).

■ **15** It is a matter of dispute whether v 15, or a greater or lesser part of it, is genuinely Hosean. The main reason underlying this dispute is the mention of Judah. It does not in fact fit the context,[138] especially in the wording of *M*: "Though you play the harlot, O Israel, let not Judah become guilty," which would also make Judah the addressee of the following warning. The final punishment of Israel already presupposed here is not in complete agreement with the foregoing accusation of the priest. For till now, Hosea has not considered the people and the priests as guilty in the same way (vv 4a, 14aα). Moreover, Hosea himself does not make the distinction between Israel and Judah which is made in the text of *M*; rather, he either sees both under the same judgment (5:10, 12–14; 6:4) or both in terms of the same hope (2:2). Such a distinction was first made by a Judaic glossator (1:7). Finally, it can hardly be proved that during Hosea's time Judah was tempted to visit the sanctuaries in the Northern Kingdom. Amos of Judah had addressed a similar warning (5:5), not to his own people, but to Israel.[139]

But only the word "Judah" should be regarded as secondary. This is suggested by the text in *G*[140] as well as by the formulation of v 15b. Although the three–part structure of the warning and the series naming the cultic places are clearly dependent on Am 5:5a,[141] it was not taken over in a rigid, literary sense; rather, it is a freely written, new composition in which the last part reveals even a modification in content.[142] If the verse is intelligible within the context of Hosea's preaching, it should not be regarded as secondary. Budde's[143] suggestion to reinterpret the consonantal text as it is presupposed by *G* (עַם זֹנֶה אתה ישראל) does not recommend itself. Rather, with *G*, we should take "You, O Israel, do not make yourself guilty" (אתה ישראל אל־תֶּאְשַׁם) as the upbeat (anacrusis) of the entire warning consisting of our lines.

Such a warning within the framework of this passage is by no means surprising. The last accusations against the priests had excused the people as a whole (vv 13b, 14b); they were even described as exempted from Yahweh's punishment (v 14aα; cf. v 4a). The recurring distinction between the guilty priests and the mislead people (cf. also vv 6, 12) has the obvious purpose of factually separating the people from the priests; this is most noticeable in the form of the address in vv 13b, 14aα. This very distinction is made in the warning (v 15) against visiting the sanctuaries. Collective thinking is overcome in a similar way in the ultimatumlike warning in 2:4f. In his early period, Hosea zealously endeavored to separate the people of Yahweh from the priests who had hopelessly given themselves over to the Canaanite cult. From a form critical point of view, the admonition derives from the parlance of judicial proceedings; its purpose is to reach a settlement.[144] Again Israel is solemnly addressed, first in the singular, then changing to the plural found already in vv 13b, 14aα; here too influence from Am 5:5 is probable. With a generally formulated saying, Hosea first attempts to separate God's people from the cult that now stands under judgment. אשם means to become culpable with regard to cultic matters; to make oneself punishable in an ultimate sense before God.[145] Hosea uses the word in this way throughout the book; in fact, it is connected exclusively with the guilt Israel has incurred by its participation in the cult of Baal (10:2; 13:1; 14:1). In order to grasp its single basic meaning, it should be noted that אשם emphasizes more the punishment that is due than the guilt presupposed by it.[146] First Hosea gives Israel a general admonition to escape the approaching punishment. To do this, they must discontinue their pilgrimages to Gilgal and Bethel. They "go" to Gilgal in the Jordan Valley near Jericho;[147] בוא is a term for the pilgrim's journey.[148] Hosea calls Gilgal—long established and well–known in Israel's history (Josh 5:2–9)—a place of wickedness also in 9:15; 12:12. One

---

139  Differently, van Gelderen, 121.
140  See textual note "w."
141  "He [Hosea] certainly listened in his youth to the hard sayings of the prophet of Judah," Buber, *The Prophetic Faith*, 110.
142  See the commentary on 13:7f and pp. xxiif.
143  Budde, "Zu Text und Auslegung [4:1–19]," 292.
144  Koehler, *Hebrew Man*, 149ff [150ff]; Job 22:21ff;

Ju 11:13b; 21:22; Jer 26:13.
145  Ju 21:22; Jer 2:3; 50:7; Lev 4:13, 22, 27, etc.
146  Cf. Zimmerli, *Ezekiel*, 508; differently, Nyberg and Koehler–Baumgartner.
147  On the location, see pp. 42f, and K. Galling, "Bethel und Gilgal, *ZDPV* 66 (1943): 145.
148  Is 1:12; Am 4:4; 5:5; cf. Hos 9:4, 10.

"goes up" (עלה) to Bethel[149] whose elevation is over 2400 feet. To this equally old and famous (Gen 28:10–22) place, Hosea gives the distorted and shameful name[150] Beth–aven, which perhaps was taken from Am 5:5 and later became popular among the Deuteronomistic circles.[151] The name first denotes the sanctuary—having fallen prey to the cult of Baal—that was situated east of the city (Gen 28:19; Josh 16:1f) near *Burj Beitîn*; and second, the entire city as "house of gloomy wickedness." It is probable that Hosea used the name in the same sense as Amos, since he also uses this word for the cultic high places (במות און 10:8) and for the city of Gilead (6:8; 12:12). On the other hand, it is uncertain whether the distorted name goes back to an original, בית און which would then mean "house of riches,"[152] or better, "house of lament."[153] T. Worden[154] thinks Hosea himself refers to the place of the rituals of lament in which the people gashed themselves.[155] Our interpretation of 4:11, viewed together with 7:14, makes Worden's suggestion worthy of consideration; we cannot agree, however, in view of the obvious similarity to Am 5:5 and reference to Gilead as the city of "evildoers" (פעלי און 6:8; cf. 12:12 [11]; 10:8).[156]

Wellhausen, Nowack, Budde, and Harper have suggested that "Beersheba" (בְּאֵר שֶׁבַע) be inserted in the last part of the warning, following Am 5:5; 8:14. This is quite arbitrary, however, in view of the text's history; this is especially true if it is likely that the saying in v 16 is Hosean in origin. Unlike Amos of Judah, Hosea would have had little reason for mentioning Beersheba, a place of pilgrimage deep in Judean territory. In-

stead, the tradition of Amos's (5:5; 8:14) three–part, plural warnings could have suggested to Hosea that he conclude the verse by giving the reason for his warning against these two sanctuaries which were situated nearby and frequently visited. There the people swear "As Yahweh lives" (חי יהוה) and thereby take a religious oath, for instance, as they enter the sanctuary, when they make covenants or during the cultic laments.[157] When Yahweh's name was called in Bethel or Gilgal, it was done with deceit,[158] since in fact Baal was worshiped there (Jer 4:2; 5:2). The formula appeared suspicious in light of the Canaanite ritual. One swore by a paganized Yahweh.[159] Thus the purpose of Hosea's warning is to prevent Israel's following the priests who have come under the influence of the religion of Canaan.

■ **16** Both the connections made by the catchwords[160] and the form of the entire passage,[161] suggest that vv 16–19 form the conclusion of the scene presented in vv 4–15. If this interpretation is correct, then it must be assumed that between v 16 and the warning in v 15, an objection was voiced by the people, similar to that which we observed in the relation of v 6 to v 7. The people likely uttered a reply, decidedly taking the priests' side instead of the prophet's. The prophetic saying is taken up once more, as the כי, in its old deictic function, indicates: "Indeed!" "That's the way it is!" "Exactly!" In such a way a speaker before the court would make a connection with the words of his opponents (Job 12:2; 2 Sam 12:5; Gen 31:31). Already in vv 10b and 12b, where there was a change from the first to third person within the speech, it was necessary to enter-

---

149 *Beitîn*, cf. *BRL*, 98ff; Noth, *World*, 72, 131, 140 [62, 102, 109].

150 Also in 5:8; 10:5; 12:5 *G* (differently *M*).

151 Cf. Josh 7:2; 18:12; 1 Sam 13:5; 14:23.

152 Van Gelderen, 122; cf. the corresponding change in the vocalization in Ezek 30:17.

153 Cf. 9:4 and Jer 16:5 "house of the cultic festival" (בית מַרְזֵחַ).

154 "The Literary Influence of the Ugaritic Fertility Myth on the OT," *VT* 3 (1953): 290.

155 Cf. 7:14; 1 Kgs 18:28; Jer 48:37; also Ju 2:1(*G!*), 5; and H. W. Hertzberg, *Die Bücher Josua, Richter, Ruth*, ATD 9 (Göttingen, 1969⁴), 155; Gen 35:8.

156 On the traditions of Gilgal and Bethel, cf. Galling, "Bethel und Gilgal," *ZDPV* 66 (1943): 140ff and *ZDPV* 67 (1964): 21ff; also E. Nielsen, *Shechem* (Copenhagen, 1955), 296ff, 310ff and Schunck, *Benjamin*, 155f.

157 Cf. Ps 24:4; Am 8:14; Jer 5:7; 12:16; Zeph 1:5; Ps 18:47; 119:106; Dtn 6:13; 10:20; Josh 23:7; cf. also the corresponding formulas of the Ugaritic ritual in which the expression *ḥy aliyn bʿl* occurs repeatedly: "Let the heaven rain oil/ The wadies run with honey/ That I may know that Aliyn Baal is alive/ That the Prince, Lord of Earth, exists," *CTCA* 6.III.6–9 (Gordon 49.III.6–9); cf. lines 2 and 20 (translation by Gordon, *Literature*); cf. Worden, "Influence," 290; Widengren, *Königtum*, 69f; for the religious oath see especially F. Horst, "Der Eid im AT," *EvTh* 17 (1957): 371 [also in his *Gottes Recht*, *ThB* 12 (München, 1961), 299].

158 Therefore *T* adds לשׁקר.

159 See the commentary on 2:18f.

160 See pp. 73f.

161 See pp. 75f.

tain the possibility that כי introduced a new speech.
The כי would not be intelligible as a causal conjunction.
The imagery of the "stubborn heifer" indicates that
Israel, previously addressed by the warning, will not
leave the "Baalized" cult of the sanctuaries. The unin-
structed people (vv 6, 14) show themselves incapable
of being instructed, in contrast to the early period (10:11;
cf. also Jer 13:18). The lack of understanding mentioned in v 11 has, in response to the prophetic word,
developed into hardness of heart. The imagery belongs
within the purview of the obduracy motif: the stubborn heifer "obstinately" fights against the laying on of
the yoke.[162]

After v 16a, v 16b is intelligible only as a question.
The reason for uncertainty here is that when this was first
written down, there was still knowledge of the speech's
inflection and of the opponent's contradiction. A. Weiser
thinks that the prophet makes use of a cultic song—
similar to Ps 23,[163]—that lauded Yahweh as the shepherd
of his people. The contradiction uttered by the people
in quoting the Psalm could have indicated their feeling
of security in his sanctuaries. If the catchword "lamb"
were also included in their objection, it could have
suggested Hosea's reply, in which he compares Israel to
a stubborn heifer. On "roomy place, [literally]" (מרחב),
which is probably a part of the quotation, cf. Hab 1:6.

■ 17   The reference to Ephraim's bond with the idols
is likewise most intelligible against the background of the
previously uttered warning (v 15) that sought in vain to
separate Israel from the idolatrous cult. חבר denotes;
alliance, league; cf. Gen 14:3. חֶבֶר in 6:9 is the band of
Priests.[164] Israel's allies are "dead idols" (עצבים), which
for Hosea may have meant the calf (8:4f; 13:2; 14:9)
or even the Asheroth (v 11) and Teraphim (3:4). "Ephraim" represents the leading tribe, or even the geo-

graphical name ("Mountains of Ephraim") in parallel
to "Israel" (v 16), as in 5:3, 5; 11:8. Ephraim appears to
have been Hosea's home,[165] where he chiefly made
his public speeches. It is therefore unnecessary to suppose
that here "Ephraim" already means the rump state
that remained after 733;[166] according to the probable
date of this passage, that is hardly possible.[167]

The exclamation "Let him alone!"[168] (הנח־לֹו[169])
might presuppose the presence of a small band of aggressive men loyally gathered around Hosea. Hosea cautions them; he knows that for the time being Israel's
hardheartedness is unyielding.

■ 18   Thus they rush headlong towards their own judgment. Verse 18 poses a number of text critical problems.
In terms of its context, the verse speaks of this incessant move towards destruction. Following Houtsma,[170]
one might read the first two words as the object of v
17b: "Let the drinking bouts be," or even as the subject
of v 18b. But the well-attested Masoretic text deserves
to be interpreted. As a prophetic perfect,[171] סר is understandable in terms of v 17b: "their beer will come to
an end!" The prophet would then point toward the
sobering effect of the approaching judgment. Nevertheless, the perfects in v 18a and b should probably be
interpreted as the same tense. This leaves only van Gelderen's suggestion that the verbs be taken in succession: "when their beer, i.e., their drinking, is past,[172]
then they commit fornication, etc." The absolute infinitives emphasize the passion of their debauchery. The
people want nothing else than that which Hosea has
proclaimed as the transgression of the priests (v 10a).[173]
In spite of the prophet's warning, they love more than
anything "the dishonor of the shameless,"[174] i.e., Israel
will not be separated from the "dishonor of the priests"
(v 7), as Hosea required in v 15; rather, they wish to

162   Cf. Zech 7:14f and F. Hesse, *Das Verstockungsproblem
im Alten Testament*, BZAW 74 (Berlin, 1955), 13.
163   Cf. Mic 7:14; Jer 31:10; Is 40:11.
164   See the commentary on 6:9.
165   See p. 5.
166   Alt, "Die Rolle Samarias bei der Entstehung des
Judentums," *Kleine Schriften* 2, 319, n. 1; differently
interpreted by Alt on page 166, n. 4.
167   See p. 76.
168   Similarly 2 Sam 16:11; 2 Kgs 23:18; Ex 32:10.
169   See textual note "y."
170   See textual note "z."
171   Hitzig, *Die zwölf kleinen Propheten*, KeH (Leipzig,

1881⁴).
172   On the use of סור, cf. Is 28:7; also 1 Sam 1:14; on
סבָא (beverage; beer made from wheat), see *BRL*
110f.
173   On אהב, see p. 35.
174   See textual note "bb."

take part in it. Both the presupposition that vv 4–19 is a unit and the close connection of v 18 with v 15 are helpful in reaching an understanding of v 18bβ.

■ **19** The word רוח, meaning both wind and spirit in Hebrew, also picks up what the prophet has said previously. While Hosea's intention in v 12 was to show the people that the priests' "spirit of whoredom" would only seduce them, now he declares that the power of this רוח has seized them like a whirlwind. צרר (also in 13:12) actually means "to wrap" (e.g., in a garment, Ex 12:34; Prv 30:4). The metaphor "wings of the רוח" adds the notion of being carried off and stormily swept away.[175] Thus in vv 16–19a Hosea presents evidence that the prople have been swept away by the false cult. Here we see the prophet's deep disappointment with his previous attempts to separate the people from the priests. At last Hosea gives the sentence, stated briefly in the closing consecutive clause: "they shall come to shame on their altars."[176] Now everyone must experience that with which the priests had been threatened long before (vv 7, 10a). The transition from a hopeful warning (v 15) to an announcement of judgment (v 19) is comparable to the transition made in 2:4f–6f.[177]

**Aim**

When we survey the deeply moving course of the prophet's struggle against pagan worship, we see that it develops out of a threat directed precisely against the priest of one of the sanctuaries. The threat discloses his basic transgression: the priest in Israel has neglected the particular duties belonging to his office, namely, attention to and teaching of the "knowledge of God." He has buried the treasure of the "instruction of his God" and thus brought about the downfall of God's people. Therefore with his house he will be rejected as priest (v 6).

In the form of a messenger speech the prophet's pointed attack provokes a dispute with his audience which is similar to the legal procedure in the city gate. The subject of the dispute is the priesthood's spirit of whoredom (v 12b) and its ill effects. Three parties in the lawsuit can be distinguished: the prophet (and his circle v 17b?) is the plaintiff; the priesthood comprises the accused false leaders (vv 4–14); the men of the people, lamented (vv 6a, 8, 12a, 13b) and warned (v 15), are those who are misled (vv 13b, 14b).

The prophet's accusation describes how the sacrificial cult (vv 7f, 10, 13a), the practice of oracles (v 12a), and the fertility rites (vv 7, 10, 13f) patterned after Canaanite custom have spread and become a part of Israel's worship as a result of this basic sin of the priesthood. Contrary to God and his word, prostitution is practiced in Israel's worship (v 10b). Thereby spiritual and carnal fornication have become inseparably entangled. The priests are assailed, therefore, not because they are priests, but because they are priests no longer. "That is not prophecy in opposition to the priesthood, but the Hebrew tradition in opposition to clerical opportunism."[178] The word of Yahweh and Baalism are locked in battle. Disregarded by the priests, the traditions of Yahweh are actualized anew by the prophet and thus reveal their guilt. In Hosea we see that "Yahwism" is more aggressive than Baalism, whose syncretism permits the use of Yahweh's name.[179] The reason for this difference lies in Yahweh's word, which calls and activates one people (v 15; cf. 2:18) and specific messengers.

As plaintiff against the priests, Hosea laments over Yahweh's people. He understands the necessity of distinguishing between the chiefly guilty leaders and those whom they mislead (cf. 2:4). It is primarily Israel who is harmed by the accused party. As the people are deprived of God's instructions, so they are exploited by the sacrificial cult (v 8), disoriented by the practice of seeking oracles (vv 11f) and misled on a large scale to unchaste, adulterous activities (vv 13f). In the course of the dispute there is a shift in its intention. The battle against the priests increasingly becomes a struggle with the people. Although the priest was initially addressed and the people were spoken about in the third person (vv 4a–b, 6a–b), Hosea turns his attention more and more to the male members of the people. In vv 13–15 he first of all complains to them, then he excuses their daughters and daughters–in–law, and finally warns them directly. In v 15—if the problems of the text and its transmission are to some extent correctly dealt with—the dramatic climax is reached.

---

175 Cf. 2 Sam 22:11; Ps 18:11 [10]; 104:3.
176 See textual note "dd."
177 See p. 44f.

178 A. Neher, *L'essence*, 296; see the commentary on 4:16.
179 Cf. Östborn, *Yahweh and Baal*, 27; cf. 30f.

A tenor of agitated struggle is to be noted in the sayings down to v 15. The announcement of Yahweh's punishment in vv 5–6, having initiated the words that follow, noticeably yields (except for the addition in v 9) to the accusation, lament, and warning which finally end in an extremely terse description of the consequences (vv 10a, 19b). No other judgment is mentioned than that which the accused prepare for themselves (v 9 offers a precise theological formulation of this). The prophet's struggle avails nothing. As in 2:4ff he disappointedly admits that his accusation and warning fail to achieve the people's return (vv 16–19a). Torn by the spirit of whoredom, they can no longer be won back (vv 11, 17f); this spirit has completely destroyed their will.[180] In the background of the written account of this scene stand the bitter experiences of the prophet. He who does not know the ancient words of Yahweh (v 6) cannot understand the new words he speaks. Only God's new actions, borne out of his strict love, can accomplish a change (2:8f, 16, 21f; 3:1–5). But this is not said here. Rather, our passage records the outcome of this fact: Whoever rejects the knowledge of God and his instructions entrusted to him brings hopeless disaster upon himself and upon those for whom he is responsible. Those who are caught by the spirit of unfaithfulness are destroyed by their own actions (vv 9, 19). Even the most avid idolatry, with its luring practices, cannot stave off hunger, death, and shame (vv 10a, 19).

Several hundred years after Hosea, a comparable attack upon pagan worship and its priests is found in Mal 2:1–9. In the presence of the accused party, a description of the true priesthood is given which is similar to Hosea's conception of it. The true priest gives trustworthy instruction, walks in harmony and uprightness with his God, and turns many from iniquity (v 6). Malachi refers to the divine covenant with these priests as the "covenant with Levi" (vv 4, 8). Malachi's language reveals in this case a Deuteronomic influence.[181] But beyond this (cf. Dtn 33:8–11), in the emphasis upon concern for the Torah, loyalty to Israel's God, and the preaching of repentence, we note an unmistakable kinship with those pre–Deuteronomic circles whose spokesman we meet in Hosea and whom we therefore have characterized as an opposition party of prophets and Levites.[182]

The word of God proclaimed by Hosea was thus discredited and finally rejected by the priests and, following them, by the people. A genuine analogy is to be found in the Gospel of Jesus Christ (cf. Jn 11:47ff; Mk 15:11f). Hosea chap. 4 is a written account of a typical event in history. As such, it should be interpreted from within the context of the history of the Gospel, which applies to people of every period. This chapter records the prophet's struggle against the inroads Baalism made among Yahweh's people and against the false leaders on behalf of those whom they misled. Under divine direction, he contended with the people of God. This passage finds its counterpart in the New Testament in the apostolic battle against the introduction of paganism and false teaching among the followers of Jesus. The New Testament believers' relationship to the Gospel (εὐαγγέλιον) corresponds in every respect to Israel's and her priests' relationship to the "knowledge of God" (דַּעַת אֱלֹהִים) in Hosea. "Do not be mismated with unbelievers . . . What accord has Christ with Belial? . . . What agreement has the temple of God with idols?"[183] It would be salutary for the church to ponder and understand this warning in the light of Hos 4. Is it not an ever–present danger that those in responsible positions of leadership give preference to every kind of activism instead of to the Word entrusted to them? Is not the final proof of guilt against contemporary man that he is "like a stubborn heifer," "completely devoted to shame"? In any case, it was said of Jesus Christ's contemporaries: "they loved darkness rather than the light" (Jn 3:19; cf. Lk 13:34). It is well and good when shame is called shame; and the deception of pride is seen for what it is; when it is plainly recognized that man can live only from "knowledge of God."

180  Cf. 5:4 and Robinson, *Cross*, 41.
181  F. Horst, *Die Zwölf Kleinen Propheten*, HAT I, 14 (Tübingen, 1964³), 268.
182  Wolff, "Heimat," 91 [224]; cf. Neher, *L'essence*, 166–75.
183  2 Cor 6:14ff; cf. Eph 4:14; 1 Jn 2:18ff.

## The Teacher of the Unrepentant

**Bibliography**

K. Budde
"Zu Text und Auslegung des Buches Hosea
(Chap. 5:1–6:6)," *JPOS* 14 (1934): 1–41.

K. Elliger
"Eine verkannte Kunstform bei Hosea," *ZAW* 69
(1957): 151–60.

# 5

**1**
Hear this, O priests!
　Give heed, O house of Israel!
　O court of the king, hearken!
　For you are responsible for justice.
　Indeed, you are a trap for Mizpah,[a]
　　a net spread upon Tabor
**2**
　　a ⟨pit[b] in Shittim⟩[c] that was
　　　dug deep.[d]
　　But I am the ⟨chastiser⟩[e] of all of ⟨you⟩.[f]

**3**
I, I know Ephraim,
　Israel is not hid from me.
　Because you,[g] Ephraim, taught[h] whoredom,
　Israel is defiled.

**a** G (σκοπία = V: *speculatio;* S: דוֹקָא = *observatio* or *observator*) reads מִצְפָּה; T (מַלְפֵּי־כוֹן = teacher) probably reads מְצַפֶּה (cf. Hab 2:1 and van Gelderen). The parallelism ("Tabor") does not support an appellative interpretation.

**b** Although M is supported by σ′ θ′ ε′, G continues the hunting imagery from v 1. Thus we read שַׁחַת with which also the verb fits better. The superfluous ה could have belonged to the following word and thus would be a misreading of ב (Weiser). Driver, *JTS* 33, 40 (Koehler–Baumgartner) interprets שַׁחַט as "lewdness."

**c** M (Buber: "dissolute" "debauchery") is entirely uncertain. The place–name שִׁטִּים (Nu 25:1) is suggested both by the parallelism with v 1bαβ and the word's spelling.

**d** The conjecture תַּעֲמִיקוּ (Robinson), which is intended to fit the context better, is unnecessary if העמיקו is understood as an asyndetic relative clause (cf. 4:14b).

**e** G (παιδευτής = V: *eruditor*) presupposes almost the same consonants (מְיַסֵּר) that occur in M. M ("chastisement"), according to Jer 2:30; 5:3; 7:28; etc., could be a misreading. The suggestion to read מוֹסֵר ("fetter"; Guthe, Weiser) as an antithesis to the foregoing seems to be genuinely prophetic language, its imagery befitting Hosea's diction; but Hosea introduces such imagery with כְּ (cf. 5:13f; 13:8f). The history of the text and the context do not support the derivation of מוסר as a hop'al participle from סור (Ehrlich, *Randglossen zur hebräischen Bibel*, Vol 5 [Leipzig, 1912; Heidesheim, 1968²]; van Gelderen: "I am a God defunct for all of them").

**f** G presupposes לָכֶם. M and G become intelligible if the original were a difficult to read לְכֻלְכָם, which would fit the context with its second person suffix; in M (third person) העמיקו, when it was no longer understood as a relative clause, could have effected the change to the third person.

**g** Should אתה be read instead of עתה (Lippl, Koehler–Baumgartner, *BH³*)?

**h** G (ἐπόρνευσεν) S T read הִזְנָה, which results in a synonymous parallelism. Nyberg (Weiser) attempts to read M as a subordinate clause: "For when you, Ephraim, committed fornication, Israel was defiled," whereby עתה would be a conjunction; how-

**4**  Their deeds do not permit (them)[i]
    to return to their God.
  For a spirit of whoredom is at work
    in their midst,
  so that they do not know Yahweh.

**5**  Israel's pride testifies against him,
  [and Israel][j] and Ephraim
  ⟨stumbles over his guilt⟩.[k]
  [Judah also stumbles with them].[l]

**6**  With their flocks and herds they shall go
    to seek Yahweh.
  But they will not find him.
  He has withdrawn from them.

**7**  With Yahweh they have dealt faithlessly,
    for they have borne bastard sons.
  Now ⟨the locust⟩[m] shall devour their
    fields.

ever, in Hosea עתה usually introduces a conclusion: cf. v 7; 7:2; 4:16; 2:12 (and the commentary).

i  Hebrew usage (cf. Gen 20:6; 31:7; Ex 3:19; 12:23) suggests that *M* is the result of haplography, the original having been יתנום מ" (A. Oettli, *Amos und Hosea. Zwei Zeugen gegen die Anwendung der Evolutionstheorie auf die Religion Israels.* BFChrTh 5, 4 [Gütersloh, 1901], Weiser; Koehler–Baumgartner).

j  A gloss, since the parallelism is meaningless judging from Hosea's diction; cf. v 3; 4:16f.

k  יִכָּשֵׁל בַּעֲוֹנוֹ. The plural forms in *M* result from the addition of וישראל.

l  Like 1:7 and 4:5aβ, a Judaic gloss which picks up the vocabulary of the original verse; עמם agrees with the secondary expansion of v 5bα.

m  *M* ("a new moon shall devour them, their fields") is highly improbable because of its questionable meaning and the verb's double object (or should it be: "with their fields"?). *S* has omitted v 7b. *G* presupposes וְאָת and translates the subject with ἡ ἐρυσίβη, the Greek for הֶחָסִיל according to 1 Kgs 8:37; Ps 78:46; Joel 1:4; 2:25, which in θ' is a translation of הֶעָשׁ in Hos 5:12. F. Dingermann ("Massora–Septuaginta," 30) conjectures that חָרָס = חֶרֶס ("itch"), but in Dtn 28:27 חרס is translated with κνήφη. I read יֹאכַל הֶחָסִיל following *G*. The suggestion to read מַשְׁחִית (Oort, "Hosea"; Robinson, Weiser) is not closer to *M* in spelling; it departs further from *G* in meaning. α' σ' θ' already presuppose חדש.

## Form

A new transmission complex begins with a summons to the leading circles and ends with v 7. A different emphasis and a genuinely new content is not found until v 8, which begins with a summons in the imperative. Yet vv 1–7 are not a uniform speech. The beginning of the passage has the form of a divine speech (vv 1–3). According to the content, the "I" in vv 2b, 3a is not the prophet (cf. 7:12, 15; 10:10; 8:4). Verses 4–7 change from the style of the messenger speech to the forms of a disputation. The messenger speech is given in direct address (cf. 4:4–6, 14aα), but it goes from the plural in vv 1–2 to the singular in v 3b (cf. 4:13f and 15b with v 15a). Throughout vv 4–7 the addressee is in the third plural. Verse 3 is important as the transition—if *M* has preserved the original text—since both those who mislead (v 3bα) and those who are misled (v 3abβ; cf. 4:6, 13f) appear side by side as the addressees.

In spite of the transition from the plural to the singular,

perhaps vv 1–7 should be viewed together, especially because of the essentially introductory character of vv 1–2, with its summons to attention, and the divine, self–introduction in the first person (v 2b). Moreover, the evidence of guilt in vv 1–2 is presented almost parenthetically, veiled in obscure metaphor. Should this not be first disclosed in vv 3ff? On the other hand, it might seem as though vv 1f hold the leading circles accountable for משפט, while vv 3ff speak of the whorelike cult of the entire people.[1] But must these be two different things to Hosea? For him משפט is not only related to the legal procedure in the gate (cf. 10:4), as in Amos (5:7, 15; 6:12), but includes, as the gift of Yahweh (2:21; 6:5), all of Israel's institutions (5:11), in particular her cultic life before God.[2] Only this inclusive sense makes intelligible the three–part address to the priests, "house of Israel,"[3] and the royal court. Like the priests in 4:4–6, these are presented at the outset as those who lead astray. They appear as such also in v 3b, although the

---

1    Weiser.
2    10:4; 12:7; similarly Robinson 22.
3    See pp. 97f.

address is in the singular.

The lack of uniformity in this passage is not to be explained as the secondary composition of originally different sayings. Rather, as in 4:4–19, parts of the prophet's speech, all belonging to the same scene, were written down shortly after it was delivered, with no transitions from one saying to the next and without any indication of interruption by the audience. Thus both the transition from the messenger speech to the disputation and the change in the addressees become understandable. This also explains the unified theme and the absence of formulas marking the transition from one saying to the next. We can assume that there were intermittent replies made by Hosea's audience before vv 3, 4, 5, and 6, since the person of the addressee changes and since there is a certain variation of the theme.

The sequence of the structural elements of this prophetic speech suggests that the traditionists' sketch presents the scene's original order of events. After the introductory address and the self–introduction of the speaker (vv 1a, 2b), the evidence for the accusation—given at first somewhat obscurely (vv 1b–2a)—is presented in vv 3 and 4 (mostly in the perfect). Verses 5 and 6 go on immediately to describe the consequences of their action (mostly in the imperfect). After the guilt is mentioned again (v 7a) the scene concludes with a precisely worded announcement of judgment (v 7b). Instruction in the law is the passage's basic emphasis, sounded by the teacher's three–part introductory "summons to receive instruction" (*Lehreröffnungsformel*).[4] Yahweh thus attests that he is Israel's instructor in the law and the one who disciplines her (v 2b). Accordingly, within the framework of the kerygmatic unit, the lament and accusation recede in relation to the material proof of guilt and the legal consequences. In 4:4–19 Hosea, as plaintiff and accuser in the name of his God, interrupts the still–pending legal process (ריב). But in 5:1–7, he speaks from the outset in the tone of proclamation (three imperatives in v 1a), for the evidence against Israel is immutable.

The poetic structure is again[5] better preserved in the first part of the passage than in the final disputation. The lines in vv 1–5 usually have three stresses. In the introduction (vv 1–2) a colon of three stresses is synthetically (v 1aβ) or antithetically (v 2b) connected with each of the synonymously structured three–stress tricola (1aα; 1b–2a respectively). The evidence for the prophet's accusation is presented in vv 3 and 4 with synonymously (v 3a) or synthetically (v 4) parallel three–stress bicola; v 3b is conspicuous because of its shorter, second part which likewise contains a synthetic parallelism (cf. v 6b). Beginning with the still clear three–stress bicola in v 5abα, the consequences of guilt are proclaimed in lines having an irregular meter, indicative of the animated climax of the entire scene. The corruption suffered by the text during the process of transmission may have increased this irregularity.

**Setting**

Chapter 5:1–7 is to be distinguished from the scene in 4:4–19, as the enlarged circle of addressees indicates. Verse 1 mentions the royal court, together with the priests and other representatives of Israel. Correspondingly, the geographical radius of the accusations is extended. Instead of the cultic places Bethel and Gilgal (4:15), situated close by, which were main points of danger to the population of Ephraim, Hosea names three cities,[6] located much farther away, as places of the leaders' particular sins. Since he refers to the "court," Hosea most likely spoke these words in Samaria.

The time of this scene was probably not long after that of 4:4–19. The key words of the accusation are the same as in 4:4–19: cf. הזנה v 3 with 4:10, 18; cf. רוח זנונים v 4 with 4:12; cf. את־יהוה לא ידעו v 4 with 4:6; cf. כשל v 5 with 4:5; cf. the allusions to sacrifices (v 6) and sex rites (v 7a) with 4:13f; cf. the distinction between those who mislead and the misled (vv 1–3) with 4:6 and 14 (and see pp. 74f and 92f). Yet there is no longer any attempt to separate the people from their leaders. Thus we may presume that the scene in 5:1–7 came shortly after 4:4–19. Nothing prevents dating both transmission complexes in Hosea's early period, during the time of Jehu's dynasty.[7] The judgment announced in v 7b might imply a catastrophe similar to that of 2:11–15 from this same period.

---

4   See below, p. 97.
5   Cf. 4:4–19; see pp. 74f.
6   See the commentary on vv 1b–2a.

7   Deden.

Alt[8] suggested that 5:1–2 presupposed the end of the Syro–Ephraimite war. This he based on the premise that the saying in vv 1–2 was originally independent of vv 3–4 and vv 5–7, and that Mizpah, Tabor, and Shittim were political centers which Tiglath–pileser III annexed in the meantime. Aside from the fact that the latter is difficult to prove and that the separation of vv 3ff from vv 1–2 is improbable[9] as a genuine saying of Hosea, these words appear to be a proclamation growing directly out of these events rather than a later historical interpretation of them. The saying declares Yahweh's word and deed against a still very present situation of guilt. It follows then that, because these towns are mentioned, 5:1f can by no means be dated after the Syro–Ephraimite war (similarly Budde).

### Interpretation

■ **1** The three–part "summons to hear" prepares Hosea's listeners for the solemn words that follow. The ancient singers began their songs with such summons of two parts (Ju 5:3; Gen 4:23); especially the wisdom teachers introduced their sayings with this summons (Prv 7:24; Ps 49:2; Is 28:23; Dtn 32:1[10]). The form was then used to introduce instruction in the law (Prv 4:1; Job 13:6; 33:1, 31; 34:2, 16; Is 49:1; 51:4) and thus also became an introduction to the sayings of the prophets (Is 1:2, 10; 32:9; Mic 1:2; Jer 13:5; Joel 1:2). In addition to the chief themes of the parallel–structured "summons to hear" discussed below, the most important catchword is "justice" (משפט v 1aβ; cf. Is 28:23–26; 32:9–16; Job 34:2–6, 16f; Is 49:1–4; 51:4); cf. "instruction" (תורה Prv 4:2; Is 1:10; 51:4); "to teach" (ירה hip'il Is 28:26); "to judge" (יכח hip'il); and "to contend" (ריב Job 13:6); also cf. "to chastise" (מוסר and יסר pi'el v 2b; cf. Prv 4:1; Is 28:26) and "to know" (ידע [לא] v 4b; cf. Job 33:1–3; 34:2–4; Is 1:2f). L. Koehler[11] called this

form a "summons of two witnesses" (*Zweizeugenruf*). But in view of the history of the form's derivation and the key words connected with it, designating it a "summons to receive instruction" is preferable. Secondarily, it can function as the summons of a witness (e.g., Is 1:2; cf. Dtn 31:28b). When a prophet began his sayings thus, he spoke with the authority of the (court's) law–teacher, though it is not always possible to distinguish between him and the plaintiff. Hosea uses the formula to introduce neither a divine (as in Is 1:2, 10; Jer 13:15) nor prophetic saying (Is 28:23); instead, the expression is part of the divine address itself. Thus he presents his God as Israel's teacher of the law. The formula usually has two parts.[12] The three parts of the formula in 5:1 do not derive, therefore, from a fixed expression.

The three different groups addressed account for this particular three–part form; the prophet allows none to escape his notice. The address to the "house of Israel" (בית ישראל) between the priests and the royal court cannot be an insertion to complete the form, nor can the words simply refer to "the people." Rather, the three stresses per line might have led to the abbreviation of a longer phrase. "(Heads) and rulers of the house of Israel" (קציני בית ישראל [ראשי]) is suggested by Mic 3:1, 9. In view of 1 Sam 11:3; 1 Kgs 21:8; Dtn 19:12, the phrase more appropriate for the Northern Kingdom would be "elders of the house of Israel" (זקני בית ישראל), those clan chieftains responsible for משפט who were occasionally assembled.[13] This would not, however, be the "princes" (שרים),[14] who more probably belong to the "house of the king" (בית המלך 3:4; 7:3, 5; cf. Jer 26:10, 17), nor the "prophets" (נביאים),[15] whom Hosea never singles out among his opponents.[16]

Hosea tells the priests, clan chieftains and the court of their common responsibility: "For you are account-

---

8    A. Alt, "Hosea 5:8–6:6. Ein Krieg und seine Folgen in prophetischer Beleuchtung," *Kleine Schriften* 2, 187, n. 1.

9    See pp. 95f.

10   Cf. the introduction to the instruction of Amenemopet, Chap. 1, (Wilson, *ANET*[2], 421); and the Babylonian "Dialogue about Human Misery," Chap. 25 (Pfeiffer, *ANET*[2], 440).

11   *Deuterojesaja stilkritisch untersucht*, BZAW 37 (Giessen, 1923), 111f.

12   שמעו || הקשיבו Mic 1:2; Is 28:23b; Job 13:6; 33:31; Prv 4:1; 7:24; Is 49:1; שמעו || האזינו Dtn 32:1; Ju 5:3; Is 1:2, 10; 28:23a; 32:9; Jer 13:15; Joel 1:2;

Ps 49:2; Job 34:2; cf. Gen 4:23; הקשיבו || האזינו Is 51:4.

13   Cf. 12:1; 10:15 (cj); 1:4, 6; also Dtn 31:28; cf. Noth, *History*, 108f [104]; F. Horst, "Naturrecht und Altes Testament," *EvTh* 10 (1951–52): 267f; [also in *Gottes Recht, Gesammelte Studien*, ThB 12 (München, 1961), 252f]; for the postexilic period, cf. Joel 1:2 and Wolff, *Joel und Amos*, 28f.

14   Lindblom, Lippl, Robinson.

15   Richter, *Erläuterungen*; Procksch, *BH*[3].

16   Cf. 6:5; 9:7; 12:11, 14; see the commentary on 4:5.

able for justice" (מִשְׁפָּט; cf. Jer 4:12; 39:5). It is clear from the syntactical parallel in Dtn 1:17aγ (cf. Jer 32:7; Ezek 21:32) that this cannot mean: "the (following) sentence of judgment pertains to you."[17] In their own way, each of the three groups of leaders are responsible for מִשְׁפָּט. According to Hosea, the priests' duty is the proclamation of divine law.[18] The clan chieftains are responsible for the local administration of justice in the city gate.[19] The royal court is perhaps the highest court (2 Kgs 15:2), but its particular duty was to defend against the enemies' infringement upon Israel's rights (5:11). In 5:1 Hosea is thinking of the cooperating legal institutions, and, with respect to the מִשְׁפָּט collectively entrusted to them (cf. Job 34:4), of all of Israel's just, salutary regulations of life that Yahweh's law provides.[20]

■ **1, 2** The leaders have not lived up to their responsibility. Instead of furthering a peaceful life in Israel, they have deceitfully trapped the people. With three metaphors drawn from hunting they are reproached as destroyers of Israel's freedom. פַּח is a trap set chiefly for birds.[21] Likewise, רֶשֶׁת is a net which catches birds (7:12), but it is also used for lions (Ezek 19:8). שַׁחַת is a pit for all kinds of game, including the gazelle, fox, and rabbit, as well as the lion (Ezek 19:4); the deeper it is dug, the more certain is its catch.[22]

Israel's leaders have the same effect ("you are"—הֱיִיתֶם) as such traps, nets, and pits: they rob the people of their freedom and life. It does not say who in particular are caught (cf. 9:8). Instead, three towns are mentioned. Mizpah might be the stronghold (*Tell en–Naṣbeh*)

situated on the border opposite the Southern Kingdom, 9 miles north of Jerusalem.[23] F. M. Abel[24] thinks Hos 5:1 refers to Mizpah of Benjamin. That the "trap for Mizpah" was a temple of Astarte built there could not be proved by the American archeological expedition.[25] On the other hand, a large number of Astarte statuettes, of the type belonging to the eighth century, B.C. (Middle Iron Age), have been discovered, which proves that the fertility cults flourished there.[26] The reference might also be to Mizpah in Gilead,[27] but here this would be less likely for Hosea, especially since with Shittim one town east of the Jordan is already mentioned: *Tell el–Hammam* is located on the eastern edge of the highlands opposite Jericho.[28] The reference to Shittim might recall the apostasy of Baal–Peor (Nu 25:1ff) mentioned in 9:10; this apostasy may have been repeated. In any case, Shittim belonged to the Kingdom of Israel at the time of Jeroboam II.[29] Tabor, the mountain peak of *Jebel et–Tor*, is located on the northeastern edge of the Jezreel Valley,[30] where it rises to a height of some 1500 feet. As a place of special cultic transgression, it also could have lured Israel away from her proper worship.[31] But it is uncertain which destruction of "justice" these "preservers of justice" are guilty of at these three locations. The following verses suggest that the transgressions were chiefly of a cultic nature. This would also clarify all three instances of hunting imagery: the leaders allured the people. This choice of imagery may have had its basis in Hosea's bitter experience, related in 4:15–19, of the people's hopeless entrapment by those who mislead them.[32]

17  Nowack, Gressmann, M. Schumpp, *Das Buch der Zwölf Propheten*, Herders Bibelkommentar x/2 (Freiburg, 1950).

18  Cf. 4:6 with 4:1f and see pp. 79f; thereto, see Horst, "Naturrecht," 268 [254]: דַּעַת אֱלֹהִים and דַּעַת מִשְׁפָּט belong together, Jer 9:3, 6; 22:15f; Dtn 33:10.

19  1 Kgs 21:8ff: Ruth 4:2ff.

20  12:7; 6:5; see the commentary on 2:21.

21  Am 3:5; Ps 124:7; Prv 7:23.

22  Cf. Prv 22:14; 23:27; on the various kinds of traps, cf. Dalman, *Arbeit* 6, 322f, 334–40.

23  Cf. A. Alt "Neue Erwägungen über die Lage von Mizpa, Ataroth, Beeroth und Gibeon," *ZDPV* 69 (1953): 1ff; on the problem of the border's location, cf. A. Jepsen, *Die Quellen des Königsbuches* (Halle/ Saale, 1953), 97 and see the commentary on 5:8.

24  *Géographie de la Palestine* 2 (Paris, 1938), 388f.

25  Cf. J. Hemple, "Chronik," *ZAW* 53 (1935): 302;

C. C. McCown–J. C. Wampler, *Tell en–naṣbeh excavated under the direction of the late William Frederic Bade* 1 (Berkeley, 1947), 8.

26  McCown–Wampler, *ibid.*, 245ff.

27  Ju 11:29, *el–Mishrifeh* N. of Gilead; cf. M. Noth, "Lehrkursus 1956," *ZDPV* 73 (1957): 32f, or *Tell Rāmith* N. of Jabbock; cf. N. Glueck, *Explorations in Eastern Palestine* 4, *AASOR* 25–28 (1951): 100ff.

28  Cf. N. Glueck, *ibid.*, 378.

29  M. Noth, "Beiträge zur Geschichte des Ostjordanlandes III: Die Nachbarn der israelitischen Stämme im Ostjordanlande," *ZDPV* 68 (1951): 49f [also in M. Noth, *Aufsätze zur biblischen Landes–und Altertumskunde* 1, ed. H. W. Wolff (Neukirchen, 1971), 474f].

30  Noth, *World*, 20, 28 [16, 23].

31  Cf. Dtn 33:19; Ju 4:6, 12, 14 also presuppose that Tabor was a holy mountain; cf. H. W. Hertzberg,

■ **2** But Israel's leaders are to learn that Yahweh, the Lord of Israel, does not remain silent. He presents himself as the מְיַסֵּר of them all.[33] This word, whose root is also preserved by the Masoretic tradition (מוסר) pictures Yahweh as Israel's teacher, who will make sure that his משפט prevails (6:5). With this self-introduction of Yahweh, the solemn, three-part introductory formula first becomes fully comprehensible. The root יסר belongs to the language of instruction in the family;[34] it especially denotes the father's instruction of his son,[35] but it can also mean chastisement. Hosea uses the word in the latter sense, but not without its basic pedagogical meaning. It appropriately designates one of the typical characteristics of the God whom Hosea proclaims (11:1ff). Yahweh establishes in Israel his righteous rules for living;[36] but his intention for those whom he chastens is life, not death,[37] for the aim of his "chastisement" is new obedience.[38] Thus יסר is a significant theme in Hosea's theology.[39]

■ **3** Without a copula, clauses in the perfect follow in v 3a; the subject is placed first and therefore is emphasized. Verse 3a gives the presupposition for Yahweh's disciplinary actions. Perhaps v 3a was spoken after Hosea's opponents disputed what he had said about the outlying cities. Yahweh is keenly aware of Israel's situation. He is not overcome by the deceptive and alluring means used by her false leaders.[40]

The object of Yahweh's knowledge is stated in v 3b, which at the same time is the reason for his disciplinary action announced here. Verse 3bα again mentions the work of the false leaders, in direct address as in vv 1b, 2a, but in the singular[41] and now without a metaphor: it is Israel's adulterous worship that deceptively ensnares her. As is usually the case, זנה hip'il has a personal object.[42] Verse 3bβ names the outcome of the misleading of the people. טמא nip'al (likewise in 6:10; cf. 9:4 hitpa'el) denotes the cultic guilt incurred by Israel, just as אשם signifies the punishableness of its cultic acts.[43] Hosea's cultic terminology derives from his positive view of the priestly order and his contact with those priests who formed the opposition.[44]

■ **4** The messenger speech, with Yahweh speaking in the first person, does not continue; instead, there is now a prophetic disputation. Verse 4 first emphasizes that the corruption brought into Israel's midst is irreparable. With this the prophet's bitter experience with the people in 4:16ff (from the scene in 4:4–19) becomes the subject of the instruction in the law he presents before Israel's leaders. Now the theme is Israel's incorrigibility. For Hosea it is no longer humanly possible for Israel to "return" from her idols to God.[45] "Their deeds" have destroyed this possibility. Total apostasy takes away freedom. נתן means "to allow, permit," also in Gen 20:6; Ezek 4:15; on this theme, cf. 7:2. The narcotic of deception produced by the cult destroys their powers of orientation.[46] In Hosea מעללים denotes only the evil deeds of Israel (7:2; 9:15; cf. 12:3; 4:9).

Verse 4b explains why Israel's deeds prevent her conversion: "a spirit of whoredom" prevails "in their midst" (בקרבם). This does not mean "it possesses them,"[47] but "it prevails *in their midst*," as surely as Israel's leaders are at work within her. In this verse קֶרֶב

---

"Die Melkisedeq-Traditionen," *JPOS* 8 (1928): 174–76; O. Eissfeldt, "Der Gott des Tabor und seine Verbreitung," *ARW* 31 (1934): 14–41, lists Greek evidence of a Baal Tabor (Ζεὺς Ἰταβύριος, Sanchunjaton in Philo Byblius, *FHG* 3, fr. 2, 7, 566); also F. M. Abel, *Géographie de la Palestine* 1 (Paris, 1933), 353ff and J. Boehmer, "Der Name Tabor" *ZS* 7 (1929): 161–69.

32  See pp. 90f.
33  See textual note "f."
34  Dtn 8:5; 21:18; Prv 4:1; 19:18.
35  Prv 31:1; Dtn 8:5; cf. 4:36.
36  Is 28:26; Jer 10:24; 30:11; 46:28.
37  Jer 30:11; Ps 118:18.
38  Dtn 4:36; 8:5f; 21:18; Prv 4:1f; 19:18.
39  Cf. 7:12, 15; 10:10; on this topic, cf. 2:8f, 16f; 3:4f and J. A. Sanders, "Suffering as Divine Discipline in the Old Testament and Post-Biblical Judaism,"

*Colgate Rochester Divinity School Bulletin* 28 (1955): 7f; 41f; 117.
40  On the juxtaposition of Ephraim–Israel, see p. 91.
41  Is the person who interrupted Hosea meant here? Cf. 4:4–6 for address to an individual.
42  Differently in 4:10, 18; see p. 82.
43  See the commentary on 4:15.
44  See p. 79.
45  See the commentary on 2:9 and 3:5.
46  Cf. 4:11f. and the commentary.
47  Nötscher.

is not the inner self of the individual,[48] but the "midst" of the people.[49] As the leaders were previously characterized as misleaders (vv 1b, 2a, 3b), so the spirit of whoredom, in the external form of Israel's leader, reigns in her midst like a deceptive foreign power.[50] The phrase "spirit of whoredom" (רוח זנונים) pictures them in their irresistible and indomitable activities. The outcome is that Israel "does not *know* Yahweh." Why does Hosea not say "love"? Would not אהב contrast better with זנה ("to fornicate") than with ידע ("to know")? He reserves אהב with a human subject for Israel's love for the cult of Baal.[51] ידע, however, characterizes that relation to Yahweh which the priests' proper services are supposed to provide (4:1, 6; 6:6). The priests' spirit of whoredom, which dominates the elders and the royal court in apparently the same manner, has destroyed Israel's knowledge of God, of his saving deeds (11:3; 2:20) and of his instructions (4:1), thereby destroying Israel's saving contact with Yahweh. The correction and reproof of Israel's leadership—previously described simply with the metaphor of the hunter's trap (vv 1b, 2a) or only indirectly by the catchwords "whoredom" and "defilement" (v 3)—has reached a decisive point: Israel's false leaders have finally separated her from her God; as a result her return to him (whom she no longer knows) is impossible because of her current way of life.

■ **5** Speaking as a witness for Israel's Chastiser, the prophet further explains the legal situation. Perhaps contemptuous words interrupted the prophet as he spoke, in turn provoking a new saying about "Israel's pride" (cf. also 7:10). The expression "testify against" (ענה ב) is reminiscent of such a rejoinder; it denotes a witness's incriminating statement against an accused person.[52] The defense incriminates itself (בפניו). The pride of Israel

and of her dignitaries is conclusive proof for the truth proclaimed: pride is the evidence of the audience's inability to repent.

Verse 5b brings the theme of v 4a to completion. Israel's deeds no longer permit her return to Yahweh; what is more, they become her own self–condemnation: "they stumble over their guilt," as one stumbles over a trap.[53] A wicked deed requires no recompense as punishment; the deed contains the seeds of its own punishment: to reject God is to reject life under his salvation (cf. Ezek 4:17). In v 5bβ the Judaic gloss is a reminder of the fact that what was once valid for Israel also applies to God's people of later generations in Judah (the same is true of 4:5, 15).

■ **6** Perhaps an arrogant interruption (see above on v 5a) of Hosea's speech made reference to the numerous sacrificial animals the people bring to sanctuaries when they "seek Yahweh" (cf. 1 Sam 15:14, 21). But Hosea reckons animal sacrifice as part of Israel's guilt (4:8, 13). In the "Baalized" sacrificial cult, "the offering is changed from being a sign of the extreme self–devotion and becomes a ransom from all true self–devotion."[54] Though they seek Yahweh, they do not find him.[55] Perhaps the expression "seeking and (not) finding" is reminiscent of specific motifs from the Baal myth of the absent divinity,[56] for Hosea elsewhere makes polemical use of the language of Canaanite rituals.[57] In the Old Testament, in any case, the phrase "seek and find God" did not originate with Jeremiah (5:1; 29:13) and Deuteronomy (4:29),[58] but with Hosea (2:9; 5:6; cf. Am 8:12b). One feigned love for "Yahweh" in the whorelike cult (cf. 2:18f and 4:15b); yet Yahweh does not let himself be found in the gatherings of the cult, but only in his own freedom. "He has withdrawn from them." As a rule, חלץ otherwise (transitive) denotes the removal of cloth-

---

48  Hosea expressed this with לֵב; see the commentary on 4:11.

49  As in Gen 24:3; Nu 5:27; 1 Sam 16:13.

50  Cf. "to lead astray" (התעה) 4:12b and the commentary.

51  4:18; 9:1; 8:9; 2:7, 9, 12, 14f; 3:1 and p. 60.

52  Ex 20:16; Nu 35:30; 1 Sam 12:3; 2 Sam 1:16; Job 32:12; cf. L. Delekat, "Zum hebräischen Wörterbuch," *VT* 14 (1964): 39f.

53  Cf. 4:5; 14:2, 10; further, 4:9; 12:3, 15 and the commentary; on the metaphor, cf. Prv 29:5f.

54  M. Buber, *The Prophetic Faith*, 119.

55  On the other hand, cf. 3:5 and the commentary.

56  Cf. *CTCA* 6.4.44 (Gordon 49.4.44) [bqt!]; Gordon, *Literature*, 46; on the cult of Ishtar: Speiser, *ANET*[2], 106–9; on the cult of Osiris: H. Bonnet, *Reallexikon der ägyptischen Religionsgeschichte* (Berlin, 1952), 569 and H. Gressmann, "Tod und Auferstehung des Osiris," *AO* 23, 3 (1923): 3ff.

57  On 2:4–17, see pp. 33f; cf. H. G. May, "The Fertility Cult in Hosea," *AJSL* 48 (1932): 77.

58  Thus Fohrer, "Zum Text von Jes. 41:8–13," *VT* 5 (1955): 244.

ing (Dtn 25:9f; Is 20:2); only here (intransitive) does "removal" mean the withdrawal of a person. But this statement, especially since it has to do with Yahweh, is genuinely Hosean (cf. 5:15a). With these words, the witness for Israel's "Chastiser" (v 2b) designates the first of Yahweh's disciplinary measures (cf. v 15; 2:9f, 16f), whose consequences are described in v 7b. Yahweh cannot be found because the people have *de facto* alienated themselves from him (v 4). Thus they stumble over their guilt (v 5b). If Israel will not avoid the pagan sanctuaries (4:15), then Yahweh withdraws his presence from them.

■ **7** The new expressions in v 7a elucidate the guilt of Israel's apostasy. The instructive intention of the prophet's words can be seen in the proof of guilt (cf. vv 3b–5) repeated here. בגד ב denotes Israel's covenant–breaking, faithless dealings (also in 6:7), like "to forsake" (עזב) in 4:10. This consists in the "begetting of bastard children." Here the sex rites are again called by name, for the "bastard sons" (בנים זרים) are the children conceived through "sexual relations with strangers" in the foreign cult.[59] The word זר conveys a vivid emotional feeling; it denotes not only the foreigner as such (7:9; 8:7; Is 61:5), but what is alien in a general sense in contrast to Israel's intimate relationship with her God (8:12; Is 1:4; Joel 4:17). In Hosea, an ethico–cultic emphasis is stronger than an ethno–political.[60] "Bastard sons" (בנים זרים) and "children of whoredom" (ילדי זנונים) are apparently synonymous for "children who owe their existence to the pagan cult."[61] If v 2a refers to Shittim, then it is evident at least for this city (in view of 9:10 and Nu 25:1ff) that from the outset of this scene, Hosea charges Israel's leaders with false leadership, especially with respect to the sex rituals (cf. הזנית in v 3b; רוח זנונים in v 4b).

In conclusion, v 7b announces Yahweh's punitive measures against this activity as a whole. Verse 7b, which was not translated by *S*, is one of the most obscure in the entire book. If the Masoretic Text be considered original, it is conceivable that there was an ancient connection between the new moon festival and rites of the sex cult, though it is no longer recognizable;[62] it perhaps suggests that children were sacrificed at the time of the new moon,[63] so that the illegitimate children, in accordance with the will of Yahweh, must die at the new moon festival.[64] Yet the impression this saying gives is that of a terrifying threat rather than an allusion to an established custom. The latter might be the case, if it were possible to view this as announcing the death of the "legitimate children"[65] as punishment for the fathering of bastard children. But this meaning of חלק is neither to be found nor to be expected; it always refers to a portion of one's possession, usually a cultivated field. Moreover, the suffix in יאכלם ("devours *them*"), occurring next to the accusative object את־חלקיהם, lends difficulty to Nyberg's hypothesis.[66] Finally, the translation "The new moon shall devour them with their legitimate children" is hardly possible, particularly in this context, since Yahweh as "Chastiser" does not threaten Israel with death. If חדש were an unequivocal designation for the New Year Festival, the interpretation of the verse would be simplified. Then, on the day when new fertility was declared, the prophet would have announced the beginning of great economic distress.[67] Since this interpretation remains vague—especially because Caquot[68] has to interpret חדש as an accusative of time ("He [Yahweh] shall devour their fields on New Year's Day")—the text in *G* should probably be considered as the original. It announces a plague of locusts,[69] a catastrophe comparable to that spoken

59  Cf. 4:13f; Is 2:6b; Jer 2:25; and pp. 86ff.

60  Cf. L. A. Snijders, "The Meaning of זר in the O.T.," *OTS* 10 (1954): 1–154; also P. Humbert, "La femme étrangère du livre des Proverbs," *RES* (1937): 49–64; *idem*, "Les adj. zar et nokri," *Mélanges Syriens* 1 (1939): 275ff, which takes issue with G. Boström (see pp. 13f).

61  See p. 15.

62  Thus G. Boström, *Proverbiastudien*, 124, with reference to Jer 2:24, though his interpretation is hardly convincing.

63  Cf. 2:13; 13:2 and O. Eissfeldt, *Molk als Opferbegriff im Punischen und Hebräischen* (Halle, 1935).

64  Cf. also Rost, "Erwägungen," 456f.

65  This is Nyberg's interpretation of חלקיהם.

66  He interprets the suffix as dative: "the new moon consumed . . . of them."

67  Cf. A. Caquot, "Remarques sur la fete de la néoménie dans l'ancien Israel," *RHR* 158 (1961): 1–18; Jacob, "L'Heritage," 257.

68  "Remarques," 16.

69  See textual note "m."

of in 2:11–15. In spite of the obscurity, it is clear that the prophet announces the chastening work of Yahweh in the form of a terror–filled event in which Israel will learn that Yahweh, the God of salvation and life, is not to be found in the rituals of the Baal cult (v 6).

### Aim

This passage does not state the goal of Yahweh's chastisement (but cf. 2:9; 3:5); its essential point is rather the basis and necessity for it, while the disciplinary measures themselves are hardly mentioned. Through his prophet, the God of Israel confronts the nation's leaders as the "teacher" ($\pi\alpha\iota\delta\epsilon\upsilon\tau\dot{\eta}\varsigma$ v 2 G) who holds them responsible for their incorrigible apostasy (vv 1–3). In the style of solemn instruction in the law, they are taught that Yahweh knows their deeds prevent them from returning to him. Precipitated perhaps by the final experiences of the preceding scene (4:1ff), this is the central theme of our passage. The practices of the pagan cult (vv 4–7a) are not a wickedness from which Israel by herself might be able to turn, for they have robbed her of the intention to genuinely repent: Israel knows Yahweh no longer (v 4b); he has withdrawn himself from her (v 6b). Thus she falls prey to her own guilt. *Conversio* and *renovatio*—insofar as the guilt is rooted in the "spirit of whoredom" of a false love—is no longer humanly possible. He who disciplines Israel makes this unavoidably clear.[70] It has become senseless to appeal to her goodwill (2:4f; 4:15). Yet Israel's God does not leave his faithless and incorrigible people to their own devices but rather addresses them through his prophet. However, he does not call upon them to improve themselves; instead, with the solemn instruction in the law concerning their guilt, he above all states the consequences of their wickedness (vv 5–7), which, in spite of all their cultic activities, mean disaster.

The background of these severe consequences is merely alluded to in this attestation of Yahweh's new manner of dealing with Israel: he withdraws both himself and his salvation (vv 6b, 7b). That this action could achieve Israel's return to him is not mentioned here, but in 3:3ff (2:8f). In this scene the accent lies upon God's disclosure of his faithless people's entanglement in a web of guilt and the consequences they must face. God's people must recognize that they cannot dissociate themselves from the history of their guilt; that without God's chastening actions they would remain hopelessly given up to the ruin of their false leaders (Heb 12:4–11). It is first stated in the Gospel of Jesus Christ (Jn 16:16ff) that God saves his unteachable people by withdrawing himself from them.

But one can also be misled away from the Gospel. Whoever is sent to a people that have become deaf to the Good News about Jesus Christ should meditate on Hos 5:1–7; he should let Hosea show him the first addressees of this passage and be cured from a false zeal to convert others. He should announce the new deed of God coupled with a sober analysis of human behavior and its consequences.

---

70   Cf. Jer 13:23; Jn 8:34; Rom 6:6; Heb 6:4–6.

**Return in the Midst of Collapse?**

**Bibliography**

A. Alt

"Hosea 5:8–6:6. Ein Krieg und seine Folgen in prophetischer Beleuchtung, *Kleine Schriften* 2, 163–87.

R. Bach

*Die Aufforderungen zur Flucht und zum Kampf im alt. Prophetenspruch*, WMANT 9 (Neukirchen, 1962), 59ff.

W. W. Baudissin

*Adonis und Ešmun* (Leipzig, 1911), 403–16.

W. Baumgartner

"Der Auferstehungsglaube im Alten Orient," *ZMR* 48 (1933): 193–214 [also in his *Zum AT und seiner Umwelt* (Leiden, 1959), 124–46].

K. Budde

"Hosea 7:12," *ZA* 26 (1912): 30–2. *Idem*, "Zu Text und Auslegung des Buches Hosea (6:7– 7:2)," *JBL* 53 (1934): 118–33.

G. R. Driver

"Hosea 6:5," *VT* 1 (1951): 246.

Th. H. Gaster

"Zu Hosea 7:3–6, 8–9," *VT* 4 (1954): 78f.

P. Humbert

"Der Deltafürst So' in Hosea 5:11," *OLZ* 21 (1918): 224–26.

F. König

"Die Auferstehungshoffnung bei Osee 6:1–3," *ZThK* 70 (1948): 94–100.

F. Nötscher

"Zur Auferstehung nach drei Tagen," *Biblica* 35 (1954): 313–19.

P. Ruben

"Hos 7:1–7," *AJSL* 52 (1936): 34–40.

H. Schmidt

"Hosea 6:1–6," *Sellin Festschrift*, ed. A. Jirku (Leipzig, 1927), 111–26.

S. Spiegel

"A Prophetic Attestation of the Decalogue: Hosea 6:5 with Some Observations on Psalms 15 and 24," *HThR* 27 (1934): 105–44.

J. J. Stamm

"Eine Erwägung zu Hosea 6:1–2," *ZAW* 57 (1939): 266–68.

N. H. Torczyner

"Gilead, a City of Them that Work Iniquity," *BJPES* 11 (1944): 9–16.

I. Zolli

"Hosea 6:5," *ZAW* 57 (1939): 288. *Idem*, "Note on Hosea 6:5," *JQR* 31 (1940–41): 79–82.

See the Bibliography for 5:1–7.

8  Blow the horn in Gibeah,
    the trumpet in Ramah!
  Sound the alarm in Beth–aven,
    ⟨terrify⟩[a] Benjamin!
9  Ephraim shall be laid waste
    on the day of chastisement.
  Among the tribes of Israel
    I proclaim what is sure.

10  The rulers of Judah act
    as men who displace[b] landmarks.
  Upon them I will pour out
    my wrath like water.

11  Ephraim is oppressed,[c]
    justice is crushed
  For he persisted,
    in following[d] what is worthless.[e]
12  But I am like pus[f] to Ephraim,
    like rottenness to the house of Judah.
13  When Ephraim saw his sickness
    and Judah his sores,
  then Ephraim went to Assyria
    and sent to the great king.[g]
  Yet he, he has no power to cure you
    or heal you of your sores.
14  For I am like a lion to Ephraim,
    like a young lion to the house
    of Judah.
    I, even I, will rend and go away,
    I will carry off, so that none
    shall rescue.

a  *G* (ἐξέστη) suggests a form of the verb חרד (Dingermann, "Massora–Septuaginta," 31: הֶחֱרַד); the parallelism suggests an imperfect, וַהֲרִידוּ (Wellhausen; Alt, "Hos 5:8–6:6"; Koehler–Baumgartner). Like α′ σ′ θ′ (ὀπίσω σου) *M* probably intends to give the message of alarm: "(They are coming) behind you, Benjamin!" (M. Buber, *Bücher der Kündigung* [Köln, 1958]); "Danger is close upon you" (C. von Orelli, *Die zwölf kleinen Propheten*, Strack–Zöcklers kurzgefasstes Kommentar zu den heiligen Schriften A. u. N.T. [München, 1908³]); or perhaps *M* characterizes those addressed as "Your followers, O Benjamin"; cf. Ju 5:14; 6:34f and Bach, *Die Aufforderungen*, 59, n. 4.

b  On סום hip'il cf. Gesenius–Kautzsch § 72ee; Grether § 45w.

c  *G* makes the verbs active (κατεδυνάστευσεν ... κατεπάτησε; cf. Am 4:1) and to the first verb adds an accusative object τὸν ἀντίδικον which forms a parallel with משפט (κρίμα): "Ephraim oppresses his opponent and treads justice under foot."

d  On the asyndesis הואיל הלך, cf. 9:9; Dtn 1:5; Zeph 3:7; 1 Sam 2:3 and Brockelmann, *Syntax* § 133b.

e  *G* (τῶν ματαίων; similarly *S T*) suggests that צַו, a synonym of שָׁוְא, is a coarse epithet which is a "sound–imitation mocking the manner of prophetic speech" (Koehler–Baumgartner); cf. Is 28:10, 13. Since the time of Duhm צָרוֹ was often the conjectured reading. Humbert, "So," thinks that שֶׁוְא, which *G* presupposes, is the Egyptian סוא ("So" 2 Kgs 17:4) = Sib'u; cf. R. Kittel, *Geschichte des Volkes Israel* 2 (Gotha, 1925⁷), 365; but according to Alt, "Hos 5:8–6:6," 174, and Bauernfeind, *TDNT* 4, 566f, this is improbable. Also cf. H. Goedicke, "The End of 'So, King of Egypt,' " *BASOR* 171 (1963): 64–66, and W. F. Albright, "The Elimination of King 'So,' " *BASOR* 171 (1963): 66.

f  According to G. R. Driver, "Difficult Words in the Hebrew Prophets," *Studies in Old Testament Prophecy*, ed. H. H. Rowley (Edinburgh, 1950), 66f and Koehler–Baumgartner, this word is probably II עָשׁ, which means "pus," "putrefaction"; cf. עָשָׁשׁ in Ps 31:11, translated in σ′ by εὐρώς; more importantly, the imagery in v 13 makes the above suggestion convincing in comparison to the customary translation "moth"; see the commentary on 5:12.

g  Perhaps יָרֵב became understood as a secret name for the Assyrian king (Koehler–Baumgartner; *G* has Ιαριμ or ιαρειβ) after the letters of the original expression מַלְכִּי רָב were incorrectly separated. The expression מלך רב (thus *Sefire* I, B, 7 = Donner–Röllig, *KAI* 1, 42) corresponds to the Akk. šarru(m) rabû(m); the close grammatical connection of the two words is expressed by the *yôd–compaginis*, without there being a construct chain; see textual note "n" to 10:6. The readings in α′ θ′ are attested by Jerome with the word *iudicem*; σ′ translates φονέα; according to Syh, θ′ reads κρίσεως; Buber suggests "quarrelsome person."

**15**    I will withdraw^h to my place,
       until they ⟨are desolated⟩^i and seek
       my face.
       When they are in distress,
       they shall ask for me.^j

# 6

**6:1**   "Come, let us return to Yahweh,
       for he has torn and he will heal us;
         ^ahe has stricken, and he will bind us up,
         2/ will preserve our life.^b
       After two days, on the third day
       he will raise us up, that we may
       live in his presence.
**3**    Let us know,^c yes, let us strive,
       to know Yahweh.
       As the dawn (breaks, so) certain is
       his going forth.^d
       He comes to us as surely as the rain,
       as the spring rain
       that ⟨refreshes⟩^e the land."

**4**    What shall I do to you, O Ephraim?
       What shall I do to you, O Judah?
       Your loyalty is like morning mist,
       like dew that vanishes early.
**5**    Therefore I strike by prophets,^f
       slay them by words of my mouth.
       ⟨My⟩^g justice then breaks forth ⟨like⟩^g
       light.
**6**    For I desire loyalty, not sacrifice;
       the knowledge of God instead of burnt
       offerings.
**7**    But they, they transgressed the covenant
       ⟨in⟩^h Adam,
       there they became unfaithful to me.

h   As in 2:9; 6:1, *G* presupposes וְאָשׁוּבָה, but in *M* we may see Hosea's occasional tendency to use asyndesis (see textual notes "d" to 5:11, "b" to 6:2, and "c" to 6:3).

i   *G* (ἀφανισθῶσιν) presupposes יֵשַׁמּוּ (Wellhausen) or יִשְׁמוּ (Procksch, Fohrer) as in 10:2 and 14:1. On the basis of the homonymy, J. Koenig sees an intentional interpretation of the original word יאשמו in *G* ("L'activité hermeneutique des scribes dans la transmission du texte de l'AT," *RHR* 162 (1962): 18ff). α' σ' θ' give a theological interpretation by translating "to do penance"; however, in Hosea אשם means "to become punishable"; see the commentary on 4:15; cf. 13:1. Or does אשם in v 15 have the nuance of "to be punished" (cf. 10:2; 14:1)?

j   *G* joins 15b with 6:1 and inserts λέγοντες = לֵאמֹר; see the commentary on 5:15.

a   The copula in וְיַךְ must have been omitted early in the text's transmission (before *G*), but it is required by the *parallelismus membrorum* (Wellhausen).

b   יְחַיֵּנוּ is the third stress of v 1b and therefore belongs to v 1 (Stamm, "Hosea 6:1–2"); on the history of the word's interpretation, cf. *G* (ὑγιάσει) and α' σ' (ἀναζωώσει).

c   One might consider וְנֵדְעָה a supplementary gloss added to create a line of three stresses (Fohrer "Umkehr und Erlösung beim Propheten Hosea," *ThZ* 11 [1955]); but for what reason would it have been added?

d   ε' and the content of 5:15a support *M*, which is less likely to be secondary than *G* (εὑρήσομεν αὐτόν), whose text is best explained as a misreading of נִמְצָאֶנּוּ. It is possible that the sentence is an asyndetic relative clause connected with יהוה: "his going forth is as sure as the dawn."

e   Although "early rain" (יוֹרֶה) in *M* would fit with "spring rain" (מלקוש), it is a misreading of the original יַרְוֶה (F. Perles, *Analecten zur Textkritik des Alten Testaments* [München, 1895], 90; Koehler–Baumgartner).

f   Since v 5a has no accusative object in *M*, *G* (διὰ τοῦτο ἀπεθέρισα τοὺς προφήτας ὑμῶν) adds one unnecessarily (cf. Is 65:1; Ps 35:5f; thus according to G. R. Driver, "Hebrew Notes," *VT* 1 [1951]: 246), and destroys the *parallelismus membrorum*. In Ugaritic the word *ḥṣb* occurs several times in the sense of "to fight" (|| *mḫṣ*): *CTCA* 3.2.6f, 19f, 23f, 29f; 7I.4, 6 (Gordon 'nt 2.6f, 19f, 23f, 29f; 131.4, 6).

g   Who would be addressed by the reading in *M* ("and your justices are light that breaks forth")? In *G S T* the original text can be recognized (וּמשׁפָּטִי כָאוֹר); the words were merely separated incorrectly.

h   The interpretation of בְּאָדָם as a place-name is made necessary by the following word שָׁם; even if שָׁם were to be interpreted as temporal in meaning (Nyberg), *M* "as Adam" (= "as the inhabitants from Adam"? thus Nielsen, *Shechem*, 290) or "as a man" is unsatisfactory.

| | |
|---|---|
| **8** | Gilead is a city of evildoers,<br>〈whose footprints〉[i] are bloody. |
| **9** | As a robber 〈lies in ambush〉[j]<br>so does the band of priests.<br>On their way to Shechem they commit<br>murder;<br>indeed, they act shamefully. |
| **10** | In the house of Israel[k] I saw<br>a horrible thing.<br>[There Ephraim played the whore,[l]<br>Israel is defiled.][m] |
| **11** | [For you also, O Judah, a harvest<br>is appointed.][n]<br><br>Whenever I restored the fortunes of my<br>people,[o] |

# 7

| | |
|---|---|
| **7:1** | Whenever I healed Israel,<br>the transgression of Ephraim was revealed<br>and the 〈wickedness〉[a] of Samaria.<br>For they deal falsely:<br>The thief breaks in,[b]<br>and the robbers raid without. |
| **2** | But they do not consider,[c]<br>that[d] I remember all their wickedness.<br>Now their deeds encircle them,<br>they occur before my face. |
| **3** | By their wickedness they make a king glad,[e]<br>by their lies the officials. |

i   *M* "tracked with blood" is grammatically uncertain; I vocalize *M* עֲקֻבֵּיהָם דָם with Sellin; (Koehler–Baumgartner).

j   The text's transmission is quite uncertain: *G S* read forms of כַּח, with different suffixes; σ′ *V* have the plural of חַךְ; *M* (infinitive construction? Gesenius–Kautzsch § 75aa) and *T* have חכה pi'el; in *G*ᵐˢˢ *S* (cf. Ziegler, *Duodecim prophetae*) a כְּ is prefixed to the next word. כַּח and חַךְ could easily be corrupted forms of חכה. The converse is less probable. Originally, the text may have read וּמְחַכֵּה כְּאִישׁ, which fits the sense of the remainder of the verse.

k   בְּבֵית־אֵל (Marti) is often conjectured because of the place-names "Adam" (v 7), "Gilead" (v 8), and "Shechem" (v 9) and because it precedes the word שָׁם (v 10b). "Israel" is therefore thought to be a premature generalization of "Bethel," as in 10:15 *G* and Am 5:6 *G*.

l   G. Richter (*Erläuterungen*) reads זְנִיתָ אפרים. But the glossator could have used the noun, which frequently occurs beginning with Jeremiah, though it is not found in Hosea (see textual note "o" to 4:10 and "p" to 4:11).

m   A gloss from 5:3 (cf. textual note "r" to 7:10), whose style is foreign to Hosea (cf. textual note "b" to 6:10); it is connected by שָׁם, in conformity with 6:7b.

n   A gloss, perhaps added in two stages; the brief addition "also Judah" (cf. 4:15) which is part of v 10 in *G*, appears to have undergone a later expansion. The Judaic glossator often introduces his additions with גם (cf. 4:5; 5:5).

o   *G* takes v 11b and the first two words of 7:1 as part of 6:11a.

a   Instead of "wickednesses," *G* presupposes רָעַת, which is more probable between עָוֺן and שֶׁקֶר; also cf. 7:3a.

b   *G* inserts πρὸς αὐτόν, prompting Oettli's conjecture that בַּיִת or בַּיְתָה has been lost; cf. Ezek 7:15a and F. Horst, "Der Diebstahl im Alten Testament," in *Gottes Recht*, ThB 12 (München, 1961), 168, n. 6. The transition from imperfect to perfect suggests that the text is corrupt, but an explanation is hardly possible.

c   Literally: "They do not speak to their heart." *G* ὅπως συνᾴδωσιν ὡς συνᾴδοντες τῇ καρδίᾳ αὐτῶν perhaps reads יֹאמְרוּ instead of יאמרו; however, *M* is supported by α′.

d   Brockelmann, *Syntax* § 144 thinks it possible that here "as often as" (כ) is constructed with a dependent genitive clause (cf. 1 Sam 2:13; Ps 74:3). Then it would have to be translated: "They do not regain their senses, though again and again I recall their wickedness." But the verse's connection with 6:11b–7:1a rules out this interpretation.

e   Since the time of Wellhausen, יִמְשְׁחוּ מְלָכִים is often read, though the text's transmission and the context do not support the conjecture.

**4**  They all commit adultery,[f]
⟨they⟩[g] are like an oven
that burns without a baker;
he ceases to stir the fire,
from the kneading of the dough,
until it is leavened.

**5**  The rulers ⟨begin⟩[h] the day of ⟨their⟩[i] king
by ⟨becoming inflamed⟩[j] from wine,
whose power enchants[k] the mockers.[l]

**6**  For they are ⟨kindled⟩[m] like an oven,
their heart ⟨burns within them⟩.[n]
All night their ⟨passion⟩[o] slumbers,
in the morning it blazes up like a
burning flame.

**7**  All of them are hot as an oven,
they devour their judges.
All their kings fall.
None of them calls upon me.

**8**  Among the nations
Ephraim mixes himself.
Ephraim is a cake
that remains unturned.[p]

**9**  Foreigners devour his strength,
but he himself is unaware.
Even gray hairs have stolen upon[q] him,
but he himself is unaware.

**10**  [Israel's pride witnesses against him][r]
And they do not return to Yahweh their
God,
nor seek him [for all this].[s]

**11**  ⟨ ⟩[t] Ephraim is like a dove,
easily deceived, without sense.
Upon Egypt they call,
to Assyria they go.

**12**  As they go,
I will throw my net over them.
Like birds of the air I will bring them down.
I will chastise[u] them according to
the report of their ⟨wickedness⟩.[v]

---

f   Sellin reads אֹנְפִים, harmonizing it with v 6 (*S T*; see textual note "o" on 7:6); but this destroys a specific emphasis provided by its connection with vv 3 and 5.

g   תנור is a masculine noun; therefore the ה in בערה is superfluous, having originally been הם, whose ם may have been omitted by haplography. *G* has "translated word for word, without giving much attention to the context;" it reads תנור בֹּעֵר לְמַאֲפֶה שָׁבַת מֵעִיר (F. Dingermann, "Massora–Septuaginta," 37).

h   Instead of "they make sick," *G S V* and *M*[mss] vocalize הֶחֱלוּ.

i   Instead of "our king" (*M*), *T* and the context make it necessary to read מַלְכָּם; in *G* a corruption within the Greek text's transmission resulted in changing ἡμῶν to ὑμῶν (cf. Ziegler, *Duodecim prophetae*, and J. W. Wevers, "Septuaginta–Forschungen," *ThR* 22 (1954), 106.

j   In accordance with *G*, an infinitive construction (חֲמֹת, Gaster, "Zu Hosea 7:3–6, 8–9," 78f) rather than the noun ("commotion") would be expected between החלו and מן.

k   Literally "draws"; cf. 11:4 and Ugaritic *mšk* = "to grasp tightly."

l   On ליץ po'lel cf. H. N. Richardson, "Some Notes on ליץ and its Derivates," *VT* 5 (1955): 166f.

m   *G* presupposes קָדְחוּ (Nowack) whose consonants are more similar to *M* than יָקַד, as suggested by Nyberg.

n   *M* ("in their ambush") could have arisen from בֹּעֵר בָּם, which is suggested by the *parallelismus membrorum* 6aα ‖ β.

o   *S T* and the following verse require אֹפֶהֶם; *M* ("their baker") vocalizes the word in accordance with v 4; *G* reads אֶפְרַיִם.

p   בְּלִי is a negation also in 2 Sam 1:21; Job 8:11; cf. Brockelmann, *Syntax* § 125b.

q   Thus J. Blau, "Etymologische Untersuchungen auf Grund des palaestinischen Arabisch," *VT* 5 (1955): 341, following the suggestion made in Gesenius–Buhl on the basis of the frequent occurrence of the vulgar Arabic *zrq* = "secretly steal upon"; this interpretation is more convincing in this context than G. R. Driver's suggestion that the word derives from II זרק = "become light" (cf. Koehler–Baumgartner).

r   A gloss taken word for word from 5:5a; see textual note "m" to 6:10.

s   This expression is not found in *S* and, since it hardly fits with the verse's poetry, it should be considered secondary; the formula is found in closing summary statements of prose narratives; cf. Job 1:22; 2:10.

t   Perhaps ויהי is a redactional connective, since it disrupts the two stress bicolon; none of Hosea's sayings begins with ויהי; on והיה see p. 48.

u   Instead of the unusual hip'il form, the pi'el form אֲיַסְּרֵם probably should be read (cf. textual note "e" to 5:2).

v   *G* τῆς θλίψεως might presuppose לְרָעָתָם (Nyberg suggests לְצָרָתם). *M* speaks of the proclamation "to

| | |
|---|---|
| 13 | Woe to them,[w] they even flee from me! |
| | Down with them, they even rebel |
| | against me! |
| | And I, should I redeem them? |
| | Though they speak lies against me |
| 14 | and do not cry to me from their hearts, |
| | but wail upon their beds; |
| | because of grain and new wine they ⟨gash⟩[x] |
| | themselves, |
| | and are ⟨completely rebellious⟩[y] against me. |
| 15 | And I, I [trained][z] strengthened their arms. |
| | But they planned evil against me. |
| 16 | They turn themselves, ⟨but⟩[aa] not ⟨to me⟩.[aa] |
| | They are like a slack bow. |
| | Their rulers shall fall by the sword |
| | because of the insolence of their tongue. |
| | That shall bring mockery on them |
| | in the land of Egypt. |

their assembly," as does α' κατὰ ἀκοῆς τῆς συναγωγῆς αὐτῶν.

w    Cf. Brockelmann, *Syntax* § 11c.

x    In G (κατετέμνοντο) and M^mss יִתְגּוֹדָדוּ can be recognized as the original reading, which is supported by the *parallelismus membrorum*. M (= S) has misread "they sojourn."

y    "They withdraw" (M) is improbable preceding בְּ; similarly G (ἐπαιδεύθησαν = יָסְרוּ; cf. v 12b, 15a and Dingermann, "Massora–Septuaginta," 40). The consonantal text, made certain by G, is probably to be vocalized יָסֹרוּ (Marti; cf. 4:16).

z    M ("I trained") is a supplementary interpretation (without a copula!) added to the shorter text preserved by G.

aa   The beginning of the line is corrupt. G (εἰς οὐθέν) and σ' (εἰς τὸ μὴ ἔχειν ζυγόν) presuppose the preposition אֶל as well as the negation which suggests אֶל-לֹא יוֹעִיל (cf. Jer 2:8, 11; ζυγόν = עַל!); after vv 7, 10, 15, it would be simpler to read וְלֹא אֶלִי or וְלֹא עָדַי (Am 4:6ff; Joel 2:12), which would also make the following simile more intelligible.

## Form

According to both form and content, 5:8 begins a new section of Hosean tradition. The two–part summons to alarm is an introductory formula, with the same function as the introductions in 4:1, 4; 5:1. It makes no connection whatsoever with the previous verses and, with the new place–names, focuses upon new difficulties, namely, those of war. It is a problem to determine how far this new transmission complex reaches. A new beginning comparable to 5:8 does not occur until 8:1. From 5:8 to 7:16 the sayings appear to be syntactically, stylistically, and thematically linked together.

In most cases it is of course relatively easy to determine the limits of the rhetorical units by noting the genres of the prophet's sayings. In 5:8f the summons to alarm introduces a threat[1] to Ephraim that is intensified by an unusual concluding formula.[2] In v 10 there follows a motive clause and threat to Judah's military leaders. A lament over Ephraim's distress in v 11a leads to further motivation and threat to both Ephraim and Judah (vv 12–14). To these sayings v 15 adds a word expressing a more hopeful outcome. A priestly penitential song in 6:1–3 interrupts the prophetic genres. In response to

the song, the divine speech uttered by the prophet commences again in 6:4; as in 5:12–14, it concerns both Ephraim and Judah. Instead of the expected "assurance that a prayer is granted" (*Erhörungszuspruch*), the divine speech is composed essentially of accusations (vv 4b, 7–10a) that are only momentarily interrupted by a threat (v 5) and by didactic sentences (v 6). These accusations are aimed chiefly at the priests (v 9). Chap. 6:10b is vividly reminiscent of 5:3b and thus it appears to have been added to v 10a to interpret the obscure word "horrible thing" (שַׁעֲרוּרִיָּה); 6:11a is a Judaic gloss bearing the same style as 5:5bβ. A new accusation against Ephraim and Samaria begins in 6:11b and 7:1a; it extends first to 7:2, but then continues further in 7:3–7 as an accusation against the officials of the court. A lament over Ephraim's fate follows in 7:8–9; it finally reaches its conclusion in the lament over Ephraim's conduct (v 10b). On the other hand, v 10a is a secondary addition taken from 5:5a (cf. 6:10b). Threats with their motivation follow in vv 11f and vv 13–16.

But this lengthy series of prophetic sayings—to be further analyzed below—by no means gives the impression that it is a later literary connection of originally

1    Cf. R. Bach, *Die Aufforderungen*, 59ff.
2    See the commentary on v. 9.

independent units. At the least, they must have belonged together in groups. When compared with 5:8–9, even 5:10 does not appear to be an independent saying whose original setting was different. The same metrical structure unites them. In each a mixed bicolon 3 + 2 is followed by a two–stress bicolon. Though 5:10 no longer speaks of Ephraim, but rather of the officials of Judah, both are mentioned in the third person. Thus the same group of people may have been addressed in vv 8–10 at one historical moment, especially since the end of v 9 already speaks of the "tribes of Israel." Since v 10 begins with היו, it is best interpreted as the prophet's response to his audience's objections raised against his words in vv 8f. It does not appear to be an independent saying from a later period.[3] The following lament over Ephraim (v 11), providing both a description and an explanation of the situation, might presuppose that the attack threatened in v 9 has in the meantime taken place. But hardly would the prophet begin a new saying only to interpret past events. Rather, he alludes to these events in his disputation in order to meet his opponents' arguments. The only remaining question is whether the threat in v 9 and the lament in v 11 can be explained in terms of the same historical situation. When they are viewed with vv 12–14, there is no doubt that this is possible. In vv 12–14, we have a fairly balanced saying (3 + 3) that places a past disaster (vv 12f) alongside a threat (v 14). Moreover, this saying concerns both Judah and Ephraim, again supporting the contention that vv 8–11 derive from the same time and situation. Verse 15 may have immediately followed v 14.[4] When we consider both form and theme, it is preferable to regard 5:8–15 as various sayings stemming from the same historical moment, rather than to divide them according to different periods.

How does the penitential song in 6:1–3 relate to what precedes? It is connected to 5:13f by the catchwords "to tear" (טרף) and "to heal" (רפא); a looser connection with 5:15aα is made by the imagery in 6:3aβ. Is the song therefore simply a simulated quotation by the prophet? The new saying beginning with v 4 apparently is a response to the penitential song. Verse 4 is more intelligible if vv 1–3 preserve genuine words which

Hosea's contemporaries, perhaps the priests, uttered in opposition to him.[5] Perhaps Hosea's opponents wanted to prove that expectations like those voiced in 5:15b were already fulfilled in the present day. The traditionists placed vv 1–3 before v 4 in order to give bold relief to Hosea's rejoinder in the question in v 4a and the rebuke in v 4b. A similar passage preceding 4:16b would have been helpful.[6] Belonging to the prophet's retort are not only the following sentences, connected by "therefore" (על־כן) and "for" (כי), but vv 7–10a as well. "And they" (והמה) never begins a new prophetic saying; but Hosea often continues his train of thought adversatively by ו and a personal pronoun (cf. 5:12, 13b; 7:13b, 15).

The question raised in 6:4 is reflected upon in a different manner in 6:11b–7:2. "Healed" (רפא) in 7:1a still recalls 6:1 (5:13b) and 7:2a looks back to 6:4b as though further critique of the penitential song (vv 1–3) follows in these verses. Therefore, at least down to 7:2, these sayings consistently take a position over against the question: Standing between past and future disaster (cf. 5:8–14), is it possible for Israel to return to Yahweh (5:15b–6:3, 4b, 7–10a; 7:2)? Is it possible for Yahweh to return to redeem Israel (5:15a, 6:4a, 5–6, 11b–7:1a)?

The accusations against the officials in 7:3–7 appear to begin a new theme. But an analysis of the historical situation would have to explain whether this new theme does not fit precisely into the same circumstances presupposed by the preceding verses.[7] That this may be the case is indicated especially by the catchword "their wickedness" (ברעתם) which connects v 7:3a with v 2, and by the theme of "not turning to Yahweh" (5:11, 13, 15; 6:4b; 7:2) which is picked up by the conclusions in v 7bβ. Even at the beginning of the prophetic dispute in 5:8–13, the subject of his proclamation centered around the problems raised by the political and military leadership. Whereas the turmoil of domestic politics is mentioned in vv 3–7, the difficulties of foreign policy dominate the lament in 7:8f, 10b and the threats with their motivation in vv 11–16. Verses 8ff contain no breaks in the structure indicative of separate prophetic sayings; moreover, these verses recall the main theme of Israel's lack of insight and her spurious return to Yah-

---

3   Alt, "Hosea 5:8–6:6."
4   H. Schmidt, "Hos 6:1–6."
5   See pp. 116f.

6   See the commentary on 4:16.
7   See pp. 110ff.

weh.[8] Nevertheless, here we must also determine whether these verses belong to the same historical period.[9] As regards the theme, the woe oracle in 7:13ff and the threat in 7:16aβ completely round off this series of sayings, for here the threats of Ephraim's devastation (which initiated the scene in 5:8f) are intensified in their application to the authorities. Accordingly, the series of sayings in 5:8–7:16 should be regarded as a kerygmatic unit.

The primary genre of this transmission complex is the divine speech. With the exception of 7:10b, Yahweh appears exclusively in the first person. There are, of course, verses without Yahweh's personal speech, such as 5:11; 6:8–9; 7:3–6, 8–9, which may be understood as disputations.

The changes in the form of address are to be explained by the prophet's animated discourse. As in 4:4 and 5:1, the scene is begun by a saying directly addressed to the audience, calling for their attention (5:8). The remainder of the prophet's words are usually in the third person of the lament or accusation,[10] of the announcement of the sentence, or of the establishment of the consequences before the assembled court.[11] It should be recognized that the announcement of judgment usually stands at the beginning of the scene and initiates the further dispute over the transgression, which is the motivation for the judgment; it is announced once again at the conclusion.

After the introductory words in 5:8, direct address in the second person occurs again only in 5:13b and 6:4. It should be noted further that 6:4 is a response to the priests' reference to the penitential song (6:1–3). Therefore v 4 momentarily uses the style of the oracle of assurance that a prayer is granted (*Erhörungszuspruch*).[12]

Insofar as a metrical structure is discernible, the sayings manifest a vivid change of meter that corresponds to the transitions within the scene. At the beginning, we find three very symmetrical strophes (5:8–10), each coupling a five–stress with a four–stress bicolon. The same prosodic structure occurs at the end of the transmission complex in 7:16aβb where there is a heightening of the theme found at the beginning. Qinah meter (3+2) occurs in 6:11b–7:1aα, 8–9, 10b; two–stress bicola in 5:11; 7:11, 13a. As usual, the meter found most frequently is the three–stress bicolon (3+3): 5:12, 13a, 14; 6:4, 6; 7:2, 3, 7. Here only those prosodic units are listed that appear in pairs. Isolated prosodic units of the above–named types (also one three–stress tricolon in 6:5) are found next to metrical arrangements that are irregular or quite difficult to determine. This is particularly true in 6:8–10 and 7:4–6, verses whose texts are more corrupt. The penitential song (6:1–3) contains primarily the three–stress colon. A three–stress tricolon at the beginning (vv 1–2aα) and the end (v 3aβb) enclose a three–stress bicolon (v 2aβb) and a two–stress bicolon (v 3aα). By deleting ונדעה, the middle part would also become a three–stress tricolon.[13] Synonymous parallelism is the most frequently occurring type (5:8, 11–14; 6:4–6, 11b–7:1, 2b, 3, 7–9, 10b, 11b, 13); antithetic parallelism is quite infrequent (7:14a, 15); freer, synthetic forms stand in between (5:9, 10; 6:7–9, 7:2a, 16).

### Setting

The form critical analysis repeatedly raised the question whether the sayings in this kerygmatic unit have their origin in the same historical situation. We have stated that after 5:8 there is no evidence of a clear break until 8:1; that, on the one hand these verses have to do with the same threat of a military catastrophe, and on the other, the same problem concerning Israel's return to Yahweh. These observations could lead one to the conclusion that the entire passage represents a literary arrangement of sayings that were originally proclaimed by the prophet on distinctly different occasions, as is the case in 2:18–25.[14] This conclusion, however, is made quite improbable by the text's transmission: all redactional formulas are absent.[15] These sayings have been

---

8   Cf. 7:8–10 with 5:15–6:4; 7:11b with 5:11, 13; 7:13–16 with 6:4; 7:2, 7.
9   See pp. 110ff.
10  5:10a, 11, 13a; 6:7–10a, 11b–7:2a, 3–7, 8–9,10b, 11, 13–16aα.
11  5:9, 10b, 12, 14, 15; 6:5; 7:2b, 12, 16.
12  Cf. Begrich, "Heilsorakel," 81–92 [217–31].
13  But see textual note "c" on 6:3.

14  See pp. 47f.
15  For the one exception, see textual note "t" to 7:11.

combined without any seams. It is therefore much more likely that they originated from the same historical occasion and that they were given written form promptly thereafter than that weeks or months originally separated them. Such was Alt's hypothesis regarding 5:8f, 10, 11, 12–14, 15–6:5. Budde ("Zur Text und Auslegung [5:1–6:67"]) and Robinson even supposed that years lay between 5:8ff and vv 11ff, as did Alt and other critics concerning 6:6 and vv 7ff. Our working hypothesis could be refuted only by compelling evidence that would link the individual sayings to various historical situations.

But precisely the opposite can be demonstrated, namely, that the sayings within this block of tradition are better interpreted in terms of one definite historical moment rather than various, widely separated events. The time was some point in 733, when Tiglath–pileser III came from the North and attacked the uppermost part of the Jordan Valley. From there he conquered, on the one side, the regions of Israel east of the Jordan (Gilead) and, on the other side, the Galilean highlands and the Jezreel Plain (Megiddo). In the previous year, during his campaign against Philistia, he had already subjugated Israel's coastal plain (Dor).[16] It is at this time that "Ephraim is oppressed, justice is crushed" (5:11). According to 5:11b, Hosea sees the basis for this calamity in the pact with the Aramaean prince, Rezon of Damascus, who, in comparison with Assyria, was weaker in military might (2 Kgs 16:5; Is 7:1ff). In the following year (732) his power was to be completely destroyed by Tiglath–pileser III. Perhaps 7:9a also refers to the Aramaean troops which, in the joint campaign against Jerusalem, consumed Ephraim's military strength (Is 7:2). Our text reflects in various aspects the time when Tiglath–pileser's attack brought about the end of the Syro–Ephraimite war.

1) King Pekah was overthrown by his own supporters.[17] A certain Hoshea ben Elah murdered him and immediately ascended the throne himself (2 Kgs 15:30).

If the prophet is thinking of this overthrow in 7:7b, the expression "all their kings fall" would be more intelligible than if connected with the murders of each of the preceding kings during the past twelve years.[18] Then Hoshea's ascent to the throne is to be seen as the background of 7:3.

2) King Hoshea immediately became a vassal to Tiglath–pileser III and paid him tribute.[19] Chap. 5:13 alludes to this incident. A few months before, the same thing was done in Judah by Ahaz (5:13a$\alpha$[1]; cf. 2 Kgs 16:7ff). But now Hosea primarily questions Ephraim's latest act of submission (5:13a$\beta$b). In addition, 7:11b ("upon Egypt they call, to Assyria they run")—because of the juxtaposition of Egypt and Assyria in this order—is intelligible only in terms of these events. We would of course expect that behind the anti–Assyrian coalition of the Syro–Ephraimite war stood Egyptian support, or at least that it was actively sought.[20] But this can be concluded as well from the flight of the Philistine Prince Hanun from Gaza to Egypt in 734.[21] In the transition from the twenty–second/twenty–third Libyan Dynasty to the twenty–fourth/twenty–fifth Ethiopian Dynasty, Egypt itself experienced widespread disruption because of internal struggles and therefore could provide no effective help.[22] As Israel had previously called to Egypt (in vain), now they run to Assyria. Precisely in this period Ephraim "mixes himself among the nations" (7:8a).

3) Immediately after the attack of Tiglath–pileser III, the revolution in Samaria, and the submission to Assyria, Hosea threatens further catastrophes. That is the essential content of his announcement of judgment. Even worse dangers (5:14f) would follow the present ones (5:11–13; 7:8f). As a result, death by the sword awaited the new leaders in Samaria (7:16a$\beta$). Moreover, the Egyptians would mock them (7:16b) because of Samaria's recent turn toward Assyria and the hope that Assyria could be of more help than Egypt. Hosea foresees a total destruction also for the heartland of Ephraim,

---

16  Cf. A. Alt, "Tiglathpilesers III. erster Feldzug nach Palästina," *Kleine Schriften* 2, 157; Noth, *History*, 259f [235]; see p. 48.

17  Cf. The Annals of Tiglath–pileser III from 734–3, Oppenheim *ANET*[2], 283, line 228.

18  Zechariah: 2 Kgs 15:10; Shallum: 2 Kgs 15:14; Pekahiah: 2 Kgs 15:25.

19  Cf. the stone tablet inscription of Tiglath–pileser III

from 734–3 in *TGI* 53, lines 17f.

20  Kittel, *Geschichte* 2, 365.

21  See the fragment of Tiglath–pileser III's Annals, Oppenheim, *ANET*[2], 284; D. J. Wiseman, *Iraq* 13 (1951): 21ff; Alt, "Feldzug," 157, 159.

22  Cf. A. Scharff and A. Mortgaat, *Ägypten und Vorderasien im Altertum* (München, 1950), 172ff; Zimmerli, *Ezekiel*, 698f.

the Samarian highlands (5:9). It approaches from South to North: Gibeah, Ramah, Bethel are alarmed in this order. Alt has shown that this can merely refer to the forward movement of Ahaz' Judean troops, which till then had been surrounded in Jerusalem by the armies of the Syro–Ephraimite coalition. Alt supposed that this advance by Judah occurred at the time when "the appearance of Assyrian troops forced both the discontinuation of the seige on Jerusalem and the dispatching of main forces to the endangered northern boundaries of Israel and the Aramaean Empire."[23] According to Alt, the saying in 5:10, which he dates at a later time, indicates that the Judean counterattack had already taken place,[24] while only with 5:11 is there mention of Tiglath–pileser III's defeat of the Northern Kingdom.[25] In 5:12–14, Alt thinks that the Syro–Ephraimite war has ended as a result of the ascension of a new king in Samaria and of subjugation to Assyria.[26]

The other historical sources at our disposal do not permit us, as Alt himself emphasizes, to state more precisely when Judah advanced northward during the course of Tiglath–pileser's intervention.[27] In view of the swiftness of Tiglath–pileser's chariots, is it not more likely that the Judeans, already hemmed in for such a long time, first went on the march after the Assyrian King had already conquered Israel's northern region? Therefore, would it not be better to suppose that 5:8f and Judah's initial counterattack belong to the same time as 5:11, 13, with their reference to the Assyrian victory? The text's history of transmission has already shown this to be the more probable view. Then 5:10 would either relate to older events or would simply mention the beginning of Judah's military advance.[28]

All things considered, our observation that 5:8–7:16 represents a kerygmatic unit is accounted for historically by the supposition that collectively these sayings belong to the disquieting days of 733. In this year Tiglath–pileser III overtook Israel's northern region; Pekah was murdered; King Hoshea usurped the throne, and

then submitted to Assyria and offered to pay tribute. There is no equal amount of textual evidence to support dating these verses at the time of Menahem, as was again recently suggested for the main part of chaps. 4–14.[29]

The significance given to the priests (6:7ff), the cult (6:6; 7:14), the political leaders (5:13; 7:3ff, 16), and the war, together with the quotation of the penitential song in 6:1–3, may suggest that an important cultic celebration in Samaria was the occasion on which Hosea spoke these words.[30] With penitence and sacrifices, the cultic event may have solemnly observed Israel's subjugation to Assyria by the new king, Hoshea (7:3, 5), whom Tiglath–pileser III had endorsed as his vassal.[31]

It is understandable that Hosea's circle[32] immediately wrote down his sayings (cf. Is 8:16; 30:8ff) because of the hostility that may have been expressed against him (7:5b; cf. 9:7). The brief period of time separating the public delivery of the words from their written form again explains the absence of all introductory or concluding formulas. Perhaps this would also clarify the reason for the poor condition of the text in various places. These sayings traveled a long and hazardous route before they became a part of the Deuteronomistic book of Hosea. Several sayings relating to certain situations may have been or become difficult to read; if knowledge of a passage's historical context had disappeared quite early, it could no longer be fully understood.

### Interpretation

■ **8** Hosea sounds a frightening call to alarm. Horns and trumpets were blown when there was danger of attack from the enemy (Nu 10:9), enabling those working in the open fields or underway with their flocks to gather in the walled city and prepare their defense.[33] With his call to alarm, the prophet speaks as Israel's watchman (cf. 8:1).

Here, the enemy who strikes such terror apparently makes its advances from south to north through Gibeah

23  Alt, "Hosea 5:8–6:6," 168–69.
24  *Ibid.*, 172.
25  *Ibid.*, 176.
26  *Ibid.*, 179ff.
27  *Ibid.*, 173.
28  See p. 114.
29  H. Tadmor, "The Historical Background of Hosea's Prophecies," in *Y. Kaufmann Jubilee Volume*, ed. M.

Haran (Jerusalem, 1960): 84–88; *idem*, "Azriyau of Yaudi," *Scripta Hierosolymitana* 8 (1961): 232–71, especially 249ff.
30  7:1; see the commentary on 7:4.
31  See the stone tablet inscriptions, *TGI*, 53, line 18; cf. Noth, *History*, 260f [236].
32  See pp. 75f.
33  Jer 4:5; cf. Joel 2:1 and Noth, *World*, 146f [114].

(*Tell el–Fūl*, 3 miles north of Jerusalem) and Ramah (*er–Rām*, 5 miles north of Jerusalem) towards Bethel (*Beitîn*, 11 miles north of Jerusalem).[34] Therefore, the danger approaches from the direction of Jerusalem on the hilly road that leads to the region of Ephraim (v 9a). All of Benjamin, including the northernmost part, is gripped by fear. At the time of Josiah, each of the settlements listed here were counted as part of Benjamin.[35] All of them may have belonged to the Northern Kingdom during the eighth century, as a result of King Jehoash's successful attack upon Jerusalem at the beginning of the century.[36] It should not be supposed that these towns were captured only weeks earlier when the Syro–Ephraimite forces were on their way to attack Jerusalem.[37] Given the conditions noted above, Hosea's alarm is more intelligible if the towns belonged to the Northern Kingdom. Tiglath–pileser's success in the North gave Ahaz courage, after several powerless decades, again to move the northern boundary in accordance with Jerusalem's old needs for protection.[38] Or, did Tiglath–pileser III himself make room for his long–time vassal, Ahaz, to advance as far as Ephraim?

■ **9**  In any case, as God's messenger, Hosea proclaims that Judah's thrust northward is preparation for Ephraim's desolation. The nucleus of the threat is in v 9a. "It appears as though Benjamin is supposed to escape attack, with the war actually taking place in Ephraim, the ancient center of the Northern Kingdom."[39] As divine judgment, it will be a "day of chastisement." L. Koehler[40] understood the "day of chastisement" (יום תוכחה) in terms of the "day of Yahweh." But the formulation is unique.[41] Perhaps Hosea chose this word to give the destruction the positive sense of Israel's "correction."[42]

The prophet's message concerns the "tribes of Israel."

In principle Hosea has in mind all of Israel, namely, the old tribal league.[43] In the entire scene he intentionally avoids the name "Israel" when he means the Northern Kingdom as such. This he reserves for those who are of Yahweh's people (7:1 ∥ 6:11 עמי) or who at least should be.[44] The Northern Kingdom, on the other hand, is exclusively called "Ephraim" (5:11; 7:8, 11), especially in parallel to the Kingdom of Judah (5:13; 6:4) or the capital, Samaria (7:1). This is all the more understandable, since its territory in the meantime had been reduced to a rump–state encompassing the middle region of the highlands west of the Jordan; it had been known as "Ephraim" for a long time.[45] Earlier as well Hosea had addressed the inhabitants of this region as Ephraim, which he placed in parallel to "Israel."[46] During the same period, like Hosea in the Northern Kingdom, Isaiah in Jerusalem also mentions the land on the other side of the national border (8:14; 9:8; cf. 7:17).

These observations should not, however, mislead us into interpreting v 9b in the past tense, as though it said that formerly in the South, as in the North, Yahweh's messengers "proclaimed what is true" concerning the approaching judgment. On the one hand, v 9a is concerned only with the catastrophe in Ephraim; on the other, we do not know whether Hosea himself, before speaking this word, expressed his views concerning Judah's war against the Northern Kingdom. Thus "I proclaim" (הודעתי, perfect as in 6:6, 10a; 7:2, etc.) has a present sense.[47] "What is sure" (נאמנה) indicates that what is proclaimed shall come to pass.[48] Generally in Hosea, as in 5:12ff and 6:4ff, it is Yahweh who speaks in the first person (cf. 2:4ff; 4:4ff; 5:1ff). This sentence intensifies the threat. It clearly brings the speech to a conclusion with a formula reminiscent of the language of the law teacher.[49] The introductory call to

---

34  Perhaps the reproachful name בית און ("Beth-aven") was first inserted here by the traditionists, for Hosea means the city, not the sanctuary; see pp. 89f.

35  Josh 18:21–28; cf. Noth, *Josua*, HAT 1, 7 (Tübingen, 1953²), 111f.

36  2 Kgs 14:8–14; cf. Noth, *History*, 236f [216f]; Jepsen, *Quellen*, 97; Schunck, *Benjamin*, 154–61.

37  Alt, "Hos 5:8–6:6," 168f.

38  Cf. 1 Kgs 15:16–22 and Alt, "Neue Erwägungen," 4ff.

39  Alt, "Hos 5:8–6:6," 170.

40  Koehler, *Theology*, 221f [211].

41  "Chastisement" (תוכחה) occurs elsewhere only in

2 Kgs 19:3 = Is 37:3, and Ps 149:7.

42  For יכח hip'il see the commentary on 4:1; for יסר pi'el, see the commentary on 5:2 and 5:15.

43  11:1; see the commentary on 2:1–3; 3:4 and 10:11.

44  6:10a; 6:10b and 7:10a are secondary in their present context; see textual notes "m" to 6:10 and "r" to 7:10.

45  Noth, *World*, 57f [49f].

46  4:16f; 5:3; see pp. 90f.

47  Cf. Am 5:21; Jer 2:2 and Brockelmann, *Syntax* § 41c.

48  Cf. 1 Kgs 8:26; Is 55:3 and Weiser, *TDNT* 6, 185.

49  Prv 22:19, 21; 1 Sam 10:8; see the commentary on 5:1.

alarm and the affirmative closing formula provide this terse announcement of Ephraim's devastation "on the day of chastisement" with a complete framework seldom found in Hosea's individual sayings.

■ **10** We should assume, therefore, that the saying in v 10 was evoked by the audience's interruption of Hosea. Responding to his mention of the "tribes of Israel" (v 9), they probably broached the subject of their hostile brothers' transgressions. Verse 10a seems to take up the opponent's objections, to which Yahweh's threat is added in v 10b.

היה כ means "to do, act like."[50] Criticized are the "rulers of Judah" (שרי יהודה), who in this case[51] are the military authorities. Their dealings are compared with the malicious deeds of those who change the boundaries of the fields. For God's covenant people, such behavior stood under the curse (Dtn 27:17), since God himself gave the covenant members their portion; especially does he defend the weaker neighbor in Israel.[52] Hence, the war between Judah and Israel is assessed in terms of justice required by Yahweh's covenant. Hosea removes himself from the suspicion that his politics favors Judah. He is the messenger of Yahweh, the God of all the tribes of Israel (v 9b). To interpret v 10a in the past tense, it would be necessary to recall events that happened more than a hundred years earlier, namely, when Asa moved Judah's boundary up to Mizpah.[53] For decades, however, this boundary appears to have been changed by Israel's counter measures.[54] Hence, היו should probably be interpreted as a perfect expressing the present tense; then the reference to moving the border would be connected with the present approach of Ahaz' troops,[55] which Hosea's audience—after his call to alarm in 5:8—may have indignantly characterized as Judah's transgression.

Yahweh will also "pour out his wrath" upon them. His wrath is to be distinguished from his essence, as a tool is distinguished from the master craftsman who uses it.[56] The wrath is compared with water, for in Palestine nothing else was "poured out" in such great measure and power as the rushing waters of the torrential winter rains. In God's name Hosea admits to his opponents that Yahweh's human instruments in the judgment cannot escape punishment for their own transgressions.[57]

■ **11** Hosea further concedes that Ephraim already has "suffered violence," namely, the violence of those very weeks when Tiglath–pileser III advanced into the northern and eastern provinces. As a result, Ephraim's "legally established orders were overthrown."[58] Again Hosea speaks of war with concepts drawn from Israel's legislation pertaining to social justice: "misplace landmarks" (הסיג גבול, see above) in v 10; here, "to oppress" (עשק) and "to abuse" (רצץ).[59] The assonance of the passive participles gives a stirring quality to the lament over the already–present distress.[60] As no other prophet, Hosea shares the burdens of his people and stands by their side (cf. 4:6, 8, 15b; 5:1).

Yet he is still his God's messenger who can immediately uncover the guilt causing his people's distress. According to v 11b, the cause lies in the fact that they have lost their political independence in a manner unworthy of God's people. "What is worthless" (צו)[61] probably refers to the Aramaean Kingdom of Damascus, with whose king, Rezon, the recently fallen Pekah had made a pact.[62] One might also think of Egypt in this connection, but in 7:11, 16 Egypt is explicitly called by name, whereas the Aramaeans, who likewise have just been attacked, are otherwise unnamed by Hosea. Thus, this expression of contempt might apply especially to them.

■ **12** Israel's existence was decisively dependent upon

---

50 Cf. 7:16; 8:8; 9:10; 11:4; 13:7; 14:6; Ex 22:24; Ezek 16:31 and C. H. Ratschow, *Werden und Wirken im AT*, BZAW 70 (Giessen, 1941), 11–3.
51 See p. 62.
52 Dtn 19:14; Prv 22:28; 23:10; Job 24:2.
53 1 Kgs 15:22; cf. Noth, *History*, 235 [215].
54 See the commentary on 5:8.
55 See p. 112.
56 Cf. 13:11; 8:5; 11:9; 14:5; Ezek 7:3 and Zimmerli, *Ezekiel*, 171.
57 Cf. Is 10:5ff, 12ff.
58 On משפט, see p. 52 and 2:21f.
59 Cf. Lev 19:13; Dtn 24:14; 28:29, 33; Am 4:1; Mic

2:2.
60 Cf. Dtn 28:33 and P. P. Saydon, "Assonance in Hebrew as a Means of Expressing Emphasis," *Biblica* 29 (1955): 294.
61 See textual note "e" to 5:11.
62 See p. 111.

its God; the political league with the Aramaeans could not guarantee its existence, a fact as true of Ephraim as of Judah. The verse's parallel structure indicates the amphictyonic (and thus prenational) orientation of Hosea's thought.[63] Yahweh uses the ancient formulas of theophany and self–introduction, expressing with awe–inspiring solemnity the determinative significance he has for his people, even though they have broken his covenant.[64] Hosea is familiar with the "I am Yahweh" formula which formed the basis of the ancient covenant (12:10; 13:4). Here, however, the expression is connected with his judgment, not his grace.

To Israel, Yahweh is like "pus" and "decay." In v 12 עשׁ ("pus"; see textual note "f" to 5:12) cannot mean "moth." This is also evident from those examples in which a moth is compared with persons; only their quickly perishable nature is characterized (Ps 39:12 [11]; Job 4:19). Moreover, the moth destroys clothing (Is 50:9; 51:8), not people. That "pus" is the correct meaning is conclusively shown in the continuation of v 13a, which speaks of "sickness" and "wound" as the consequence of Yahweh's theophany of judgment. "Rottenness" (רקב) also destroys people, not things. According to Hab 3:16; Prv 12:4; 14:30, it affects the bones. The imagery "proves how little the language of the prophets was checked by 'aesthetic' or 'dogmatic' considerations."[65] On the contrary, when the God of salvation becomes the judge of his covenant–breaking people, the prophet's imagery demands the listeners' attention and is intentionally unambiguous.[66]

In contrast to v 14, v 12 is a statement strictly in the present tense which, by its adversative connection with the negative explanation given in v 11b, interprets positively the lamentable condition mentioned in v 11a. Yahweh, not Tiglath–pileser III, is the Lord of his-

tory. Israel has to recognize that he is at work in historical events.

■ **13** But Israel saw it otherwise. Naturally Ephraim could not fail to recognize his "sickness" (חלי), since, after the coastal plain was taken, both Galilee and Transjordan were overthrown. Similarly, Judah had already seen itself dangerously wounded from the siege laid to Jerusalem by the troops of the Syro–Ephraimite coalition.[67] Yet Samaria's diagnosis was incorrect. It considered Assyria the actual cause of its difficulties, and therefore sent messengers to the "great king,"[68] Tiglath–pileser III. This both Ephraim and Judah had done, one after the other,[69] but Hosea is concerned primarily with Ephraim. For this reason, no reconstruction of "Judah" in parallel to Ephraim in v 13aβ is necessary.[70] The address in the second person plural (לכם–מכם) in v 13b indicates that here the prophet addresses his remarks directly to his audience. This means that he is thinking above all of the recent submission of young King Hoshea. The direct address underlines what is important to Hosea in the entire context: the latest political move in which Ephraim has become Assyria's vassal is not a solution to the problem. The order "Ephraim–Judah" in v 13a should not be pressed historically. There is no other reason to consider this a reference to Menahem's payment of tribute for Ephraim five years before, in 738.[71] Rather, the sequence corresponds to that in v 12, thereby giving predominant interest to Ephraim (v 13aβb).

The imagery of sickness has continued to this point to explain the present affliction (v 13aα), its true cause (v 12), and the futility of the attempts to find a solution (v 13aβb). Further "chastisement" (תוכחה v 9a), threatened at the beginning of this scene, is made necessary by the false path Israel has taken. She has not

---

63   Cf. vv 9b, 10 and see p. 113.
64   Cf. Lev 18:2b; Ex 20:2 and see W. Zimmerli, "Ich bin Jahweh," *Festschrift A. Alt*, ed. G. Ebeling, BHTh 16 (Tübingen, 1953), 179–209 [also in his *Gottes Offenbarung*, ThB 19 (München, 1963), 11–40]. Concerning the change from אני (vv 12, 14b; 5:2; otherwise occurring exclusively in Ezekiel, the Holiness Code and the Priestly Writings) to אנכי (vv 14a; 12:10; 13:4; otherwise occurring exclusively in the Elohist and Dtn [except for 12:30]); cf. *ibid.*, 193, n. 2; further, see K. Elliger, "Das Gesetz Leviticus 18," *ZAW* 67 (1955): 24f.
65   Hempel, *Worte*, 308.
66   See the commentary on 1:9.
67   The imagery of sickness and bodily wound representing distress in times of war also occurs in Is 1:5ff and Jer 30:12f.
68   See textual note "g" to 5:13.
69   See p. 111.
70   Alt, "Hos 5:8–6:6," 177f; Harper, 277; Weiser, 53.
71   2 Kgs 15:19f; Noth, *History*, 257 [233].

turned to her true "Chastiser," Yahweh. Now he will show that he is not only the hidden cause of Israel's sickness, but her overwhelming opponent.

■ **14** Again the formula of self–introduction[72] gives the reason (כי) why it is useless to seek Assyria's help. And once more both kingdoms are mentioned. This makes it clear that beyond the beginning of impending disaster, namely, Ahaz' northward advances (v 8), Hosea expects the total destruction of Ephraim (v 9a) as of Judah (v 10b). In this annihilation Yahweh will be like a "lion." שחל (also cf. 13:7) and כפיר denote especially powerful, hungry young lions.[73] No less boldly than in v 12, Yahweh speaks of himself in theriomorphic terms: he will "rend" and "carry [them] off," so that none shall stand in his way. The threat is uttered in v 14b, with verbs in the imperfect; for Hosea's audience, it corresponds to the threat in v 9a. Here we naturally think of Assyria's continued rending of Israel—on down to the overthrow of Samaria—and the annexation of the land into the Assyrian provincial system. The final clause ("so that none shall rescue" [ואין מציל]) emphasizes that this announcement of judgment is simply the reverse side of the confession of Yahweh as Israel's only redeemer (cf. 2:12b). Hosea was the first to have compared Yahweh's essence and his deeds so directly with those of wild animals. Amos compared only his voice with the roaring of a lion (1:2; 3:8). Perhaps this suggested the metaphor to Hosea.

■ **15** With the catchword "I will withdraw" (אלך), v 15 continues still another motif from the imagery of v 14. With his prey, the lion withdraws himself to his "place" (מקום) of hiding. In addition to this metaphor, the threat may contain motifs from the Canaanite myth of the disappearing God.[74] The metaphor is not continued with further reference to the fate of the prey. Instead, it is Yahweh's departure that results in the destruction of land and people (Ps 104:29). Hosea does not state where Yahweh himself dwells. Like the lion metaphor, only a part of the myth is used. Both serve—

only in passing—to elucidate Yahweh's disciplinary measures ("day of chastisement" יום תוכחה v 9a). The preliminary conclusion (v 15aβb) states the purpose of Yahweh's "discipline." In the temporal purpose clause with "until" (עד אשר), we see how the prophets used concepts drawn from a cyclic nature–mythology to speak of Yahweh in historical and eschatological terms. Withdrawing himself from his people, Yahweh leaves them to the continuing events of war, until Ephraim's devastation, as threatened in v 9a, is completed. "They are desolated" (יֶשְׁמוּ)[75] is reminiscent of "laid waste" (לִשְׁמָה) in v 9a. In the course of the war, what had been announced during the time of Jeroboâm II (2:12) will be fully accomplished.

What previous attacks from the enemy had been unable to do (v 13) must be achieved by total destruction: Israel shall seek the craftsman instead of his tools. They shall "seek his face," but not by sacrificing at the appointed times in the Canaanite cult (5:6); rather, from the wilderness they shall return to Yahweh, the God of the Covenant as Hosea had already promised in his early period (3:5). This is the sense of "to seek" (בקש), as it is interpreted by its parallel "to ask for" (שחר pi'el), which belongs to the noncultic language of Wisdom.[76] Also in the Psalter (63:2; 78:34) the word שחר describes the direct seeking of Yahweh by one in great affliction.[77] The proclamation of an approaching "day of chastisement" and burning anger is intended to turn Israel to Yahweh.

■ **6:1–3** A penitential song now follows v 15. But this is not the kind of "turning to Yahweh" Hosea meant, as is shown by 6:4ff on the one hand and by 14:3f on the other. Verses 1–3 have been thought to be a song which the prophet composed and attributed to the people as a sign of their fleeting repentance.[78] But this is not the case, as the absence of an introductory formula[79] and the content of vv 1–3 indicate. It is more probable that these verses are a penitential song the priests sung

72  See the commentary on v 12.
73  L. Koehler, "Lexikologisch–Geographisches," ZDPV 62 (1939): 121.
74  See the commentary on 5:6 and May, "Fertility Cult," 83.
75  See textual note "i" on 5:15.
76  Job 7:21; 8:5; 24:5; Prv 1:28; 7:15; 8:17.
77  The expression is much too solemn to have ever served as an introductory formula. It should not, therefore, be taken as the beginning of 6:1–3, as G intends; cf. textual note "j" to 5:15.
78  Alt ("Hosea 5:8–6:6"); Schmidt ("Hosea 6:1–6"); and Lindblom, in his review of Hosea (BK XIV) ThLZ 87 (1962): 835.
79  Cf. 8:2; 10:3; 14:3; on ישחרנני see the commentary on 5:15.

during these very times of danger.[80] The first part of the song is connected with the previous verses by means of catchwords.[81] This makes vv 1–3 most appropriate as a rejoinder to Hosea's words, prefaced by the remark: "The expectations you have for the future (5:15b) are materializing among us now!" It might be supposed that a more direct connection exists between 5:8–15 and 6:1–3, since the expectation of Yahweh's reappearance in 6:3 does in fact correspond with his departure in 5:15a. In this case it would have to be presumed that Hosea's sayings in 5:8–15 prompted the song and perhaps an entire day of repentance. Then 6:4ff would be part of a later scene on this very day. However, except for the catchword relationship noted above, the language and imagery of the penitential song give it the appearance of being independent. It should probably "be understood entirely in terms of the popular piety which had been influenced by the Canaanization of the Yahweh cult."[82] In a different way it had also made an impression on Hosea's own proclamation.[83] Consequently, the connection established by catchwords and similar thoughts is accounted for by common presuppositions.

The traditionists probably added the song to the sayings of Hosea which they had fixed in writing because it appeared indispensable for understanding the following question. Similarly, the words of Amaziah in Am 7:10–13 were transmitted and preserved as a help in understanding Amos' saying in 7:14–17. But, corresponding to the characteristic way Hosea's sayings were transmitted in chaps. 4–14, any introductory or concluding formula is absent here.[84]

The motifs of lament, confession of guilt, avowal, and penitence occur in brief form only in the cohortatives at the beginning of each of the two strophes (vv 1aα, 3aα). Of form critical importance is that these motifs give way to longer expressions of confidence and trust in the main parts of both strophes (vv 1aβ–2, 3aβb). These words sound like a kind of self–appeasement, especially since Yahweh is not directly addressed.

■ **1** In this song, Israel sees herself as a people which is obedient to the prophet. The song takes up not only an important keyword (שׁוּב) from his preaching (2:9; 3:5; 5:4) but also his future expectations (5:15aαβ) in the cohortatives at the beginning of each strophe (vv 1aα, 3aα). Moreover, in the expressions of trust it picks up the imagery of a wounded man attacked by wild animals, making it a part of the confession (noted as missing in 5:13) that Yahweh has torn and stricken them. This confession is filled with confidence that he will also heal and bind up (cf. Dtn 32:39; Ezek 30:21; Job 5:18).

■ **2** "He will preserve our life" (יְחַיֵּנוּ) in v 2a is probably part of the last three stresses in v 1.[85] The verses concern one who has been wounded but is still alive. Here, therefore, חיה pi'el does not mean "to make alive";[86] rather, it has its usual meaning of "preserve alive."[87] The following temporal clauses then form the first line of the three–stress bicolon that closes the first strophe. The line is tautological:[88] "after two days" = "on the third day." On the third day, that is, in a short time, Yahweh again will "raise up" from their sickbeds (Ps 41:4, 11) those who have been wounded and cared for. It is then certain that they "continue to live in Yahweh's presence." The expression originates from the idea that in death one is separated from Yahweh.[89] Accordingly, a resurrection from the dead is not spoken of.

### Resurrection on the Third Day

To be sure, in terms of the history of religion of the ancient Orient and of the New Testament Hos 6:2 has been considered evidence for a resurrection on the third day.

The cultures surrounding Israel did in fact speak of resurrection. For Byblos, Lucian[90] attests to the myth of Adonis' resurrection; on the day after sacrifices were made in his behalf, it is reported that he came to life again: μετὰ δὲ τῇ ἑτέρῃ ἡμέρῃ ζώειν τέ μιν μυθολογέουσι. Concerning the Egyptian god,

---

80  Cf. Josh 7:6ff; 1 Sam 7:6, and H. Gunkel–J. Begrich, *Einleitung in die Psalmen* (Göttingen, 1937), 117ff.

81  For טרף and רפא in v 1, cf. 5:13b, 14b; on the imagery of sickness, cf. 5:12f.

82  Hentschke, *Stellung*, 91.

83  See the commentary on 5:15.

84  See pp. 75f.

85  Stamm, "Hosea 6:1–2," 267.

86  Luther; cf. Dtn 32:39.

87  Nu 31:15; Josh 9:15; Is 7:21; cf. Koehler–Baumgartner, 293a.

88  Stamm, "Hosea 6:1–2," 268.

89  Ps 6:6; 30:10; 88:11ff; cf. von Rad, *TDNT* 2, 844ff; and Th. C. Vriezen, *Theologie des AT in Grundzügen* (Neukirchen, 1957), 173.

90  *De Syria dea*, § 6.

Osiris, Plutarch[91] reports that he died on the seventeenth of Athyr and was found alive on the nineteenth of Athyr.[92] On the cult of Tammuz, which was not unknown in Israel,[93] we note the fragments of an ancient Sumerian poem about Inanna's descent into the nether world for three days and three nights.[94]

When the early church of the New Testament wanted scriptural proof for Jesus' resurrection "on the third day" (1 Cor 15:4; cf. Lk 24:7) hardly another passage was as appropriate as Hos 6:2.[95] To be sure, the Targum only speaks of "the days of comfort to come in the future" and the "days of resurrection" instead of noting the number of days; perhaps the intention was to make Hos 6:2 unusable as a proof-text for the early Christians.[96] It should be noted, however, that neither the New Testament, nor the Apostolic Fathers, nor the ancient apologists cite

Hos 6:2 as a proof-text. Tertullian was the first to use it as such.[97] Following the Church Fathers, Luther also thought Paul (1 Cor 15:4) was referring to Hos 6:2; his exposition of the passage reads: "He will make alive. He is speaking of Christ's resurrection." [Trans.]. (*Vivificabit Loquitur de resurrectione Christi, WA* 13, 27). Calvin, however, preferred to interpret it in an ecclesiological sense.[98]

---

The ancient song in vv 1–3 merely voices the expectation that a sickly nation will be put on the road to recovery by Yahweh, and in the shortest possible time. The set length of time, "after two days, on the third day," if at all reminiscent of the myth of the gods' resurrection,[99] is used at the most in a proverbial sense.[100] This is evident from the fact that the statement (1) is made

---

91  *De Iside et Osiride* 13, 356C; 19, 366F.
92  Cf. Baudissin, *Adonis*, 408ff.
93  Ezek 8:14; cf. Zimmerli, *Ezekiel*, 219f.
94  S. N. Kramer, "Ishtar in the Nether World according to a New Sumerian Text," *BASOR* 79 (1940): 18–27; W. F. Albright, *From the Stone Age to Christianity* (New York: Doubleday, 1946), 144f; F. Nötscher, "Zur Auferstehung nach drei Tagen," 314ff; H. Schmökel, *Heilige Hochzeit und Hoheslied* (Wiesbaden, 1956), 31; additional bibliography on this subject may be found in G. Fohrer, "Umkehr und Erlösung beim Propheten Hosea," *ThZ* (1955): 167, and W. von Soden, "Sterbende und auferstehende Götter," *RGG*³ 1, 688f; on Al'iyan Ba'al of Ugarit, see pp. 38ff.
95  *G* reads: "On the third day we shall be raised and shall live in his presence": ἐν τῇ ἡμέρᾳ τῇ τρίτῃ ἀναστησόμεθα καὶ ζησόμεθα ἐνώπιον αὐτοῦ.
96  Cf. Delling, *TDNT* 2, 948–50.
97  *Adversus Marcionem* IV 43 1f (C. Chr. Tert. op. I, 661): It was very meet that the man who buried the Lord should thus be noticed in prophecy, and thenceforth be "blessed;" since prophecy does not omit the (pious) office of the women who resorted before day-break to the sepulchre with the spices which they had prepared. For of this incident it is said by Hosea: "To seek my face they will watch till daylight, saying unto me, Come, and let us return to the Lord: for He hath taken away, and He will heal us; He hath smitten, and He will bind us up; after two days will He revive us: in the third day He will raise us up." For who can refuse to believe that these words often revolved in the thought of those women between the sorrow of that desertion with which at present they seemed to themselves to have been smitten by the Lord, and the hope of the resurrection itself, by which they rightly supposed that all would

be restored to them? [Trans.]. (*Oportuerat etiam sepultorem domini prophetari ac iam tunc merito benedici, si nec mulierum illarum officium praeterit prophetia, quae ante lucem conuenerunt ad sepulcrum cum odorum paratura. De hoc enim per Osee: et quaerent, inquit, faciem meam; ante lucem uigilabunt ad me dicentes: eamus et conuertamur ad dominum, quia ipse eripuit (dixit) et curabit nos, percussit et miserebitur nostri, sanabit nos post biduum, in die tertia resurgemus. Quis enim haec no credat in recogitatu mulierum illarum uolutata inter dolorem praesentis destitutionis, qua percussae sibi uidebantur a domino, et spem resurrectionis ipsius, qua restitutuiri se arbitrabantur.*)

*Adversus Iudaeos* XIII, 23 (C. Chr. Tert. op. II, 1389: Why, accordingly, after His resurrection from the dead, which was effected on the third day, did the heavens receive Him back? It was in accordance with a prophecy of Hosea, uttered on this wise: "Before daybreak shall they arise unto Me, saying, Let us go and return unto the Lord our God, because Himself will draw us out and free us. After a space of two days, on the third day"—which is His glorious resurrection—He received back into the heavens (whence withal the Spirit Himself had come to the Virgin) [Trans.]. (*Cur itaque post resurrectionem eius a mortuis, quae die tertia effecta est, caeli eum receperunt secundum prophetiam (ab) Osee emissam huiusmodi: ante lucem surgent ad me dicentes: eamus et reuertamur ad dominum deum nostrum, quoniam ipse eripiet et liberabit nos post biduum in die tertia. Quae (est) resurrectio eius gloriosa de terra in caelos eum recepit, unde et uenerat ipse spiritus ad uirginem*). Cf. S. V. McCarland, "The Scripture Basis of 'On the Third Day,'" *JBL* 48 (1929): 124–37.
98  *CR* 42, 320f.
99  Thus H. G. May, "Fertility Cult," 84f.
100  Baudissin, *Adonis*, 410.

about the people, not about a god and (2) is related to the recovery of a wounded person, not the resurrection of a dead one.[101] Yahweh "is not a god who dies and rises, but is the living God."[102]

■ **3** The second strophe, however, more clearly echoes mythical motifs. First, the introduction in the cohortative —especially with the word "let us seek" (נרדפה)—recalls the motif of seeking the absent or sleeping God.[103] The similies of the breaking of dawn, of the seasonal return of the first autumn showers (גשם), and of the late spring rains (מלקוש) reveal nature–mythical thinking influenced by the Canaanite religion. The confidence of Israel's hope is emphasized by the series of similies.[104] If Israel celebrated this day of repentance during the dangerous period of 733, its hope may have been nourished by Tiglath–pileser III's recognition of King Hoshea ben Elah as his vassal.[105]

■ **4** Hosea responds to the recitation of the penitential lament in the first person style of divine speech, similar to the priests in the cult when they give assurance that a prayer has been granted.[106] Here we would least expect to find the messenger formula, which is generally absent in Hosea. The salvation oracle, in contrast to the prophetic saying, ordinarily does not contain such a formula. The traditionists apparently understood Hosea's sayings throughout as a kind of priestly proclamation, to which the messenger formula is alien.[107] This might account for the surprising absence of the formula in Hosea; it also suggests that the traditionists were members of priestly opposition groups.[108]

The content of the answer given the priests, even in the opening question, is quite unusual. God is pictured struggling with himself (cf. 11:8). This is in complete accord with Hosea's particular manner of proclamation, which alternates between sympathetic lament and biting accusation.[109] As in 5:10–14,[109a] God addresses himself to all of the tribes of Israel. He acknowledges that Israel's repentance is proof of her חסד, namely, her loyalty to the bond between them,[110] her devotion and fidelity to him.[111] But Israel's covenantal loyalty is far too unsteady. That חסד in vv 4 and 6 means the love "Ephraim and Judah should have for each other"[112] is ruled out by the context, where the relationship between Ephraim and Judah plays no role; the main theme, rather, is turning to Yahweh.[113]

Hosea uses a simile drawn from nature which corresponds to the song's second strophe: "You think God should promptly appear like the dawn. But your own faithfulness to the covenant immediately disappears again." "Morning mist" (ענן־בקר) denotes ground fog which, like early dew, disappears with the sun's rising.[114] Thus both are appropriate metaphors for describing Israel as fleeting and changeable. Why is Israel characterized in such a way? In view of the song (vv 1–3), it must be that her confession of guilt is deficient[115] and that her confidence rests too much in the laws of nature, resulting in the confusion of Yahweh with Baal. The following verses further elucidate the ground of Yahweh's rejection.

■ **5** "Therefore" (על־כן) first introduces the consequences Yahweh draws from the inconstancy of Israel's covenant loyalty, an inconstancy yet to be described.

---

101 The carefulness of Tertullian's application of the proof–text is seen in the fact that he attributes these words to the women on Easter morning; see note 97.

102 J. Hempel, "Ich bin der Herr, dein Arzt," *ThLZ* 89 (1957): 820; *idem*, "Heilung als Symbol und Wirklichkeit im biblischen Schrifttum," *NAG* (1958): 271ff.

103 1 Kgs 18:27; see the commentary on 5:6 and 5:15.

104 Note especially the word "sure" (נכון) in v 3aβ.

105 See p. 112.

106 Cf. Ps 85:9 and J. Begrich, "Heilsorakel," 81–92 [217–31]; Gunkel–Begrich, *Einleitung*, 137.

107 Cf. Begrich, "Heilsorakel," 87; also Seierstad, *Die Offenbarungserlebnisse*, 208f.

108 See pp. 75f, 79f.

109 See the commentary on 5:10, 11 and on 4:4–15.

109a See pp. 113f.

110 See the commentary on 2:21.

111 Cf. A. R. Johnson, "Hesed and hāsîd," *NTT* 56 (1955): 100–12.

112 Thus A. Jepsen, "Gnade und Barmherzigkeit im AT," *KuD* 7 (1961): 269.

113 5:15; 6:1ff, 7; see pp. 128ff.

114 R. B. Y. Scott, "Meteorological Phenomena and Terminology in the Old Testament," *ZAW* 64 (1952): 21, 24; and Dalman, *Arbeit* 1, 193f.

115 Cf., on the contrary, 14:3f, and also 7:2.

Through his prophets, Yahweh struggles to overcome it.[116] The perfect verbs and the plural noun suggest that the verse refers to the earlier prophets in the Northern Kingdom, such as Ahijah of Shilo, Elijah, Micaiah ben Imlah, and Amos, as well as to Hosea's own proclamation (5:8f, 14).[117] These perfects clearly portray prophecy's function in the void between Israel's breaking of the covenant (v 4b) and the breaking forth of Yahweh's plan for their salvation (v 5b). The prophets are instruments of Yahweh because they proclaim "the words of his mouth."[118] This corresponds to the fact that the first person in Hosea's sayings is always the "I" of Yahweh. The prophet's words are deadly weapons.[119] Hosea may be thinking of the immediately preceding destruction of Israel's army by Tiglath–pileser III's chariots as the fulfillment of an earlier prophecy;[120] at the same time, however, he probably refers to the still greater catastrophe he himself has just proclaimed (5:8f, 14).

Though Yahweh "slays" Israel because of her inconstant loyalty, his intention is not to destroy her; rather, he wants those rules for living which he provides again to take effect. The intended results are described by the imperfect verb "to break forth" (יצא). The comparison of "justice" (משפט) with the breaking forth of the "(sun) light" denotes its superiority and constancy over against Israel's loyalty (חסד v 4), which is like a passing cloud.[121] Yahweh's משפט[122] is compared with Israel's, and, as seen in 2:21, the word has a related meaning in both applications. In v 5 משפט denotes right relationships within a community,[123] and thereby is related first of all to Yahweh's own words and deeds. Since these are the foundation of Israel's rules for living, they also renew her existence and her conduct (5:11). To achieve genuine renewal in Israel, the "day of chastisement" (5:9) announced by the prophet cannot be spared this people whose repentance is only momentary.

■ **6** The intention of the prophet's sermon of judgment, in accordance with Yahweh's present struggle with Israel, is to save Israel by a revitalization of Yahweh's משפט. This is evident from v 4 as well as from the didactic sentence in v 6. The saying reaches a climax in v 6 insofar as it concludes both the critique of Israel's repentance (v 4), and the interpretation of the prophetic judgment speech (v 5) with the same basic explanation. The perfect verb "I desire" (חפצתי) expresses the universal validity of Yahweh's will. Like "to be pleased with" (רצה), חפץ belongs to the theme of the cultic "reckoning" of the priests.[124] Yahweh states what is acceptable to him. The verse has the appearance of a citation from a specific didactic tradition (cf. 1 Sam 15:22) which clarifies its own position by means of negation. Parallel to "not" (לא), the "rather than" (מן) has a privative meaning and likewise a negative force.[125] Not meal and burnt offerings (cf. 4:8, 13f; 8:13), but "loyalty" (חסד) and "knowledge of God" (דעת אלהים) are the objects of Yahweh's delight. The verse's connection with v 4 indicates that here חסד chiefly denotes the faithful, covenantal relationship to Yahweh which is neither compatible with the politics of coalition (5:11b), nor with submission to a greater nation (5:13), nor with the civil war between Ephraim and Judah (5:8, 10). The concept of חסד indicates how completely the right covenant relationship with God forms the basis of the Old Testament ethos (cf. v 4 and 4:1f). The parallel concept דעת אלהים shows that this relationship to God—indeed, this communion with the God who is active, who gives and speaks—is the foundation of everything. This cognitive idea in the phrase "knowledge of God" makes clear that God's covenant loyalty can be "known" from the revelation of his word (4:1f, 6) and his work (11:1–3; 2:10; 13:4). Since it is knowledge of him who is the continually efficacious God of Israel, it creates a relationship between Israel and her God. To know him is to experience him and to live in communion with him in trust and obedience. For Hebrew thought, these existential components are inseparably bound to the cognitive functions, all of them in turn

---

116 On "to hew" [literally], (חצב) in Ugarit, see textual note "f" to 6:5.

117 Cf. H. W. Wolff, "Heimat," 84f, [233f]; see the further discussion by Rendtorff, "Erwägungen," 149f, 153ff.

118 אמרי־פי; cf. Is 30:2; Jer 1:9; 15:19.

119 Cf. Am 7:10; Is 9:7; Jer 5:14; 23:29; Is 49:2; 55:10f.

120 E.g., Am 2:13–16; 4:2; 5:27.

121 This metaphor finds further application in Ps 37:6.

122 Concerning the original suffix משפטי, see textual note "g" to 6:5.

123 Cf. Fahlgren, ṣᵉdāqā (Uppsala, 1932), 129f.

124 Is 1:11; Mal 1:10; Ps 51:18; see R. Rendtorff, "Priesterliche Kulttheologie und prophetische Kultpolemik," *ThLZ* 81 (1956): 342.

125 Cf. Prv 8:10; Gesenius–Kautzsch § 119w; differently

belonging to the structure of דעת.[126]

It is clear that with this didactic statement Hosea discloses the significance of Israel's cult as well as her history. In the kind of worship he desires, Yahweh is not satisfied with pious rituals. In genuine worship God's relationship to his people is experienced, for there his deeds in history and his instructions for life are "re-presented." Such worship—entirely different from the ritual of sacrifice and penitence cited here—would have an effect on Israel's political relationships with foreign powers and with her brother, Judah. According to Hosea's thinking, when Israel collapses, the priests ought to recite the stories of the exodus from Egypt (2:17b; 11:1ff), or the stories of the wilderness wanderings (9:10; 13:5) and the gift of the land (2:10, 17a). As long as Israel does not regard her history and worship as bound up exclusively with the God proclaimed in Israel, Yahweh will chastise her still further with the severe weapon of prophecy, which makes her history a history of judgment. Of importance to Hosea is the relationship between Israel and her God, who acts on her behalf. Therefore, the nuance of difference between his didactic statement and a surprisingly similar sentence from Egyptian wisdom is not unimportant. "More acceptable is the character of one upright of heart than the ox of the evildoer. Act for the God, that he may act similarly for thee. . . ."[127]

This basic statement about the will of Yahweh in v 6 reads like a manifesto of the prophetic-Levitic opposition party, which we assumed stands in the background of 4:6.[128] This group struggles simultaneously against the cultic practices and the political current in Israel. We saw already in 5:1 that an official alliance of priests and court officials long since stood opposed to them. Now, in the cultic solemnities following the critical period of Israel's collapse, this again becomes apparent.

■ **7** The "catalogue of sins"[129] in vv 7–10a makes clear that the official priests do not follow the will of God described by v 6; and that, for this very reason, the publicly declared repentance in 6:1–3 is insufficient. "But they" (והמה) makes an adversative connection with v 6.[130] Similar to the transgressions of 5:1b–2, the deeds for which accusation is made here can no longer be explained in detail. This observation alone makes it probable that Hosea had in mind certain contemporary events rather than older instances from the remote past received as tradition.

To be sure, the first example of "Adam" might suggest an event connected with the period of the conquest (cf. Ps 78:60b!). "Adam" recalls the ancient region of the present–day *Tell ed–Damje* situated at the mouth of the Jabbok River, which is mentioned in Josh 3:16 as well.[131] In this case, at the time the Jordan was crossed there would have been a breaking of the covenant in Adam comparable to the incident at Baal–Peor mentioned in 9:10. Yet other traditions, while referring to the latter, know nothing of the former. Moreover, in this passage Hosea apparently does not otherwise go further back into Israel's history. Hence, v 7 probably refers to some recent action by the cultic community which demonstrated its unfaithfulness to the covenant. Verse 7b shows that here "covenant" (ברית) does not mean some treaty, but refers rather to Israel's relationship to Yahweh: "they dealt faithlessly with me." The catchword ברית names the presupposition for loyal conduct within the community designated by משפט in v 5 and by חסד and דעת אלהים in v 6. That ברית occurs at the beginning of the "catalogue of sins" suggests that vv 7ff belonged originally with vv 4–6. The word denotes the binding relationship between Yahweh and Israel to which "God in his free sovereignty purposely committed himself as Lord to be responsible for the protection and well–being of his people."[132] For Hosea the basis of the covenant is the exodus from Egypt (12:10; 13:4; 11:1; cf. Jer 31:32) and the wandering in the wilderness (9:10). Connected with the covenant is Yahweh's giving of the "Torah" (8:1, 12; 4:1f, 6). Al-

H. Kruse, "Die 'dialektische Negation' als semitisches Idiom," *VT* 4 (1954): 385–400.

126 Cf. Wolff, "Erkenntnis," 426ff and Vriezen, *Theologie*, 104f.

127 "The Instruction for King Meri–ka–re," Wilson, *ANET²*, 417, line 129; cf. S. Morenz, *Ägyptische Religion* (Stuttgart, 1960), 103f; 142f.

128 See pp. .79f

129 Weiser.

130 See p. 109.

131 Cf. N. Glueck, "Three Israelite Towns in the Jordan Valley: Zarethan, Succoth, Zaphon," *BASOR* 90 (1943): 5f.

132 F. Horst, "Recht," 67 [283]; cf. the commentary on 2:20.

though Israel can "make no legal claim" upon the "covenant promises," "God has the legal right to make demands upon all who are bound by the terms of the covenant."[133] This is presupposed by the accusation in v 7, but it does not describe to what extent the covenant was broken.

■ 8  The transgressions committed in Gilead are also unspecified (cf. 12:12). The city lies in the highlands, some 6 miles south of Jabbok and 15 miles east of the Jordan.[134] פֹּעֲלֵי אָוֶן can mean "evildoers" of various kinds, but in the Old Testament, the word פָּעַל—popular in the Phoenecian language—is always suggestive of enmity against Yahweh or is connected with the pagan cults.[135] The meaning is that deeds committed in Gilead left traces of blood behind them. It has been thought that "traces" (עָקֵב) is an allusion to an unknown Jacob tradition.[136] But again, it is more probable that Hosea refers to recent transgressions. Thus פֹּעַל אָוֶן could recall objectionable military and political dealings[137] as well as specific cultic transgressions (cf. Prv 30:20) which Hosea otherwise designates by the word זְנוּנִים. Then "traces of blood" might refer to child sacrifice.[138]

■ 9  "The way to Shechem" is the third place mentioned in the catalogue. Verse 9 expressly accuses the "band of priests" (חֶבֶר כֹּהֲנִים). We may presume, in view of the context, that it is chiefly the same priests who are accused in vv 7 and 8. This group of thieves is guilty of murder. חֶבֶר, an Aramaic loan word, is also found in the vocabulary of the people at Mari (ḫibrum). It denotes a smaller sociological unit: an alliance, association, or community.[139] Perhaps Hosea uses this foreign word in

a disparaging sense.[140] The deeds are designated as זִמָּה, which usually means indecent conduct. Similar to v 8, this might refer to a specific act in the Canaanite cult. However, the details in v 9a make it more probable that the action was of a political or cultic–political nature. This may have been some brutal assault against the priestly (Levitic) and prophetic opposition (cf. 9:7–9) who could have had their chief residence in the old amphictyonic center of Shechem.[141] It remains to be observed that Hosea polemicized against Bethel, Gilgal, Mizpah, Tabor and Samaria, but never against Shechem. E. Meyer has already drawn attention to this fact.[142] Dtn 27:14 mentions the service the Levites performed at the amphictyonic center in Shechem. In 1 Kgs 12:1, the city is still considered the locus of the attitude that Israel remained a united whole, an attitude shared by Hosea in his own way (2:1–3; 5:10ff). Shechem was unlike Dan and Bethel (1 Kgs 12:29), where calf worship was established, and non–Levitic priests (according to 1 Kgs 12:31) were appointed. Finally, it was a city of refuge (Josh 20:7), thus providing still another reason for the accusation, since people were robbed on their way to its asylum (cf. Dtn 19:3). It can no longer be determined whether the priests were thereby involved in a revolt against the throne.[143] Here it is also unlikely that Hosea was referring to such ancient events as those mentioned in Gen 34; 49:5ff.[144]

■ 10  Verse 10a gives the impression of being a summary statement, provided "Bethel" is not the correct reading.[145] This final sentence is helpful in answering the basic question whether the list of transgressions in vv 7–9

133 Horst, "Recht," 67 [283].
134 *Khirbet Jelʿad*; cf. M. Noth, "Beiträge zur Geschichte des Ostjordanlandes I," *PJ* 37 (1941): 59ff [also in his *Aufsätze zur biblischen Landes– und Altertumskunde* 1, ed. H. W. Wolff (Neukirchen, 1971), 355ff.
135 P. Humbert, "L'emploi du verbe pāʿel et de ses dérivés substantifs," *ZAW* 65 (1953): 35–44; cf. Is 31:2 and Prv 30:20 and see the commentary on 4:12ff concerning Hosea's criticism of the cult with the catchword זְנוּנִים.
136 Recently Nielsen, *Shechem*, 291.
137 Is 31:2; according to 2 Kgs 15:25, there were fifty men of Gilead who were co–conspirators in Pekah's plot of 734.
138 See the commentary on 5:7.
139 M. Noth, "Die Ursprünge des alten Israel im Lichte neuer Quellen," *AFLNW* 94 (1961): 16, 30 [also in his *Aufsätze zur biblischen Landes– und Altertumskunde*

2, ed. H. W. Wolff (Neukirchen, 1971), 252; 263f]. In Ugaritic *ḥbr* means the "companion," *CTCA* 6.VI.48 (Gordon, 62.48).
140 Cf. its meaning as "curse" in Dtn 18:11; Ps 58:6; Is 47:9, 12 and the use of חבר in 4:17.
141 Cf. Wolff, "Heimat," 94, n. 70 [249, n. 70].
142 *Geschichte des Altertums* 3 (Stuttgart, 1954³), 16f; 2² (1953³), 311f.
143 Alt, "Hosea 5:8–6:6," 186 and see below.
144 Nielsen, *Shechem*, 291.
145 See textual note "k" to 6:10.

refers back to deeds of the remote past or to recent political or cultic sins. The perfect, typical of Hosea,[146] can express events which are current or recent (but cf. 9:10). The nominal clauses in vv 8 and 9aα as well as the imperfect in v 9aβ support, in this context, a present interpretation of the perfect verbs (also in vv 7 and 9b). "Horrible thing" (שַׁעֲרוּרִיָּה, cf. Jer 18:13) suggests cultic rather than political transgressions. Additional support for this is found in (1) the connection of the accusations in vv 7–10a with v 6; (2) the express mention of the priests in v 9; (3) the interpretative gloss in v 10b that is reminiscent of 5:3.[147] Alt[148] supposes that "in a genuinely Hosean fashion these verses portray the progress of a revolution that began in Gilead and continued on over the Jordan (Adam) toward Shechem, etc." But, in addition to the observations noted above, other evidence tells against this: (1) the order of those places named; (2) the fact that for each town a particular transgression is mentioned, with no recognizable connection with what precedes it.

■ **11a** The Judaic gloss[149] is difficult to interpret (is "appointed" [שָׁת] to be translated impersonally?). The language is that of the exile: "harvest," denoting judgment in the sense of "last hour," is also found in Jer 51:33.[150] Together with the other Judaic glosses (5:5bβ; 4:5aβ, 15aβ²; 1:7) and the redactional superscriptions in 1:1 and 4:1a, v 11a demonstrates how important the book of Hosea had become for Judah during the period of the exile.[151]

■ **6:11b–7:2** The next verses—perhaps evoked by the audience's response that Yahweh has forgiven Israel's transgression when she cried out to him—begin with the tone of a lament.[152] This tone remains in the new accusations, continuing on to the perfects in 7:2b. The accusations apparently allude to the list of transgressions in 6:7–10: cf. "they deal falsely" (פָּעֲלוּ שֶׁקֶר) in 7:1a with "evildoers" (פֹּעֲלֵי אָוֶן) in 6:8; "robbers" (גְּדוּד) in 7:1b with "robber" (אִישׁ גְּדוּדִים) in 6:9. But beyond this the accusations connect the passage 6:7–7:2 with 5:8–6:6 in that Yahweh's question in 6:4a—evoked by the penitential liturgy (6:1–3)—is considered in a new light in 6:11b–7:1, and in the fact that the genuineness of Israel's repentance is further tested (cf. 7:2 with 5:15; 6:4b–6). Moreover, it is stated that if Yahweh were to fulfill Israel's self-confident expectations, it would not lead to the salvation he intended; cf. 6:11b–7:1a with 6:1–3.

■ **6:11b–7:1** Hosea's God comes to a decision on the basis of the history of his mighty acts. "Restore the fortunes" (שׁוּב שְׁבוּת v 11b), parallel to "healed" (רפא), denotes the restoration of the people's wounded body (cf. 5:13; 6:1), an event which happened repeatedly in the course of Israel's history. In this passage, the expression should be interpreted in the sense of *restitutio in integrum*,[153] rather than in the sense of suspension of imprisonment for guilt.[154] "To heal" (רפא) includes the meaning of "forgive" (cf. 14:5), for which concept Hosea uses no other word.[155]

What occurred when Yahweh helped Israel out of distress? There was new "transgression" and "wickedness." Samaria, an independent city–state, as capital of the land (also 10:5, 7; 14:1) was responsible for the political decisions under discussion. It stands parallel to Ephraim, as do Jerusalem and Judah in Isaiah (3:8; 5:3). "They deal falsely." Instead of the more usual עָשָׂה שֶׁקֶר (2 Sam 18:13; Jer 6:13; 8:10) Hosea again uses the word פָּעַל, which implies hostility toward Yahweh.[156] Within the larger context, the expression can mean deceptive repentance (6:1–4) as well as treacherous political alliances (5:11b, 13). Considered in terms of

---

146 See the commentary on 5:9.
147 See textual note "m" to 6:10.
148 "Hos 5:8–6:6," 186, n. 1.
149 See textual note "n" to 6:11.
150 Cf. Joel 4:13 [3:13]; the motif already occurs in Am 8:2.
151 Cf. E. Janssen, *Juda in der Exilszeit*, FRLANT 69 (Göttingen, 1956), 88ff; 91.
152 On "my people" (עַמִּי), cf. 4:6, 8, 12 and see pp. 78f; further, cf. 5:10 and the commentary.
153 Thus according to E. L. Dietrich, שׁוּב שְׁבוּת. *Die Endzeitliche Wiederherstellung bei den Propheten* BZAW 40 (Giessen, 1925), who derives שְׁבוּת from the root שׁוּב.
154 Thus E. Baumann, "שׁוּב שְׁבוּת. Eine exegetische Untersuchung," *ZAW* 47 (1929): 17–44, who considers the root to be שׁבה. Concerning the difficulty of the phrase's interpretation see R. Borger, "Zu שׁוּב שְׁבוּ/ית," *ZAW* 66 (1954): 315f.
155 J. J. Stamm, *Erlösen und Vergeben im AT* (Bern, 1940), 81.
156 See the commentary on 6:8.

the immediate context, the former meaning is the more likely, especially since the expression is related to the cult also in Jer 6:13; 8:10. But for Hosea it should not be separated from the latter. Earlier as well as now (6:7–10a), whenever Yahweh has mercy on his people, their pious outward appearances are not followed by appropriate deeds; rather there is theft and robbery within and without.

■ **2** Such deeds are characteristic of their lack of genuine, reflective repentance.[157] Israel has not considered that Yahweh's judgment intends to tear her loose from her wickedness and return her to the covenant (cf. 6:5). The penitential song (6:1–3), rejected in the course of this scene, is considered fleeting (6:4b) because any sign of confession of guilt is absent (in contrast to 14:3–4). Thus there is neither a liberation from the false path that has been taken, nor a genuine return to Yahweh's covenant. "Now" (עתה) introduces the conclusion that must be drawn and, as the outcome, is to be lamented: their deeds encircle them.[158] As in 4:9; 5:4, 5b, man is pictured as captive to the principle of that fateful sphere which he creates for himself by his own actions.[159] Yet this does not work itself out independently,[160] but "before Yahweh's face." Appearing before him are not those who in their distress seek communion with him (5:15; 6:6), but those who are caught in and circumscribed by their own deeds. They make necessary the further chastisement announced by the prophet (5:9, 14).

■ **3–7** In the course of this scene, the repetition of the catchword "wickedness" (7:1, 2) and the reproach against their "false dealings" (v 1) may have provoked a counter–question from the audience: How could such a reproach against a chastened people be justified at this time, when they demonstrated their repentant attitude? This may have given Hosea reason to begin a new reproach concerning the recent events of King Hoshea's enthronement and the murder of his predecessor, Pekah.[161] In the disputation, he begins by making an accusation, giving the evidence for their "wickedness"

and "deceit" (v 3). Then he uses the metaphor of a baker's oven (תנור vv 4, 6, 7a) for these deeds in order to formulate—in the style of a divine speech—the main point of the accusation at the end (v 7bβ), which also connects this part of the scene with the whole passage.

■ **3** The "wickedness" that "makes the king glad" probably refers to the violent overthrow of the king which the prophet has condemned. Since Pekah's anti–Assyrian politics were unsuccessful, a new political line of submission was attempted by King Hoshea, who was prepared to become Assyria's vassal. With the deposition of the king, his court's military and civil "officials" (שׂרים) are also replaced. The coronation is a day of joy (1 Sam 11:15b; 2 Kgs 11:14). "Make glad" (ישׂמחו), which should not be replaced by the less–vivid conjecture יְמָשְׁחוּ[162]—a verb that fits poorly with the second object, שׂרים—emphasizes the arrogance (vv 4–7) of those accused. We can no longer ascertain whether the priests mentioned previously[163] are reproved here as supporters of the revolt. The "wickedness" and "lies" (כחשׁ also occurs in 10:13 and 12:1) consist in the fact that in the midst of the collapse, attempts were made to manipulate domestic policy (cf. 5:11b, 13) instead of turning to Yahweh in new obedience and worship (6:6; 7:1).

It is hardly possible to see Baal and his mythological court[164] behind the figures of the king (מלך) and his officials (שׂרים). This is clear from the context (cf. v 7bα) as well as from Hosea's general cultic and political point of view and vocabulary (cf. 3:4; 8:4; 13:10f). J. Begrich's[165] analysis already has criticized this interpretation sufficiently.

■ **4** The word "they all" (כלם) includes those circles reproved in v 3 for deposing the old king and also the newly invested court. That they are called "adulterers" fits well the accusation of "deception" (v 3; cf. v 1a) and Hosea's metaphorical language (3:1; 4:13f). As in the cult, political dealings are also carried on in unfaithfulness toward Yahweh (cf. v 7bβ with 2:15). These

---

157 On "heart" (לב) see the commentary on 4:11.
158 Cf. 5:4 and the commentary.
159 See the commentary on 4:11 and Koch, "Vergeltungsdogma," 12.
160 On היה see the commentary on 5:10.
161 See pp. 111f.
162 See textual note "e" on 7:3.
163 Cf. 6:9; and the commentary.

164 Nyberg, also Östborn, *Yahweh and Baal*, 34, 37.
165 "Zur Frage der alttestamentlichen Textkritik," *OLZ* 42 (1939), 481f.

idolatrous passions are compared with glowing embers of an "oven" burning unattended—insofar as the condition of the transmitted text allows us to understand it. The "oven" (תנור) was usually cylindrical in form and up to three feet in length. Its walls sloped upward, with an orifice at the top. When the wood was ignited early in the morning (v 6b), the oven could burn like a flaming torch (Gen 15:17). After the fire burned for hours, dough that had been kneaded with yeast and left standing for several hours was shaped into flat cakes and slapped on the oven's inside walls and baked. Practically every house had its own oven (Lev 26:26), but the court[166] and the large cities[167] had professional bakers.[168] Therefore, the mention of the bakers would be more intelligible if this scene took place in the royal city of Samaria (cf. 7:1) rather than elsewhere.

■ 5 Wine influences the "mockers," adding fire to their heated emotions. The "mockers" (לצצים) are probably those who garrulously deride the prophet (cf. 9:7). The expression suggests that Hosea had to submit to interruptions in the course of this scene. "The day of ⟨their⟩ King" may indicate the celebration of the day when Tiglath-pileser's vassal ascended the throne. Hosea maintains an obvious distance: "their king."[169] Throughout the uncertain text, one senses a spirit of arrogant commotion that followed the Assyrian invasion, the murder of the king, the payment of tribute, and the acceptance of the murderer as the vassal king. Wickedness and deception feed on drunken frenzy.

■ 6 This verse continues to describe the emotional frenzy of the activity. An oven burns slowly during the night, if at all; but it "blazes up brightly in the morning" when a new pile of wood is kindled. Similarly the "passions"[170] of Israel's leaders are quickly inflamed. Does Hosea refer to the recent enthusiasm in the court following the depressing weeks of catastrophe (v 5a)? Or does he mean the agitation kindled by his appearance as prophet among those who wanted to sleep off their drunken bout (v 5b)? Or, with a new application of his metaphor, does Hosea look back to the revolt's beginning, which suddenly broke out into the open from a secret conspiracy (v 7a)? The text remains obscure.

■ 7 Comparing the heated passions once again to an oven, the continuation in v 7 clearly relates to the palace murder, which at the same time is pictured as the work of a famished wild animal: "they devour their judges" (cf. "devour" [אכל] in 2:14; 13:8). Thus the metaphor of the oven is applied in a variety of ways: it denotes the heated passions of Israel's adulterous desertion of Yahweh (v 4); the glowing enthusiasm of the enthronement celebration; the fervent agitation of the disputes (v 5); and finally, the flare-up of the confusion attending the deposition of the king (v 7). In v 7 the prophet moves on from an actual event—which we discern only with difficulty—to a more general and fundamental description.[171] In the year 733, one could look back upon a series of revolts against the throne: within a period of twelve years, four kings were overthrown.[172] In Hosea "judges [literally]" (שפטים) simply appears to be another word for (a group of) "leaders" (שרים),[173] perhaps especially important royal officials who would necessarily be deposed along with their king.

The brief nominal clause concluding the verse states what continued to be valid: none of the kings' murderers call upon Yahweh. This again picks up the "red thread" that continues throughout the entire scene. As Assyria (5:13) and then Egypt (7:11) were sought instead of Yahweh (cf. 11:7; 2:18), so the new kings are called upon instead of Yahweh. Once more Hosea portrays his God as one whose love has been disappointed (2:15; 5:15; 7:1). Judgment must then become even more intense (5:9, 14; 6:5; 7:2) to accomplish Israel's return to Yahweh (5:15).

■ 8 The catchword "Ephraim among the nations" seems to begin a completely new series of prophetic sayings. The domestic-political theme of "revolt against the throne" is replaced by problems involving foreign policy. But at the probable time of this scene's occurrence, both

---

166  1 Sam 8:13; Gen 40:1ff; 41:10.
167  Jer 37:21; Neh 3:11.
168  Cf. Dalman, *Arbeit* 4, 88ff; 104ff; *BRL*, 75ff; Noth, *World*, 159f [125f]; A. G. Barrois, *Manuel d'Archéologie Biblique* 1 (Paris, 1939), 320ff.
169  See textual note "i" to 7:5.
170  See textual note "o" to 7:6.
171  Cf. the similar transition from 6:7–9 to v 10a.
172  See p. 111.
173  See textual note "z" to 13:10.

themes are inseparably dovetailed. King Hoshea had killed Pekah at the advance of Tiglath–pileser's troops because his political alliance with Aram, Philistia, and Egypt would have to be dissolved in favor of submission to Assyria. Following the prophet's accusation in 7:3–7, the new king's advisers could have quickly asked Hosea: What else could we have done than turn from Aram, Philistia and Egypt and go to Assyria, thereby deposing Pekah? But these are only suppositions to explain the transition to a new theme. Yet two points can be made. (1) V 8 does not in essence begin a new theme; rather, the prophet returns to the scene's initial theme in 5:8–13, which in the meantime led to particular arguments with the groups of priests (6:1–7:2) and royal officials (7:3–7). (2) The metaphorical language in v 8 indicates that the simile of the oven connected with the theme "revolt against the throne" is still in effect.

Usually, when Hosea replies to his opponents' objections, he indicates his sympathy by beginning with a lament (vv 8–9: cf. 5:11; 6:11b–7:1a). Ephraim has "mixed" himself among the nations, as oil is mixed with dough.[174] This metaphor is quite appropriate for the way Israel was politically and militarily "mixed together" with Aram and Judah with Egypt and Assyria in 733.

Verse 8b develops a new aspect of the metaphor. The flat cakes of bread thrown on the hot stove must be turned quickly lest they burn.[175] The purpose of the metaphor is probably to say that the necessary return to Yahweh is still wanting (v 10b). Ephraim undisturbedly remains lying on the wrong side, though the consequences will be painful.[176]

■ **9** What is more, "foreigners devour his strength."[177] This may refer not only to the Aramaean troops in league with Israel who marched through the land in 733 on their way to conquer Jerusalem and "camped in Ephraim,"[178] but also to the Assyrians who, having entered the coastal province of Dor in the previous year, now enter the provinces of Meggido and Gilead. During the upheavals of 733, when one disaster was succeeded by another, "gray hairs have stolen upon [many],"[179] for they have suddenly aged from fright. Hosea chiefly laments the fact that though Israel has fatefully lost her strength and vitality, none is aware of it. The expression "and he knows it not" (והוא לא ידע), twice repeated, becomes understandable within the same context as Hosea's reproof of the drunken frenzy and delirium surrounding the recent confirmation of their vassal king (vv 3–5).

■ **10** The interpolater, who has inserted an older saying of Hosea's (5:5a) here as he did in 6:10b, traces Israel's lack of insight into her true situation back to her stubborn "pride."

Verse 10b might also be a secondary insertion taken from 5:4a, 15, especially since "Yahweh their God" occurs here instead of the divine speech in the first person[180] found in the surrounding context. However, the two lines in v 10b appear to be much more independent of possible parallels than v 10a; in addition they constitute a *Qinah* strophe which is consonant with vv 8–9. Although the disputation style does not match the following saying, it does correspond well with vv 8–9, to which the gloss[181] "for all this" (בכל־זאת) correctly refers, since the theme of vv 8–9 prepares for v 10b.[182] The transition from singular (vv 8f) to plural (v 10b) frequently occurs within the speech units (cf. 5:13, 14f; 6:4). The explanation for this is that only with the accusation does the prophet leave aside the singular in v 8b required by the metaphor. In any case, however, it should be noted how well v 10b fits with the kerygmatic theme of the entire scene (cf. 5:13, 15; 6:4b, 6; 7:2, 7, 14, 16). If this saying should not originally belong within this scene, it nevertheless appropriately expresses the point of the prophet's accusations.

■ **11** Continuing the theme "Israel among the nations" (v 8a), a new saying (vv 11–12) uses the imagery of a "foolish dove" to describe Ephraim's relationship to the nations.[183] For Hosea, practical ungodliness is tanta-

---

174 "Mix" (בלל) Ex 29:2; Lev 2:5; in v 4 Hosea spoke of the preparation of dough.
175 Dalman, *Arbeit* 4, 35f.
176 Wellhausen.
177 On "foreigners, strangers" (זרים) see the commentary on 5:7.
178 Is 7:2; see p. 111.
179 See textual note "q" to 7:9.

180 7:7, 12; see p. 110.
181 See textual note "s" to 7:10.
182 See above.
183 On "simple, easily seduced" (פתה), see p. 41; on "heedless, with no sense of direction" (אין לב), see pp. 41f.

mount to stupidity and instability (cf. 4:11f).[184] This becomes apparent in Israel's seesaw politics. The call to Egypt for help, followed by submission to Assyria, does not fit the period of change from King Pekahiah to King Pekah.[185] Pekahiah had probably continued the policies of his father, Menahem, who had to pay tribute to Tiglath–pileser III beginning in 738.[186] Pekah's politics, on the other hand, were anti–Assyrian.[187] Nor do these political maneuverings—going first to Egypt, then to Assyria—fit with the events of 724;[188] at the most, they would correspond with what occurred soon after Shalmaneser V's accession to the throne (727), but we have little information concerning this.[189] But they certainly would fit the year 733.[190] The simile of a fluttering bird (also in 11:11) appears repeatedly in the Annals of Tiglath–pileser III from the same year.[191]

■ **12** A new announcement of judgment is directed against Israel's current practice of seesaw politics among the great powers. The announcement returns to the threat at the beginning of this scene (5:9, 14): Yahweh will "spread out his net" and catch them.[192] This suggests the devastation of Ephraim's heartland (5:9). Similar to 5:9, ("chastisement" [תוכחה]), the punishment is announced as a disciplinary measure.[193]

■ **13** The cry of woe, which seldom occurs in Hosea,[194] indicates that the sayings in this scene are reaching a climax. After the first stage of weighing the evidence (6:4) and then examining Israel's transgression, Yahweh reaches a decision. Unlike the previous sayings, this cry of woe only speaks of Israel's relationship to Yahweh. She flees (נדד [also in 9:17]) before Yahweh and disobedi-

ently rebels against him. "Rebel" (פשע [also in 8:1]) designates rebellion in a nonreligious sense;[195] in this context it signifies opposition to divine authority and attack upon God's lordship.[196] Yet Israel expects Yahweh to liberate such rebels from their calamity. The brief adversative clause—"and I am supposed to redeem them"—apparently returns again to the expectations and expressions of trust voiced in the penitential song (6:1–3), which had caused Yahweh's inner struggle (6:4a) over Israel's fate. Yet, after consideration of the attitude of the priests and the worshipers (6:7–7:2), the dealings of the court (7:3–7) and its foreign policy (7:8–12), the words of repentance are exposed as "lies."[197] It is of course Yahweh's will to save his people. But it is precisely this, his saving will and his covenant loyalty, which set in bold relief the shamefulness of Israel's deceitful attempts at saving herself (cf. 6:11b–7:1). Here the word "to redeem" (פדה [also in 13:14]), originally belonging to the sphere of commercial law, similar to "to heal" (רפא 5:13; 7:1; cf. 6:1), means deliverance from physical danger.[198] With respect to the use of this term for the deliverance from Egypt, Deuteronomy (7:8; 9:26; 13:6; 21:8) apparently stands in a tradition which is first found in Hosea.[199] If there is to be a true liberation of Israel, a new relationship to Yahweh must be established first by his judgment. The "destruction" denoted here by שד recalls 5:9a, "desolation" (שמה). The disputations draw to a close. Evidence has now been publicly presented which provides the motivation for the initial threats.

■ **14** That we rightly saw a criticism of Israel's prayers

---

184 Cf. K. Barth, *Church Dogmatics* IV, 2, tr. G. W. Bromiley (Edinburgh: T. and T. Clark, 1958), 409ff [460ff]: "We are forced to the rather unusual and hazardous statement that sin is also stupidity, and stupidity is also sin. By stupidity we mean, of course, that which the Bible describes and condemns as human folly" (411).

185 Thus Procksch.

186 2 Kgs 15:19f; Noth, *History*, 257 [233].

187 See pp. 111f.

188 2 Kgs 17:4; Noth, *History*, 261f [237].

189 2 Kgs 17:3; G. Ricciotti, *The History of Israel* 1, (Milwaukee: Bruce, 1955), 353f; W. von Soden, "Assyrien," *RGG*³ 1, 652.

190 See pp. 111f.

191 Cf. *TGI*, 51 (line 203 of the Annals); 53 (line 12 of a stone–tablet inscription); Alt, "Feldzug," 157 (fragments from the Annals, line 17).

192 Concerning the imagery, cf. 5:1 and the commentary; it was already used in the great hymn to Shamash to characterize divine judgment; see A. Falkenstein–W. von Soden, *Sumerische und Akkadische Hymnen und Gebete* (Zürich, 1953), 243.

193 On "discipline, chasten" (יסר) see the commentary on 5:2.

194 It is found elsewhere only in 9:12.

195 1 Kgs 12:19; Is 1:2; cf. Koehler, *Theology*, 169 [159].

196 Horst, "Naturrecht," 263 [247f].

197 With "lies" (כזבים) cf. "falsehood" (שקר 7:1); "lies" (כחשים 7:3); and "treacherous bow" (קשת רמיה 7:16).

198 Cf. Stamm, *Erlösen*, 14, 87f.

199 Stamm, *Erlösen*, 19; see also Mic 6:4.

behind v 13b is confirmed by v 14. This verse adds that Israel, according to the whole manner of her prayers, is not worshiping Yahweh but rather the gods of Canaan.[200] In an international treaty from the middle of the eighth century, the Assyrian Assurnirari V supposes that his treaty partner Mati'el of Arpad does not march out with his troops "with his whole heart" (*a–na ga–mur–ti libbi* [*bi*]–*šu*), which means here "not in complete loyalty."[201] Once again Hosea's criticism of the cult shines through. Instead of calling to Yahweh deliberately and with humble obedience, they howl lustily (ילל hip'il) from their adulterous beds[202] during their rites of fertility.[203] They gash themselves, as was customary in the rituals of the Baal cult.[204] People cut themselves when they lamented over some difficulty (1 Kgs 18:28), especially over death (Dtn 14:1; Lev 19:28; Jer 16:6). By these actions Israel demonstrated how stubborn[205] she is toward Yahweh. Of principal concern in the fertility rites was "grain and new wine." It is understandable that these rites were practiced anew in the present festivals of lamentation over military disaster not only because foreign troops themselves took of Israel's food,[206] but also because Tiglath–pileser III probably divested the Samarian highlands of its most important source of grain, the Jezreel Valley.[207]

■ 15 Yahweh is deeply grieved by the foreign cults in that he alone had "strengthened the arms" of Israel (cf. 2:10; 11:1ff). The glossator interprets this "strengthening of the arms" in the sense of Job 4:3 and in the spirit of Hosea's theology (5:2; 7:12; 10:10; cf. especially 11:3), as Yahweh's work of educating Israel (יסר pi'el). By contrast there are plotters in Israel who purposely "plan evil" against Yahweh. In every sentence from v 13 on, Hosea regards the sum total of Israel's transgressions as a personal attack upon Yahweh, especially upon his love (13bα, 15a).

■ 16 In the light of our interpretation of vv 13–16, the corrupt text in the beginning of v 16a should probably read: "they turn [themselves] to." Of course, Israel "turns" from Egypt to Assyria (5:13; 7:11); from Pekah to Hoshea ben Elah (7:3ff), and also to a god patterned after a Canaanite model (6:1–3; 7:14). But the one necessary turning to Yahweh never occurs.[208] In this respect Israel is a "deceitful bow." G. R. Driver[209] has shown that קשת רמיה is a feeble and useless bow; it appears to be capable of shooting, but the arrow does not reach its target.[210] Ps 78:57 (note "they twisted," נהפכו) uses the same metaphor. With this expression this scene's accusation is definitively formulated.

At the conclusion, the threat which initiated the entire scene (5:8f) is repeated. In v 16, however, the content of the threat is not about the land's devastation, but the death of its leaders by the sword. "Because of the insolence of their tongue:" זעם means "curse"; in this instance it is probably the curse against the prophet (cf. 7:5b) uttered by those from courtly circles; this can be read between the lines, e.g., in 5:10; 7:3, 8. Their resistance against the divine word spoken by the prophet will not prevent, but will ultimately provoke divine judgment. Even Egypt will hold them in derision when it learns that Israel's strategy of turning from Egypt to Assyria[211] could not save her from total disaster.

### Aim

The threat of a total military destruction of Israel provides the basic thrust of the kerygma of this scene. The catastrophe will surpass all previous blows against Israel, for its heartland, Ephraim—up to this time unscathed—will also be attacked (5:9, 14; 7:13, 16). It is made clear that judgment comes not only upon the Northern Kingdom, but upon all Yahweh's covenant people as such (5:10, 12–14; 6:4, 11b). Human agents of Yahweh's judgment are only indirectly visible (5:8, 10a; 7:16aβ); once Yahweh speaks expressly of the prophets' words as those of his own mouth (6:5); in another instance he mentions the pouring out of his own wrath (5:10)! Otherwise, Yahweh himself always executes the punishment: pictured as a ravenous lion, he will not

---

200 On "from their heart" (בלבם) see pp. 38ff and also the commentary on 7:2.
201 On the text and its interpretation see E. Weidner, *AfO* 8 (1932–33): 20f.
202 On "bed" (משכב), cf. Is 57:8; Ezek 23:17; Song 3:1; also, May, "Fertility Cult," 78ff.
203 See the commentary on 4:13f.
204 See textual note "x" to 7:14.
205 See textual note "y" to 7:14.
206 See the commentary on 7:9.
207 See p. 48.
208 See textual note "aa" to 7:16; "to me" (אלי) occurs as a catchword in 7:7, 14; similarly in v 10b; 5:15.
209 "Problems of the Hebrew Text and Language," BBB1 (1950) 53.
210 Cf. Koehler–Baumgartner.

let the prey from his clutches (5:14); like a hunter of birds, he stretches out his net and brings down the dove in its attempts to escape (7:12). It is already evident from this imagery that in his zeal Yahweh is less intent on Israel's destruction than on drawing her away from the foreign nations. They cannot help her; in the end, they will only hold her in contempt (5:11b, 13b; 7:11b, 16b). Yahweh's judgment is unambiguously described not as the ultimate but as the penultimate judgment (5:15). Accordingly, the concepts of chastisement (5:9) and discipline (7:12) characterize its purpose.

The announcement of judgment opens this turbulent scene and also dominates its conclusion; however, it occupies less space than the accusations, which assail the audience again and again with well–known facts of their guilt elucidated by appropriate metaphors. The heart of the accusation consists in this: though Israel, in her previous experience of catastrophe, had made strategic moves in both foreign (5:11b, 13; 7:11) and domestic policy (7:3ff), she had failed to do what was of decisive significance for Yahweh's covenant people, namely, to return to him (5:15; 7:7b, 10b, 14a, 16a cj.). This is the crucial guilt around which most of the sayings in this scene revolve, especially after the audience's objections called for the further reasons for the accusation. It was alleged by them that, with their political maneuvers, they had also performed religious exercises (6:1–3; cf. 7:14). An examination of their claim reveals that the crimes against the community (6:7–10), the court's revolt (7:3–7), and the change from one foreign ally to another (7:11–12) prove that their turning to Yahweh was much too superficial (6:4b); indeed, it was deceptive (7:13b; cf. vv 1a, 3, 15a). What is lacking is not the readiness for service and sacrifice, but, according to 6:6, loyalty (חסד) to Yahweh and the knowledge and acknowledgment of him as the God of Israel, whose lordship extends over all areas of life (דעת אלהים). What is lacking is not religious trust (6:1–3), but the recognition and confession of their transgression against Yahweh (7:2a). Hence the climax of the accusation indicates that Yahweh's people, with all their fervor in political and religious undertakings, have rejected him as their God. The sayings culminate in personal laments: "they

deal faithlessly with me" (6:7); "they stray from me;" "they revolt against me" (7:13); "they are ⟨rebellious⟩ against me" (7:14);[212] "they plan evil against me" (7:15). Yahweh does not expect achievements in place of those unfaithful acts, but rather that they turn to him and wait upon his action. That they fail to do this is indicated by the other series of Yahweh's personal laments; "none of them calls upon me" (7:7); "they do not cry to me" (7:14); "they do not turn to me" (7:16).[213] From this it becomes clear that Israel's actual guilt is that she has grieved the God of the covenant (6:7). This guilt comprises all her acts of transgression, since they were committed in the face of his love as he demonstrated it again and again by saving her from danger (6:11b), healing her (7:1), redeeming (7:13), and strengthening her (7:15). Israel has turned away from God's proven covenant loyalty. Herein lies the decisive point of the accusation and the basic motivation for Yahweh's judgment.

For Yahweh it is insufferable that Israel should continue her present attitude toward him. God's love is the *leitmotif of his judgment*, whose purpose it is to win his people back. This becomes evident in Yahweh's sympathetic lament over the misery which already exists in Israel (5:11a; 7:8f). For this reason he struggles within himself: has not Israel experienced enough chastisement (6:4)? But it is not enough, if he really intends to liberate Israel from her hopeless ways and wickedness (7:1–2). Without genuine knowledge of God (6:6), i.e., without both a clear recognition of guilt (7:2a) and a new relationship to him in all spheres of life, the previous catastrophe and the attempt at a new beginning remain a futile, even fatal, undertaking. Hence, Yahweh's love, which seeks to bring Israel back to her first love, has to proceed with judgment until Israel seeks him in the midst of her distress (5:15). It should be noted that any admonition to return is absent. By herself, Israel is totally incapable of return (7:2). God must deal further with her and will himself effect her return to him. "It is notable that especially those prophets who place decisive importance on God's love, namely, Hosea and Jeremiah, are the most radical in their description of divine wrath."[214] The punishment is executed with ex-

---

211  See pp. 111f and the commentary on 7:11.
212  See textual note "y" to 7:14.
213  See textual note "aa" to 7:16; cf. 5:15; 6:6; 7:2a,

10b.
214  Vriezen, *Theologie*, 131; cf. J. Fichtner, *TDNT* 5, 403f; Hos 5:12, 14; Jer 13:12–14.

treme sympathy because its goal is to return Israel both to a knowledge of God as lord of her history and to a bond of loyalty with him (5:15; 6:6). The prophet's words have a twofold purpose: (1) to bring Israel to a knowledge of her guilt by announcing divine judgment; and, (2) to disclose the purpose of the judgment. Through his messengers, God rigorously struggles to make his justice and covenant ordinances "break forth like light" (6:5).

This "sword of the Spirit, which is the word of God,"[215] should be wielded and endured in the church of the New Testament as well. According to Mt 9:13 (cf. 12:7) Jesus sends the "righteous" Pharisees to the book of Hosea to study the didactic sentence in 6:6, lest they criticize him for eating with tax collectors and sinners.[216] Thus God's pilgrims of the New Covenant harm only themselves if they do not listen carefully to the words of this passage. For they, too, must endure trials similar to those suffered by God's people of the Old Testament; they, too, are capable of misunderstanding the purpose of political catastrophes. Even as they keep Jesus' cross and resurrection before their eyes, their roots lie—no less than in the Old Testament—in God's healing love and saving power. Yet as God's people march through history, they can misunderstand the purpose of the judgments which come upon the church of Jesus Christ also in the midst of political upheavals. The church seeks new points of orientation through changes in political alliances and through religious formalities, instead of confessing the guilt involved in all her political unions, instead of recognizing the deception that grows out of her customs and innate confidence,

instead of being liberated by and for the Lord, who alone is the Lord of all powers and the physician of all who are ill, instead of trusting in his deeds and obeying his words. The message of Hosea can also help Christendom return to its first and only love.

The church should especially ponder two points. First, Hosea speaks to individuals only as members of the entire nation; the call to repentance of John the Baptist and Jesus was also spoken in the plural: μετανοεῖτε, ("repent," Mt 3:2; 4:17). "Far from weakening it, it is the plural which constitutes it a genuine seriousness. Behind this plural there stands the seriousness of the great cause of God in the world."[217] It is not a Christian interpretation of the text if we merely individualize it and forget that the path Christianity takes must be taken as the new "people of God" (cf. 1 Pt 2:8f).

Second, Hosea had to struggle with a calculated resistance to his indictment that was religious as well as political. There are times when one must oppose an overly secure faith, like that reflected in 6:1–3,[218] with its shrewd intention to shape history to its own ends. In the New Testament era as well, the wrath of God is provoked by man's attempts to deal with periods of severe catastrophe by a coalition of political strategy and religious zeal. In all spheres of life, God wants his liberated people to acknowledge the guilt of false hope and disobedience; he wants them to look for help in the power of his love and he wants them to do his will. According to Hosea, only such a community of God has "heart," i.e., the ability to orient themselves rationally in this world.[219]

---

215  Cf. Eph 6:17 and Heb 4:12 with Hos 6:5.
216  Cf. E. Lohmeyer, *Das Evangelium des Markus* (Göttingen, 1951), 251 and G. Bornkamm, "Enderwartung und Kirche im Matthäusevangelium," in *The Background of the New Testament and its Eschatology, in Honour of C. H. Dodd* (New York: Harpers, 1956), 234f. On the different meaning given to 6:6 by its quotation in Matthew, cf. H. Braun, "Das AT im NT," *ZThK* 59 (1962): 19.

217  Barth, *Church Dogmatics* IV 2, 566.
218  See pp. 116–19.
219  See the commentary on 7:2, 11, 14.

**Sow the Wind and Reap the Whirlwind**

**Bibliography**

H. Cazelles
"The Problem of the Kings in Os 8:4," *CBQ* 11 (1949): 14–25.

J. de Fraine
"L'aspect religieux de la royauté israélite," *AnBibl* 3 (1954): 147–53.

H. Torczyner
"Dunkle Bibelstellen," *Vom Alten Testament* (K. Marti: Festschrift), BZAW 41 (Giessen, 1925): 277f.

# 8

1  **The trumpet to your mouth!**[a]
    **As a**[b] **vulture (it comes) over Yahweh's house,**
        **because they transgress my covenant**
            **and rebel against my instruction.**
2  **(Of course) they lament over me:**
        **"My**[c] **God!"—"We [Israel]**[d] **know you!"**
3  **(But) Israel rejects the**[e] **good.**
        **An enemy shall pursue him.**[f]

a   "Palate" (חֵךְ) also stands parallel to "lips" in Prv 5:3; 8:7, meaning "mouth" (Song 5:16; 7:10), just as *ḥanakun* does in later Arabic (Nyberg). *G* (εἰς κόλπον αὐτῶν ὡς γῆ) found a corrupt text and read אֶל־חֵכָּם ּכְעָפָר.

b   As a rule, comparisons call for the definite article; cf. Is 1:18 and Brockelmann, *Syntax* § 21cβ. The suggestion to read שֹׁפֵרְךָ נֹצֵר (*BH³*): "Your horn to your mouth, O watchman over Yahweh's house," removes the necessary protasis from the יַעַן"–clause. The trumpet of alarm is blown because of danger from the enemy, not because a law is broken. *M* is supported by *G* and the noteworthy parallel in *T* ("O prophet, call out with your palate as with the trumpet! Say: Behold, as the eagle flies upward, so a king with his troops comes up and advances against the house of Yahweh's sanctuary, because they transgress my covenant . . .").

c   *S* ("our God") harmonizes the word with the plural verbs.

d   *M* adds ישראל in apposition to the subject; *G S* offer the shorter and probably original text. This briefer text also speaks against the otherwise illuminating assumption of an exchange of יהוה at the end of v 1b with ישראל at the end of v 2 (Torczyner, "Bibelstellen," 277).

e   On the absolute in Hebrew, cf. Brockelmann, *Syntax* § 21cγ. טוב meaning "word" (cf. R. Gordis, "Hos 14:3," 88ff) would be possible in view of תורתי (v 1), but the way the thought of v 3 is continued makes this suggestion unlikely, as in 3:5 (see p. 63).

f   Concerning the form of the suffix, which presupposes the connecting vowel *a* with the imperfect (instead of the usual יִרְדְּפֵהוּ), cf. Gesenius–Kautzsch § 60d, Beer–Meyer 2, § 84, 2a. An intentional onomatopoeia apparently led to the selection of the darker sounding ō. *G* (ἐχθρὸν κατεδίωξαν) misread the unusual suffix as an affix of the third plural (van Gelderen suggests יְרָדְפוּ) and accordingly made אויב the accusative (cf. 2:9; 12:2). But with Israel as the subject, a verb in the perfect singular, as in v 3a

**4** They make kings, but without my will.
    They set up officials,ᵍ
    but without my knowledge.
From their silver and their gold
    they make idols for themselves,
    so that it shall be destroyed.ʰ

**5** ⟨Throw away⟩ⁱ your calf, O Samaria!
    My wrath burns against them.
How long do they remain incapable of
    purity?

**6** But theyʲ are from Israel!
That a craftsman has made.
    It is not God.
Rather, the calf of Samaria
    shall be broken into pieces.

**7** Indeed, they sow the wind
    and mowᵏ the whirlwind.
Grain with no head
    yields no bread.ˡ
Were it to yield,
    foreigners would swallow it.

**8** Israel is swallowed up.
    Now theyᵐ are among the nations
[as] a worthlessⁿ thing.ᵒ

**9** For by themselves they have gone up to
    Assyria.
    A wild ass keeps to himself,
    Ephraim pays off its lovers.

**10** Even if they receiveᵖ a whore's wages
    among the nations,

---

g The unusual form of שרר hipʻil (instead of הַשִׂרוּ) could derive from Hosea's preference for assonance with the accented parallel 4aα∥β; cf. v 3b.

(ונח), would be expected. Thus *M*, supported by *S T V*, deserves preference as *lectio difficilior*.

h *G S T* presuppose יְכָרֵתֿ, therefore relating it to the more obvious word עצבים; but this destroys the ironic sense of the result clause. Weiser thinks the clause is an "addition" but offers no compelling reasons.

i חנז is presupposed by *G* (ἀπότριψαι), α' (ἀπώσθησον), and θ' (ἀπόρριψαι); σ' (ἀπεβλήθη) and ε' have vocalized the verb as a passive: חנז or זָנַח. *M* ("he rejects") harmonizes the word with the vocalization in v 3a; in this case Yahweh would have to be the subject, which, in view of the divine speech in the context (v 5aβ; cf. v 4a), is improbable. The direct address, as indicated by עגלך suggests the imperative of *G* α' θ'; moreover, the question posed in v 5b marks the transition to a more lively manner of speech. The free conjecture אֶזְנַח (Wellhausen, Sellin) or זַנְחָתִּי (*BH*³; Robinson) appears even less justified, since v 5aβ in no case presents a genuine parallel to v 5aα.

j This elliptic nominal clause can dispense with a subject, "since in the context of discussion it is presupposed" (cf. K. Oberhuber, "Zur Syntax des Richterbuches," *VT* 3 [1953]: 8).

k Literally: "harvest," in the sense of "to gather, bring in" (Koehler–Baumgartner); in the Hebrew the assonance of יזרעוריקצרו should be noted.

l Here the assonance in Hebrew has developed into complete rhyme (see p. 135); literally: "The grain with no head produces no flour." On the negation בלי ("destruction"), cf. Brockelmann, *Syntax* § 52bβ. Instead of לו and יעשה, *BH*³ suggests feminine forms corresponding to קמה, but the agreement of gender is probably broken, since in the metaphor of empty grain stalks the application is to Israel; cf. vv 7bβ, 8a. Van Gelderen gives consideration to whether קמה is masculine here (Sellin) or whether it is a misreading of קָמָה (Gen 41:5, 22).

m See textual note "k" to 9:16.

n חָפֵץ ("pleasure," "delight") occasionally has the meaning "precious," "valuable" (Prv 3:15; 8:11); cf. Deden.

o כלי ("vessel," "instrument") pales to the meaning "thing" if the object is to be characterized primarily by its material or quality (Gen 24:53; Ex 3:22); thus the expression כלי אין חפץ בו denotes here the opposite of כלי חמדה ("precious thing" 13:15) and of כְּלֵי תִפְאָרֶת ("pieces of jewelry") in Ezek 16:17.

p *G* (παραδοθήσονται) probably read יֻתְּנוּ (Nyberg, Dingermann, "Massora–Septuaginta," 43) (נתן hopʻal); however, the climax, indicated by גם כי, makes it nevertheless more probable that *M* is to be interpreted as נתן qal in the sense of "to receive a harlot's wage" (Nyberg, van Gelderen).

I will now gather them up,
so that they soon ⟨writhe⟩ under the
burden[q]
of the officials' king.

**11** Indeed, Ephraim has multiplied altars.
He uses them for sinning.[r]
Altars for sinning!

**12** Though I write for him the multitude[s]
of ⟨my instructions⟩,[t]
they are regarded as something alien.

**13** ⟨Sacrifices they love, and⟩[u] they sacrifice,
flesh ⟨they love⟩, and they eat;
Yahweh takes no delight in them.[v]
Now he will remember their guilt
and punish their sins.
They shall return[w] to Egypt.

**14** Israel has forgotten his maker
and built palaces.
And Judah has multiplied walled cities.
But I will send fire upon his cities
so that it devours their castles.

q *M* is absolutely incomprehensible: חָלַל הֵחֵל מִן
hipʿil) means "to begin with" (Ezek 9:6); יַחֵל דְּבָרוֹ
means "he breaks his word" (Nu 30:3); משׂא can
mean "burden" or "utterance." מִמַּשָּׂא was already
read by αʹ (ἀπὸ ἅρματος) and σʹ (ἀπὸ φόρου). *G*
(καὶ κοπάσουσι μικρὸν τοῦ χρίειν βασιλέα καὶ
ἄρχοντας) reads וְיֶחְדְּלוּ מְעַט מְמְשֹׁחַ מֶלֶךְ וְשָׂרִים;
וְיֶחְדְּלוּ is also confirmed by σʹ (καὶ μένουσιν) and θʹ
(καὶ διαλείψουσιν); מְשֹׁחַ by θʹ and וְשָׂרִים by αʹ *S*
*T V.* No other emendations are required if וְיָחִילוּ
("to be in labor," "to writhe"; or with Hoonacker
וְיֶחֱלוּ "to become weak," "sick") is read as the verb
form. *S* basically supports *M*. See pp. 143f.

r Nyberg vocalizes לַחֲטֹא and interprets the parallels
as a pun ". . . sin-offering altars . . . altars for sinning," by presuming that the unit consists of two
lines. But the prosodic unit appears to have three
lines, as in vv 8f, 13, despite the 'athnāḥ; cf. also Buber.

s רֻבּוֹ (Ketib with an ancient case ending, according
to C. Brockelmann, *Handbuch der Orientalistic* III
[Leiden–Köln, 1964], 1, 62, and Grether § 53w;
differently Gesenius–Kautzsch § 90k and Beer–
Meyer 1 § 45, 3d) is quite probably to be preferred
to the Qere רֻבֵּי, an unusual plural form.

t *G αʹ* read תּוֹרָתֶי, which, next to רבו is probable but
not necessary, as 9:7bβ indicates (רֹב עֲוֹנְךָ = πλῆθος
τῶν ἀδικιῶν)

u The sequence of consonants הבהבי in *M* is unintelligible; αʹ (θυσίας φέρε φέρε θυσιάξουσιν) translates uncomprehended forms of יהב, which θʹ (θυσίας
μεταφορῶν ἐθυσίσαν) painstakingly attempts to
correct (cf. D. Barthélemy, *Les devanciers d'Aquila,* VT
Suppl 10 [Leiden, 1963], 256). In its expanded text
(. . . θυσιαστήρια τὰ ἠγαπημένα. διότι ἐὰν θύσωσι
θυσίαν . . .) *G* preserves the reminiscence of the root
אהב. Cf. Thomas, "Love," 63, n. 6. Since the time of
Duhm and Marti זֶבַח אֲהָבוּ וַיִּזְבְּחוּ (or: זְבָחִים) is generally read in order to reconstruct the *parallelismus
membrorum*; on the sentence's construction, cf. Mic
2:2a.

v Verse 13aβ is frequently considered secondary, but
without sufficient reason; see p. 136.

w *G* recognizes the relationship of v 13bβ to 9:3bα
and adds the words of 9:3bβ to v 13.

## Form

Here, 8:1, begins a new transmission unit. This is evident
from the excited opening command to sound the alarm.
Unlike 5:8 this command is addressed to an individual.
When a new king was announced or the army had to
retreat, the military commander sounded the trumpet.[1]
Accordingly, the person addressed here is not the prophet
but rather a military officer. That it is not the prophet[2]
is demonstrated by the fact that the large number of
imperative opening calls in the book of Hosea address
either Israel as a whole (9:1; 14:2 [4:1]), definite groups
of leaders (5:1, 8 [2:4]), or an individual leader (4:4
cj.); however, Hosea himself is nowhere addressed in the
transmission complex of chaps. 4–14.

1 2 Sam 2:28; 18:16; 20:22; 2 Kgs 9:13; 1 Kgs 1:34;
cf. Ju 3:27; 6:34; 7:18.

2 H. Frey, *Das Buch des Werbens Gottes um seine Kirche*
(Der Prophet Hosea), Die Botschaft des Alten Testaments, 23, 2 (Stuttgart, 1957); M. J. Buss, *The Prophetic Word of Hosea*, BZAW 111 (Berlin, 1969).

The call to alarm introduces a threat with its motivation (vv 1aβ–3) which is completely self–contained.[3] Threats in their briefest form open and conclude this saying. The initial threat evokes fear with sinister, enigmatic metaphors (v 1aβ); the concluding threat tersely states that the vulture is the "enemy" (v 3b). Three sentences (vv 1bα, 1β, 3a) in the more involved middle section (vv 1b–3a) name the guilt which has brought on the approaching disaster, while intercepting the words Israel offers as an excuse (v 2). Corresponding to the summons of alarm addressed to the military officer is the threat, with its motivation, which is uttered in a declarative style (third plural); cf. 5:8f. This saying (1–3), which begins the entire scene presented here (4ff), is in the form of the Yahweh speeches in 4:4–6; 5:1f, 8f.

Verses 1–3 are best understood as the beginning of this scene. Similarly, the following sayings are better understood when they are thought of as having been initially transmitted with vv 1–3. These sayings are thematically connected throughout, often by means of catchwords. The beginning of each saying indicates that they all belong to the same scene. Rejoinders from Hosea's audience probably were spoken between each saying. A new beginning does not occur until 9:1, where a new addressee is named, with new vocabulary and theme. On the other hand, the sayings in vv 4–14 have the same theme as vv 1–3, and they are closely meshed either syntactically or by catchwords.

The personal pronoun "they" (הם) at the beginning of v 4 connects an accusation with the previous verses. Verse 4 does not belong to the threat in vv 1–3 which is a rounded off, rhetorical unit; yet it is not independent of vv 1–3. For the addressee, given in v 1a as "house of Yahweh," with the accusation made in the third person plural already in vv 1b–2, is not designated anew.[4] There are also other instances where (ו)המ(ה) appears at the continuation of a scene: 4:14aβ; 6:7; 8:9, 13bβ. The general accusation that Israel has rejected the covenant, the Torah, and the "good" in vv 1b, 3a is

concretely pictured in v 4 with a reference to a godless monarchy and idolatrous cult. Thus the replies made by Hosea's audience may have evoked the prophet's accusations.

The theme of the calf in Samaria in vv 5–6 indicates that these verses form a unit. This saying begins with an exhortation addressed to Samaria, providing the imperative read by G[5] is original. Considered form critically, the exhortation is a "proposal to reach a settlement" (*Schlichtungsvorschlag*). Like other speech forms used by Hosea, it has its original setting in the legal process.[6] It is therefore worthy of note that the prophetic exhortation has its origin in the "proposal to reach a settlement." This would explain its occurrence after the previous accusations and threats of judgment, and the immediately following proclamation of the burning anger "against them." The third plural in v 5aβ presupposes the foregoing sayings in vv 1f, 4, even though the singular address denotes the beginning of a new rhetorical unit. "Throw away," "reject" (זנח) in verse 5 picks up the catchword in v 3a; the "calf" (v 5) picks up the theme of idols in v 4b. This juxtaposition of a summons in the singular and the statement made in the third plural (v 5a) recalls the same juxtaposition in v 1; now, however, the addressee is designated as "Samaria." This, together with the third plural, probably refers to the responsible circles of leaders, as in v 1.[7] The actual threat (imperfect) does not occur until v 6b, following the declaration of Yahweh's wrath in v 5aβ (perfect). But v 6b lacks special stress; rather, it is introduced as a motivation (כי) for a didactic demythologizing of the idol (v 6a). Prior to this, as frequently occurs in Hosea, a lament is uttered.[8] Thus the introductory exhortation, as an attempt to reach a settlement, has its motivation in an agitated statement of wrath (v 5aβ), a lament (vv 5b, 6aα) and a didactic sentence (v 6aβ). Because of the concluding threat, the exhortation becomes an urgent summons (cf. 2:4f). The connection of forms which derive from a genuine dialogue marks a climax within the scene.

3    Cf. Wolff, "Begründung," 9 [18].
4    Concerning the characteristics of the beginning of a unit, cf. M. J. Buss, *Prophetic Word*, 28ff.
5    See textual note "i."
6    Cf. Boecker, *Redeformen*, 117–21: For the plaintiff's proposal of a settlement prior to bringing a legal matter before the court, cf. Josh 22:19a; Gen 13:8f; Ju 11:13b; for the assembled court's proposal during

the legal dispute, cf. Ju 21:22; 1 Kgs 3:25; for the defendant's, cf. Job 19:21; Jer 26:13a; in Hosea, cf. 2:4b; 4:15; see p. 89.

7    Cf. "house of Israel" in 5:1, as the clan chieftains; see the commentary on 5:1.
8    "How long?" vv 5b, 6aα; the question belongs to the form of the "proposal to reach a settlement": Gen 13:9; Josh 22:16–18.

The two sayings that follow in v 7a and 7bα have a sapiential structure. Both may be quotations from ancient proverbial material. End rhyme as in v 7bα very seldom occurs; but cf. the complete rhyme of words in 12:9 עָוֹן־אוֹן[9] and Prv 11:2 in addition to the sporadic end rhyme with suffixes and inflections;[10] this occurs also in Hos 2:7b.[11] Like the rhyme of the quotation in 2:7—which is presumably the citation of hymnic material[12] —here the rhyme probably does not stem from the prophet himself, especially since a correction is made in v 7bβ. Similarly, v 7a with its assonance, takes up a traditional proverb.[13] Chapter 10:12f provide a glimpse of the prophet's independent utilization of traditional metaphors.

The כִּי which introduces the two sayings indicates that they are intended to be understood as contributions to a discussion.

### The Deictic Function of כִּי

The כִּי at the beginning of the saying is a clear example of the particle's ancient function as a deictic or demonstrative interjection.[14] We have already noted the deictic כִּי in 4:16.[15] To the passages listed in the discussion of 4:16, Boecker[16] has in the meantime added 1 Sam 29:8 (cf. 26:16, 18; Hos 4:1bβ). As an emphatic particle, כִּי occurs at the beginning of a dialogue held in the context of a legal dispute (also Hos 8:9a, 11a). Thus it is incorrect to see in vv 6f a stringing together of causal clauses,[17] which would not correspond with the prophet's style. The threefold occurrence of כִּי in vv 6f is exemplary. If we attempt to find a uniform English translation, only the following exclamations would be suitable: "Indeed!" "Verily!" "Really!" "That's it!" But in individual instances, the important nuances are provided by the context. Thus in v 6a following the question, it is adversative ("but"); v 6b gives the

motivation ("for"); in v 7a, at the beginning of the reply, it has a deictic–emphatic sense, with a contradictory, scornful undertone: "Exactly!"

How did these proverbs, which have their origin in the agricultural sphere, come to be placed in the context of this scene? It is presumable that the previous threat against the idol was answered with a reference to its usefulness in the fertility rites of the agricultural year. Perhaps cultic songs about seed time and harvest, grain and meal had been previously sung, such as occurred before 4:16 and in 6:1–3 (2:7b), to which Hosea countered with his own ironic quotations. That these quotations belong in this context is indicated by the correction appended in v 7bβ; it recalls the threat of the first saying in v 3b.

The approaching distress announced in v 7b ("they would swallow it" יִבְלָעֻהוּ) is lamented in v 8 with the same catchword ("is swallowed" נִבְלַע) as though it has already taken place. It is characteristic of Hosea to revert from a threat to a lament (cf. 5:9, 11; 4:5b, 6). This may have been evoked by his audience's objection that Israel had already suffered enough. Yet this expression of the prophet's sympathy immediately goes on to disclose the causes of Israel's danger (v 9), and then proceeds to a new threat (v 10a) which states the purpose of the judgment (v 10b). Again, this train of thought is characteristic of Hosea (cf. 5:11a; b, 12–15aα; 15aβb; 4:6; 7:8–12). Just as vv 5–7 elucidate the accusation against the cult in v 4b and had connected it with the introductory threat (vv 1, 3; cf. 6b; 7bβ), so vv 8–10 continue the accusation against political maneuvers in v 4a and likewise place them under Yahweh's judgment (v 10aβ).

With a deictic–emphatic כִּי, v 11 begins a new saying

9 See the commentary on 12:9.
10 Ex 29:35a; Nu 10:35; Ju 14:18; 1 Sam 18:7; Is 7:11b; Jer 8:20; Ps 55:7; 75:7–8; 146:4–5, 7–9; cf. K. G. Kuhn, *Achtzehngebet und Vaterunser und der Reim* (Tübingen, 1950), and the review by K. Galling, *VF* (1951–52): 221–23.
11 See textual note "b" to 2:7.
12 See the commentary on 2:7.
13 Cf. provisionally Sir 7:3: "Sow not in the furrows of unrighteousness / Lest thou reap it sevenfold" (trans. R. H. Charles, *The Apocrypha and Pseudepigrapha of the Old Testament*, Vol. 1 [Oxford: Clarendon Press, 1913¹; 1963²], 338).
14 Brockelmann, *Syntax* § 159a; Beer–Meyer 2, § 114, 2; Th. C. Vriezen, "Einige Notizen zur Übersetzung des Bindewortes *ki*," BZAW 77 (1958): 266–73.
15 4:10b, 12b; see the commentary; cf. also 13:15.
16 Boecker, *Redeformen*, 32; 152.
17 Robinson, Weiser.

(see above on v 7a). The theme of false worship (vv 1b, 4b, 5f) is now developed with regard to the sacrifices. This saying is still a part of the same scene. First, it is introduced by כי, which indicates a change of speaker in the dialogue. Again, Hosea probably replies to objections voiced by his listeners, who, in attempting to justify themselves, called Hosea's attention to the large number of sacrificial altars.[18] Second, the mention of "my instructions" (v 12) refers back to the basic accusation in v 1bβ; vv 12 and 11 belong together, as seen by the correspondence of "many" (רב) in v 12 and "multiply" (הרבה) in v 11: the countless number of instructions are despised in favor of the countless altars for sacrifice. A lament (v 12) again occurs between the two accusations (vv 11, 13a), though it is not sympathetic to Israel as in v 8; instead it is a sorrowful lament by the God whom Israel has rejected, likewise typical in Hosea.[19]

There is disagreement as to the ending of the unit. Is v 13aβ still a part of it, even though in this judicial verdict (cf. 6:6; 8:6a)—almost didactic in style—Yahweh is not the speaker but is spoken about in the third person, and even though it does not fit the context of bicola? The change from the first to the third person referring to Yahweh is found already in v 1 and frequently occurs in Hosea,[20] especially where a transition is made to didactic formulations (2:22; 6:4–6; 7:10). Also the rhythmic structure of chap. 8 is otherwise uncertain (vv 4b, 5); it contains tricola (vv 8f, probably v 11 also; v 13b) which often occur in Hosea, especially in introductory and concluding passages.[21] It cannot be said with certainty whether the present literary form precisely reflects that of Hosea's speech, or whether it goes back to the traditionists. It is probable, however, that the form remained the same after it had been fixed in writing, for v 13aβ is cited together with v 13bα already in Jer 14:10. We regard v 13bα as original in its present context, even though it also occurs in 9:9b. Also in 10b, "now" (עתה) introduces the threat (cf. v 8b). That a brief resumption of the announcement of punishment occurs at the end of a detailed accusation, corresponding to v 3b, is not unusual in this scene (vv 6b, 7b, 10aβ). But the prophetic speech in v 13b would seem to require the word "Yahweh" (יהוה) in v 13aβ, since verse 12b is divine speech. A pronouncement of the sentence in the perfect is also juxtaposed with an announcement in the imperfect in v 5f.

Verse 14 bears the characteristics of a secondary addition: the imperfect consecutive verbs, similar to those in 7:10 and 4:9, differ remarkably from the style of the entire scene. Moreover, v 14b is noticeably reminiscent of Am 1f (with respect to the transition from prophetic to divine speech). This makes the connection of 8:14 with the Judean redaction of Amos (2:4f!) worthy of consideration.[22] On the other hand, the parallel position of Judah and Israel and above all, the correlation of forgetting the creator with the building of palaces and fortresses appears to be Hosean. The catchword "multiplied" (הרבה) fits particularly well in this scene (v 11; cf. 10:1; 4:7). Chap. 4:15 also recalls a saying of Amos, but it need not be regarded secondary in Hosea. The content of the accusation in 14a and of the threat in v 14b fits quite well with the scene's main theme (cf. vv 1b, 3a and vv 1aβ, 3b). Thus, in view of the verse's peculiar formulation, two items remain to be considered: (1) whether the traditionists later added v 14 to a first sketch of this scene, and in so doing perhaps combined Hosea's thoughts with formulations found in Amos; (2) whether, as the dispute ran its course, Hosea found it necessary to change his style.

## Setting

The literary combination of this scene (8:1–14) with 5:8–7:16 was certainly intentional. The similarity of the call to alarm in 8:1 and 5:8 suggests that they both belong to the similar period of military and political turmoil. The danger from the enemy mentioned in 8:1aβ, 3b is reminiscent of 5:9a, 10a, 7:16aβ; the arbitrary attempt to redeem the situation by revolution against the

18 Cf. 4:7 and the commentary; 6:1–3, 4ff and the commentary.

19 2:10, 15; 5:15; 7:7, 13, 14, 16 (cj.); 4:1bβ, 6bβ, 7; 6:4, 6; 8:1b.

20 See p. 16.

21 2:4a, 5b, 8, 16; 4:4a, 11f, 14aβb; 5:15aβb; see pp. 33 and 75.

22 Thus R. Tournay's review of *Dodekapropheten 1. Hosea*

(BK XIV/1), *RB* 69 (1962): 272.

23 See p. 112.

24 Weiser.

25 vv 5, 6; see the commentary.

throne (8:4) and the prayerful cry to God (8:2) recall
7:3–7 and 6:3. The subjugation to Assyria mentioned in
v 9a corresponds to 5:13a (7:11). The certainty that
Israel is given over to a more powerful enemy (8:7b, 8)
is also clearly expressed in 7:8f. Hosea considers Israel's breach of covenant the cause of the catastrophe.
The formula "transgress the covenant" (עבר ברית)
occurs only in 8:1b and 6:7. This emphasizes once again
that the literary relationship of these two scenes corresponds with their historical relationship.

Accordingly, the date of the sayings in chap. 8 is
roughly the same time of the year 733 as in the preceding
section.[23] This was after Tiglath–pileser III's successful
military operation in the northern region of Israel (v 8),
after Hoshea ben Elah's revolt against the throne (v 4a)
and his submission to Assyria (v 9a). There is no basis
on which to separate vv 8–10 from its context and, with
Deden et al., to date it at the time of King Menahem
(738). The sayings are too reminiscent of 5:11a, 13a; 7:8f.
That there is mention of only one calf in the national
cult of Samaria (vv 5, 6) is explained by the loss of Galilee, and with it the calf of the sanctuary in Dan (1 Kgs
12:29) to Tiglath–pileser in 733.[24] Hosea sees the approach of a new and even greater danger, perhaps during
the spring of that bitter year when there was anxiety
over the harvest (v 7b). If v 14a adds further recollections
of this scene, then a certain amount of time separates
this scene (8:1–14) from the previous one (5:8–7:16). In
comparison with the always–present danger of Assyrian
advances from the north, the military hostilities of the
Syro–Ephraimite war with Judah (5:10f) have completely receded into the background. In Hosea's view,
Judah and Israel will receive the same judgment (cf.
earlier 5:12–14; 6:4).

This scene takes place in Samaria,[25] which is more
obvious than in the preceding scene.[26] A gathering
of people may have presented the opportunity for Hosea
to dispute with the leading circles of the royal residence, similar to 5:1.

### Interpretation

■ **1** The initial words are apparently addressed to a
military leader responsible for announcing danger from
the enemy.[27] The summons is quite agitated, as the absence of an imperative verb indicates. Hosea speaks
as though he, from an extreme outpost, is reporting directly to headquarters news that requires new decisions
(Hab 2:1; Ezek 33:1ff; Is 58:1) and the sounding of
an official alarm.

The following nominal clause also conveys this excitement. The כ prefixed to the subject כנשר still possesses
a nominal function: "Something like a vulture." The
vulture is a metaphor for swiftness,[28] for dangerous vo-
racity[28a] and majestic superiority.[29] This vulturelike
enemy sweeps down upon "Yahweh's house." With such
a phrase, Hosea does not refer to a temple (which one?),
but to the land as Yahweh's property, as in 9:15 and
perhaps 9:8.[30] In the Annals of Tiglath–pileser III the
Northern Kingdom of Israel is called *bit humria*.[31]
"House of Yahweh" (בית יהוה) might be a prophetic
parallel to the political expression "House of Omri"
(בֵּית עָמְרִי). Hosea conceives of the land as Yahweh's possession (2:10; cf. Jer 12:7; Zech 9:8). Probably the
expression was current already in those circles concerned
with the amphictyonic traditions, since it is unem-
phasized and appears within the Yahweh speech.[32] In
the Egyptian lists of Asian countries we find such corresponding names as Beth–Anath, Beth–Dagon, Beth–
Horon, Beth–Olam, etc.[33]

After the brief call to alarm, there follows in vv 1b–3a
a longer statement of the cause for the approaching
disaster. Israel ignored Yahweh's covenant promises in
her historical existence among the nations.[34] That
Yahweh is the sovereign guarantor of the covenant is indicated here more clearly than in 6:7 by the suffix "*my*
covenant" (בְּרִיתִי), i.e., the obligations assumed by Yahweh for the good of Israel, and its parallel "*my* instruction" (תורתי), the covenant ordinances he establishes.
The ancient prophetic circles of the Northern Kingdom

---

26  See p. 112.
27  See pp. 133f; on the sounding of the trumpet at the
    approach of danger, see p. 97.
28  Jer 4:13; 2 Sam 1:23; Lam 4:19.
28a Hab 1:8; Prv 30:17; Job 9:26.
29  Ezek 17:3; Ex 19:4; Dtn 32:11.
30  On בית as "arable land," "settled region," cf. E.
    Täubler, *Biblische Studien: Die Epoche der Richter* (Tü-
    bingen, 1958), 278f.
31  Oppenheim, *ANET*², 284.
32  See p. 16.
33  Wilson, *ANET*², 242; cf. R. P. Hugues Vincent,
    *Jérusalem de l'Ancien Testament*, 2 (Paris, 1956),
    612, n. 3; however, this should be compared with
    Amarna Letter 290 in Albright, *ANET*², 489.
34  On ברית see pp. 50f.

appear to have already made the accusation that the divine covenant was scorned (1 Kgs 19:10, 14). Any connection between the covenant concept and the Sinai tradition, as supposed by O. Procksch,[35] is nowhere else visible in Hosea;[36] here such a connection might be assumed, if at all, only on the basis of the parallelism of "covenant" (ברית) and "instruction" (תורה).

---

### תורה (Torah) in Hosea

In Hosea Torah (תורה, "instruction") is always more than simply the individual instructions given by the priest (Jer 18:18; Dtn 17:11; 33:10), as 4:6 has already indicated.[37] This word denotes the entire disclosure of Yahweh's will, already fixed in writing, which goes back to God's own hand (8:12). This disclosure is not a presupposition of the covenant, but a consequence of it. It describes that attitude and conduct appropriate to the covenant (חָסָד) which Hosea mentions in 4:1f in his allusion to apodictic law. In this respect, the Torah can also mediate the entire "knowledge of God" (4:6). Thus Hosea inaugurates a comprehensive understanding of the Torah, which was later presupposed by Deuteronomy (17:19; 31:9f; 1:5), and was further developed in Ps 1 in the direction of "Holy Scripture;"[38] in the New Testament "Torah" occasionally designates the entire Old Testament.[39]

---

Israel's protest against the Torah is a dispute against the claim of God to be her only leader (13:4), whose saving purposes are mediated through his covenant. Thus Israel dashes head-on into a threatening disaster. Significantly, what is said of Torah here and in v 12 was said of Yahweh himself in 6:7; 7:13. In his Torah Yahweh acts for Israel's salvation. Rebellion against the Torah is therefore rebellion against the God of the covenant (cf. 4:6; 6:6).

■ **2** Therefore Yahweh is not satisfied by a merely correct cultic invocation of his name. Israel's misunderstanding of the knowledge of God becomes evident in her prayers of lamentation. With the word "to cry out" (זעק) the person called to is generally denoted by אֶל ("to"), as in 7:14; לִי ("to me," v 2) is unusual. However, it should not be supposed that לִי is a corruption of אֵלַי, since זעק ל also occurs in 1 Chr 5:20. Moreover, as a rule ל with זעק indicates the reason for the lament; cf. Is 15:5; Jer 48:31. The prophet's formulation, with לִי placed first in the sentence, probably reflects the sense intended by the worshipers he quotes, who defend themselves against the accusation of breaking the covenant: "because of me they cry." The imperfect יִזְעָקוּ between the perfects in v 1b and v 3a denotes present, repeated acts in contrast to the completed facts which give the motivation for the judgment. The invocation "my God"[40] could have been a genuine response to the proclamation of covenant law (12:10; 13:4), if Israel had not at the same time rejected "*the good*" (v 3).

■ **3** "Good" (טוב) is a comprehensive word, which, according to v 1b, must certainly also mean conduct in conformity with the covenant, such as the prophet sees lacking in 4:1f and 6:4ff. Amos uses the word in contrast to "evil" (רָע 5:14f). In Hosea's parlance it also includes the gifts of the covenant, the healthy, pleasant, free life, without hunger or danger. Israel experienced all this with its God in the early days of her existence (2:9b); she will again obtain this in the end time when she returns to Yahweh (3:5b). In her rejection of the promises and ordinances of Yahweh's covenant, Israel has not thrown off something that is a difficult restraint; instead, she has given up the protection of her life by God's law (4:1–3) and therefore the security before all the enemies surrounding her as well. Thus v 3a provides v 1b with an "evangelical" interpretation.

Verse 3b, which is immediately connected with the motivation in vv 1b–3a, picks up the threat in v 1a. The subject "enemy" (אויב) is placed first in the clause, and thus emphasizes the bad exchange which Israel has made. The "enemy" in pursuit of Israel no doubt clarifies the obscure reference to the vulture (v 1). But the prophet has no interest in more closely defining the

35   *Theologie des Alten Testaments* (Gütersloh, 1949), 527, and Vriezen, *Theologie*, 66.
36   See p. 121.
37   See the commentary.
38   H. J. Kraus, *Psalmen*, BK XV/1 (Neukirchen, 1960), 4f.
39   Rom 3:19; 1 Cor 14:21; Jn 10:34; 12:34; 15:25; cf. E. Würthwein, "Gesetz," *RGG*[3], 2, 1513; *idem*,
       "Der Sinn des Gesetzes im Alten Testament," *ZThK* 55 (1958): 259f.
40   See the commentary on 2:25.

enemy. He proclaims his God's judgment as the result of Israel's apostasy. It is this proclamation which deserves attention and explication.

■ **4** Israel's apostasy is elucidated in v 4 in two directions. Here both of the accusations give an answer to the question: In what respect has Israel rejected the "good" of Yahweh's covenant?[41] Verse 4a mentions the struggles against the throne. Nyberg and Cazelles think that in view of v 10b and the context, v 4 has to do with the worship of a major deity (מלך) of the Canaanites, and his divine court (שרים). But in this case, מלך hip'il and שרר hip'il would have a different meaning than that usually found in the Old Testament.[42] Hosea's contemporaries hardly would have related his words to the Canaanite pantheon. The accusation's decisive accent—"without my will," "without my knowledge"—is meaningful only in relation to the installation of kings and royal officials. Lies and treachery (7:3) rather than calling upon Yahweh (7:7) dominate the accession of a new king. "Without my will" (לא ממני) means that the plan and initiative of Israel's God (Is 30:1) were not considered in the selection of the king. "Without my knowledge" (ולא ידעתי) indicates that the royal officials were neither selected by Yahweh, nor given his approval (1 Kgs 1:11, 18; cf. 2 Sam 5:3). If we note this main point of the accusation, it becomes clear that Hosea does not reject the monarchy as such, nor does he criticize the monarchy in the Northern Kingdom because he favors Jerusalem kingship.[43] Rather, he judges the way in which a new king was set on the throne.[44] Once more he "evaluates [the monarchy] in terms of the ancient charismatic royal ideal."[45] Again we see Hosea as one of the links in the chain of the Northern Kingdom's prophetic figures,[46] such as Ahijah of Shiloh (1 Kgs 11:29ff) or Elisha (2 Kgs 9:1ff), who designated kings in Yahweh's name. In this corrupted situation, he now speaks as a prophet who was not consulted and, as a charismatic, accusingly states that there has been no legitimation of the rulers. Israel, who is threatened by enemies, is to blame for the installation of her kings, for she has disregarded Yahweh's covenant and his law.

The *idols* (v 4b) in Israel's cult are the second evidence of her guilt. Just as the kings are established by men, without Yahweh, so the idols are fabricated by men.[47] עצבים is first of all a neutral word for "image," from the root I עצב, "to form." But usually it contains an undertone of contempt because of its similarity in sound to words from the root II עצב ("to hurt, pain, grieve").[48] Where Hosea speaks of idols in the plural (also in 4:17; 13:2; 14:9), he probably had in mind, in addition to the calf idols in Dan and Bethel, the many other cultic idols throughout the land,[49] and especially the plaques and statuettes in private use.[50] They use "their silver and their gold" for their idols, though these goods are gifts from Yahweh (2:10). Perhaps the result clause ironically insinuates that the expensive objects are used in order to be destroyed. In any case it notes that destruction is the ultimate consequence. "So that" (למען) may introduce a result clause as well as a purpose clause.[51] Of concern here are the factual results. Israel should know that all worship of idols is doomed for destruction.[52] According to divine law, destruction from Yahweh comes above all upon the idolaters themselves. This explains the early conjecture "*they* will be cut off" (יכרתו).[53] But the singular form is part of the sentence's irony: the use of precious metal in disobedience against Yahweh results in its destruction (cf. 2:11–15; 9:6b). Perhaps this had already happened to the calf in Dan in 733. Hosea is in agreement with apodictic law (Ex 20:3f; 34:17; Lev 19:4); the making of idols contradicts

---

41 See p. 134.
42 See Koehler–Baumgartner; Nyberg: "They have created a מלך for themselves"; G. R. Driver's etymological interpretation is even less likely ("Problems of the Hebrew Text and Language," in *Alttestamentliche Studien: Festschrift F. Nötscher*, ed. H. Junker and J. Botterweck, BBB 1 [Bonn, 1950], 50).
43 Thus van Gelderen, 277; Östborn, *Yahweh and Baal*, 55.
44 Cf. de Fraine, "L'aspect."
45 Alt, "Hos 5:8–6:14," 126.
46 See the commentary on 6:5.
47 Harper, 314; van Gelderen, 278.
48 C. R. North, "The Essence of Idolatry," BZAW 77 (Berlin, 1958): 154.
49 Ju 17f; 8:22ff.
50 Cf. *BRL*, 200ff; A. Parrot, "Le Museé du Louvre et la Bible," *CAB* 9 (1957): 38–82; B. Gemser, "Bilder und Bilderverehrung," *RGG³*, 1, 1271f.
51 Cf. D. Michel, *Tempora und Satzstellung in den Psalmen* (Bonn, 1960), 173f.
52 Lev 20:3, 5, 6; Dtn 4:3; Ezek 14:7f; cf. Zimmerli, *Ezekiel*, 303ff.
53 See textual note "h."

the will of God. This stands opposed to ancient Oriental thought in which the destruction of idols was sacrilege against the divinity. The idol "helped one to subordinate the divinity to himself, not to subordinate himself to the divinity."[54] Thus already for Hosea, the subordination of the monarchy to Yahweh (cf. Dtn 17:14ff), as well as the renunciation of idols (Dtn 4:23), is a part of the covenant with Yahweh (v 1b).

■ **5** The worship of idols and of Baal together constitute the worship of foreign gods. The exhortation[55] in v 5 makes this evident; here the prophet's struggle for Israel's return to Yahweh begins anew. Instead of rejecting the blessings of Yahweh's covenant, Samaria ought to reject its calf. The connection of v 3a with v 5a by the catchword "reject," "throw away" (זנח) should be noted. Those circles representative of the royal city now are directly addressed: "Samaria!" Neither here nor elsewhere[56] does Hosea use the word to denote the geographical area of Samaria. The broader use of the word cannot be found until after the Assyrian conquest of the city in 721. This corresponds with Assyrian usage whereby a province was named according to its capital city.[57]

But where was the calf of Samaria located? We possess no evidence that a calf ever stood in Samaria. Indeed, it is to be concluded from 2 Kgs 10:26f that the Baal temple, erected by Ahab according to 1 Kgs 16:32, never contained the calf idol. Thus, after Jehu's destruction of this temple and its transformation into latrines (2 Kgs 10:27), it is even less probable that the calf idol would have stood, for instance, in an official temple of Yahweh or even in a "private Canaanite cult of the old inhabitants of the city."[58] Thus we can hardly postulate the existence of such a cultic image in the city of Samaria only on the basis of the combination of the two words

"calf of Samaria" in Hos 8:5, 6. Moreover, the statement in Am 8:14 is too obscure to support this thesis. Hos 10:5 is decisive evidence against this, for there the inhabitants of Samaria are represented as worshipers of the calf in Bethel.[59] Thus the "calf of Samaria" (עגל שמרן) is to be conceived of as the idol Jeroboam I erected in Bethel (1 Kgs 12:29).[60] Nor according to 2 Kgs 10:29 was it destroyed by Jehu, but was officially worshiped, uninterruptedly, down to the time of Hosea according to 2 Kgs 14:24; 15:9, 18, 24, 28. Accordingly, the "calf of Samaria" should be understood as another expression for "royal sanctuary" and "temple of the kingdom" designating the temple of Bethel (Am 7:13). The singular (calf) confirms the presumed period when Hosea delivered this saying: the calf of Dan, if it indeed had at one time a similar meaning for the capital city, ceased to exist after the invasion of Tiglath–pileser.[61]

What was the shape of the "calf" (עגל)? The word denotes a young bull at the peak of its youth. It probably did not have a scornful ring, although the word also denotes a helpless calf, dependent upon its mother.[62] Already in Ugarit it could be compared with Baal: "As with the heart of a cow toward her calf [ᶜgl], as with the heart of a ewe toward her lamb, so is the heart of 'Anat toward Baal;"[63] in *CTCA* 3.3.41 (Gordon 'nt 3.41) ᶜgl il probably means the god Yamm, Baal's enemy.[64] Hence the word is official cultic terminology rather than an intentional expression of derision, especially since Ex 32:4, 8, etc.; Dtn 9:16, 21, and 1 Kgs 12:28, 32 use the same word. The image was probably constructed of a wooden center overlaid with gold leaf,[65] since it could be burned (Ex 32:20). Noth provides the justification for using Ex 32 to clarify the matter.[66] Also compare the word "splinters" in v 6 (see below). There is no agreement as to the type of idol it was. Otto Eissfeldt[67] suggests

---

54 K. H. Bernhardt, *Gott und Bild* (Berlin, 1956), 155; cf. 70; also C. R. North, "Essence," 158ff.

55 Concerning the nature of the exhortation as a proposal to reach a settlement, see p. 134.

56 See the commentary on 7:1.

57 2 Kgs 23:19; cf. Noth, *World*, 101 [79].

58 Cf. Alt, "Stadtstaat," 294ff; differently, Noth, *History*, 232 [212]; Harper, Robinson.

59 On the text, see p. 171.

60 Albright, *Archaeology*, 160; van Gelderen; Weiser.

61 See pp. 136f.

62 Is 11:6; Jer 31:13; *CTCA* 15.1.5 (Gordon 128.1.5).

63 *CTCA* 6.2.7–9 = 28–30 (Gordon 49.2.7–9 = 28–30);

translation in Gordon, *Literature*, 45.

64 Cf. Schmidt, *Königtum*, 36f.

65 Thus recently, A. Kuschke, "Goldenes Kalb," *RGG*³, 2, 1689.

66 Noth, *Pentateuchal Traditions*, 142–45 [157–60].

67 Eissfeldt, "Lade," 190–215.

that it was "a staff crowned with the image of a calf,"[68] used as a standard to lead the cultic procession. It represented God as one who goes before his people as their leader: "This is your god, O Israel, who brought you up out of Egypt" (Ex 32:4; 1 Kgs 12:28). To be sure, the only comparable material Eissfeldt is able to cite is a mosaic of shell from Mari.[69] On the other hand, there is evidence from the eighth century that in the region of Syria the calf commonly served as a pedestal for the gods, especially the storm god.[70] Not to be excluded from consideration here is the picture of an idol with the body of a human being and the head of an animal, as may be seen from the calf image from *Tell el–Asch'ari*.[71]

The bull has been conceived of as the pedestal for an idol especially because of the calves of Bethel and Dan. They were of course erected in opposition to Jerusalem's ark (1 Kgs 12:27f) and, like it, could have served as the empty throne for the divinity, who was intentionally left unrepresented.[72] This may have been Jeroboam I's understanding of it. On the other hand the following must be considered: the cultic invocations "Behold your god" (הִנֵּה אֱלֹהֶיךָ 1 Kgs 12:28) or "This is your god" (אֵלֶּה אֱלֹהֶיךָ Ex 32:8); Hosea's antithesis: "It is not God" (לֹא אלהים הוא 8:6a); the manner in which El is pictured in Ugarit as a bull;[73] the fact that Baal's offspring is a bull;[74] finally there is the image of the bull in *Tell el–Asch'ari* mentioned above. Certainly in Hosea as well, it is unquestionable that the calf was more than just a pedestal for the divinity. For Hosea's thought, probably too little is claimed when it is said that the bull is an attribute or symbol of the divinity and its strength. Hosea presupposes much more than the customary idea that the divinity itself was pictured and represented by the image of the calf. Thus the worship of the calf image is itself evidence that the covenant has

been broken. The thematic parallel in Ex 32 confirms the connection of vv 1b and 5 in Hos 8.

Following the exhortation directly addressed to the leaders, a statement in the perfect tense concerning Yahweh's wrath serves to intensify the exhortation and provides its motivation. אַף is the word Hosea uses most frequently for God's wrath (11:9; 13:11; 14:5). It occurs only with the first person suffix, thus in the context of the divine speech (likewise "wrath," עֶבְרָה in 5:10; 13:11b), which continues on uninterruptedly from v 1. This divine wrath is poured out over all of Israel (third plural suffix). The expression "my anger burns against them" appears incongruent with the exhortation, "Reject your calf, O Samaria!" The explanation for this may be that the former expression has become a fixed part of the motifs in the apostasy narratives and their corresponding paraeneses.[75] The chief reason for divine burning anger is generally Israel's turning to foreign gods.[76]

The exhortation, moreover, is accompanied by the lament: "How long do they remain incapable of purity." The question "how long" (עַד־מָתַי) is one of the motifs of the lament;[77] "purity" (נִקָּיֹן) likewise belongs to the asseveration of innocence which accompanies the lament (Ps 26:6; 73:13; Gen 20:5). לֹא יוכל, which means "unable, incapable of," is characteristic of Hosea (5:13). The lament juxtaposed with the expression of divine wrath indicates how jealous judgment and grieving, expectant love for Israel struggle within Hosea's God.

■ **6** The cry "But they are from Israel!" belongs to v 5b. It suggests hope of a return from the midst of a Canaanite milieu. If understood in this way[78] the sequence of the consonants certainly better fits the context of an animated argument than would the reading: "For who is the calf of El" (כִּי מִי שֹׁר אֵל).[79] "Bull" (שׁוֹר) appears strange

---

68 Eissfeldt, "Lade," 210.
69 Eissfeldt, "Lade," 209.
70 *ANEP*, 500; 501; 531; *AOBAT*, 345.
71 K. Galling, "Das Stierbild von tell–el–asch'ari," *ZDPV* 69 (1953): 186f, Table 6.
72 Cf. recently, G. von Rad, *Old Testament Theology* 1, tr. D. M. G. Stalker (New York: Harper and Row, 1962), 58.
73 Cf. Pope, *El*, 35.
74 *CTCA* 5.5.18ff (Gordon 67.5.18ff); *CTCA* 10.3.1ff; 17ff; 32ff (Gordon 76.3.1ff, 17ff, 32ff); see pp. 38f.
75 Ex 32:10f; Nu 25:3; Dtn 11:17; Josh 23:16.
76 J. Fichtner, *TDNT* 5, 402–3.

77 Ps 6:4; 13:2f; 35:17; 79:5; 80:5; 89:47; Zech 1:12; cf. Gunkel–Begrich, *Einleitung*, 230; C. Westermann, "Struktur und Geschichte der Klage im Alten Testament," *ZAW* 66 (1954): 53 [also in his *Forschung am Alten Testament*, ThB 24 (München, 1964), 276].
78 See textual note "j."
79 Tur Sinai, *Encyclopaedia Biblica*, The Bialik Institute, 1 (1950): see under *'abbîr*.

after "calf" (עֵגֶל) in vv 5a, 6b (otherwise, שׁוֹר is used in Hosea only for sacrificial animals; cf. 12:12), nor does "El" (אֵל) as a proper noun fit with 2:1; 11:9; cf. 12:1, since for Hosea the cult of the calf means worship of Baal (13:1f).

Only a "pure" Israel belongs to the God of the covenant. But the idol "is not God," because it is the product of human skill and therefore stands at man's disposal. This conclusion in the didactic sentence is the presupposition for the scorn heaped upon the foreign idols also in Is 2:8, 20; 40:19f. The calf cannot offer man divine help, since it has been helplessly appointed for destruction (v 6b) as the prophet announced. The hapaxlegomenon שְׁבָבִים is related to the Middle Hebrew word שָׁבַב ("to hew")[80] and to the Arabic *sabba*, "to cut," or *sebība* "chips," "splinters," and probably means "wooden chips" or "splinters."[81] Only the strict rejection of the calf of Samaria—it is expressly mentioned again in the verse's conclusion, as in the initial exhortation (v 5a)—can arrest the divine wrath. Thus at the end also this threat, an expansion of the foregoing didactic sentence, intensifies the prophet's attempt to reach a settlement.

■ 7  The sapiential sayings[82] which are now brought into the discussion emphasize the indissoluble connection between a present action and its future consequences.[83] The order God has established in the world can be demonstrated to Israel's farmers by using the harvest as an example (v 7a). The deed is the seed that sprouts up in abundance for harvest. Here, רוּחַ, a gentle breeze, is a catchword used in Wisdom for unstable, helpless vanity.[84] Trust in cultic and political maneuvers thus leads to self–deception (cf. 12:2), just as surely as the calf of Samaria will be shattered. סוּפָה is a destructive whirlwind which, like the harvest, grows out of the seed of a gentle breeze. The law of correspondence[85] as well as the law of multiplication[86] applies to sowing and harvest. The threat posed by the enemy's advance (vv 1, 3) may have partly helped determine Hosea's use of these sapiential sayings. With the wind and vanity of their idol worship, Israel brings upon itself a whirlwind of disaster.

The second saying (v 7bα)[87] elucidates the objective side. A dry stalk of grain yields no meal. Likewise, Israel waits in vain for dead cultic objects to provide it with life. The second saying appears to state metaphorically the interpretation of the matter which Hosea goes on to develop in what follows (v 7bβ). The grain standing in the fields is irretrievably poor. If it should nevertheless yield a harvest, the attacking enemy will devour it. The word זָרִים designates foreigners who are not so much enemies as simply those whose ways are alien to Israel, who do not belong to Yahweh's covenant. The meaning is almost that of "heathen."[88] The announcement of judgment remains noticeably indefinite: the prophet cannot say precisely whether total crop failure or the enemy will rob the people of their food. Nor does he call the enemy by name, as before (v 3).

■ 8  On the transition from v 7 to v 8, see page 135. With his audience, Hosea laments that the announcement of judgment is almost fulfilled; this is very probably a reference to the Assyrian invasion of Galilee and Gilead in recent weeks of 733. Israel's surrender to the enemy makes it despicable among the nations.[89] Israel no longer possesses anything desirable or precious (חֵפֶץ is used in this sense in Prv 3:15; 8:11). Later, Jehoiachin in exile (Jer 22:28) and Moab consigned to death (Jer 48:38) are likewise characterized as such a contemptible vessel. With these words Hosea nearly intones a dirge. Israel is a precious, desirable, notable people among the nations only as her God's free covenant people.

■ 9  Israel herself relinquished her freedom in that she "went to Assyria." "They" (הֵמָּה) emphasizes that Israel took the initiative in offering tribute, even before Assyria's conquest forced its necessity. Thereby Hosea places immediately after the lament (v 8) an explanation of the distress: Hoshea ben Elah submitted to Assyria

---

80  G. Dalman, *Aram.–neuhebräisches Handwörterbuch* (Frankfurt, 1938³), 412.

81  Jerome suggested "cobweb": *in aranearum telas erit vitulus Samariae.*

82  See pp. 172f, especially on the connection made by כִּי.

83  H. Gese, *Lehre und Wirklichkeit in der alten Weisheit* (Tübingen, 1958), 33ff, 42ff.

84  Eccl. 1:14, 17; Prv 11:29; Job 7:7.

85  As in Prv 11:18; 22:8; Job 4:8; Gal 6:7; 2 Cor 9:6; Mt 13:24ff.

86  Sir 7:3; Mt 13:8.

87  On its rhyme, see p. 135.

88  See the commentary on 5:7; 7:9 and 8:13 (cf. Lam 5:2; Dtn 28:33; Ps 109:11).

89  See textual note "n."

in 733.[90] The connection of v 9 with v 8 made by "for" (כי) is correctly understood only if the particle is interpreted as adding an explanation rather than motivation in a strict sense. If the people of God look to Assyria for help, that nation will devour them.

The sentence "a wild ass wanders alone," contrary to the Masoretic division of the verse, is to be taken with v 9b. It states nothing about Assyria, but rather is related antithetically to Ephraim, as the pun "wild ass–Ephraim" (פרא–אפרים) confirms.[91] It is, of course, not denied that a wild ass is a gregarious animal. With its herd, it remains withdrawn from other animals and people.[92] By contrast, Israel not only goes after her lovers; she even goes so far as to pay them off. Nyberg[93] interpreted תנה hip'il to be a derivate of "whore's wages" (אֶתְנָה).[94] The whore Ephraim who surrenders herself is not even worth enough to her political "lovers" to receive a harlot's wages from them. She has to pay them! With this, Hosea transfers his metaphor of the prostitute from the cultic sphere to that of Israel's foreign policy. Thus the כי–clause explains Israel's worthlessness among the nations.[95] Tiglath–pileser III provides an elucidation of King Hoshea's "gifts for the lovers" when he reports that 1000 (?) talents of silver were paid as tribute.[96] It is also possible that Hosea utilizes well–known political jargon. An international treaty between Assurnirari V (755–46) and Mati'el of Arpad reads: "If the person in question has not observed the treaty–stipulations of Assurnirari, . . . thus let him indeed be a whore, (let) [his] army indeed (be) women. Like a whore, may they receive [their wages] (?) at the place in their city. May land after land approach them."[97] Here breach of treaty is characterized as whoredom.

■ **10** After v 8 has lamented the disaster and v 9 has explained it in terms of Israel's guilty conduct, v 10 continues with a threat of judgment (v 10a) and a statement of the judgment's purpose (v 10b). The punishment will ensue, "even if" Ephraim, in its prostitution among the nations, would "receive" a "whore's wages"[98]

instead of paying it (v 9)—which is contrary to all custom. "I will now gather them up." The threat is uttered in the form of a messenger speech, with Yahweh speaking in the first person. A suggestive metaphor announces the approaching disaster as a "gathering" (קבץ; cf. 9:6). The reference is to a gathering together for judgment (Zeph 3:8; Joel 4:2 [3:2]), a "gathering" of the sheaves to the threshing floor to be threshed (Mic 4:12f), or a "mixing together" of metals in a melting furnace (Ezek 22:19f). Yahweh does not allow his people to mingle in among the nations (cf. also 2:2).

The continuation in v 10b in any case describes the outcome of Yahweh's intervention. G[99] conceives of the consequences in terms of domestic politics, and is reminiscent of v 4a: Yahweh's judgment will put an end to the arbitrary enthronement of the kings (cf. also 7:3ff). But beginning with v 8, the context has to do only with foreign policy. How might the smooth, understandable text presupposed by G have become corrupt in M with such difficult words? H. Cazelles[100] suggests a connection between "burden," "utterance" (משא) and "to take up" (נשא) in Am 5:26 and conceives of a procession with Assyrian idols, whereby "king" (מלך) would denote "King Assur" and "leaders" (שרים), his subordinate divine princes. Then ויחלו following M could derive from חלל hip'il: "they desecrate themselves" by bearing in the procession the god–king of Assyria and his subordinate gods.

Yet Hosea hardly would have proclaimed such a worship of foreign gods as the consequence of Yahweh's judgment (v 10aβ). Moreover, the connection with v 4a and especially with vv 8f makes it necessary to interpret מלך as a political figure. If the Assyrian (or even Canaanite, according to Nyberg, "Problem"; see pages 124; 139) divinities should be meant here, then in view of Hosea's otherwise clear diction, one would expect an unambiguous definition, as in Am 5:26. Thus I would ask whether the difficulties presented by the text and the context—which should be considered together—

90   Cf. 5:13aβ and the commentary.
91   Cf. 9:16; 14:9; and the commentary on 2:24f; van Gelderen, 291.
92   On the zoological definition of "wild ass" (פרא), cf. P. Humbert, "En marge du dictionnaire hébraïque," ZAW 62 (1950): 202ff.
93   Nyberg, "Problem," 250.
94   See the commentary on 2:14; cf. also "whore's fee" (אֶתְנָן) in 9:1.
95   On this subject cf. 5:13; 7:11; 12:2.
96   Oppenheim, ANET², 284a.
97   Cf. E. Weidner, AfO 8 (1932–3): 23.
98   See textual note "p."
99   See textual note "q."
100  Cazelles, "Os 8:4," 14–25; cf. the commentary on 8:4.

would not be minimized if first מלך שרים were left standing without a copula. Corresponding to "great king" (מלכי רב) in 5:13,[101] it would then refer to the great king of Assyria (cf. "king of kings" [מֶלֶךְ מְלָכִים Ezek 26:7]). In this connection it should be noted that Akk. šarru in the plural denotes the viceroys.[102] משׂא would then denote the burden of tribute (cf. 2 Ch 17:11) and would precisely take up the thought of vv 9, 10a. Perhaps M is a misunderstanding only of the vocalization of וְיָחִילוּ. "To have labor pains," "to writhe" (חיל) is often used for political danger (Mic 4:10; Jer 4:19; 51:29; Ezek 30:16); "to writhe under," "tremble before" (חיל מן) occurs frequently: Jer 5:22; Dtn 2:25; 1 Sam 31:3; Joel 2:6. Here, as in 1:4, "a little" (מעט) is used as an adverb denoting time: "soon." The entire verse is genuinely Hosean. In his tribunal Yahweh hands over to the difficulties of foreign rule those who surrendered themselves to foreign powers (cf. 5:11; 7:8f, 16; also 4:17ff; 5:5).

■ 11  A deictic "indeed" (כי) indicates a new departure in the speech. To Israel's apostasy from the covenant mentioned in v 1b, vv 11–13 now add further proof of Israel's transgression, namely, the cultic sacrifices. When Hosea mentions the multiplication of sanctuaries for offering sacrifices,[103] we see that he finds the expansion of the sacrificial centers to be an innovation. "He uses them for sinning." "To be" (היה) occurs frequently in Hosea in a dynamic sense that emphasizes "the reality of an event which is in itself incredible";[104] it also occurs in 5:9.[105] The statement is so astonishing and filled with excitement that its main catchwords are repeated: "Altars for sinning!"[106] The basic meaning of חטא as "to miss the mark"[107] is audible here, as v 12 immediately indicates.

■ 12  Yahweh's instructions are avoided by recourse to the sacrificial cult. That v 12 interprets v 11 is shown by the connection made by the catchwords "multiply–multitude" (רבו–הרבה). Hosea himself knows of a multitude of instructions in the form of written tradition. This provides us with evidence for a written tradition of ancient covenant law for the middle of the eighth century. That the law had been put into writing "increases its authority,"[108] especially since it was written by God himself (Ex 24:12; 34:1). The opposition to calf worship in Israel's tradition is attested by the especially important text of Ex 32:15–16. But to Israel, these divine instructions appear to be "strange."[109] These words may reflect the tension between the official priests and those (Levitic) circles of traditionists with whom Hosea was closely associated. The sequence of tense: אכתוב (imperfect)—נחשבו (perfect) indicates, as in v 13a, that the statement in the imperfect placed first in the sentence represents a relative clause which has an adverbial sense, and is subordinate to the main clause in the perfect.[110] Apparently, the sacrificial cult so zealously promoted by Hosea's contemporaries played no role in the written tradition which he presupposes here.[111] On this basis the fundamental severity of Hosea's criticism of the sacrificial cult has to be understood.

■ 13  Unlike Hosea, his contemporaries have great interest in the festivals of sacrifice. In contrast to עוֹלָה, זֶבַח denotes the sacrifice in which only a part of the animal is burned; but the main distinction lies in the fact that it was eaten in a common meal by the participants in the cult. During the preexilic period it was "the customary sacrifice at the numerous cultic places."[112] Delight in eating meat has supplanted attention to Yahweh's covenant requirements. They cannot count on

101  See textual note "g" to 5:13.
102  Koehler–Baumgartner; šar šarrâni frequently occurs as a title for the Assyrian kings from Tiglath–pileser I to Ashurbanipal; P. Chéminant, Les prophéties d'Ez. contre Tyre. Thèse (Paris, 1912). During the same period the title šar [kal] malkē occurs with Tiglath–pileser I on the cylinder of Qal'at Sherqāt 1,30 [KB 1, 16], and similarly with the name of Asshurnasirpal Annals 3, 127 [KB 1:114].
103  Cf. 4:7; 10:1; cf. the commentary on 4:7.
104  Cf. Ratschow, Werden, 66f.
105  Cf. 1:9; 5:1; cf. the commentary on 5:9.
106  See textual note "o" to 9:7. On the archeological findings relating to places of sacrifice, cf. K. Galling, "Altar," RGG³ 1, 253f and Albright, Archaeology, 41f.
107  See pp. 80f.
108  G. Gloege, "Bibel III," RGG³ 1, 1145.
109  On זו see the commentary on 5:7. The "strange god" is mentioned in Dtn 32:16; Is 17:10; 43:12; Ps 44:21; 81:10.
110  Cf. Nyberg, "Problem," 253.
111  Cf. the allusions to the decalogue in 4:1; also 4:6ff; see the commentary on 6:6 and 8:1.
112  Cf. L. Rost, "Erwägungen zum israelitischen Brandopfer," BZAW 77 (1958): 177–83.

Yahweh's acceptance[113] of their offerings. With great solemnity, Hosea proclaims Yahweh's rejection. In language borrowed from the sacrificial system of the priests, Hosea declares their practices to be illegitimate. By repudiating the numerous places of sacrifice Hosea again indicates his close relationship to the fathers of Deuteronomy (cf. 12:5ff).

The threat follows the verdict and is introduced by "now" (עתה) as in v 10a. In the disputation style Hosea proclaims that it is Yahweh who indicts Israel before the court. The basic meaning of זכר is "to remember." In the judicial sphere the hipʻil has the special meaning of "to inform," "to make known," "to make a statement in a court proceeding" (Is 43:26). This corresponds to the basic meaning "to express," "to say" of the Akk. zakāru.[114] The word זכר can introduce the dismissal of an indictment[115] as well as the indictment itself.[116] In Ezekiel "remembrance of guilt" (מַזְכִּיר עָוֹן 21:28 [23]; 29:16) denotes the office of the plaintiff. The word is also connected with עון in 1 Kgs 17:18; Nu 5:15. Hosea probably uses an expression borrowed from the legal procedure; it is not surprising that it occurs again in 9:9. Since Yahweh is not the plaintiff but rather the judge in v 13, זכר has the qal form as in 2 Sam 19:20. B. S. Childs[117] also regards זכר as a legal term. When Yahweh accuses Israel of transgression, it becomes—by virtue of his "remembering"—a present and a future reality. As judge he then also calls her to account[118] for her offenses.

### עון (guilt) and חטאת (sin)

In addition to 8:13, "guilt" (עָוֹן) stands parallel to "sin" (חַטָּאת) in 4:8[119] (9:9) (12:9, חֵטְא) and 13:12. עון signifies especially a wicked (7:1 ∥ "wicked" [רָעָה] 9:7) offense committed in any sphere of life which makes one culpable and punishable (5:5; 14:2, 3). It occurs 10 times in Hosea. On the other hand, the noun חַטָּאת is found only 5 times; only in 10:8 is it not parallel to עון. In 10:8, significantly,

it means a cultic offense, for which Hosea quite frequently uses the verb חטא (4:7; 8:11; 13:2; also in 10:9).

After the announcement of disaster in general terms, a precise description follows in the third line of the tricolon in v 13b: "They shall return to Egypt." These words should not be considered a secondary addition. The introduction of the guilty party with the pronoun "they" (המה), which is placed first in the sentence, is typical of Hosea's style (3:1; 4:14; 6:7; 7:13; 8:4, 9; 9:10; 13:2); the tricolon structure fits the prosody of the saying (vv 11, 13a). But to what does this threat refer? Is Egypt thought of as the current world power or as the classical land of oppression? Or does Hosea actually mean Assyria, which is expressly mentioned in v 9 and is quite probably meant in vv 1a, 3b, 7b, 10 as well?

### "Egypt" in Hosea

Hosea mentions "Egypt" a total of 13 times: 5 of these unequivocally recall the beginning of the saving history (2:17; 11:1; 12:10, 14; 13:4), while 5 are parallel to Assyria (7:11; 9:3; 11:5 [G], 11; 12:2). In the three remaining examples (7:16; 8:13; 9:6) Egypt appears alone; however, there is no clear or even exclusive reference to its connection with the saving history. In several passages (9:3; 11:5 [G]; 11:11) Egypt and Assyria stand parallel. One might at first suppose that Egypt, typical of Israel's saving history, merely stands for Assyria, the contemporary world power. But this interpretation is not possible in 7:11, since the metaphor of the dove fluttering to and fro is meaningful only if Egypt, the same as Assyria, is mentioned as a contemporary political power.[120] Likewise in 12:2 Israel's treaty partner, Assyria, stands next to her trade partner, Egypt, to whom she delivers oil. If we take only this into account, it is more likely that the three other passages also place Egypt and Assyria parallel as current political powers, providing the statements themselves permit such an interpretation. Passages 9:3; 11:5 [G], 11:11 are different from 7:11 and 12:2 in that they do

---

113  רצה is the technical term; Am 5:22; Mic 6:7; Lev 1:3; 19:5; 22:19; see the commentary on 6:6.
114  Koehler–Baumgartner.
115  Gen 40:14; Lev 26:45; Ps 132:1; Neh 5:19; Jer 2:2.
116  Ezek 21:28 [23]; 29:16; 1 Kgs 17:18; Nu 5:15; cf. H. Boecker, *Redeformen*, 106–10.
117  *Memory and Tradition*, StBTh 37 (London, 1962), 32f; differently, Schottroff, "Gedenken," 207, 235ff. Cf.

7:2: "I remember all their evil works" (כָּל־רָע עָתָם זָכַרְתִּי).
118  On פקד see p. 40.
119  See p. 81.
120  See pp. 126f.

145

not make a reproach for a past offense, but rather announce future judgment (9:3; 11:5 [*G*]) or salvation (11:11). The remaining three instances which mention Egypt (7:16; 8:13; 9:6) are also sayings concerning the future; thematically, they, too, are related to 9:3; 11:5 [*G*], 11, in that they directly mention "Israel's return to Egypt" (9:3; 11:5 [*G*], as in 8:13) or at least presuppose it (11:11, as in 7:16; 9:6). With respect to these six passages, it must therefore be decided whether all of them, like 2:17, announce future events in the light of ancient saving history or in relationship to concrete political events of that time. In view of 7:13[121] the latter is certain first of all for 7:16: in contemporary Egypt, which Israel left and turned to Assyria, Israel will be held in derision after Assyria has fully destroyed her. Perhaps the Israelite refugees will hear this mockery. Apparently 9:6 speaks of such groups that fled to Egypt. When Ephraim collapses, only one course of action remains for those willing and able to escape the Assyrians—to flee to Egypt like Hanun, the Philistian prince of Gaza, in 734.[122] Following the attack on Jerusalem in 587, some of the Judeans also fled to Egypt (Jer 43). After 727 Hoshea ben Elah officially sent messengers to Egypt for help.[123] In 733 Hosea sees unfaithful Israel confronting a historical dilemma: either Israel will be destroyed by Assyria, or she must flee to Egypt for help. In such a context the sayings in 9:3 and 11:5 [*G*] are also to be understood (cf. Is 7:18; 11:11, Mic 7:12). The catchword "return" (שׁוב) is used in 9:3 and 11:5 (*G*) for the turn toward Egypt, as in 8:13b. Although it would hardly be used for Israel's turn to Assyria, the catchword שׁוב in v 13b, especially in this pregnant declaration of the return to Egypt, also alludes to Israel's saving history, which otherwise is so important in Hosea (cf. 2:17).

Thus Hosea sees the ultimate destruction of Israel's military power (vv 1, 3), her sanctuary (v 6), and her economy (v 7) as a result of Tiglath–pileser's assault; the people who remain will suffer under the burden of tribute (v 10b). Likewise, those who wish to continue enjoying their sacrificial celebrations must flee to Egypt. When this flight is described as a "return," it likewise of course means that the history of salvation (2:17; 11:1) is brought to an end (Dtn 17:16). And precisely in this the judgment ordained by Yahweh is completed.

■ **14** Although the style of v 14 suggests that it is a sec-

ondary addition,[124] the thoughts contained in the first half of the verse are best understood as authentic. Hosea also laments that Israel has "forgotten" her God in 2:15;[125] 4:6; 13:6. To be sure, Hosea does not otherwise call Yahweh Israel's "*creator*"; yet in 11:1, Israel is Yahweh's son, and none other than Yahweh has loved, strengthened, and protected him (11:2ff; 2:10; 10:11; 9:10; 2:5), beginning with the time of his youth. Precisely comparable formulations do not occur until Deutero–Isaiah (51:13; 44:2). But the statement about the forgotten creator stands here in a particular context: Israel glorifies herself and seeks to secure her existence by building fortified cities. היכלות may denote palaces—especially the royal palace (1 Kgs 21:1; 2 Kgs 20:18)—as well as temples (1 Sam 1:9; 3:3). The latter is not to be unconditionally excluded in Hosea, for in such royal temples (cf. Am 7:13) Israel turned away from the God she has known from the period in the wilderness (2:8f [6f], 16f [14f]) and submitted herself to the Canaanite cult. Beyond this, Hosea sees a danger in the civilization of the cities in general (cf. also 10:14; 11:6). He does not on principle reject the building of houses, as the Rechabites do (Jer 35:7), but he takes note of the extent of their luxury and the size of their fortifications, indications that Israel has forgotten her God.[126] They *multiply* their fortifications just as they have their altars. The division made between the palaces in Israel and the fortified cities in Judah should probably be understood as a stylistic feature, not as factual. The prophet's criticism has its roots in premonarchic, ancient Israelite belief in Yahweh, and therefore applies to Israel as well as Judah; similarly 5:10, 12–14; 6:4; 10:11.

As in v 10aβ the threat (v 14b) is formulated as a divine speech. Like 4:15, it is dependent upon Amos, although its formulation has no exact prototype in the sayings of Amos addressed to the foreign nations (cf. Am 1:4, 7, 10, 14; 2:2). Moreover, for the first time this particular threat is directed to both Israel and Judah. Am 2:4f provides an example of later Judaic simulations of early prophetic sayings. On the whole, the threat is also unlike the later Judaic glosses in Hosea (cf. 1:7; 4:15; 5:5; 6:11). The different suffixes should be noted: "*his* cities" are probably the cities of the people of both

121  See pp. 127f.
122  See p. 111.
123  2 Kgs 17:4; Noth, *History*, 261f [237]. Cf. 11:5;

12:2; 13:15; and see p. xxi.
124  See p. 136.
125  See p. 40.

Israel and Judah; "*her* castles" are those of the cities.

The description of the disaster corresponds to the expectations of the enemy's attack in vv 1a, 3b, and to the resulting devastation in vv 6b, 7b. Israel's only choice is either to pay unbearable tribute (v 10b?) or to "return to Egypt" (v 13b).

### Aim

This scene has been entirely shaped by the approaching danger from Assyria's troops which draw near with terrifying speed (vv 1a, 3b). The sanctuaries will be destroyed (v 4b, 6b), the harvest plundered (v 7b), and the cities completely burned (v 14b); in short, Israel will be devoured by a ravenous vulture (v 8). Placed under heavy tribute, she will soon writhe in pain (v 10b?; see textual note "q"). The only alternative remaining is to return to Egypt (v 13b), the land from which Yahweh first called the youth, Israel (11:1; cf. 2:17).

All of this indicates that the end of the saving history is imminent. Yahweh himself controls and effects this, for he gathers his people for judgment (v 10aβ) and pronounces the sentence (v 13b). It is his own anger (v 5b) that destroys the sanctuaries and burns down the cities (vv 6, 14).

Yahweh's wrathful judgment, however, does not essentially dominate the chapter. But Hosea no longer entertains the hope that the end of the saving history can be delayed. Not once does the call to "return" to Yahweh appear in this passage, although it runs throughout the previous scene like a red thread.[127] The exhortation in 5a[128] and the entreating question in vv 5b–6aα, together with the didactic sentences in vv 6aβγ and 7abα, are the final attempt to awaken Israel to reason. Nevertheless, they indicate that Hosea still cannot give up contending with his people.

This is shown especially by the fact that the accusations occupy a much larger space than the announcements of judgment (by contrast, cf. 9:1–6). Here the chapter's peculiar accents are to be found. We sense the intense involvement in the prophet's animated speech. Even the initial saying in vv 1–3 is dominated by the accusation, with the decisive catchwords occurring in v 1b. Israel has put an end to the history of God's covenant. This is

the beginning of Hosea's dispute with his audience, whom he quotes already in v 2. The rest of the arguments Hosea advances essentially provide elucidation and motivation for his general reproach that the covenant has been broken. Hosea demonstrates this with six instances of Israel's conduct: (1) by the way a new king is installed, insofar as it is done without consulting God's will (v 4a); (2) by the making of idols, which results in the destruction of God–given natural resources (v 4b); (3) by venerating the calf, for man's technology is thereby worshiped as God (vv 5–6); (4) by political submission to Assyria, whereby Israel loses her special worth among the nations (v 8); (5) by the sacrificial system, in which the guiding principle is human lust rather than God's will (vv 11–13); (6) by expanding the number of cities, whereby Israel forgets her creator (v 14).

In any case the accusation is supported by the complaint that Israel rebels against Yahweh. It is characteristic of this scene that breaking the covenant is spoken of as transgression of the Torah;[129] it is treated as something alien to Israel (v 12), especially in the cult. Were the Torah able to make a salutary as well as a material effect on the whole of Israel's life, then it would be to Israel's "good" (v 3a).[130] Again, we are able to sense the depth of Hosea's sorrow. It is evidence of God's own suffering, who is regarded as an alien and an enemy in Israel and thus is rejected (v 1b). At the same time it indicates his sympathy with Israel, for she destroys the best thing she possesses, namely, the possibility of a life of freedom. On the whole, sorrow over the fact that Israel brings her saving history to an end is more strongly expressed than the threat of its end. Nevertheless, no other road lies ahead except that which leads to judgment.

This chapter represents a high point in the prophet's struggle against pagan worship. But in significant contrast to 4:4–19 and 5:1–7, chap. 8 is at the same time concerned with Israel's political attempts to create security for herself, which is also a rejection of God's covenant with his people. This reminds us of Paul's anathema against those who proclaimed a "different Gospel" (Gal 1:6ff). Whenever Christianity, "having begun with the spirit," is tempted "to end with the flesh" (Gal

---

126  Archeological material on the fortification of cities may be found in Barrois, *Manuel* 1, 127ff.
127  On 5:8–7:16, see pp. 109f, 128f.
128  See textual note "i."
129  V 1b; see pp. 137f.
130  See pp. 138f.

3:3), the prophets can render a special help. Especially this chapter discloses the wrong path taken by God's New Testament people whenever they place a false authority over themselves; whenever they succumb to the idolatry of their accomplishments; whenever they seek help in their own works; whenever they give in to unbelief; whenever they take delight in their "worship services" instead of hearing and obeying the will of God; whenever they delude themselves with self–glorification and a false self–confidence, instead of placing their future in the hands of their Creator.

Hosea's precise references to the historical events of his time are a stimulation for the Church of Jesus Christ to ascertain the similar temptations of its own time, so that it either returns to the narrow way of the gospel within this world or else perceives that its own way leads to judgment. If we hear and understand chap. 8 in this way, many of its details begin to speak to us anew, especially the words of v 8b. It states that the people of God retain their worth among the nations and for the nations only as long as they draw this–worldly, historical consequences from God's covenant promises and instruction (compared to this, the confession made within the context of its "worship services" [v 2] means little). When they no longer exist as the living church of their living Lord, they will be overcome by the world powers. Thus Hosea's accusation and threat to the ones who despise God's covenant and his word enable us to understand better the New Testament's cry of woe to the rich and satisfied, to those who "laugh now" and who are praised by men (Lk 6:24ff).

**The End of the Festivals**

**Bibliography**

M. J. Buss
"A Form–Critical Study in the Book of Hosea with Special Attention to Method," diss. Yale University (New Haven, 1958), 179–89; *idem, The Prophetic Word of Hosea*, BZAW 111 (Berlin, 1969).

R. Dobbie
"The Text of Hosea 9:8," *VT* 5 (1955): 199–203.

A. H. J. Gunneweg
*Mündliche und schriftliche Tradition der vorexilischen Prophetenbücher als Problem der neueren Prophetenforschung.* FRLANT 73 (Göttingen, 1959), 89–90, 101–2.

D. W. Harvey
"Rejoice not, O Israel," in *Israel's Prophetic Heritage, Essays in Honour of J. Muilenberg* (New York: Harper and Row, 1962), 116–27.

P. Humbert
"Laetari et exultare dans le vocabulaire religieux de l'Ancien Testament," *RHPhR* 22 (1942): 185–214; now also in his *Opuscules d'un hébraïsant* (Paris, 1958), 119–45.

S. Mowinckel
" 'The Spirit' and the 'Word' in the Pre-exilic Reforming Prophets," *JBL* 53 (1934): 204–5.

G. Quell
*Wahre und falsche Propheten* (Gütersloh, 1952), 10–15.

J. P. Seierstad
*Die Offenbarungserlebnisse der Propheten Amos, Jesaja und Jeremia* (Oslo, 1946), 188–89.

H. W. Wolff
"Hoseas geistige Heimat," *ThLZ* 81 (1956): 85–87, 92 [also in his *Gesammelte Studien*, ThB 22 (München, 1973²), 235–38, 246.

# 9

**1**
Do not rejoice, O Israel!
⟨Do not exult⟩[a] like the peoples!
For you go a–whoring away from your God.
You love a harlot's fee
on every threshing floor
heaped with grain.[b]

**2**
Threshing floor and winevat shall[c] no longer befriend[d] them;
the new wine shall deceive them.[e]

a  *G* (μηδὲ εὐφραίνου = אַל־תָּגֵל; similarly *T S V*) preserves the *parallelismus membrorum* that one expects here (see "Form"). *M* ("until exultation") is unusual; yet cf. Job 3:22 (van Gelderen).

b  דָּגָן is missing in *S*; perhaps it skipped over it to the next word, גֹּרֶן.

c  A verb with two subjects is usually in the singular. (Brockelmann, *Syntax* § 132).

d  On רעה II, cf. Koehler–Baumgartner; Nyberg, 68; and J. Fichtner, *TDNT* 6, 312f, and also 12:2; Prv 13:20; 28:7; 29:3. *G* (οὐκ ἔγνω αὐτούς) need not presuppose the more common יָדַע, but it could have read רעה II, as in Prv 12:20 (Is 44:20?). *T V* support *M; S* supports at least the consonantal text.

e  *G S T V* presuppose בָּם (as do several *M*^mss), as the context itself suggests. Does *M*, with the third feminine singular suffix, refer to the whore Israel on the basis of v 1?

| | |
|---|---|
| **3** | They shall not dwell in Yahweh's land. |
| | Ephraim must return[f] to Egypt, |
| | and in Assyria they[g] shall eat unclean food. |
| **4** | They shall not pour out wine to Yahweh, |
| | their sacrifices[h] shall not please[i] him. |
| | Like mourners' bread (it shall be) for them; |
| | everyone who eats of it shall be defiled. |
| | Indeed, their bread (serves) their gullet.[j] |
| | [It shall not come into Yahweh's house.][k] |
| **5** | What will you do on the day of meeting, |
| | on the day of Yahweh's feast? |
| **6** | For behold, when they flee[l] from the devastated (land),[m] |
| | Egypt shall gather them in, |
| | Memphis shall bury them. |
| | Precious is their silver[n]— |
| | weeds shall inherit them, |
| | thorns (shall grow) in their tents. |
| **7** | The days of punishment have come, |
| | the days of vengeance are ⟨imminent⟩.[o] |
| | Israel may ⟨cry⟩:[p] |
| | "The prophet is a fool! |
| | The man of the spirit is mad!" |
| | Because great[q] is your guilt, |
| | ⟨ ⟩[r] is great ⟨the⟩[r] hostility. |

f  *G* (κατῴκησεν) incorrectly read יָשַׁב because of v 3a (cf. Harper); the absence of a preposition before מצרים does not support *G*. σ′ *V* confirm *M*; cf. W. L. Holladay, *The Root šûbh in the OT* (Leiden, 1958), 29, n. 42.

g  When a noun has a collective sense, a singular verb frequently changes to a plural as the sentence continues, as in 6:4; 7:11; 8:5, 8; 9:16, etc.; cf. Ex 1:20; 33:4 (Gesenius–Kautzsch § 145g).

h  *M* (note the accent) *G V* read זבחיהם with the following colon, with the result that יי becomes the subject of the plural יערבו. This, plus the symmetry of the lines, supports the division already found represented by *S*.

i  יַעַרְכוּ (suggested by many critics since Kuenen, e.g., Nowack, *BH*[3], Harper, Robinson, Frey) as a transitive would produce a more precise parallel to 4aα, but *G T V* support the less frequent verb form in *M*.

j  On the meaning of נפש, see the commentary on 4:8.

k  Probably a gloss; see the commentary on 4:4.

l  The clause in the perfect is a circumstantial clause which is asyndetically constructed with the following statements in the imperfect; cf. Brockelmann, *Syntax* § 139.

m  *G* (ἐκ ταλαιπωρίας Αἰγύπτου) destroys the sense by separating מצרים from what follows, making "Memphis" the subject of "gather" and מחמד (misread as the place-name Μαχμας) the subject of "bury."

n  Literally: "Costliness (is the quality of) their silver."

o  The reading קָרְבוּ (according to *S*) is supported by the rule of alternation in parallelism; the second באו may have arisen from a mutilation of קרבו. To be sure, Hosea occasionally utilizes word repetition to achieve a crescendo effect (cf. 6:4; 7:8, 9; 8:11; 11:8; see Buss, "A Form–Critical Study" 116); however, this is not consistent throughout the book. Here *S* should be preferred as *lectio defficilior*; cf. also Ezek 7:7b, 12.

p  Since the work of van Hoonacker יֵרַע has generally been accepted as the correct reading because of the context. *G* (κακωθήσεται = וַיֵּרַע) presupposes almost these same consonants. α′ (ἔγνω) and σ′ (γνώσεται), like *T*, already know *M* ("shall experience").

q  Literally: "because of the abundance of your guilt."

r  I read רַבָּה הַמַּשְׂטֵמָה; nor do *G S* presuppose the copula ו; the article ה probably became lost by haplography. The clause in *M* ("and great is a hostility") makes the sentence somewhat unclear. Buber translates *M*: "By the multiplication of your iniquity, also the greatness of your opposition," but here ו . . . עַל—translated as "by . . . also"—is problematic and the absence of the article before משטמה also remains unexplained. The subordination of both clauses to עַל (Sellin, Weiser) is difficult syntactically and according to the contents, especially since they are not parallel to each other. L. Koehler (by letter) would move v 7bβ behind הַשִּׁלֵּם.

8     The watchman[s] of Ephraim
        is with ⟨God⟩.[t] [Prophet][u]
        A trap[v] (lies) upon all his paths,
        Hostility (rages) in the house
          of his God.

9     They deeply corrupt[w] themselves
        as in the days of Gibeah.[x]
        He shall remember their guilt,
        he shall punish their sins.

s   "To lie in wait" (צפה) (Sellin; Dobbie, "Hos 9:8") occurs elsewhere only in Ps 37:32, where it is followed by ל instead of עַל. With van Gelderen I read צפה אפרים, following G (σκοπὸς Ἐφραιμ) and V (speculator Ephraim). On the difficulties presented by v 8a, see the commentary.

t   According to G (μετὰ θεοῦ = עם אלהים) the form of the suffix in M ("my God") may be secondary, perhaps resulting from textual corruption: it does not harmonize with אלהיו in v 8bβ (where G likewise has not translated the suffix, nor in 9:17 and 8:2). Sellin's frequently adopted suggestion (e.g., by Robinson, Weiser, Frey) to read עִם אֹהֶל נָבִיא has no support in the transmitted text. R. Dobbie's conjecture (אֶל־חַיֵּי נביא) is even further removed from the consonantal text (Dobbie, "Hosea 9:8"); cf. textual note "s."

u   The gloss נביא is supposed to clarify the subject of v 8a; it also provides an antecedent for the suffixes in v 8b.

v   Literally: "a fowler's trap."

w   The relative verb העמיקו is constructed asyndetically with the following main verb (V: profunde peccaverunt); cf. textual note "d" to 5:11 and Gesenius-Kautzsch § 120g.

x   G (τοῦ βουνοῦ) makes reference to the cultic high places, as in 4:13 and 10:8; the name Gibeah is not found in G in 5:8 and 10:9. α' and σ', however, translate γαβαα just as in 10:9.

## Form

The direct address in the prohibitive form and the mention of the addressee "Israel" (v 1a) mark the beginning of a new scene. In vv 2–4 the third person plural replaces the second person singular of the initial addressee. Direct address occurs again in v 5, now in the plural, which changes once more to the third person plural in v 6. In v 7bβ direct address (singular) occurs for the last time ("because of the greatness of *your* guilt") within the context of the reporting style which speaks about Israel (v 7a) and Ephraim (vv 8f). A different kind of passage begins only in v 10; it does not contain the vivid alternation from second to third person as found in vv 1–9. How is this alternation to be explained?

Before we turn to this question, let us note that vv 1–9 have a certain cohesion due to the absence of the messenger style. Verse 10 returns immediately to the divine speech in the first person, which has occurred previously in 8:1–5, 10, 12, 14b. In the intervening passage (vv 1–9) the sayings are entirely in the disputation style in which the prophet mentions God (vv 1a, 8ab) or Yahweh (vv 3a, 4a [b], 5b) only in the third person.

The sayings in vv 1–6 obviously are closely related by a common theme: Is the harvest festival truly the festival of Yahweh? This is the basic issue of the heated dispute. As noted above, vv 7–9 bear the same style as the preceding verses. Moreover, not only the threats in vv 7–9 are similar to those of vv 1–6, but in the dispute concerning the prophetic office, these verses first become fully intelligible as a conclusion to this scene, in which the prophet's disruption of the festival provoked insults from his audience.

Those who are accused and threatened are directly addressed, but then they are spoken of in the third person. How is this to be explained? The passage is neither an uninterrupted, composed speech, nor is it a genuine literary form. Rather, it is evident that the transitions in the passage are to be clarified only in terms of a public, verbal dispute. In addition to the speaker, at least two additional groups are involved. The question remains open, however, as to how one might imagine the relationship of those directly addressed to those who are spoken of in the third person. It is conceivable that the addressees are those groups responsible for the festival celebrations: the priestly circles would especially rejoice over the harvest, the "harlot's fee" (v 1); it is they who have to make "preparation" for the festival (v 5); for Hosea, their guilt stands in the foreground (v 7bβ). The third person would then refer to other groups comprising the entire people. This was the explanation for the juxtaposition of the second and third persons in 4:4–19. There in the legal proceedings the accused are distinguished from the injured party.[1] In 9:1–9, however, there is no description of two different groups. "Israel" (vv 1, 7), as a designation of the leaders of the cult, can hardly be placed in antithesis to "Ephraim" (vv 3, 8) as a designation of the entire people. But then only the other explanation remains, namely, the assumption that the second and third persons designate the very same groups; that the prophet, as plaintiff or judge, turns to the defendants themselves and then speaks about them to the assembled court. The latter could be represented by Hosea's disciples, who were also the traditionists of his sayings.[2] It is significant that the punishment is always announced in the third person (vv 2ff, 6, 7a, 9), whereas the accusation, in the course of the legal proceedings, is made in direct address (vv 1, 7b). But here it should be noted that v 7bβ is an answer to the counter-charge. The question: "What will you do . . .?" (v 5) is also a part of the vigorous argument between the opponents in the case. Here the question is preceded by the threat in vv 2–4—similar to other passages[3]—with the accusation in the third person.

With respect to the details, we have to assume that, where there are no smooth transitions from verse to verse, Hosea's audience has made defensive objections as his legal opponents. Such objections are directly cited in v 7bα. Hence it is conceivable that after the accusation in direct address (v 1), they referred to a good harvest as proof that their worship of God justifies them. The prophet answers this with the threat of imminent disappointment (vv 2ff) in the neutral style of an announcement of disaster. It must be assumed that between vv 6 and 7 the prophet's threat was provocatively and optimistically rejected with the words of the vehement

insult taken up in v 7bα. J. Lindblom, who is otherwise inclined to regard the prophet's words as revelation that has been given written form, even supposes that in 9:1–9 "the speech was composed in public in order to be immediately delivered."[4] The traditionists regarded only the words spoken by Hosea as worthy of transmission.

The rhythmic structure of the verse is unusually balanced. To be sure, I find the four–line strophe, which Buss[5] represents as the predominate form of the strophe in Hosea, only in the conclusion in v 9. But it is uncertain whether, in comparison to 8:13bα, v 9b is a part of the oral proclamation of this passage.[6] Possibly a four–line strophe occurs in v 4aβb, if v 4bβ is considered Hosean.[7] On the other hand, strophes composed of bicola and tricola are easily recognizable (cf. the arrangement of the sentences in the translation): vv 1, 2–3, 4a–bα. In vv 5–6 two tricola follow a bicolon. These verses provide an emphatic conclusion to the rhetorical unit of three strophes which begins in v 2. Again, two strophes follow in vv 7a–bα, 7bβ–8; each contains bicola and tricola, while the conclusion in v 9 is a third strophe of two bicola.

The urgency with which Hosea speaks can be perceived only when one hears the effect created by this structure of bicola and tricola. The words roll over Hosea's audience like the waves of the surf. Synonymous parallelism is dominant in the bicola; in the tricola, one line usually stands synthetically parallel to the other two.

Although the individual lines usually have three stresses, lines of two stresses clearly occur at the end of both the larger rhetorical units (vv 2–6; 7–9), i.e., in vv 6 and 9. Several of these whiplike lines of two stresses are found in the initial strophes in vv 1 and 2. The traditionists responsible for the sketch of this scene have here preserved what is probably a truer picture of Hosea's powerful, poetic diction than is found in any other passage.

1    See pp. 74f.
2    Cf. Jer 2:9–13; Is 5:3–7 and Boecker, *Redeformen*, 71–94, 143–59.
3    Is 10:3; Jer 5:31; cf. Prv 25:8; Job 9:12.
4    Lindblom, 143; see above p. 75.
5    Buss, *Prophetic Word*, 39.
6    See the commentary on 9:9.
7    See the commentary on 9:4.

## Setting

As the introduction (v 1a) indicates, the prophet's accusations and threats disrupt the jubilant rejoicing of an important harvest festival. According to v 5, the gathering might be the week–long Autumn Festival celebrated at the conclusion of the vintage, [7a] called "the festival of Yahweh" in Ju 21:19; Lev 23:39. It was characterized by a particular joyfulness (Ju 21:21; Lev 23:40; Dtn 16:14).

In Hosea's time these great festivals were probably held at the main threshing floors (v 1, cf. also Dtn 16:13). Before one of Samaria's gates there was a threshing floor that also served as a gathering place for important cultic celebrations. [7b] Here there was room for the festive dances (Ju 21:21). Verses 1–9 provide no basis for the hypothesis that Hosea spoke these words in Samaria. This scene might also have taken place in Bethel, Gilgal, or Shiloh. Yet there is no evidence against Samaria as the setting.

Since the *date* of this text is not much later than the previous scene, which unquestionably took place in the capital, there is good reason to believe that the prophet also spoke these words in Samaria. [7c] In the traditionists' written account, the threat of a return to Egypt in v 3bα recalls 8:13bβ; the words announcing Yahweh's retribution in v 9b recalls 8:13bα. Whereas the exact wording of the verses in chap. 8 is not repeated, there are no grounds for supposing that v 3bα and v 9b are merely literary additions to chap. 9. Above all, the content of the threat is the same: Assyria shall devastate the land and deport those unable to escape to Egypt (cf. vv 2, 3, 6 with 8:5b, 7b, 10a, 13b, 14b). Thus it is conceivable that the date of this scene is the Autumn Festival in 733, or at least in one of the years immediately following. There is as yet no indication of an official approach to Egypt, such as that made by Hoshea ben Elah, probably after Tiglath–pileser's death in 727 (2 Kgs 17:3f). On the other hand, the people have survived the terror struck by the Assyrian invasion in the spring of 733 and the period of the throne revolts. Exuberant rejoicing again spreads throughout the land, since the harvest is apparently plenteous (v 1).

## Interpretation

■ **1** Hosea begins another speech by calling for his listener's attention with a startling cry (cf. 5:8; 8:1). He calls all festal shouts to halt with an expression which is a literal contradiction to the hymnic summons and priest's cultic instruction. [8] In the Old Testament the word–pair שׂמח—גיל ("rejoice—exult") occurs for the first time in Hosea. The expression is at the same time evidence for the originally Dionysian character of the Canaanite fertility cult, which is a counterpart to the rituals of lamentation. [9] The "rejoicing" is expressed by noisy applause and enthusiastic commotion (cf. Ju 16:23; 2 Sam 6:12). As is still recognizable in *M* [10] the "exultation," expressed by shrill, unrestrained screams, characteristically progressed toward a climax. It is evident from 10:5b that the screams are a special part of calf worship. Thus it is not surprising that גיל, as it is first used by Hosea, is found neither in the Pentateuch, nor in the Deuteronomistic History, and that the prophets Amos, Micah, Jeremiah [11] and Ezekiel strictly avoid the word; Isaiah uses it once (9:2). Later in Joel 1:16; 2:23 there is more evidence that the word–pair belongs primarily to the harvest festival. *V* captured the climax implicit in the two words by translating: *noli laetari Israel, noli exsultare sicut populi* ("rejoice not, O Israel, exult not as do the nations"). [12]

With the word "Israel" the official cultic community is addressed (as in 4:15; 8:2, 3, 6), which is the chosen community of Yahweh (9:10; 10:1; 11:1; 12:14; 13:1; 14:2). The word "Ephraim" probably could not be used here, since it primarily denotes the inhabitants of the area of Ephraim as a people (cf. 5:13; 8:8, 10). Because of what God has done for "Israel" in her history, she cannot allow herself to follow the customs of the nations. [13] But like a prostitute [14] Israel has fallen away

---

7a   See the commentary on 2:13 and E. Kutsch, "Erwägungen zur Geschichte der Passafeier und des Massotfestes," *ZThK* 55 (1958): 31f.

7b   1 Kgs 22:10; for Jerusalem, cf. the threshing floor of Araunah the Jebusite: 2 Sam 24:18.

7c   8:5, see p. 137.

8   Cf. the parallelism "rejoice—be glad" in Ps 14:7; 16:9; 32:11, etc.; also Joel 2:21, 23; Zeph 3:14.

9   See the commentary on 7:14.

10   שׂמח אל־גיל; see textual note "a."

11   48:33 (Moab) is secondary.

12   Cf. P. Humbert, "Laetari et exultare."

13   See the commentary on 7:14.

14   On זנה see pp. 15f.

from the One who elected her. The word עַמִּים in this context takes on the sense of "heathen," which is usually expressed by גּוֹיִם.[15] Again Hosea takes as his starting point Israel's distinctness from the nations; he does this in a different manner in 8:8, 10.[16] Whatever Israel may do, her actions will be judged otherwise than the deeds and actions of the nations, among whom there is no "apostasy" from their gods (cf. Jer 2:10). What the nations do naturally is "whoredom" for Israel.

Israel's "whoring" is evident chiefly in her activities on the threshing floors. There her "love of the harlot's fee" is found, a perverse, lustful kind of love.[17] The word "harlot's fee" (אתנן) should probably be understood as a fixed *energicus* verb form[18] (derived from אֶתְּנַן, "I will give") and, like the unique form אֶתְנָה,[19] always denotes a harlot's hire. Dtn 23:19 expressly mentions the "hire of a harlot" (אֶתְנַן זוֹנָה); likewise Mic 1:7.[20] Israel is given her hire by her lovers, the Baals, on the "threshing floors."[21] Apparently the threshing floors also served as places of worship,[22] particularly because these areas had a high elevation and were exposed to the wind; without exception, they were situated near the towns and were common property of the community.[23] This would explain why the winevat is not yet mentioned with the threshing floor in v 1 as it is in v 2. Hosea no longer directly names the Baals as Israel's idols as he did in his early period (cf. 2:15, 18f). Perhaps during the perilous times of 733 the people regarded themselves more emphatically as worshipers of Yahweh (cf. 6:3; 8:2; 9:4, 5). However, they did not submit themselves to him as the Lord of Israel's entire life (6:4; 8:3); instead, they sought their own carnal pleasure and economic gain. Thus they indeed partook of the gifts of the land, but they did not receive them from the real Provider (7:14; 2:10). In the prophet's eyes, these alleged worshipers of Yahweh are still faithless idolaters of Baal; their cultic feasts are heathen activities that must be vigorously destroyed.

■ **2** In the face of the prophet's words forbidding such exultation, his listeners may have made mention of the blessings of heaven, which they believed to be divine confirmation of their past actions. Then the prophet begins a new saying (v 2) in the style of the announcement of disaster.[24] Now he names the "winevat" (יקב) along with the threshing floor. The winevat was carved out of rock and consisted of a basin in which the grapes were trodden; connected with this was a deeper pit that received the juice. The word יקב denotes chiefly the latter,[25] where the grape juice is collected. The vat could be used for grape juice as well as for olive oil.[26] Perhaps v 2a refers primarily to the olive oil—together with the grain of the threshing floor—since the new wine is expressly mentioned in v 2b and since Hosea otherwise speaks of the triad grain, new wine, and olive oil.[27]

The threshing floor and winevat shall not "befriend[28] them" by giving of their grain and wine, but shall deceive[29] them instead. They will not deliver what they now promise. The possibility held out in 8:7bβ has become a reality: the harvest has matured, but Israel will not enjoy its produce. The unusual formulation of v 2 is not grounds for interpreting the threat of disaster as a harvest failure, which would create difficulties in understanding the prophet's words forbidding joy at the harvest in v 1a.

■ **3** Accordingly, v 3 introduces an explanation of v 2, not a new threat. Those who presently rejoice over the threshing floor and winevat shall not enjoy their produce, because they will be taken to foreign lands. "They shall not dwell in Yahweh's land." Israel has gone a–whoring away from Yahweh (v 1) and this is the conse-

15 Bertram, *TDNT* 2, 365f; Strathmann *TDNT* 4, 34f.
16 See pp. 142f.
17 Cf. W. Eichrodt, *Theology of the Old Testament* 2, tr. J. A. Baker (Philadelphia, Westminster, 1967), 291 [*Theologie des Alten Testaments* 3 (Göttingen, 1939), 31]; Eichrodt, however, overlooks the fact that Hosea also uses "to love" (אהב) in every instance that speaks of Yahweh's love; see the commentary on 3:1.
18 Thus H. Bauer–P. Leander, *Historische Grammatik der hebräischen Sprache des Alten Testaments* 1 (Halle, 1922), 487 and Beer–Meyer § 40:1.
19 2:14; see the commentary.
20 On Ezek 16:31f, see Zimmerli, *Ezekiel*, 359.
21 Cf. 2:7, 9f, 11f and the commentary.
22 See p. 153 ("Setting"); in addition, cf. Ju 6:37ff; 2 Sam 6:6.
23 Dalman, *Arbeit* 3, 67ff; Barrois, *Manual* 1, 314f.
24 See "Form" on p. 152.
25 Dalman, *Arbeit* 4, 354ff and see diagrams 100–11; *BRL*, 538; Barrois, *Manual* 1, 330.
26 Joel 2:24; but cf. Dalman, *Arbeit* 4, 207.
27 See the commentary on 2:10; in 2:11 [9] and 7:14 only grain and new wine are mentioned.
28 On רעה II see textual note "d" and cf. רֵעַ in 3:1; see the commentary, p. 60.
29 On כחש see the commentary on 4:2.

quence. In the divine judgment, Israel learns that Canaan is "*Yahweh's land*"; in her apostasy to the Baals, she had refused to believe this. "Yahweh's land" (אֶרֶץ יְהוָה) in v 2 is the first occurrence of this phrase in the Old Testament; like the expression "house of Yahweh" (בֵּית יהוה) in 8:1 and 9:15 (cf. 9:8), it is also peculiar to Hosea. Later the expression occurs in Jeremiah.[30] It corresponds to the expression "the land is mine" (לִי הָאָרֶץ Lev 25:23), which gives the basic theme of ancient Israel's body of law dealing with the tenure of land.[31] Yahweh owns the land; he can therefore give it to whomever he will. If he removes Israel from his land, he also removes her from fellowship with him and from his care. Indeed, he takes away the opportunity for Israel legitimately to worship him[32] after she has despised this opportunity.

The ancient saving history now comes to end in that Israel reverts to the life which preceded her original relationship with Yahweh. "Israel shall return to Egypt." As v 6 indicates, this sentence takes on an immediate significance in its context: some of the people will have to immigrate to Egypt,[33] while others will be removed to Assyria. The expression "to eat unclean food" means food produced in an "unclean" land which belongs to foreign gods, not to Yahweh.[34] A bas–relief[35] found at Nimrud illustrates how people were deported from a city conquered by Tiglath–pileser III: Assyrian troops lead away men carrying small bundles over their shouldders, with their sheep and goats going before them.

■ 4  Do the sentences contained in v 4 relate to the present cultic celebrations or to the threats upon the cult as such? The former is possible, since according to the antithesis in v 4a and 4b, their sacrifices are "not for Yahweh" but "for their gullet." In this case v 4 would be another interpretation of the phrase "whoring away

from Yahweh" in v 1aβ. Then it would have to be assumed that after v 3 Hosea's audience raised an objection to the prophet's threat against the sacrifices offered at this very festival. Verse 4 would be an invective uttered by Hosea in reply. Nevertheless, the smooth continuation both of the imperfect verbs and of the same general tone in v 4 give it the appearance of a threat which thus sets forth vv 2–3. As v 3 interprets v 2, so v 4 explains the content of v 3. The deportees, far removed from Yahweh's land, will no longer be able to pour out drink–offerings to Yahweh. Sacrifices that would have pleased Yahweh will no longer be offered in a foreign land. Here "to be pleasing" (ערב) is a technical term from the cult, as in Jer 6:20; Mal 3:4.[36] The food to be eaten in exile will taste like the "bread of mourners."[37] It is unsuitable for the cult (Dtn 26:14); anyone who eats of it is not fit to participate in cultic worship. It is only for the "gullet," i.e., it only satisfies the hunger of the deportees.[38]

---

The sentence "it shall not come into Yahweh's house" is meaningless for the exilic period; nor does it seem to fit the situation in Palestine during the time of Hosea. The many places where sacrifices were offered[39] stood in the open. The context (v 3) also indicates that for Hosea, "defilement" is anywhere outside of "Yahweh's land." If v 4bβ is considered Hosean, "Yahweh's house" would have to be understood in the sense of "Yahweh's region" in accordance with the usage in 8:1 and 9:15.[40] However, v 4bβ is probably a gloss which states, again in the language of the Deuteronomic cultic regulations, that a harlot's hire brings defilement (cf. Dtn 23:19; Ex 23:19). It may have had its origin in the redaction of Hosea.[41]

---

■ 5  With his threat of deportation Hosea makes doubtful any future celebration of the Yahweh festival; he has

30  Jer 2:7; 16:8; cf. Ezek 38:16; Joel 1:6; 4:2 [3:2].
31  See Alt, "Ursprünge," 327f; von Rad, "Promised Land and Yahweh's Land," in *The Problem of the Hexateuch and Other Essays*, 87f; Wildberger, "Israel und sein Land, *EvTh* 16 (1956): 407f.
32  1 Sam 26:19; Ju 11:24; 2 Kgs 5:17.
33  See the commentary on 8:13 and K. Galling, "Das Königsgesetz im Deuteronomium," *ThLZ* 76 (1951): 136.
34  Am 7:17; on Ezek 4:13, cf. Zimmerli, *Ezekiel*, 127f.
35  *ANEP*, 366.
36  Cf. von Rad, *Theology* 1, 261.
37  Cf. Ezek 24:17 *G*; Jer 16:7 *G*; on Job 42:10, cf.

Fohrer, "Zur Vorgeschichte und Komposition des Buches Hiob," *VT* 6 (1956): 254. On this topic, see J. Scharbert, "Schmerz," 123f.
38  See textual note "j."
39  See the commentary on 8:11 and 9:1.
40  See the commentary on 8:1.
41  Cf. R. E. Wolfe, "The Editing of the Book of the Twelve," *ZAW* 53 (1935): 93.

already announced judgment (vv 2–4) upon the present festive exultations (v 1). The phrase "day of meeting" (יום מועד) is the appointed day of convocation which, synonymous with "feast of Yahweh" (חג יהוה, cf. 2:13 [12]), probably means the great Autumn Festival of the Yahweh covenant.[42] As a festival of Yahweh, it is by all means possible that it was celebrated in the presence of the calf (cf. Ex 32:5). "To do on . . ." (עשה ל) sig-nifies the preparation of the offerings for the cult (cf. 2:10bβ [8bβ]; Ex 10:25; 2 Chr 24:7). The sacrifices shall no longer be placed at the disposal of the priests who are responsible for the cult. The festive assembly becomes a gathering for judgment.

■ 6 Those who now celebrate in unrestrained joy will be removed from their homeland. Here שד denotes the "devastation" of the land and the fortified cities wrought by an army (10:14, 2; 7:13; cf. 12:2). The people who are not deported shall immigrate. Egypt[43] will gather them in (cf. קבץ pi'el in 8:10). This "gathering" in Egypt will mean the complete destruction of the festive con-vocations belonging to Israel's history of salvation. It is a gathering unto death; the parallelism of "gather" and "bury" also occurs in Jer 8:2 and 25:33. In Hosea's time, Memphis, with its huge graveyard, had been fa-mous for 2000 years because of its pyramids from the Fourth Dynasty. The city was situated 15 miles above the peak of the Nile Delta. It will become the grave even of those who expect to be saved by Egypt.[44]

For the cult nothing will remain of the silver which had been used in the worship of Baal (8:4b). The "weeds" will "inherit" the silver in this universal devastation; a wild growth of vegetation will cover the forsaken land and even "thorns" will spring up in the "tents." The "tents" refer especially to those of the pilgrims attending the festival. Hence in v 6 we see once again that all

festive exultations hasten to meet their end.

■ 7 The prophet's disruption of the festive celebrations probably evoked defensive words from his audience similar to those found in Amos (7:10ff) and Isaiah (28:7ff).[45] Hosea makes his reply first by summarizing his threat in terse, drumming sentences. In the pro-phetic perfect tense, he declares that the disruption was originated by Israel herself, for the coming days are days of testing and punishment for Israel's transgressions.[46] These are days of vengeance and recompense.[47] In Hosea's announcement of divine judgment, he uses con-cepts taken from the punishment of criminal offenses in civil law.[48] Testing and requital each has its appointed date, its day (Is 10:3; Am 3:14), its time (Jer 8:12; 10:15) and year (Jer 11:23; 23:12). Hosea also speaks of the (single) "day of chastisement" (5:9), the "day of war" (10:14). But in v 7 he says "days," for he is thinking (v 3, 6) of that larger historical context which had be-gun with the advances of Tiglath–pileser III. The twofold occurrence of the phrase ("days of punishment," "days of vengeance") resolutely emphasizes the definitive character of the prophet's declaration.[49]

When Israel insults the prophet, she simply provides further evidence of her own guilt. Verse 7bα is to be interpreted as a quotation of the people's scornful words, following most modern critics.[50] This obtains even if "he cries" (יריע) were not to be read for "he knows" (ידעו) in v 7aβ.[51] In his zealous proclamation a prophet often quotes the words of his opponents without indi-cating it by an introductory formula.[52] An אויל is a "blockhead," especially a "foolish talker" (Prv 10:8, 10); משגע means dovelike, incessant cooing,[53] the enthu-siastic babbling (2 Kgs 9:11; Jer 29:26) of a "madman" no longer accountable for his action (1 Sam 21:14–16 [13–15]). Hosea sees himself condemned with other

---

42  See "Setting" on p. 153; cf. 1 Sam 1:3, 19, 20; 1 Kgs 8:2, 65; 12:32.

43  See the commentary on v 3bα.

44  Cf. Noth, World, 263f [208f], 287f [228]; H. Bonnet, Reallexikon der ägyptischen Religionsgeschichte (Berlin, 1952), 446ff.

45  Cf. also 4:16 and the commentary; also Janssen, Exilzeit, 85f.

46  On the expression "days of punishment" (יום פְּקֻדָּה) cf. Is 10:3; Jer 8:12; 10:15; 11:23; 23:12; 46:21; 48:44; 50:27; 51:18; Mic 7:4; also יום פָּקְדִ in Am 3:14; פקד in Hos 1:4; 2:15; 4:9, 14; 8:13 and p. 40.

47  Cf. Is 34:8; Mic 7:3f; Ex 21:36.

48  Horst, "Recht," 73f [289f].

49  Concerning the free adaptation of v 7aα in 1QS 3:14f, cf. P. Wernberg–Möller, "Reflections on the Biblical Material in the Manual of Discipline," StTh 9 (1956): 57.

50  Wellhausen, Sellin, Harper.

51  See textual note "p."

52  In addition, 6:1–3; 4:16b; 5:11a (cf. Alt, "Hosea 5:8–6:6," 176, n. 5); cf. Is 22:13; 28:9f and Wolff, Zitat, 19 [47].

53  Cf. Arab. saǧaʿa, Koehler–Baumgartner.

prophets of the Northern Kingdom such as Elisha (2 Kgs 2:23; 9:11) and Amos (7:12f, 16).[54] Hosea's opponents, those professional optimists, encircle him, noisily shouting him down with insults born of their hatred and of their unrepentent self–justification.[55] The reason for their abusive language probably lies in Hosea's persistent threats and also in his unusual conduct (as portrayed in chap. 3) despite the apparent normalcy of life in Israel. "Man of the spirit" is likely a popular name for the "Man of God"[56]—well–known in the Northern Kingdom—for he was said to be overcome by the Spirit of God.[57] In these contexts the spirit means especially the "impulse to speak."[58] It is significant that this characterization of the prophet appears in his quotation of the people's words. Like the other preexilic, writing prophets, Hosea does not speak of himself as a person filled with the "spirit." His proclamation has its orientation in Yahweh's action in history, in the tradition of knowledge of him and his Torah, and above all in the new revelation of Yahweh's clear word to the prophet. However, Hosea does not intentionally distinguish himself from the line of those prophets who were known as "Men of the Spirit," e.g., Elijah (1 Kgs 18:12), Micaiah ben Imlah (1 Kgs 22:21f), or Elisha (2 Kgs 2:9).[59]

Rejected as a "Man of the Spirit," Hosea with critical presence of mind inserts this quotation; the insulting words were born out of an intensely hostile situation. The word "hostility" (מַשְׂטֵמָה) occurs in the Old Testament only in Hosea; like "to bear a grudge" (שָׂטַם) and "to cherish animosity" (שָׂטַן), it probably belongs to the language of the legal dispute. The word denotes total opposition.[60] The people's attack is aimed at God's "lawyer," who presents the lawsuit of his God (cf. vv 7a and 9b with 4:1, 4). Now 1QS 3:23 speaks of the dominion of the מַשְׂטֵמָה of the Angel of Darkness; cf.

1QM 13:11; CD 16:5 (מלאך המשטמה); in Jub the word משטמה is a name for Satan.[61] This development is conceivable only when the word had denoted an extreme antagonism from the very outset. The hostility of Hosea's opponents is the evidence of their "great guilt." This they have achieved by their unwillingness to repent and by their rejection of Yahweh's plaintiff and messenger of judgment.

■ **8** Verse 8a is one of the most difficult passages in Hosea. Is it a statement about the people or the prophet? That is, does it relate to v 7bβ or to v 8b? According to the vocalization of the first two words in *M*, Ephraim is spoken of as a צֹפֶה. However, the meaning of the verb required by the context, "to lie in ambush," is not attested for צפה followed by the preposition "with" (עם).[62] Thereby all attempts to emend "with God" (עם אלהי) are also rendered improbable.[63] M. Buber follows *M*, in that he understands "Ephraim" to be a vocative.[64] Verse 8a appears to be connected with v 8b, since the suffixes in v 8b (נביא ["prophet"] was not in the original text) are comprehensible only if v 8a speaks of the prophet. Yet the first person speech of the prophet ("my God") would not likely precede v 8b, which speaks of the prophet in the third person ("in the house of *his* God"); in v 8a *G* simply reads "God." Furthermore, the vocative "O Ephraim," which is in an unusual position in the sentence, is not continued in v 8b. Hence, we must attempt to understand the text in terms of *G*. According to it, Hosea, in dispute with his people, calls himself "Ephraim's watchman." The צפה is one who keeps watch from a tower.[65] With his calls to alarm, Hosea had assumed this duty (5:8; 8:1). It is, therefore, not surprising that he was the first to speak of the prophetic office as that of a watchman and that Jeremiah (6:17) and Ezekiel (3:17; 33:2, 6, 7) follow his lead

---

54  See p. 120.

55  G. Quell, *Wahre und Falsche Propheten* (Gütersloh, 1952), 15.

56  אִישׁ הָאֱלֹהִים Ju 13:6; 1 Sam 9:6; 1 Kgs 12:22; 17:18, 24; 2 Kgs 5:8, etc.

57  1 Sam 10:6; 1 Kgs 18:12; 22:21f; 2 Kgs 2:9, 16; cf. Is 61:1.

58  J. Hänel, *Das Erkennen Gottes bei den Schriftpropheten* BWANT NF 4 (1923), 168.

59  But cf. Mowinckel, "Spirit," 204–5.

60  Cf. von Rad, *TDNT* 2, 73, and especially F. Horst, *Hiob*, BK XVI/1 (Neukirchen, 1968), 13f.

61  Koehler–Baumgartner *Suppl*, 169.

62  See textual note "s."

63  See textual note "t."

64  Buber: "He who is a scout, O Ephraim, is a messenger of my God, a proclaimer—the fowler's trap is upon all his ways."

65  1 Sam 14:16; 2 Sam 13:34; 18:24–27; 2 Kgs 9:17–20.

in this, as they do in other respects.[66] At a time when he is personally rejected and silenced as a mad babbler, the prophet Hosea now speaks about himself, although he avoids the first person style. In the objective manner of the legal dispute, he attests that the watchman of Ephraim is "with God." He abides in the presence of God, as Moses (Ex 34:28) and Samuel (1 Sam 2:21) once did, and as every prophet is supposed to do, according to Deuteronomy;[67] cf. also the Deuteronomistic historian's view that the kings' hearts should be "wholly with Yahweh,"[68] and Mic 6:8.[69]

The prophet who is "with God" warns and awakens Israel and then finds himself pursued "on all his paths" like a wild animal. With this phrase, Hosea summarizes two decades[70] of his experiences in various locations as a prophet. When he names the "house of his God" as the place of this hostility, it can hardly be interpreted as evidence that Hosea belonged among those certified prophets of the official sanctuaries.[71] Against such an interpretation speaks the following: (1) Hosea rejected the official sanctuaries (4:15; 8:11–13) and therefore he hardly would have referred to them as "house of my God"; cf. also Am 7:13. (2) "Yahweh's house" in 8:1 and 9:15 means "Yahweh's land" (9:3). (3) The parallel phrase "on all his ways" suggests that his persecution ensued over a large area. Here בית means "area," "region."[72]

■ 9 In the following "judicial sentence" the comparison made with "the days of Gibeah" (ימי הגבעה) indicates that Hosea's experience of rejection, like his mission (6:5), is not considered something unique. There is no reference here to the cultic high places, as Humbert following G indicates.[73] In that case the plural גְּבָעוֹת, as in 4:13 and 10:8, would be expected. In Hosea the singular "Gibeah" is always a reference to the city (5:8;

10:9). Therefore Hosea draws on a unique event of the past in order to make a comparison, as in 2:5 [3], 17 [15]; 12:10 ("as in the day" [כיום] or "days" [כימי]). There is no allusion to Saul's accession to the throne. Although Saul came from Gibeah (1 Sam 10:26; 11:14), the history of his accession is not connected with Gibeah, but with Gilgal[74] and perhaps Mizpah (1 Sam 10:17). Furthermore, the monarchy is not mentioned in this entire scene, nor would such a reminiscence provide a meaningful context for the prophet's persecution. Rather, we are reminded of the story in Ju 19–21 which tells of the appalling crime committed against a sojourning Levite by Benjamites in Gibeah. Much like the prophets and Hosea himself, the Levite experienced brutal treatment at the hands of certain men. Hosea demonstrates his familiarity with traditions which conceivably were at home in Levitic circles. The opposition party formed by Levites and prophets of Hosea's time makes understandable the use of such traditions.[75] From its earliest period, Israel's history is shot through with ruinous deeds. The word for "bring harm" (שחת pi'el, Koehler–Baumgartner) describes less the kind than the effects (cf. 11:9) of Israel's actions. Israel works destruction and ruin, once against the Levite, so now against the prophet. Yahweh, however, will judicially prosecute their transgressions. V 9b has the same formula of threat as 8:13bα;[76] but it therefore need not be secondary, especially since "now" (עַתָּה) is not present in v 9b. A passage which concluded with an accusation would not be in accord with Hosea's style. In any case, the sketches of each scene usually conclude with an announcement of judgment (4:3, 19; 5:7; 7:16; 8:13b, 14b). The idea contained in v 7a is repeated in v 9b; here—as frequently—brief, suggestive threats provide the framework for concrete descriptions of Israel's guilt (cf. 8:1–3).

66    Cf. also Hab 2:1; Is 52:8; 56:10; Is 21:6 and H. Bardtke, "Der Erweckungsgedanke in der exilisch–nachexilischen Literatur des Alten Testaments," BZAW 77 (Berlin, 1958), 19ff, who interprets the prophets' work as that of awakening, alarming their people.
67    Dtn 18:13: "You shall be wholly with Yahweh" (תָּמִים תִּהְיֶה עִם יהוה).
68    1 Kgs 8:61; 11:4; 15:3, 14. שָׁלֵם עִם־יהוה
69    "Walk humbly with your God" (הַצְנֵעַ לֶכֶת עִם־אֱלֹהֶיךָ).
70    Cf. 2:6ff; 4:16 and the commentary.
71    Recently, Gunneweg, Tradition, 101f.

72    See p. 137. On "trap," "snare" (פַּח) see p. 137; on "hostility" (מַשְׂטֵמָה) see p. 157.
73    Humbert, "La logique," 160.
74    1 Sam 11:15; also according to Hos 9:15; see the commentary.
75    Cf. Wolff, "Heimat," 90ff [242ff].
76    See p. 145.

## Aim

The words of this scene appear to be a kind of parting address. In the first section the threat of judgment (vv 2–4, 6) is much more comprehensive than the accusation (v 1b). The prohibition against all festive exultation (v 1a) and the question in v 5 ("What will you do?") hardly indicate a tone of sympathetic lament; rather they strengthen the devastating consequences announced by the prophet; Israel will be removed from Yahweh's land—thus experiencing final separation from Yahweh—to the unclean land of Assyria (vv 3, 4) and to the graves of Egypt, in which her entire history of salvation will also be buried (v 3bα, 6; see the commentary). The end of Israel's festivals means the end of her saving history. But this end is brought on by an Israel who terminates her relationship of trust in her God by forsaking him like a whore.

In the second section this predominating announcement of a final judgment is merely emphasized by the sharply formulated words of v 7a (and v 9b), which, to be sure, stand within a new context. It should be noted that the prophet's negation of the festive celebrations—also a negation of Israel's future—provoked a stinging rejection of him by his audience. The opposition Hosea faced may have been something similar to Amos' banishment from Bethel (Am 7:10ff). The prophet offers no defense against the outcries of "Fool!" With deliberate objectivity and a stinging reply, he demonstrates that the hostility against him reveals Israel's guilt in its fullest dimensions. What is said and done against him merely verifies his accusation that Israel is faithless toward her God; he answers her conduct with the threat of divine judgment. Hence the prophet takes leave of his people, placing them into God's hands. By announcing that the rejected God of the covenant is the coming Lord of judgment, the prophet opens himself to the charge of "Fool!"

This is reminiscent of the apostle Paul. His apostolic legitimacy was placed into question and his manner of speaking of the cross of Christ was dismissed as "foolishness" ($\dot{\alpha}\phi\rho o\sigma\acute{v}\nu\eta$ 2 Cor 11:1, 16, 21; 12:6, 11). In Corinth he was handed over to opponents superior to him. His message for them, however, was that in weakness and foolishness, divine strength and wisdom are revealed on earth.[77] He gained this knowledge from Jesus Christ: "For he was crucified in weakness, but lives by the power of God. For we are weak in him, but in dealing with you we shall live with him by the power of God" (2 Cor 13:4).

The early Christian Church saw Israel, who had once stood face to face with Hosea, confronted by Jesus of Nazareth with a similar decision. With the words "days of vengeance" ($\dot{\eta}\mu\acute{\epsilon}\rho\alpha\iota$ $\dot{\epsilon}\kappa\delta\iota\kappa\acute{\eta}\sigma\epsilon\omega s$) Lk 21:22 also is reminiscent of Hos 9:7. All prophecies of judgment upon those who alienate themselves from the God of love and who despise his messengers find their fulfillment when the despised Savior becomes the Judge (Mk 3:22–30), when the persecuted messengers of Jesus (Lk 21:12ff) experience the "days of vengeance" (vv 20ff).

The words of Hosea first begin to speak with their greatest urgency in the context of the message of Jesus Christ. Those who rejoice in thinking they can escape divine judgment confront the "No!" of the God of all history when they no longer have fellowship with him. If the rejection of Hosea and his message calls forth divine judgment, how much more so the rejection of Jesus Christ, God's ultimate Word spoken to man. In the weakness and foolishness of the Cross he offers strength and wisdom to all who come to him and do not turn away adulterously. The words of Hosea in this passage have been surpassed in that Jesus of Nazareth, the crucified, offers anew the full love of God to Israel and to all who live without faith. Yet these words possess a certain power, for those who reject God's love and despise his messengers will find no refuge from the approaching storm. "Who as preacher would place a no–man's–land between us and the prophets and with Schleiermacher declare *ex cathedra* that we have nothing to teach about the wrath of God?"[78]

77    2 Cor 11:30; 12:9; cf. E. Käsemann, "Die Legitimität des Apostels," *ZNW* 41 (1942): 54.
78    G. Quell, *Wahre und falsche Propheten* (Gütersloh, 1952), 14.

## Ephraim's Glory Has Vanished

**Bibliography**

R. Bach
  "Die Erwählung Israels in der Wüste," unpub. diss. Univ. Bonn (Bonn, 1952).
H. Braun
  " 'Der Fahrende,' " *ZThK* 48 (1951): 32–38.
O. Henke
  "Zur Lage von Beth Peor," *ZDPV* 75 (1959): 155–63.
N. Lohfink
  "Hate and Love in Osee 9:15," *CBQ* 25 (1963): 417.

# 9

**10** Like grapes in the wilderness,
  I found Israel.
  Like a first fruit on the fig tree
  [in[a] its first season][b]
  I discovered your[c] fathers.
  But when they came to Baal–peor,
  there they consecrated themselves to shame,
  there they became detestable like their ⟨friend⟩.[d]

**11** Ephraim is like a flock of birds;
  His glory takes flight.
  No childbirth! No fruitful womb!
  No conception!

**12** Even if they bring up their sons,
  I will make them childless, (so that) no man (remains).
  Indeed! Woe to them also,
  when I turn away from them.[e]

**13** Ephraim, as I see,
  ⟨has exposed his sons to the hunt⟩.[f]

a  ב *essentiae* (Grether § 89k; Brockelmann, *Syntax* § 106g).

b  *S* does not yet contain this explanatory gloss on בכורה. If the phrase were original, it would have to modify תאנה. Then it would designate the tree's initial bearing of fruit, which is not attested elsewhere. (M. Buber, *The Prophetic Faith*, 117, translates "a fig tree which produces fruit for the first time.") In *G* (πρόϊμον) and σ′ (πρόδρομον) the word also modifies "early fig"; cf. *G*'s version of Is 28:4; Jer 24:2, and the commentary of Theophylact of Achrida (Ziegler, *Duodecim Prophetae*, 95); see pp. 163f.

c  *G* (αὐτῶν = אֲבוֹתֵיהֶם; thus Sellin) schematically harmonizes the word with its context; but the remaining translations in the Hexapla support *M* with ὑμῶν.

d  In *M* the word is vocalized as an infinitive with suffix: "like their loving"; *G* (ὡς οἱ ἠγαπημένοι) presupposes כָּאֲהֻבִים. Perhaps אֹהֲבָם (cf. 3:1) or מְאַהֵב (cf. 2:7–15) should be read, if *M* is not more representative of Hosea's thought; see pp. 165f.

e  I read בְּשׁוּרִי derived from שׁוּר II (Sellin, Koehler–Baumgartner, 957) "to depart" (שׁוּר with מִן occurs in Song 4:8 "to descend from"; feminine participle שָׁרוֹת in Ezek 27:25 "caravans"). *M* is reminiscent of the synonymous "to turn aside" (סוּר); following *S*, Nyberg suggests Arab. *t̠ʾr* ("to take vengeance"); however, in this form the word is foreign to the Old Testament.

f  *G*'s reading (εἰς θήραν παρέστησαν τὰ τέκνα αὐτῶν) offers the meaning which is more probable in this context; it presupposes something like לְצַיִד שָׁת לֹד בָּנָיו (Koehler–Baumgartner, 967). θ′ is also worthy of consideration: εφραιμ καθὼς εἶδον εἰς πέτραν πεφυτευμένοι οἱ υἱοὶ αὐτοῦ. The Achmimic translation is similar: *vidi ephraim sicut rupem in qua filii eius plantati sunt.* Although these versions also presuppose בָּנָיו, they otherwise support *M*. They continue the imagery of barrenness insofar as they picture the sons of Ephraim "planted in rock," which is prob-

Now Ephraim must lead[g]
   his sons to the butcher.[h]

**14** Give them, Yahweh
   —what will you give them?—
   give them a childless[i] womb
   and dry breasts!

**15** All their wickedness (became visible)
   in Gilgal;
   indeed, then I became their enemy.
   Because of their evil deeds
      I will drive them out of my house.
   I will love them no more.
      All their leaders are false leaders.[j]

**16** Ephraim is stricken,
   their[k] root is withered.
      They shall yield fruit[l] no[m] longer.
   But if they should give birth,
      I will slay the dearest children of their
      womb.

**17** Let my[n] God reject them.
   For they have not listened to him.
   They shall become wanderers
      among the nations.

ably a reference to completely unfertile ground rather than to graves carved in the rock. In this case, however, either אֶל־צוּר (Ezek 17:8) or עַל־צוּר (Ezek 17:22), rather than לְצוּר, would be expected (on the imagery, also cf. Ezek 19:13). Connected with the misreading of בְּנֶה for בָּנָיו $M$ already understood צור as the name of a city (likewise in $V\ S\ T$): "Ephraim, as I see, (goes) to Tyre, planted in the pasture." Therefore, $M$ is probably the youngest, $\theta'$ and Achmim the middle, and $G$ the oldest phase in the history of the text's transmission.

g  V 13b contains a noun clause whose predicate, an infinitive $+$ לְ, characterizes the event as imminent and inescapable (Brockelmann, *Syntax* § 25eβ, 47; cf. Gesenius–Kautzsch § 144hk).

h  $G$ (εἰς ἀποκέντησιν) and $S$ presuppose "slaughter" (הֲרֵגָה); $\alpha'$ supports $M$.

i  $G$ approximates this meaning with ἀτεκνοῦσαν; Koehler–Baumgartner translates "miscarrying."

j  Note the alliteration; literally: "Rebels."

k  See textual note "g" on 9:3.

l  On the alliteration, see the commentary on 9:16.

m  The infrequent בְּלִי (Ketib) is to be preferred to the usual בַּל (Qere); (cf. 7:2); especially since Hosea often prefers בלי, as in 4:6; 7:8; 8:7 (cf. textual note "p" on 7:8 and note "l" on 8:7.

n  $G$ (ὁ θεός) presupposes אלהים (cf. 9:8a, b).

## Form

It has long been observed that a deep caesura occurs between 9:9 and 9:10. Critics noted that one major difference in the historical retrospect which, though it has occurred once or twice previously (6:7? 9:9), now stands in the foreground and is especially predominant in the present dispute (vv 10, 15).[1] But it should also be emphasized that Hosea's direct address and vigorous disputes with his audience—repeatedly observable from chap. 4 to their climax in 9:1–9—suddenly give way to a more reflective manner of speech.[2] These differences in the tradition before and after 9:10 make it initially probable that the climax of the disputes in 9:7–9 also reflects a decisive break in Hosea's prophetic activity. Insulted (9:7) and persecuted (9:8), the prophet likely had to discontinue his work in public, at least temporarily.

To whom, then, are these following sayings addressed? Who was responsible for their written form and who

transmitted them?

Here, too, there are neither introductory nor concluding formulas to help answer these questions. Therefore we rely on a form critical analysis to aid our understanding of the text.

Verse 10 contains first of all a historical retrospect of the wilderness and conquest periods, which marked the beginning of Israel's apostasy to the Baal cult and was constitutive of her present situation. Those who were precious in Yahweh's sight have become detestable. This brief historical account might be an entirely independent saying in the form of a lament.[3] Yahweh speaks in the first person, lamenting over the fathers of Israel. The addressees are considered their sons ("your fathers"), although they are not expressly mentioned as such (cf. 2:4). Verses 11f are unquestionably a rhetorical unit. Ephraim, and thus contemporary Israel, is the new subject, now spoken of in the third person; after v 10 the direct address (second person) is no longer used. The

1  Cf. only Wellhausen, 121 and O. Eissfeldt, *The Old Testament; an Introduction*, tr. P. R. Ackroyd (New York: Harper and Row, 1965), 386 [*Einleitung in das*

2 

3 

*Alte Testament* (Tübingen, 1964³), 520].

2  Cf. van Gelderen, 312.

3  Robinson.

narrative tense (perfect) of v 10 is replaced by imperfects (and a perfect consecutive) in vv 11a and 12a which, with vv 11b and 12b, are to be understood as threats. In v 13, Ephraim is named anew as the subject of the description of guilt (v 13a G; similar to v 10) and of the immediately following threat (v 13b; similar to vv 11f). The threat of extinction is the theme which connects the two sayings in vv 11–13. Like v 10, both are formulated as Yahweh speech; they lament and threaten (contemporary) Ephraim.

After the prophet's prayer in v 14—quite unusual in the book of Hosea—the Yahweh speech continues in vv 15f. It begins in v 15aα with an account of Ephraim's initial past transgressions. The suffixes indicate that v 15 was inseparably connected with the preceding verses in the transmission of the passage.[4] In v 15aβ, b, a threat of expulsion from the land (elucidating v 11a) follows in the imperfect. A further threat is uttered in v 16 which is set off from the previous verse: Ephraim is mentioned anew, and the threat is couched in the language of lament (v 16aα; similar to 8:8–10). After the threat of deportation in v 15, v 16 clearly recalls the extinction theme in vv 11b–13. The divine speech changes to prophetic speech in v 17, as found only in v 14. Nevertheless, v 17 should not be taken with the following verses; 10:1 begins another unit, as indicated by the new mention of Israel and the different imagery and theme, whereas the suffix in ימאסם connects v 17a with v 16.

The prophet's words in v 17 reflect—as the phrase "my God" indicates—more a dialogue with God than a discussion with his audience. To be sure, the verb is a jussive, instead of the direct address (imperfect) of prayer as in v 14. In view of the preceding divine speech in vv 15–16, v 17 is better interpreted as a wishful prayer—parallel to the sequence vv 10–13 and 14—than as prophetic proclamation.

This, 9:10–17, is thus a transmission unit which is knit together by style and theme; the unit has a two–part, parallel structure: vv 10–14; vv 15–17.

The connection of v 10 with vv 11ff is, to be sure, the least intelligible. Nevertheless, the combination of Israel's past and present in v 15, as well as Hosea's general manner of proclamation, make it unlikely that v 10

would have mentioned Israel's former transgressions apart from a reference to the consequences facing the present generation. Moreover, the word "their glory" (כבודם) appears to connect v 11 antithetically with "shame" (בשת) and "detestable" (שקוצים) in v 10. But the direct address to the audience ("your fathers," v 10) occurs only in this instance within the entire transmission unit. How is this to be explained?

The question brings us to the basic form critical problem of this passage. What kind of an *event* would explain how these forms of speech have become a transmission unit?

First, let us state the results of the analysis of the details made above. Verses 10–17 are distinguished from all other preceding transmission units in 4:4–9:9: here we find none of the prophet's disputes with his audience which regularly intersperse those units. In their place, the prophet's prayer to Yahweh is found twice (vv 14, 17). Otherwise, the passage is exclusively a divine speech (vv 10–13; 15–16). This juxtaposition of divine speech and prophetic prayer, whereby the two are related, occurs only in accounts of prophetic visions and auditions (cf. Am 7:1–6; Is 6:8–11). Therefore, vv 10–17 should also be understood as the sketch of an audition account.

This also explains the unique form of address "your fathers" in v 10. The prophet is included with his people as in 1:9, where—though he alone is addressed in v 9a—v 9b includes him and his people with the second person plural. But here prophet and people are taken together only in v 10a, which speaks of the election of the fathers. In the following verses, the words are addressed to the prophet concerning the guilt and punishment of the people, who are spoken of in the third person. In the hour of divine judgment, the prophet stands on the side of his God (v 17a).

Like the sketches of previous scenes, the language of vv 10–17 is that of elevated speech with a free rhythm. Bicola predominate (vv 10a, 12–15). In those verses where the language is especially excited, the longer tricolon is found (vv 10b, 11, 16a, 17). Short lines of two stresses occur more often than those of three; only one three–stress bicolon (v 13a) is found among the many two–stress bicola (vv 10a, 12b, 13b, 14a, 15). In all

4    *Contra* Sellin, Weiser, *et al.*

remaining prosodic units, particularly in the tricola, lines of two and three stresses appear to be combined. Synonymous parallelism is unquestionably predominant in this passage. The second member often elucidates or heightens the first (vv 10bβ, 11, 12, 14–16). In the tricola, one member is synthetically parallel to the other two which are synonymous to each other (vv 10bα, 11a, 16a). In v 17 the lines are synthetically parallel.

### Setting

Who was responsible for giving this transmission unit its written form? This audition account (9:10–17) is distinct from the comparable *memorabilia* in chaps. 1 and 3 (cf. Am 7:1ff; Is 6) just as the sketches of the scenes in 4:4–9:9 are distinct from the collection of sayings in chap. 2.[5] The account has no introduction or concluding formulas and there is a lack of smoothness in the transitions in style and thought within the passage. In this respect, the type of transmission here is the same as that of the sketches of the prophet's words in 4:4–9:9. Therefore, these verses probably were not written by the prophet himself; the traditionists are best conceived of as those members of the opposition party who had especially close ties with Hosea.[6]

The account of the audition given before this inner circle would make the change to the jussive verb in the second prayer (v 17) quite understandable. Within the context of such an account, the distinction between a desire expressed in prayer and the proclamation style is obliterated in the Hebrew. The obvious lack of smoothness and continuity in the structure need not be attributed to Hosea himself, nor to a later literary rearrangement of the text. A better explanation is that the text received its shape from the traditionists who heard Hosea's words firsthand and put them into writing. For this reason alone, it is not advisable to place v 16b behind v 11a (cf. *BH*[3]), especially since v 16b also connects with v 16a.

For the first time, Hosea's words are addressed exclusively to the circle who transmitted his sayings. This circle was especially conversant with Israel's traditions; at Hosea's mention of Baal–peor or Gilgal they were immediately able to recall precise details connected with those places. A similar historical allusion appeared only once previously; it was, significantly, at the conclusion of the last scene in 9:9. There, referring to the "days of Gibeah," Hosea is shown to be alienated from his people.[7] The preceding context in 9:7–9 explains why Hosea's audience is now reduced to a smaller group. The literary affinity of 9:7–9 and vv 10–17 suggests that only a short period of time separated them. Thus, e.g., the "flying away" of Ephraim in v 11 (cf. v 15) recalls the flight to Assyria and Egypt in 9:3. This audition account would then confirm our interpretation that at sometime after 733, the leaders and many of the people became so hostile toward Hosea that he could no longer speak publicly. The closing sentence alludes to this: "They have not listened to him" (v 17). Now he addresses his words to the inner circle of the opposition who were devoted to the traditions of premonarchic Israel and of the older prophets from the Northern Kingdom.[8] Moreover, this sketch of the prophet's audition indicates that his public rejection led him to a new, personal struggle with his God. Out of this struggle arose his concurrence with God's will to bring judgment on Israel (vv 14, 17). In this respect, our passage is one of the historical antecedents of Jeremiah's confessions, particularly those confessions which are combined with a divine oracle (Jer 15:15–21). The inner struggles of the troubled prophet probably led him to ponder seriously the election traditions (v 10a) and the other historical traditions of Israel (vv 10b, 15).

### Interpretation

■ **10** With a very eloquent simile the divine speech begins by recalling Yahweh's first encounter with Israel. The expression "grapes in the wilderness" represents "imagery which almost borders on the fantastic."[9] Yet the words are intended to be heard as such. במדבר ("in the wilderness") should not be changed to בַּסְּמָדָר with Sellin. There is no basis for this in the history of the text's transmission, and the word's meaning "bushel of berries" is quite uncertain.[10] The phrase points out how unexpected and joyful an event it was. This is confirmed by the parallel בכורה, the early fig which ripens at the end of May on the sprouts from the preced-

5  See pp. 33 and 75.
6  See p. 75.
7  See the commentary on 6:7.

8  Sellin, 7; 19f; Lippl, 9.
9  Bach, "Erwählung," 18.
10  See Koehler–Baumgartner.

ing year. It is especially tender in comparison to the תאנה, the fig that first ripens on the sprouts of the current year late in August.[11] Upon discovery of such a first fruit, one immediately devours it with delight.[12] Yahweh *saw* them, which means here "detect, discover," as in Is 28:4 (cf. Ezek 16:6), in strict parallelism to the preceding verb "to come across, to find" (מצא); cf. 12:5b. These expressions serve to characterize the initial act of the entire event of the election of Israel (cf. the "finding of David" in Ps 89:21). "Israel" undoubtedly means the "fathers" during the wandering in the wilderness.

## Israel and Ephraim

Only in v 10, 11:1, and 12:14 does "Israel" (ישראל) so unambiguously denote the tribal league of the early history which Yahweh elected. Now Hosea designates the present Northern Kingdom only with "Ephraim" (vv 11, 13, 16 as is found throughout the book after 5:11–14; on Hosea's diction in his early period, cf. the commentary on 4:17 and also 5:3, 5; even until 5:9 "Ephraim" is still used to denote above all the geographical or tribal region). There was no time when the official political terminology corresponded to that of the prophet; in 1 and 2 Kings, the Northern Kingdom is never called "Ephraim." When Hosea places "Israel" parallel to Ephraim, it is obvious that he usually means the people of Yahweh (4:15; 5:9; 8:2, 3, 6, 14; 9:1; 10:1; 13:9; 14:2, 6) and not merely the "inhabitants of the Kingdom of Israel" in distinction to Judah.[13]

This election tradition, which is connected with the wilderness period, not with Egypt,[13a] has been designated by R. Bach[14] as the "discovery tradition." It is special material that supplements the Pentateuchal traditions. The tradition is attested only by the allusions to it in Dtn 32:10; Jer 2:2f and further by its amplification in Ezek 16:1ff.[15] It again provides evidence that Hosea was allied with circles which, in a sense esoterically, preserved traditions that were otherwise little known. Unique to their view of the election in the wilderness is that Yahweh's choice of Israel is motivated by her "preciousness." When he found this people, they were according to his "taste." With this moving expression of divine gratitude for human love and devotion (cf. Jer 2:2), the first words of the audition are heard by the prophet who had been repudiated by his people. He is unable to correlate the ancient election tradition with Yahweh's present rejection of Israel.[16]

The prophet immediately perceives that this tradition merely serves as backdrop before which Israel's shameful apostasy appears even more incomprehensible and dreadful. "And the God who has met this treachery suffers, as His prophet suffers, betrayed by his wife."[17] Israel first betrayed God when she came in contact

---

11  Dalman, *Arbeit* 1, 379.
12  Is 28:4; Jer 24:2; Mic 7:1. In his commentary, Theophylact of Achrida offered this explanation for the unusual expression chosen by *G*: Σκοπὸν δὲ ὀνομάζει τὸ πρώϊμον σῦκον, ὃ πάντες ἀποσκοποῦσιν, ὡς πρῶτον φανέν (Ziegler, *Duodecim prophetae*, 95).
13  Cf. on the other hand, Rost, *Israel*, 25–29.
13a 2:17; 11:1; 12:10, 14; 13:4; see pp. 43f.
14  Bach "Erwählung."
15  See Zimmerli, *Ezekiel*, 345ff; in addition, see the commentary on 10:11 and 13:5.
16  Concerning the problem of the correspondence of inspiration and tradition, cf. Seierstad, *Die Offenbarungserlebnisse*, 207f: "The content of the divine speech points to mental reflections which derive from Hosea's own historical consciousness. This phenomenon is in conformity with the essence of inspiration (in the psychological sense). Inspired mental activity is generated only on the basis of, and in a positive or negative relation to, ideas and kernels of thought, which somehow already exist in the historically and humanly conditioned psyche of the person said to be inspired. These ideas may arise from a conscious spiritual life, from individual or collective spiritual instincts. Such inspiration becomes genuinely divine revelation only when there is a contact of spirit with spirit in the religious person. This revelation completely takes over, initiating and directing the mental productivity of the human mind—according to its principles—and therefore is that which dominates the person, creating his actual experiences by teleologically actualizing concepts and trains of thought. . . . Also these prophetic sayings which reflect upon Israel's history probably 'came' to Hosea with all the characteristics of a divine speech, exactly as the evidence in chaps. 1 and 3 shows."
17  Buber, *The Prophetic Faith*, 118.

with the Canaanite cult of Baal. Baal–peor (בעל פעור) is the name of a god (Nu 25:3) who was worshiped on Mount Peor (Nu 23:28),[18] after which the city Beth–peor (בֵּית פְּעוֹר) was named (Dtn 3:29; 4:46; 34:6; Josh 13:20). It is improbable that בעל פעור is a shortened form of בית בעל פעור ("house of Baal–peor"), although one expects an אֶל before the personal name. The city of בית פעור has been identified with a *Khirbet esh–Shech Jājil*,[19] which is no longer known to us today.[20] New investigations render it probable that it was located where the present–day *Khirbet 'Ajūn Mūsa* is situated, 3 miles west of *Tell el–Hammâm* ( =Shittim).[21] This is approximately 12 miles east of the northern end of the Dead Sea, 4 miles west–northwest of *Ḥesbân*, on a summit south of the Roman way, immediately north of the pump–works *'Ajūn Mūsa* which supply water for *Mâdebā*. The ruins reveal the remains of a small but strong Moabite fortress.[22]

There "they consecrated themselves to shame." The first meaning of נזר nip'al is "to submit oneself to abstentions," as the "Nazarite" (נָזִיר) does.[23] Hosea was the first to use this word to denote union with a foreign god through the assumption of certain obligations (*G*: ἀπηλλοτριώθησαν). Accordingly, Ezekiel speaks of "separating oneself from Yahweh" (14:7).[24] Nu 25:1–5 (J) states that Israel "yoked herself" (וַיִּצָּמֶד) to Baal–peor (cf. Ps 106:28). On the basis of Nu 25:6ff and 31:16,[25] it is not certain whether this refers to the first encounter with the sex rites of Canaan in the region of Moab; but it is certainly probable in terms of Hosea's thought, especially since the subsequent threats in vv 11–13, 16 are best understood as threats against the practice of the fertility rites. For Hosea these rites are the distinguishing marks of the Baal cult.[26] Hosea's reminiscence of Baal–peor could have had a historical kernel

in Israel's early period, when Moabites and Israelites together visited the sanctuary of Baal–peor which was situated on their border.[27]

With such a "consecration" they give themselves up to "shame" (בשת). בשת should not be considered a secondary substitute for בעל, since the parallelism suggests alternation in the terminology after "Baal–peor."[28] Moreover, "shame" belongs to Hosea's view of the subject (cf. 2:7; 10:6). It is more likely that the substitution of בעל for בשת in other instances was made because of Hosea's usage.[29] Actions make the man. Whoever allies himself with the god of shame becomes despicable himself. "Detested thing" (שקוצים) is used later mostly for heathen idols;[30] Hosea, however, means the fathers of Israel who became loathsome in Yahweh's sight. Jer 13:26f indicates that the sex rites also stand in the background.[31] Finally, the comparison with "like their friend" (כאהבם) also refers to these rites. The Baals are called "lovers" (מְאַהֲבִית) in 2:7 [5], 9 [7], 12 [10],[32] but cf. also "who loves" (אֹהֶבֶת).[33] Accordingly, with *G* one might wish to vocalize the word as a participle,[34] with the result that the partners in the cult would be compared with each other: "Tell me whom you love, and I will tell you who you are." But the more unusual infinitive would also represent Hosea's thought: One's actions determine who he is (cf. 5:4). With his last statement in v 10 Hosea has caught his age in the mirror of history. The history of Israel's fathers has left its imprint on the race down to the present generation.

■ 11 Hence the transition to the remark concerning "Ephraim" is no sudden shift for Hosea. When he compares Ephraim with a "bird," the imagery first of all depicts Israel's fluttering away from Yahweh toward another goal—in the direction of the great political powers in 7:11f—here, toward the cult of Baal (v 10b). But

---

18 See pp. 39 and 98.

19 M. Noth, "Israelitische Stämme zwischen Ammon und Moab," *ZAW* 60 (1944): 19f [also in *Aufsätze zur biblischen Landes–und Altertumskunde* 1, ed. H. W. Wolff (Neukirchen, 1971), 398f].

20 Henke, "Beth Peor," 160.

21 See p. 98.

22 Cf. N. Glueck, *Explorations in Eastern Palestine* II, AASOR 15 (Pennsylvania: Univ. of Penn., 1935), 110f; Henke, "Beth Peor," 160ff; A. Kuschke, "Das Deutsche Evangelische Institut für Altertumswissenschaft des Heiligen Landes: Lehrkursus 1959," *ZDPV* 76 (1960): 26f.

23 Nu 6:2, 5f; Ju 13:5, 7; 16:17; Am 2:11f.

24 See Zimmerli, *Ezekiel*, 301f.

25 On these passages, see Noth, "Stämme," 23ff, 28f [402ff].

26 See the commentary on 4:10.

27 Cf. Noth, "Beiträge," 47 [472f].

28 Sellin, Harper.

29 2 Sam 2:8, etc.; see Koehler–Baumgartner, 158.

30 Koehler–Baumgartner.

31 Cf. Fahlgren, *ṣedākā*, 33ff and North, "Essence," 155.

32 See p. 35.

33 3:1; see textual note "a" on 3:1.

34 See textual note "d."

now the imagery is descriptive not of the guilt but of the punishment. Like a flock of birds, Ephraim has become flighty, so that its glorious unity is scattered in every direction. "Glory" (כבוד) is used to form a contrast with "shame" (בשת) and "detestable things" (שקוצים). Whatever made the grape and early fig Israel esteemed, glorious, and delightful in Yahweh's sight, whatever accounted for her honorable election by Yahweh, it shall disappear. The following words interpret כבוד in concrete terms as a large number of offspring.[35] "Fly (עוף hitpoʻel) occurs in the Old Testament only in this verse. The prophet's conception of the action has determined the form of the verb: As a people Israel will "fly away," "fly upward," in that she "takes flight"[36] partly toward Assyria, partly toward Egypt. The verse's continuation describes the flight of Ephraim's glory in a different way: the threefold מן–privativem[37] abruptly announces that the springs of life will dry up. In the climax which traces new life from birth to pregnancy (="fruitful womb") to conception, even the germination of further life in Ephraim is denied. The "glory of Ephraim" means—in addition to a harmonious community life—especially the increase of life. The way this is expressed here reflects the intensity of the audition.

■ 12  This verse heightens the threat and includes those children who may still grow up—which is no longer possible according to v 11.[38] Even these children provide no future hope, for they too will be snatched from their mothers, which may imply death by slaughter, deportation, or in flight. The dreadful threat of v 11b has now attained its goal: "no man" (מאדם) [remains]; cf. Is 6:11. On their way toward this goal, the very lives of those threatened here are overshadowed by woe. The word "to them" (להם) refers to the childless mothers and fathers. The death of growing children is more tragic than barrenness. What is more grievous for parents than this? Their God withdraws from them.[39] Worse than childlessness is godlessness—in the sense of his inaccessibility. Only when God withdraws himself is there

no longer hope in the continuation of the saving history, which began with God's drawing near, his discovery and election of Israel (v 10a).

■ 13  This text and its transmission are also problematic.[40] According to G it probably says that Ephraim, in God's view and judgment, has exposed his children to mortal danger. The simile of the "hunt" most likely refers to military expeditions which Ephraim had arbitrarily undertaken, for instance, in the joint advance it made with Damascus against Jerusalem, provoking Assyria's counter–attack (734–3); or perhaps it recalls Ephraim's change in allegiance from Assyria to Egypt after the death of Tiglath–pileser III, thus challenging Shalmaneser V (727 and the years following). Ephraim has to face the consequences of its politics: its sons are led to a new slaughter, or, in the harsh language of the prophet, "to the butcher."[41]

■ 14  The prophet responds to the words he perceived in the audition with a call to Yahweh. The form of his petition indicates how he wavers in his struggle between affirmation of the divine voice threatening death and his compassion for his people, how he grapples with the election of the rejected and the proclaimed rejection of the elected (v 10; cf. Ex 32:11–14). Like Amos (7:2, 5) and Isaiah (6:11), Hosea is unable to consent to the will of God without first posing a counter–question. Nor can he let God's will go unheeded in his counter–petition. His petition: "Give them, Yahweh!" had to be followed immediately with the question: "What will you give them?" He can do no more than choose between the threats—each more severe than the last—revealed to him in the audition: Ephraim will be scattered (v 11a); his mothers will be barren (v 11b); their children will die (vv 12a, 13); Yahweh will withdraw (v 12b). He takes up only one of these threats when he cries: "Give them a childless womb and dry breasts!" It is as though he chose this as the least evil, or perhaps as a punishment which could not be avoided, since the women must no longer participate in the fertility rites of the Baal cult. On

---

35  Cf. Prv 11:16; also Is 5:13 and von Rad, *Theology*, 229.

36  Cf. 9:3 and the more detailed description in the same audition in vv 15aβ, 17b.

37  See p. 120.

38  Concerning the style of "irreale Synchorese," cf. H. Gese, "Kleine Beiträge zum Verständnis des Amosbuches," *VT* 12 (1962): 436f.

39  See textual note "e." Concerning God's withdrawal of himself, cf. 5:6, 15 and the commentary.

40  See textual note "f."

41  On the grammatical construction, cf. textual note "g."

the other hand Hosea hopes that death in war, deportation, flight, and Yahweh's withdrawal will not come to pass. It is as though Hosea, like David in 2 Sam 24:12ff, chooses the punishment in which Israel yet remains in Yahweh's hand. The dreadfulness of the threatened judgment is lessened in that barrenness—otherwise the most horrible curse—would now be a sign of God's gentleness (Job 3:11–16). Hence the context makes it necessary that Hosea's harsh petition be understood as an inconspicuous intercession. The way Hosea intercedes for his people, though it is entirely bound up with the proclamation of God's will, shows that he cannot relinquish his struggle for God's mercy. This provides an absolutely unique opportunity for a fleeting glimpse at Hosea's dialogue with his God. It confirms the way in which he suffers with Israel while remaining obedient to God, as evidenced by the sympathetic laments which are often interwoven through his accusing speeches.[42]

■ **15** The new sequence of words spoken by Yahweh appears to continue the dialogue with the prophet. Verse 15 still speaks of those already mentioned (3rd plur. suff.), whose punishment Hosea has just called into question. The repeated series of threats, with a new motivation, becomes even more distinct. The motive clause is very terse and refers only to *Gilgal* as the center of all wickedness. In 4:15, Hosea like Amos, had warned against going to Gilgal. It is possible to translate the nominal clause in v 15 in the present tense, but the perfect tense (to be understood as inchoative) of the motive clause—"there I began to hate them"—is at the same time a forceful reminder of Gilgal's history. Thus the second series of divine speeches begins, like the first series (v 10), with a historical reminiscence. It is not impossible that the sequence "Peor–[43] Gilgal" represents a series which the traditionists of Hosea's words knew from the itinerary of the Conquest tradition.[44] Yet we have no knowledge of a corresponding event from the period of the conquest. On the other hand, the beginnings of the monarchy under Saul, and his subsequent rejection,

are in fact connected with the name of Gilgal (1 Sam 11:15; 15:12, 21). The mention of the political leaders in v 15b$\beta$ also suggests a connection with Saul. It is even probable that, in the course of the audition, the "evils" of the political sphere were mentioned together with the apostasy of the cult of Baal. In Hosea's public sayings both themes appeared side by side (lastly in chap. 8). This "evil" in Gilgal gives the impression of some immediately present transgression, like the guilt of Peor. Again Hosea draws upon history, not as past event, but as that which dominates the present and provides its foundation. If Gilgal is in fact a reminiscence of the history of Saul, then the criticism of the monarchy in v 15 is more comprehensive than in 7:3–7; 8:4a.[45] Israel's history illustrates the depth of her guilt, which—in contrast to her attempts at returning to Yahweh (cf. 6:4b)—is by no means ephemeral.

Yahweh becomes her enemy (שׂנא). Hosea uses the word שׂנא only here. It makes understandable the profusion of threats (vv 11–13) uttered in response to Israel's complete wickedness. And it explains why Yahweh cannot place restraints on his judgment as Hosea has requested. Yahweh will not revoke his decision to drive Israel from the land.[45a] The land is called "Yahweh's house," as in 8:1.[45b] Yahweh became displeased with Israel in Gilgal. His love held sway in spite of his displeasure, but there was no response to his love.[46] So his love will continue no longer.[47] Israel's leaders[48] rebelliously and obstinately reject the God of the covenant,[49] as their rejection of the prophet in the scenes in 5:8–8:14 has indicated (cf. 9:17a$\beta$). Obstinacy against the word of the covenant God is the very sin which provokes his complete judgment.

■ **16** Included in this judgment is the punishment of barrenness, which is the minimal judgment the prophet

---

42   See pp. 93 and 129.
43   Shittim, see page 165.
44   Cf. Mic 6:5b and Wellhausen, 124; concerning the centrality of Gilgal in the Conquest tradition, cf. H. J. Kraus, "Gilgal: Ein Beitrag zur Kultusgeschichte Israels," *VT* 1 (1951): 181–99; further, see H. Wildberger, *Jahwes Eigentumsvolk*, ATANT 37 (Zürich/Stuttgart, 1960), 60.

45   See p. 165 and the commentary on 13:10.
45a  See the commentary on v 11a; cf. also 8:3, 13; 9:3, 6.
45b  See the commentary on 8:1.
46   Hosea never uses the word אהב of Israel's love for Yahweh; see p. 60.
47   Cf. the expression in 1:6 with v 15b$\alpha$.
48   On שׂרים see the commentary on 3:4.
49   On סרר see the commentary on 4:16.

had accepted. This punishment, first described in the perfect, is a present reality. Ephraim is already a felled tree whose roots are drying up.[50] All future fecundity is powerfully negated; cf. vv 11b, 14b. The alliteration "Ephraim–fruit" (אפרים–פרי), as that in v 15b "leaders–false" (שריהם–סררים) should be noted. It points to the repetition of the theme from the first part of the audition, which heightens the statement's significance. The pun "Ephraim"—פרי at the same time carries the meaning (cf. Gen 41:52): "The fruitful land will become fruitless" (cf. also 14:9).

Verse 16b repeats the threats of barrenness from vv 12a, 13b and increases their severity: on the one hand, it is Yahweh himself who will slay the children; on the other, the "sons" (v 13b) are called the "treasure of their womb." This repetition of the threats in vv 11–13, now more precisely stated, denies the prophet's intercession hidden in v 14.

■ 17 The prophet now speaks a second time (cf. v 14); after the repeated threat has subdued his intercession for Israel (cf. Am 7:7ff after vv 1–6) he can only agree unreservedly to the harshness of God's will. "My God" Hosea says of Yahweh who has compelled his obedience and from whom he cannot escape.[51] But Israel no longer claims him as her God (cf. 2:25; 14:4). While the elect turn from Yahweh, the prophet continues officially to represent the people of God in the midst of their apostasy. The catchword "rejection" now summarizes Yahweh's judgment upon them.[51a] Perhaps this again recalls the tradition of Saul's rejection in Gilgal (1 Sam 15:23), especially since he, too, was rejected for disobeying the word of God proclaimed to him. This alludes to the prophet's own rejection, which stands in the background of the audition.[52] "They do not listen to Yahweh"—that is their real guilt. The punishment they incur reminds today's reader of Cain's sentence— "You shall be a fugitive and a wanderer" (נָע וָנָד Gen 4:12). נדד denotes a restless wandering; this was previously expressed by the imagery of flighty birds (v 11a; cf. v 15aβ). It is a consequence of straying from Yahweh, and, in this respect, incurred punishment. They shall wander "among the nations" (cf. 7:8; 8:8). "Here emerges the shadow of the eternal Jew."[53]

## Aim

This passage is a sketch, with no introductory or concluding formulas, of the prophet's audition account. We have noted in the background a contention in the dialogue between Hosea and his God. At the conclusion a twofold presupposition is recognizable: (1) the determined rejection of the prophetic word by the people and its leaders (cf. v 17aβ with 9:7f); (2) the prophet's inner struggle to reconcile the election traditions with his commission to proclaim judgment (cf. v 14 with v 10a).

The beginning of the divine speech establishes first of all that Israel was once precious in Yahweh's sight. It is not said that Yahweh planted the grapevine or fig tree, Israel.[54] Rather, in its context this peculiar statement about Yahweh's discovery of Israel's preciousness merely emphasizes that in the wilderness period Yahweh was delighted with what he found (v 10a). It was a time when Israel existed for no one else (cf. 2:16 [14]); again, this is not to say that none beside Yahweh cared for Israel (2:9 [7]). Within the context everything centers upon Israel's relationship to her God. Israel's apostasy to idols (v 10b) and her wicked rebellion and disobedience against Yahweh (vv 15, 17a) have distorted this relationship. With this her glory (v 11a) gives way to loathsome shame (v 10b).

The particular message of this passage has three parts:

1. Israel's guilt is traced far back into her history. Its beginning is found in her seductive encounter with the first sanctuaries of Baal–peor in the arable land (v 10b); its complete development was attained in Gilgal, probably with the history of Saul and thus with the beginnings of the monarchy (v 15). Prosperity and security were thereby sought independently of Yahweh. This disclosure of the history of Israel's apostasy is nothing other than the unveiling of the very present time. Israel's guilt, with its historical roots, is shown to be ripe for judgment, insofar as Yahweh's love (vv 10a, 15b) and call are no longer met by response and obedience (v 17).

2. Yahweh's judgment seems to be the very conclusion of his love; it is the outpouring of his hatred (v 15) which the rebellious nature of Israel has provoked. In this

---

50  On "to be smitten, stricken" (הֻכָּה) cf. Jon 4:7f; Ps 121:6; Mt 21:19.
51  Cf. Eissfeldt, "Mein Gott," 5f.

51a  Cf. 4:6 and the commentary.
52  9:7–9; see p. 163.
53  Braun, " 'Der Fahrende,' " 36.

respect, the judgment is Yahweh's personal action against Israel (v 16b). But the question of the totality of the judgment remains to be discussed. Never before in Hosea has judgment become so central a theme as it does in this audition and dialogue. The prophet's attempt to place limits on Yahweh's judgment is rejected. Israel's apostasy from Yahweh destroys her future. The disobedient become barren and childless (vv 11b–13, 16). Those who have strayed from Yahweh shall wander among the nations, with neither a future history nor salvation (vv 11a, 17b). Alienated from God, not only does Israel's glory turn into shame, but her life ultimately gives way to extinction. The message of judgment thus discloses the seriousness of the decision between obedience or disobedience to God's wooing call of love. "The idea of tragedy is absolutely missing."[55]

3. This message develops out of the prophet's victory over himself. The diastatic tension between him and his God in v 14 should be noted. In his inner struggle the prophet, although with hesitation, makes intercession for Israel.[56] The divine judgment is repeated, now more intense, bringing Hosea to a solitary, complete affirmation, as it was probably reported to the small circle of

those who formed the opposition. The prophet, who has overcome his inner conflict, becomes certain of two things: first, that the rejection of his message by the people is at the same time a rejection of "his God"; second, that total judgment of those who have abandoned Yahweh is merely the converse of election.

At the end of the passage, the picture of Israel restlessly wandering among the nations is reminiscent of the typical actuality of these words, especially for Israel. Hosea's message of judgment, as subsequent history shows, proved to be only the beginning of that judgment the "daughter of Jerusalem" brought upon herself in the crucifixion of Jesus of Nazareth.[57] No less does this judgment place the new community of God—gathered from all nations—before this decisive question: Are they the grapevine which bears delicious fruit because they hang on the vine which is Christ (Jn 15:1ff)? Or are they the fig tree, cultivated and fertilized again and again, which nevertheless bears no fruit and is therefore cut down (Lk 13:6ff)?

---

54   Thus Buber, *The Prophetic Faith*, 117.
55   Cf. H. Braun's development ("'Der Fahrende,'" 36) of the distinction between Hosea's message and the fate of Sophocles' Oedipus, who is literally a $\pi\lambda\alpha\nu\acute{\eta}\tau\eta\varsigma$ like the $\pi\lambda\alpha\nu\^{\eta}\tau\alpha\iota$ of Ephraim in v 17 G.
56   See the commentary on v. 14.
57   Cf. $\dot{\epsilon}\kappa\beta\acute{\alpha}\lambda\lambda\epsilon\iota\nu$ in Lk 19:45 with Hos 9:15 *G*; Lk 23:28ff; see p. 168.

### Shattered Altars

**Bibliography**

W. F. Albright
"The High Place in Ancient Palestine," VTSuppl 4 (1957): 242–58.

G. Fohrer
"Der Vertrag zwischen König und Volk in Israel," *ZAW* 71 (1959): 17.

P. Humbert
"En marge du dictionnaire hébraique," *ZAW* 62 (1950): 200.

H. Torczyner
"Dunkle Bibelstellen," BZAW 41 (1925): 278.

# 10

1    Israel was a luxuriant[a] vine.
        He yielded fruit[b] accordingly.
    The more fruit he produced,[c]
        the more he supplied for the altars.
    The fairer his land became,[c]
        the more beautifully he made his pillars.

2    Their heart is false.[d]
        Now they are guilty.[e]
    He himself will shatter their altars,
    and destroy their pillars.

3    Indeed, now they will say:
        "We have no king!
    For we feared not Yahweh.
    What can the king do for us?"

4    ⟨Uttering⟩[f] words—
        Committing perjury—
        Making treaties—
    So justice[g] sprouts like a poisonous herb
    along the furrows of the field.

a    Although גֶפֶן is usually considered feminine, בּוֹקֵק modifies it as an attributive adjective. In matters of agreement, the meaning is more important than the form (cf. Brockelmann, *Syntax* § 28bβ). Here, as in the continuation, the prophet refers to Israel. In v 1 בּוֹקֵק should be interpreted in the light of the Arab. *baqqa* ("to branch off, split, spread"); thus Humbert, "En marge"), since a "degenerating" (Koehler–Baumgartner), "rampantly growing" (Lippl) vine is not fruitful (cf. Is 65:6); v 1b of course presupposes that the vine is productive.

b    It appears unnecessary to deviate from "to make like" (שׁוה I pi'el; cf. Ps 18:34) in this simile; also cf. *V: fructus adequatus est ei.* "To place" is the meaning of שׁוה II, not "to produce." *G* (εὐθηνῶν) probably did not read "enlarged" (יִשְׁגֶּה) (Oettli, Harper; Koehler–Baumgartner), but rather יִשְׁלָה, as in Jer 12:1; Lam 1:5; cf. Ps 73:12.

c    רב and טוב are infinitives within nominal clauses which are made into comparative clauses by the prefixed כ (cf. Nyberg, 72).

d    חלק I denotes smoothness, especially a flattering tongue (Ps 5:10 [9]; 12:3; Prv 28:23); חלק II (passive intransitive means "apportioned") is attested by α′ σ′ (ἐμερίσθη), *V* (*divisum est*) and *T*; the transitive meaning in *G* (ἐμέρισαν καρδίας αὐτῶν) seems to fit the sense even less, since the subject remains unclear; to take the subject from v 2b (הוּא)—simply in view of the sequence of the tense in v 2—hardly reproduces the original text.

e    On the meaning of אשם, see pp. 89f on 4:15; *G* (ἀφανισθήσονται) and *V* (*interibunt*) presuppose יָשֹׁמּוּ or יֵשַׁמּוּ, as in 5:14 and 14:1.

f    Instead of *M* ("they have spoken"), *G* still read דבר (λαλῶν), which probably should be vocalized דַּבֵּר in parallel to the following infinitives (Brockelmann, *Syntax* § 46b).

g    With no substantiation, Fohrer ("Vertrag," 17) reads "bloodshed" (מִשְׂפָּח) as in Is 5:7; but cf. Am 6:12.

**5** Samaria's inhabitants[h] worship[i] the ⟨calf⟩[j]
of Beth–aven.
Indeed, its people mourn for it.
Its priestlings[k] exult[l] because of its
splendor.
Indeed, it departs from it.

**6** ⟨They will⟩ also ⟨carry⟩[m] it to Assyria
as a gift for the ⟨great king⟩.[n]
Ephraim brings disgrace upon himself.[o]
Israel is ashamed because of his plan.[p]

**7** Samaria is destroyed.[q]
Its king (is swept away) like a twig
on the water.

**8** The high places of transgression,
of Israel's sin,
will be destroyed.
Thorns and thistles grow on their
altars.
They will say to the mountains:
"Cover us!"
and to the hills: "Fall on us!"

h   It is uncertain whether G (οἱ κατοικοῦντες) presupposes the plural שְׁכְנֵי (Koehler–Baumgartner). *M* could be an old collective noun (*status constructus* of שָׁכֵן); cf. Nyberg, Gispen.

i   Both α′ (ἐσεβάσθησαν) and σ′ (ἐφοβήθησαν) suggest גור III (Koehler–Baumgartner: "to be afraid of" with לְ = "for"); in Ps 22:24 [23] and 33:8 the word stands parallel to other verbs denoting cultic worship: הלל piʻel; כבד piʻel; ירא. G (παροικήσουσιν) is reminiscent of גור I, which does not fit with v 5b.

j   G θ′ and the suffixes in v 5b require the reading לְעֵגֶל. The reading in α′ reflects a knowledge of *M* ("calves").

k   G (καθὼς παρεπίκραναν), not comprehending the foreign word (וּכְמָרָיו), conjectures וּכְמָרוּ; α′ (τεμενίτης) clearly distinguishes between these "members of the temple" and the legitimate priest, whereas its predecessors leave the word untranslated (χωμαρειμ); cf. D. Barthélemy, "Les devanciers d'Aquila," *VT* Suppl 10 (1963): 86.

l   To read the opposite of יגילו (*BH*³: יְיֵלִילוּ; Nötscher, Robinson: יָחִילוּ) is opposed by the unanimous transmission of the word.

m   G S T presuppose יוֹבִילוּ, and also the pronominal object אֹתוֹן, which cannot be construed as a nominal subject ("its sign") because of the verse's content. Does *M* ("it is brought") originate from this misunderstanding?

n   See textual note "g" on 5:13. In an Aramaic inscription from *sefire* of almost the same date, the title מלך רב is used for the treaty partner of King Matiʻel of Arpad; cf. M. A. Dupont–Sommer, *Les inscriptions araméennes de Sfiré* (Paris, 1958), 61 (I: B: 7) and Donner–Röllig, *KAI* 2, 253.

o   On the expression לקח בשנה, cf. Ezek 36:30: לקח חֶרְפָּה and Jer 20:10: לקח נִקְמָה.

p   The suggested reading עֲצַבּוֹ (עָצָב = "idol" in Is 48:5) instead of עצתו (Wellhausen; Koehler–Baumgartner) would then recall v 5, but without considering the transition to v 7.

q   Or, in view of G (ἀπέρριψε Σαμάρεια βασιλέα αὐτῆς; cf. *V*: *transire fecit Samaria regem suam quasi spunam super faciem aquae*) is נִדְתָה the correct reading? נדה piʻel should be interpreted, on the one hand, according to the Akk. *nadū* "to throw" and on the other, according to the Middle Hebrew "to expel": "Samaria has 'rejected' its king." *M* ("reduced to silence") is to be retained only if, with Wellhausen, the verse division is made with שֹׁמְרוֹן, whereby the participial form would presumably be a threat, which is unusual (cf. 4:5f; 10:15).

## Form

A new subject, "Israel," and a different theme mark the new unit which begins with 10:1. From v 1 to v 8 Israel is spoken of only in the third person. The direct address form, which last occurred in an isolated context in 9:10[1] and several times in 9:1–9, does not occur again until v 9. Chap. 10:1–8 is further marked as a distinct unit by the total absence of Yahweh's speaking in the first person, which was an essential characteristic of 9:10–13, 15–16, and which occurs again in 10:9f. Finally, the passage appears to be an unusually complete unit, particularly with respect to its contents. It deals mainly with the places of worship, while the theme of kingship appears in vv 3 and 7. The conclusion (v 8), which announces desolation of the high places of worship and sacrifice, returns to the initial theme, according to which the numerous altars (v 1) were threatened (v 2b). Significantly, the main catchword "altars" (מזבחות) recurs in vv 1, 2 and 8. Furthermore, the disclosure of Israel's transgression dominates the first part (vv 1–2a, 3–5), while the threat is first developed (vv 6–8) after its preliminary announcement in v 2b.

How are the text's form critical peculiarities to be interpreted? Here Yahweh does not speak in the first person and thus the form of the messenger speech is totally absent; nor is the audience directly addressed (second person). This, with the clear unity of the theme, points to the reflective character of the passage. Such a speech was most conceivably delivered before the prophet's inner circle, to whom we attributed the audition account in 9:10–17.[2] Nor in 10:1–8 is there any indication that Hosea's opponents voiced objections to his words. First in 4:4–19 the units of transmission were distinguished by supposing that Hosea's audience interrupted his speech. In the meantime M. J. Buss[3] pointed out that this method could not be applied to all of the units, especially to the genuine unit in 10:1–8.[4] In point of fact, this passage is best understood as a rhetorical unit.

Chap. 10:1–8 represents the development of a type of prophetic speech which is reflective or *didactic* in nature. As in the messenger speech and the disputation, both guilt and punishment are mentioned; however, there is no direct argumentation with the persons involved. Rather, this type of speech is delivered within the closed circle of the prophet's intimates (Is 8:16), who were faced with strong opposition as well. Together with them, Hosea is in search of understanding as he looks back to Israel's historical roots (v 1) and then views her present undertakings (vv 4f). He further describes to his circle what Israel can expect in the future (vv 2f, 6–8).

Synonymous parallelism was predominant in the sketches of Hosea's public speeches. But here, corresponding to the reflective nature of the didactic speech, this parallelism has diminished. It clearly occurs at the beginning (vv 1, 2b) and the end (v 8), whereas a synthetic train of thought takes precedence in the other verses. The prosaic character of the passage is evident in other respects. Above all, the short lines of two or three stresses in synonymous parallelism diminish remarkably (they occur only in vv 2b, 4b, 6b, 8b). Instead, longer sentences are interconnected by a certain correspondence of thought; clearly constructed lines of five stresses occur only in vv 1b and 8a.

### Setting
Although this didactic speech is plainly distinguishable from the audition account in 9:10–17, there are certain points of transition between the two passages. Israel's historical development is compared with a growing vine in 10:1. This recalls the simile in 9:10, where Israel's fathers are said to be "like grapes in the wilderness." The beginning of 10:1 appears to have been suggested by the imagery in the opening lines of the audition account; however, the scene developed here is no longer about the vanishing of Israel's precious vitality (as in 9:11–13; 16f) but rather about the destruction of her cultic places. Thus a difference in content corresponds to the different form, even though 10:1–8 presents more of a supplement which has essentially the same purpose as 9:10–17. This supplement was of particular interest to the opposition party of prophets and Levites.

In another respect the difference and the similarity of the two units is even more remarkable. In correspondence to the first person divine speech in 9:10–17, Yahweh is referred to only as "he" in 10:2b. Yahweh is explicitly named only in the quotations in v 3b. "He" (הוא) in v 2b has its antecedent in the transmitted text of 9:17.[4a] Together with the previous observations, this not only suggests that the time of 10:1–8 is not long after 9:10–17, but that 9:10–10:8 probably form a single transmission unit. In the units of transmission previously delineated,

---

1   See the commentary.
2   See p. 48.
3   Buss, "A Form-Critical Study," 111.

4   *Ibid.*, pp. 105–10.
4a  Cf. van Hoonacker.
5   See the commentary.

Yahweh is introduced either in the first person of the messenger speech (4:4; 5:2, 10; 8:1) or expressly by name (4:1, 9:1). If this didactic speech probably followed soon after the audition account, it is likely that both speeches were recorded together by the circle of traditionists.

These sayings contain several allusions to historical events which provide criteria for their date. Since v 3 probably refers to the future, it offers no help; the same is likely true of v 7.[5] But in v 7 the mentioned vacillation between broken agreements and treaties gives us concrete information. The connection of v 3 with v 4b should at least be considered a reference to inner political turmoil of the revolts against the throne. In addition, v 6a presupposes that tribute has recently been paid to "the great king" of Assyria. Finally, v 6b speaks of a plan which, according to the context, may have to do with matters of foreign policy. This is often related to the breaking of Israel's vassal treaty with Assyria and the move toward closer ties with Egypt, as mentioned in 2 Kgs 17:1ff; the allusion to broken treaties in v 4a might also refer to this. However, 7:11 gives evidence of similar foreign intrigues in the years 734–33.[6] The expression "this also will be brought to Assyria" in v 6a appears to have been formulated in a time when large payments of tribute were still remembered by everyone (cf. 8:9b). Moreover, if we add to this v 4a, which at least may also allude to treacherous domestic politics, then the only time left to be considered is that of Hoshea's revolt against Pekah.

Hence this didactic speech may be best understood if we date it at the time when the disturbances of 733 had begun to recede in the public mind. People again devoted themselves to cultic activities (vv 1, 5), as is evident from the mention of the harvest festival in 9:1ff. The people rejected the prophet's threats from recent months as madness (9:7f). Driven from public view (9:8), the troubled, solitary prophet withdrew to the small circle of the opposition.[7] He instructed them to keep a close eye on Israel's former and present transgressions and bravely to face Yahweh's inevitable judgment upon the newly revived cultic practices. In this connection, it is hardly coincidental that with the quotation of the words the people are soon to speak, his statements reach a climax in vv 3 and 8b. Among his intimates the prophet still feels the pressure of the people's rejection (9:7; cf. 4:16; 6:1–3; 8:2; 10:4). He draws the attention of his circle to the fact that God's judgment will awaken a completely different voice in the people (cf. 14:2ff).

### Interpretation

■ 1 Hosea's words are motivated by what he sees as he looks back to Israel's history: the abundant gifts she has received ultimately led to her destruction, for she misuses them in the pagan cult. Here it is not said that these gifts come from Yahweh, as it was in connection with the use of Israel's abundant silver for the making of idols (2:10b; 8:4b); nor is it mentioned when he speaks of her satiety from the good pasture (13:6) which made Israel forget Yahweh. Yet this is a self–evident presupposition for Hosea in his sayings about the abundant grapes on the vine and the goodness of the land (cf. 2:10a [8a]; 11:2–4; Jer 2:21). The accent, however, lies upon the abundance of life in the land as it was known in Israel during the last decades under Jeroboam II. This luxury misled Israel into giving too much attention to her altars. Hosea repeatedly takes up the subject of the large amount of grain; the numerous priests (4:7), soldiers (10:13) and places of sacrifice (also in 8:11); the multitude of fortresses (8:14); the profusion of transgression and hostility (9:7), of falsehood and violence (12:2). The roots "to be abundant" (רבב and רבה) occur nine times in Hosea to characterize the enormity of Israel's wrong; twice the words characterize the abundance of Yahweh's gifts (2:10; 12:11).[8] The productivity of the rich land promotes the artistic fashioning of the pillars.[9] The time is long past when Israel harmlessly adapted the *maṣṣēbôth* to their worship, where they functioned as memorials (Josh 24:26f; Gen 31:13; 35:20). The inroads into Israel made by Canaanite religion and culture disclosed their connection with

---

6   See the commentary on 7:11.
7   See the commentary on 9:10ff.
8   Concerning the altars as places of sin, cf. 8:11 and

the commentary; for Hosea's criticism of the *maṣṣē-bôth*, cf. the commentary on 3:4.
9   Cf. Sellin.

the fertility rites.[10] For this reason Deuteronomy, following Hosea, expressly prohibited them[11] as "*maṣṣēbôth* of the Canaanites."[12]

■ **2** Why do the numerous altars and the beauty of the *maṣṣēbôth* make Israel culpable? "Their heart is false."[13] The people may have learned—otherwise than in an earlier period—to call on Yahweh in time of need (cf. 2:18f [16f] with 6:3; 8:2); yet they are not oriented[14] toward him, for they do not seek the will of Yahweh but rather their own opportunities for religious mastery of their own fate; they seek the pleasure of cultic celebration (cf. 4:7–13; 8:11–13). They have not given their heart to Yahweh in uprightness. The antithesis to "false," "divided" (חלק) may be "faithfulness" (אֱמֶת), "trustworthiness" (אֱמוּנָה) and "loyalty" (חֶסֶד; cf. 2:21f [19f]; 4:1; 6:6; on this subject also cf. 10:4) rather than "undivided" (שָׁלֵם),[15] although the Deuteronomistic expressions "with all your heart" and "heart wholly true to Yahweh" should be noted.[16]

Thus Israel deserves the punishment it receives.[17] "Now" (עתה) frequently introduces the threat as here; cf. 5:7; 8:10, 13. The prophet announces nothing less than imminent judgment. It is *Yahweh* who brings judgment upon Israel. The word "he" (הוא) cannot possibly mean Israel.[18] The singular pronoun is distinguished too clearly from the three plural forms in vv 1bβ, 2a, which characterize Israel's deed in the immediately preceding context. Yahweh[19] treats the altars like the animals that are not to be sacrificed in the legitimate cult:[20] "He 'will break the neck of their altars.'"[21] This first suggests breaking off the four horns from the altar (Am 3:14). Similarly, he demolishes the artistically made *maṣṣēbôth*. With "to devastate" (ישדד) Hosea again uses—and not for the last time (cf. 10:14)—the catchword "devastation" (שד); with it he had twice

announced the gruesome devastation of the land in the year of Assyria's attack on Northern Israel, from which people could escape only by fleeing to a distant land (7:13; 9:6). Even the sanctuaries, the last places of asylum, will be destroyed.

■ **3** If careful note is taken of how v 3 is connected with v 2, then it is to be expected that the sentence introduced by "indeed, now" (כי עתה) and formulated in the imperfect, like v 2aβb, is an explication of the "now" in v 2aβ, which announces the impending judgment.[22] If Hosea was thinking of words already spoken at the present, he would have—as always in such cases—connected a perfect verb with the עתה (cf. 7:2; 8:8; 5:3 M). The prophet expects that in this judgment (v 2b) Israel will spurn her present king Hoshea—as she had previously rejected Pekah and his predecessors (7:3–7) —without humbly inquiring into God's will (8:4). But no more will Israel install a new king according to her own will, since the approaching catastrophe will make it clear to Israel that only a charismatic monarchy— one in which Yahweh's word designates the king—can help her. Whoever receives the acclamation of a people not filled with the fear of Yahweh will, in the approaching devastation which will also devour the holy places, be recognized as worthless to Israel. After the difficult months of preaching only judgment and waiting in vain for the people's return, for the first time the rejected prophet, speaking to an intimate circle of those faithful to Yahweh, alludes to a hope that the land's complete devastation will awaken in the people an acknowledgment of their guilt.[23] If v 3 is interpreted as a quotation of popular opinion which had already been expressed, then it must be separated from v 2 and connected with a group who "wish to excuse their own lawlessness with the weakness of the king,"[24] who, for

10  Cf. G. Pilhofer, "Phallische Kulte," *EKL* 3, 178.
11  Dtn 16:22; Cf. Lev 26:1 and Noth, *Laws*, 53f [73f].
12  Dtn 12:3; cf. Ex 23:24; 34:13.
13  See textual note "d."
14  On לֵב cf. p. 128.
15  Cf. the ancient version cited above in textual note "d."
16  Dtn 6:5; 1 Kgs 8:61; 2 Kgs 20:3, etc.; cf. Weiser, *TDNT* 6, 188.
17  On "to offend," "to be guilty" (אשם), see textual note "e."
18  Marti: "When man becomes disappointed, he destroys his gods"; cf. Is 2:20; similarly other commentators.
19  Concerning the relationship to 9:17, see "Setting" on pp. 172.
20  Such as the ass, Ex 13:13; 34:20.
21  Buber, *The Prophetic Faith*, 119.
22  Cf. the commentary on 2:12; also cf. 8:10.
23  See pp. 48f.
24  Robinson.

example, do not consider themselves to be under the authority of the new king, Hoshea ben Elah "after the murder of Pekah."[25] But this is not in accord with the prophet's view that he also would have supported the king only indirectly, even one such as Hoshea ben Elah. Thus the syntactic connection of v 2 and 3 noted above requires that v 3 be interpreted as a word the prophet expects the people to speak in the future (cf. v 8b).

■ **4** The prophet hopes that Israel will confess her guilt. This gives him cause to present a new picture of the present transgressions—especially those which are connected with the monarchy, and for which there was an expected compensation through increased cultic activity. The content of this verdict picks up his statement about the false heart in v 2aα: he strings the transgressions together in a series of infinitives in v 4a as in 4:2. The phrase "uttering (empty) words" denotes meaningless political agreements also in Is 8:10 (cf. Is 58:13). "Calling on God's name with deceit."[26] What this means in relation to the palace revolts is elucidated by 7:3–5. Also the expression "making treaties" primarily relates to the "treaty between king and people"[26a] which had been broken repeatedly during Hoshea's reign.[27] Only in a derivative sense do vv 3 and 4b refer to treaties with foreign nations (cf. 12:2; 5:13; 8:9), which is not completely impossible preceding v 6.

Yet v 4b especially draws attention to the injustice[28] of the land's institutions. Here Hosea freely makes use of a saying from Amos, similar to what we observed in 4:15 and 8:14. The prophet declares that justice sprouts like poison. In the light of Am 5:7 and 6:12 this means: the salutary institution of justice changes into a poisonous weed; justice is deceitfully misused. The ancient expression "along the furrows of the field"[29]—

which also occurs in 12:12b like a fixed formula—seems to compare the faithfulness of the fathers with the faithlessness of this generation.

■ **5** Israel worships her calf instead of promoting loyalty and justice.[30] As in 4:15 and 5:8, Bethel bears the disgraceful name coined by Amos: "house of wickedness."[31] The "inhabitants of Samaria" means the residents of the capital city.[32] At the ancient sanctuary, the national cult performs its rites more and more after the manner of the Canaanites. "To be afraid of" (גור) denotes the official cultic worship.[33] In addition, the word "to mourn" (אבל) may refer chiefly to the rituals of lament and mourning for Baal, perhaps even to the cultic wailing over the death of Baal in the myth.[34] This might correspond to the priests' ecstatic "shouts."[35] However, if the calf has already been surrendered as a trophy of war or as tribute, the mourning would already allude to the loss of it. A ritual lament before the image of the calf becomes an act of mourning for the loss of the image. The sudden change of thought first becomes apparent in the concluding sentence of the verse: "for it (its splendor) departs from it." In bitter irony these words give the reason for the priests' cultic exultation. For the first time in the Old Testament the priests are designated by the foreign word כְּמָרִים; later in Zeph 1:4 and 2 Kgs 23:5 the word is reserved for those who have committed themselves to the pagan cult of Baal. The word is occasionally used for a certain class of priests (eunuchs?), but in Phoenician and Aramaic it denotes priests in general.[36] The "glory" (כָּבוֹד)[37] of the calf, which is the object of the priests' exultation, means the calf's costly, magnificent gold. Like the images of the nations, (Is 46:1f; Jer 48:7; 49:3; Dan 11:8), the idols of Israel cannot escape deportation (cf. Is 10:10f).

---

25 Weiser.
26 On "to curse" (אלה), see the commentary on 4:2.
26a 2 Sam 3:21; 5:3; cf. Fohrer, "Vertrag," 1–22.
27 See p. 111.
28 On "justice" (משפט) see the commentary on 2:21.
29 שָׂדִי is more archaic than שָׂדֶה; cf. Koehler–Baumgartner.
30 See textual note "j."
31 See p. 90.
32 See the commentary on 8:5.
33 See textual note "i."
34 See the commentary on 7:14f and Widengren, *Königtum*, 63; cf. Ju 2:1, 5; Gen 35:8.

35 On ניל, see the commentary on 9:1.
36 Textual evidence is given in Jean–Hoftijzer, *Dictionnaire des Inscriptions sémitiques de l'ouest* (Leiden, 1960), 122: כמר II; cf. J. Lewy, "Zur Amoriterfrage," *ZA* 38 (1929): 243–45 and W. F. Albright, *From Stone Age to Christianity* (New York: Garden City, 1957), 234, n. 46; Koehler–Baumgartner.
37 Cf. כבוד in 9:11; the word occurs only in these two instances in Hosea.

■ **6** The conclusion of v 5 already announces the disaster. In vv 6–8 Hosea clearly explains to his colleagues in the opposition group how he conceives of Yahweh's judgment. The idol will be surrendered to the "great king" of Assyria as payment of tribute. "Carry" (יבל hipʿil) denotes the giving of gifts or payment of tribute also in Ps 68:30; 76:12; Zeph 3:10 (the hopʿal is used for the passive in Is 18:7; 12:2).[38] In return for this, Ephraim is disgraced, which is caused by Ephraim's own "plan." עֵצָה means political plan in Is 30:1 as well. After king Hoshea's revolt, it was hoped that faster submission to Assyria would prevent Israel's complete destruction.[39] The total lack of success with this kind of politics brings outright shame upon Ephraim.

■ **7** The participial expression within a threat in the imperfect (or perfect consecutive verbs; cf. vv 6, 8) is unusual. The sentence appears to be an interpretation (supplementary?) of the shame mentioned in v 6b. The shame is brought on by the downfall[40] of Samaria, the capital and royal residence. This Hosea had expected since the failure of the Syro–Ephraimite war. Now he expressed this directly to his circle of intimate friends. The shame also results from the fact that the king, like a piece of wood washed away by a flood, will be driven off by the Assyrian troops which inundate the land. The annals of Tiglath–pileser III contain a fragment in which a description of the Samarian overthrow of Pekah is compared to a storm: "Pekah, their king, they overthrew (gap) like a thunderstorm . . ."[41] This rather obscure statement about the action taken by the Samaritans against their king could fit quite well with the textual variants offered in *G V* discussed in textual note "q." However, the context suggests instead that this was a serious overpowering and sweeping violence (cf. also Is 8:7f), which would soon overcome Hoshea ben Elah as well.

■ **8** In any case, the continuation in v 8 announces a catastrophic devastation of the land. In the larger context, the ruin of the cultic places is of greater significance than the elimination of the king and his residence.

Like Bethel, which was called "house of wickedness" (lastly in v 5), all sanctuaries on the high places are now spoken of as "high places of wickedness"; indeed, the opposition party directly calls them "Israel's sin," which corresponds to Hosea's words in 4:7 and 8:11.[42] In Ugaritic there is evidence that בָּמָה still means "back," "ridge." In the Old Testament it can mean "high ground" and is increasingly used to designate those places of worship foreign to Yahwism. Even if the "high places" had a connection with burial rites, and if the *maṣṣēbôth* were understood in an earlier period as memorial stelae,[43] for Hosea they would hardly indicate a special "high place for lamentation."[44] Rather, the word refers to the classical locations of the idolatrous cults. "Bamah has become a fixed theological concept."[45] As special centers for religious observance, these locations will be turned into a wilderness: thornbushes will overrun the altars, the costly ornaments will be carried off (vv 5f), and the entire land will be desolate and bare (9:6).

The announcement of judgment upon altars and *maṣṣēbôth* in v 2b is heightened by a quotation of words yet to be spoken, which reveal the effect of the catastrophe upon the people. The same is also true in v 8. In dread of destruction, the inhabitants of Samaria "will say to the mountains: 'Cover us!' and to the hills: 'Fall on us!' " Those who survive will desire to live no longer and therefore they cry out for a great earthquake. It seems better to them to be crushed and buried by falling rocks than to have to live with no refuge among the destroyed sanctuaries. Divine judgment cannot be endured. Isaiah speaks in a similar fashion of those who look for protection in the gaps, in the rocks, and in the holes in the ground when the day of Yahweh comes (Is 2:10, 21). It is no longer possible for Hosea to conceive of a place for the protection of Israel (cf. Am 6:9ff).

**Aim**
These sayings revolve around the transgressions and the fate of the cultic places (vv 1f, 5, 8). Criticism of the

---

38  Cf. D. J. McCarthy, "Hos 12:2, Covenant by Oil," *VT* 14 (1964): 219–21.

39  5:13; 8:9; see pp. 111f.

40  On דמה II nipʿal, see p. 78.

41  Translation of *TGI*, 52, line 228f. Oppenheim, *ANET*², 283: ". . . their king [. . . like a] fog/snowstorm. . . ."

42  Concerning the furnishings of the high sanctuaries, see p. 86.

43  Albright, "High Place," 242–58; cf. K. Galling, "Erwägungen zum Stelenheiligtum von Hazor," *ZDPV* 75 (1959): 1–13.

44  See p. 90.

45  Schwarzenbach, *Terminologie*, 13; 1 Kgs 14:23.

cult must have stood in the foreground for those of the opposition who gathered around Hosea. This is especially understandable if the (Levitic) priestly opposition groups were members of this circle.[46] The guilt and fate of domestic and foreign politics is inseparably connected with the cult (vv 3–4, 6–7). Above all Hosea now draws a line that goes from Yahweh's abundant gifts (v 1) to Israel's "false heart" (vv 2a, 4, 5) and finally to the complete catastrophe of Israel's self–secure plans (vv 2b, 6–8a). The prophet's dispute with the people over their cultic behavior and the hostile propositions they advance has a continuing effect. By quoting their future words, he reflects their reaction to the coming judgment: they will admit that their loss of sovereignty results from their lack of fear in Yahweh (v 3); they will cry out that the devastation of the land and its sanctuaries is more than they can bear (v 8b).

Thus Hosea spoke, giving strength to the small circle of the faithful. He shows them the final end of those who reject the prophetic word of judgment. Ultimately, they will prefer death to life (v 8b; cf. Jer 8:3; Rev 9:6). Hosea's circle is to keep this in mind even though the present cultic activity is richer, more varied and creative than before (vv 1, 5). No attention to the places of worship, no lament, no rites of exultation can make up for not living according to the will of God (vv 2a, 4). Whoever worships the calf (v 5) instead of Yahweh—the God who elected Israel and made her increase—and whoever follows his own plans (v 6b) instead of Yahweh's instructions has chosen death over life. Thus Hosea nourishes that circle from which the Deuteronomic theology and paraenesis later grow (cf. Dtn 30:15–20).

The second generation of New Testament documents offers a new interpretation of Hosea's words. According to Luke, Jesus said to the women of Jerusalem who, wailing and lamenting, accompanied him on his way to the cross: "Do not weep for me, but weep for yourselves and for your children" (Lk 23:27ff). Hosea's word concerning those who said to the mountains: "Fall on us!" still has to be implemented in Israel if she "refuses to let the death of Jesus, who was obedient unto death, turn her from her own schemes and goals."[47] Israel's decision under Hosea was only a prelude to Israel's last decision before the crucified and resurrected Christ, in whom the offer of salvation to Israel came with finality.

According to John's Revelation the same decision confronts "the kings of the earth and the great men and the generals and the rich and the strong and everyone, slave and free" (Rev 6:15), i.e., all mankind, with no exceptions. With the same words Hosea once announced, they will all cry out to the mountains and the rocks: "Fall on us and hide us from the face of him who is seated on the throne, and from the wrath of the lamb" (Rev 6:16). This prospect gives strength to the persecuted community (6:10f), a small group threatened by the superior power of a world hostile to Christ.

In times of persecution this didactic speech of Hosea was recognized as a helpful signpost. Whenever Christianity adulterates the gift of life given it in Christ by false religious fads and political schemes, Hosea's words take on a new relevancy. Then Christianity will not only have to repeat the isolated quotation in the last saying, (v 8b), but it will also have to acknowledge that the entire passage exposes the misleading path it can take even when the gospel is proclaimed in the church.

---

46 See pp. 79 and 121.
47 K. H. Rengstorf, *Das Evangelium nach Lukas*, NTD I, 2 (Göttingen, 1937), 251.

## War—The Fruit of False Trust

**Bibliography**

R. Bach
"Die Erwählung Israels in der Wüste," unpub. diss. Univ. of Bonn (Bonn, 1952).

G. Farr
"The Concept of Grace in the Book of Hosea," *ZAW* 70 (1958): 98–107.

M. H. Goshen–Gottstein
" 'Ephraim is a well–trained heifer' and Ugaritic *mdl*," *Biblica* 41 (1960): 64–66.

J. C. von Kölichen
"Der 'Lehrer der Gerechtigkeit' und Hos 10:12 in einer rabbinischen Handschrift des Mittelalters," *ZAW* 74 (1962): 324–27.

J. Rieger
*Die Bedeutung der Geschichte für die Verkündigung des Amos und Hosea* (Giessen, 1929), 76–77.

E. Robertson
"Textual Criticism of Hos 10:11," *Transact. Glasgow Univ. Or. Soc.* 8 (1938): 16–17.

# 10

9  Since the days of Gibeah
   you[a] have sinned, O Israel.
   **There they have remained.**
   Surely[b] in Gibeah
   **war shall overtake them**
   **because of the transgressors.[c]**

10  I ⟨have come⟩[d] to[e] chastise[f] them.
   **Nations shall mass against them,**
   **when they are chastised[g] for their**
   **double iniquity.[h]**

a   *G* (ἥμαρτεν) and *V* (*peccavit*) harmonize the word with the third person in 10:1–8 and perhaps vocalize it as in v 8: חַטַּאת ישראל = "since the days of Gibeah (there are) the sins of Israel."

b   An asseverative לֹא (comparable to Latin *nonne*) has developed from its use in the rhetorical question ("shall they not reach . . .?"), as R. Gordis has shown ("Studies in the Relationship of Biblical and Rabbinic Hebrew," *Louis Ginzberg Jubilee Volume* [New York, The American Academy for Jewish Research, 1945], 181–83; cf. *idem*, "Hosea 14:3," 89).

c   Literally: "Sons (= companions) of unrighteousness"; Koehler–Baumgartner (707) derives עלוה from the root עלה II which is not attested in the Old Testament; however, it should probably be explained as metathesis of עַוְלָה (cf. v 13a) and thus interpreted as a substantive from the root עול I ("to deal unjustly") (cf. Koehler–Baumgartner 687; W. H. Gispen, *Het Boek Hosea*, COT (Kampen, 1953).

d   *G* (ἦλθον: a corruption of ἦλθεν within the Greek text's transmission; cf. Ziegler, *Duodecim prophetae*) presupposes בָּאתִי. *M* ("in my desire") would have been connected with v 9, or the following copula should be deleted (thus Harper, who conjectures בְּעָבְרָתִי). In a supposedly original reading באתי, it remains unclear how the *wāw* in *M* became placed after the *'aleph*.

e   The change from perfect to imperfect with a *wāw–copulative* is indicative of a purpose clause; cf. Brockelmann, *Syntax* § 135b, and see the commentary on 2:8bβ.

f   Perhaps (וְ)אֶיְסָרֵם should be read, as in 7:12; see

**11**    And[i] Ephraim (was surely) a trained heifer
           that loved[j] to thresh.
         When[k] I passed by
           her fair neck,[l]
         I wanted to harness Ephraim,

textual note "u" on 7:12 and Koehler–Baumgartner, 387. On *M* (יסר qal) cf. Gesenius–Kautzsch § 60a, 71.

g    *G* (ἐν τῷ παιδεύεσθαι αὐτούς) presupposes בְּהֻסְרָם (or בְּיָסְרָם according to Robinson), as do *S* and *V;* *M* (qal infinitive construct of אסר: "when they are bound," likewise *T*) mechanically harmonizes the consonants with v 10a (Dingermann, "Massora-Septuaginta," 51). Accordingly, had *M* intended to read בְּאָסְרָם "when I chastise them"? Concerning the dependence of a clause (instead of the usual infinitive) on the preposition בְּ, cf. Brockelmann, *Syntax* § 145a.

h    Qere = עֲוֹנֹתָם, which is presupposed by *G S V.* Ketib = עֵינֹתָם, in the sense of "before both their eyes" (H. G. A. Ewald, *Die Propheten des Alten Bundes* [Göttingen, 1867–8²]; cf. 2:12: "in the sight of") is, according to both the grammar and the context, highly improbable. The interpretation "their sources" (עֵינֹתָם) is more probable; accordingly, לִשְׁתֵּי would be explained as a misreading of the infinitive construct of שתה, perhaps originally לִשְׁתּוֹ (cf. Bauer–Leander, 427; Nyberg, 79, considers שְׁתֵי an Old North Hebrew infinitive construct); see the commentary on v 10.

i    *G V* do not translate the copula.

j    On the *yôd-compaginis* attached to a participle in the *status constructus*, cf. Gesenius–Kautzsch 90 kl and Beer–Meyer 1 § 45, 3d; see textual note "s" on 8:12; perhaps the *yôd* is added because of the meter (P. Joüon, *Grammaire de l'Hebrew Biblique* [Rome, 1947 § 93n], Robertson, "Hos 10:11") suggests אָהַבְתִּי, but this makes the beginning of v 11aβ (וְאָנִי) obscure.

k    The compound noun clause (verbal clause with an inverted subject) in v 11aβ functions as a circumstantial clause. It is subordinate to v 11b, which consists only of imperfect verbs, and has the sense of a temporal clause; cf. Gesenius–Kautzsch § 142a and L. Koehler," Syntactica IV," *VT* 3 (1953): 301ff. The insertion of a וְעַתָּה before אַרְכִּיב (Harper) is unnecessary; it would interrupt the progress of the sentence.

l    On the interpretation of the *status constructus* form, cf. Brockelmann, *Syntax* § 77. Nyberg (33f, 80) considers טוּב צַוָּארָה a noun clause which, as an asyndetic relative clause preceded by עַל, is changed to a substantive: "... by her, whose neck possessed beauty" = "... by the fair-necked" (thus Bach, "Erwählung"). Under the obvious assumption that the words form a normal construct chain, the same conclusion is reached when it is recognized that for the Hebrew, one part of the body can represent the whole and signify its outstanding characteristic; cf. A. R. Johnson, *Vitality*, 88, and Th. Boman, *Hebrew Thought Compared with Greek*, tr. J. L. Moreau (Philadelphia: Westminster, 1960), 101ff.

Judah would plow,[m]
Jacob[n] harrow:[o]

12 "Sow[p] according to righteousness,
    (thus)[q] you will reap according[r] to
    loyalty.
    Break up the fallow ground of
    ⟨knowledge⟩[s]
    and seek[t] Yahweh,
    until the ⟨fruit⟩[u] of righteousness
    comes to you."

m    *G* (παρασιωπήσομαι) read אַחֲרִישׁ, harmonizing it with the first person form of ארכיב, and understood it (from the root חרשׁ II) as a threat against Judah ("I will omit mention of"; cf. v 13a: παρεσιωπή-σατε ἀσέβειαν).

n    לו (like לכם in v 12aα; cf. v 12bβ) as a kind of *dativus ethicus* is best left untranslated; cf. Brockelmann, *Syntax* § 107ef.

o    Here *G* (ἐνισχύσει) also misinterprets in that it probably read יִשָׂרֶה (cf. the same translation in 12:4, 5). *M* is made certain by the parallelism of the three verbs in v 11b and the unity of metaphor in vv 11–13a.

p    See textual note "n."

q    The content requires that this be interpreted as a result–clause expressing a promise, similar to v 12bβ (עד־יבוא); cf. Brockelmann, *Syntax* § 3.

r    Literally: "according to the expression of"; cf. Brockelmann, *Syntax* § 107 ld; *G* (εἰς καρπὸν ζωῆς) incorrectly read לְפְרִי חַיִּים.

s    *G* (φωτίσατε ἑαυτοῖς φῶς γνώσεως) and *T* presuppose דָעַת. This fits the inner structure of the parallel clauses better than *M* ("and time"), which derives from a rather late misreading of ד as ו; on the parallels צדקה ‖ חסד ‖ דעת, cf. 2:21f; 4:1; 6:6; on φῶς γνώσεως (*G*) as Gnostic terminology (*Corpus Hermeticum* 10:21; already in TestLevi 4:3; 18:3); cf. G. Stählin, *Jesus Christus, das Licht der Welt: Festschrift Stohr* (Mainz, 1960), 73f.

t    The infinitive with ל stands in apposition to דעת and explains its nature and purpose; cf. Brockelmann, *Syntax* § 15g.

u    *G* (ἕως τοῦ ἐλθεῖν γενήματα δικαιοσύνης ὑμῖν) probably read פְּרִי (Koehler–Baumgartner, 403), which it frequently translates with γεν(ν)ημα(τα) (Is 3:10; 65:21; Jer 7:20; Dtn 26:10; 28:4, 11, 18, 42, 51; 30:9), although in Hosea, *G* translates פְּרִי otherwise with καρπός (9:16; 10:1; 14:9) as in the immediate context (v 13; cf. also textual note "r"). Therefore the Hebrew text presupposed by *G* may also have read תְּבוּאָה. Nevertheless, פְּרִי as the correct reading would more easily explain (1) the vocabulary in v 13a, which in other respects presents a strict antithesis to vv 11b–12 and (2) the misreading in *M* (וְיֹרֶה): "and he teaches" = *V: qui docebit vos iustitiam* (ירה II hip'il "to cause to rain" is not attested in the Old Testament; cf. Koehler–Baumgartner and Dalman, *Arbeit* 1, 122); וְיֹרֶה presents a premature interpretive break with the metaphor which probably derives from the common late–Jewish expectation of an eschatological teacher; cf. Wolff, *Joel und Amos*, 75f on Joel 2:23; cf. especially CD 6:11 with b. Bechoroth 24a!; וְיֹרֶה apparently still presupposes דָעַת in v 12bα. In each of the first three cola the metaphor comes first (sow, reap, break up), then the interpretation: righteousness, loyalty, knowledge. Correspondingly, first the metaphor "fruit" and then the interpretation "righteousness" is to be expected in the fourth colon.

180

13    (But)ᵛ you have plowed unrighteousness,
         you have reaped transgression,
            you have eaten the fruit of lies.
         Indeed, you trusted in your ⟨chariots⟩,ʷ
            in the multitude of your warriors.

14    Thus tumult of war shall ariseˣ among
         your tribes
         so that all your fortresses shall
            be destroyed,ʸ
         as Shalmanᶻ destroyed Beth–arbelᵃᵃ
            on the day of battle,
            when a mother over sons was
               shattered.

15    Exactly thus ⟨shall I do⟩ᵇᵇ to you,
         O house of ⟨Israel⟩,ᶜᶜ
            because of your greatᵈᵈ wickedness.
         At dawn shall be utterly silenced
            the king of Israel.

v    *G* (ἵνα τί) connects v 13a with vv 11b–12, although
      the other witnesses of the text do not contain a cor-
      responding לָמָּה. It fails to recognize the direct con-
      nection which the shorter and certainly original
      text of *M* makes with v 11b, for it does not recognize
      that v 12 has the nature of a quotation; see p. 182.

w    *G* still read בְּרִכְבְּךָ (originally ἅρμασι, according to
      Ambrose), whereas *G*ᴮ already theologized (ἁμα-
      ρτήμασιν; cf. Ziegler, *Duodecim prophetae* and Mic
      5:9); similarly, *M* generalizes ("upon your way"),
      as do *S V*, misreading רכב as דרך. Yet, in view of
      the parallel phrase ("in the multitude of your war-
      riors") *G*'s reading probably translates the original;
      the form *drkt* ("rule, dominion": J. Aistleitner,
      *Wörterbuch der ugaritischen Sprache* [Berlin, 1963], 82f,
      where examples are noted) which occurs, frequently
      in Ugaritic, should probably not be considered the
      equivalent of the Hebrew דרך without further evi-
      dence.

x    א in קָאם is a secondary linear vocalization (cf.
      *Bauer–Leander*, 404; Gesenius–Kautzsch § 72p).

y    The singular (hop‘al of שדד), supported by *G* (οἰχή-
      σεται), may be original and, after the כָל-, considers
      the fortresses a unit; cf. Is 64:10; Prv 16:2; *V* already
      translates with a plural (*vastabuntur*).

z    *G* (Σαλαμαν) and σ' (σάλμαν) support *M*, so that
      the Hexaplaric variant σαλμα (Ziegler) can by no
      means provide evidence for the proposed reading,
      שַׁלּוּם (2 Kgs 15:10, 13–15), which appears just as
      arbitrary as *G*⁷⁶⁴'s interpretation: Shalmaneser. *G*
      introduces Σαλαμαν with ὡς ἄρχων, thus misread-
      ing כשר as כְּשַׂר.

aa   σ' (ἐν τῷ οἴκῳ τοῦ αρβεηλ) supports *M*; *G* (ἐκ τοῦ
      οἴκου Ιεροβααλ) apparently presupposes יְרֻבַּעַל (Ju
      8:29, 35, etc.) instead of ארבאל; likewise *V* (*Salmana
      a domo eius qui iudicavit Baal*), but Ιεροβοαμ = יָרָבְעָם
      (Hos 1:1; 1 Kgs 11:26–31; 2 Kgs 14:23–29) already
      occurs in *G*ᴮ and other *G*ᵐˢˢ.

bb   *G* (ποιήσω) read אֶעֱשֶׂה, probably preserving the ori-
      ginal text, which corresponds with v 14aα. *M* ("has
      done") regards "Bethel" as the subject, probably
      the reason for the misreading in this context (see
      textual note "cc"). *M* is already presupposed by *S*
      and *V*.

cc   Thus *G*. *M* reads "Bethel." Aside from the context,
      this is improbable merely because Hosea usually
      calls Bethel בֵּית אָוֶן ("Beth–aven" 4:15; 5:8; 10:5;
      12:5 *G*).

dd   Literally: "because of the wickedness of your wick-
      edness"; concerning the paranomasia of a genitive
      connection having a superlative meaning, cf. Brock-
      elmann, *Syntax* § 79b; *G* (ἀπὸ προσώπου κακιῶν
      ὑμῶν) has a shorter text, without רַעַת, which is pos-
      sibly original. But Hosea likes to use the superlative;
      cf. 9:7 רֹב עֲוֹנְךָ; 7:2; 9:15 כָּל־רָעָתָם. *V* (*a facie mali-
      tiae nequitiarum vestrarum*) supports *M*.

## Form

After the climax describing the approaching catastrophe in 10:8, v 9 begins a new passage, with a new address to Israel which again mentions the guilt that brings her judgment. The next new unit apparently does not begin until 11:1, which has a different theme and names Israel anew. As in 9:10 and 10:1, 10:9 and 11:1 commence with a historical retrospect. Yet one might also ask whether v 11 represents a new beginning similar to that in 11:1. There a different kind of historical reminiscence is expressed concerning Ephraim (v 11). Against this one could argue that the beginning of the transmission units usually name "Israel" rather than "Ephraim" as the subject of the prophet's proclamation;[1] but of more importance is the fact that the new saying (v 11) is connected with the foregoing verses by a *waw* copulative.[2] The determining factor lies in the observation that the catchword "war" (מלחמה)—which does not occur elsewhere in Hosea's announcement of disaster —occurs after v 9 first in v 14 and then is actually developed in vv 14f. Yet vv 14f are not to be separated from v 13b, while כי joins v 13b to the previous saying in vv 11–13a. Finally, the saying which might appear to begin with v 11 is connected to vv 9–10 by the peculiar catchword "injustice" (עולתה v 13a) which appears in v 9 in the form עלוה.[3] Thus in the first place both the syntax and the catchword connections indicate that vv 9–15 are a transmission unit.

To these remarks several form critical observations should be added. Direct address is almost completely absent in 9:10–10:8; nor are there, at first, any forms indicative of direct address in 11:1ff. Yet in this unit Israel is addressed in the second person from the outset (v 9a), and then throughout vv 12–15, where singular (vv 9a, 13b, 14) forms alternate with plurals (vv 12, 13a, 15). Moreover, the divine speech in the first person appears in each of the different parts of this unit (vv 10a, 11, 15 *G*), but is not present in 10:1–8. Nevertheless it is precisely this variety of the forms of address—

different from the didactic speech in vv 1–8—which requires that various rhetorical units be distinguished.

Israel is addressed in the singular only at the beginning of the accusation in vv 9–10; on the other hand, as soon as the transition is made to the announcement of disaster, Israel is spoken of only in the third person plural. Concerning the alternation of second and third person in the forms of speech before the court, see pp. 74f and p. 134 on 8:1–14.

The imagery drawn from agricultural life in vv 11–13a indicates that these verses constitute a rhetorical unit. In the style of an account, this unit begins by describing the previous history of Ephraim; the audience is not directly addressed (plural) until the accusation in v 13a. Verse 12 is a part of the preceding account. This verse admonishes ancient Israel, which is now described as "yoked" for plowing and harrowing; the accusation against the present generation in v 13a is made in terms of this agricultural imagery. Verse 12 is not an interpolation, dependent on Jer 4:3,[4] that interrupts the connection of v 11 with v 13a; rather it makes the proper connection between them. The strictly parallel content of the statements indicates that v 12 leads to v 13a, not that it originates from Jer 4:3.[5] Nor should v 12, therefore, be regarded as an independent admonition. To be sure, its style is that of an independent exhortation, clearly structured in a multimembered series of imperatives, with parallels in Hosea only in 4:15,[6] 12:7 and 14:2f. Though similar to those passages which are only slightly reminiscent of the exhortatory style, v 12 is subordinate to a different form.[7] As the quotation of a previously spoken exhortation, it appears within the account of the previous history of Ephraim, who is now accused of disobedience (v 13a). Hence vv 11–13a also become understandable as a unit in terms of the speech forms used in the forum.[8] This peculiar saying, proceeding from a description of the praiseworthy history of Ephraim to a severe accusation, becomes understandable when, following v 10, Hosea's audience

---

1  Cf. lastly 9:10; 10:1, 9; previously, 5:1, 9; 8:3; 9:1; later on 11:1; 14:2; differently, however, in 12:1 and 13:1.
2  Not, however in *G*; see textual note "a."
3  See textual note "c."
4  Thus Guthe.
5  See p. 186.
6  See p. 77.

7  See the commentary on 2:3, 2:4f and 8:5f.
8  Concerning the report on a defendant's previous actions used to initiate the words of accusation, cf. first of all Jer 2:1ff and Boecker, *Redeformen*, 105ff.

retorted by referring to the election traditions.

Verses 13b–15 present a new rhetorical unit, as the transition from the second person plural in vv 12–13a to the second person singular clearly indicates. Within this unit, whose structure consists of a threat–and–motive clause, there is a transition from the previous imagery to the subject itself; here the catastrophe brought on by war briefly alluded to in vv 9b–10 is further described. The כי, in its deictic function as a demonstrative particle, connects vv 13b–15 with the foregoing saying. This connection could have been made by the traditionists, who wanted above all to ellucidate the accusation in v 13a with the new saying in v 13b. But the כי, as is also probable in 4:10b, 12b, 16; 8:7, 9, 11, could also mark the beginning of the prophet's words after his audience expressed an objection.[9] The address changes abruptly to the singular; its probable explanation is that an important representative of the royal court in Samaria raised an objection to Hosea's words; cf. v 13b: "Your chariots," "your warriors"; v 14: "among your people," "all your fortresses." Then it is not likely coincidental that the threat ends with a reference to the king (v 15b), immediately preceded by a solemn word to the "house of Israel" (בית ישראל v 15a G). This is conspicuous in comparison to the usual "Israel" (ישראל) in Hosea; as in 5:1,[9a] it probably should not be interpreted as simply "the people," but rather suggests here the "dynasty of the kingdom of Israel."

Hence, with its three prophetic sayings this transmission unit again has all the characteristics of those previous sketches of Hosea's public orations that were found in 4:4–9:9.[10]

A poetic structure is clearly recognizable only in the middle section of 11b, 14aα, where the balanced lines repeatedly express one train of thought. In the prosodic units consisting of three synonymous lines in vv 11b, 12a and 13a, we find that the first and third lines have two stresses, while the second line has three. The transition to the brief lines of two stresses in v 13a (after the seemingly calmer exhortation quoted in v 12) coincides with the accusation that now has a whiplash effect. The metrical structure at the beginning of the threat and motivation sounds similarly harsh. The accusation is

a forceful two–stress bicolon (v 13b) followed by the threat, a wordy, rolling, three–stress bicolon (v 14aα); in the continuation the lines increase in length. They have no recognizable rhythm and, like the first saying in vv 9–10, they seem almost to be prose.

## Setting

Where could these sayings have been proclaimed? Verses 13b–15 suggest that circles of political leaders from the royal court are present. Therefore Hosea most likely spoke these words in Samaria.

What is their date? The prophet begins with the same reminiscence of the "days of Gibeah" which closed the scene in 9:1–9. According to 9:7f and our analysis of 9:10–10:8[11] there was probably a period of time when Hosea did not speak publicly. If we take this into consideration it might be possible that this scene (10:9–15) occurred at the same time as that reported in 9:1–9, which belongs to the period preceding Hosea's withdrawal from public view. But certain factors tell against this: 10:9–15 is also clearly related to 10:1–8, as can be seen, for example, by a comparison of v 15b with v 7 and vv 12–13a with v 4b. In addition, we have noted that the historical retrospect that first appears in 9:9 was not developed further until the time the rejected prophet withdrew from public view (9:10, 15; 10:1). Now, in 10:9–15 the historical retrospect has become more intense (v 9, 11f). Hence nothing speaks against the assumption that the traditionists' literary order of these units corresponds to the chronological order of the scenes.

We do not know how long Hosea remained publicly silent. The fact that the catchwords in 9:9 are repeated in 10:9 suggests a shorter rather than a longer period of time. After 733 political turmoil seems to have further diminished.[12] People felt increasingly secure against the hostile attacks (v 9b), especially in view of their own military strength (v 13b). They were heading in the direction of the year 727, when Shalmaneser V succeeded Tiglath–pileser III. At that time it was thought that the Assyrian yoke could be completely thrown off (2 Kgs 17:4).

9    See p. 135.
9a   See the commentary on 5:1 (and also 1:4?); cf., however, p. 19.
10   See p. 75f.
11   See pp. 172f.
12   See p. 153 on 9:1–9.

## Interpretation

**■ 9** The first words of Hosea recorded here by the traditionists seem to have been provoked by ironic questions, perhaps uttered by members of official circles. They may have inquired about the outcome of his alarm of war in Gibeah, one of the southernmost towns of the Northern Kingdom. He had sounded the alarm in the midst of the deep crisis following the collapse of the Syro–Ephraimite war and the Assyrian attack in the north in 733 (5:8). Did the prophet, for instance, still think that "in Gibeah the war would overtake them"? Would he still regard as God's word his comparison of his own rejection with the "deeply corrupted actions" of the "days of Gibeah"?[13] An elucidation of the development of such arguments is found in Is 5:18f. It would be conceivable that Hosea answered such pointed questions by emphatically repeating the accusation which had concluded his last public scene. Now he not only says: "As in the days of Gibeah," but "since the days of Gibeah you have sinned. There they have remained." In v 9 עמד means "to persist in the same attitude," "remain unchanged."[14] It is the opposite concept of "return," which Hosea has long since called for.[15] Thus for Hosea history was of utmost importance because past historical events are typical for and determinative of the present time. There is even less reason here than in 9:9 to consider this a reference to the beginning of the monarchy. Gibeah was certainly Saul's royal residence,[15a] but it was not the place of Israel's guilt in connection with the inception of the monarchy.[16] On the other hand, Hosea's words become understandable in the light of Benjamin's terrible offense against the sojourning Levite—a shocking transgression against divine law in Israel (Ju 19:30)—together with the destructive war of retribution that followed (Ju

20:34, 48). Since Gibeah's former guilt is also its present guilt, the city's former disaster will come once again to Gibeah, despite the mockery the proph enemieet'ss make of him.[17] The בני עלוה are the rebellious agitators.[18] The word עלוה, like עולתה,[19] denotes the "perversity" and "baseness" seen in apostasy (Ezek 28:15f) and hostility (Ps 89:23; 2 Sam 7:10); as revolt against the legitimate sovereign, it was a capital offense (2 Sam 3:34). Thus Yahweh's judgment comes upon present Israel as the "people of Gibeah"; similarly Isaiah called Jerusalem "people of Gomorrah" and her leaders "rulers of Sodom" (Is 1:10).

**■ 10** Yahweh presents himself as the teacher who disciplines his people.[20] He does not instruct them with precepts but with historical data.[21] He is the commander–in–chief of the nations that gather to attack Israel. Hosea independently developed the same theology of world history as Isaiah (10:5).[22] The "assembly" of the nations means that Yahweh "gathers" them to begin the new battle of Gibeah (cf. אסף in Ju 20:11, 14). As Yahweh once intervened for Israel against the gathering nations (Ju 6:33) as they came forth to war, he now comes against his own people on the new "day of Yahweh."[23] Hosea designates the foreign nations by the word עמים also in 7:8; 9:1. It is less probable that he means that the Assyrian troops are recruited from the various nations (cf. 2 Kgs 17:24); rather, with the obscure, suggestive plural[24] his purpose is to attest to the superior power of Israel's teacher, who has his eyes focused on Israel's "double iniquity." What is the meaning of "double"? It could hardly refer to the two calves of Dan and Bethel,[25] since Dan plays no recognizable role in Hosea.[26] Nor does v 9 indicate that Benjamin's crime and the sins connected with the monarchy's beginnings are juxtaposed as a double misdeed of Gi-

---

13 See the commentary on 9:9.
14 Cf. Jer 48:11; Lev 13:5, 37; Dan 10:17; Ps 19:10 [9].
15 שוב; cf. 5:4, 15; 7:16; see p. 129.
15a 1 Sam 10:26; 11:4; cf. A. Alt, "Die Urgestalt des Reiches Israel," *Kleine Schriften* 2, 31.
16 On Gilgal, see the commentary on 9:15.
17 See textual note "b" on the asseverative question "Shall it not overtake them?" These words are understandable in the context of the dispute.
18 Cf. "base fellows" (בְּנֵי־בְלִיַּעַל) in Ju 19:22; 20:13.
19 See textual note "c."
20 On יסר see the commentary on 5:2.
21 Bertram, *TDNT* 5, 606f.
22 Cf. H. W. Wolff, "Das Geschichtsverständnis der alttestamentlichen Prophetie," *EvTh* 20 (1960): 218–35 [also in his *Gesammelte Studien*, ThB 22 (München, 1964), 289–307].
23 This expression does not occur in Hosea; cf. Am 5:18–20; Is 2:12.
24 See the commentary on 8:1, 3.
25 1 Kgs 12:28f; cf. Gispen.
26 See the commentary on 8:5; 10:5.

beah.[27] Rather, Hosea's view of Israel's present history suggests that Gibeah's former sin is doubled by Gibeah's present guilt ("There they remained" v 9). Yet the text of v 10bβ remains uncertain.[28] It is possible that the verse refers not to the causes but to the effect of Yahweh's judgment: foreign nations will drink from Israel's springs, a motif reminiscent of 7:9.

■ **11** In the course of the prophet's speeches he frequently addresses himself to his audience's views (does he respond to objections voiced by them?).[29] Now he clothes in new imagery the election traditions that have apparently troubled him since 9:10. Although once a useful "heifer," Ephraim has long been "a stubborn cow" (4:16). מלמדה probably means "trained, practiced, broken in," rather than "teachable."[30] The following words emphasize that she pleased Yahweh and was therefore useful to him. She "loved to thresh." Here threshing is thought of without a threshing sledge or cart wheel.[31] The animal can therefore run about freely, even frisk about playfully (Jer 50:11) and eat unhindered (Dtn 25:4). It is this cheerfully industrious young animal that Yahweh encounters. In v 11 "pass by" (עבר) does not mean to spare as Yahweh passes by[32] but to discover as Yahweh comes upon the heifer (cf. Ezek 16:6, 8), which corresponds to the "finding" motif in 9:10.[33] As he goes by, the "beauty of her neck" arrests his attention. טוב does not mean her pleasant form as such but her visible strength and power.[34] Accordingly it is Israel's appropriate usefulness, as in 9:10, which Yahweh's election presupposes in this tradition. He observes that this animal with such a neck is capable of more than simply threshing. Thus Yahweh yokes the animal so it can pull the wagon and the plow. Whereas חרש "to plow" means to break up the ground, שׂדּד signifies the cultivation of the land with a harrow to flatten the

surface for planting.[35] Each of the three various actions described has a different subject. Each part of v 11b is essential, corresponding to the three imperfect verbs in v 12 and the three parallel perfects in v 13a, even though the occurrence of "Judah" is surprising between Ephraim and Jacob.[36] Moreover, I see no basis in the text's history or in Hosea's own thought for the view that "Judah" is the correction of an original "Israel" made by the Judaic redactor.[37] There is sufficient evidence for Hosea's view of Israel as an entirety.[38] If he holds this view of Israel at the present[39] it is even more true of Israel's unity in the past. If "Judah" is considered original after "Ephraim," the third name "Jacob" becomes even more intelligible. Chap. 12:3ff [2:ff], 13 [12] show that Hosea has a knowledge of the Jacob tradition. In 12:3ff he sees Israel's essence in this particular patriarch. In 10:11 Jacob may denote the old tribal league, together with the tribal names that came to designate the two kingdoms. The name of Jacob, father of all the tribes, unlike "Israel," is not used exclusively for one of the kingdoms.

With these metaphors, Hosea pictures Israel's election as an election to service. The concept of election means to commission someone with a greater task,[40] in this case the cultivating of the arable land. This task apparently was determinative in Hosea's choice of imagery. The wilderness should be considered the place of the election, as in 9:10, even if the threshing heifer as such, like the grapes, does not belong there.

■ **12** The commission that is inseparably connected with Israel's election is expressed in v 12. Yahweh commands that the seed be sown with a view towards the future harvest, and that the plowing be done in expectation of its produce. Verse 12 states more clearly than v 11 that it is not Israel's agricultural life in itself that is

27 Weiser.
28 See textual note "h."
29 E.g., 5:10f, 8:8; see pp. 113f and 136.
30 Cf. Jer 31:18; Sir 51:17; Ps 51:15; Is 40:14, and Goshen–Gottstein, "Ephraim."
31 Cf. Is 28:27f; cf. Dalman, *Arbeit* 3, 107.
32 Harper.
33 Thus Bach, "Erwählung"; but also cf. Zimmerli, *Ezekiel*, 349.
34 Cf. Th. Boman, *Hebrew Thought Compared with Greek*, tr. J. L. Moreau (Philadelphia: Westminster, 1960), 87f, and also textual note "l" and the commentary on 3:5.

35 Cf. Dalman, *Arbeit* 2, 189ff; G. E. Wright, *Biblical Archaeology* (Philadelphia: Westminster, 1957), 180; Is 28:24f; Job 39:10.
36 Contra S. Mowinckel, *Prophecy and Tradition* (Oslo, 1946), 71f, *et al.*
37 Thus Nyberg, 83.
38 See the commentary on 5:9ff.
39 Concerning the future, see the commentary on 2:2.
40 Cf. Th. C. Vriezen, *Die Erwählung Israels nach dem Alten Testament*, ATANT 24 (1953).

meaningful, but rather her life in community with the lord of her election (cf. Is 1:3). Therefore the chief concepts which express life in accordance with the covenant are used here. Taken by itself, the expression sow "according to righteousness" (לצדקה) could be a picture of the right, appropriate care taken to obtain "good" seed (Mt 13:24, 27) which is removed from the weeds.[41] Whether or not Hosea had this in mind at all, he surely was thinking of Israel's entire conduct in accordance with Yahweh's covenant, as the following words indicate (cf. 2:21). Everything Israel undertakes in the land, which is a gift to her from Yahweh (2:10), should be done in accordance with her relationship to her God (cf. 10:4b). The צדקה is the "saving sphere," the "power–charged field" and "highest value of life, upon which all of life rests when it is in accord with order."[42] He who "sows" according to this order will harvest "according to loyalty"[42a] and will therefore experience the goodness of the covenantal God through what he "harvests" in life.[43] If the second imperative is read as a second exhortation, then חסד would have to be understood more in the sense of the generosity required of Israel at the harvest, particularly with regard to the poor (Lev 19:9f; 23:22; Dtn 24:19). But this interpretation corresponds to Hosea's thought less than the idea of Israel's relationship to God, which is seen by the usage of חסד in 6:4, 6; 12:7; 2:21; 4:1.[44] Verse 12bβ interprets the second imperative as a promise. Hosea does not mean "merit" in a sense of the effect of one's deed; rather, he refers to life within the saving covenant, which is determined completely by Yahweh's election. In addition to the words צדקה and חסד, this is indicated especially by the following words about "breaking the fallow ground of knowledge by seeking Yahweh."[45] The metaphor of "breaking up the ground"

refers to the plowing either of virgin land or land that has lain fallow and thus needs to be weeded and broken up. This results in an especially fruitful harvest.[46] This new plowing which is to bring Israel a life of wholeness is a plowing of the knowledge of God.[47] This phrase is more closely defined as the "knowledge of seeking Yahweh." That "Yahweh" occurs within the divine speech is understandable from the exhortation;[48] moreover, it is also explained by the use of the fixed formula "to seek Yahweh."[48a] Claus Westermann[49] has demonstrated that, whereas the word שאל is connected with the priest's administration of the oracle (cf. 4:12), "to inquire of Yahweh" (דרש את־יהוה), especially in Northern Israel, denotes the turning to Yahweh in some distress, such as sickness or danger of military attack. In these instances it is always a prophetic figure, a "man of God," who is sought out and who communicates the divine answer.[50] It is important to note "that the inquiry addressed to the deity denoted by the word דרש takes place only through a prophet."[51] This again indicates that Hosea is connected with the particular prophetic traditions of the Northern Kingdom. The phrase is a fixed formula in the theology of the opposition party. In v 12 Israel is offered virgin land (cf. 12:11f) from which she can gather the "fruit of righteousness"[52] as the harvest. Thus Hosea speaks of Yahweh's guidance of Israel to the arable land: he instructs her to anticipate the gifts of her calling as she lives according to his ordinances. The purported relationship of the last line to the Baal myth[53] is not based upon the text. Nor does the presumed secondary text of M refer to rain, but to the teachings that correspond to the knowledge of seeking Yahweh.[54]

■ **13a** The cutting, terse accusation is expressed in terms of the ancient covenantal instructions.[55] Here "plow-

41 Cf. 2 Sam 4:6 G and Dalman, *Arbeit* 2, 201.
42 F. Horst, "Recht," 75 [291]; v. Rad, *Theology* I, 317ff; see p. 52.
42a See textual note "r."
43 On "loyalty" (חסד), see the commentary on 2:21. On the relationship of sowing to harvest, see the commentary on 8:7.
44 See the commentary on 4:1 and 6:6; also see textual note "q."
45 See textual note "s."
46 Prv 13:23; cf. Dalman, *Arbeit* 2, 137f; with the same meaning, the word *nr* has been found in Ugaritic (*CTCA* 16.3.10 [Gordon 126.3.10]); cf. Gray, *KRT*,

72.
47 Cf. 4:1, 6; 6:6 and the commentary.
48 See "Form" on p. 182; cf. 12:7; 14:2; 4:15.
48a Cf. 4:6; 6:6 and the commentary on 1:2.
49 "Die Begriffe für Fragen und Suchen im Alten Testament," *KuD* (1960): 2–30.
50 E.g., 1 Kgs 22:5ff, 2 Kgs 3:11; 8:8ff; 22:13ff.
51 Westermann, "Begriffe," 20.
52 See textual note "u."
53 Cf. Worden, "Influence," 296.
54 See textual note "u."
55 See "Form," pp. 182f.

ing" takes the place of "sowing," since plowing and sowing—unlike our own practice—belong together in order to cover the grain with the earth.[56] Instead of sowing in accordance with the covenant, Israel planted godless unrighteousness in contradiction of her election. "Unrighteousness" (רֶשַׁע) denotes the opposite of "righteousness" (צדקה), just as "unrighteous" (רָשָׁע) is a perfect antithesis to "righteous" (צַדִּיק).[57] Accordingly, now Israel will harvest in its present existence the very opposite of Yahweh's covenant loyalty (חסד), namely, the "perversity"[58] of its apostasy, and instead of taking pleasure in the fruit of a life of wholeness, they must reap the "fruit of lies." According to the context, "lie," "deceit" (כחש) does not refer primarily to one's relationship to his neighbor (as in 4:2; 7:3) but to the covenant with Yahweh (as in 12:1). As the corresponding third line in v 12 indicates they practice and experience deceit by rejecting the "knowledge of seeking Yahweh," i.e., the directions given by his prophet. Instead the people devotedly seek answers from the priestly oracles which have come under Canaanite influence.[59] They sacrifice in the sanctuaries influenced by Baal worship (2:9; 5:6) and, above all, expect help from their own political tactics (7:3, 10).

■ **13b** The new saying that begins in v 13b[60]—perhaps evoked by a question from Hosea's audience—explains the preceding metaphor as the seed of false trust in military strength, whose harvest is inevitably war. And war in turn produces the fruit of a great devastation. Here בטח means "trust" in the sense of "to feel secure"; the basic meaning of the word denotes the condition of security.[61] This feeling of security is based on factors of military strength. The "chariots"[62] were the most fearsome weapons of that time. Known since the Hyksos period, the chariot became greatly sig-

nificant in the neo–Assyrian era.[63] According to Shalmaneser III's "Monolith Inscriptions" of 854–3, Israel was able in its time to call upon more chariots (2,000) than all the other Syro–Palestinian kingdoms, even more than Damascus (1,200) and Hamath (700).[64] Israel's former glory was still remembered and was nourished again and again. Even in the spring of 721, when Samaria was conquered after the long years of catastrophic defeats, Sargon II found 50 of the subjugated chariots good enough to incorporate into his royal militia.[65] The intent to interpret דרך in M as *dominium, potentia* on the basis of the Ugaritic *drkt*[66] is without significance for this verse in view of the variant in G parallel to גבורים.[67] The large number of trained professional soldiers can fight better than a levy of farmers.[68] They also serve as the king's bodyguard. If members of the royal court replied to Hosea after his words in v 13a,[69] then this elucidation of the apostasy from Yahweh's covenant (v 13b) becomes especially understandable. Hosea's accusation was picked up by the circle of traditionists and later finds expression in the "law of the king" in Dtn 17:16.

■ **14** Israel's trust in her military strength results in the alarm of war. שָׁאוֹן first denotes the roar (שׁאה II) of waters (Is 17:12f) and then the noise of fighting at the beginning of battle, the tumult of a multitude, and the summons to fight (cf. Is 13:4; 17:12; Jer 51:55). The "tumult of war" shall arise "among your people" ( = "against your forces"?).[70] Trust in a false object reaps only great desolation in the land. This Hosea has repeatedly announced since 7:13 with the word "destroy" (שׁד 9:6; 10:2); now in a prolix statement he uses it to denote a total annihilation.

The comparison with the destruction of "Beth–arbel" by Shalman, which must have been meaningful to

---

56  Dalman, *Arbeit* 2, 180–85.
57  Cf. Kraus, *Psalmen*, 8f; concerning the reminiscence of this verse in 1QS 3:2, cf. P. Wernberg–Møller, "Notes on the Manual of Discipline (DSD) I 18, II 9; III 1–4, 9, VII 10–12, and XI 21–22," *VT* 3 (1953): 198, and *ThSt* 9 (1956): 54.
58  On עולתה and עלוה, see the commentary on v 9.
59  See the commentary on 4:12.
60  See "Form," p. 183.
61  בָּטַח; cf. Ju 18:7 and A. Weiser, *TDNT* 6, 191.
62  See textual note "w."
63  *BRL* 420; *ANEP*, 356–61; *AOBAT*, 130.
64  Oppenheim, *ANET*², 278f; *AOT*, 340f; *TGI* 145f.
65  Oppenheim, *ANET*², 284; *AOT*, 349; *TGI*, 54.
66  S. Bartina, *Verbum Domini* 34 (1956): 202–09.
67  See textual note "w"; cf. the critical position taken by H. Zirker, "דרך = potentia?" *BZ* NF 2 (1958): 291–94.
68  Cf. גבורים in 2 Sam 20:7; 23:9; Jer 26:21.
69  See pp. 182f.
70  Nu 20:20; 21:33; Josh 8:3, 7; 11:7; Ju 5:14. Concerning the fortresses, see the commentary on 8:14.

Hosea's contemporaries, is unfortunately no longer intelligible. For the longest time, critics have been able to offer nothing more than conjectures.[71] With reference to the variant readings in *G*, Cheyne, Sellin, *et al.*, suggested the reading כְּשֹׁד שַׁלּוּם בֵּית יְרֻבְעָם, thus connecting the verse with the murder of Zechariah, the son of Jeroboam, by the usurper Shallum. But 2 Kgs 15:10 says nothing about a "battle" with such devastating consequences as Hosea mentions here. Others interpreted "Shalman" as an abbreviation for Shalmaneser V (727–22), who was thought to have destroyed Beth–arbel in the march against Samaria. Again, there is no evidence for this. Our dating of the passage[72] does not support such a late time. It still seems best to consider "Shalman" as the Moabite king Salamanu, named by Tiglath–pileser III in a list of those who paid him tribute.[73] In addition, Am 2:1–3 could also be cited; however, this passage does not refer to that area where Beth–arbel is usually thought to be located, namely, in Northern Transjordan, modern *Irbid*, which is barely 12 miles N.W. of *Tell Rāmît* (Ramoth of Gilead).[74] Beth–arbel might have been an important city somewhere in the area between Israel and Moab, which—like the city Abel of Beth–maacha near Dan mentioned in 2 Sam 20:18—was given the name "Mother over Sons"[75] and was totally destroyed. רטש pi'el means the dashing in pieces of children upon rocks in Ps 137:9; 2 Kgs 8:12; pu'al in Is 13:16; Nah 3:10; cf. also Hos 14:1.

■ **15** Israel's God prepares exactly this (ככה) kind of disaster for those who depend upon their own power instead of his covenant, for this is their "great wickedness" (cf. vv 12f). Even the king of Israel will be silenced once and for all,[76] i.e., he shall perish "at dawn," the very beginning of the day of battle.[77] In point of fact Hoshea ben Elah was to be taken captive by Shalmaneser V before the seige of Samaria began (2 Kgs 17:4; cf. Hos 10:7).

### Aim

Thus the scene draws to a close with a terrifying description of the destructive battle which was mentioned already in v 9b. "War" (מלחמה)—this is the passage's unambiguous theme. It is apparent even in the introduction that war is announced to those who feel themselves secure, who mockingly rejected the previous threats.[78] The nations' war against Israel shall serve the purposes of her "Chastiser" (v 10). In the midst of this great event involving all nations, Yahweh carries on a discussion with Israel over his saving history. Against the background of election history, this is clear from the invective in the middle of the scene (vv 11–13a). Because of Yahweh's delight in Israel, he once called her to serve him (v 11) and thus to be cared for by him (v 12). Through her covenant, through seeking his instructions, and in the sphere of his kindness, Israel was to reap and enjoy the fruit of her saving fellowship with him (v 12). But Israel turned away from his instructions and promises and, after the manner of the nations, sought her security in the political development of her own power. Thus in the catastrophe of her own politics she has to learn in an entirely new way that salvation is found in Yahweh alone. The history of the ancient covenant people comes to a complete halt. For those who believed themselves to be secure, Hosea thus made it unavoidably clear that the refusal of worship in accordance with the divine covenant and the substitution of self–deception for seeking God's will lead to destruction. The elect can live only from their God and his word, which creates fellowship and provides life (v 12). Trust in power–politics becomes the seed of death.

---

71   See textual notes "z" and "aa."

72   See "Setting," pp. 183.

73   Oppenheim, *ANET*², 282; *AOT*, 348; cf. A. H. van Zyl, *The Moabites* (Leiden, 1960), 23, 149f, 183, and H. Donner, "Neue Quellen zur Geschichte des Staates Moab," *MIOR* 5 (1957): 165f.

74   Cf. M. Noth, "Beiträge zur Geschichte des Ostjordanlandes. I. Das Gebiet Gilead als Siedlungsgebiet israelitischer Sippe," *PJ* 37 (1941): 92 [also in his *Aufsätze zur biblischen Landes– und Altertumskunde* 2, ed. H. W. Wolff (Neukirchen, 1971), 382, and N. Glueck, *Explorations in Eastern Palestine* 4, *AASOR* 25–28 (1951), 153f.

75   "Settlements of the emigrants of the mother–town" Koehler–Baumgartner, 59, 159.

76   On דמה II pi'el, see the commentary on 4:5.

77   Cf. 1 Sam 11:9–11; 2 Chr 20:16–20; Is 17:14 and J. Ziegler, "Die Hilfe Gottes am Morgen," *BBB* 1 (1950): 285f.

78   See p. 183.

In 2 Cor 9:10 Paul uses the expression "harvest of righteousness" ($\gamma \epsilon \nu \acute{\eta} \mu \alpha \tau \alpha \ \tau \hat{\eta} s \ \delta \iota \kappa \alpha \iota o \sigma \acute{\nu} \nu \eta s$ [פרי צדק]) taken from Hos 10:12b, and thus repeats the promise offered those against whom Hosea has brought his accusation. "God will increase the harvest of your righteousness." Paul uses the ancient promise in order to rouse the Christian community to trust in the seed her Lord has supplied. In doing so, she would become free to aid with generous gifts the poor among God's new covenant people. By refusing to secure his own existence through greediness, the believer can vouchsafe his "obedience in professing the gospel of Christ" (v 13); in contributing generously to the collection for Jerusalem he shows evidence of his genuine trust in the Lord.

With this brief example Paul suggests to God's new covenant people that in the light of the judgment upon the elect of the old covenant they reach a clear understanding of the promise and also of the danger under which they themselves stand. From Paul they had surely learned that there is apostasy from the Gospel also in the era of the new covenant, when Jesus Christ has suffered the total judgment of God; that "the unrighteous will not inherit the kingdom of God" (1 Cor 6:9; Gal 5:21); rather, that the people of the new covenant will be asked in all seriousness about "the fruits of the spirit" (Gal 5:22).

A careful study of all three sayings in this scene makes this very earnestness clear to us. These passages teach us to recognize the danger of false security which is typical for all who are called as the new people of God to do good among the heathen nations. These words plainly warn us against using the sword (Mt 26:52) in disobedience of God's word, especially after the world's Reconciler commanded his disciples "to put the sword away." In trust only in the crucified and resurrected Word, the Lord of all nations, these words call us to take "love, joy, peace, patience, kindness, goodness, faithfulness, gentleness, self-control" (Gal 5:22) and let these "fruits" mature in us as the "harvest of righteousness" which grows out of the "seed of covenant loyalty."[79]

---

79    See the commentary on v 12.

## Love's Consequences

**Bibliography**

H. v. d. Bussche
"La ballade de l'amour méconnu. Commentaire d'Osée 11:1–10," *Bible et Vie Chrétienne* 41 (1961): 18–34.

K. Galling
"Vom Richteramt Gottes," *DTh* 6 (1939): 86–97.

H. J. Kraus,
"Hosea 11:1–9," (Second Sunday after Christmas) *Göttinger Predigtmeditationen 1952–3* (Göttingen, 1953), 33–38.

✓ J. L. McKenzie
"Divine Passion in Osee," *CBQ* 17 (1955): 287–99f.

G. Östborn
*Yahweh and Baal*, LUÅ NF 1, 51, 6 (Lund, 1956), 51–53, 82–86.

J. Reider
"Etymological Studies in Biblical Hebrew," *VT* 2 (1952): 121.

ᵥ D. Ritschl
"God's Conversation, An Exposition of Hosea 11," *Int* 15 (1961): 286–303.

E. Rohland
"Die Bedeutung der Erwählungstraditionen Israels für die Eschatologie der alttestamentlichen Propheten," diss. Univ. Heidelberg (Heidelberg, 1956), 49–54.

Th. Sprey
"[Syr.] משבה–תיבותא," *VT* 7 (1957): 408–10.

# 11

1  When Israel was young, I loved him;
   out[a] of Egypt I called my son.[b]
2  (Yet) ⟨as I⟩[c] called them,
      they strayed from ⟨me⟩.[d]
   ⟨They⟩[d] sacrificed to the Baals,
      to the graven images
         they sent up the smoke of sacrifice.

a   The temporal interpretation: "since (the days) in Egypt" (van Hoonacker; Buber) attempts to harmonize the verse with v 2a *M* (see textual note "c"); however, Hosea's diction does not support this: cf. 11:11 and 12:14 with 10:9.

b   *M* is confirmed by α′ σ′ θ′ *S V*; cf. also Mt 2:15 and thereto A. Baumstark ("Die Zitate des Mt.-Ev. aus dem Zwölfprophetenbuch," *Biblica* 37 [1956]: 296–313), who supposes that the quotation in Mt originates "from a lost, ancient Targum of the prophets having essentially the same nature as the old Palestinian Pentateuch Targum." *G* (τὰ τέκνα αὐτοῦ) presupposes בָּנָיו, thus harmonizing the singular "Israel" (v 1a) with the plural ("them") in v 2.

c   בְּקָרְאִי corresponds with *G* (καθὼς μετεκάλεσα); also vv 1 and 3 lead one to expect a statement by Yahweh. Similarly, the following כְּ (v 2aβ) suggests that a כְּ was prefixed to the verb (cf. 4:7 and Is 55:9 in 1QIsᵃ). *M* ("they called" = *V*), after the כְּ was dropped, probably misread י as ו. Who is supposed to be the subject in *M*; Egypt or the prophets (Gispen)? Buber translates "They immediately go to

**3**     Yet it was I who taught[e] Ephraim to walk
          and ⟨I⟩[f] who took them in ⟨my⟩[f] arms.
          But they did not perceive
              that I cared for them.
**4**     With humane cords I drew them,
              with ropes[g] of love.
          And I was to them
          as those who lift a ⟨small child⟩[h]
              to their cheek,
          and I bent down[i] to him,
              to feed[j] ⟨him⟩.[k]

d     מִפְּנֵיהֶם is attested by *G* (ἐκ προσώπου μου· αὐτοὶ . . .). As a result of the corruption of the verse's first word, *M* ("from them") has misread the same consonants (see textual note "c").

e     H. Englander, "Rashi's Grammatical Comments," *HUCA* 17 (1942–3): 473: "R. correctly notes that תִּרְגַּלְתִּי is an anomalous form, and then correctly observes that the text's word is equivalent to הרגלתי"; cf. Gesenius–Kautzsch § 55h (a tip'el form); Joüon § 59e (denominative); Koehler–Baumgartner *Suppl.*, 185.

f     *M* is unintelligible. According to *S T V*, וָאֶקָּחֵם עַל־זְרוֹעֹתָי would be expected; *G* also presupposes that the subject is the first person (ἀνέλαβον αὐτὸν ἐπὶ τὸν βραχίονά μου), but because of "Ephraim," it chose a singular instead of a plural object ("as frequently is the case," Dingermann, "Massora–Septuaginta," 53).

g     The unusual plural form occurs elsewhere only in Ex 28:14, 25; 39:18, where it means an artistically woven cord; the customary form עֲבֹתִים denotes ropes used as fetters: Ju 15:13f; 16:11f; Ezek 3:25; 4:8.

h     The original עוּל (thus van Hoonacker, Sellin, Buber) received the more usual vocalization of "yoke" in *M* (α' *S V*). Perhaps this was suggested by the mention of cords and ropes; but neither חֶבֶל nor עֲבֹת (but instead מוֹסֵר in Jer 2:20; 5:5; 27:2; 30:8; on Sir 30:53, cf. Dalman *Arbeit* 2, 113) are ever found together with עֹל; nor does 4a make a transition from the similie of Israel as the father's child to the simile of an animal (as in 4:16; 10:11). The simile in *G* also remains in the human realm: ὡς ῥαπίζων ἄνθρωπος = כְּמֹרֵט (Reider, "Studies," 121), or כְּמָכָה ⟨אָדָם⟩. Reider's suggested reading, which adds three words unknown in Biblical Hebrew and also provides a view entirely foreign to Hebrew man, is unacceptable ("I will be like foam of the sea [כְּמֹר יָם] that caresses their cheeks [יְעַלְעֵל] and carefully I place my confidence in him"). See pp. 199f.

i     Close to אוֹכִיל, *M*'s reading (נטה hip'il imperfect) is probably the original reading, for the transition to the iterative imperfect is customary in this context (cf. vv 2b, 3a, 7b; on 4:13 see p. 86). אט is hardly to be interpreted as deriving from *אטט ("tenderly against him," thus Gispen, following Ewald), for the adjective's construction is different both with verbs (always after them, e.g., 1 Kgs 21:27; usually לְאַט: Gen 33:14; Is 8:6) as well as with persons (לְ, 2 Sam 18:5; עַם, Job 15:11). In Hosea the asyndeton of the following אוֹכִיל is not unusual (cf. vv 8a, 9a; 9:9; 10:11b, 13; 12:4b).

j     On the verb form cf. Bauer–Leander § 53x.

k     Instead of לֹא (*M*; is the "not" a mistake in hearing?)

5　He returns[l] to the land[m] of Egypt,
　　　but Assyria is (and remains) his king.
　　　For they refuse to return.

6　Thus the sword surges[n] throughout his cities
　　　and destroys his braggarts,[o]
　　　it devours[p] because of their schemings.

7　But my people are bent[q] on apostasy
　　from me,[r]
　　　to ⟨Baal⟩[s] they ⟨call⟩,[t]
　　　(but) ⟨he⟩[t] by no means[u] ⟨raises
　　them⟩[v] up.

read לוֹ, which is attested by $G$ ($αὐτῷ$) and is to be
taken with v 4. $M$ states that instead of the (negated)
return to Egypt, Israel will become subjugated to
Assyria; again, however, this does not correspond to
Hosea's thought (7:11; 8:13b; 9:3, 6; 11:11; 12:2;
see pp. 145f). Or should one think of a לֹא of asesver-
ation, as R. Gordis ("Studies," 181–83) suggests for
this passage (see textual note "b" on 10:9).

l　$G$ ($κατῴκησεν$) read שָׁב, as in 9:3 (see textual note
　　"f" on 9:3). $σ'$ $V$ support $M$.

m　$G$ read אפרים instead of אל־ארץ, perhaps influenced
　　by 9:3; but Hosea has ארץ מצרים also in 2:17;
　　7:16; 12:10; 13:4; on the other hand, 11:1 (v 5 $G$)
　　has מצרים, as is usually the case.

n　חול (qal perfect consecutive) = "dance round
　　dances" as in Ju 21:21 designates a whirlwind in Jer
　　23:19; 30:23; thus $T$ $α'$ ($ἔπεσεν$) interpreted the
　　form in $M$ as well; cf. J. Scharbert, "Schmerz,"
　　21–26 and the commentary on v 6. $G$ ($ἠσθένησε$) and
　　$σ'$ (Jerome = $vulnerabit$), presuppose "to become
　　sick, weak" חלה [I]ʾ, similarly $S$. $V$ ($coepit$) thinks
　　of "to begin" חלל nipʿil) in contrast to "to com-
　　plete" (כלה piʿel v 6aβ).

o　Literally: "idle talk"; בד (II) (Job 11:3, etc.; see
　　Koehler–Baumgartner) is to be preferred to בד (I)
　　plural "sticks" (bar? stave?) because of the parallel
　　("schemings" v 6b); on this subject, cf. 10:4, 6.

p　$G$ ($φάγονται$) perhaps read וְאָכְלוּ = "as a result,
　　they will be destroyed." Dingermann, "Massora–
　　Septuaginta," 55) explains $M$ as a "mechanical
　　harmonization" with the previous verbs. The paral-
　　lel formulation can just as easily be original. $T$ $σ'$
　　($καταναλώσει$) $V$ ($comedit$) support $M$.

q　תלא qal (passive participle) = "to hang" (cf. Dtn
　　28:66; 2 Sam 21:12) is also presupposed by $G$ ($ἐπι-
　　κρεμάμενος$); cf. J. Ziegler, "Studien zur Verwertung
　　der Septuaginta im Zwölfprophetenbuch," $ZAW$
　　60 (1944): 111 and Josh 10:26 תְּלוּיִם.

r　It is not impossible that $G$ ($ἐκ τῆς κατοικίας αὐτοῦ$—
　　the noun is incorrectly derived from ישׁב and under-
　　stood as מוֹשָׁבוֹ), in view of the suffix, attests to the
　　original text (לִמְשׁוּבָתוֹ = "to his unfaithfulness,"
　　thus Dingermann, "Massora–Septuaginta"); cf.
　　especially 14:5 and Jer 2:19; 3:22; 5:6. In any case,
　　the meaning of "apostasy" is assured better by the
　　language of the Old Testament and the context than
　　the assumption that the word speaks of "Yahweh's
　　return" to his people (May, "Fertility Cult," 83f; see
　　the commentary on 5:15).

s　The text of v 7b remains completely obscure. I read
　　בַּעַל with Sellin, which is strongly suggested by the
　　antithesis to v 7a. $α'$ $σ'$ $T$ $V$ read "yoke" (עֹל) as in v
　　4. The meaning and syntax of $M$ ("they call up-
　　wards to him"; similarly Ewald, Buber, Gispen,
　　Joüon § 103a) remain obscure, especially with re-
　　gard to the continuation in v 7bβ (see textual notes
　　"t" and "v").

t　Following Sellin, I read יְקָרְאוּ הוּא, thus changing
　　the word's suffix in $M$ ("they call to $him$") into the

8    How shall I surrender you, O Ephraim?
      give you up,[w] O Israel?
   How can I surrender you like Admah?
      treat you like Zeboim?
   My heart turns against me,
      my remorse[x] burns intensely.[y]

9    I will not execute
      my burning anger,
   I will not again
      destroy Ephraim.
   For I am God
      and not a man,
   the Holy One in your midst,
      and I will not become enraged.[z]

10   [They shall follow after Yahweh.
      He will roar like a lion.
   Indeed, he, he will roar,
      so that the sons shall come trembling
         from the sea.]

11   They shall come trembling from Egypt,
      like (fluttering) birds
   and like doves from the land of Assyria.
      I will ⟨return⟩[aa] them to their houses,
      [says Yahweh].

        pronominal subject of the following clause, which would refer to בעל in v 7bα (see textual note "s"). Perhaps M resulted from the corruption of בעל to על. With this interpretation, the subject stays the same as in v 7a; in M the subject is indefinite; it is surprising that the object (הו)—if it takes up the preceding "my people" in v 7a—is singular, since the previous verb תלואים is plural.

u   Cf. Ps 33:15; Koehler–Baumgartner: "thoroughly" or "entirely"; see textual note "y."

v   Perhaps α′ (ἅμα οὐκ ὑψώσει αὐτούς) presupposes an original verb form יְרִימֵם; cf. also G (οὐ μὴ ὑψώσῃ αὐτόν). The corruption of the context in M has concealed the suffix among new vowels.

w   "To deliver over to" מגן (I), as in Gen 14:20.

x   The conjecture רַחֲמָי (Wellhausen; recently Koehler–Baumgartner, 609) based on its occurrence with נכמרו in Gen 43:30 and 1 Kgs 3:26 destroys the terseness of the *parallelismus membrorum* and is supported only by θ′ (τὰ σπλάγχνα τοῦ ἐλέους). α′ σ′ (παράκλησις) have translated the word the same as in Zech 1:13; Is 57:18 M. G (μεταμέλεια) and V (*poenitudo*) incorporate a sense of the abstract plural that is not attested elsewhere.

y   Literally: "entirely," "totally"; see textual note "u."

z   "Excitement" עיר (II), also in Jer 15:8; on the grammatical construction, cf. 1 Sam 25:26 (בוא בדמים = "to be guilty of blood," i.e., murder). Or, is the word a truncated form of עֶבְרָה (cf. 13:11; 5:10)? אבואבעיר has been considered an incorrectly spelled dittography of אֲבָעֵר: "I will not burn down, desolate" (lastly, McKenzie, "Divine Passion," or as אבוא לְהָעֵר (Weiser); אבוא מַבְעִיר is also worthy of consideration; cf. 7:4. G (εἰς πόλιν) V (*civitatem*) and S translate with the "city."

aa   וַהֲשִׁיבוֹתָם (= G: ἀποκαταστήσω αὐτούς) is supported by the preposition עַל (2 Sam 16:8; 1 Kgs 2:32; Is 46:8), which does not fit with M ("I will cause them to live"); cf. 12:10b (ישב hipʻil with בְּ). Or, as in 8:1, does Hosea refer, with בית, to the inherited "property," the ancient "area of settlement"? See p. 137.

## Form

Chapter 11 is a homogeneous unit, separate from the previous and following context. Not a single catchword connects it with 10:9–15; the direct address to Israel predominating there is almost lacking here. The new unit begins with a completely novel and much more intensive historical retrospect. It is equally evident that a new passage begins in 12:1, where the subject is named anew and the theme clearly changes.

    Yet in what sense is 11:1–11, in view of its internal structure, to be considered a *unit*? First of all, vv 1–7

are clearly dovetailed by copulae (vv 3, 6, 7); by the use of personal pronouns in the singular (vv 1, 4b, 5a, 6a) or plural (vv 2, 3, 4a, 5b, 6b, 7) for "Israel" (v 1), "Ephraim" (v 3), or—at the climax of the passage—for "my people" (v 7a); finally, by the unity of the theme: Israel has responded to Yahweh's love with obstinate renunciation from the very beginning (vv 2, 3, 5, 7).

    The entire passage is a *historico–theological accusation,* as the summary statement in v 7a indicates. The genre already occurs in Am 4:6ff, and also in Is 9:7ff.[1] Here it is structured in analogy to a legal complaint made by a father against his stubborn son.[2] Verses 5–6 are not introduced as an announcement of judgment; rather, they belong to the description of the consequences of Israel's reactions and Yahweh's new actions. This is indicated also by the tenses employed; compare the transitions from vv 1–2a to v 2b and from v 2b to v 3 with those from v 4 to v 5 and from v 5 to v 6.

There is no clear change in the passage until vv 8f, where Israel–Ephraim are mentioned anew and directly addressed for the first time in the chapter. Neither copula nor catchword connects vv 8f with the previous verses. Should vv 8f be separated from the foregoing context?[3] As to the form, it should be noted first of all that the first person divine speech continues, and that the singular address recalls the singular forms of the metaphorical personifications in vv 1, 3a, 4b, 5a, 6a. As to the content, the statement in v 9aβ: "I will not *again* destroy Ephraim" (לא אשוב), is intelligible only against the background provided by the previous measures taken to liberate and discipline Israel mentioned in vv 1–7.[4] It must also be asked whether the basic message (that Yahweh cannot destroy Israel because he is God and not man, the Holy One) would be fully comprehensible without the loving will of Yahweh so strongly emphasized in the first verses.[5]

But the accused party spoken of in the third person in vv 1–7 changes to direct address in vv 8f. How shall this be explained? We noted previously that such a change occurs with the transition from the accusation to the proposal to reach a settlement (*Schlichtungsvorschlag*). The accusation is brought before the court, whereas the proposal to reach a settlement is addressed directly to the defendant, especially during an animated dispute.[6] Now in vv 8f a particularly impassioned speech is recorded, as indicated by the repetitions and especially the tone set by the first word איך. This word belongs to the lamentation,[7] but it can also introduce a self-accusa-

tion (Prv 5:12); finally, this word can also be followed by a first person imperfect when there is a transition to a self–caution: "How might I . . ."; "How could I . . ."; "How should I. . . ."[8] In these expressions, איך is less indicative of the beginning of a speech than it is of a certain change within it, providing an adversative undertone. W. Rudolph[9] therefore translates the word in Jer 9:6 with "however." In our passage, the self–caution is combined with an address to the defendant within the context of a legal dispute. Here the caution—immediately after the accusation brought against the opponent's former actions—gives the "proposal to reach a settlement" the definite form of a *declaration of amnesty* (*Strafverzichterklärung*, cf. Gen 13:8f). Thus the defendant witnesses the plaintiff's own inner struggle as he first utters a self–caution (v 8a) and then waives the punishment (v 9b).

The abrupt change in vv 8f therefore should not be interpreted in such a way as to require the separation of these verses from vv 1–7. Yahweh's self–caution and remission of punishment in vv 8–9 presuppose a discussion of Israel's former deeds in vv 1–7; similarly, the long complaint in vv 1–7, with the summary statement in v 7a: "My people are bent on apostasy from me," expects the proclamation of Yahweh's future actions. In the book of Hosea, such a proclamation is always found in each of the transmission units. Hence, according to our form critical observations, it is not only possible but quite probable that vv 1–9 should be regarded as a rhetorical unit.

Yahweh's first person speech is not continued by v 10 but by v 11. Israel is spoken of in the third person in v 11 (as in vv 2–4a, 5b, 6b, 7) instead of in the direct address found in vv 8a, 9b, which was already interrupted by the third person in v 9aβ. Thus the promise of salvation (second person) changes to a declaration of salvation (third person).[10] There is no reason to question the authenticity of v 11, since the combination of Egypt and Assyria, like the metaphor of the dove, are typically

1 On Ezek 16 and 20, cf. W. Zimmerli, *Ezekiel*, 344, 439f.
2 Cf. Dtn 21:18–21; Is 1:2ff; Rohland, "Erwählungs- traditionen," 53.
3 Cf. Buss, "A Form Critical Study," 107f.
4 See pp. 201f.
5 See p. 202.
6 Cf. 1 Kgs 3:22, 26b, and p. 134; see also H. J.

Boecker, "Anklagereden und Verteidigungsreden im Alten Testament," *EvTh* 20 (1960): 398–412, especially 404.
7 Mic 2:4; Jer 48:38; Ezek 26:17; 2 Sam 1:19, 25, 27.
8 E.g., Gen 39:9; 44:34; Ps 137:4; Jer 9:6.
9 *Jeremia*, HAT I, 12 (Tübingen, 1958²).
10 Cf. 2:18–25 and the commentary.
11 See the commentary on v 11.

Hosean.[11] Then v 11 would also belong to the rhetorical unit of vv 1–9. In vv 1–7 Israel's deeds follow regularly upon Yahweh's actions. Thus in v 11, after the proclamation of an abrupt change in Yahweh, the statements about its future effects on Israel is not unexpected. On the other hand, it would be surprising if Israel were not the subject of the statement once again, as is now the case in v 11a. Nevertheless, from beginning (v 1) to end, Israel's conduct remains encircled by Yahweh's action: in v 11b Yahweh is once again the subject.

In this chapter only v 10 makes statements about Yahweh in the third person. As to their content, they are understandable as commentary on v 11, especially on the word "they tremble" (יחרדו). This trembling is (1) elucidated as "following after Yahweh": v 10a$\alpha$; (2) as the result of Yahweh's roaring like a lion: v 10a$\beta$, b$\alpha$. (3) The word itself is used to supplement the subjects of v 11a: not only those of the Egyptian and Assyrian diaspora return to Yahweh, but also those of the western diaspora: v 10b$\beta$. Whereas vv 1–9, 11 correspond in general with the course of Hosea's orally delivered speech, the commentary in v 10 must have been inserted by the traditionists. The two notations in v 10a might utilize genuine words of Hosea, since he uses the lion metaphor for Yahweh also in 5:14; 13:7. But the diction is reminiscent of Amos: the words אריה ("lion") and שאג ("roar") never occur in Hosea, but they are found in Am 1:2; 3:4, 8. Hence the traditionists may have utilized prophetic sayings known since the time of Amos for the purpose of elucidating the connection of vv 9 and 11. With its repetitions (שאג as in v 10a, חרד as in v 11a) the third addition in v 10b also appears to be a supplement. To those returning from Egypt and Assyria (v 11) it adds the phrase "the sons from the sea," which is unknown in Hosea's other sayings and, according to v 5, is not to be expected from Hosea in this context. But it would surely fit the time of Hosea;[12] its formulation is not of a demonstrably later date. Thus v 10 may represent a supplement added by the traditionists; this is confirmed by its notable lack of poetic diction in comparison to vv 9 and 11.[13] In its relation to the theme of this chapter, v 10 is most similar to the addition in 8:14.[14]

The genuine material in vv 1–9, 11 manifests an unusual continuity in that it traces the life of Yahweh's son Israel from his earliest youth into his future. Any indication of a discussion between Hosea and his audience is completely absent. It is Yahweh who speaks. Israel is addressed only momentarily as seen in those verses where the most excitement is generated (vv 8a, 9b). The traditions from Israel's earliest times, transposed into the metaphor of fatherly love, stand prominently in the foreground.[15] In each of these respects our passage is related to 9:10–17. Like 9:10–17, an audition account seems to form the basis of this passage, which is clothed in the lively expressions of a lawsuit in the city gate. Coinciding with the abrupt change in Yahweh's attitude, there is a sudden transition to the direct address of Israel, which is at the same time an address to the prophet —as in 9:10[16]— who is Israel's intercessor. Hosea and his circle, whose theology is rooted in the election traditions, and who also suffer under Israel's distress, await Yahweh's word of mercy. It is not inconceivable that between vv 7 and 8 the prophet entreated Yahweh's forgiveness, as Amos did in 7:2, 5 (cf. 9:14). Nevertheless, according to our form critical observations on v 8[18] it would not be required.

There is a different tone in v 8, as the meter itself indicates. The description of Israel's history in vv 1–7 consistently exhibits longer prosodic units that border on prose. A distinct synonymous parallelism occurs only in vv 2b$\beta$, 3a, 4a, 5a and 6a; to each of these verses further sentences are joined in a synthetic parallelism. The clear parallel structure in vv 8–9 is quite distinct from the foregoing verses. Here the internal parallelism is strictly carried through in six bicola; after four synonymously parallel bicola in vv 8 and 9a, two antithetic bicola follow in v 9b, producing a heightening affect. In accordance with the tone of lament in the self–caution, the prosodic units begin with the qinah–meter (3+2, v 8a) changing to a three–stress bicolon (v 8b), and finally to a longer four–stress bicolon (v 9a) which declares Yahweh's complete salvation. The motivation is expressed in concise two–stress bicola (v 9b) in which the emphasis of each word is increased by a distinct alliteration. The ולא repeated at the beginning of both of the second halves of the last two bicola produces a

---

12  See the commentary on v 10.
13  See pp. 195f.
14  See p. 136.

15  See the commentary on vv 1–4.
16  See the commentary on 9:14.
18  See p. 194.

particular accentuation. This style corresponds with the repetition of אֵיךְ at the beginning of both bicola in v 8a and picks up the לֹא at the beginning of each line in the immediately foregoing bicolon in v 9a. The repetition of these initial catchwords in v 8a and 9b further indicates the external parallelism of each prosodic unit, which is added to an internal parallelism of the lines. The two bicola in vv 8a and 9b are synonymously parallel, while those in vv 8b and 9a are synthetically parallel.

Thus vv 8–9 manifest an unusually strict poetic character that is nevertheless entirely determined by the context. The self–caution of Yahweh in the first two bicola (v 8a) is followed by the self–disclosure of his saving will in the two longest bicola in the middle (vv 8b, 9a). These bicola conclude with a sharply accented, tersely formulated motivation whose theme is the holiness of God (v 9b).

Whereas v 10 is devoid of any metrical structure, v 11 again presents a three–stress tricolon.[19] The first two lines are synonymously parallel to each other; the third line is synthetically connected to them. This formation corresponds to the tricola in vv 3 and 6.

## Setting

There is no indication of a direct disputation in these verses. It is therefore most conceivable that, as in 9:10–10:8, this divine speech was delivered before the circle of those who belonged to the opposition group composed of prophets and Levites. They were intensely interested in Israel's previous history and in the question of the nation's future. The abbreviated, sketchy nature of the passage, especially recognizable in the transition from v 7 to v 8 and from v 9 to v 11, would suggest that the account was written by this circle. These traditionists were most likely responsible for the additions made in v 10.

The historical retrospect closely connects this chapter with the preceding passages beginning with 9:10. The nature of chap. 11's transmission shows it to be related to all the units beginning with 4:1. But the message concerning the end of Yahweh's wrath and judgment and of the kindling of his pity has parallels in the previous material only in chaps. 2 and 3 and later in 14:2–9.[20] Yet

an important distinction should not be overlooked. In 2:4–17; 3:1–5, the impending judgment is described as an approaching deed of Yahweh which serves the purposes of his love; it will return Israel to Yahweh and thus lead to a new salvation (2:8f, 16f; 3:4f). In chap. 11 on the other hand, the anguish brought on by judgment already dominates the past and the present (vv 4–7), although there are no visible signs of Israel's return (vv 5b; 7a). Yahweh's own change in attitude, in which his holy love shines through, provides the motivation for the salvation that now approaches. In this decisive point, which is closely related to the present historical situation, chap. 11 stands much closer (1) to the saying in 14:5 concerning Yahweh's spontaneous love which heals Israel's unfaithfulness; and (2) to the supplements to chap. 2 (vv 18–25; 1–3).

Form critical considerations also indicate important differences between chaps. 11 and 2:4ff. In view of these differences, the two chapters should not be connected too closely with each other. To be sure, both chapters are a continuous divine speech in the first person, and the primary forms of speech are those of the legal procedure.[21] But in other respects, chap. 11 exhibits neither the kind of thematic unity and homogeneous structure of 2:4–17, nor the arrangement of individual sayings as found in 2:18–25. Instead, the nature of its transmission is like that we have observed in the sketches contained in 4:4–10:15: although there is distinct unity of theme and setting within the transmission units, there are observable tensions in what formally gives the impression of a seamless chain of rhetorical units. This is evidenced by the jaggedness of the transitions and by the form of address.

Thus the routes taken by the transmission of these two related chapters were certainly different ones. In chap. 2 a redactor supplemented a written document from Hosea's early period with some of his later sayings.[22] In chap. 11 the prophet's audition account has been recorded by his disciples.

It should also be noted that the "says Yahweh" (נְאֻם־יְהוָה) formula which concludes the divine speech in

---

19   נְאֻם־יהוה belongs outside the meter; see pp. 196f.
20   Cf. 2:7 with 11:2; 2:9bβ with 11:1, 3, 4; 2:17b with 11:11; 2:20bβ with 11:11b; 2:25 with 11:8; 3:1b

with 11:1, 4; 3:5b with 11:11a; see pp. 47f.
21   See pp. 32, 47.
22   See pp. 11f.

11:11 occurs elsewhere in Hosea only in 2:15, 18, 23.[23] But there the expression has been added to the beginning of two different sayings (2:18, 23), and it is also used to emphasize the personal speech of Yahweh at the transition from the proof of guilt (2:15b) to the proclamation of Yahweh's consequent actions (2:16–17). In chap. 11, however, the formula marks the conclusion of the transmission unit in an entirely different way. The traditionists to whom we attribute chaps. 4–11 never use this formula of divine utterance elsewhere. Therefore it is presumable that in chap. 11 this formula originates from the same redaction that introduced this large complex of sketches of Hosea's speeches with the formula: "Hear this word of Yahweh, O sons of Israel" in 4:1a.[24]

The text provides us with minimal criteria for determining its date. Verse 11 certainly presupposes more than a mere delegation of diplomats sent to Egypt and Assyria (thus 7:11). It would appear as though at least a considerable part of the population were living in foreign lands. And it is conceivable that, parallel to the Assyrian deportation, many people fled to Egypt. The earlier threats (cf. 9:3, 6) and announcements of new military struggles (10:6–8, 14f) very likely were being fulfilled as Hosea received these words from Yahweh and then proclaimed them (cf. vv 5f). It should be further noted that Israel's turning to Egypt and Assyria is no longer placed parallel, as in 7:11 (9:3); rather, v 5 attests to Assyria's supremacy as unshakable; Assyria is no longer spoken of as a superior power whose help Israel seeks (5:13; 8:9).[25]

It is possible that chap. 11 belongs to the time of Shalmaneser V's reign (727–2), when Israel's new turn toward Egypt provoked Assyria's retaliation (2 Kgs 17:4). It hardly recommends itself to date the passage later than 724 or even 721.[26] First, chap. 11 is closely connected, as noted above, with chaps. 9–10,[27] which belong to the period between 733 and 727. Second, it is also related to 2:18–25, which must have originated soon

after 733. In view of these considerations the most likely period would be the first half of the reign of Shalmaneser V, perhaps at the beginning of his punitive measures, especially since Samaria itself is not yet expressly mentioned as a beseiged or even a conquered city (v 6).

### Interpretation

■ **1** Hosea goes further back into the first stages of Israel's history than he does in 9:15 or 10:1, 9. He specifically mentions Israel's very beginning, which is only presupposed by the other historical retrospects. Here, in contrast to the tradition taken up in 9:10 and 10:11, Yahweh elected Israel by calling him out of Egypt. Hosea expresses the election as the "ascending" (עלה qal 2:17 [15]) or the "leading up" (עלה hip'il 12:14 [15]) from Egypt (cf. 12:10 [9]; 13:4). The tradition is part of Israel's original creed. In accordance with his use of metaphor, Hosea gives this traditional confession a completely new shape. At the time of Israel's initial relationship with Yahweh (Ju 19:30), he was a child (cf. נְעוּרִים in 2:17 [15]). נער can be an infant (Ex 6:2), a child that is weaned,[28] or a young, still dependent person (Jer 1:6f; Gen 18:7). If the word in v 11 is supposed to denote something more than the time of Israel's beginning, at the most it would refer to his helplessness,[29] but in no case to his usefulness (as in 9:10; 10:11). The first event in the life of young Israel worthy of report is that Yahweh loves him.[30] With this metaphor Hosea was the first to use the word "love" (אהב; also cf. v 4) as an interpretation of the election of God's people. In so doing, he has unsurpassably elucidated what Amos before him wanted to say with the word "to know" (ידע), a less vivid word for "election." Hosea's catchword passes through his circle of traditionists into Deuteronomy's sermon.[31]

Yahweh's love for helpless young Israel was demonstrated not only by his deliverance of him from Egypt, but at the same time by his "call," as a father calls "his

---

23  See pp. 40f.
24  See p. 36.
25  See p. 200.
26  Robinson.
27  In addition, cf. 10:6bβ with 11:6b.
28  Gen 21:12; see the commentary on 1:8.
29  Cf. vv 3f, 2:4 and the commentary.
30  Cf. 9:15b and pp. 60f.

31  Dtn 23:6; 7:8, 13; 10:15; 4:73; cf. Wildberger, *Eigentumsvolk*, 111ff.

son." As the following verses make clear, this laid the foundation for an intimate relationship of care, guidance, and obedience. Jeremiah explains this aspect of the deliverance from Egypt as the making of a covenant (31:32). Hosea interprets the covenant concept already handed down to him by the analogy of the relationship of a father to an adopted son,[32] and combines it with the Exodus tradition.

That Israel is here called "son" of Yahweh emphasizes the personal relationship of love described in vv 1a and 3f. Israel is to be closely and inseparably united with Yahweh. This intimate togetherness means that Israel is Yahweh's personal property and "holy people." The Deuteronomic School also reflects this relationship when it addressed Israel as "Yahweh's sons" (Dtn 14:1). The idea of parentage, procreation, and creation is far removed.[33] As the next verses indicate, especially the concept of education is combined with the idea of Yahweh's love. In this sense Isaiah (1:2ff; 30:9) and Jeremiah (3:14, 19, 22; 4:22; 31:9, 20) also spoke of Yahweh's sons.[34] What is the background of this prophetic saying which speaks of Israel as God's son? Since the time of ancient Egyptian Wisdom, spiritual sonship was a concept essential to the ancient oriental ideas of raising and educating children.[35] An eighth century Phoenician gate inscription by Azitawadda of Karatepe, king of the Danunites, stated: "Yea, every king considered me his father because of my righteousness and my wisdom and the kindness of my heart."[36] Thus, according to the courtly concepts at the time of Hosea, not only righteousness and wisdom, but "goodness of the heart" belonged to the fatherly image. In the next century an oracle addressed to Esarhaddon of Assyria assured him that his prayer had been granted in these words: "Fear not, Esarhaddon! I, the god Bel, speak to you. The beams of your heart I strengthen, like your mother, who caused you to exist. Sixty great gods are standing together with me and protect you. The god Sin is at your right, the god Shamash at your left; sixty great gods stand round about you, ranged for battle. Do not trust men! Turn your eyes to me, look at me! I am Ishtar of Arbela; I have turned Ashur's favor unto you. *When you were small, I sustained you*. Fear not. . . ."[37] These words are very similar to those found in v 1. Here we find the concept of the king as God's son, known in Egypt since the third millennium, i.e., since the fourth dynasty of the Old Kingdom.[38] A thousand years later, the concept appears in Mari in an oracle of Adad in the following form: "Am I not Adad, the Lord of Kallassu, who raised him (Zimrilim) on my knees. . . ."[39]

In spite of these similarities, it is improbable that Hosea borrowed the concept of Israel as Yahweh's son from the wisdom tradition or the traditions of the court and cult, developing it further antithetically. Hosea's world of thought is that of Canaanite myth and cultus which had exerted its influence upon Israel. According to Canaanite concepts, the father and mother deity belong together.[40] Hosea freely forms and develops his concepts as he struggles against the Canaanite religion. Already in 2:4 [2], speaking as the lawful husband of his wife, Israel, he addresses her children, and in 2:6f [4f] he calls them "bastard sons."[41] By contrast, the eschatological people of God are designated as the "sons of the living God,"[42] probably by Hosea himself. There is no evidence that 11:1ff is an adaptation of preexisting formulas; rather, it is very likely that Hosea is again struggling against the myth of Baal (vv 2, 7b).[43] In his polemic against Canaanite myth and religion, Hosea speaks of early Israel as the legitimate son of God.[44] Then he freely develops the metaphor, guided

---

32  6:7; 8:1; cf. Horst, "Recht," 283.

33  Otherwise in Dtn 32:6, perhaps also in Ex 4:22f, where Yahweh's "first born son" is mentioned in parallel to "Pharaoh's first born son."

34  In addition, cf. Is 43:6f; 63:16; Mal 1:6; 3:17; and Quell, *TDNT* 5, 971–74.

35  Cf. H. Brunner, *Altägyptische Erziehung* (1957), 10ff and *passim*.

36  בצדקי ובחכמתי ובנעם לבי; Untere Torinschrift I, 12f, according to A. Alt, "Die phönikischen Inschriften von Karatepe," *WO* I, 4 (1949): 274; likewise *WO* II, 2 (1955): 178; trans. Rosenthal, *ANET* Suppl. (Princeton: Princeton University Press, 1969), 218; cf. Donner–Röllig, *KAI* I, 5.

37  Pfeiffer, *ANET*², 450 (italics added by the author).

38  Bonnet, *Reallexikon*, 382.

39  A. Lods, "Une tablette inédite de Mari," in *Studies in Old Testament Prophecy*, ed. Rowley (Edinburgh, 1950), 103ff.

40  Kapelrud, *Baal*, 65, and also Pope, *El*, 47f; in the Old Testament, cf. Jer 2:27.

41  See the commentary on 2:4ff.

42  2:1; see the commentary.

43  See the commentary.

44  As in the marriage metaphor, where the legal rather than the sexual aspects are important (see page

above all by the traditions of Israel's history.

■ **2** The second sentence at once indicates how Hosea traverses Israel's history. Apostasy follows directly upon Yahweh's liberating call out of Egypt.[45] As in 9:10, v 2 also presupposes that already with the conquest the still youthful Israel gave himself to the cult of Baal.[46] The offerings are burnt before the idols. פָּסִיל is primarily a neutral designation for an object that is "hewn" or "carved," a stele. Therefore Dtn 7:25 and 12:3 expressly say "graven images of their Gods" (פְּסִילֵי אֱלֹהֵיהֶם).[47] In v 2 the parallel "Baals" (בעלים) indicates the interpretation of פסילים as "carved images" or "idols" to be correct.[48]

■ **3** This verse is connected antithetically to v 2 (G), for "but I" (ואנכי) contrasts with "they" (הם) at the beginning of v 2b; cf. the similar placement of הם in 4:14aβ; 8:9. The pluperfect can be expressed by the perfect tense: "Though I had taught them to walk. . . ." After Yahweh's call to freedom (v 1b) the key word "love" in v 1a is further elucidated in v 3, so that the apostasy to the Baals becomes quite incomprehensible: Yahweh helped Israel grow to independence (cf. Is 1:2); in his tender youth Yahweh bore him in his arms and protected him. Israel, however, did not listen to the call of the one who led him out of Egypt, nor did he give attention to the care provided by Yahweh's fatherly actions. Israel should have understood this as his "healing." If v 3a is to be understood in the pluperfect, then, like v 1, it would further describe the divine delivery from Egypt in the metaphor of the father and son relationship and v 3 would not refer to Yahweh's guidance through the wilderness. "To heal" (רפא) is better understood in connection with the liberation from Egypt than as Yahweh's "care"[49] of Israel in the wilderness. In 5:13 (6:1) and 7:1 Hosea also uses the word for deliverance

from "political" disaster. Yahweh, not the Baals, was the physician who saved Israel from the deadly peril in Egypt. In the Pentateuch, the word רפא occurs only twice; first in the secondary development of the theme "guidance through the wilderness" in Nu 12:13. There the word is used in a narrative concerning Moses prophetic office (cf. Hos 12:13 [12]); he interceded in Miriam's behalf after she had been struck by leprosy.[50] The word is found a second time in Ex 15:26, a Deuteronomistic passage in which Yahweh categorically refers to himself as Israel's physician. In Hosea, too, the Exodus–Conquest traditions are connected by the wilderness tradition; cf. v 4 with 13:4–6.

■ **4** In this survey of Israel's history, v 4 presupposes the period of the wandering in the wilderness and the conquest. But in view of the textual difficulties, it should be asked whether v 4 continues the metaphor of Israel as God's "son," or whether an animal metaphor replaces this imagery. Hosea's simile in 4:16 pictured Israel as a stubborn cow; in 10:11 the metaphor of the young heifer harnessed for plowing described the journey into the arable land.[51] Yet it is unlikely that the metaphor changes in v 4. Otherwise, why the emphasis upon "humane" cords and ropes "of love"? The suggestion to interpret אַהֲבָה here and in Song 3:10[52] as "leather" is made untenable by the parallel phrases עבתות אהבה ‖ חבלי אדם. There is of course a similarity here to the leading of cattle by ropes.[53] But v 4 emphatically speaks of a different kind of leading: the leading of young people who can easily go astray (cf. Ps 32:9 and especially 2 Sam 7:14). As his father, the God of Israel had great difficulty in bringing him to his goal. His leading and directing was accompanied by his constant nurture. This is also expressed by M, which speaks of "easing the yoke from their jaws before feeding them."[54]

15), here the concept of Yahweh's care and nurture rather than that of procreation is significant.

45 Or, according to M: apostasy from Yahweh results from the calls of other people (or gods) to Israel; see textual note "c."

46 On "Baals" (בעלים), see pp. 38ff; on "to sacrifice" (זבח), see pp. 144f; on "to send up sacrifices in smoke" (קטר), see p. 40.

47 Cf. Lev 26:30 and Kurt Galling, "Erwägungen zum Stelenheiligtum von Hazor," *ZDPV* 75 (1959): 12.

48 On this topic, see the commentary on 8:4.

49 Thus Robinson, 26, on 7:1, who interprets the word as the care of a physician and refers to Jer 51:8, 9.

50 Cf. Noth, *Pentateuchal Tradition*, 127 [140].

51 See the commentary on 10:11.

52 Thus G. R. Driver, *Canaanite Myths and Legends* (Edinburgh: T. & T. Clark, 1956), 133.

53 Dalman, *Arbeit* 2, 133.

54 Dalman, *Arbeit* 2, 99f: "Although the yoke, with its hooks and ropes, does not hinder chewing, an oxen coupled and yoked with a second animal can hardly lean down to the food placed before it. The yoke is therefore removed for feeding. Instead of the neck, the jaws are mentioned, for it is not the freedom (as in Is 10:27) but the feeding of the animal released from the yoke that is of concern. Nevertheless, it is

But when *M* is made intelligible by Dalman's explanation, Hosea's meaning is hardly recognizable. It is not a yoke which v 4a presupposes; rather, continuing v 3aα, it speaks of the loving guidance of man. This would suggest that v 4aβ is the completion of what is expressed in v 3aβ. Thus v 4aβ would not only mean: "I took them in my arms," but: "I was like one who lifts a small child to his cheek," namely, an exceedingly gentle father.[55] This further demonstration of the father's love should be understood in the light of v 3b. When the father's help was not comprehended, he became even more loving: "I bent down and fed them." What an expressive picture of divine condescension! In the way Hosea has freely developed this self–contained metaphor, we see how he is actually guided by the main themes of the credo: in the background of v 4 stands the theme of Yahweh's "guidance through the wilderness into the arable land," which is even more distinct in 2:10, 16f; 13:5f.[56]

■ **5**  For the third time (cf. vv 2, 3b) the three–part declaration of Yahweh's love (vv 1, 3a, 4) is unappreciatively rejected by those who—though Yahweh has called, led, and loved them—desire to "return to Egypt."[57] According to v 5 Hosea's thoughts have reached the present situation; he is probably concerned about the vain attempts to shake off Assyrian domination after Tiglath–pileser's death by dependence upon Egypt.[58] The prophet's words express Israel's desire to return to the situation which preceded the beginning of their salvation history (v 1); their wish to return to Egypt is found already in the Yahwist's narrative in the Pentateuch (Nu 14:4). Hosea has come to the final section of his description of the accused party, not to the announcement of punishment. This is indicated by (1) the parallels in vv 2b and 3b and (2) the motive clause in

v 5b, which is to be viewed together with the summary judgment in v 7b. The refusal to return to Yahweh explains their desire to return to Egypt. Verse 5aβ is not synonymously parallel to v 5aα; the sentence describes not an act but a condition, whose sense is concessive or adversative: "Although Assyria is his (lawful) king"; or even better: "But Assyria is (and remains) his king." Then the sentence adjoined in v 5b is intelligible as a motive clause: because Israel refuses to make a genuine return, the return to Egypt is useless. Assyria, in the person of the new king Shalmaneser V, is ready to exercise its supremacy once again.

■ **6**  The statements following in v 6 are a further description of the present situation, for they portray the impending disaster brought on by Shalmaneser V.[59] Since 733 Israel's cities had suffered enough of the sword's wrath. The fifth layer of archaeological excavation at Hazor in 1955–8 showed examples of the destruction wrought by Tiglath–pileser III.[60] The word חול, meaning the enraged slashing or swishing of a sword, is found in an ancient Aramaic inscription upon a statue which Barrakab of Yadi (Zinjirli), a contemporary of Tiglath–pileser III, erected for his father, Panammu.[61] The sword first strikes the boastful plan makers.[62] But Samaria is not yet mentioned (in contrast to 14:1). In point of fact, even before he besieged Samaria, Shalmaneser V was able to take king Hoshea prisoner and occupy the remainder of the land.[63] Although it cannot be determined with certainty, it is possible that Hosea has included these recent events in the unhappy story of Yahweh's love for his son. In any case, to Hosea the political disaster is merely the obverse side of Israel's refusal to return to his God. This is indicated by the position of v 6 between vv 5b and 7a.

■ **7**  Although the anguish of war shattered the nation's

not without significance that the yoke is inconceivable apart from a harness which encloses the neck and touches the jaws."

55  This seemingly involved statement is not unusual for Hosea; cf. 5:10a and also 4:4b *M*. Incidentally, instead of עַל, מֵעַל is usually used to indicate the removal of the yoke from the animal's jaws. Cf. Gispen, and see textual note "h."

56  See the commentary on 13:5f.

57  See pp. 145f.

58  2 Kgs 17:4; see p. 197.

59  See p. 197.

60  Cf. the preliminary report in *BA* 19 (1956): 6; 20

(1957): 39; 21 (1958): 41ff; 22 (1959): 10; and also the final reports by Yigal Yadin *et al.* (*Hazor* 1 [Jerusalem, 1958], 19, *passim*).

61  Cf. M. Lidzbarski, *Handbuch der nordsemitischen Epigraphik* 1 (Berlin, 1898), 442, Panammu–Inschrift table 23, line 5; also found in Donner–Röllig, *KAI* I, 39, No. 215, 5; on this matter, cf. Scharbert, "Schmerz," 23.

62  See textual note "o" and 10:6; 7:16.

63  2 Kgs 17:4; Noth, *History*, 261f [237].

obstinate plans, there was no change in their attitude.
Verse 7 summarizes the prolonged history of Israel's
stubbornness: "My people are bent on apostasy from
me." But Yahweh's zealous love has not yet diminished,
as the twofold first person suffix indicates: "*my* people"[64] and "apostasy from *me*"; the pain of unrequited
love, a theme which occurred in Hosea's early sayings[65] is found again. Once more Baal seems to be Yahweh's actual rival[66] as was already evident in v 2b.
Hosea refuses to interpret the official lament over political
danger—like all the priests' cultic activity—as a turning
to Yahweh.[67] This grieves the God of Israel for he
sees through the futility of their pious efforts. "He [the
Baal] cannot raise them up." The text's uncertain
transmission, however, makes it difficult to interpret. Our
suggested understanding of it perhaps finds further
support in the word "raise" (רום pi'el) which, at the conclusion of the disappointed father's lament, picks up
the imagery of vv 1–4, if it is used here as in Is 1:2. Yet
the passage actually no longer deals with the raising
of children but with the raising–up of those who have
been cast down. Thus the historico–theological accusation is completed, probably in the tone of a passionate
lament which is perceptible in v 7a and in vv 2, 3b, 5 as
well.

■ **8** In this respect, Yahweh's fervent self–caution not to
destroy Israel totally is not surprising here.[68] Here
נתן means complete surrender, giving up, as in Ps 44:12;
Mic 5:2; cf. Ju 6:13; Dtn 2:31; מגן has the same meaning.[69] In spite of his obstinate ways, Israel is not totally
lost. Above all, Yahweh has not given him up; rather, he
attempts to bring him back by his disciplinary measures, although in vain (cf. vv 4f, 6f). The other occurrences of Admah and Zeboim in the Old Testament
are found only in connection with Sodom and Gomorrah:

Gen 10:19 (J); 14:2, 8; Dtn 29:21f. WisdSol 10:6,
following Gen 14, calls them the "Five Cities." Hosea
refers to a tradition attested in Dtn 29:21f, which tells
how Yahweh's burning anger overcame these cities, totally destroying all life and the possibility of renewed
life. Hosea had not conceived of a total annihilation in his
earlier threats of war,[70] but such a threat stands in
the background in 9:6, 11ff; 10:6ff, 15ff. Now, on the
other hand, at the time when the worst difficulties
are befalling Israel, Hosea lays the foundation for the
certainty that Yahweh will never conclusively surrender
Israel. Israel will not be completely "overturned"[71]
as the cities mentioned here; rather, there will be an
"overturning," i.e., a change, in Yahweh's heart. Yahweh, the "Holy One in your midst"[72] takes the place
of Israel's "righteous" people. Yahweh's will[73] is directed
against himself, i.e., against his wrath (v 9a). In the
phrase "my heart turns against me" (נהפך לבי בקרבי),[74]
בקרבי is replaced by עלי which has a hostile sense.[75]
The rarely used word "remorse" (נחומים) (found elsewhere only in Is 57:18; Zech 1:13) emphasizes the
turning point in Yahweh's will attested in v 8. Therefore
נחומים should not be emended to רחמים.[76] His remorse (over his wrathful intention to judge) "grows hot,"
i.e., it provokes and dominates him; thus the better–
known expression "his heart yearns" (נכמרו רחמיו Gen
43:30; 1 Kgs 3:26) is given an independent modification.
Again and again we see the God of Hosea in conflict
with himself over Israel.[77]

■ **9** After the three bicola in v 8, which radiate the
excitement of an impassioned outburst, the final, divine
resolve is presented in two long lines in v 9a. Each line
begins with a decisive "not" (לא) to indicate Yahweh's
change of heart. The לא is echoed in both of the following tersely formulated motive clauses by a twofold

---

64 See p. 79.
65 See pp. 40f.
66 See textual note "s."
67 See the commentary on 6:1–4; 7:14; 9:1.
68 On "how" (איך), see p. 194.
69 See textual note "w."
70 See the commentary on 5:9.
71 Cf. הפך in Gen 19:25; Dtn 29:22.
72 Cf. בקרבך in v 9b with Gen 18:24b and see Galling,
   "Vom Richteramt Gottes," *DTh* 6 (1939): 96f; on
   the diction, cf. Dtn 6:15.
73 On "heart" (לב), see the commentary on 4:11.
74 In Lam 1:20 the words denote painful remorse;

cf. H. J. Kraus, *Klagelieder*, BK 20 (Neukirchen,
   1968³).
75 Cf. Josh 10:5 and Brockelmann, *Syntax* § 110b.
76 See textual note "x."
77 E.g., 6:4; see the commentary; cf. the earlier words
   of Am 7:3, 6 and thereafter the Deuteronomistic
   tradition of Jeremiah's sayings: 26:3, 13, 19, etc.; on
   this theme, see especially Jer 31:20.

ולא.[78] Yahweh's burning anger is expressly mentioned in 8:5.[79] It is not to rule over Israel's history. To understand this sentence, it should be kept in mind how Hosea had proclaimed Yahweh's judgment during recent years, and perhaps especially that, because of the election traditions, he had expected a liberation from the pronounced disaster even earlier.[80] Now he can declare a new word from his God, at least among those who, like him, think of Israel in terms of Yahweh's entire history with his people: "I will not again destroy." What does אשוב mean? Had Yahweh once before brought about Israel's destruction? Certainly not in the sense of vv 8f. What had befallen Israel up to this time was the consequence of Israel's own intentional actions, the harvest of what had been sown (4:9; 8:7; 10:13). Also in the historical retrospect contained in the accusation, the recent political troubles were not presented as the result of Yahweh's wrath, but as the consequences of Israel's refusal to return (vv 5f). Israel's situation would be totally different if Yahweh were to destroy with the heat of his wrath rather than to draw with cords of love. Therefore the *verbum relativum* שוב cannot indicate a second destructive action. שוב denotes, however, not only the repetition of an action, but also the restoration of previous conditions, or the nullification of a deed.[81] Thus in 2:11 Hosea says that Yahweh will take back the land's produce which he has given Israel. Likewise, v 11 refers to returning to destruction of those whom he had called out of Egypt, the place of destruction (9:6), whom he had since lead continually with his love. This Yahweh had done, although his love had to be expressed in the form of disciplinary measures in response to all Israel's disappointing actions. Hence v 9a demonstrates that Yahweh's original will to love his people remains dominant.

The motive clause states that God proves himself to be God and the Holy One in Israel in that he, unlike men, is independent of his partner's actions.[81a] Remaining completely sovereign over his own actions, he is not compelled to react. The Holy One is the totally Other, who is "Lord of His own will, who does not execute the fierceness of his anger . . . . in His decision He is independent and free. Holy means superior, almighty."[82] It is important to note that the concept of Yahweh's holiness, appearing only once in Hosea, provides the foundation not for his judging will but for his saving will, to which he had committed himself from the very beginning of Israel's saving history. Similarly, it is not until the prophecy of Deutero–Isaiah that the uniqueness of Yahweh's saving restoration of his despondent people is said to be founded upon his holiness (Is 40:25ff). However the closing sentence in v 9bγ may have read,[83] for the fifth time after vv 8bα, β, 9aα and β it emphasizes that Yahweh will not execute his fierce anger, nor will he come to destroy Israel.

■ 11 Accordingly, the final period of the nation's history is not to be dominated by the consequences of Israel's deeds (vv 5–7); rather, the future will be determined by Yahweh's decision to let his love rule. Now Hosea proclaims the return of an anxious people who are to return home trembling from foreign lands (cf. 3:5): Israel will no longer seek false political alliances;[84] the threat of weakness and death in Egypt and Assyria (7:16; 8:8f, 10, 13b; 9:3, 6) is rescinded. The people are to achieve a peaceable life in the land (cf. 2:17, 20). The preposition על ("to [lit. 'on'] their houses") quite probably is not a continuation of the metaphor of the bird that again finds his nest,[85] since in v 11b Hosea leaves the metaphor and speaks of the people themselves. He most probably uses "house" (בית) again in the sense of (native) residence as in 8:1; 9:15 (8).[86] Hence, Yahweh's love finally prevails, achieving its goal of peace: Israel is delivered from Egypt.

The closing formula,[87] probably added by the redactor, emphasizes in conclusion that this prophecy of salvation is a "saying of Yahweh." The formula does not occur in any of the other sketches within the transmission complex beginning with 4:1. Therefore, it is prob-

78   Concerning the poetic structure of vv 8 and 9, see pp. 195f, "Form."
79   See p. 141.
80   See the commentary on 9:10 and 10:11.
81   Cf. Nowack; also W. L. Holladay, *The Root šûbh in the OT* (Leiden, 1959), 69f.
81a  Concerning the word אל in the antithesis (ולא־איש), cf. Is 31:3; Ezek 28:2.
82   Koehler, *Theology*, 52 [34].
83   See textual note "z."
84   Cf. 8:8f; 7:11, where the dove imagery already occurred; see pp. 126f.
85   Cf. Ps 84:4 with Sellin.
86   See the commentary on 8:1.
87   See pp. 196f.
88   See pp. 194f.

ably a concluding note by the redactor of the sketches in 4:1–11:11, especially since chap. 12 begins as though chap. 11 does not exist; we previously noted a similar break between chap. 4 and chaps. 1–3.

■ **10** In this verse we found three explanatory supplements to v 11 which the traditionists drew from a store of prophetic traditions.[88] "They will follow after Yahweh" elucidates the elliptic expression "trembling from" in v 11a. The triumphs of Yahweh's holy love will be met (cf. 2:9) by the discipleship of those who now look to the Baals (vv 2, 7; cf. 2:7, 15) and to foreign powers for help (v 5; cf. 5:11, 13; 7:11). Israel's return to the homeland brings salvation only if it is accompanied by following Yahweh. The "turn" within Yahweh (v 8b) effects Israel's return to Yahweh.

"He will roar like a lion." This second notation explains how Yahweh's rejection of his own wrath has consequences for Israel. The calling father (vv 1f) now roars like a lion, with a voice that cannot be overheard. Though he does not call Israel to judgment,[89] Israel returns home only in terror (cf. 3:4f).

"Indeed, he will roar, and his sons will come trembling from the sea." The statement undoubtedly has the characteristics of oral discourse in Hosea's style.[90] Although the content does not fit the context,[91] the words are not inconceivable in Hosea's time: there were surely enough deported Israelites in the coastal regions (Am 1:3 [9]; cf. 8:12). The formulation is unique and has no model in texts of a late date, even though the subject of a scattered Israel's return home is first clearly expressed in such texts (e.g., Is 11:11). It is therefore not impossible that v 10b, like the additions in 3:5b[92] originates from a later Judaic eschatology of salvation.

### Aim

Hosea's proclamation in chap. 11 embraces the entire history of God's son, Israel. His past and present life is placed within the framework of a lamenting kind of accusation which considers Israel's obstinate apostasy his response to Yahweh's deeds of love (vv 1–7). Unlike the historico–theological accusations which precede and follow chap. 11, the accusations here do not issue into a new threat. Rather, the plaintiff's self–caution leads

first to an express rejection of the judgment (vv 8–9), and then to the proclamation of a new exodus from foreign lands (v 11).

The historico–theological complaint raises the question: What is to determine Israel's future, Israel's own rejection of Yahweh or Yahweh's love? The answer—at first surprising—refers to Yahweh as God, who is not man but the Holy One. God demonstrates that he is the Holy One in that his remorse overcomes his wrath, and thus creates a new life of security for Israel.

Of great theological significance in this chapter is its disclosure that Israel's election and guidance is founded upon God's love (vv 1, 4); this love is not some inconstant characteristic but proves to be the incomparable, holy essence of God himself. Yahweh cannot set aside his love just as he cannot set aside his divinity. His love shows itself in a multitude of calls and actions: though his love is disappointed, it helps Israel further; rejected, it trains and nourishes him (vv 1–4); as suffering love (vv 5–7), it struggles against the divine wrath and thus bears the anguish of neglect within itself (vv 8–9), thereby arriving at the ultimate development of its power (vv [10] 11). Thus the prophet is much less a witness and plaintiff against Israel's history than he is a witness to the divine love which struggles with Israel as within itself.

The enormous accomplishment of the prophet's audition account first becomes clear when it is compared to the decree of Deuteronomic law (Dtn 21:18–21): the rebellious son must be stoned to death. In chap. 11, however, the obstinate son, Israel, learns that the father suffers under his refusal to return; that the father turns his wrath into a new expression of divine love. Moreover, God's ultimate, powerful, liberating action will free Israel, his son, once and for all.

We must say the same thing about the prophet's words as Paul said about the sending of God's son, Jesus Christ: "God has done what the law . . . could not do" (Rom 8:3). This was noted also in relation to Hos 3:5.[93] There, too, "love" was the key word. But in two respects chap. 11 says even more. First, divine love embraces the entire life of the people of God, from their earliest beginnings on into the future, which means to say that Israel exists

---

89  Cf. Am 1:2; 3:4, 8; Hos 5:14; 13:7; Jer 25:30.
90  "Indeed" (כִּי) is followed by a pronoun as subject, as, e.g., in 4:14; 5:14; 8:9.
91  See p. 224.
92  See p. 63.
93  See pp. 62–3.

only by the love of his God. Second, 11:8f reveals that the basis of this love is the holiness of God himself, so that man's unfaithfulness and obstinacy cannot change Yahweh's love into anger. The struggle between God's love and his wrath takes place in God himself, in that the destructive "overturning" and "burning" of judgment against Admah and Zeboim now takes place in God's heart instead of in Israel.[94] God, the "Holy One in the midst" of Israel averts the catastrophe for his own sake, since as in Sodom, ten just men cannot be found in Israel. Thus Abraham's intercession in Gen 18:17–33 is unexpectedly fulfilled. In contrast to Hosea's earlier sayings in 2:8f, 16f; 3:1–5, Yahweh's judgment and mercy stand in conflict. In the preview given by those passages, God's judgment stood in the service of his love. Now, as Yahweh contains his smouldering anger, only opposition to his salvation is expressed, but his love emerges to overpower it.[95]

Only a short distance separates this idea from the words of John: "God is love" (1 Jn 4:8, 16) and their substantiation found in the sending of the Son to atone for our sins (v 10); nor is it far removed from Paul's message: "Where sin increased, grace abounded all the more" (Rom 5:20).

In Hos 11, however, it must be recognized that Hosea knows of only one goal of the power of God's love: Israel's peaceable settling in her own land. This is the result of Yahweh's liberation and deliverance of Israel from the dominion of the nations. Moreover, this love is given only to the son, Israel. Finally, it must be seen that the prophet's words only promise what John and Paul speak of as the historical fulfillment of this promise in Jesus Christ.

Although chap. 11 is thus limited and preparatory, it nevertheless has a paradigmatic significance for all peoples who are "fellow heirs, members of the same body and partakers of the promise in Christ" (Eph 3:6). These words of Hosea, especially because of their concreteness, help each generation to believe anew the miracle of God's completely free, constantly efficacious and purposeful love. This love is the actual channel of life for every individual, for all of mankind. It nourishes men from the heart of God himself, i.e., from the incomparable divine essence of God (vv 8b, 9b). This chapter makes clear to what extent the Old and New Testaments legitimate each other.[96]

94  See the commentary on v 8b.
95  On the relationship of the change in Yahweh to the change in the situation, see p. 196.
96  Von Rad, *Theology* 2, 372–77.

**Betrayal of the Prophetic Word**

## Bibliography

P. R. Ackroyd
"Hosea and Jacob," *VT* 13 (1963): 245–59.

A. Bentzen
"The Weeping of Jacob, Hos 12:5a," *VT* 1 (1951): 58–59.

M. Gertner
"The Masorah and the Levites. Appendix on Hosea 12," *VT* 10 (1960): 241–84.

H. L. Ginsberg
"Hosea's Ephraim, more Fool than Knave. A New Interpretation of Hosea 12:1–14," *JBL* 80 (1961): 339–47.

E. Jacob
"La femme et le prophète. À propos d'Osée 12:13–14," *Hommàge à W. Vischer* (Maqqél shâq éd, 1960), 83–87.

D. J. McCarthy
"Hosea 12:2—Covenant by Oil," *VT* 14 (1964): 215–21.

Ch. W. Reines
"Hosea 12:1," *JJSt* 2 (1950–1): 156–57.

Th. C. Vriezen
"Hosea 12," *NThSt* 24 (1941): 144–49; *idem*, "La tradition de Jacob dans Osée 12," OTS (1942): 64–78.

R. Vuilleumier
"La tradition cultuelle d'Israël dans la prophétie d'Amos et d'Osée," *Cahiers théologiques* 45 (1960): 73f.

C. Westermann
"Das Hoffen im Alten Testament: Eine Begriffs-untersuchung," *ThV* 4 (1952): 19–70 [also in his *Forschung am AT*, ThB 24 (München, 1964), 219–65].

E. Zolli
"Il significato de *rd* e *rtt* in Osea 12:1 e 13:1," *Rivista degli Studi Orientali* 32 (1957): 371–74.

# 12

1 [11:12] With lies Ephraim encompasses me,
    with treachery the house of Israel.
    But[a] Judah still goes with[b] God,
    is loyal to the holy ones.

a    The inverted sentence order alone—with "Judah" placed first—next to the statement about Ephraim in v 1a requires an adversative interpretation. *G* places καὶ Ιουδα with v 1a; also in other respects *G* differs widely with *M* in v 1b; see textual note "b."

b    The consonantal text in *M* is basically supported by *V*: *Iudas autem testis* (עֵד) *descendit* (ירד) *cum deo et cum sanctis fidelis*; the Achmimic translation is similar. α' attests רד with the translation ἐπικρατῶν (רדה). On the other hand, the text *G* used (νῦν ἔγνω αὐτοὺς ὁ θεός, καὶ λαὸς ἄγιος κεκλήσεται θεοῦ) was either quite corrupt or incorrectly read: "Now God has recognized them and they shall be called the holy

2 [12:1] Ephraim befriends[c] the wind
and chases the east wind all day.
[Lies and violence[d] he multiplies].[e]
With Assyria they make an alliance,
to Egypt ⟨they deliver⟩[f] oil.
3 [2] [g]Yahweh has a lawsuit with ⟨Israel⟩,[h]
to call Jacob to account according
to his ways;
according to his deeds
he will requite him.
4 [3] In the womb he tricked his brother,
in his wealth[i] he strove against God.
5 [4] But ⟨God⟩[j] [angel] proved himself lord
and prevailed.
He wept and made supplication to him.
In Bethel[k] he finds him
and there he speaks with ⟨him⟩:[l]

people of Yahweh" (עַתָּ יְדָעָם אֵל וְעַם קְדוֹשׁ יָהּ נֶאֱמָר). The *parallelismus membrorum* supports the well–attested, though difficult–to–understand, text in *M*.

c Cf. textual note "d" on 9:2.

d *G* (κενὰ καὶ μάταια) probably read "falsehood and deceit" (כָּזָב וָשָׁוְא).

e This sentence does not fit the context, for the two prosodic units in v 2 are strictly parallel; it is best explained as an interpreting gloss that adds the chapter's key thoughts (cf. v 1a) to v 2.

f יוֹבִילוּ is required by *S*, the *parallelismus membrorum*, and the consonantal text, insofar as the ו at the beginning of v 3a is less necessary than at the end of v 2b. The vocalization of *M* resulted from the separation of ו from the last word in v 2. In spite of this separation *G* (ἐνεπορεύετο) still presupposes יוּבָל. Perhaps *G*'s reading was caused by haplography of the ו.

g See textual note "f." *G* (καὶ κρίσις) supports *M*.

h *M* ("Judah") probably originates from the book's Judaic redaction (cf. 4:15; 5:5; 6:11, where, however, the technique of redaction is different; see p. xxxii); the unusual copula preceding לפקד was probably added at the same time (but cf. Am 8:4; Ps 104:21). "Jacob" must represent either Israel as a whole (cf. 10:11; 12:13) or the Northern Kingdom (Is 9:7f; 17:3f; Mic 1:5). The combination of ל + פקד, expressing purpose, requires that the accused party be the same in v 3a as in v 3b.

i און = "strength" (thus also the Greek translations, except for *G*: ἐν ἰσχύι; *V*: *in fortitudine*), "wealth" (cf. especially v 9) contrasts the sin of Jacob's manhood with his first sin (cf. v 4a). *G* (ἐν κόποις) apparently translates אָוֶן, as in Mic 2:1; Hab 1:3; 3:7; Zech 10:2; cf. Hos 12:12 *M*.

j σ′ (κατεδυνάστευσε), *V* (*invaluit*), as *M*, derive וישר from שרר, not from שרה (v 4b, as do *G* and α′). The vocalization in *M* as well as a preposition different from that in v 4b support the former. But "to rule over" is expressed by שרר עַל (Ju 9:22). And why should an "angel" rather than God be Jacob's opponent? On Vriezen's interpretation, see p. 212. Would not מלאך at least require the definite article? Yet it seems questionable whether here Jacob is still the subject; if so, the following words (v 5a$\beta$) are unintelligible. Hence, it seems quite probable that the preposition אֶל represents an incorrect reading of an original אֵל caused by placing the marginal gloss מלאך into the text (cf. Gertner, "Masorah," 277, 281). Nor does Hosea mention angels elsewhere.

k As in 4:15; 5:8; 10:5, 8, *G* reads Ων; accordingly Ziegler (*Duodecim prophetae*, 130) regards אָוֶן as the original reading, since otherwise *G* simply would have transcribed the word (βαιθηλ), as it does in Am 3:14; 4:4; 5:6 (twice); 7:10, 13; Zech 7:2; in Hos 12:5 α′ σ′ θ′ also have transcribed בֵּית־אֵל. But at the least, it is just as possible that *G* has harmonized v 5 with the previous passages in Hosea as it is that *M* later changed the original reading only in v 5. The

6 [5]    [And Yahweh is the God of hosts,
      Yahweh is his name!]

7 [6]    "But you (full of trust)ᵐ shall return
      to your God,
      shall preserve loyalty and justice
      and wait continually upon your God!"

8 [7]    In the merchant'sⁿ hand are false scales;
      he loves injustice.ᵒ

9 [8]    But Ephraim says:
      "Indeed, I have become rich,
      I have made my fortune;ᵖ
      ᑫall my gains bring me no guilt
      that would be sin."ᑫ

10 [9]    But I am Yahweh, your Godʳ
      from the land of Egypt;
      I will again make you dwell in tents
      as in the days of meeting.

11 [10]    I spoke toˢ the prophets,
      I gave vision upon vision.
      Through the prophets I make
      proclamation.ᵗ

12 [11]    (Even) if Gilead was wicked,
      then they truly have become useless.
      In Gilgal they sacrifice bullocks,ᵘ
      thus their altars shall also become
      stone heaps
      on the furrows of the field.

13 [12]    Jacob fled to the land of Aram,
      Israel became a servant for a wife,
      for a wife he became a herdsman.

14 [13]    But by a prophet Yahweh brought up
      Israel out of Egypt,
      by a prophet he was tended.

15 [14]    Ephraim has bitterly grieved.ᵛ
      He will make him accountable
      for his bloodguilt;
      his Lord will return to him
      his reproach.

variant reading בּיתי (Gᴬ μου) is attested as early as Tertullian: *in templo meo me invenerunt et illic disputatum est ad eos* (*Adversus Marcionem* IV, 39; Ziegler, *Duodecim prophetae*, 129).

l   *G S* and the context make it necessary to read עִמּוֹ rather than *M* ("with us"; *V: "nobiscum"*), which is traceable to a misunderstanding of the suffix in the preceding word, יִמְצָאוּנ. Concerning the numerous variant readings of *G* in v 5, cf. Ziegler, *Duodecim prophetae*, 129f.

m   שׁוּב בּ should be understood as *constructio praegnans*; in addition to שׁוּב, a second verb is implied which is constructed with בּ, e.g., האמין (Jon 3:5; Ps 78:22) or בטח (Ps 56:5, 12); cf. the usage of בּ in Ps 69:7 and see textual note "b" on 1:2; שׁוּב with בּ that indicates direction occurs in 1 Kgs 2:33; Ob 15.

n   α′ clarifies כנען with the word μετάβολος ("trader," as in Zech 14:21; Is 23:8; cf. Ziegler, *Duodecim prophetae*), likewise *T* ("merchants"); cf. Koehler–Baumgartner, 444b.

o   Literally: "to oppress"; עשׁק occurred previously in 5:11. Most critics (Koehler, Weiser, Lippl) regard לְעַקֵּשׁ "to pervert," "to defraud" as the original reading.

p   α′ (ἀνωφελές; likewise in v 12) and *S* read אָוֶן, as *G* in v 4 (see textual note "i").

q   *G* has translated the words: יְגִיעָיו לֹא יִמָּצְאוּ לוֹ עַל־ עָוֹן אֲשֶׁר חָטָא, thus already adding an announcement of punishment to the accusation in vv 8, 9a. But there is no clear indication of a transition to the announcement of punishment until v 10 (וְאָנֹכִי); thus it is more probable that v 9b continues the Ephraim speech from v 9a. *V* confirms *M*, except for the last word (*peccavi*).

r   *G* adds the words ἀνήγαγόν σε, which translates הֶעֱלִיתִיךָ in Ex 20:2 (cf. Jer 7:22; 11:4 *G*) or הוֹצֵאתִיךָ in v 14; Ex 32:4; 1 Kgs 12:28; cf. *G*'s even longer supplement in 13:4 (see textual note "i" on 13:4).

s   עַל expresses the speaker's superiority; דִּבֶּר עַל also occurs in 2:16; 7:13.

t   This word is uniformly attested, but its meaning is uncertain. "To silence" (4:5, 6; 10:7, 15) seems unlikely because of the parallel clauses (but cf. 6:5). It is conceivable that the word is a *terminus technicus* for the "telling of parables" (Buber), or better, for the proclamation of God's plans (cf. דמה I in Koehler–Baumgartner).

u   *G* (ἄρχοντες) reads שָׂרִים.

v   Is a phrase with the verb's accusative object missing? Or should a suffix be added to the verb: הִכְעִיסוֹ (Procksch) or הִכְעִיסַנִי (Lippl)?

## Form

Chapter 12 does not presuppose what has been proclaimed in 11:8–11. Now Ephraim's guilt is expressed in a different way as deception and betrayal of its God, the theme that makes this chapter a kerygmatic unit. The key word "treachery" (מרמה) in v 1a—found only in chap. 12—occurs again in v 8 and remains the dominant subject until v 15. There, Ephraim's bitter provocation and abuse is expressed by the similar sounding word "bitterly" (תמרורים). In the meantime, the theme of "deception" is developed with reference to Ephraim's bargaining spirit (vv 2, 8f), to Jacob (vv 4f, 13), and Gilgal (v 12).

Thus the accusation (vv 1a, 2, 4, 8f, 12a, 13, 15a) unquestionably predominates the entire chapter. It is intensified by reference to Yahweh's words (vv 5b, 7, 10a, 11) and deeds (vv 5a [cj.], 14), which show Ephraim's own deeds to be all the more false. The difference in Judah's conduct, at least according to the present text, is also indicated in v 1b. This rather lengthy proof of Israel's guilt—judged in terms of saving history—then leads to the rather tersely formulated threats of Yahweh's judgment, which are stated concretely only in vv 10b and 12b. In the decisive sentences that provide the framework (vv 3, 15b) the threats simply declare a general kind of retribution. In this connection, v 15bβ picks up the words "he will requite him" (ישיב לו) from v 3bβ, thus emphasizing the thematic unity also of the announcement of judgment.

Nevertheless, chap. 12 does not represent a rhetorical unit. After vv 1–2, v 3 appears to begin a new saying (cf. 4:1), although its continuation immediately picks up the theme of the previous accusation. After vv 4f, this new saying ends temporarily with the quotation of an exhortation in v 7.[1] A new accusation against Ephraim begins in v 8. The saying might have been evoked by the audience's objections, who perhaps maintained that the cited admonition had been obeyed. Yet the כי—so characteristic of a change of speaker in the sketches of Hosea's sayings[2]—is absent here. Nor is it found at the beginning of the subsequent sayings in chaps. 12–14. This again poses the question raised in connection with the transition from vv 1f to vv 3ff noted above: is the literary connection of these sayings different from that found in chaps. 4–11? The saying in vv 8f, which begins with an accusation, changes to a first person divine speech in v 10, with a threat in v 10b. Connected by a simple copula, v 11 recalls Israel's saving history, and v 12a introduces new evidence of guilt, with a description of

the consequences in v 12b. A fifth saying commences in v 13, which again lacks the obvious terseness of a new beginning found only in v 3. Its style seems to indicate that it is a continuation of the foregoing, but there is no reference back to v 12, nor are there grounds for supposing that an objection was voiced between vv 12 and 13. Only the content shows that the foregoing theme continues, especially since Jacob is named again. Verse 14 is formulated in complete antithesis to v 13, and thus vv 13 and 14 form a rhetorical unit. Verse 15a sums up the accusation—not only of the final saying but of the entire chapter—in one statement of judgment; v 15b presents an equally comprehensive announcement of judgment which refers back to v 3b. Thus the theme of Ephraim's offensive deceit of his God is brought to a conclusion after it has been treated in five loosely connected rhetorical units. Chapter 13:1 begins with a different kind of accusation.

The sayings are mostly formulated as words of the prophet; they speak of God in the third person (vv 1b, 3–5, 7, 14f) and their basic tone is set by the disputation style. Divine speech in the first person occurs only in vv 10 and 11. It should not be assumed as self–evident that the first person in v 1a is Yahweh, for the style of v 1b is that of a disputation, not a messenger speech.[3] The one encompassed with Ephraim's lies could well be the prophet (cf. 9:7f), who expects true followers more likely in Judah than in Israel.[4] Nevertheless, it seems unusual that the prophet would speak here in the first person. This occurs with certainty only in 3:1 and 9:17; it is unlikely, on the other hand, in 5:9.[5]

Both the unusual prophetic lament and the content indicate that a new kind of transmission complex begins in 12:1. It assumes that what remains of the Northern Kingdom has ultimately closed its door to prophetic truth, but a certain openness is still to be found in Judah. Verse 1a suggests that this final transmission complex in the book is similar to the first in chaps. 1–3 in that it presupposes a nucleus of sayings that were either written or dictated by the prophet himself.[6] This would also clarify the above observation that the sayings in 12:1ff are connected in a different fashion than the sketches of

---

1 See the commentary on 12:7.
2 See p. 135; cf. also 9:4, 6; 10:3, 5, 13.
3 See pp. 209f.

4 See pp. 210f.
5 See the commentary.
6 See pp. 11f.

the scenes found in chaps. 4–11.[7] Yet there is a similarity to the secondary additions found there, as for example in 8:14 and 11:10 (cf. 12:3, 11, 13).

The rhythmic structure of the individual sayings is quite like the other sayings in Hosea; it presupposes that these sayings were proclaimed orally. A distinct synonymous parallelism is found in the three–stress bicola in vv 1–2aα, b, 4 and 15b; it also occurs in the three-stress tricola in vv 3 and 7, which begin and end the second saying, and in v 11. The meter of the remaining verses is difficult to determine, in spite of the obvious elevated style (especially in vv 5 and 13f).

### Setting

If we are correct in assuming that chap. 12 begins a transmission complex distinct from that of chaps. 4–11, the sayings of this chapter nevertheless could have originated from the same period as some of the other sketches of Hosea's sayings: v 1 is reminiscent of 9:7f; v 2b recalls 7:11 or 11:5. Since Gilead has apparently been captured by Tiglath–pileser,[8] and Ephraim again swings between Assyria and Egypt, the time is possibly the beginning of Shalmaneser V's reign.[9] In the meantime a considerable wealth (v 9) had promoted disloyalty to Yahweh.

The sayings collected here were most likely proclaimed near the Judean border[10] in the area of Bethel (v 5) or Gilgal (v 12).

### Interpretation

■ 1   Those accused are the inhabitants of the rump state "Ephraim"[11] and their official representatives, the members of the "house of Israel."[12] They have "encompassed" their powerful opponent as one surrounds a fortress[13] or encircles his worst enemy.[14] Their weapon

is "lies"[15] and "treachery" (מרמה), as is said of Jacob in Gen 27:35 (J) and repeatedly of the enemy in Lamentations.[16] Who is meant, Yahweh or the prophet?[17] In Hosea and elsewhere כחש (4:2, 7:3) and מרמה (12:8) concern the neighbor; only in one instance does the reference concern Yahweh (Ps 17:1). Thus the terminology of this sentence is best understood as a complaint uttered by the deceived and oppressed prophet (cf. 9:7f). This interpretation is supported by the fact that the immediately following verses contain no words spoken by Yahweh in the first person, and that the entire chapter, except for vv 10 and 11, speaks of God in the third person.[18] Of course, Yahweh, who speaks through the prophet, is affected as well. Indeed, later in vv 11 and 14, it is emphasized that Yahweh's will is at work in the prophet. If the main theme, the betrayal of the word of Yahweh spoken through his prophet, is alluded to from the beginning then vv 11 and 14 become more intelligible within the context of this chapter.

This view finds further support in the transmitted text of v 1b, although its interpretation is not without difficulty. It has largely been considered corrupt: originally a further statement about Israel, the Judaic redaction applied the words to Judah.[19] Now v 1b is said to speak of Judah's worship of the Canaanite God אֵל (El) and of its loyalty to El's heavenly court of "holy ones" (קְדשִׁים),[20] or even to the קְדשִׁים, the male cult prostitutes.[21] Of course the Old Testament knows elsewhere of אֵל and the קְדושִׁים, his royal counselors who encircle him.[22] The Yehimilk Inscription from the tenth century B.C. mentions Ba'alšamēm and the "Lady of Byblos" together with "the assembly of the holy gods of Byblos."[23] Like the temple prostitutes in Hosea, which he calls קְדשׁות in 4:14, the qdšm appear along side the priests in the Ugaritic lists.[24] This interpretation of v 1b

---

7   See p. 208.
8   See the commentary on v 12.
9   Cf. "Setting" of chap. 11, p. 197.
10   See p. 210 on v 1b.
11   See the commentary on 5:9.
12   "Clan chieftains"; cf. 5:1 [1:4; 10:15] and the commentary.
13   Josh 6:3f; 2 Kgs 6:15.
14   Ps 18:16; 22:13, 17; 88:17; 118:10–12.
15   On כחש, see the commentary on 4:2.
16   Ps 5:7; 10:7; 35:20; 36:4; 38:13; 43:1; 55:12, 24; 109:2; cf. 2 Kgs 9:23; Jer 9:5.
17   See p. 208.

18   See p. 208.
19   Wolfe, "The Editing of the Book of the Twelve," *ZAW* 53 (1935): 91.
20   Nyberg; Pope, "El," 13.
21   Sellin; Weiser.
22   Ps 89:8; cf. v 6; Dtn 33:3; Zech 14:5; Job 5:1; 15:15; cf. Ex 15:11 *G*.
23   מפחרת אל גבל קדשם, with אל in the plural *status constructus*; Donner–Röllig, *KAI*, No. 4, lines 4f; cf. vol. 2, 7; Eissfeldt, "Ba'alšamēm," 3; and W. Röllig, "El als Gottesbezeichnung im Phönizischen," *Festschrift G. Friedrich* (Frankfurt, 1959), 407.
24   *CTCA* 77.3; 71.73 (Gordon 63.3; 113.73).

assumes that Yahweh is the speaker in v 1a.

The following considerations, however, tell against this: (1) The inverted sentence order emphasizes the subject by placing it first. This makes sense only if the subject is not identical with the subject in v 1a, thus making an intentional distinction. This observation supports the "But Judah" (ויהודה) found in most of the texts and versions, but not the conjectured "But he" (והוא) which has been proposed[25] in place of "But Israel" (וישראל),[26] a suggested reading made impossible after the immediately preceding "the house of Israel" (בית ישראל). (2) Hosea often uses the adverb "still" (עד), which can denote the continuation of an action, to emphasize an antithesis (cf. 2:18, 19; 14:4, 9). The placement of עד immediately after the subject makes it more probable that the activity of this subject is viewed in contrast to that of another subject. Thus v 1b does not speak of a different action by the same subject. This also supports the reading "Judah" but not the suggested reading "Israel." (3) Hosea never uses "El" (אל) to designate a Canaanite divinity; it unequivocally refers to the God of Israel in 11:8, a text which probably dates from the same period as chap. 12.[27] The original text of 12:5aα probably also contains the word אֵל.[28] If Hosea had referred to the divine king of Canaan, he would have used the word "Baʻal" (בַּעַל 2:15, 18f; 11:2; 13:1). But if אל denotes Yahweh as God, then the sentence makes sense only if Judah is its subject. (4) In need of clarification, however, is the nature of the subject's behavior in relation to אֵל. This brings us to the disputed meaning of רוד. Nyberg[29] has drawn attention to the Arabic r'd "to change pasture";[30] this might fit Jer 2:31 and Gen 27:40; however, the text in M is uncertain in both passages. Zolli[31] mentions, among other things, the Syriac rdʼ ("to run, flow, live, to set out") whereas

Reines[32] notes the Akk. redu: "to follow, pursue." In v 1 the connection of רוד with עם ("with") is probably not to be any more narrowly defined than a kind of dealing with God. That its meaning is positive is clear from the parallel word "is loyal" (נאמן), which denotes a relationship of loyalty. If רוד denotes a certain discipleship to אל, its subject can only be Judah, not Israel, even though the precise meaning of רוד is uncertain. (5) But who are the "holy ones" (קְדוֹשִׁים) to whom Judah is loyal? In view of our remarks concerning אל, the conjecture "male cult prostitutes" (קְדֵשִׁים) is impossible in the sentence's parallel structure. Hosea neither mentions nor alludes to the idea of a divine council.[33] In terms of Hosea's theology, the interpretation of קדושים as a majestic plural may be more probable; then it could be understood in analogy to "Elohim" (אלהים).[34] But in Josh 24:19 קדושים stands in an attributive relationship to אלהים, whereas in Prv 9:10 and 30:3 the word is more likely a genuine plural.[35] To ascribe to Hosea only the usage of the word as a majestic plural is inadvisable, for in 11:9 the singular קָדוֹשׁ is parallel to אל. The only remaining possibility is that קדושים means the people, as the pious among God's people are called in Ps 34:10 and Dan 7:21.[36] But it also appears that already in an earlier period especially the Levites were so designated.[37] In addition, Elisha as a "man of God" was once called a "holy one" (2 Kgs 4:9). We must therefore consider the possibility that Hosea is referring to the circle of prophets and Levites closely associated with him[38] as the "Holy One." Though they are persecuted in Israel, they are still able to find refuge in Judah (cf. Am 7:12). This again lends support to our assumption that in v 1a the prophet initially laments over his own oppression. Perhaps his personal afflictions, as well as Shalmaneser V's recent military advances, forced him

25  Sellin, Weiser.
26  Nyberg.
27  See p. 209; in addition cf. 2:1.
28  See textual note "j."
29  Nyberg, 92.
30  G. R. Driver, PEQ 79 (1947): 125, defines it: "to be restless" with reference to the Akk. râdu "tremble"; cf. Koehler–Baumgartner, "to roam."
31  Zolli, "Significato."
32  Cf. W. Reines, "Hos 12:1," JJSt (1950–1), 156–57.
33  Ps 89:8, etc.; see p. 209.
34  Cf. Josh 24:19; Prv 9:10; 30:3, and Brockelmann, Syntax § 19c.

35  Cf. M. Noth, "The Holy Ones of the Most High," in The Laws in the Pentateuch and Other Studies, tr., D. R. Ap–Thomas (Philadelphia: Fortress, 1966), 217 [Gesammelte Studien, 276f].
36  Ibid., 218, 227ff [277, 287ff].
37  2 Chr 35:3; cf. Nu 3:12; Ps 16:3, and Kraus, Psalmen, 121ff.
38  Wolff, "Heimat," 83–94 [232–50].
38a  Also cf. the assonance in v 2bα with 5:11; 8:7.

into the vicinity of the Judean border, around the area of Bethel (cf. v 5), so that, as once in 733 (5:8–10), he is easily able to obtain information from the other side of the border.

■ **2** The participial clauses in v 2a concerning Ephraim stand in precise antithetical parallelism to the same kind of clauses about Judah in v 1b. The emphasis upon "Ephraim," which precedes the verb, is intelligible only if it follows "Judah" in v 1b. The accusation is given a "lashing" intensity, even by the sound of the words, as indicated by the threefold alliteration of the predominant ר of the word אפרים in the phrase רעה רוח ורדף.[38a] This becomes more evident, however, from the verse's content: the rump state's only remaining friend is the wind, i.e., nothingness.[39] Ephraim only chases after the East wind, the sirocco,[40] which is powerful enough to parch and destroy everything.[41]

The following prosodic unit (v 2b), which forms a chiasmus to v 1a, gives an interpretation of the metaphor. To "chase after the east wind" refers to the treaty Hoshea ben Elah made with Assyria (5:13; 8:9) in 733, with its obligation to pay tribute.[42] The friendship with the wind is the recent, fateful relationship with Egypt after the death of Tiglath–pileser III; the oil Israel sent made the agreement official. Verse 2bβ is an exact parallel to v 2aα insofar as oil is the gift of allegiance that ratifies the making of a treaty, especially by a vassal.[43] Deuteronomy (cf. 7:2; 17:16) takes up the battle begun by Hosea (cf. additionally 7:11; 10:4, 6; 14:4) against the politics of treaty making with foreign powers.

■ **1, 2** These verses, in effect, say that Ephraim, in his reliance upon treacherous political ties with the great powers (v 2b), betrayed the prophetic word of God (v 1a) and thus betrayed himself (v 2a). The prophet's complaint, which expresses an unusual hope in connection with Judah, has been placed at the beginning of a literary unit. The reason for this may have been that the prophet, in view of the impending disaster for the Northern Kingdom, wrote down his oral proclamation

to preserve it for a watchful circle of followers in Judah.

■ **3** The accusation (vv 1–2) is followed by a loosely connected saying which officially initiates Yahweh's lawsuit[44] with an anticipated threat.[45] If the above–noted assumption concerning v 1b is correct, then it is not surprising that in v 3a "Israel" was replaced by "Judah" quite early.[46] The judgment speech originally addressed to the Northern Kingdom is now intended to be a warning for Judah. There was good reason for this, since the original saying called Israel "Jacob." It thus emphasized not the geographical aspect which separated Israel from Judah but the common history of salvation which united them.[47]

■ **4** Thus Yahweh's lawsuit with Jacob begins once more in the presence of Israel. The Israel of Hosea's time is unmasked by reference to her forefather. The prophet recites Israel's history and thus uncovers the deception she now practices.

The assonance noted in v 2 is now used to interpret the name of Jacob, disclosing his very nature: "Jacob"— "deception" (יעקב—עקב). Jacob "tricked his brother in the womb." The original meaning of the "typical Mesopotamian—West Semitic name *Jaḥqub–ila*" ("May God protect")[48] is unknown by Hosea as well as by the Pentateuchal traditions. Although Hosea apparently is acquainted with much of the content of these traditions, he introduces some significant changes. The Yahwist's narrative of the birth of the twins Jacob and Esau derives the name Jacob from עָקֵב (Gen 25:26), since he grasps Esau's "heel." This narrative mentions nothing about a "deception." Rather, that Jacob takes hold of his brother's heel is considered to be fulfillment of the foregoing promise (v 23) concerning his superiority. "Jacob" is first connected with "to deceive"

---

39   See the commentary on 8:7.
40   Noth, *World*, 27 [27].
41   Cf. 13:15; Ps 103:15f; Is 40:6f; Ezek 17:10, and Zimmerli, *Ezekiel*, 383.
42   See the commentary on 8:9.
43   Cf. Ps 68:32 and McCarthy, "Hosea 12:2," 219; also E. Kutsch, "Salbung als Rechtsakt," BZAW 87 (Berlin, 1963) 66–69; on יבל hip'il, cf. 10:6 and the

commentary.
44   Cf. 4:1bα and the commentary.
45   Cf. 4:9b and the commentary.
46   See textual note "h."
47   Cf. 10:11 and the commentary.
48   M. Noth, "Mari und Israel," in *Geschichte und Altes Testament. Festschrift Alt*, ed. W. Zimmerli (Tübingen, 1953), 142f [also in Noth, *Aufsätze* 2, 225].

(עקב) by the words of Esau[49] in the later narrative of the underhanded way Jacob obtained his father's blessing. Later on the same connection is found in Jeremiah (9:3). By boldly tracing Jacob's cunning dealings back to the story of his birth, Hosea pursues "the sin back to his unconscious actions" with "an almost uncanny consistency."[50] Hosea speaks not of Esau's deception, but of that of "his brother," for he wants to unmask Jacob's present guilt. He may have in mind the enmity between Ephraim and Judah,[51] or even the treachery he himself experienced as a prophet as reported in this chapter (vv 1, 13f).

In any case, the verse's continuation deals with the rejection of God's word and the struggle against the prophet's proclamation of it (9:7f): "In his wealth he strove with God." This alludes to the tradition of Jacob's wrestling at Jabbok in Gen 32:23ff. "Strength" (אוֹן) may denote man's procreative powers (Gen 49:3). In view of this, באונו in parallel to בבטן could be translated: "in the womb . . . as a man. . . ." Or should the word be interpreted as "wickedness" (אָוֶן) in accordance with G[52] since the verse speaks of guilt? The word stands parallel to "deception" (מרמה) in Ps 36:4 [3] and also occurs in v 12. Yet the word's suffix and its connection with the Jacob tradition, as well as its context within chap. 12, make it most likely that here אוֹן denotes wealth, as in v 9. Jacob wrestled with God as one who had become rich (Gen 32:5, 11, 22f). Ephraim now exults over his riches in opposition to the word of his God (vv 9, 2b).

■ **5** The continuation of the Jacob story in v 5aα brings with it enormous difficulties and has led to the most contradictory attempts to resolve them. The causes of the problem lie not only in the variety of layers in the transmission history of Gen 32:23–33, but especially in the inner tension within this extremely brief sketch. (1) In M the verb form וַיָּשַׂר from שׂרר ("to reign") combined with the preposition אֶל is unknown and remains inexplicable. (2) The suggested vocalization וַיָּשַׂר (from שׂרה ["to strive"])[53] is unacceptable because this same verb would hardly occur with אֶת in v 4b and with אֶל in v 5a. It is arbitrary to read אֶת in both cases.[54] (3) There is tension between the content of v 5aα and v 5aβ. Why should the victor Jacob weep and make supplication? The text does not state that these actions represent his craftiness. To make such an allusion, the sentences would have to be rearranged. Vriezen[55] suggested that the two sentences represent a dialogue between people and prophet: in v 5aα the people correct the prophet (v 4b), then vice versa in v 5aβ; in vv 5b–6 the people again speak. There is, however, no basis in the text to support his hypothesis. The continuation in the narrative tense (imperfect consecutive v 5aα) tells against this. The tension between vv 5aα and 5aβ remains unresolved. In this context Hosea's formulation of the statements is pregnant and specific. Therefore they should not be interpreted as though Hosea intentionally alludes to Gen 32 simply because there Jacob's struggle (v 29b) is found connected with his petition (vv 27b, 30a). We have already observed how Hosea freely makes use of tradition. (4) The same observation applies to vv 4b and 5aα if we find a tension between these verses: in v 4b Jacob strives with God, whereas in v 5aα the angel is the subject. To interpret this with reference to Gen 32, where Jacob's partner is first said to be "a man" (v 25) and then "God" (vv 29, 31), incorrectly assumes that here the prophet is bound to tradition. It also fails to recognize the freedom and the clarity of the prophet's intention. In no other instance does Hosea mention angels.[56]

As far as I am able to determine, the verse takes on clarity within its context only if we draw the consequences from the last observations above. Thus מלאך would have to be a gloss, carefully added for the purpose of elucidating אלהים in v 4b in the light of a tradition related to that in Gen 32:25. This provides us with an unambiguous text[57] without the difficulties noted above. The subject is אֵל which Hosea uses to designate the

---

49  Gen 27:36; in the immediately preceding verse (35) Jacob's deed is characterized as "deception" (מרמה), the key word of chap. 12.
50  K. Elliger, "Der Jakobskampf am Jabbok," *ZThK* 48 (1951): 28.
51  Cf. 2:3 and the commentary.
52  See textual note "i."
53  Robinson.
54  Weiser.
55  Th. C. Vriezen, OTS 1 (1942): 65.
56  See the commentary on v 1bβ.
57  See textual note "j."

deity also in v 1b and 11:9 (2:1). In v 5 אֵל follows אלהים (v 4b) because of the alternating style and perhaps because of the meter.[58]

Thus Hosea says that he who acts deceptively, who cunningly fights against God and man, will encounter his Lord and victor in Yahweh. Now v 5aβ becomes intelligible: Jacob wept and made supplication because Yahweh had defeated him. It is not surprising that Jacob, once again the subject as in v 4, is not named anew, for in the lawsuit Jacob is normally the subject anyway. The statement about God in v 5aα was necessary for the understanding of the passage.

The continuation of the verse again uses the tradition freely. Accordingly God finds[59] Jacob in Bethel and answers his supplication. It is probable that here the tradition from Gen 28:10–22 (JE) has been combined with that from Gen 32:23–33 (J); this is confirmed especially by v 7;[60] but also cf. Gen 35:1–5, 7 (E).

In v 5 Hosea has begun to disclose not only the present but the future of his audience with the help of the Jacob stories: Yahweh will prove himself both Lord and victor, as he had once with Jacob. Israel, however, should take the course of its ancestor: weeping and supplication, submission and repentance. In Bethel Yahweh's word will once again come to those willing to return. It is hardly surprising that *M* changed the original "there he spoke with *him*"[61] to read: "there he spoke with *us*." Hosea also changes the narrative tense in vv 4 and 5a to the imperfect in v 5b. What is yet to be said deals primarily with the present and the future. It is likely that for this reason v 7 is in the form of a quotation which contains the ancient words addressed to Jacob.

■ **6** But the next verse in the transmitted text contains a doxology which has been inserted into the passage. It has been supposed[62] that here Hosea himself inserted a reminiscence of the Moses tradition (Ex 3:15). But this is unlikely, particularly because the plerophoric divine name in v 6 appears strange next to אלהים in vv 4 and 7, "Yahweh" in v 3 (cf. v 10), and אֵל in v 5 (cj.); moreover, it has no parallel in Hosea. Above all, such doxological insertions are also found in Amos.[63] These are "doxologies of judgment" and should be understood in terms of the administration of sacral law (Josh 7:19). The person who heard these words of Yahweh spoken by Hosea acknowledged Yahweh's holiness (cf. Ps 30:5; 97:12) and at the same time confessed his own sins. As in Amos, Yahweh is designated as "God of hosts" to emphasize his absolute power.[64] Yet the redaction in both Hosea and Amos is not the same: (1) Here we have "Yahweh, God of hosts" (יהוה אלהי הצבאות) whereas in Amos either אלהי does not occur (9:5a) or צבאות lacks the definite article (4:13b). (2) In Hosea the final word is זכרו, whereas Amos has שְׁמוֹ (4:13b; 5:8a; 9:6b). To be sure, in the doxologies, זֵכֶר has almost surely the same meaning as שֵׁם (cf. Prv 10:7; Ps 135:13; Ex 3:15); but זכר more strongly emphasizes the re–presentation that occurs "from generation to generation" each time the name of the God of Israel is invoked.[65] (3) There is also a distinction in the content. The doxology in the tradition of Hosea's sayings occurs before an ancient word from Yahweh is proclaimed anew (after v 5b!); in Amos, however, the doxology comes after the announcement of judgment (4:12; 9:4; cf. 5:6ff).

Hosea and Amos therefore probably did not undergo a relatively late, common redaction. Rather, the addition in v 6 more likely originates with the specific tradition of the third transmission complex of Hosea's sayings (chaps. 12–14) and its new proclamation in the area of Judah.

---

58 If we count the syllables by the alternating method, there are three accented syllables each in v 5aα and v 5aβ; cf. F. Horst, "Die Kennzeichen der hebräischen Poesie," *ThR* 21 (1953): 97–121.

59 Concerning מצא as a word signifying election, cf. 9:10 and the commentary.

60 See the commentary on v 7.

61 I.e., Jacob; see textual note "l."

62 Buber, *The Prophetic Faith*, 116f [167]; Gertner, "Masorah," 279.

63 4:13b; 9:5f; cf. F. Horst, "Die Doxologien im Amosbuch," *ZAW* 47 (1929): 45–54 [also in his *Gottes Recht*, ThB 12 (München, 1961), 155–66].

64 Cf. O. Eissfeldt, "Jahwe Zebaoth," *Miscellanea Academica Berolinensia* II/2 (1950), 128–50 [also in his *Kleine Schriften* 3 (Tübingen, 1966), 103–23]; von Rad, *Theology* 1, 18f.

65 Ps 102:13; 135:13; cf. Schottroff, "Gedenken," 292–9.

**■ 7** Introduced in v 5b, the exhortation in v 7 is to be heard in reverence and humility, according to v 6. The three–part exhortation is a preliminary climax to the prophet's utilization of the Jacob tradition. The quotation contained in v 7 is now an exhortation that is entirely appropriate to the contemporary situation of Hosea's audience (10:12f). The tradition presupposed by Hosea's words is found in Gen 28:15, 21, which relates how Jacob returns from a foreign land with the help of his God. By comparison, v 7 is concerned not with Israel's return *to* God,[66] but with the *how* of her return, as the preposition ב indicates:[67] only the God of Israel can make this possible. Therefore, Hosea requires a new loyalty to him and his ordinances.[68] Hosea speaks of anxiously waiting[69] for Yahweh only here. "Continually" (תמיד) emphasizes constancy in contrast to Israel's flighty nature, which is lamented in 6:4. The insertion of the doxology in v 6 indicates that the quotation in v 7, based on the Jacob tradition, was recognized as an exhortation having contemporary validity and significance.

Verse 7 has been considered a later paraenetic addition because its formulation resembles Ps 37:34; 25:5, etc.[70] Nevertheless the verse probably stems from Hosea: (1) The introduction of a citation into the tradition in 10:12 is parallel; (2) the tricolon is typical for Hosea's diction; (3) the language is demonstrably Hosean, apart from תמיד.

**■ 8** It becomes evident in v 8 that Hosea used the ancient exhortation (v 7) especially to disclose Israel's present guilt, much like 10:12.[71] כנען denotes nothing other than contemporary Ephraim, which is filled with a Canaanite spirit of harlotry and commerce. For ancient Israel, trade belonged to foreigners. The commercial cities of Phoenicia, whose region was especially designated by the word "Canaan," "the land of red purple,"[72] were centers of trade.[73] The "false scales" (מאזני מרמה) are almost proverbial in prophecy and Wisdom.[74] Thus the word "deception" (מרמה) from v 1a appears again; there, as in v 8, it has to do with the "oppression"[75] of the neighbor.

**■ 9** By quoting the defendant, the prophet offers proof of guilt with words from the defendant's own mouth. The quotation further develops the accusation.[76] Wealth led to injustice just as injustice led to wealth. It was this same wealth (און) which had once led Jacob to struggle against God;[77] his unjust service had made him rich (cf. v 13). But Ephraim denies that there has been any injustice. מצא און forms a wordplay with לא מצא עון in v 9b. Since עון sounds similar to און the relative clause is necessary to establish that this transgression is unequivocally sin[78] against Yahweh. Ephraim's economic gains are in conflict with his trust in Yahweh and Yahweh's requirement of loyalty in the community (v 7). His wealth enables him to make treaties which betray the divine word uttered by the prophet (v 2). The quotation in v 9 on the whole suggests how the prophet's rejection (v 1a), which he laments as "betrayal" and self–deception, is to be understood.

**■ 10** Yahweh answers Ephraim's self–assertion ("I am rich") with the self–introduction formula: "I am Yahweh, your God, from the land of Egypt" (cf. 11:1),

---

66  Cf. "to" (אֶל) in 2:9; 5:4; 6:1; 7:10, 16 (cj.); 14:3; עד in 14:2.

67  Cf. ב *instrumenti* in 12:14; see textual note "m."

68  On the two concepts "loyalty and justice" (חסד ומשפט) in Hosea, cf. 2:21 [19]; 6:4f and the commentary on 2:21.

69  On קוה as a designation for tensely (cf. קו = "stretched line") awaiting Yahweh, cf. C. Westermann, "Das Hoffen im Alten Testament," *ThV* 4 (1952): 25 [also in *Forschung am AT*, *Gesammelte Studien*, ThB 24 (München, 1964), 225]; P. A. H. de Boer, "Étude sur le sens de la racine *qwh*," *OTS* 10 (1954): 225–46; J. van der Ploeg, "L'espérance dans l'AT," *RB* 61 (1954): 481–507.

70  Recently, C. Westermann, "Hoffen," 57 [253], n. 69.

71  See p. 182.

72  Noth, *World*, 52 [45].

73  Ezek 16:29; 17:4 and W. Zimmerli, *Ezekiel*, 380.

74  Am 8:5; Prv 11:1; 20:23; cf. Mic 6:11; its opposite, the "just scale" (מאזני צדק), is mentioned in Job 31:6; Lev 19:36; cf. Prv 16:11 and K. Galling, "Handel," *RGG*[3] 3, 57.

75  On the word עשק and its relation to the established social order, see p. 114.

76  Cf. C. Westermann, *Basic Forms of Prophetic Speech*, tr. H. C. White (Philadelphia: Westminster Press, 1967), 61.

77  V 4b; on the subject, see also 13:6!

78  On חטא, cf. 13:2; 8:11; 4:7, and pp. 80f, 145.

79  Cf. 13:4 and 4:1f; cf. also Zimmerli, "Jahwe," 196 [28]; K. Elliger, "Ich bin der Herr, euer Gott," in *Theologie als Glaubenswagnis. Festschrift K. Heim* (Hamburg, 1954), 9ff [also in his *Kleine Schriften*, ThB 32 (München, 1966), 211ff].

with which he had proclaimed his clear instructions for the conduct of life in Israel.[79] Now, after the accusation summarizing the previous history of the defendant,[80] he speaks as judge in the lawsuit (v 3). With the word "I will make you dwell" (אוֹשִׁיבְךָ) Yahweh threatens to return Israel to the tents in which she once lived. This alludes to the exhortation from the Jacob tradition (v 7a). Those who refuse to return (שׁוּב) with trust in Yahweh must leave the commercial prosperity of Canaan and be resettled (ישׁב hip'il) in the poverty of nomadic life. The context does not suggest the meaning of "festive tents"[81] even though the "days of meeting" are mentioned. The "tent of meeting" (אֹהֶל מוֹעֵד) of the Priestly Document can in no case be the presupposition for the reference to "tents."[82] To be sure, it could be asked whether the מוֹעֵד does not mean "time of the festival" as in 2:13 and 9:5 (cf. 2:11), thus being a reference to Israel's living in tents, as she did especially during her festivals, which is presupposed by 9:5f.[83] Nevertheless, it is more likely that Hosea means the tradition of Yahweh's first "meeting" with Israel in the desert.[84] This is also supported by the fact that, in his sayings about Israel's future, Hosea uses "as in the day(s)" (כִּימֵי or כְּיוֹם) to introduce analogies drawn from Israel's early history, not from the present (2:5, 17; 9:9; cf. 10:9). Incidentally, this tradition has already appeared in 2:16f and 13:4f in connection with the Egypt tradition as in 12:10.[85] To postulate a tent festival in Hosea's time lacks sufficient evidence and is unnecessary.[86] The content of this threat is similar to the announcement of the new wilderness situation in 2:11ff, 16f; 9:15, 17.

■ **11** By recalling the prophetic proclamation of God's will, v 11 elucidates Israel's present guilt just as v 7 did by referring back to the ancient exhortation to Jacob. These two verses are similar also in their external struc-

ture; both are three–stress tricola in synonymous parallelism.[87] As in 6:5, Hosea is probably thinking of the line of prophets in the Northern Kingdom—whose forefather is ultimately designated as Moses (12:14)—who in various ways were agents of Yahweh's justice.[88] They are active still in Hosea's time, as the transition from the perfect verbs in v 11a to the iterative imperfect in v 11b suggests. But v 11 does not explain what will happen when Israel returns to a nomadic life, as v 10b threatens; instead, it elucidates the new proof of guilt offered in v 12a.[88a]

■ **12** Here Israel's sacrificial worship is again mentioned; it has nothing in common with Yahweh's desire for "loyalty and justice" (חֶסֶד וּמִשְׁפָּט v 7bα) and thus for "knowledge of God" (דַּעַת אֱלֹהִים).[89] The text, especially difficult in its first part, perhaps recalls that Gilead in Transjordan became particularly known as a wicked place through its bloody transgressions (cf. 6:8, where אָוֶן also occurs; cf. 10:8); and that in the meantime Gilead had also been punished by Tiglath–pileser's attack in the Transjordan area.[90] שָׁוְא means the futility of deceit, especially in Israel's pagan worship (Ps 24:4; 31:7; Jer 18:15). Whoever participates in this deceives himself and becomes nothing (Job 15:31 !). The theme begun in v 1a is continued by related catchwords. Through their rejection of the divine word spoken by the prophet (v 1a, 11; cf. 7) the people have fallen prey to the deceitfulness of the cult, of politics (v 2), and of commerce (vv 8f). Thus the altars will become heaps of stone (v 12b; cf. 2:8f; 4:19; 8:13; 9:6, and especially 10:8).

■ **13** A new saying begins in v 13 which clearly belongs with v 14. The narrative style corresponds less to the immediately preceding context than to the first mention of the Jacob tradition in vv 4f. But the content of the

---

80  Vv 4–9; cf. 11:1–7 and pp. 193f.

81  Cf. 9:6; cf. A. Alt, "Zelte und Hütten," *Kleine Schriften* 3, 242.

82  Cf. Ex 25:22; Sellin; Gertner, "Masorah."

83  See p. 156.

84  9:10; see the commentary; cf. also 2:5; 10:11.

85  On 11:1–4, see pp. 198f.

86  Cf. H. J. Kraus, *Worship in Israel*, tr. Geoffrey Buswell (Oxford, 1966), 132 [156].

87  On "to speak urgently to someone" (דִּבֶּר עַל), cf. 2:16 and the commentary. On "I make proclamation" (אדמה), see textual note "t."

88  Cf. 6:5f and the commentary.

88a  In a similar way 6:5 belongs to 6:6.

89  Cf. v 11 with 4:6; 6:6; 8:11f and the commentary. On Gilgal, see p. 89; on Gilead, p. 122. Concerning the location of Gilead, see M. Noth, "Gilead und Gad," *ZDPV* 75 (1959): 36ff [now in Noth, *Aufsätze* 1, 489ff].

90  The Assyrian province of *Gal–'a–za* was probably named after the administrative headquarters in Gilead; cf. Alt, "Das System der assyrischen Provinzen," *Kleine Schriften* 2, 202ff; see p. 209.

new saying is quite similar to the theme of true and false worship dealt with in vv 11f. The reference to Jacob's servitude "for a wife" (cf. Gen 29:15–30) is not for the purpose of demonstrating his love, as in Gen 29:20, nor to legitimate this manner of obtaining a wife (cf. Josh 15:16f, 1 Sam 17:25). Nor does it present an early stage of the patriarch's humility, since he unassumingly worked as a laborer, whereby the first birth of Israel would be placed before a second spiritual one (v 14).[91] Even less does v 13 portray Jacob's servanthood as an opportunity for divine redemption. In this case, it would remain unintelligible why Jacob's activity is emphatically mentioned, while nothing is said of his slavery in Egypt before v 14.[92] Instead, similar to vv 4f, Hosea emphasizes Jacob's deceit of his God. This is done by two catchwords: (1) perhaps by Jacob's flight to "*Aram*" and his work in the capacity of servant, which might allude to Israel's submission to foreign powers;[93] (2) more clearly, by Jacob's slaving "for a wife" (באשה), emphasized by virtue of its repetition. How would this repetition accent a reprehensible act after v 12, unless it alludes to the sex rites practiced in the cult?[94] The patriarch of Israel had begun his disgraceful association with the foreign woman in Aram and thus became the prototype of the condemned priesthood.[95] The patriarchal tradition known to us from J is alluded to only by the catchwords "to serve" (עבד Gen 29:20, 30) and "to tend," "to watch" (שמר Gen 30:31), but it is not recognizable in the context.

■ **14** Yahweh's deed stands in strict antithetical parallelism to Jacob's reprehensible deed. A twofold occurrence of "by a prophet" (בנביא) contrasts with the repeated "for a wife" (באשה). Thus God's efficacious "service" to Israel opposes Jacob's false worship "services"; however, it is also his purpose to liberate and to uphold Israel through the prophetic word (cf. v 11; 6:5). In addition, the correspondence of the last word in both prosodic units (vv 13 and 14) is probably intentional. Deceitful Israel has herself "tended" (שמר) sheep; liberated by its God, Israel is "tended" (נשמר) by the prophet. This means that the "ministry" and proclamation of divine law is placed in antithesis to the false "practices" of the sex rites.[96]

It cannot be denied that here "prophet" means Moses, since a connection is made with the Exodus from Egypt. This receives indirect support by the fact that the Deuteronomic circles, whose beginnings can be traced to Hosea, call Moses a prophet (Dtn 18:15f); at the same time he is regarded as the head of the Levites (Ex 32:25ff; Ju 18:30; Ex 2:1). Apparently Moses was first called a "prophet" by Hosea and his circle of supporters. They regarded him as the spiritual head of their opposition group comprised of prophets and Levites.[97] The theme of the chapter (vv 1, 11) makes it understandable that he is named only according to his office as prophet. The reference to Moses as prophet may point to an essential historical connection of eighth century prophecy with the charismatic leaders of Israel's early years.[98]

God's action through Moses not only stands in contrast to Jacob's deeds, but ensues from them, just as God's victory follows the battle at Jabbok in vv 4f, and his answer responds to Jacob's supplication (vv 5, 7). Likewise, Israel's present deceit will be overtaken by God's new deeds alluded to already in vv 10 and 12b. As Jacob represents Israel's false path in history, so the prophet symbolizes Yahweh's guidance of Israel.[99]

■ **15** The final verse of the passage expresses again the certainty of God's impending judgment. Initially the transmitted text[100] abruptly makes a summary statement of the guilt: "Ephraim has bitterly grieved." הכעיס is a

91 Thus e.g., Calvin; cf. E. Jacob, "La femme," 84.
92 *Contra* Ackroyd, "Hosea and Jacob," 246f.
93 Cf. 5:11b and the commentary; cf. also 12:2.
94 Cf. 4:14 and the commentary.
95 On the usage of שמר, cf. 4:10f: שמר זנונים; see textual note "o/p" to 4:10.
96 Ex 18:13ff; 20:18ff; also cf. שמר in v 7bα!
97 Wolff, "Heimat," 93f [247f]; G. Fohrer, "Levi und Leviten," *RGG*³ 4, 336f; H. Strauss, "Untersuchungen zu den Überlieferungen der vorexilischen Leviten," unpublished dissertation, University of Bonn (Bonn, 1960).
98 Cf. Rendtorff, "Erwägungen," 149, 160ff; R. Smend,

*Yahweh War and Tribal Confederation*, tr. M. G. Rogers (Nashville: Abingdon, 1970), 78ff [*Jahwekrieg und Stämmebund*, FRLANT 84 (Göttingen, 1963): 87ff].
99 Cf. E. Jacob, "La femme," 85f; *idem*, "Der Prophet Hosea und die Geschichte," *EvTh* 24 (1964): 286.
100 Cf. textual note "v."
101 Dtn 4:25; 9:18; 31:29; Ju 2:12; 1 Kgs 14:9, 15; 2 Kgs 17:11; 21:6; 23:19; Jer 7:18f; 8:19; 11:17, etc.
102 Cf. Lev 20:9, 11, 12, 13, 16, 27; Ezek 18:3 and H. Graf Reventlow, "Sein Blut komme über sein Haupt," *VT* 10 (1960): 311–27.

catchword in the theology of Deuteronomy, Jeremiah, and the Deuteronomist.[101] It always points to the provocation of Yahweh by pagan worship. In his summary accusation we see the prophet again moved with sorrow. Israel's transgression deeply grieves the heart of Hosea's God (cf. 2:15b).

The announcement of judgment follows, concluding the passage in parallel statements: "He will leave his bloodguilt upon him," i.e., he will let it weigh heavily upon him. With this expression Hosea makes use of a cultic legal formula that announces the punishment.[102] Israel's provocation of Yahweh is thus characterized as bloodguilt (cf. Lev 17:4), a transgression deserving death. But "the bloodguilt" does not take effect independently; rather, "his Lord" puts it in force, and also lets his "reproach" fall back upon Ephraim himself. Picked up from v 3bβ, "requite to him" (ישיב לו) rounds off the sketch of the lawsuit speech.[103] Israel's transgression against her God is again characterized as personal injury with the word "reproach" (חרפה). Only here does Hosea call Yahweh Ephraim's "Lord," who, as his "master" (אדניו), has the last word of judgment, even after all Israel's renunciations.

**Aim**

The path through these individual sayings has shown us the chapter's tightly woven, clearly stated unity of theme. To be sure, there is a lack of smoothness in the transitions between the sayings stemming from Yahweh's lawsuit with Israel. But the theme of the chapter is remarkably unified, as may be seen even in the prophet's choice of vocabulary. The statement about retribution at the beginning of the lawsuit (v 3bβ: "according to his deeds he will requite him" [כמעלליו ישיב לו]) recurs at the end (v 15bβ: "his Lord will requite him . . ." [ישיב לו אדניו]). These expressions make it immediately evident that the prophet's certainty of God's new actions also dominates his proclamation in chap. 12. These new actions are announced by a terse yet lucid statement given prominence by the divine speech form (v 10; cf. 12b). Here in the middle of the passage, plainer than in the sayings which surround it as a framework, the prophet proclaims: Israel shall be led back to a pov-

erty–stricken, nomadic way of life.

This announcement has its motivation in the proof of Israel's guilt which predominates the majority of these sayings. Here again Hosea's selection of vocabulary is indicative of the passage's unity. The chapter is introduced by the words "lies" and "treachery" against God and his messenger.[104] The lament over the prophet's (final?) rejection in Ephraim (vv 1–2) appears to have been the reason these sayings from the lawsuit (vv 3–15) were fixed in writing.[105] Although the catchword "treachery" (מרמה) in the introductory lament recurs in v 8, it is of more significance that the words "grief" (הכעיס) and "reproach" (חרפה) in the concluding summary accusation (v 15) correspond with the passage's basic thrust, which is also seen in the words about "trickery" (עקב) and "contention" (שרה) in v 4, as in those of "wickedness" (און) and "uselessness" (שוא) in v 12.

These words unequovically state that Israel's guilt is not simply that she has violated a set of general precepts; rather, Israel has grievously and deceitfully rejected the person of her God. This is confirmed by the fact that Israel's sins are set forth repeatedly (vv 7, 11, 14) as resistance to the proclamation of God's word; as decisive and utter abuse of the *prophetic word*. It is not fortuitous that chap. 12, more powerfully and in greater detail than any other chapter, speaks of God's proclamation through the prophets (v 11) and of Moses as the prophet who led Israel out of Egypt (v 14). The introductory lament (v 1a) is therefore best interpreted as Hosea's lament over the personal attacks he endured, of which the quotation in v 9 provides an elucidation.[106] Rejection of the prophetic word grieves the God of Israel.

The history of the people of God continues into the future not by disregard of the prophetic voice but only by following the direction that voice proclaims. To follow a different way is to chase the wind and emptiness (vv 2, 12), even though Israel may rely ever so strongly upon her own skill, wealth, strength, and piety (vv 2b, 4, 8f, 12f). We have seen that the brief words announcing God's forthcoming actions dominate, providing the framework for the more detailed descriptions of Israel's guilt. The recollections of Israel's early history in chap. 12 should be considered in view of this genuine history

---

103 Cf. 4:9 and the commentary.
104 V 1a; see p. 209.
105 See p. 211.

106 See pp. 209ff and 214.

of the future, which future is the God of Israel himself. Israel's past discloses both her present and her future, for also her past was dominated by God's word to Israel; her past was life in his presence.

Compared to all of the historical retrospects in the book, here the difference lies in the detailed re–presentation of the *Jacob story* (vv 4–5; 7, 13). Also its content is essentially different. Previously Hosea has shown that Israel's history prior to the conquest was a history of obedience (10:11; 2:17) and of pure joy to Yahweh (9:10). In going back further to the time of the patriarchs, however, chap. 12 paints a dismal picture of the foul deeds preceding the beginnings of the saving history in Egypt and in the wilderness. Jacob is essentially represented as a prototype of Ephraim's present guilt.[107]

What is Hosea's purpose? Surely it is not only to make some kind of analogy, to hold up a mirror to the past; for he apparently has a genuine interest in history. His interest lies in the fact that Jacob's history of guilt is overcome by Yahweh's saving history. The sequence of reminiscences of Jacob's servitude in Aram and the deliverance from Egypt in vv 13–14 makes this especially clear. But also in the Jacob history itself, continued after v 4 in vv 5 and 7, we see that Jacob's God demonstrates his Lordship over his cunning opponent;[108] that in response to his supplication God shows him a way into the future (vv 5aβ, b, 7).

In this chapter Hosea's proclamation does not depart from the central thought that Yahweh demonstrates his Lordship, even to present, guilt–laden Israel.[109] Only by way of suggestion does the threat in v 10b, the climax of the chapter, go beyond this. The threat that Israel will again live "in tents" attests that Israel's present cultic (v 12b) and economic life (vv 8f), with its political relations to foreign nations (v 2), will be totally destroyed. That period of Israel's history, which was so influenced by Canaanite culture and religion, comes to an end. Above everything this means: all hindrances to hearing the prophetic word will be removed; a con-

text will be created in which Yahweh and his prophets confront Israel anew, like the earlier "days of meeting."[110] Nevertheless, Hosea does not yet speak of a new phase of the saving history. This is precisely what Hosea's use of the Jacob and Moses stories shows: the history of man's apostasy indeed prepares its own end (vv 2a, 3b, 12b, 15b), but not the end of God's actions and thus of saving history itself (vv 4f, 10, 13f).

The call to new obedience to the prophetic word by genuine *return* comes only indirectly (vv 5, 7, 11, 14). This call had an increased significance for the tradition of these words in Judah, which perhaps already began when these sayings were given written form; the reference to Judah in v 1b suggests such a conclusion. The prophets and Levites who formed the opposition became increasingly oriented toward Judah as destruction approached the Northern Kingdom; there they held up Ephraim's march toward catastrophe as an example for the Southern Kingdom. This resulted in the Judaic redaction of the book, recognizable in v 3a[111] and in the doxological response of the congregation in Judah when it heard Hosea's words.[112] Thus chap. 12, which is concerned with Israel's history has in turn a history of its own.

As a segment in the further development of saving history this passage achieves a significance similar to that of the Jacob and Moses stories in Ephraim's history at the time of Hosea. It provides Old Testament models for man's behavior and for God's action in Jesus Christ. Moreover, this text is an aid in (1) laying bare the offenses committed by those who misjudge or who reproach the witnesses to Jesus Christ.[113] (2) It helps us in our expectations of the future by directing us only to the saving history—to which the prophetic and apostolic word attests—of the Lord of all history, whom we recognize in Christ (vv 3, 4, 10, 14, 15; cf. Mk 1:15). Finally, (3) it helps us put our confidence not in our own skills, strength, and piety, but in the superior power of the Lord (vv 2, 5–7, 8f, 12; Rev 3:17–19).

---

107 See the commentary on vv 4 and 13.
108 See the commentary on v 5aα.
109 V 15b; אדני‎ occurs only here in Hosea.
110 See the commentary on 12:10.
111 See textual note "h."
112 V 6; see the commentary.
113 Vv 1, 4, 11, 12, 13; cf. Gal 1:6–9; 2 Th 2:14; Lk 10:16).

**Israel's Revolt Against Her
Deliverer Leads to Death**

**Bibliography**

J. L. McKenzie
"Divine Passion in Osee," *CBQ* 17 (1955): 287–99.

H. G. May
"The Fertility Cult in Hosea," *AJSL* 48 (1932):
76–98.

E. Sellin
"Hosea und das Martyrium des Mose," *ZAW* 46
(1928): 26–33.

M. Testuz
"Deux fragments inédits des manuscrits de la Mer
Morte," *Semitica* 5 (1955): 38–39.

R. Vuilleumier–Bessard
"Osée 13:12 et les manuscrits," *Revue de Qumran* 1
(1958/59): 281–82.

E. Zolli
"Il significato di *rd* e *rtt* in Osea 12:1 e 13:1,"
*Rivista degli Studi Orientali* 32 (1957): 371–74.

# 13

1   When Ephraim spoke (there was) terror;[a]
     he was ⟨exalted⟩[b] in Israel.
       He incurred guilt with the Baal and
        died.

2   And now they sin further:
     they make for themselves a molten
       image
     from their silver ⟨according to the
       type⟩[c] of the idols.
     All of it[d] is the work of craftsmen.
       They say to[e] themselves:
        "Those who sacrifice[f] men[f] kiss
         calves."

3   Therefore they shall be like morning mist,
     like dew that vanishes early,[g]
     like chaff ⟨blown⟩[h] from the threshing
       floor,
     like smoke (that rises) from the window.

a   Unique in the Old Testament, this word is now attested in 1QH 4, 33, with the same meaning as that
found in α′ (φρίκην), σ′ θ′ (τρόμον), *V* (*horror*). *G*
misread it as the more familiar תרת and made it the
object of נשא; the latter is also done by α′ σ′; cf.
רֶטֶט in Jer 49:24.

b   There is no certain evidence (Na 1:5; Hab 1:3) for
the intransitive meaning of the qal form (Gispen; cf.
Gesenius–Buhl). The following הוא rather suggests
a nominal clause parallel to v 1aα and thus the nip'al
participle נִשָּׂא (Oort, Marti); *S* (Wellhausen, Harper) presupposes נָשִׂיא; thus also Zolli, "Significato,"
who interprets רתת on the basis of the Arabic *ratt*
("ruler") as an explanatory gloss on נָשִׂיא.

c   Literally: "according to the model" (כְּתַבְנִית), corresponds with *G* (κατ' εἰκόνα), *V* (*quasi similitudinem*)
and Is 44:13, whereas *M* ("according to their insight" or "technical skill") can only be explained
with uncertainty as an abbreviated form of כתבונתם
(Gesenius–Kautzsch § 91e).

d   Literally: "its entirety"; the singular suffix proves
the necessity of taking the verse's third line of three
stresses as an appositive to the second line.

e   Cf. 7:2.

f   Nor did the ancient versions consider the grammatical construction a *genitivus explicativus* ("sacrificing
men," i.e., "men who sacrifice"). אדם is usually
regarded as the accusative object; to be sure, *G*
(θύσατε) *V* (*immolate*) presuppose זִבְחוּ, which simplifies the grammar.

g   Concerning asyndeton and the adverbial function
of the first participle, cf. Grether § 87n; Joüon § 177g;
also P. Wernberg–Møller, "Observations on the
Hebrew Participle," *ZAW* 71 (1959): 65.

h   Read יְסֹעַר pu'al, which is required by מץ as its subject, instead of the po'el ("he blows") in *M*.

| | |
|---|---|
| **4** But I am Yahweh your God[i] | |

**4** But I am Yahweh your God[i]
 from the land of Egypt.
 You know no God but me,
 there is no savior besides[j] me.
**5** I ⟨fed⟩[k] you in the wilderness,
 in the land of drought.[l]
**6** And in accord with[m] their pasture
 they were filled;
 they were filled, and their heart was
 lifted up.
 Therefore they forgot me.
**7** So I became[n] like the[o] lion to them,
 like a[o] panther I[p] will lurk
 along the way.
**8** I will attack them like a[q] she—bear
 who[r] is robbed of her young,
 and tear open the enclosure of their
 heart.
 Then ⟨the dogs shall devour them⟩,[s]
 wild beasts shall mutilate[t] them.

i  *G* inserts: "Who founds the heavens and creates the earth, whose hands created all the hosts of heaven, and I have not instructed you to follow them; and I delivered you"; cf. the previous insertion in 12:10 (textual note "r" on 12:10).

j  On negatives used as prepositions, cf. Brockelmann, *Syntax* § 118.

k  *G* (ἐποίμαινόν σε) attests רְעִיתִיךָ, similarly *T S V*, which *M* also presupposes in v 6a. *M* ("I knew you"), influenced by v 4b, misread ר as ד and added a second ' (from the preceding word אֲנִי).

l  *G* offers a free interpretation (ἐν γῇ ἀνοικήτῳ); Koehler–Baumgartner ("country of fever") relates the word to the Akk. *la'ābu* ("to punish with fever"); but cf. Gesenius–Buhl and v 6, where regions of hunger, not of disease, are indirectly presupposed.

m  כמרעיתם has the grammatical sense of a nominal circumstantial clause; this renders the following imperfect consecutive understandable with no change required in the text. According to *S* (literally: וּרְעִיתִם), the vocalization כְּמוֹ רְעִיתִים might be possible; כְּמוֹ רְעוֹתָם is also worthy of consideration.

n  *G* (καὶ ἔσομαι) and *V* (*et ego ero*) have already harmonized this continuation (imperfect waw–consecutive) of the narrative tense from v 6 with the following imperfect forms (cf. Keil).

o  Unlike v 3a; 5:12, 14; 14:6, here the particle of comparison has no article, as often occurs, e.g., in 13:8; 14:9; Nu 23:24; Job 16:14; cf. Joüon § 137i.

p  *G S* read אַשּׁוּר, the more familiar vocalization, which would be supported by שָׁם (v 8b) only if v 8a did not separate v 7b from v 8b, and if שָׁם could not be interpreted in a temporal sense as well (see p. 227). If אַשּׁוּר is read, at the beginning of the verse וָאֱהִי must be replaced by וַאֲנִי because of the parallelism.

q  See textual note "o."

r  Concerning the absence of the feminine ending when a word is naturally feminine, cf. Brockelmann, *Syntax* § 16a.

s  *G* (καὶ καταφάγονται αὐτοὺς ἐκεῖ σκύμνοι δρυμοῦ) presupposes a plural subject in the third person, perhaps יֹאכְלוּם שָׁם כְּלָבִים. The subject in the parallel v 8bβ supports *G*. *M* ("and then I will devour them like a lion" = *V*) is understandable as a misreading because of v 8a; in no other instance does Hosea use the word לָבִיא for a lion (cf. v 7 and 5:14); the return to the lion simile, which was left after v 7a, seems strange as well.

t  Actually "split, rip open" (14:1); here בקע is used, as in 2 Kgs 2:24.

u  *S* attests שַׁחֲתוֹךָ. *M* ("he destroys you") perhaps incorrectly has the subject of v 8b continue as the subject of v 9a. *G* (τῇ διαφθορᾷ σου, Ισραηλ, τίς βοηθήσει;) interprets the word nominally: "Who will help you in your destruction?" *V* is similar (*perditio tua Israel: tantummodo in me auxilium tuum*).

v  *M* ("for in me, in your help" or "indeed, with me, with your help [he destroys you]"[?]) remains obscure. According to *G* (see textual note "u") and *S*,

9  ⟨I⟩ᵘ will destroy you, O Israel.
 ⟨Who will help you?⟩ᵛ
10 ⟨Where⟩ʷ then is your king,
 that he may save you,
 ⟨and⟩ˣ all your ⟨rulers⟩ʸ
 that they may ⟨help⟩ᶻ you,
 of whom you said:
 "Give me king and rulers!"?
11 I gaveᵃᵃ you a king in my anger,
 and I tookᵃᵃ him away in my fury.
12 Ephraim's transgression is bound up,
 his sin is preserved.
13 When the pangs of birth come for him,
 he is an unwiseᵇᵇ son.
 At the proper time,ᶜᶜ he does not
  present himself
  at the mouth of the womb.ᵈᵈ
14 Shall I redeem them from the power of
 Sheol?ᵉᵉ
 Shall I ransom them from death?ᵉᵉ
 Whereᶠᶠ are your thorns,ᵍᵍ O Death?
 Whereᶠᶠ is your sting,ʰʰ O Sheol?

  מִי בְעֹזְרֶיךָ (cf. Ps 118:7 and Grether, § 89g) should probably be read. *M* becomes explicable if we assume that בִּעְזֹרֶךָ developed from כִּי עֶזְרְךָ as a result of dittography (cf. Nyberg, 102); then כִּי might introduce a noun clause which is the subject of another clause: "It has led to your destruction, O Israel, that your help was in me" (cf. Brockelmann, *Syntax* § 159a).

w *G* (ποῦ) *V T* have read אַיֵּה or they understood אֱהִי as הַיָּא (likewise probably *M* [metathesis?]), for אֵפוֹא primarily follows interrogative particles (cf. אֵיה אֵפוֹא in Ju 9:38; Is 19:12; Job 17:15 and Brockelmann, *Syntax* § 55b); cf. also v 14b.

x *S* presupposes וְכֹל rather than the reading of *M* ("in"), which is connected with its misreading of the following noun; see textual note "y."

y שָׂרֶיךָ (Houtsma, "Bijdrage tot de kritiek en verklaring van Hosea," *ThT* 9 [1875]: 73) is presupposed in v 10bβ and restores the corresponding parallelism expected in v 10a: מַלְכְּךָ ‖ שָׂרֶיךָ. *M* ("in all your cities") may be an ancient misreading (see textual note "x").

z וְיִשְׁפְּטֶךָ (Procksch, Lippl) completes the parallelism with וְיוֹשִׁיעֶךָ (cf. textual note "y"). *G* still presupposes parallel verb forms (διασωσάτω σε ... κρινάτω σε). *M* ("and your judges") is a result of the preceding incorrect reading and is similar to the diction of 2 Sam 7:7 (text according to 1 Chr 17:6), 11; 15:4.

aa *G* σ' θ' presuppose imperfect consecutive verbs; but the imperfects in *M* denote repeated actions that continue into the present; cf. Brockelmann, *Syntax* § 42d; Hos 4:13; 11:2b, 4γ.

bb Cf. Brockelmann, *Syntax* § 13b.

cc The Hexaplaric and the Lucianic recensions of *G* probably read "because now" (כִּי עָתָּ [διότι νῦν]).

dd Literally: "the place where the sons burst forth."

ee The context requires that the clauses, like 4:16b and 7:13b (see p. 91), be understood as questions. In addition to the word order, the audience would perceive that they are questions, primarily from the accent upon the words in oral speech; cf. Brockelmann, *Syntax* §§ 53, 54a; Joüon § 161a; Beer–Meyer § 111c.

ff α' σ' (ἔσομαι) θ' (καὶ ἔσται) *V* (ero) derive אֱהִי from היה; *G* (ποῦ) reads as in v 10a; see textual note "w."

gg Cf. Koehler–Baumgartner II דֶּבֶר; the word is usually understood to mean "plague"; the parallel קֶטֶב ‖ דבר also occurs in Ps 91:6; see pp. 164f. *G* (ἡ δίκη σου) need not be a corrected spelling of νίκη made within the Greek text's transmission (Nyberg, 104f; he supposes that the Hebrew text used by *G* contained an infinitive construct of נבר = "to conquer"; cf. 1 Cor 15:55); rather, it is a translation of דָּבָר (Quell, *TDNT* 2, 174; cf. Ziegler *Duodecim prophetae*); accordingly, α' translates ῥήματα; θ' has δίκη.

hh Read *qŏṭŏbkā* (from קֶטֶב; Gesenius–Kautzsch § 93q) by analogy to the syllabic division of gutturals.

| | |
|---|---|
| | Compassion[ii] is unknown to my eyes. |

**15** Indeed! Though he ⟨flourishes⟩[jj]
    among ⟨the reeds⟩,[jj]
    the eastwind shall come as Yahweh's wind,
    which rises from the wilderness.
    Then his fountain shall be ⟨exhausted⟩,[kk]
    then his spring shall run dry.
    It shall plunder the ⟨treasury⟩[ll]
    of every costly possession.

**14:1**
**[13:16]** Samaria must bear her guilt,[mm]
    for she has rebelled against her God.
    They shall fall by the sword,
    their children shall be dashed in pieces,
    their pregnant women[nn] ripped open.

ii    H. Engländer, "Rashi's Grammatical Comments," *HUCA* 17 (1942–3): 473, "R. on נֹחַם notes that the מ is a root letter and correctly notes that this form is like נֹעַם. R. then notes that if the text word were derived from נח the form would be נֵחָם."

jj    *M* ("he flourishes among brothers") is traceable to a misunderstanding of the infrequent word אָחוּ (Gen 41:2, 18; Job 8:11; cf. Ugaritic 'aḥ = "meadow" and F. Horst, *Hiob*, BK XVI, 131f); *M* is the result of taking מ from the original מַפְרִיא and joining it to אח. This misinterpretation of "reeds" as "brothers" requires changes in the text. *G* (διαστελεῖ) *S V* presuppose יַפְרִיד ("indeed, he separates brothers from one another"), which, as an allusion to the deportation, nevertheless remains a possibility (Dingermann, "Massora–Septuaginta," 63), although it would be necessary to bracket the phrase as a gloss (May, "Fertility Cult"); cf. v 1a in the light of the following threats; cf. textual note "kk."

kk    וְיֵבַשׁ is more probable than *M* ("and he will be ashamed of himself," which is explicable in view of the misunderstanding in v 15a) because of the parallel ויחרב and also from *G* (ἀναξηρανεῖ = וְיוֹבִישׁ?) *S* and *V*. The new fragment from the Dead Sea (Testuz, "Deux fragments," 38–9) also reads יבש instead of שׁיבוֹ. This becomes even more significant, for in 14:1a of the fragment, a ו denoting a vowel letter occurs in the word ובאלוהיה, which is absent in *M*. To be sure, *G* here reproduces causative forms —also for the neighboring verbs—after it mistook יהוה for the subject in v 15bα (ἐπάξει καύσωνα ἄνεμον κύριος); as a result, עָלָה had to be misread for a preposition (ἐπ' αὐτόν = עָלָיו or עָלֶיהָ).

ll    *G* (τὴν γῆν αὐτοῦ καί) reads the more familiar אַרְצוֹ and must therefore dissolve the *status constructus* form.

mm   *G* (ἀφανισθήσεται) misreads תִּשַּׁם (as in 5:15; 10:2): "she shall be desolated."

nn    The later syntax requires וְהָרִיּוֹתָם תְּבֻקַּעְנָה, but agreement of subject and predicate was often neglected, especially with a third plural feminine (Gesenius–Kautzsch § 145u).

## Form

Chapter 13:1 begins a different accusation against Ephraim, who is named anew; no stylistic or thematic connections with the previous chapter are recognizable in the following verses. A new and completely different theme is not found until 14:2, where Israel is the new addressee.

The various rhetorical units in 13:1–14:1 can be distinguished with little difficulty. To begin with, vv 1–3 form a clearly structured judgment speech. The motivation occurs first (vv 1–2); it mentions the defendant's earlier deeds (v 1) as well as the "present" guilt of which he is accused (v 2). "Therefore" (לכן) introduces the announcement of punishment in the form of a verdict that stipulates the consequences of the guilt.[1] The accused party is always spoken of in the third person. The "I" of Yahweh's personal speech does not appear.

It is otherwise in v 4. Although the new saying is connected with the foregoing verses by the copula, and the addressee is not mentioned again,[2] the beginning of a different rhetorical unit is clearly recognizable. The self–introduction formula, in which Yahweh speaks in the first person, does not initiate an announcement of disaster, as in 12:10. Rather, this formula—here resembling its usage in the proclamations of divine law, as in 12:10—occurs in a form corresponding to Dtn 5:6. To be sure, the proclamation of the divine will in v 4 has been changed into a kind of "hymnic self–praise" that lauds Yahweh's uniqueness for Israel. Verse 4bα might of course be understood as a prohibition reminiscent of apodictic law, but the parallel noun clause in v 4bβ suggests an indicative interpretation of v 4bα; compare the arrangement of the clauses with Ex 20:3.[3] This "self–praise" introduces further details of the plaintiff's deeds (v 5), leading finally, by way of the earlier history of its defendant, to the guilt in question, guilt which arose from the defendant's common experiences with the plaintiff. Thus vv 4–6 are a part of the plaintiff's speech. The address to the second person in vv 4–5 stems from the use of the traditional self–introduction formula and from the lively dispute which calls the opponent's attention to the known facts of the case. The direct address to the defendant is also part of the dispute previous to its presentation before the court.[4] When the case passes from the preliminary hearing to the actual accusation in v 6, it is made before the court in the third person form. Verse 7 is probably a part of the accusation in that it, like vv 1b and 13, reports how the previous penalties were unsuccessful. This would assume that $M$, not $G$ $S$, preserves the original text.[5] The transition to the announcement of punishment is made, at the latest, in v 8. Thus vv 4–8 belong together as a complex judgment speech (with a lengthy preliminary report) in the form of a first person divine speech.

Although the divine speech continues in vv 9–11, Israel is the new addressee; the direct address continues through v 11. This passage is a threat of judgment in a special form which, by means of scornful expressions,[6] emphasizes the irrevocability of the punishment. As a rhetorical unit, vv 9–11 should quite probably be set off from v 8a, where the defendant is spoken of in the

strict form of the announcement (third person). However, if the threat, formulated in expressions of scorn but without a motivation clause, were to be considered a completely independent saying within the context of an accusation, it would be entirely without analogy. The direct address form is best accounted for by supposing that Hosea's listeners voiced an objection which optimistically rejected the proclamation of Yahweh's intervening punishment and its destructive consequences (v 8a, b).

It would appear that v 12 begins a completely new unit. In vv 12–13 the guilt is established and Ephraim is named once again. In v 14, first the false hopes are rejected, perhaps hopes which the audience expressed after v 13.[7] This might also account for the transition from the third person singular in vv 12f to the third person plural in v 14, which occurs elsewhere as well (vv 14–15; 14:1a–b). Then the announcement follows, which is developed in v 15–14:1. In 14:1a the verdict is briefly expressed once again. Yet, despite this formal independence, I am reluctant to separate completely 13:12–14:1 from the previous verses. Neither theme nor structure of the saying permits this. The announcement (v 14) takes up not only the first person form, corresponding to vv (4–)8–11, but also the interrogatory style of the words of scorn (cf. v 14a with v 10a). More significantly, there is an allusion to the theme characteristic of chap. 13—in contrast to the earlier chapters—insofar as in this last saying (13:12–14:1), all the heaped–up transgression is viewed together with the previously executed but fruitless punishment.[7a] Moreover, in an otherwise unusual manner, the decreed judgment is the death penalty.[7b] Finally, with the word "bear guilt" (אשם), the summary of the verdict in 14:1a picks up the introductory accusation in 13:1b; the threat, with the word "rip open" (בקע) repeats a word that appears elsewhere in Hosea only in 13:8b. Thus 13:1–14:1 surely presents a transmission unit in line with the sketches of the prophet's sayings. It contains at least four

1 As in 2:8, 11, 16; Is 5:13, 24 and Am 7:17, עַל־כֵּן introduces the announcement in 4:3; Is 9:16; Jer 5:6. See Boecker, *Redeformen*, 149–59 and the commentary, pp. 65f; also C. Westermann, *Basic Forms of Prophetic Speech*, tr. Hugh Scott (Philadelphia: Westminster, 1967), 149.

2 By contrast, cf. the headings to the sketches of the prophet's words in 9:1 and 10:9.

3 See the translation above and cf. Zimmerli, "Jahwe," 186f [18f].

4 Boecker, *Redeformen*, 26ff; 57ff.

5 See textual note "n."

6 "Where now is your king?" Cf. Ju 9:38; Ps 115:2.

7 Cf. 4:16b and the commentary.

7a Cf. vv 12f with 13:1f and v 6f.

7b Cf. vv 14b, 15b, with vv 8, 9a, and also with 13:16, 3.

distinguishable rhetorical units: vv 1–3, 4–8, 9–11, 12–14:1.

Whereas 13:1–14:1 is closely related to chap. 12 in several respects, it is distinguished from the sketches contained in 4–11: (1) At least in two instances (vv 9–11, 12ff) the individual sayings are connected only according to their theme; the connections are not recognizable from the style alone.[8] (2) Exactly like 12:15, the closing verse (14:1) summarizes the verdict and penalty by repeating the chief catchword from the beginning (v 1).[9] (3) Unlike the transmission units in chaps. 4–11, 12 and 13 do not begin with a divine speech. (4) It may be significant that the expression "And I am Yahweh your God, from the land of Egypt," in addition to 13:4, is found only in 12:10 in Hosea. Finally, it should be noted that "therefore" (לכן), which introduces the verdict stipulating the consequences of the guilt, in addition to 13:3, occurs only in 2:8[6], 11[9], 16[14].

The metrical structure of the passage, once again, is only partially clear. Tricola are found primarily at the beginning (v 1?) and end (v 14:1b), and at the climax of the rhetorical units[10] where one line normally stands synthetically parallel to two synonymously parallel lines. Furthermore, clearly recognizable prosodic units are usually three–stress bicola in synonymous parallelism: v 2a, b; v 3a, b (four synonymous lines, as in 11:8!); vv 7, 8a, 14a; in addition there is a two–stress bicolon in v 15bα². These clearly distinguishable prosodic units present metaphors that impress themselves on the mind. Several asymetrical prosodic units, usually with a shorter second line, are striking because of their clear synonymous parallelism: vv 10a (cj.), 11, 15bα¹.

Hosea's metaphorical language possesses a bold quality (vv 7f, 13, 14bα) and an intuitive power (vv 3, 15). The style of the legal process gives his words a certain rhetorical vitality. Moreover, there are cultic elements (v 4) as well as scornful (vv 10a, 14a) and authoritative questions (v 14bα). These various elements are discussed below in detail in "Interpretation."

## Setting

We have noted that this scene's accusations differ from earlier ones in that they repeatedly allude to previous threats upon Israel's life which did not lead to her renewal: 13:1, 7, 13.[11] In the light of this, it must be concluded that the great danger of 733 lies far in the past and that a phase of relaxed political tension has led to a new increase of transgression (vv 2, 12) which went hand in hand with political optimism (vv 14a, 15a). This optimism seems to have been especially strengthened by Israel's dependence upon Egypt after the year 725.[12] However, Hosea already sees the dangerous storm approaching from the East under the leadership of Shalmaneser V (cf. vv 15b, 3, 8, 9 with 2 Kgs 17:5). Indeed, with its questions and pronouncements in vv 10 and 11, this scene is correctly understood only if King Hoshea ben Elah had already been imprisoned by the Assyrians.[13] The seldom mentioned city[14] of Samaria (otherwise only in 7:1; 8:5; 10:5, 7) and the unique announcement of its inhabitants' death points to the same period when the seige on the capital was approaching or had already begun. Accordingly, the sayings from this scene were very probably proclaimed around the year 724. In point of fact, in none of the preceding scenes[15] had the prophet so powerfully spoken of Ephraim's irrepressible destruction. In comparison to the accusations, the threats (vv 3, 8–11, 14–14:1) occupy a disproportionately larger space than even in chap. 12 (vv 3, 10b, 12b, 15b), to say nothing of their insistence and harshness.

Yet in chap. 12 we saw the preliminary stage of the situation as it now stands.[16] We found reason to suppose that at the time of those sayings, Hosea was no longer in Samaria, but had been driven to the southern border. The sayings in 13:1–14:1 would be more understandable if they were proclaimed in this area than in the capital. The structural relationship between the sketches in 12 and 13:1–14:1 indicates that both sections are different kerygmatic units which belong together as one transmission complex.[17]

---

8   See p. 208.
9   See p. 217.
10  Is v 2b a two–stress tricolon? Verse 6 has a graduated
    parallelism and a shortened closing line which is a
    kind of echo (cf. 2:15b [13b]). Verse 14b is a three–
    stress tricolon.
11  Cf. the idea of "double guilt" expressed in 10:10
    (text is uncertain) and see the commentary.

12  2 Kgs 17:4; see the commentary on v 15a.
13  2 Kgs 17:4b; see the commentary on 10:3.
14  See p. 140 and Alt, "Stadtstaat," 299f.
15  On 10:1–8 see pp. 172f.
16  See pp. 208f.
17  See pp. 223f.

## Interpretation

■ **1** Once again the accusation begins with a reminiscence of Israel's previous history.[18] According to what is probably the original text,[19] v 1 speaks of Ephraim's preeminence in all of Israel as it was represented, e.g., by the Ephraimites Joshua (Josh 24:30) and Jeroboam I (1 Kgs 11:26; 12:20). But for Hosea "Ephraim," having long ago ceased to mean the tribe, denotes the region of Mount Ephraim,[20] where the royal residence of Samaria is located. From there, in the last two decades, issued many a political decision which brought "terror" to the other areas of the Northern Kingdom and also to Judah, so that "hearts shook as the trees of the forest shake before the wind" (Is 7:2; 2 Kgs 16:5). In his superiority Ephraim "incurred guilt through Baal," i.e., he contaminated the cult.[21] Ephraim will die out (4:10; 9:11ff, 16f) because he worshiped Baal, from whom he expected the growth and increase of life. This Hosea had repeatedly threatened.[22] In the meantime it has in fact happened: "and he died." Hosea probably looks back to the year 733 when Tiglath–pileser had torn to pieces the kingdom and the body politic. He referred to this as rape and abuse in 5:11; 8:8 says "Israel is devoured."[23] According to Israelite thought, a person who was imprisoned, oppressed by the enemy, or extremely ill was already overcome by the power of death. This often finds expression in the lamentations and hymns of thanksgiving.[24]

■ **2** In view of this it is not surprising that he who has entered the realm of death, "the utmost degree of uncleanness" (cf. Nu 9:6; 19:11ff), who can no longer offer praise to Yahweh,[25] "continues to sin." That is, Ephraim continues to fail Yahweh in his pagan worship.[26] After the catastrophe of 733 the people made idols with a new intensity, especially molten calf images patterned after Canaanite models; 8:4b–6 already presupposed such activity in an earlier period.[27] New in v 2 is that (1) the word מסכה—also used in Ex 32:4, 8 for the calf—denotes a molten image. The singular noun probably does not refer to a certain image, but rather to the oft–recurring design of small bronze statuettes overlaid with silver.[28] This is indicated by the plural forms "idols" (עצבים) and "calves" (עגלים). Also new (2) is the cultic precept—probably cited with irony: "those who sacrifice men should kiss calves." The words disclose the complete absurdity of the fertility rites. Human sacrifice is presupposed here, namely, the offering of the firstborn conceived in the sacral forests.[29] At the same time the idol receives the cultic kiss (1 Kgs 19:18). Such a death of children whom God loves (11:3f), accompanied by the veneration of a man–made calf idol is the height of perversity (Rom 1:22f). Such are the actions of those who enter the death realm of the pagan cult of Baal.

■ **3** The penalty introduced by לכן, immediately continuing v 2b, announces the judgment as the inevitable consequence of Ephraim's conduct. Whoever attempts to gain his life through Baal will lose it. He destroys himself, as the four similes of quickly vanishing objects makes clear. The first two similes also occur in another context.[30] They need not be considered secondary in v 3 simply because they also occur in 6:4b. They fit well with the meter and structure of the saying; cf. the repetition of 8:13bα in 9:9b.[31] A third simile of evanescence is added to that of morning mist and dew: chaff quickly blows away when tossed into the wind that howls across the threshing floor.[32] The fourth simile is that of smoke; as it rises from the chimney it promptly dissolves into nothing. "Window" (ארבה) can also denote the small opening in the pigeon loft,[33] as well as a

---

18  Cf. 9:10; 10:1, 9: 11:1ff; 12:3ff [2ff], 11f [10f], 13f [12f].
19  See textual notes "a" and "b."
20  See pp. 91, 153.
21  On "to be guilty" (אשם) see p. 89; on the worship of Baal cf. 1:2; 2:7ff [5ff]; 18f, [16f]; 4:10f; 9:10; 11:2 and the commentary on each passage.
22  מות qal ("to die") only in 13:1; hip'il in 2:5; 9:16.
23  Cf. 7:9; 2 Kgs 15:29 and p. 111.
24  Cf. v 14; on this topic see Chr. Barth, *Die Errettung vom Tode* (Zollikon, 1947), 102ff; G. von Rad, *Theology* 1, 387ff.
25  "Man's most characteristic mode of existence," von

Rad, *Theology* 1, 275f, 369.
26  "To miss," "to sin" (חטא) cf. 4:7; 8:11 and the commentary.
27  See pp. 139ff; cf. H. Schrade, *Der verborgene Gott* (Stuttgart, 1949), 170–74.
28  Cf. 8:4b (2:10bβ [8bβ]) and the commentary.
29  See pp. 14, 86f; cf. Jer 32:35; Lev 18:21; Dtn 18:10; 2 Kgs 16:3; 21:6; Ezek 16:20ff; 23:37; Ps 106:37–39; see Zimmerli, *Ezekiel*, 357.
30  Cf. 6:4b and the commentary.
31  See p. 158.
32  See p. 154; Is 17:13; Ps 14; Dalman, *Arbeit* 3, 126–39.
33  Is 60:8; Barrois, *Manuel* I, 341f.

window opening to the outdoors (Eccl. 12:3). Each of the similes serves to announce that the destruction will be total and corresponds therefore with 9:11.

■ **4**  In the sketch of this scene, a new saying follows in v 4. Perhaps it is the prophet's response to his audience's mention of the election traditions. In the style of the traditional proclamation of divine law, Hosea solemnly announces to his audience in direct address that Yahweh is the only God Israel knows; that besides him she has no helper.[34] This verse does not repeat a demand upon Israel, but rather praises the God who alone is her savior (cf. Is 43:11; 45:21).

■ **5**  This "self–praise" of the God of Israel continues in v 5, which connects the Wilderness with the Exodus tradition. "I" (אֲנִי) takes the place of the preceding "I" (אָנֹכִי), as in 5:14.

■ **6**  The "self–praise" spoken by the plaintiff in v 5 prepares for the evidence of guilt presented in v 6. Like a shepherd, Yahweh brought Israel into the land; there she became satiated.[35] The graduated parallelism accents this satiety and emphasizes its result, namely, the proud lifting up of Israel's heart. The intended goal of the report, the direct accusation, is first presented as the consequence introduced by "therefore" (עַל־כֵּן): Yahweh is forgotten. This thought also occurs in 2:15 where, similarly, its final position in the verse gives it a strong accent.[36] The expression forms a contrast to the right knowledge of God (cf. 13:4b). Like the phrase "knowledge of God," the idea of "forgetting" him refers to God's acts of salvation. The pride of Israel's heart has alienated her from God.

In the development of the accusation in vv 4–6 there first occurs a train of thought which the Deuteronomic paraenesis repeatedly uses by appropriating the main catchwords, although in Deuteronomy it is considerably expanded and is given the form of an exhortation (Dtn 8:11–20; 6:12–19 [11:15f]). Here we again recognize in Hosea one of the fathers of the early Deuteronomic movement. The same summary of the saving history

in Jeremiah (2:5ff) displays less dependence on Hosea.

■ **7**  According to M[37] v 7a is a report which (like v 1a) is still a part of the preliminary facts of the new announcement. Already in 733 the God of Hosea had declared himself a rending lion (שַׁחַל in 5:14). The shepherd had become the fatal enemy of his herd (c)᾽ 1 Sam 17:34; 1 Kgs 13:24). The mention of the lurking panther[38] has an imperfect verb also in M and thus applies to the present. שׁוּר means "to watch"; here it is used in the sense of "to lie in ambush." Unlike 14:9 the word has no accusative object, as in Jer 5:26. The idea is that Yahweh waits attentively, a thought expressed in 5:15 in a similar context. Various actions by Yahweh are pictured by different animals, each according to its own characteristics.

■ **8**  Not until v 8a does Hosea clearly proclaim Yahweh's judgment for the immediate future, as indicated by the new simile of the bear and by the two imperfect verbs placed at the head of their clauses. It would appear as though Hosea follows Amos' words concerning the day of Yahweh (5:18f): Those who think they can escape the lion will be met by a bear. However, both the structure and the vocabulary of Hosea's saying shows that he formulated it independently. For "lion" Amos has אֲרִי instead of שַׁחַל.[39] Like v 3 this saying also threatens Israel with total destruction, although here the imagery is much more gruesome. Yahweh himself is the attacking she–bear; robbed of her young, she is enraged. פָּגַשׁ describes not only a sudden encounter (1 Sam 25:20) but also a hostile attack (Ex 4:24). A picture of a bear ready to attack, its paws outstretched, may be seen in reproduction no. 511 of the seals in O. Weber's publication.[40] The "she–bear robbed of her cubs" (דֹּב שַׁכּוּל) is a metaphor for extreme danger also in Wisdom;[41] in apocalyptic[42] the bear is a voracious animal that tears open the chest (cf. also 2 Kgs 2:24). The expression "enclosure of their heart" (it occurs only here in the Old Testament) also appears to mean the chest, whose ribs protect the heart, the seat of life.[43] When it is "ripped

---

34  See p. 223.

35  Cf. 2:10, 15b and Wolff, "Wissen um Gott," 540 [190].

36  See pp. 40, 223.

37  See textual note "n."

38  The "striped" leopard; cf. Koehler–Baumgartner *Suppl*, 172.

39  See the commentary on 11:10.

40  D. Weber, *Altorientalische Siegelbilder* (Leipzig, 1920); cf. also *AOBAT*, no. 36 and M. Noth, "The Understanding of History in Old Testament Appocalyptic," in Noth, *Laws*, 208 [268].

41  Prv 17:12; 28:15; 1 Sam 17:34–37; 2 Sam 17:8.

42  Dan 7:5: "It had three ribs in its mouth between its teeth."

43  See pp. 83f.

open," the person is completely lost. Never before in Hosea has Yahweh pictured himself as such a drastic danger to Israel. Unlike v 8b, even 5:14 does not present such totally destructive consequences. However, I consider it improbable that the verse states that Yahweh himself devours his prey.[44] שָׁם (used temporally, as in Ps 36:13; 132:17) indicates what follows: after the she-bear has calmed her rage and killed her foe, wild beasts (and "the dogs") will make sure that no limb remains intact[45] and that nothing remains.

■ **9** When Yahweh becomes Israel's opponent she finds only enemies; none can help her. This thought, for which v 8 was the preparation, is expressed in direct address (second person singular) as a divine speech. Perhaps v 9 was evoked by the audience's reference to help from some political power (Egypt? v 15a [Cj.]; 12:2). In Jer 4:7 the word שׁחת denotes the destruction wrought by the lion. Hosea has already used the word in 11:9 for Yahweh's judgment. The perfect[46] expresses the event as irrevocable.[47] What was previously stated in 13:4 and earlier in 2:12b; 5:14bβ is repeated in v 9 with different words: Israel can find no help outside of Yahweh nor against Yahweh.[48]

■ **10** Apparently Israel has just lost her previous help.[49] Shalmaneser V has taken Hoshea ben Elah prisoner, along with other important political and military leaders. By sheer persistence Israel had persuaded Yahweh

to give her a king. It seems that the group of prophets and Levites gathered around Hosea was already acquainted with that tradition—later taken up into the Deuteronomistic history—which told how kingship was "wrested" from Yahweh.[50] In this verse it becomes quite plain that the roots of Hosea's criticisms of kingship go deeper than the present grievances.[51] Almost like the Baal cult (cf. v 4 after vv 1–3), kingship from the outset was in opposition to Yahweh's lordship. Before Hosea's time, such opposition is attested only in 1 Sam 10:27 and in Jotham's fable, recorded in Ju 9.[52]

■ **11** In Hosea's view, kingship was only granted to Israel in Yahweh's wrath (cf. 9:15). The imperfect verbs refer to all the kings from Saul to Hoshea ben Elah, whom Yahweh in his wrath has just stripped of his royal office.[53]

■ **12** Although v 12 sounds like a new saying, it is fully intelligible only in the context of the previous verses, whose references to a long chain of transgressions reach back to the beginnings of kingship (v 10), and even to the conquest (v 6); in the last decade Israel's guilt has reached such proportions that Yahweh's disciplinary measures are in vain (13:1f, 7). Verse 12 says that Ephraim's transgression and sin[54] are "bound up," like a legal document which is bound together,[55] and that they are "preserved"[56] like a treasure, lest they be diminished. This saying is directed against those who

---

44   *M*; see textual note "s."

45   Here בקע pi‘el "to split" means "to rip into pieces"; on this thought, cf. 14:1 and textual note "t" to 13:8

46   See textual note "u."

47   Cf. 10:15; 9:7; 4:19; Brockelmann, *Syntax* § 41; Beer–Meyer § 101, 4.

48   See textual note "v." Calvin (*CR* LXX, 485) recognizes the actual excitement of the saying (based on the Hebrew text: "He has destroyed you, O Israel, because your help is in me"): "Surely I would never be lacking to you, but you close the door to me, and with your wickedness, you drive away my grace from reaching you. It follows, therefore, that you now perish through your own fault" [Trans.]. (*Et certe ego numquam tibi deessem, sed tu mihi occludis januam et repellis malitia tua gratiam meam, ne ad te usque perveniat. Sequitur ergo, te nunc perire propria culpa*). Cf. Luther (*WA* 13, 62, on v 9: "destroy"): "There begins the scoffing. You are lost. Your plans accomplish nothing. I will make sure that you see that you are nothing. I will show you that you must flee to

me for refuge" [Trans.]. (*Ibi incipit insultatio; es ist mit dir verloren, tua consilia nihil faciunt, ich wills mit dir machen, ut videas te nihil esse, ad me confugiendum esse monstrabo*).

49   See p. 224, "Setting."

50   1 Sam 8:6; cf. A. Weiser, "Samuel und die Vorgeschichte des israelitischen Königtums," *ZThK* 57 (1960): 144ff [also in his *Samuel* (Göttingen, 1962), 25ff].

51   Cf. 3:4; 7:3ff; 8:4; 9:15, and pp. 139, 167.

52   Cf. K. H. Bernhardt, "Das Problem der altorientalischen Königsideologie im AT," VT Suppl. 8 (1961): 139ff.

53   See pp. 114, 141, on אף as panting in anger and on עברה as the outbreak of wrath; here both are instruments used by Yahweh.

54   On the parallel of עון and חטאת see p. 145.

55   צרר in Is 8:16; cf. Job 14:17; 1 Sam 25:29.

56   צפן Ps 27:5; 31:20; cf. Ezek 7:22.

still dismiss the prophet's threat with optimistic expectations, who regard the question of their guilt as settled. The guilt, however, remains in effect, as though it were laid away in a nonrevisable legal record which the guilty party cannot obtain (cf. Jer 32:10–15). Thus v 12 might as easily conclude the foregoing as well as begin the following threats; but the defendant is spoken of in the third person, which relates the verse closer to v 13 than to v 11.

■ **13** Now a different metaphor describes the history of Ephraim's transgression, especially that of the last decades. The imagery of the "mother's birth pangs" is used for the first time in prophecy in connection with approaching disaster.[57] But in v 13 the metaphor is given a peculiar twist. Ephraim is pictured not as a woman giving birth but as the child who is to be born. He is boldly called an "unwise son" (here the interpretation mingles with the metaphor), i.e., he is an inept, inexperienced child who is unaware of what "the hour" requires. The truly wise man knows when the time is right (cf. Eccl 8:5). But Ephraim did not appear at the mouth of the womb at the time ordained by Yahweh. Drawn from Wisdom (as 8:7), this imagery expresses the same ideas found in the sayings about Israel's refusal to return at the time of judgment.[57a] Behind the metaphor stands the certainty that Yahweh sends judgment which, like the pangs of birth, is to bring Israel new life (cf. Is 66:7–9). That "no sons were born" is not a sign of their rejection for Hosea (as in 2 Kgs 19:3); rather, it points to the guilt of the unwise son who has rejected the "knowledge of God" (דעת אלהים vv 4–6; cf. 6:6).

■ **14** In the course of the accusation, v 14 presents a different metaphor. Perhaps the indictment in v 13 was countered with the objection that Yahweh could act as Israel's true "midwife," since he can command the powers of "Sheol" and "death." Or like 4:16b,[58] v 14a[59] may call into question another response to Hosea from the audience; they possibly quoted a cultic hymn which was influenced by Canaanite thought and mythology. The word "to redeem" (גאל) does not otherwise occur in Hosea's vocabulary. "To ransom" (פדה) is found again only in 7:13b, in a similar rhetorical question.[60] In the light of v 13 this quotation may well allude to the idea that the womb threatens to become a grave and a place of the dead.[61]

Hosea leaves the questions with which he dismissed the words of his opponents (v 14a) and asks an authoritative question (v 14bα). This fills the concept of "Sheol" and "death" with new meaning. In the threat now issued by the prophet, they represent the foreign powers which menace Israel's life.[62] These nations stand under the commanding authority of Israel's God (cf. 10:10). If those hostile nations punish Israel with the "thorns" and "stings" of the drover or foreman, then the imagery of tormenting and distressing death is clear (cf. Josh 23:13; Nu 33:55; Ju 8:7). To be sure, only in Ps 91:6 are "thorn" (דבר) and "sting" (קטב) mentioned in connection with a humanly wielded weapon ("arrow" in v 5). In most cases these words denote pestilence,[62a] which would naturally fit here as the instrument of death and Sheol as well. In each instance Yahweh refuses to be "compassionate." Hosea distinguishes between "compassion" (נחם) and "regret, remorse" (נחמים 11:8).

■ **15** With a deictic כי[63] the prophet returns to the unwise son Ephraim—last mentioned in v 13bα— referring to him by the word "he" (הוא). In the presumably original text[64] a new metaphor pictures him as "flourishing among the reeds." "Reeds" (אחו) is an Egyptian loan word[65] that probably alludes to the time when Israel attempted to cut her ties with Assyria by becoming dependent upon Egypt.[66] Yet the "east wind" (cf. 12:2a) is not quiet for long. It is "Yahweh's wind" (cf. 8:7a; Is 40:7), summoned by him as an instrument of death's power (v 14bα). The storm of Assyrian troops approaches from the wilderness (cf. 8:1; Is 5:26–30). Hosea continues to clothe his threat in metaphor. The

---

57  Cf. Jer 6:24; 22:23 and then Is 26:17 and thereafter the apocalyptic literature.

57a  Cf. 5:4; 11:5; cf. especially 5:8–7:16 with 5:15; 6:4; 7:2, 10, 16 (cj.).

58  See the commentary.

59  See p. 223, "Form."

60  גאל occurs parallel to פדה also in Jer 31:11; Ps 69:19; on this theme, see Ps 103:4.

61  Cf. Jer 20:17; Job 3:11; 10:18; further, cf. Ps 139:13, 15 and Kraus, *Psalmen* 2, 920.

62  See the commentary on 13:1b; cf. Is 28:15.

62a  See textual note "gg."

63  See p. 135.

64  See textual note "jj."

65  F. Horst, *Hiob* BK XVI/1 (Neukirchen, 1969²), 132.

66  Cf. 12:2b and "Setting," p. 224.

sirocco[67] will dry up every fountain and spring; although Ephraim believes he will flourish from the waters of the Nile, he will be overcome by the scorching heat of death. The imagery continues until v 15bα. Now, in v 15bβ, on the horizon appear the plundering troops of Shalmaneser V, who will leave nothing of value behind them.[68] What Hosea threatened in vv 3 and 8 in metaphorical language now becomes clearly expressed.

■ **14:1** In the summary presented in the closing verse[69] Hosea speaks even more plainly. Now the royal city of "Samaria" is hit. Her rebellion against God has made her guilt[70] final. The new word Hosea uses to designate her revolt, מרה, is synonymous with סרר (4:16; 9:15), and can denote the obstinacy (Dtn 21:20; Ps 78:8) of the unmanageable son (11:1ff). The profusion of metaphors in the previous verses yields to hard facts announcing death in the summary of the verdict as well as in the three–part announcement of punishment: "They shall fall by the sword" (cf. 7:16). After the sword has made its way from city to city (11:6), it now strikes the inhabitants of the capital. The prophet already foresees the three–year seige of the city (2 Kgs 17:5). Even the most helpless among the people will be subjected to Assyria's brutality: the children shall be "dashed in pieces";[71] pregnant women will be "ripped open" (cf. 13:8). Thus in the conclusion Hosea returns to the theme of childlessness and extermination (4:10; 9:11–16). Baal, the Canaanite god of fertility, brings Israel ultimately to her death (cf. 13:1).

**Aim**

Once again we see all the characteristics of a scene in which Hosea spoke publicly. The deepest shadows of the approaching, final catastrophe fall across this scene. Seldom before has the prophet summoned forth death so directly as he does here (v 14; cf. v 1); never before has he spoken openly of death so comprehensively and with such intuitive description and assailing force.[72] In three, ever–widening onslaughts, the prophetic sayings each voice the same intention of destruction (vv 3, 8, 15–14:1).

The passage is like a final reckoning, a last word from the messenger, before the ultimate collapse of what remained of an independent nation of Israel. With the collapse of its last fortress, the 150–year–old royal city, it falls to Assyria's sword, nay more, to the attack of Yahweh. Hosea shows that the approaching political catastrophe is a *catastrophe of the saving history*. Only as such can the destruction be understood in relation to the God of Israel. Therefore, as he threatens with death, the prophet once again attests to Israel's beginnings with the words of divine "self–praise" (vv 4–5). Hosea shows that Israel's guilt consists in her pride during times of plenteous "pasture" (v 6); in her obstinate independence and actions of self–assistance (v 10); in her deafness to the recent judgment upon her idolatry (vv 1, 7, 12f).[73]

The path leading to new life for Israel does not pass by her guilt, as the people evidently thought.[74] Her guilt is bound up and preserved (v 12). No political alliance[75] can provide a helper who could stave off Yahweh's intention to destroy an Israel that denied her only helper (v 4) through the fertility cults (v 2) and political tactics (vv 9ff). Because Ephraim rebels against the God who wants to save Israel, the ancient saving history comes to an end for the Northern Kingdom with the fall of Samaria (14:1).

For the New Testament as well, the path to new life does not pass by guilt or death. The difference, however, is that guilt and death are overcome for Israel—and at the same time for all nations—through Jesus Christ. Therefore in 1 Cor 15:55 Paul could cite Hosea's words in 13:14bα according to G. Paul takes the command which summons death for Israel and makes it a mockery of death because God "gives us the victory through our Lord Jesus Christ." Hos 13 can indirectly help the world recognize the new, ultimate gift of God in Christ, which is given to all men in unconditional forgiveness

---

67   See the commentary on 12:2.
68   On "to plunder" (שסה), cf. 2 Kgs 17:20; Is 17:14; Jer 30:16.
69   See p. 223, "Form."
70   On "to be guilty" (אשם), see p. 26.
71   See pp. 188.
72   Cf. only the audition account in 9:10–17 and 10:9–15.

73   See p. 228.
74   V 14a; see the commentary.
75   Cf. v 15a and the commentary.

and with the seal of Jesus' resurrection from the dead.

In light of this, Hos 13 also takes on a new and direct contemporary significance. Christianity endured the first persecutions and it saw war and the power of destruction march through the world even after the time of Christ. But these Christians now viewed death and its realm—which in Hos 13:14 stood under the command of Yahweh—under the power and authority of the exalted Christ, as the allusion to Hos 13:14 in Rev 6:8 indicates. Yet not merely this one verse but the entire chapter can help the Christian recognize the seriousness of the statement: "It is a fearful thing to fall into the hands of the living God" (Heb 10:31), especially if one begins to "outrage the Spirit of grace" (v 29). The Lutheran Confessions have therefore readily emphasized the words of Hos 13:9 in the following translation: "Israel, thou hast plunged thyself into misfortune, but in me alone is thy salvation" (*Perditio tua ex te est, Israel, tantummodo in me salus tibi*).[76]

Jesus of Nazareth did not come to establish safety and security but rather to call to discipleship and faith. The New Testament community proclaimed that the whole world can find life in him, but he who shuns him is headed for death. For those who "outrage the spirit of grace" the saving history of the New Testament can also come to an end, as the ancient saving history ended for Samaria in 721. Samaria was not all of Israel, and the end of its history was not the end of God's way. Nevertheless, each generation should take seriously Hosea's words as a warning, lest it, too, become like Samaria.

---

76  Solid Declaration 11.7 (cf. 62), *The Book of Concord*, ed. Theodore G. Tappert (Philadelphia: Fortress, 1959), 617.

### The Healing of Spontaneous Love

#### Bibliography

B. W. Anderson
"The Book of Hosea," *Int* 8 (1954): 301ff.

G. R. Driver
"Difficult Words in the Hebrew Prophets," *Studies in OT Prophecy*, ed. H. H. Rowley (Edinburgh: T. & T. Clark, 1950): 67f.

R. Gordis
"The Text and Meaning of Hosea 14:3," *VT* 5 (1955): 88–90.

A. Peter
"Das Echo von Paradieserzählung und Paradiesmythus unter besonderer Berücksichtigung der prophetischen Endzeitschilderung," unpub. diss. Univ. of Würzburg (Würzburg, 1947).

H. Wh. Robinson
*The Cross of Hosea* (Philadelphia: Westminster, 1949), 59ff.

Th. Sprey
"[Syr.] משובה-תיבותא," *VT* 7 (1957): 408–10.

M. Testuz
"Deux fragments inédits des manuscrits de la Mer Morte," *Semitica* 5 (1955): 38–39.

# 14

*Song of Songs 2 : 4*

**2 [1]**  Return, O Israel,
 to Yahweh your God.
  For you have stumbled upon your guilt.

**3 [2]**  Take words with you
 and return to Yahweh.
  Say to him:
 "Will you ⟨not⟩[a] take away guilt?
 Accept the word.[b]
  We offer the ⟨fruit⟩[c] of our lips.

**4 [3]**  Assyria shall not save us,
 we will not ride upon horses,
nor will we any longer say: ⟨Our god⟩[d]
 to the work of our hands.
  [Since in you an orphan finds mercy.]"[e]

a  *G* (μή) still presupposes בַּל; concerning the asseverative meaning (= *nonne*) of the particle, cf. Gordis, "Hos 14:3," 89, and Ps 16:2; see textual note "b" on 10:9. It is possible to understand *M* ("whole") as a misreading, but syntactically it is hardly conceivable as the original reading, even when regarded as a "noun used as an adverb followed by a genitive clause" ("as often as you forgive iniquity," Brockelmann, *Syntax* § 144, Nyberg, 107f; see textual note "d" on 7:2), since it does not fit with what follows.

b  Cf. Gordis, "Hos 14:3," 89f: טוֹב = דְּבָה (Neh 6:19; Ps 39:3a). Or: "Accept what is good" (?); cf. Prv 13:2; 12:14.

c  *G* (καρπὸν χειλέων) reads פְּרִים שְׂפָתֵינוּ. The enclitic מ is an archaic Canaanite case ending; cf. R. T. O'Callaghan, "Echoes of Canaanite Literature in the Psalms," *VT* 4 (1954): 170f; Beer–Meyer § 45 l. It is unnecessary to place the מ with שפתנו (= מִשְׂפָּתֵנוּ); thus recently M. Mansoor, *Revue de Qumran 3* (1961), 391f. The context shows that *M* ("as young bulls") is a misreading.

d  *G* translates Θεοὶ ἡμῶν.

e  *G* reads יְרֻחַם and distorts the meaning thus: ὁ ἐν σοὶ ἐλεήσει ὀρφανόν. θ is similar to *M*, likewise the Fragment from the Dead Sea: ירוחם (Testuz, "Deux Fragments"). As an abbreviated form of יַעַן אֲשֶׁר as in 1 Kgs 3:19; 8:33, etc., אֲשֶׁר (θ': ὅτι) appears to

| 5 [4] | I will heal their apostasy.[f] |
| | I will love[g] them spontaneously.[h] |
| | [For my anger has turned away from him[i]]. |
| 6 [5] | I will be as dew to Israel; |
| | he shall flower like a lily, |
| | [j]shall strike root[k] like the forest |
| | of Lebanon;[l] |
| 7 [6] | his shoots shall spread out, |
| | that his splendor[m] may be like the olive tree, |
| | his fragrance like the forest of Lebanon.[n] |
| 8 [7] | ⟨They shall⟩[o] again dwell in ⟨my⟩[p] shadow, |
| | shall grow grain.[q] |
| | His[r] fame ⟨shall⟩[s] flourish like a vine, |
| | like the wine of Lebanon.[t] |

be a secondary prose connecting particle; cf. Gesenius–Kautzsch § 158b. A different sentence (Hosea's?) expressing trust has been added to the penitential prayer (see p. 235).

f  $G$ (τὰς κατοικίας αὐτῶν) misunderstands the Hebrew, as in 11:7; see textual note "r" on 11:7.

g  The Achmimic and Sahidic translations offer an interpretation: *miserebor*.

h  $V$: *spontanee* (cf. 1 Pt 5:2); with $G$ (ὁμολόγως) cf. ὁμολογία = נדבה in Dtn 12:6, 17; cf. Am 4:5; Ezek 46:12 for the freewill offering.

i  $G$ (ἀπ' αὐτῶν) harmonizes the sentence—recognizable as a gloss by the nonagreement of the suffix—with its context. $G$ interprets v 5a in terms of 11:9a, and in view of 13:11 (8:5; 9:15; cf. Is 9:16aα).

j  The Dead Sea Fragment has no copula (Testuz, "Deux Fragments").

k  Literally: "his roots."

l  The interpretation offered by $T$, Buber, and all versions; today "as the poplar" (כַּלִּבְנֶה) is generally conjectured (cf. 4:13); thus Koehler–Baumgartner, Sellin, Robinson, Lippl, Weiser.

m  $G$ (κατάκαρπος) freely interprets $M$: the "splendor" of the olive tree is its abundant fruit.

n  See textual note "l."

o  $G$ (καθιοῦνται) presupposes יֵשְׁבוּ instead of $M$'s reading ("inhabitants"); ן ($G$ adds καί) is unnecessary after יֵשְׁבוּ, which is to be understood as a *verbum relativum* (Grether § 87n); cf. Gen 26:18; 43:2; on ישׁב in Hosea cf. 11:11 $M$; 12:10; cf. 2:20b; $M$ ("the inhabitants of his shadows return") uses the infrequent connection of a *status constructus* with a preposition (cf. Is 9:1b; Grether § 72m).

p  Within the context of the divine speech (cf. 6:5) בְּצִלִּי is more probable than "his shadow" ($M$); this reading is more meaningful also in the light of the comparison of Israel with Lebanon in v 8b, even though v 8b makes the misreading in $M$ intelligible.

q  For this expression, cf. Gen 19:34; Is 7:21; 2 Sam 12:3. $G$ (ξήσονται καὶ μεθυσθήσονται σίτῳ [later $G$–witnesses read στηριχθήσονται; cf. Ziegler, *Duodecim prophetae*]) reads וְחָיוּ and therefore has to interpret דגן as an instrumental dative (likewise $V$). $G$ probably added the second verb independently, for otherwise the sentence would have said nothing about the new flourishing of life. This verb should not be used as a basis for reconstructing an expansion of the original text (Robinson adds וְיִרְוְיוּ).

r  L. Koehler, "Emendationen," BZAW 41 (1925): 177, suggested the reading "the thought of me" (זִכְרִי). This appears to be improbable because of the foregoing parallel statements; cf. especially הוֹדוֹ in v 7aβ.

s  $G$ (καὶ ἐξανθήσει ὡς ἄμπελος τὸ μνημόσυνον αὐτοῦ) requires the singular יִפְרַח.

t  E. Osty (*La Sainte Bible* [Am, Hos] 1960²) reads חֶלְבּוֹן instead of לְבָנוֹן with no support from the transmission of the text. According to Ezek 27:18 and the Assyrian inscriptions, "wine of Helbon" was

9 [8]  What ⟨has⟩ Ephraim ⟨ ⟩ᵘ any more to do  
with idols?  
I, I will answerᵛ and look after him.ʷ  
I am like a luxuriant juniper,  
on me fruit is to be found for you.

famous; cf. Zimmerli, *Ezekiel*, 655. But the great fruitfulness of Lebanon surely was no less known; cf. Na 1:4 and the commentary on vv 6, 7, 8.

u   *G* (αὐτῷ) reads לוֹ; *M* ("What have I yet to do with idols?") is intelligible only if the beginning of the verse would read וַיֹּאמַר אֶפְרַיִם (thus *S T*); Ephraim, not Yahweh, was "united with idols" (4:17). But the continuation can be understood only as a divine speech and demonstrates that *S T* added the phrase for purposes of clarification. Therefore "Ephraim" should be understood as *casus pendens*, which is again referred to by לוֹ (Grether § 95c).

v   *G* (ἐταπείνωσα = עִנִּיתִי) supposed the word to be ענה II, as in 2:17; 5:5; 7:10; cf. E. Kutsch, עֲנָוָה ("Demut"): Habilitationsschrift Univ. Mainz (Mainz, 1960), 32.

w   *V* (*dirigam eum*) presupposes וַאֲאַשְּׁרֶנּוּ: "I lead him in the straight way" (Koehler–Baumgartner); *G* (ἐγὼ κατισχύσω αὐτόν) recognizes a clear sequence of thought in v 9bαʰ: "I have humbled him, and I will strengthen him." In view of the completely parallel sentence in 6:1aβ, this reading would be acceptable if a corresponding root שׁור III could be identified. In view of *G*, Nyberg suggested "I conquer him" (וַאֲשֹׁרֶנּוּ [אֲשׁר]). Driver reads "I affirm it" ([אֲשֹׁרֶנּוּ] שׁרר) (cf. Job 33:3, 14, 27) which would introduce v 9b. Wellhausen's suggestion is much too audacious: "[I am] his Anat and Ashera" (עֲנָתוֹ וַאֲשֵׁרָתוֹ); (Sellin's response: ". . . more ingenious than correct"). With *M* the word should be provisionally regarded the same as that found in 13:7.

## Form

In 14:2–9 a prophetic summons (vv 2–4), which speaks of Yahweh in the third person, is connected with a divine speech (vv 5–9). Verses 2–4 are not a penitential liturgy in the strict sense, but rather a prophetic summons to recite this liturgy. The penitential prayer itself[1] does not follow upon the prophet's exhortation to return to Yahweh; instead, the prophet merely recites the prayer before the people, and in response to the confession of sins yet unspoken by them, he proclaims healing that is, in fact, a healing of their impenitence. Thus the exhortation is formulated completely in the light of the oracle of salvation (*Erhörungszusage*). The announcement of healing (v 5) is actually the central point of the text. It is the presupposition for the entire passage, as is also made evident by Jeremiah's version of it in 3:22 and 4:1.

The form critical distinction between vv 2–4 and v 5 makes this even clearer. In v 5 the divine speech in

the first person speaks of the people in the third person. This is the style of an audition account of a divine decree (cf. Ps 85:9ff; 126:5f), not of an assurance of salvation, which is formulated in direct address (as in Jer 3:22; cf. Hos 6:4). On the basis of the decree he is about to announce, the prophet himself addresses Israel in the second person in vv 2–4: "Return, O Israel, to Yahweh your God!"[2] The prayer the prophet recites before the people mainly concentrates upon strict renunciation.[3]

The divine answer given in v 5 is the kernel of the entire passage. Introduced by the summons to return in vv 2–4, it is followed by a more involved development of the consequent actions of God's love. As the threat follows the verdict (cf. 14:1), so the announcement of abundant life follows the avowal of Yahweh's saving intentions. Formulated in the style of a solemn announcement of the judicial sentence, v 5 continues to speak of the people in the third person plural. In contrast to

---

1   Cf. Josh 24:14ff; Ps 85; 126:4ff.                1 Kgs 8:46ff.  
2   Cf. 2:1–3, also 8:5a (cj.), and the commentary.  
3   Cf. Josh 24:14ff; Ju 10:14ff; 1 Sam 7:3ff; Gen 35:2ff;

v 5, however, vv 6–8 refer to "Israel" mostly in the singular. The imagery of these verses is reminiscent of the motifs found in love songs.[4] Cf. "blossom like the vine" (פרח הגפן) in v 8 with Song 6:11; 7:13; "fragrance like the forest of Lebanon" (ריח לבנון) in v 7 with Song 4:11; 2:13; 4:10; 7:9, 14; "wine" (יין) in v 8 with Song 1:2, 4; 4:10; 5:1; 7:10; "dwell in my shadow" (ישׁב בצלי) in v 8 with Song 2:3; "lily" (שׁושׁנה v 6) in the sense of a living plant, occurs elsewhere only in Song, where it is found seven times.[5] The divine speech addresses Israel in the second person—like the prophet's words in vv 2f—only in v 9b. This direct address in v 9b is made understandable by the exhortatory tone of the immediately preceding (textually uncertain) v 9aα, similar to the exhortation in vv 2f. Formulated as a question, v 9aα is entirely dominated by the salvation oracle, as are vv 2f. The oracle's announcement form (third person) becomes a direct assurance of salvation (second person) in the conclusion (v 9b). Our division of the text (v 5; vv 6–8; v 9) is confirmed by the mention of "Israel" in v 6a and "Ephraim" in v 9a.

The words promising healing and salvation are given increased significance within the passage by the abundance of typically Hosean metaphors, expressed in beautiful prosodic units of mostly synonymous lines containing two or three stresses (vv 5–8). The renunciation (v 4) and the assurance of salvation in v 9b are of a similar structure. The vivid introduction (vv 2–3), with its direct address in terse tricola, is set off from the bicola which are formulated in a style of proclamation.

## Setting

This great announcement of salvation contains no clear criteria on which to base its date. But it is probably best understood at the time when the end of the Northern Kingdom was in view. The fall is as good as complete (cf. the perfect in v 2b with the imperfect in 5:5bα), since it has now become apparent that neither Assyria nor the Canaanite cult can help Israel (vv 4, 9a). The expression in v 9a: "What has Ephraim any more (עד) to do with idols," especially indicates with the word עד that a turning point has been reached which puts the entire past into question. Therefore, it is conceivably the

time of Shalmaneser V, when Samaria's end was near.

The theme of 14:2–9 is closely related to that of chap. 11. It should be noted that the same important catchwords occur in both passages: "to return" (שׁוב vv 2f, 8; cf. 11:5, 11 *G*); "apostasy" (מְשׁוּבָה v 5; cf. 11:7); "to heal" (רפא v 5; cf. 11:3); "to dwell" (ישׁב v 8; cf. 11:11 *M*). In chap. 14 the final hour is somewhat nearer, for Egypt (cf. v 4 with 11:5, 11) has disappeared from view and words of accusation have fallen completely silent. God's inner struggle, which the audience witnessed in 11:8f, has given way to a straightforward proclamation of salvation.

In terms of its transmission, however, chap. 14 stands nearer to chaps. 12–13, and not simply because of the present literary arrangement of the three chapters. The forms of speech in chap. 11 were completely understandable as forms derived from the legal procedure in the city gate. In chap. 14, however, the forms reveal a somewhat stronger cultic influence. Perhaps it is significant that יהוה אלהיך occurs in Hosea only in 12:10; 13:4 and 14:2. This transmission complex (chaps. 12–14) seems to have received its present shape from a new proclamation of these words in the context of worship (cf. v 12:6), perhaps in the area near the Judean border (cf. 12:1b, 3a *M*). In any case, it is especially suitable for such purposes.

In view of its original audience, 14:2–9 should be set off from 12:3–14:1. The characteristics indicative of a public dispute have disappeared. In any event, 14:2–9 belongs to a later date; Hosea probably spoke these words before the inner circle of the opposition group, to whom the entire transmission complex, together with 12:1–2, was entrusted.

## Interpretation

■ **2** The exhortation is an invitation to those who have already stumbled; unlike the exhortations in 2:4f; 4:15; 8:5a (cj.) (cf. 10:12; 12:7), the purpose here is not to snatch Israel away from a threatening judgment. The disaster has already taken place.[6] But Yahweh, the God of Israel desires a new beginning, for it was not Yahweh but Israel's guilt that brought her collapse. The prophet's summons to return comes from the God

---

4   Cf. the commentary on 2:9, where such imagery has already occurred.

5   See p. 236.

6   Cf. v 2b with 5:5 and the commentary.

7   V 5; see pp. 233f and cf. H. W. Wolff, "Das Thema Umkehr in der alttestamentlichen Prophetie," *ZThK*

who has already revealed his saving will to his prophet.[7]

■ **3** What must Israel bring with her as she returns? For a long time Yahweh had withdrawn himself from the pilgrimages and their animal sacrifice (5:6). The only appropriate offerings are "words" which renounce every proffered accomplishment and all help from a foreign nation, as well as every attempt at self–help. Although v 3bα is not unambiguous,[8] the phrase נשׂא עון, with Yahweh as its subject, is textually certain. It vividly expresses the expectation that Yahweh "carries (off)" and thus removes their sins, so that they no longer harm guilty Israel.[9] With their prayer, the worshipers offer the "fruit of their lips,"[10] namely, the following promise of renunciation (v 4). If טוב does not also mean "word"[11] then it paraphrases the "fruit of the lips" as proverbial goodness (Prv 13:2; 12:14). But that is the renunciation of everything except Yahweh himself and his deeds.

■ **4** As in the ancient Yahweh cult, the idols are rejected (cf. Gen 35:2ff; Josh 24:14ff). In the eighth century the idols took on new forms: (1) The great foreign power, Assyria, from whom help was erroneously expected again and again (5:13; 8:9); (2) Israel's own military strength, her horses, which refer to her chariot corps,[12] the essence of her martial forces;[13] (3) the calf image of the Baal cult which, though the "work of our hands" (8:6; 13:2), was worshiped as "our God" (8:6).[14] In the solemn disavowal of the gods she presently worships, Israel renews her original confession of faith in Yahweh as her only savior, the comforter of the helpless (13:4; cf. Ju 10:14–16; Ps 33:16ff).

In the present text the אשׁר–clause,[15] which concludes the prayer, corresponds to the expression of confidence which closes the complaint (Ps 10:18; 60:14). In v 4 after the renunciation, the אשׁר–clause takes over

the function of a confession (cf. Josh 24:16f). The language (רחם; cf. 1:6; 2:25) and outlook (cf. 9:10; 11:1ff) appear to be Hosean. With no father the orphan is given up to injustice and violence;[16] motherless, he is in need of kindness and support in his weak and helpless situation.[17]

The prayer Israel is to offer in the future, in which she will turn to Yahweh, is different from her present penitential songs (cf. 6:1–3; 8:2). Those wordy expressions of trust, with the basic tone of self–appeasement,[18] are replaced here by Israel's repentant self–surrender to her God in the renunciation of false help.[19]

■ **5** Hence this penitential prayer, induced by Israel's acknowledgment of her guilt, finds no rejection, as in 6:4; 8:3; rather, it is followed by Yahweh's promise to heal her apostasy. Formulated in view of the promise, the prayer is spoken by the prophet as an explanation which anticipates the promise. Up to this point Israel has remained true only to her "apostasy" (מׁשׁובה; cf. 11:7). She will not and cannot leave it (5:4; 7:2; 11:5). Israel has irretrievably given herself over to apostasy as to a sickness unto death (cf. Prv 1:32!). Yahweh now shows that he is the physician who not only can help her in external necessity (5:13; 6:1; 7:1), but who can above all heal her obstinacy.[20] It should be noted carefully that Hosea speaks in a basic and positive way of Israel's forgiveness in the approaching time of wholeness as Yahweh's comprehensive succor and support of life in Israel. The verse continues: "I will love them freely."[21] "Spontaneously" (נדבה) emphasizes the *free will offering* noble spontaneity of love that presupposes no accomplishments whatsoever on Israel's part.[22]

■ **6** Replete with rich and colorful metaphors, the following verses attest to the efficacy of God's love. In the previous words of judgment, Yahweh was pictured

---

48 (1951): 141 [also in Wolff, *Gesammelte Studien*, 142f].

8 See textual note "a."

9 Cf. Ex 32:32; 34:7; Is 33:24; see J. J. Stamm, *Erlösen*, 67f; W. Zimmerli, "Die Eigenart der prophetischen Rede des Ezechiel. Ein Beitrag zum Problem an Hand von Ez 14:1–11," *ZAW* 66 (1954): 9 [also in his "*Gottes Offenbarung*," *ThB* 19 (München, 1963), 158f].

10 Cf. Is 57:18f; Prv 10:31; 12:14; 18:20; PsSol 15:3; 1QH 1:28f; Heb 13:15.

11 See textual note "b."

12 This does not mean "cavalry"; cf. *BRL*, 425.

13 Is 30:16; 31:3; 36:8; Dtn 17:16.

14 See p. 142.

15 See textual note "e."

16 Ex 22:21f; Dtn 27:19; Is 1:17.

17 On רחם see the commentary on 1:6.

18 See the commentary on 6:1–3.

19 Cf. 10:3 and the commentary.

20 On "heal" (רפא), see the commentary on 6:11b–7:1.

21 On "to love" (אהב), see pp. 60 and 35.

22 On this subject, cf. 11:1 and the commentary. On v 5b see textual note "i."

as a lion, a leopard, and an angry bear (5:14; 13:7f); now he compares himself to the "dew." Whereas these animals endanger and destroy, dew promotes life and growth (Dtn 33:13). One does not see the dewdrops fall and yet they are there. The inhabitants of Palestine know how necessary the dew is for the constant growth of plant life, for "in the rainless season dew alone moistens the ground."[23] In the evening and morning hours it may be precipitated so heavily by a westerly wind that it becomes unpleasant to be outdoors. But without the dew, neither melons, grapes, nor fruit could grow.[24] Since Hosea has spoken of Israel's death (13:1ff, 8; 14:1 [13:16]), it is significant that he uses the imagery of the dew, for later dew and resurrection are connected (Is 26:19).

The dew will cause Israel to bloom "like the שׁושׁנה." This is probably not the "white lily," which is essentially a garden flower. Rather, in a broader sense, the word denotes a flower with large (1 Kgs 7:26) cup-like blossoms which, like the varieties of iris, may flourish in the desert valleys and among the thornbushes (Song 2:1f).[25] Nourished by the healing and life-bringing love of Yahweh, his people will blossom forth anew like this flower. While the metaphor of the lily extols the miracle of new life and beauty of the future Israel, the phrase "he shall strike root like the forest of Lebanon" points to the durability and strength of Yahweh's new creation. At least since the time when Solomon sent thousands of woodsmen into the forest of Lebanon to prepare lumber for his buildings (1 Kgs 5:28), Lebanon was considered in Israel to be the ideal forest. She praised its mighty cedars as planted by Yahweh (Ps 104:16), who alone could splinter their wood (Ps 29:5). Their proverbial height (Is 2:13; Ps 92:13) is matched by their mighty roots spoken of in v 6. The lily and Lebanon are themes found in love songs.[25a]

■ **7** Refreshed by Yahweh, the tree of Israel shall put forth young "shoots," which signify the abundance of new life. Israel's "splendor" is said to be like the olive tree. The tree's fruitfulness, "the rich abundance of its tender branches, and the crisp foliage growing above its strong trunk are a picture of the highly satisfied life."[26] "His fragrance" is a second reminiscence of Lebanon (cf. Song 4:11). "In the regions where the mulberry, olive and fig tree grow, the ground is covered with myrrh, thyme, lavender, sage, cistrose, styrax, with fragrant shrubs and herbs which fill the air with pleasant odors, particularly when the wanderer treads upon them."[27] This new life, therefore, is not only strong and fruitful, but is also provided with pleasures that awaken a feeling of intense well-being. Again, the mood suggested is that of the love song.

■ **8** The expression "sitting in the shade" also belongs to the love song,[28] whether the shade be that of an olive tree or a cedar (Ezek 17:23), as *M* reads, or in the shade of God himself,[29] under the cover of his protection and goodness. Israel's poetic language tells of the pleasantness of sitting in the shade of the mighty, be it the king (Lam 4:20; cf. Ju 9:15) or Yahweh (Ps 17:8; 36:8; 91:1; 12:15, etc.).[30] In terms of the announcement of salvation, the expression may especially refer to the delight of sitting in the shade of one's lover (cf. Song 2:3). After Yahweh's people had to live again in the wilderness (9:3; 12:10), Yahweh gives them a new "dwelling" in the rich, sheltered, arable land (cf. 2:17, 20b; 11:1). The land's chief product is "grain" (2:10; 9:1f), followed by wine and oil. But here the vine is mentioned, like the olive tree in v 7, as a metaphor for the "fame," i.e., the "reputation," of Israel herself which continually makes her worthy of remembrance and mention (זכר). For a second time (cf. v 6) פרח is used to signify the "sprouting" of new life from the dew and the shadow of Yahweh's healing love. For a third time (cf. vv 6, 7) Lebanon is mentioned, now because of its famous wine. Finally, Israel once again becomes the precious vine it was supposed to be from the very beginning of her history (cf. 10:1 and Is 5:1ff). According to 10:1 the comparison of Israel with the vine is by no means unusual for Hosea.[31]

---

23  Noth, *World*, 31 [26].
24  Cf. Dalman, *Arbeit* 1/2, 514–19.
25  Dalman, *Arbeit* 1/2, 357ff.
25a The lily: Song 2:1, 16; 4:5; 5:13; 6:2, 3; 7:3; Lebanon: Song 4:12, etc.; see p. 234.
26  Cf. Jer 11:16; Ps 52:10 and Dalman, *Arbeit* 4, 164.
27  H. Guthe, "Libanon," *RE*[3] 11, 436.
28  See textual note "o"; cf. 4:13.

29  See textual note "p."
30  Cf. Kraus, *Psalmen*, 132, 836.
31  *Contra* Peter, "Echo."
32  "What have I to do with you?" Ju 11:12; 1 Kgs 17:18; 2 Kgs 3:13; 2 Chr 35:21; cf. 2 Sam 16:10; 19:23; 2 Kgs 9:18f; the ו preceding the second ל is absent in Jer 2:18 also.

■ **9** After the announcement of Israel's new life of salvation which Yahweh himself brings, v 9 looks once again at the Ephraim of the present, a defeated remnant of a kingdom. The form of the question (מה with a twofold ל) is unusual, but it is probably best interpreted by analogy to the expression מַה־לִּי וָלָךְ.[32] Ephraim's association with the idols (4:17; 8:4; 13:2) is definitively called into question by Yahweh's love, which creates a completely new life in Israel. The rhetorical question has the function of an indirect exhortation that is entirely dominated by the proclamation of salvation. What follows in v 9 is given the precise form of an oracle of assurance that a prayer will be granted.[33] Yahweh's basic answer to Ephraim's prayers is supplemented by a permanent "looking after," "beholding," "attention."[34] If Hosea has used the same word here as in 13:7, he then further declares that Yahweh, who grants Israel's prayer and thus saves her, is also constantly awake, looking out for his people (cf. Nu 24:17; Job 7:8).

The God of Israel provides her with more than his word and his attention. In the last "I am" saying in Hosea, the prophet declares in a final, bold metaphor that Yahweh himself is the gift of salvation to his people: he is described as a luxuriant "cypress"[35] or as a (Phoenician) "juniper."[36] רענן emphasizes the full abundant foliage of the tree, which was regarded as the archetype of ever–enduring existence. *G* has "thick foliage" (πυκάζουσα).[37] Furthermore, it is thought of as a fruit tree. Thus it can hardly be disproved that a type of tree of life is conceived of here.[38] On Babylonian cylinder seals and palace reliefs the tree of life is often portrayed as a kind of palm which bears pineapple–shaped fruit.[39] Among the Phoenicians the cypress was known as a holy tree.[40] Verse 9 is the only instance in the Old Testament in which Yahweh is compared to a tree. Once again Hosea's polemical theology—now in dispute with the trees and oracles of the Canaanite cult, which were connected with the sex rites (cf. 4:12f)—leads to a unique formulation whose intention is similar to the marriage parable of his early period. In contrast to the syncretism of Canaanite religion, Hosea declares that the fertility and vitality Ephraim vainly sought in its Canaanite cult is to be found in his God alone. The word "your fruit" (פריך) may again be a wordplay on "Ephraim" (אפרים), as in 9:16.[41]

**Aim**

The source of light that illuminates the entire passage burns in v 5. The spontaneous love of Israel's God, who negated his own wrath in 11:8f and thus removed the divine judgment upon Israel, is proclaimed in v 5 as the power of life that heals the deathly illness of Israel's apostasy. The completely unambiguous expression "I will love them spontaneously" provides the motivation for divine redemption. The basis for the salvation of God's people does not lie somewhere external to Yahweh. It is found neither in the prophet's intercession[42] nor in God's sympathy for his needy people,[43] nor in the outbreak of Israel's good intention (13:1ff, 12ff; 14:1). The very opposite is the case. Israel has cast to the wind all exhortations and judgments and, stumbling over her own guilt (v 2b), of her own accord heads toward death (12:15; 14:1). To be sure, Yahweh's compassion repeatedly came to expression in the earlier sayings,[44] but Israel's distress never led to mercy's triumph. Nor was the prophet in fact able to intercede for Israel. After the death sentence upon old Israel,[45] only the free will of God's holiness (cf. 11:9b; 3:1b) shall set in motion a completely new history of the people of God.

The first fruit of this prophetic insight proclaimed in v 5 is the completely new kind of invitation to *return* in vv 2–4. It has nothing in common with the earlier ultimatumlike admonitions (2:5; 4:15; 8:5 [cj.]) in which the prophet vainly attempted to snatch his people away from their guilty path at the last moment. Hence the call to return to Yahweh is an invitation entirely founded upon the certainty that Yahweh will cure Israel's apostasy and liberate the people from their guilt. The

33  Is 49:8; Ps 118:5 and see the commentary on 2:23f.
34  On שׁור, see the commentary on 13:7; concerning the text's uncertainty, see textual note "v."
35  Dalman, *Arbeit* 1/1, 259.
36  Koehler–Baumgartner.
37  Cf. R. Gradwohl, *Die Farben im Alten Testament*, BZAW 83 (Berlin, 1963), 33.
38  Cf. Gen 3:22 for a tree of life pictured as a fruit tree.
39  Cf. Peter, "Echo," 184f.
40  F. Lundgren, *Die Benutzung der Pflanzenwelt in der alttestamentlichen Religion*, BZAW 14 (Berlin, 1908), 31.
41  See the commentary.
42  See pp. 168f.
43  See the commentary on 6:4 and cf. Am 7:2, 5.
44  See p. 135.
45  See the commentary on 13:1.

summonses in vv 2f have the same function as the oracle of assurance in v 5.[46] Accordingly, the content of the penitential prayer is also different from that in 6:1–3 and 8:2. The prayer is related to Yahweh's readiness to forgive (v 3b) and at the same time renounces every help from Israel's idols (v 4a). Rejection of the pagan gods means return to the God who loves spontaneously. As the "fruit of our lips," this renunciation is a sacrifice of thanksgiving offered to the God of redemption (cf. Heb 13:15).

After Israel's apostasy is healed, which Yahweh's forgiveness achieves, the regenerated people of God are to have a new life (vv 6–9). The "I" of Yahweh encloses (vv 6a, 9b) the description of this new life. The simile of the dew as well as of the green cypress attests that he is the mysterious but always trustworthy source of Israel's new existence. The description of Israel's new sprouting and growth indicated by the catchword פרח in vv 6a and 8a is the longest part of the passage. The imagery of flora from arable land, heightened to the very utmost by the threefold reference to Lebanon, graphically presents the indestructible permanence of this new life (v 6b), its fruitful abundance (vv 7f), and especially its miraculous nature (v 6aβ) and exquisite comfort (v 7). "It is a remarkable fact that the same prophet who thinks so emphatically in terms of saving history can at the same time move Yahweh's relationship to Israel over into the horizons of an almost vegetable natural growth and blossoming, where all the drama of the saving history ebbs out as if in a profound quiet."[47] This may be accounted for by the language drawn from the ancient love songs.[48] This is the earliest example of Luther's "Where there is the forgiveness of sins, there is life and salvation." The prophet irresistibly transports his audience into the climate and atmosphere of a life of complete wholeness. A particular mark of this prophetic announcement of salvation is the certainty that no goodness is lacking where God's spontaneous love creates a repentant people; that his action also reaches into the concrete and physical side of life, where he, like the dew, awakens life out of dead soil. In this sense, our text anticipates somewhat the miracles of Jesus recorded in the New Testament. "The normal Christian of the West . . . does not understand or trust the luxury, even if it is that of God Himself. There might be some hope if only he were not so proud of the fact. From the point of view of the Gospels and their attestation of the epiphany of the Son of Man it is quite right that he should be continually surprised by this superfluity of the grace of God. . . . But it is not right that he should be rigid in relation to this superfluity."[49]

46   Cf. Jer 3:22; Is 43:24f, and pp. 233f.
47   von Rad, *Theology* 2, 146.
48   See pp. 217f.
49.  C. Barth, *Church Dogmatics* IV/2, tr. G. W. Bromiley (Edinburgh: T. & T. Clark, 1958), 247 [German 273].

**The Traditionist's Conclusion**

**Bibliography**

K. Budde

"Der Schluss des Buches Hosea," in *Studies Presented to C. H. Toy* (New York: Macmillan, 1912), 205–11.

# 14

**10 [9]**    Who is so wise that[a] he understands
         these things?
      so discerning that he knows them?
      Indeed, the ways of Yahweh are straight.
      Righteous ones walk in them.
      But rebels stumble in them.

**a**   The *wāw*–copulative (with imperfect) introduces a result clause after questions as well as after negative clauses; cf. Gesenius–Kautzsch § 166a. *G V* also translate v 10a as interrogatives. Contrariwise, Brockelmann, *Syntax* § 157 considers מי חכם a relative clause: "Whoever is wise, let him consider; whoever is prudent, let him take note"; but the only parallels he lists are אֲשֶׁר–clauses.

## Form

Verse 10 contains two different kinds of clauses: a double question combining a longer and a shorter line into a bicolon; a didactic sentence in the form of a three–stress tricolon, with the initial line followed by two lines in antithetic parallelism.

Wisdom teachers often employ concluding questions like those in v 10a (cf. Eccl 8:1; Ps 107:43). We also find such questions added to the sayings of Jeremiah in 9:11. They belong to a period when the prophetic traditions had long since been preserved as literature and their interpretation had become problematic.

The didactic proposition in the second sentence (v 10b) intercepts the provocative double question. The connection made by the deictic כִּי, which we have often found in the book,[1] leaves open the possibility that v 10b did not originally belong with v 10a. Its vocabulary and antithetic structure are also typical of Wisdom (cf. Prv 10:29; 24:16b).

## Setting

Merely the fact that this closing verse is concerned with the problem of interpretation and actualization indicates that it stands quite far removed from Hosea's lifetime, and also from the original draft of the different transmission complexes. The close relationship of its questions with Jer 9:11 and Ps 107:43[2] would point at least to the exilic period, if not to postexilic times. The vocabulary of the final didactic sentence is found in the Deuteronomistic history,[3] and the single instance of the plural "ways of Yahweh" (דרכי יהוה) occurs in a passage in Ps 18 which appears to be Deuteronomistic.[4] Yet this formulaic, sapiential material—at least the final two lines—appears to have been composed as a special conclusion to the book of Hosea. Its author uses the typically Hosean word "stumble"[5] in closing; also cf. "to rebel" (פשׁע) in 7:13 and 8:1; by contrast, Wisdom literature usually places "wicked" (רָשָׁע) in opposition to "righteous" (צַדִּיק).

## Interpretation

**■ 10**   Here the "one who is wise" already refers to the interpreter of the written Hosean traditions. The gift of wisdom is necessary to discern and understand them. Only he who understands the prophet's words proves deserving of the name "wise man."

---

1   See pp. 131f.
2   Cf. Kraus, *Psalmen*, 737.
3   "To walk in the way of Yahweh" (דֶּרֶךְ יְהוָה לָלָכֶת בָּם Ju 2:22); cf. Dtn 8:6; 10:12; 11:22, 28; 19:9; 26:17; 28:9; 30:16; 31:29.
4   V 22; cf. Kraus, *Psalmen*, 146.
5   כשׁל qal: 4:5; 14:2; nip'al 5:5.

The principle of interpretation should be the acknowledgment that the ways of Yahweh are just.[6] Here the "ways of Yahweh" (דרכי יהוה) refer to the ways Yahweh commands, which are to be observed as such (Ps 18:22 [21]).[7] These ways are just (cf. 1 Sam 12:23; Acts 13:10) and in every case good. Whoever follows these righteous directions is therefore considered just and stands upon the right paths; whoever rebels against them[8] shall stumble upon them (cf. Is 8:14f).

**Aim**

The last verse of the book indicates that the prophet's words are correctly understood later on as well only by him who perceives that the ancient "ways of Yahweh" are meaningful instructions in the present and that they are a summons to understand and to follow. Every reader is called upon to decide between discipleship or revolt and thus between walking or stumbling. The question: "Who is wise?" is presumably only the writer's preliminary cry of distress over the difficulty of understanding the transmitted text. With a kind of protest against the perils inherent in the earliest attempts at interpreting of the Hosean tradition,[9] his essential purpose is to call forth an intensive searching of these words, that it might lead to the discovery and the following of the way of Israel's God as the way of the present and of the future.

---

6    Cf. Michaelis, *TDNT* 5, 55.
7    Cf. "the way which I have commanded you" (הַדֶּרֶךְ אֲשֶׁר צִוִּיתִי) in Dtn 31:29; cf. the passages in Dtn, listed on p. 239 under "Setting," which place Yahweh's commandments parallel with his ways.
8    See the commentary on 7:13.
9    Cf. the first indications of this in 12:6 and see p. 213.

**Bibliography**
**Indices**

## 1. Studies in Old Testament Prophecy

Fohrer, G.
"Neuere Literatur zur alttestamentlichen Prophetie," *ThR* 19 (1951): 277–346; *ThR* 20 (1952): 193–271; 295–361; *ThR* 28 (1962): 1–75; 239–97; 301–74.

Heschel, A. J.
*The Prophets* (New York: Harper and Row, 1962).

Lindblom, J.
*Prophecy in Ancient Israel* (Oxford: Blackwells, 1963²).

Meyer, R., J. Fichtner, and A. Jepsen
"Propheten II," *RGG*³ 5, 613–33.

von Rad, G.
*Old Testament Theology* II, "The Theology of the Prophetic Traditions," tr. D. G. M. Stalker (New York: Harper and Row, 1965).

Rendtorff, R.
"προφήτης," *TDNT* 6, 796–812.

*Idem*
"Prophetenspruch," *RGG*³, 5, 635–38.

## 2. History of the Interpretation of the Minor Prophets

Krause, G.
*Studien zu Luthers Auslegung der kleinen Propheten,* BHTh 33 (Tübingen, 1962).

Werbeck, W.
"Zwölfprophetenbuch," *RGG*³ 6, 1970.

## 3. Commentaries on the Minor Prophets

Augé, R.
*Profetes Menors,* La Bíblia, versió dels textos originals i commentari XVI (1957).

Bewer, J. A.
*The Book of the Twelve Prophets,* Harper Bible (New York: Harper and Row, 1949).

Bleeker, L. H. K., G. Smit
*De kleine Propheten,* Text en Uitleg, 3 vols. (Gronigen, 1926–34).

Brown, S. L.
*Hosea,* WC (London, 1932).

Coppens, J.
*Les douze petits Prophètes* (Paris, 1950).

Deden, D.
*De kleine Profeten,* BOT, 3 vols. (Roermond, 1953; 1956).

Duhm, B.
"Anmerkungen zu den zwölf kleinen Propheten," *ZAW* 31 (1911): 1–43; 81–110; 161–204.

*Idem*
*Die zwölf Propheten, in den Versmassen der Urschrift übersetzt* (Tübingen, 1910).

Edghill, E., G. Cooke, G. Stonehouse, and G. Wade
*Obadiah, Joel, Jonah,* WC (London, 1925).

Ehrlich, A. B.
*Randglossen zur hebräischen Bibel,* 5 (Leipzig, 1912; Hildesheim, 1968²).

Ewald, H. G. A.
*Die Propheten des Alten Bundes* (Göttingen, 1867–68²).

Gressman, H.
*Die älteste Geschichtsschreibung und Prophetie Israels (von Samuel bis Amos und Hosea),* SAT 2, 1 (Göttingen, 1921²).

Guthe, H., K. Marti, J. W. Rothstein, E. Kautzsch, and A. Bertholet
*Die Heilige Schrift des Alten Testaments (Hosea bis Chronik),* 2 (Tübingen, 1923⁴).

Haller, M.
*Das Judentum: Geschichtsschreibung, Prophetie, und Gesetztgebung nach dem Exil,* SAT 2, 3 (Göttingen, 1925²).

Harper, W. R.
*Amos and Hosea,* ICC (Edinburgh: T & T Clark, 1905).

Hitzig, F., H. Steiner
*Die zwölf kleinen Propheten,* KeH (Leipzig, 1881⁴).

van Hoonacker, A.
*Les douze petits Prophètes,* ÉtBi (Paris, 1908).

Jepsen, A.
*Bibelhilfe für die Gemeinde* (Stuttgart, 1937).

Keil, C. F.
*Biblischer Commentar über die zwölf kleinen Propheten* (Leipzig, 1888³).

Kroeker, J.
*Die Propheten oder das Reden Gottes,* Das Lebendige Wort (Giessen und Basel, 1932).

Laetsch, Th.
*The Minor Prophets,* Bible Commentary (St. Louis: Concordia Publishing House, 1956).

Lehrman, S. M., S. Goldman, and E. Cashdan
*The Socino Books of the Bible* (Bornemouth, 1952²).

Lippl, J., J. Theis, H. Junker
*Die zwölf kleinen Propheten,* HS 8, 2 vols. (Bonn, 1937, 1938).

Mauchline, J., H. C. Phillips, J. A. Thompson,

N. F. Langford, H. E. W. Fosbroke, S. Lovett,
J. D. Smart, W. Scarlett, R. E. Wolfe, H. A. Bosley,
C. L. Taylor, H. Thurman, D. W. Thomas, W. L.
Sperry, Th. C. Speers, R. C. Dentan, J. T. Cleland,
*The Twelve Prophets*, IB 6 (New York and Nash-
ville: Abingdon Press, 1956).

Marti, K.
*Das Dodekapropheton*, KHC (Tübingen, 1904).

Mitchell, H. G., J. M. P. Smith, and J. A. Bewer
*Haggai, Zechariah, Malachi, Jonah*, ICC (Edinburgh: T & T Clark, 1912).

Mowinckel, S., N. Messel
*De Senere Profeter oversatt*, De Gamle Testamente
(Oslo, 1944).

Nötscher, F.
*Zwölfprophetenbuch*, Echter–B (Würzburg, 1948).

Nowack, W.
*Die kleinen Propheten*, HK (Göttingen, 1922³).

von Orelli, C.
*Die zwölf kleinen Propheten*, Kurzgefasster Kom-
mentar zu den heiligen Schriften Alten und
Neuen Testamentes, eds. H. Strack, O. Zöckler
(München, 1908³).

Osty, E., A. George, J. Trinquet, A. Feuillet,
and A. Gelin
*La Sainte Bible* (Paris, 1957–60).

Procksch, O.
*Die kleinen prophetischen Schriften*, Erläuterungen
zum Alten Testament, 2 vols. (Stuttgart, 1910;
1929²).

Ridderbos, J.
*Korte Verklaring der Heiligen Schrift* (Kampen,
1932–35).

Riessler, P.
*Die kleinen Propheten* (Rottenburg, 1911).

Rinaldi, G.
*I Profeti minori*, 1 (Torino, 1953), 2 (1959).

Robinson, Th. H., F. Horst
*Die Zwölf Kleinen Propheten*, HAT 1, 14 (Tübingen,
1964³).

Schmidt, H.
*Die grossen Propheten*, SAT 2, 2 (Göttingen, 1923²).

Schumpp, M.
*Das Buch der zwölf Propheten*, Herders Bibelkommentar 10, 2 (Freiburg, 1950).

Sellin, E.
*Das Zwölfprophetenbuch*, KAT 12, 2 vols. (Leipzig,
1929²; 1930³).

Smith, G. A.
*The Book of the Twelve Prophets*, Expositor's Bible
(New York: Armstrong, 1928²).

Smith, J. M. P., W. H. Ward, and J. A. Bewer
*Micah, Zephaniah, Nahum, Habbakkuk, Obadiah and
Joel*, ICC (Edinburgh: T & T Clark, 1911).

Vellas, B. M.
ΕΡΜΗΝΕΙΑ ΠΑΛΑΙΑΣ ΔΙΑΘΗΚΗΣ,
5 vols. (1947–50).

Weiser, A., K. Elliger
*Das Buch der zwölf Kleinen Propheten*, ATD 24–25, 1

(Göttingen, 1967⁵), 2 (1967⁶).

Wellhausen, J.
*Die kleinen Propheten* (Berlin, 1963⁴).

## 4. The Text of the Minor Prophets

### a / Hebrew
Buhl, F.
"Einige textkritische Bemerkungen zu den kleinen
Propheten," *ZAW* 5 (1885): 179–84.

Freehoff, S. B.
"Some Text Rearrangements in the Minor
Prophets," *JQR* 32 (1941–42): 303–08.

Gese, H.
"Die hebräischen Bibelhandschriften zum Dode-
kapropheton nach der Variantensammlung des
Kennicott," *ZAW* 69 (1957): 55–69.

Milik, J. T.
*Discoveries in the Judean Desert*, 2 (Oxford: Clarendon Press, 1961).

V(ogt), E.
"Fragmenta Prophetarem Minorum Deserti
Iuda," *Bibl* 34 (1953): 423–26.

### b / Greek
Barthélemy, D.
*Les devanciers d'Aquila: Première publication intégrale
du texte des fragments du Dodécapréphéton*, VTSuppl
10 (Leiden, 1963).

*Idem*
"Redécouverte d'un chaînon manquant de
l'histoire de la Septante," *RB* 60 (1953): 18–
29.

Dingermann, F.
"Massora–Septuaginta der kleinen Propheten,"
diss. Univ. of Würzburg (Würzburg, 1948).

Kaminka, A.
*Studien zur Septuaginta an der Hand der zwölf kleinen
Propheten*, Schriften der Gesellschaft zur Förde-
rung der Wissenschaft des Judentums 33 (Frankfurt, 1928).

Kahle, P.
"Die im August 1952 entdeckte Lederrolle mit
dem griechischen Text der kleinen Propheten und
das Problem der Septuaginta," *ThLZ* 79 (1954):
81–94.

Procksch, O.
*Die Septuaginta Hieronymi im Dodekapropheton:
Festschrift Universität Greifswald* (Greifswald,
1914).

Schuurmans–Stekhoven, L. Z.
*De Alexandrijnsche Vertaling van het Dodekapropheton*
(Leiden, 1887).

Vollers, K.
"Das Dodekapropheton der Alexandriner,"
*ZAW* 3 (1883): 219–72; *ZAW* 4 (1884): 1–20.

Ziegler, J.
*Beiträge zum griechischen Dodekapropheton* (Göttingen, 1942).

*Idem*

*Duodecim prophetae*, Septuaginta Vetus Testamentum Graecum 13 (Göttingen, 1943).

*Idem*

*Die Einheit der Septuaginta zum Zwölfprophetenbuch*, Beilage zum Vorlesungsverzeichnis der Staatlichen Akademie zu Braunsberg im Winter Semester 1934–35 (Braunsberg, 1934).

*Idem*

"Der griechische Dodekapropheton–Text der Complutenser Polyglotte," *Bibl* 25 (1944): 297–310.

*Idem*

"Studien zur Verwertung der Septuaginta im Zwölfprophetenbuch," *ZAW* 60 (1944): 107–31.

*Idem*

"Der Text der Aldina im Dodekapropheton," *Bibl* 26 (1945): 37–51.

### c /Latin

Panyik, A.

"A Critical and Comparative Study of the Old Latin Texts of the Book of Ezekiel and the Minor Prophets," Thesis, Princeton University (Princeton, 1938).

Stenzel, M.

"Altlateinische Canticatexte im Dodekapropheton," *ZNW* 46 (1955): 31–60.

*Idem*

"Das Dodekapropheton der lateinischen Septuaginta: Untersuchungen über die Herkunft und die geschichtliche Entwicklung der lateinischen Textgestalt des nichthieronymianischen Dodekapropheton," diss. Würzburg Univ. (Würzburg, 1949).

*Idem*

"Das Dodekapropheton in Übersetzungswerken lateinischer Schriftsteller des Altertums," *ThZ* 9 (1953): 81–92 (Part 5 of the previously cited diss.).

*Idem*

"Die Konstanzer und St. Galler Fragmente zum altlateinischen Dodekapropheton," *Sacris Erudiri* 5 (1953): 27–85.

### d /Syrian

Sebök (Schönberger), M.

"Die syrische Übersetzung der zwölf kleinen Propheten," diss. Leipzig Univ. (Leipzig, 1887).

### e /Coptic

Grossouw, W.

*The Coptic Versions of the Minor Prophets*, Monumenta biblica et ecclesiastica 3 (Rome, 1938).

Schulte, A.

"Die koptische Übersetzung der kleinen Propheten," *ThQ* 76 (1894): 605–42; *ThQ* 77 (1895): 209–29.

Ziegler, J.

"Beiträge zur koptischen Dodekapropheton–Übersetzung," *Bibl* 25 (1944): 105–42.

### 5. Individual Studies on the Minor Prophets

Bruno, A.

*Das Buch der Zwölf: Eine rhythmische und textkritische Untersuchung* (Stockholm, 1957).

Budde, K.

"Eine folgeschwere Redaktion des Zwölfprophetenbuchs," *ZAW* 39 (1921): 218–29.

Driver, G. R.

"Linguistic and Textual Problems: Minor Prophets," *JTS* 39 (1938): 154–66; 260–73; 393–405.

Gaster, Th. H.

"Notes on the Minor Prophets," *JTS* 39 (1937): 163–65.

Jepsen, A.

"Kleine Beiträge zum Zwölfprophetenbuch, *ZAW* 56 (1938): 85–100; *ZAW* 57 (1939): 242–55; *ZAW* 61 (1945–48): 95–114.

Richter, G.

*Erläuterungen zu dunklen Stellen in den kleinen Propheten*, BFChrTh 18, 3–4 (Gütersloh, 1914).

Wolfe, R. E.

"The Editing of the Book of the Twelve," *ZAW* 53 (1935): 90–130.

### 6. History of the Interpretation of Hosea

Coleman, S.

"Hosea—Concepts in Midrash and Talmud," diss. Univ. of Bloemfontein (Bloemfontein, 1960).

Kroeze, J. H.

"Joodse exegese," *GThT* 61 (1961): 14–33.

### 7. Commentaries on Hosea

Cheyne, Th. K.

*Hosea with Notes and Introduction* (Cambridge, 1884).

Frey, H.

*Das Buch des Werbens Gottes um seine Kirche: Der Prophet Hosea*, Die Botschaft des Alten Testamentes 23, 2 (Stuttgart, 1957).

van Gelderen, C., W. H. Gispen

*Het Boek Hosea*, COT (Kampen, 1953).

Lindblom, J.

*Hosea, literarisch untersucht* (Åbo, 1927).

Nowack, W.

*Der Prophet Hosea erklärt* (Berlin, 1880).

Nyberg, H. S.

*Hoseaboken* (Uppsala, 1941).

*Idem*

*Studien zum Hoseabuche*, UUA (Uppsala, 1935).

Peiser, F. E.

   *Hosea: Philologische Studien zum Alten Testament* (Leipzig, 1914).

Schmoller, O.

   *Die Propheten Hosea, Joel und Amos*, Theologisch-homiletisches Bibelwerk (Bielefeld, 1872).

Scholz, H.

   *Commentar zum Buche des Propheten Hosea* (1882).

Simon, A.

   *Der Prophet Hosea erklärt und übersetzt* (1851).

Snaith, N. H.

   *Amos, Hosea and Micah*, Epworth Preacher's Commentaries (London, 1956).

Wünsche, A.

   *Der Prophet Hosea übersetzt und erklärt mit Benutzung der Targumin, der jüdischen Ausleger Raschi, Aben Ezra und David Kimchi* (Leipzig, 1868).

## 8. General Studies on Hosea

Anderson, B. W.

   Studia Biblica XXVI, "The Book of Hosea," *Int* 8 (1954): 290–303.

Bach, R.

   "Hosea," *EKL* 2, 201–03.

Birkeland, H.

   "Profeten Hosea's forkynnelse," *NTT* 38 (1937): 277–316.

Böhmer, J.

   "Das Buch Hosea nach seinem Grundgedanken und Gedankengang," *NThSt* 10 (1927): 97–104.

*Idem*

   "Die Grundgedanken der Predigt Hoseas," *ZWTh* 45 (1902): 1–24.

Crane, W. E.

   "The Prophecy of Hosea," *Biblica Sacra* 89 (1932): 480–94.

Gunkel, H.

   "Hosea," *RGG²* 2, 2020–23.

Hall, Th. O.

   "Introduction to Hosea," *Review and Expositor* 54/4 (1957): 501–09.

Houtsma, M.

   "Bijdrage tot de kritiek en verklaring van Hosea," *ThT* 9 (1875): 55–75.

Oettli, S.

   *Amos und Hosea: Zwei Zeugen gegen die Anwendung der Evolutionstheorie auf die Religion Israels,* BFChrTh 5, 4 (Gütersloh, 1901).

Oort

   "Hosea," *ThT* 24 (1890): 345–64; 480–505.

Owens, J. J.

   "Exegetical Study of Hosea," *Review and Expositor,* 54/4 (1957): 522–43.

Plöger, O.

   "Hosea," *RGG³* 3, 454.

*Idem*

   "Hoseabuch," *RGG³* 3, 454–57.

Robinson, H. W.

   *Two Hebrew Prophets: Studies in Hosea and Ezekiel* (London and Redhill: Lutterworth Press, 1948).

*Idem*

   *The Cross of Hosea* (Philadelphia: Westminster, 1949).

Rust, E. C.

   "The Theology of Hosea," *Review and Expositor* 54/4 (1957): 510–21.

Steinspring, W. F.

   "Hosea, The Prophet of Doom," *Crozer Quarterly* 27 (1950): 200–07.

Valeton, J. J. P.

   *Amos en Hosea* (Nijmegen, 1894).

Wolfe, R. E.

   *Meet Amos and Hosea* (New York: Harper and Row, 1945).

## 9. Specific Problems in Hosea

Budde, K.

   "Zu Text und Auslegung des Buches Hosea 1. 2.," *JBL* 45 (1926): 280–97; chap. 3, *JPOS* 14 (1934): 1–41; chap. 4, *JBL* 53 (1934): 118–33.

Seesemann, O.

   *Israel und Juda bei Amos und Hosea nebst einem Exkurs über Hosea* 1–3, Theologische Habilitationsschrift, Univ. of Leipzig (Leipzig, 1898).

Waterman, L.

   "Hosea, Chapters 1–3, in Retrospect and Prospect," *JNES* 14 (1955): 100–09.

## 10. The Text of Hosea

Grossouw, W. K. M.

   "Un fragment sahidique d'Osée 2:9–5:1," *Muséon* 47 (1934): 185–204.

Nyberg, H. S.

   "Das textkritische Problem des Alten Testaments am Hoseabuch demonstriert," *ZAW* 52 (1934): 214–54.

Testuz, M.

   "Deux fragments inédits des manuscrits de la Mer Morte," *Semitica* 5 (1955): 37–38, Table 1.

Vuilleumier, R.

   "Osée 13:12 et les manuscrits," *Revue de Qumran* 1 (1958): 281f.

## 11. The Life of Hosea

Allwohn, A.

   *Die Ehe des Propheten Hosea in psychoanalytischer Beleuchtung*, BZAW 44 (Giessen, 1926).

Batten, L. W.

   "Hosea's Message and Marriage," *JBL* 48 (1929): 257–73.

Dijkema, F.

   "De profeet Hozea," *NThT* 14 (1925): 324–43.

Gordis, R.

   "Hosea's Marriage and Message," *HUCA* 25

(1954): 9–35.

May, H. G.
"An Interpretation of the Names of Hosea's Children," *JBL* 55 (1936): 285–91.

North, F. S.
"Solution of Hosea's Marital Problems by Critical Analysis," *JNES* 16 (1957): 128–30.

Robinson, Th. H.
"Die Ehe des Hosea," *ThStKr* 106 (1935): 301–13.

Rowley, H. H.
"The Marriage of Hosea," *BJRL* 39 (1956): 200–33.

Rudolph, W.
"Präparierte Jungfrauen?" *ZAW* 75 (1963): 65–73.

Schmidt, H.
"Die Ehe des Hosea," *ZAW* 42 (1924): 245–72.

## 12. Form–Critical Studies of Hosea's Prophecy

Boecker, H. J.
"Anklagereden und Verteidigungsreden im Alten Testament," *EvTh* 20 (1960): 398–412.

*Idem*
*Redeformen des Rechtslebens im Alten Testament*, WMANT 14 (Neukirchen, 1970²).

Buss, M. J.
"A Form–Critical Study in the Book of Hosea with Special Attention to Method," diss. Yale Univ. (New Haven, 1958).

*Idem*
*The Prophetic Word of Hosea: A Morphological Study*, BZAW 111 (Berlin, 1969).

Elliger, K.
"Eine verkannte Kunstform bei Hosea," *ZAW* 69 (1957): 151–60.

Frey, H.
"Der Aufbau der Gedichte Hoseas," *WuD* Neue Folge 5 (1957): 9–103.

Westermann, C.
*Basic Forms of Prophetic Speech*, tr. Hugh Clayton White (Philadelphia: The Westminster Press, 1967).

## 13. Ancient Israelite Traditions in Hosea

Ackroyd, P. R.
"Hosea and Jacob," *VT* 13 (1963): 245–59.

Dürr, L.
"Altorientalisches Recht bei den Propheten Amos und Hosea," *BZ* 23 (1935): 150–57.

Humbert, P.
"Osée le prophète bedouin," *RHPhR* 1 (1921): 97–118.

Jacob, E.
"Der Prophet Hosea und die Geschichte," *EvTh* 24 (1964): 281–90.

Peters, N.
"Osee und die Geschichte," Vorlesungsverzeichnis der Philosophisch–Theologischen Akademie Paderborn (Paderborn, 1924).

Rendtorff, R.
"Erwägungen zur Frühgeschichte des Prophetentums in Israel, *ZThK* 59 (1962): 145–67 ["Reflections on the Early History of Prophecy in Israel," tr. Paul J. Achtemeier, in *History and Hermeneutic, Journal for Theology and the Church* 4, eds., R. W. Funk and Gerhard Ebeling (New York: Harper and Row, 1967), 14–34].

Rieger, J.
*Die Bedeutung der Geschichte für die Verkündigung des Amos und Hosea* (Giessen, 1929).

Sellin, E.
"Die geschichtliche Orientierung der Prophetie des Hosea," *NKZ* 36 (1925): 607–58; 807.

*Idem*
"Hosea und das Martyrium des Mose," *ZAW* 46 (192?): 26–33.

Vriezen, Th. C.
*Hosea, profeet en cultuur* (Gronigen, 1941).

Vuilleumier, R.
*La tradition cultuelle d'Israël dans la prophétie d'Amos et d'Osée*, Cahiers theologiques 45 (Paris, 1960).

Wolff, H. W.
"Hoseas geistige Heimat," *ThLZ* 81 (1956): 83–94 [Reprinted in his *Gesammelte Studien zum Alten Testament*, ThB 22 (München, 1973²), 232–50].

## 14. The Theology of Hosea

Baumann, E.
" 'Wissen um Gott' bei Hosea als Urform von Theologie?" *EvTh* 15 (1955): 416–25.

Baumgartner, W.
"Kennen Amos und Hosea eine Heilseschatologie?" *SThZ* 30 (1913): 30–42; 95–124; 152–70.

Behler, G. M.
"Divini amoris suprema revelatio in antiquo foedere data (Osee c. 11)," *Angelicum* 20 (1943): 102–16.

Buck, F.
*Die Liebe Gottes beim Propheten Osee*, (Rome, 1953).

Caquot, A.
"Osée et la Royauté," *RHPhR* 41 (1961): 123–46.

Dumeste, M. L.
"Le message du prophète Osée," *Vie Spirituelle* 75 (1946): 710–26.

Eichrodt, W.
" 'The Holy One in Your Midst': The Theology of Hosea," *Int* 15 (1961): 259–73.

Francisco, C. T.
"Evil and Suffering in the Book of Hosea," *Southwestern Journal of Theology* 5 (1962–63): 33–41.

Feuillet, A.

"L'universalisme et l'alliance dans la religion d'Osée," *Bible et Vie Chrétienne* 18 (1957): 27–35.

Fohrer, G.

"Umkehr und Erlösung beim Propheten Hosea," *ThZ* 11 (1955): 161–85.

Giblet, J.

"De revelatione amoris Dei apud Oseam prophetam," *Collectanla Mechliniensia* 34 (1949): 35–39.

Hellbardt, H.

*Der verheissene König Israels: Das Christuszeugnis des Hosea*, BEvTH 1 (München, 1935).

Jacob, E.

"L'Héritage cananéen dans le livre du prophète Osée," *RHPhR* 43 (1963): 250–59.

McKenzie, J. L.

"Divine Passion in Osee," *CBQ* 17 (1955): 287–99.

*Idem*

"Knowledge of God in Hosea," *JBL* 74 (1955): 22–27.

Maly, E. H.

"Messianism in Osee," *CBQ* 19 (1957): 213–25.

May, H. G.

"The Fertility Cult in Hosea," *AJSL* 48 (1932): 73–98.

Östborn, G.

*Yahweh and Baal: Studies in the Book of Hosea and Related Documents*, LUÅ Neue Folge 1, 51, 6 (Lund, 1956).

Oettli, S.

"Der Kultus bei Amos und Hosea," *Greifswalder Studien, Festschrift Cremer* (Greifswald, 1895): 1–34.

Schwarz, V.

"Das Gottesbild des Propheten Oseas," *Bibel und Liturgie* 35 (1961–62): 274–79.

Snaith, N. H.

*Mercy and Sacrifice: A Study of the Book of Hosea* (London: SCM Press, 1953).

Wolff, H. W.

"Erkenntnis Gottes im Alten Testament," *EvTh* 15 (1955): 426–31.

*Idem*

"Guds Lidenskap i rettsstriden med Israel," *TTK* 33 (1962): 74–82.

*Idem*

"Guilt and Salvation: A Study of the Prophecy of Hosea," *Int* 15 (1961): 274–85.

*Idem*

" 'Wissen um Gott' bei Hosea als Urform von Theologie," *EvTH* 12 (1952–53): 533–54. [Reprinted in his *Gesammelte Studien*, ThB 22 (München, 1973[2]), 182–205].

\* Numbers in parentheses following page citations for this volume refer to footnotes.

## Designer's Notes

In the design of the visual aspects of *Hermeneia*, consideration has been given to relating the form to the content by symbolic means.

The letters of the logotype *Hermeneia* are a fusion of forms alluding simultaneously to Hebrew (dotted vowel markings) and Greek (geometric round shapes) letter forms. In their modern treatment they remind us of the electronic age as well, the vantage point from which this investigation of the past begins.

The Lion of Judah used as a visual identification for the series is based on the Seal of Shema. The version for *Hermeneia* is again a fusion of Hebrew calligraphic forms, especially the legs of the lion, and Greek elements characterized by the geometric. In the sequence of arcs, which can be understood as scroll-like images, the first is the lion's mouth. It is reasserted and accelerated in the whorl and returns in the aggressively arched tail: tradition is passed from one age to the next, rediscovered and re-formed.

"Who is worthy to open the scroll and break its seals . . ."
Then one of the elders said to me
"weep not; lo, the Lion of the tribe of David,
the Root of David, has conquered,
so that he can open the scroll and
its seven seals."
Rev. 5:2, 5

To celebrate the signal achievement in biblical scholarship which *Hermeneia* represents, the entire series will by its color constitute a signal on the theologian's bookshelf: the Old Testament will be bound in yellow and the New Testament in red, traceable to a commonly used color coding for synagogue and church in medieval painting; in pure color terms, varying degrees of intensity of the warm segment of the color spectrum. The colors interpenetrate when the binding color for the Old Testament is used to imprint volumes from the New and vice versa.

Wherever possible, a photograph of the oldest extant manuscript, or a historically significant document pertaining to the biblical sources, will be displayed on the end papers of each volume to give a feel for the tangible reality and beauty of the source material.

The title page motifs are expressive derivations from the *Hermeneia* logotype, repeated seven times to form a matrix and debossed on the cover of each volume. These sifted out elements will be seen to be in their exact positions within the parent matrix. These motifs and their expressional character are noted on the following page.

Horizontal markings at gradated levels on the spine will assist in grouping the volumes according to these conventional categories.

The type has been set with unjustified right margins so as to preserve the internal consistency of word spacing. This is a major factor in both legibility and aesthetic quality; the resultant uneven line endings are only slight impairments to legibility by comparison. In this respect the type resembles the hand written manuscript where the quality of the calligraphic writing is dependent on establishing and holding to integral spacing patterns.

All of the type faces in common use today have been designed between 1500 A.D. and the present. For the biblical text a face was chosen which does not arbitrarily date the text, but rather one which is uncompromisingly modern and unembellished so that its feel is of the universal. The type style is Univers 65 by Adrian Frutiger.

The expository texts and footnotes are set in Baskerville, chosen for its compatibility with the many brief Greek and Hebrew insertions. The double column format and the shorter line length facilitate speed reading and the wide margins to the left of footnotes provide for the scholar's own notations.

Kenneth Hiebert, Designer